MW01492860

The Oxford Handbook of
Media and Social Justice

OXFORD LIBRARY OF PSYCHOLOGY

The Oxford Handbook of Media and Social Justice

Edited by

Srividya Ramasubramanian

and

Omotayo O. Banjo

OXFORD
UNIVERSITY PRESS

OXFORD
UNIVERSITY PRESS

Oxford University Press is a department of the University of Oxford. It furthers
the University's objective of excellence in research, scholarship, and education
by publishing worldwide. Oxford is a registered trade mark of Oxford University
Press in the UK and certain other countries.

Published in the United States of America by Oxford University Press
198 Madison Avenue, New York, NY 10016, United States of America.

© Oxford University Press 2024

Library of Congress Cataloging-in-Publication Data
Names: Ramasubramanian, Srividya, 1975– editor. | Banjo, Omotayo O., editor.
Title: The Oxford handbook of media and social justice /
[editors] Srividya Ramasubramanian, Omotayo O. Banjo.
Description: New York : Oxford University Press, 2024. |
Series: Oxford library of psychology series |
Includes bibliographical references and index. |
Identifiers: LCCN 2024022816 | ISBN 9780197744345 (hardback) |
ISBN 9780197744369 (epub) | ISBN 9780197744376
Subjects: LCSH: Social justice. | Mass media.
Classification: LCC HM671 .O93 2024 | DDC 302.2301—dc23/eng/20240614
LC record available at https://lccn.loc.gov/2024022816

DOI: 10.1093/oxfordhb/9780197744345.001.0001

Printed by Marquis Book Printing, Canada

MIX
Paper | Supporting
responsible forestry
FSC
www.fsc.org
FSC® C103567

CONTENTS

Section III • Methods and Meaning-Making

Section IV • Resistance and Revisioning

ACKNOWLEDGMENTS

This book started as a seed of an idea planted in our minds by Nadina Persaud, our incredibly supportive acquisitions editor at Oxford University Press. During the past 3 or 4 years of working on this project, we as co-editors have had numerous hurdles, such as a global pandemic, cross-country transition, and multiple family illnesses. However, Nadina kept us enthusiastic and energized about the handbook. As a fellow immigrant woman of color, she immediately saw the value of our project, continuously advocated for us, and checked in on our progress periodically without ever being overbearing. Thank you, Nadina!

Sincere and deep thanks to our research assistants—Shannon Burth, Melody Wilson, Soleil Andrews, and Maitreyee Shilpa Kishor—for helping us at every stage of the process. Through color-coded spreadsheets, multiple Google folders, careful proofreading, and constant reminders to contributors, they kept us on track and organized. Miraculously, we are here at the finish line exactly on the date that we proposed to do so. Without their labor and care, this project would not have been completed smoothly and on time.

We are sincerely grateful to our mentor, the one and only Dr. Mary Beth Oliver, whose lifelong support and encouragement has been vital to our successes. At Penn State University, she gave us a strong foundation on media effects and identity that have helped us become the media scholars that we are today. She allowed us a lot of freedom and flexibility to explore various methods and theories from critical perspectives that we found meaningful. Through her personal examples, she taught us to center care and excellence, which we have tried our best to emulate in our collaboration. We are thankful to all our mentors, well-wishers, collaborators, scholar–activists, and teachers who have made our work possible. In particular, Srivi acknowledges her students and collaborators at Media Rise, The Difficult Dialogues Project, and CODE^SHIFT for their unflinching support for social justice scholarship. More broadly, we thank all the numerous activists throughout the world doing incredibly courageous work under challenging and even dangerous circumstances.

We are also incredibly thankful to our contributors, without whom this volume would be impossible. Thank you for lending your intellectual minds, your passion, and your conviction and values to this space in collaboration with like minds and like hearts. May your academic, scholarly, and activist endeavors continue to reap goodness for you and generations to come.

Srivi thanks her parents Ramasubramanian and Lalitha, husband Gautam, son Sankalp, and sister Srinithya for their love, care, and undying support. Tayo thanks her parents Bolaji Oyefeso and Lanre Banjo for giving her a heart for justice and her daughter Morayo AdeYara for being her most personal reason to fight for it.

NOTES ON CONTRIBUTORS

Rukhsana Ahmed (PhD, Ohio University) is Associate Professor in the Department of Communication and Research Associate at the Center for the Elimination of Minority Health at the University at Albany, State University of New York. Her research examines the role of communication, culture, media, and technology in shaping health outcomes among marginalized communities and promoting broader organizational and social changes and innovations in local, national, and international health contexts. She is the Chief Editor of "Health Communication," a specialty section of *Frontiers in Communication*. She is the co-editor of *The Palgrave Handbook of Communication and Health Disparities* (forthcoming).

Ama Boatemaa Appiah-Kubi is a PhD candidate with the Department of Communication Culture and Media Studies at Howard University. Her research lies at the nexus of gender and feminist media studies, social movements, and media and cultural studies. Her research examines Ghanaian women's and queer persons' engagement with different forms of media through critical Afrocentric theories and methodologies. Specifically, she explores their representations, representational activism, resistance, identity formation, and negotiation. Implications of her research provide a better understanding of how marginalized groups are represented, but mainly how they adopt, internalize, negotiate, and challenge hegemonic forces of patriarchy, heteronormativity, imperialism, and colonialism.

Godfried A. Asante (PhD, University of New Mexico) is an Associate Professor at the School of Communication at San Diego State University. His research primarily focuses on human rights, queer Africanness and intercultural communication. He has published several essays on LGBT rights and queer epistemologies in Ghana in journals including *Howard Journal of Communications, Communication Theory*, and *Women Studies in Communication*.

Hanan Badr (DPhil, Universität Erfurt) is Full Professor at the Department of Communication, University of Salzburg in Austria. As Chair for the Public Spheres & Inequalities Unit, her research centers de-Westernizing communication research, activism, journalism, and migration in times of power imbalances. She is co-editor of *Arab Berlin* (with Nahed Samour; Transcript, 2023). She is Associate Editor of *Journal of Communication*; Chair of Activism, Communication and Social Justice Interest Group at the International Communication Association; and Kluge Fellow at the Library of Congress.

Omotayo O. Banjo (PhD, Pennsylvania State University) is a Professor in the School of Communication, Film, & Media Studies as well as Associate Dean of the Grad College at the University of Cincinnati. Her work focuses on African diasporic entertainment, identity, and belonging. She is a critical media effects scholar who has used different methodologies from textual analysis of post-racial entertainment media to transnational audience reception research and co-viewing effects. She is a McNair alum, a Fulbright award winner, and engaged scholar, having presented her work to policymakers and tech experts.

Thomas J Billard (PhD, University of Southern California) is an Assistant Professor in the School of Communication and, by courtesy, the Department of Sociology at Northwestern University. They are the founding Executive Director of the Center for Applied Transgender Studies in Chicago and Editor-in-Chief of the Center's flagship journal, the *Bulletin of Applied Transgender Studies*. Dr. Billard's research spans political communication, the sociology of social movements, and transgender studies. They are the author of *Voices for Transgender Equality: Making Change in the Networked Public Sphere* (Oxford University Press, 2024) and co-editor of *Public Scholarship in Communication Studies* (with Silvio Wasibord; University of Illinois Press, 2024).

Shannon Burth (MA, Syracuse University) is a Doctoral Student in the Newhouse School of Public Communication, where she is pursuing a PhD in Mass Communication. Her research interests include media literacy, entertainment media, representation, diversity, equity, access, and inclusion.

Charisse L'Pree Corsbie-Massay (PhD, University of Southern California) is an Associate Professor of Communications at the S. I. Newhouse School of Public Communications at Syracuse University. She investigates how media affects the way we think about ourselves and others as well as how we use media to affect the way others think about us. She is the author of *Twentieth Century Media and the American Psyche* (Routledge, 2021) and *Diversity and Satire: Laughing at Processes of Marginalization* (Wiley, 2023) and hosts a pop trash podcast entitled *Critical and Curious*.

Marissa Joanna Doshi is an Associate Professor of Communication at Hope College. Her research draws on feminist perspectives to examine the creative and cultural dimensions of media and technology use. Her secondary research interests include intercultural communication and issues of representation in mass media. Her research has been published in journals such as *Communication Research*, *Journal of International & Intercultural Communication*, *International Journal of Communication*, and *Women's Studies in Communication*. At Hope College, she teaches courses on transnational feminisms, cultural studies, media writing, and social media activism.

Mohan J. Dutta is the Dean's Chair in Communication and the Director of the Center for Culture-Centered Approach to Research and Evaluation at the School of Communication, Journalism and Marketing at Massey University.

Uttaran Dutta (PhD, Purdue University) is an Associate Professor in the Hugh Downs School of Human Communication at Arizona State University. His research focuses on sustainable development and social change in marginalized communities, specifically on the importance of culture, communication, design, and innovation in transforming the lives of people who are socially, politically, and economically underserved. He has published articles and chapters in communication journals and books and presented his research at communication conferences.

Shinsuke Eguchi (PhD, Howard University) is a Professor in the Department of Communication and Journalism at the University of New Mexico. Their research interests focus on global and transcultural studies, queer of color critique, intersectionality and racialized gender politics, Asian/American studies, and performance studies.

Christine Ngā Hau Elers completed her PhD in 2023 in the CARE Center School of Communication, Journalism and Marketing, exploring "Communicating Māori Health and Wellbeing in a Whakapapa Paradigm: Voices from the Margins." She is from Ngāti Kauwhata Iwi in the Manawatū, Aotearoa New Zealand.

Katie Ellis is Professor in Internet Studies and Director of the Centre for Culture and Technology at Curtin University. She was Curtin's researcher of the year in 2020 and is series editor of *Routledge Research in Disability and Media Studies*. Her research is located at the intersection of media access and representation and engages with government, industry, and community to ensure actual benefits for real people with disability. She has authored or edited 17 books and numerous articles on the topic of disability and the media, including most recently the monograph *Disability and Digital Television Cultures* (Routledge, 2019).

Swarnavel Eswaran is a Professor in the Department of English and the School of Journalism at Michigan State University. His documentaries include *Nagapattinam: Waves from the Deep* (2018), *Hmong Memories at the Crossroad* (2016), *Migrations of Islam* (2014), and *Unfinished Journey: A City in Transition* (2012). His research focuses on Tamil cinema's history, aesthetics, politics, contemporary digital cinema, and concomitant changes. His books include *Tamil Cinema Reviews: 1931– 1960* (Nizhal, 2020) and *Madras Studios: Narrative, Genre, and Ideology in Tamil Cinema* (SAGE, 2015). His fiction feature *Kattumaram* (Catamaran, 2019) is currently on the film festival circuit.

Ololade Faniyi is an African feminist activist-scholar and PhD student in Women's, Gender, and Sexuality Studies at Emory University. Her research employs a feminist data lens and participatory digital ethnography to the study of Nigerian feminist/ queer social-political activism, African feminist digital cultures, alternative political communication, digital/data technologies, and digital humanities. She serves as an African advisor for FRIDA, The Young Feminist Fund, and is a graduate fellow for the Atlanta Interdisciplinary Artificial Intelligence network. Her sole and collaborative works have been published in *Feminist Media Studies, Communication, Culture and Critique, and Women's Studies Quarterly*.

Radhika Gajjala is Professor of Media and Communication and of American Culture Studies at Bowling Green State University. Her books include *Digital Diasporas: Labor* *and Affect in Gendered Indian Digital Publics* (Rowman & Littlefield, 2019); *Online Philanthropy in the Global North and South: Connecting, Microfinancing, and Gaming for Change* (Lexington Books, 2017); *Cyberculture and the Subaltern* (Lexington Books, 2012); and *Cyberselves: Feminist Ethnographies of South Asian Women* (Roman and Littlefield, 2004). She has co-edited *The SAGE Handbook of Media and Migration* (SAGE, 2019), *The Routledge Companion to Media and Class* (Routledge, 2019), *Cyberfeminism 2.0* (Lang, 2012), *Global Media Culture and Identity* (Routledge, 2011), *South Asian Technospaces* (Lang, 2008), and *Webbing Cyberfeminist Practice* (Hampton, 2008). She has also been co-editor of the journal *Ada: A Journal of Gender and New Media* and continues with the Fembot Collective as Managing Editor. She is currently working on a book on gendered Global South activist digital publics. She heads the research lab for "Tooling Around: Situated Data Analytics, Digital Humanities, Digital Archiving and Data Feminism," which is a team of collaborators who are examining feminist approaches to the implementation of computational tools in digital humanities and social science.

Andrea Gambino (PhD, University of California, Los Angeles [UCLA]) is a Research, Design, and Instructional Consultant at the Friday Institute for Educational Innovation (North Carolina State University). Her dissertation examines how secondary teachers' positionalities and exposure to critical social theories guide their trajectories as social justice educators and their critical media literacy pedagogies. Her research and teaching draw on her experiences implementing critical media literacy as a tool for advancing social and environmental justice with secondary students in North Carolina and postsecondary students at UCLA. She received Teacher of the Year twice in North Carolina as well as UCLA's Academic Senate Distinguished Teaching Assistant Award, Dissertation Year Fellowship, and the School of Education and Information Studies' George Kneller Humanitarian Award.

Leandra Hinojosa Hernández (PhD, Texas A&M University) is Assistant Professor in the Department of Communication at the University of Utah. She is widely recognized for her work at the intersections of journalism and media ethics, health communication activism, and social justice. Her recent projects explore the interrelated nature of reproductive in/justice and gender violence in American and Latin American contexts. Her research is published in *Health Communication, Communication Research, Women's Studies in Communication, Frontiers in Communication, QED: A Journal in GLBTQ Worldmaking, Departures in Critical Qualitative Research*, and *Communication Teacher*.

Dal Yong Jin is a Distinguished SFU Professor and a Global Professor at Korea University. His major research and teaching interests are on digital platforms and digital games, globalization and media, transnational cultural studies, and the political economy of media and culture. He has published numerous books, journal articles, and book chapters, including *Korea's Online Gaming Empire* (MIT Press, 2010), *New Korean Wave: Transnational Cultural Power in the Age of Social Media* (University of Illinois Press, 2016), and *Artificial Intelligence in Cultural Production: Critical Perspectives on Digital Platforms* (Routledge, 2021). He is the founding book series editor of *Routledge Research in Digital Media and Culture in Asia*, and he has been directing the Transnational Culture and Digital Technology Lab since 2021.

Ralina L. Joseph is a scholar, teacher, and facilitator of race and communication. She is Presidential Term Professor of Communication; Founding Director of the Center for Communication, Difference, and Equity; and Associate Dean of Equity & Justice in the Graduate School at the University of Washington. She is the author of three books on race and communication and is currently writing *Interrupting Privilege: Radical Listening, Talking Race, and Fighting Racism*, a book of essays based on her public scholarship.

Krittiya Kantachote is an Assistant Professor of Sociology at Srinakharinwirot University, Thailand. Her research interests include gender, migration, labor, and economic sociology. She does both qualitative and quantitative research. Her current research includes the quality of life in Thailand, gray divorce in Thailand, and migrant domestic workers and the TikTok application.

Satveer Kaur-Gill is an Assistant Professor at the Department of Communication Studies at the University of Nebraska–Lincoln. Her research examines how population groups with unequal access to health, social, and digital resources experience health disparities. One of her current projects examines how precarious migrant workers use TikTok to create health resources digitally for help-seeking, information sharing, and advocacy.

Jessica Keeley is a PhD candidate within the field of psychology at Curtin University. Her research focuses on social perceptions of people with disability, particularly within the context of familial maltreatment. During her time as a student, Jessica has received several accolades and awards, including the Australian Psychological Society College of Community Psychologists Postgraduate Student Conference Award in 2020. She is currently a researcher on the Child Disability team at Telethon Kids Institute.

Adam Key (PhD, Texas A&M University) is an Associate Professor of Communication at Kansas State University–Salina. His primary research interest is the discursive production of deviance. In particular, he is interested in how systems of education and carcerality normalize majority groups while producing minoritized groups as deviant. Prior to his current role, he spent 8 years teaching inside prison walls for Lee College's Huntsville Center, where he taught more than 1,000 incarcerated students, founded and coached an undefeated prison debate team, and hosted the first TEDx event held inside a Texas prison. He is author of *The Rhetoric of Resistance to Prison Education* (Routledge, 2021) and other works in *Review of Communication, Communication Studies, Journal of Autoethnography, QED: A Journal in GLBTQ Worldmaking*, and *Journal of Bisexuality.*

Keisuke Kimura (PhD, University of New Mexico) is an Assistant Professor of Applied Communication and Critical Race and Ethnic Studies in the Department of Interdisciplinary and Communication Studies at Miami University. His research and teaching interests revolve around critical intercultural studies, politics of identity, race, gender and sexuality, digital media, Japanese popular culture, and transnationalism. His recent work can be found in *Journal of International and Intercultural Communication*, *Journal of Intercultural Communication Research*, *Journal of Hate Studies*, and *QED: A Journal in GLBTQ Worldmaking*.

Elisha Lim researches the intersection of social media, theology, and critical race theory and is working on a book called *Pious* about the rise in distorted identity politics, from ethnic fraud and polarizing populism to hyperbolic corporate solidarity statements. They have written about algorithms and identity economics in academic journals and the media (*The Daily Beast, hyperallergic, Document Journal*, and *TEDxUofT*) as well as in their upcoming graphic novel, *8 Dreams About You*.

Tanya Loughead (PhD, Catholic University of Leuven, Belgium) is a philosopher and activist in Buffalo, New York. She is Professor in the Department of Philosophy at Canisius University, where she is also President of the American Association of University Professors chapter and director of Women & Gender Studies. She specializes in contemporary continental philosophy and has published on the works of Maurice Blanchot, Emmanuel Levinas, Simone Weil, Angela Davis, and Sara Ahmed, among others. She has written two books, *Critical University* (Lexington Books, 2015) and *Politics of Maturing* (Lexington Books, 2023).

Minnie McMillian is a Doctoral Student at Syracuse University pursuing her PhD in social psychology. Her research, more broadly, focuses on exploring manifestations of racism for those from historically marginalized communities.

Kelly Merrill Jr. (PhD, The Ohio State University) is an Assistant Professor in the School of Communication, Film, and Media Studies at the University of Cincinnati. His primary research interests are at the intersection of health communication and communication technology. In particular, he is interested in responses to stigmatization and discrimination in health and across technologies among racial, ethnic, sexual, and gender minorities. Furthermore, his research investigates the use of communication technologies for social, physical, and mental health benefits.

Wunpini Fatimata Mohammed (PhD, The Pennsylvania State University) is an Assistant Professor in the Department of Communication at Cornell University. She is co-editor of the book, *African Women in Digital Spaces: Redefining Social Movements on the Continent and in the Diaspora* (with Msia Kibona Clark; Mkuki Na Nyoka Publishers, 2023). She is the book review editor of *Cultural Studies*. She is an activist-scholar whose research focuses on feminisms, decolonization, and social movements. She has won top paper awards from the International Communication Association, the Association for Education in Journalism and Mass Communication, and the International Association for Media and Communication Research.

jas l. moultrie is a storyholder, filmmaker, and doctoral candidate studying communication at the University of Washington, Seattle. Her interests include Blackness, madness, performance, memory, and creative nonfiction. While making space for her selves within the academy, she is building a literacy project for and by Black young people to amplify joy, well-being, and encourage healing.

Tomide Oloruntobi (PhD, University of New Mexico) is an Assistant Professor of Intercultural Communication in the Hugh Downs School of Human Communication at Arizona State University. At the intersection of rhetoric, cultural, and media studies, his research broadly focuses on global trans/intercultural studies, decolonization, African (transnational) communication, film, Black diaspora studies, audience studies, and mis/disinformation in the Global South. His research has appeared in *Journal of International & Intercultural Communication, Howard Journal of Communications*, and *QED: A Journal in GLBTQ Worldmaking*.

Seulgi Park is a PhD candidate in the Department of Communication at the University at Albany, State University of New York. Her research focuses on health communication and health disparities issues for immigrant populations, especially Korean immigrants. She is interested in health literacy and communicative engagement of immigrant patients in health care.

Srividya Ramasubramanian (PhD, Penn State University) is Newhouse Professor & Endowed Chair at Syracuse University. She is widely recognized for her pioneering work on data justice, critical media effects, media literacy, and anti-racism dialogues. With Erica Scharrer, she has co-authored *Quantitative Research Methods in Communication: The Power of Numbers for Social Justice* (Routledge, 2021). She is the editor of *Communication Monographs* and the Director of CODE^SHIFT (Collaboratory for Data Equity, Social Healing, Inclusive Futures, and Transformation).

Anthony R. Ramirez (PhD, Texas A&M University) is an Assistant Professor of Communication Studies at the University of Houston–Downtown. He is a national award-winning instructor and the Assistant Director of the Center for Latino Studies at the University of Houston–Downtown. His research focuses on Latinx/e identity and representation of the U.S.–Mexico border in popular culture and media. His work has been featured in *Migrants and the COVID-19 Pandemic: Communication, Inequality, and Transformation* (with Srividya Ramasubramanian; Palgrave Macmillan, 2023) and *Race/Gender/Class/Media: Considering Diversity Across Audiences, Content, and Production* (Routledge, 2023).

Anamik Saha is a Professor of Race and Media in the School of Media and Communication at the University of Leeds. His research is on issues of race, culture, and media, with a particular focus on creative and cultural industries and issues of "diversity." He is author of *Race and the Cultural Industries* (Polity, 2018); *Race, Culture and Media* (SAGE, 2021); and co-author of the Arts and Humanities Research Council–funded industry report "Rethinking 'Diversity' in Publishing" (with Sandra van Lente; Goldsmiths Press, 2020). His new book *The Anti-Racist Media Manifesto*, co-authored with Francesca Sobande and Gavan Titley was published in 2024 (Polity). He is an editor of *European Journal of Cultural Studies*.

Paola Sartoretto is an Associate Professor in Media and Communication at the School of Education and Communication, Jönköping University, Sweden, where she coordinates the international Master of Social Science in sustainable communication. Her research interests are in the intersection between communication, political participation, and social change, with a focus on communication among marginalized groups. She has also conducted research in collaboration with social movements in Brazil and co-edited the anthology *Media Activist Research Ethics* (with Sandra Jeppesen; Palgrave, 2020) in the International Association for Media and Communications Research series *Global Transformations in Media and Communication Research*.

Jeff Share (PhD, University of California, Los Angeles) teaches in the School of Education and Information Studies at UCLA. His research and practice focus on preparing educators to teach critical media literacy for social and environmental justice. He worked as an award-winning photojournalist for a decade and then taught bilingual elementary school for 7 years in the Los Angeles Unified School District. Since 2007, he has taught teachers, teacher credential candidates, and university students how to think critically about media and how to teach critical media literacy. The second edition of his book, *Media Literacy Is Elementary: Teaching Youth to Critically Read and Create Media* (Lang) was published in 2015. He is co-author of *Teaching Climate Change to Adolescents: Reading, Writing, and Making a Difference* (with Richard Beach and Allen Webb; Routledge, 2017) and *The Critical Media Literacy Guide: Engaging Media and Transforming Education* (with Douglas Kellner; Brill, 2019). He is a Fulbright Specialist who has taught critical media literacy in Argentina, China, Germany, India, and Mexico.

Cheryll Ruth R. Soriano is Professor and Research Fellow in the Department of Communication, De La Salle University. Her published work examines the intersections of digital cultures, marginality, and social justice. Her current research explores digital communication and transformations in labor and organizing in the platform economy. Her books include *Asian Perspectives on Digital Culture: Emerging Phenomena, Enduring Concepts* (edited with S. S. Lim; Routledge, 2016) and *Philippine Digital Cultures: Brokerage Dynamics on YouTube* (with E. Cabalquinto; Amsterdam University Press, 2022).

David Stamps (PhD, University of California, Santa Barbara) is an Assistant Professor at Bentley University. His research aims to understand the psychological and behavioral effects of identity-focused interpersonal interactions and individuals' exposure to and engagement with media. Inherent in this work is a recognition that issues of class, gender, race, ability, geographic location, and sexuality meaningfully impact these relationships.

Jasmina Tacheva is a writer and scholar–activist splitting her time between the United States and Bulgaria. She is Assistant Professor in the School of Information Studies at Syracuse University, where she teaches courses on the politics and ethics of data and artificial intelligence. She graduated from the State University of New York at Buffalo with a PhD in management and is currently working on her second doctorate in comparative literature at the same institution. Her main interest is at the intersection of technology and queer and transnational feminist theory, and her work in this area has appeared in journals such as *Big Data & Society*.

Ruth Tsuria is an Associate Professor at Seton Hall University's School of Communication, Media, and the Arts. Her research, which investigates the intersection of digital media, culture, and feminism, has been published in various prestigious academic outlets, such as *International Journal of Communication* and *Social Media + Society*. She is the recipient of the Inaugural Digital Religion Research Award for her contributions to the field of digital religion. She received the 2023 Researcher of the Year Award for her impressive publication record, which includes 23 articles and book chapters, and two edited books. Her most recent book is *Keeping Women in Their Digital Place: The Maintenance of Jewish Gender Norms Online* (Penn State University Press, 2024). In addition, she is the Editor-in-Chief of the *Journal for Religion, Media, and Digital Culture*.

Angharad N. Valdivia is Research Professor/Emeritus at the Institute of Communications Research and also Professor Emeritus in the Department of Latina Latino Studies at the University of Illinois. Her Latinx and Latin American studies research combined with gender and media studies research straddles political economy and cultural studies, further enhanced by an intersectional and transnational approach. Her books include *A Latina in the Land of Hollywood* (University of Arizona Press, 2022); *Feminism, Multiculturalism and the Media* (SAGE, 1995); *A Companion to Media Studies* (Wiley-Blackwell, 2006); *Latina/o Communication Studies Today* (Lang, 2008); *Mapping Latina/o Studies* (co-edited with Matthew Garcia; Lang, 2012); *Latina/os and the Media* (Polity Press, 2010); and *The Gender of Latinidad: Uses and Abuses of Hybridity* (Wiley-Blackwell, 2020). She served as editor of *Communication Theory* and the *International Encyclopedia of Media Studies*. She is a Fellow of the International Communication Association.

Erique Zhang (PhD, Northwestern University) is an Assistant Professor in the School of Communication at Simon Fraser University. Their research draws on feminist media studies, Asian American feminism, queer and trans of color critique, and fashion studies to interrogate how media representations of transgender women reproduce normative beauty ideals and how trans women and femmes of color navigate these norms in their everyday lives. They are a co-founder of the Center for Applied Transgender Studies, Assistant Editor of the *Bulletin of Applied Transgender Studies*, and an affiliate of the Center for Critical Race + Digital Studies.

SECTION I

Introduction

CHAPTER

1

Perspectives, Positionalities, and Paradigms in Media and Social Justice Scholarship

Omotayo O. Banjo *and* Srividya Ramasubramanian

Media scholarship on social justice issues has historically been fragmented across subfields of communication in siloed ways, leading to deep but unnecessary divides between social scientists and scholar–activists. The *Oxford Handbook of Media and Social Justice* explores and broadens interdisciplinary, critical, and mixed methodological approaches to media and social justice scholarship. We argue that media scholars need to explicitly engage with social justice issues in the ongoing global context of escalating pandemic inequalities, global media asymmetries, rising populist authoritarianism, transnational hate networks, online White supremacist ideology, political attacks on critical scholarship, and an urgent climate change crisis.

Why Us and Why Now?

At time of writing, Hamas has launched an attack on Israel, and there are global protests in opposing Israelis' long record of militant acts against the Palestinians. Russia continues its invasion of Ukraine for the 20th month. The escalating conflict in the Democratic Republic of Congo has led to an uptick in sexual assaults on displaced women. Artificial intelligence (AI) has threatened just about every industry from education to entertainment, impacting laborers and shifting our definitions of work. In the United States, there are movements to revise history in ways that negate the very real impact of the enslavement of Africans on American Black people's trauma and interracial relations. Books that invite critical inquiry about systemic inequities are being banned. Senate bills surveilling education about inequality in the United States, removing support systems for underrepresented students at universities, and prohibiting protest on controversial issues—a First Amendment right—are being passed or considered. All of these are resonant of previous dark eras of our time. If there was ever a time to educate and engage on matters of social justice, it is now.

We come to know about these horrific events through writers and broadcasters whether on terrestrial networks or social networking sites. We come to experience and engage and connect with others through storytellers whether in film or on TikTok. We rage. We weep. We repost and retweet. We wrestle in discourse with one another because no matter how distant the event, we are—all of us—impacted by it. Whereas the work of the industry might be to inform the public, as media scholars we inadvertently carry a responsibility to explore, unpack, and translate these impacts that as embodied people we experience psychologically, culturally, and sociologically as individuals and in the community. Who best to examine these questions? And how much more equipped are we when we entangle epistemologies, marry methods, and innovate our research in ways that respond to social problems?

In addition to the pressing moment we find ourselves in, what makes this handbook especially unique is that our collection is co-edited by immigrant faculty of color and scholar–mothers. As scholars of color, we would be remiss to ignore the ways in which media and media research tend to ignore the plight of people who look like our ancestral community and, by extension, other groups who have been marginalized and muted. Furthermore, as scholar–activists, we are compelled to employ our work as tools against systems of oppression, beginning within our field, so that we might make room for and empower others to use their scholarship to call down injustice. Given our unique positionalities in the discipline of communication and media studies, which is characterized by normative Whiteness, the chapter contributors for this volume represent minoritized voices and perspectives based on race, ethnicity, nationality, gender, and sexual orientation. Last, but more important, as mothers, we desire to model for our children what it can look like to use the power of one's words and position, talents and treasures to advocate for justice. And even more, we desire a more durable world for our own children.

Power in Perspectives, Positionalities, and Paradigms

To have a more holistic and interdisciplinary view of the relationship between media and social justice issues, this handbook includes a range of methods, paradigms, and approaches. These range from critical to postpositivist to postmodernist perspectives, as well as qualitative to quantitative to policy research. We also include Indigenous, intersectional, postcolonial, and feminist critical cultural approaches to media and social justice scholarship. In so doing, this volume takes a multimethod approach that incorporates both humanistic and social scientific perspectives.

Another unique contribution of this book is the inclusion of quantitative and empirical perspectives on social justice scholarship. Typically, social justice and media have been part of the realm of critical cultural communication scholarship, whereas quantitative studies of communication and media have been disconnected from social justice. Indeed, issues such as objectivity, categorization, validity, and reliability are often viewed as misaligned with social justice research, which takes up a postpositivist approach to analyzing data. More recently, we, along with other scholars within communication sciences, have led the quantitative criticalism movement, which takes a critical approach to media effects and media psychological research (Ramasubramanian & Banjo, 2020; Scharrer & Ramasubramanian, 2021). As pioneers in these methodologies that combine, blend, and merge various paradigms such as postpositivism, critical theory, and transformative paradigms in unique and meaningful ways, we are uniquely positioned within communication and media studies to connect and bridge various methods and subfields under the umbrella of media and social justice, through this handbook.

In this volume, we not only look at the problems and concerns from a critical perspective but also provide examples and case studies of activism and collective action from different areas of the world. The enormity and urgency of these complex contemporary social justice issues facing the world today mean that social justice activists, scholars, and storytellers need a readily available compendium of cutting-edge scholarship on media and social justice. This handbook is a collection of leading voices of media researchers and scholars committed to social justice throughout the world, many of whom have been thinking and writing about their issues within their specific cultural and national contexts for many years. We hope that this anthological bouquet of theories, methods, and case studies brings meaning to not just the creators of the collection but also those who engage with it, through their lens and values.

Overview of the Handbook

This book is organized into three main sections that cover theory, methods, and application. Each chapter in this book presents an overview of a brief history, key concepts, contemporary debates and dialogues, references to published works by leading scholars and thought leaders, and future directions on each of these topics. The handbook explores intersecting identities, social structures, and power networks within media ownership, representation, selection, uses, effects, networks, and social transformation. These theories, methods, and practices expose media and digital divides, polarizations, marginalizations, exclusions, alienations, invisibilities, stigma, and trivializations. Yet, they also showcase how individuals and communities have agency through refusal and resistance. We end with a re-visioning of the role of media and technology in our shared futures through reckoning, restoration, and reparation for collective healing and flourishing. Taking this inclusive approach to scholarship is essential as our disciplines become increasingly diverse, with students and scholars from throughout the world, many of whom have experienced multiple stigmatizations and generational violence due to colonialism, imperialism, heteropatriarchy, White supremacy, and related factors.

Section II, Approaches and Analytic Frameworks, covers multiple theoretical frameworks that introduce key concepts, debates, limits, and challenges within existing media scholarship. These then serve as the launching pad for sharing innovative theories, methods, case studies, and practices to address complex, cross-cutting, and contemporary social justice issues. Beginning with Dal Yong Jin's "Political Economy of Communication in the Digital Platform Era," (Chapter 2), the author frames questions of media and social justice with a paradigm that clarifies economic constraints. Moreover, the author suggests that because political economy analyzes the power relationships between politics and economics, it is essential to discuss the shifting power (im)balances between Western platforms and non-Western platforms, as well as the platform owners and users. By emphasizing a few primary areas concerning digital platforms, this chapter discusses the shifting media ecology in which digital platforms play a vital role in the early 21st century.

Anamik Saha further advances our conversation by providing essential clarifications of key terms that enable us to reframe our approach to social justice within the industry. In his work titled "The Limits of Diversity and Popular Anti-Racism: The Need for Reparative Justice in the Cultural Industries" (Chapter 3), the author advocates for the reimagining of reparative justice, critiquing the commodification of race within cultural industries and questioning the way diversity discourse unintentionally perpetuates racial inequalities. In Chapter 4, we revisit our foundational work on "Critical Media Effects: A Framework for Bridging Critical Cultural Communication with Media Effects Research," which was originally published in the *Journal of Communication*, emphasizing the connection between critical epistemologies and positivist methodologies. This approach allows us to comprehensively account for the multifaceted layers of identity, systems, and contexts that constitute the populations of interest in our studies.

In Chapter 5, "Black Audience and Media Resistance," David Stamps offers valuable insights into our perceptions of Blackness and the way we view Black entertainment and Black audiences, portraying them as more than just forms of art but as catalysts for activism. Chapter 6, "How Do You Shift That? Dialoguing Social Justice, Activism, and Black Joy in Media Studies" by jas l. Moultrie and Ralina L. Joseph, shines a spotlight on a series of dialogues among influential scholars in Black media and communication, including luminaries such as Herman Gray, Beretta E. Smith-Shomade, Kishonna Gray, and Robin Means Coleman, to name a few. The authors meticulously define key concepts derived from the wisdom of these distinguished scholars. They also carefully dissect the boundaries within which these Black academics challenge the hegemony of White supremacy in academia while simultaneously embracing the concept of Black joy.

The following frameworks center on the multilayered and complex identities that have traditionally been essentialized in media research. Angharad N. Valdivia traces the historical evolutions of the study of people with Hispanic and Latinx heritage. In "Latine Media

Studies: From Near Omission to Radical Intersectionality" (Chapter 7), Valdivia identifies a stage of theoretical development, which signifies maturation in our study of representation and audience identification. Keisuke Kimura and Shinsuke Eguchi, in "Queer of Color Approaches to Critical Cultural Media Studies" (Chapter 8), champion a framework that centers intersectional knowledge as a significant starting point for scholars to question and critique media practices that alter, shape, and reinforce situated meanings. In their chapter, "Queer and Transgender Media Studies" (Chapter 9), Erique Zhang and Thomas J Billard explore research that moves the field of queer and trans media studies beyond film and television and argue for the collaborative efforts of empirical and humanistic work to capture the complexity of issues in the contemporary media landscape.

Continuing a discussion of intersectionality and queer identities, Ruth Tsuria (Chapter 10) uses a dialectic approach within digital spaces to examine how various religious identities intersect with gender and sexuality. In "Digital Religion and the Negotiation of Gender/Sex Norms," Tsuria identifies tensions by which anonymity might enable minority voices and perspectives yet participatory culture might "cancel" these alternative voices by strengthening fundamental religious approaches to gender and sexual norms. Finally, in Chapter 11, "Critical Disability Media Studies," Katie Ellis and Jessica Keeley present a theoretical synthesis of research and conceptualizations of disability, culture, and the media from which scholars might use to highlight how representation impacts the way people with disabilities experience social justice.

In Section III, Methods and Meaning-Making, we delve into various approaches for exploring questions related to media and social justice research. Our journey commences with Chapter 12, "Critical Discourse Analysis," by Marissa Joanna Doshi. This chapter delves into the utility of critical discourse analysis as a framework for identifying the origins of social injustice and the ways in which these injustices are challenged. Subsequently, the remaining chapters underscore the pivotal role of data in defining and operationalizing the concepts of social justice and social justice work.

Chapter 13, "Data Justice: The Role of Data in Media and Social Justice" by Srividya Ramasubramanian, Shannon Burth, and Minnie McMillian, highlights how data offer invaluable insights into comprehending the lived experiences of marginalized communities. Similarly, Jasmina Tacheva and Tanya Loughead, in their chapter "Justice Informatics, Justice for Us All: Liberation from Techno-Ideology" (Chapter 14), identify the digital space as one colonized by dominant ideologies that inadvertently perpetuate injustices rooted in patriarchy and White supremacy. They introduce the concept of "justice informatics" as a framework through which scholar–activists can dismantle the impact of "techno-ideology."

Whereas much of the social justice work has focused on liberating media studies from Western philosophy and White supremacy, Hanan Badr presents thoughtful considerations. In response to calls for de-Westernizing communication studies, Chapter 15, "Researching Closed Fields: What We Can Learn from Analyzing So-Called Constrained, Inaccessible, and Invisible Media Contexts," encourages scholars to grapple with the complexities of investigating closed research—research that centers difficult-to-reach, often non-Western communities—while also engaging in self-reflective practices. This chapter advocates for nuanced research that reshapes our criteria for excellence; promotes interdisciplinary collaboration between communication studies and area studies; and invites diasporic scholars, with their unique epistemic perspectives, to play a more significant role in knowledge production.

In concluding this section on methods, Ololade Faniyi and Radhika Gajjala's work, "Digital Archives and Unexpected Crossings: A Data Feminist Approach to Transnational

Feminist Media Studies and Social Media Activism" (Chapter 16), employs a feminist computational analysis approach to digital archives research, demonstrating how social networks transcend closed borders. Drawing on global stories of discrimination against Muslim women, the authors underscore the significance of networked conversations on X (formally known as Twitter) and their ability to transcend geopolitical boundaries.

After establishing a foundational understanding of social justice and social justice research, encompassing various forms and perspectives through which we engage with our questions, the next section introduces case studies for the practical application of these concepts. In Section IV, Resistance and Revisioning, authors tackle questions related to diverse populations, including the U.S. working class, prisoners, diasporic communities, and ethnic minorities throughout the world. Through these case studies, we aim to identify common experiences of oppression and empowerment across different contexts, such as entertainment, social networks, technology, and health.

Beginning with Chapter 17, "Mediated Socioeconomic Injustice: Representations of Poor and Working-Class People in Mainstream Media," Charisse L'Pree Corsbie-Massay scrutinizes the broader concept of the American Dream and its contribution to socioeconomic disparities among U.S. citizens. She calls upon scholars and activists to reconsider their perceptions of classism and how they engage with and challenge these notions. Similarly, Swarnavel Eswaran's "Challenging Caste Hierarchies in Tamil Cinema" (Chapter 18) delves into classism within the context of an ethnic group in India, deconstructing Tamil-produced films to showcase how they challenge caste hierarchies. Furthermore, this chapter highlights the empowering use of storytelling in Dalit cinema to question prevailing power structures. Adam Key, in Chapter 19, "Media Representations, Incarceration, and Social Justice," offers a framework to critically understand and challenge biases against prisoners and criminals, on both macro and micro levels, through the lens of "convictism."

The subsequent chapters address issues related to immigrants and transnational communities. In Chapter 20, "Heroes of the Border: Using Counternarratives to Break Border Stereotypes and Create Superhero Narratives," Anthony R. Ramirez explores how Latina/o critical communication theory can be applied to examine comic books and graphic novels that center on immigration and Mexican immigration into the United States. In Chapter 21, "Media Creation and Consumption as Activism Among African Transnational and Diasporic Communities," Omotayo O. Banjo and Tomide Oloruntobi investigate the collaborative efforts between Black and African storytellers, fostering connections between African transnationals and diaspora communities, including second-generation Americans and Black Americans. Offering analyses of shows such as *Bob Hearts Abishola* and *LoveCraft Country*, the authors suggest that the creative agentic work of transnational and diasporic creatives is a form of social activism and by supporting this work Black audiences throughout the world engage with entertainment through affective investments.

In Chapter 22, "Subaltern Digital Cultures: Precarious Migrants on TikTok," Elisha Lim, Satveer Kaur-Gill, and Krittiya Kantachote discuss how domestic workers in Singapore use TikTok to resist soft violence, economic indenture, and commercial erasure. They critically evaluate TikTok for social justice, challenging assumptions about creators and users, while examining how platform business models both support and repress subaltern communities.

In "Media and Mental Health Interventions Among Migrants: Addressing the Disparities" (Chapter 23), Rukhsana Ahmed and Seulgi Park highlight the effectiveness of media- and technology-based mental health interventions in improving mental health outcomes among migrant groups. Similarly, Chapter 24, "Health Media Activism: Latin American Organizing in Response to Feminicides" by Leandra Hinojosa Hernández, draws our attention to feminicides—the murder of women because of their gender—and explores the ways in which Latin American activists have employed digital interactivity and hashtag feminism to respond to this violence. Relatedly, Kelly Merrill Jr.'s chapter, "Using Artificial Intelligence to Address Health Disparities: Challenges and Solutions" (Chapter 25), discusses the role that AI has played in perpetuating discrimination in health care and explores the role of AI in addressing health disparities, focusing on accessibility, usability, algorithmic bias, privacy, and trust.

The remaining chapters illustrate the ways in which marginalized, muted, and oppressed communities throughout the world use media platforms as subversive tools of resistance. In Chapter 26, "Pedagogies of Resistance: Social Movements and the Construction of Communicative Knowledge in Brazil," Paola Sartoretto provides a historical perspective on communication's role in political resistance throughout different political eras in Brazil. Social movements have strategically employed communication technologies, becoming both political actors and media activists. The next chapter illustrates the way pedagogy can operate at an institutional level. In "Emboldening Democratic Pedagogies About Media and Justice Through Critical Media Literacy and Peer Teaching" (Chapter 27), Andrea Gambino and Jeff Share detail their experiences teaching critical media literacy during the pandemic, emphasizing critical awareness, skills, and disposition. Students were encouraged to design and facilitate lessons, fostering critical media analysis and action. The authors found that incorporating peer teaching with critical media literacy offers opportunities for improved learning and teaching for social and environmental justice, both online and in-person.

Two subsequent chapters discuss the weaponization of various platforms for resistance. Chapter 28, "Alternative Cultures of Resistance and Collective Organizing in the Platform Economy" by Cheryll Ruth R. Soriano, examines the collective resistance emerging from digital labor platform workers in the Philippines. In Chapter 29, "LGBT Activism, Social Media, and the Politics of Queer Visibility in Ghana," Godfried A. Asante, Wunpini Fatima Mohammed, and Ama Boatemaa Appiah-Kubi explore how Ghanaian activists in the LGBT community use social media to navigate the tensions between political visibility and personal safety.

The following chapters focus on how Indigenous communities in South Asia and Australia leverage media for social justice. Uttaran Dutta, in "Indigenous Environmental Media Activism in South Asia" (Chapter 30), explores environmental activism among Indigenous communities, spanning nonmediated and mediated spaces. In Chapter 31, "Indigenous Media Organizing," Mohan J. Dutta and Christine Ngā Hau Elers explore the nature of Indigenous media as spaces of raising claims to social justice from the framework of Indigenous rights.

In Section V, Conclusion, we offer our concluding thoughts for reflection. By no means do we intend to offer solutions to the crises that plague our world. Instead, we aim to offer food for thought, in hopes that our ruminations about these issues, coupled with our skills as scholars and compassion as activists, might shift our theorizing, explorations, publications, and prescriptions of our social problems. We hope that these intellectual shifts might lead to more nuanced discourse that engages questions of positionality, power, and agency in ways that subvert dominant ways of knowing, understanding, and, therefore, being.

Social Justice Research: A Network of Mutuality

The work of social justice is collaborative and requires participation from a wide range of positionalities, and as such this handbook includes work from various authors from different paradigms and perspectives. As noted by the late Dr. Martin Luther King, Jr. in his widely published open letter "Injustice anywhere is a threat to justice everywhere. We are caught in an inescapable network of mutuality, tied in a single garment of destiny. Whatever affects one directly, affects all indirectly" (King, 1963). The questions of injustice cover a host of communities, from minoritized ethnic identity to muted queer identities and marginalized socioeconomic groups. These questions also extend to women, religious communities, persons with disability, and any other members of our society who have been systemically disempowered. Our work as media scholars is to uncover these issues and identify the ways the media can be used as a tool to enact justice and empower communities. Each of the contributors to this volume demonstrates the importance of this work and models for us the multiple ways we can engage questions of injustice to all communities threatened by abuses of power.

As you review each chapter, we hope first that this work can cultivate compassion, as "an absence of compassion can corrupt the decency of a community, a state, a nation" (Stevenson, 2015, p. 18). Second, as scholars, we hope that you will be inspired and motivated to re-envision media scholarship in ways that not only explore intellectual curiosities but also consider the agency of your population of interest as significant to the narratives we tell with our research. We acknowledge that this work is not easy. Writer Iejomua Oluo suggests that real change is impossible until "we identify where our privilege intersects with somebody else's oppression" (Oluo, 2018, p. 65). We contend that the work of self-reflection and reflexivity, the work of theoretical elaboration, and the work of methodological flexibility is not easy, but it is certainly necessary. It is necessary for our discussions about these difficult situations, and it is necessary for how we help others understand the nuances of the social problems we face. We may not be able to eradicate our social ills, but with what power we have as educators, researchers, and storytellers, we can significantly impact the narratives that shape reality. We invite you to consider the possibilities that await.

References

King Jr, M. L. (1963). Letter from Birmingham Jail (1963). *Martin Luther King Jr., Malcolm X, and the Civil Rights Struggle of the 1950s and 1960s: A Brief History with Documents.* Retrieved on June 9, 2024 from https://mrwaddell.com/files/apgletter.pdf.

Oluo, I. (2018). *So you want to talk about race.* Seal Press.

Ramasubramanian, S., & Banjo, O. (2020). Critical media effects framework: Bridging critical cultural communication and media effects through power, intersectionality, context, and agency, *Journal of Communication, 70*(3), 379–400. doi:10.1093/joc/jqaa014

Scharrer, E., & Ramasubramanian, S. (2021). *Quantitative research methods in communication: The power of numbers for social justice.* Routledge.

Stevenson, B. (2015). *Just mercy. A story of justice and redemption.* Spiegel & Grau.

Approaches and Analytic Frameworks

Political Economy of Communication in the Digital Platform Era

Dal Yong Jin

Political economy of communication, primarily referring to the relationship between communication systems and the broader social structure of society, particularly capitalism (Jin, 2019), has been one of the significant perspectives in communication studies. In the early 21st century, people throughout the world heavily rely on media and communication, from news to entertainment to digital culture, and political economy focuses on the increasing role of media and communication in people's daily lives. Given the continuing emergence of digital media technology and its role as a critical component of economic, social, and cultural development (Wasko, 2018), the study of political economy of communication has grown a great deal. Political economy of media produced numerous important critiques of the ways in which media were entangled with state and business power in capitalist societies (Hesmondhalgh, 2017).

Political economy of media and communication can generally be traced back to the early 1920s and the Frankfurt School. The fleeing of several Frankfurt School members to the United States in the 1920 and 1930s became a critical historical juncture to academically connect Europe and North America (Babe, 2009; Jin, 2018). Scholars in this tradition attempt to analyze the production, distribution, and consumption of media resources with a primary focus on ownership and power relations (Fuchs & Mosco, 2016; Jin, 2018; McChesney, 2008; Mosco, 2009; Wasko et al., 2011; Winseck & Jin, 2011). Inspired by Marx's ideas of viewing capitalism as an unjust system, political economy focuses on media biases and how they affect the collective consciousness of people throughout the world. "The subject of a critique of the political economy is the critical theory-based empirical analysis of capitalism" (Knoche, 2021, p. 328).

Since the mid-20th century, traditional media, such as newspapers, broadcasting, and film, have become significant in people's daily activities. As McChesney (2008) aptly stated, "Political economists of media do not believe the existing media system is natural or inevitable to change. They believe the media system is the result of policies made in the public's name but often without the public's informed consent" (p. 12). In particular, as the media and technology industries have expanded during the past two decades, scholarship on these industries has similarly proliferated and engaged with the evolving economic, social, and cultural conditions of media work. Many scholars have revisited Karl Marx's readings, reassessing his foundational ideas about topics such as exploitation, necessary labor time, and surplus labor time in light of the expansion of social media platforms, digitally networked technologies, and new professional identities (Dyer-Witheford & de Peuter, 2009; Fuchs, 2014; Holt & Perren, 2019).

Political economy continues to critique modern capitalism. This crucial tradition has had a significant impact on research in media and communication because "the media industries play a central role in modern societies, as industries in their own right and as the major site of the representations and arenas of debate through which the overall system is imagined and argued over" (Wasko et al., 2011, p. 2). What is essential is that the political economy of media and communication is deeply related to digital media and the platform technologies-driven new media, which are the significant parts of modern capitalism.

Because the political economy of media started with the cultural industry and relevant government policy, this chapter identifies the change and continuity in the cultural sector toward an understanding of information and communication technologies and/or the digital media-driven communication environment. As political economy analyzes the power relationships between politics and economics, it discusses the shifting power (im)balances within the broader society and its media environment. It critically and historically discusses the shifting media ecology within which digital platforms play a vital role in the early 21st century.

Genealogy of Political Economy of Media

Leading political economists of media describe the basic epistemological and ontological principles of political economy through a few primary dimensions: history, social totality, moral philosophy, and social praxis. First, political economy prioritizes understanding social change and historical transformation. Political economists, including Karl Marx, have examined "the dynamic forces in capitalism responsible for its growth and change" (Mosco, 2009, p. 26). Second, political economy maintains that "the discipline should be firmly rooted in an analysis of the wider social totality. This means that political economy spans the range of problems," including social class, media policy, and market economy (Mosco, 2009, p. 28). Third, political economy highlights ethical and normative inquiries (McChesney, 1999; Mosco, 2009; Winseck & Jin, 2011). In other words, political economy commits to moral philosophy. It explicitly raises basic moral questions such as justice, equity, fairness, and public good (Golding & Murdock, 1991; Wasko et al., 2011). Fourth, political economy believes in social praxis, which is "an idea with deep roots in the history of philosophy and one which has found several paths to communication studies, including Marxian theory, the Frankfurt School of critical thought, and the action-research tradition best embodied in sociology" (Mosco, 2009, p. 34).

Among these, *moral philosophy* has been significant because it is closely related to our primary value of social justice. As Mosco (2009) notes,

> Moral philosophy refers to social values and conceptions of appropriate social practices. The goal of this particular form of analysis is to clarify and make explicit the moral positions of economic and political economic perspectives, particularly because moral viewpoints are often masked in these perspectives. (p. 32)

Moral philosophy in tandem with a moral economy approach is

> strongly normative—they seek not only to identify moral principles but also to make informed judgments about what is good and bad, right and wrong, just and unjust, exploitative and non-exploitative and so on in the realm of economic life. (Hesmondhalgh, 2017, p. 207)

The emphasis on the normative does not mean that moral economy should ignore empirical approaches:

> From a methodological point of view, it must be stressed that the studies under the political economy umbrella combine theoretical elaboration and empirical observation. The two components are indispensable, and theoretical reflexivity is regularly accompanied by field surveys, which explains the importance afforded to the social sciences. . . . Such a broad perspective clearly distinguishes political economy from many other academic approaches and particularly from the work of media professionals or publicists. (Miège, 2019, pp. 74–75)

Returning to the moral philosophy discussion, it is clear that

> a moral economy approach can be seen as a contribution to political economy, rather than as an attempt to supersede it. Moral economy can serve to develop a more adequate and nuanced political economy by exploring normative questions that are often repressed. (Hesmondhalgh, 2017, p. 207)

These concerns are ideal for analysis through the *critical political economy framework*, which

> seeks to understand not just the nature of the various industries involved but also insists on seeing them in their relevant historical and social contexts. As such, political economy begins with the recognition that there are not merely economic concerns but political and moral concerns as well. (Nichols & Martinez, 2019, pp. 1–2)

The political economy of communication is interested in not only understanding the production and distribution of media content but also how we might resist the problems presented by the capitalist control of media and communication (Garnham, 2000; Mosco, 2009; Nichols & Martinez, 2019). Critical political economy is broadly concerned with power relations in society (Mosco, 2009). "Each of these impacts has become a crucial focus of examination for critical political economists because they represent key power relationships, both within particular industries, between industries, and between those industries and institutions and the broader public" (Nichols & Martinez, 2019, p. 2).

Major Approaches to the Political Economy of Communication

There are numerous focuses of interest in the political economy tradition, and political economists emphasize a few subjects that have fallen under various rubrics, including neoliberalism, the transformation of the contemporary media industry in tandem with capitalism, globalization, ownership concentration, communication policy, media industry studies, production studies, and creative industries. In the early 21st century, there have been various approaches to the political economy of media and communication; however, a few approaches are outstanding. To begin with, radical political economies have been influential. In North America, the contemporary origin of the critical political economy of media coincided with two prominent political economists. One is Dallas Smythe (1981), who developed *audience commodity theory*: The economic relationship, which is the primary driver of media as an industry, is one whereby audiences—or specifically the attentive capacities of audiences—are sold to advertisers. The other is Herbert Schiller (1969, 1992), who advanced *cultural imperialism theory*, emphasizing the one-way flow of cultural content from the West to the East, particularly from the United States to other countries, which expanded and maintained the asymmetrical economic, political, and cultural power relations between the United States and other countries.

Later, between the end of the 20th century and the early 21st century, two theoretical frameworks emerged under the umbrella of critical political economy. On the one hand, there is a *monopoly capital school*, with media scholar Robert McChesney (1999) stressing the public good characteristics of journalism and media goods more than neoclassical economists (Winseck, 2011). On the other hand, there is a *digital capitalism approach* that Dan Schiller (2000, 2023) mainly developed. He stated that networks are "directly generalizing the social and cultural range of the capitalist economy as never before" (Schiller, 2000, p. xiv). The critical traditions of research on digital technologies ask people to think about how "asymmetrical power relations that may appear to be locked into a particular pathway are, in fact, contingent and subject to alteration" (Mansell, 2017, p. 4298). This particular approach is relevant to our contemporary media environment as artificial intelligence (AI), digital platforms, and social media, as well as their implications for individuals and society, are increasing.

Most of all, the capitalization of the cultural and media industry is of growing importance for the entire economy and society as a whole because it also has an essential function in people's lives and the national economy, including the digital economy with the growth of new media industries (Knoche, 2021). While information and communication

> play an increasing role in world trade to the benefit of mainly American companies and firms (notably the Big Five: Facebook, Apple, Alphabet, Microsoft, and Amazon), this tendency, incontestably, is accompanied by what must be regarded as a marked evolution towards a multi-polarization of the world, initiated especially by the BRIC countries (Brazil, Russia, India, and China). (Miège, 2019, p. 74)

Indeed, one of the most decisive phenomena has been the rapid rise of digital technology since the early 21st century. Several digital platforms, including Apple, Alphabet, Facebook (now Meta), and Netflix, have become dominant players in many parts of the global economy. "The power of these platforms does not come from their intervention in production itself, but from their continuous and unrestrained action in the measurement of audiences, ranking of preferences, construction of reputations, and predictive analytics" (Miège, 2019, p. 80). Therefore, it is crucial to pay attention

> to the evolution of the platforms as well as the overall platform economy that is emerging online. In response to the data-driven global strategies of these information and communication giants—a process considered to be part of informational–communicational capitalism—we can expect profound changes in the capitalization of culture and media. (Miège, 2019, p. 80)

Political Economies of the Media in the Digital Platform Era

In the 21st century, political economy of communication has emphasized the significant role of digital platforms in our contemporary capitalist society. As well documented, platform studies have grown in scope and substance in the past decade, connected to much of the work in distribution studies. The role of digital platforms, big data, AI, and algorithms has come to "define much of the industry's digital distribution strategies during this time" (Holt & Perren, 2019, p. 36). Political economy of the media in the 2020s must pay attention to these new fields of study because they are not only providing new looks toward our understanding of digital media but also developing new capitalism based on the monopolistic concentration of ownership and therefore capital accumulation in their hands (Jin, 2018). Scholars in this area have also used their work to interrogate the sovereignty, values, and source of control and power in our digital culture represented by big data, AI, and algorithms (Holt & Perren, 2019). A few non-Western countries have developed their own platforms and relevant digital cultures; however, these non-Western countries have not constructed a balanced global order. The asymmetrical relationship in platform technologies between the United States and developing countries has consequently intensified. Western-based mega-digital platforms monopolize capital gains, and only a few U.S. platform owners enjoy benefits, resulting in the expansion of the global divide (Jin, 2015).

Under this circumstance, three significant new approaches—known as platform imperialism theory, platform capitalism theory, and platformization theory—have emerged during the past 10 years. Among these, *platform imperialism* (Jin, 2013, 2015; Steinberg, 2017), which was introduced in the early 2010s, mainly emphasizes an asymmetrical relationship of interdependence between the West, primarily the United States, and many developing countries, characterized in part by unequal technological exchanges and therefore capital flows, which implies technological and symbolic domination of U.S.-based platforms that have greatly influenced the majority of people and countries. *Platform capitalism*, introduced by Srnicek (2016), shows how the fundamental foundations of the economy are rapidly being carved up among a small number of monopolistic platforms and how the platform introduces new tendencies within capitalism that pose significant challenges to any vision of a postcapitalist future. *Platformization*, mainly introduced by Helmond (2015) and developed by Nieborg and Poell (2018; Nieborg et al., 2019), focuses on the rise of the platform as the dominant infrastructural and economic model of the social web and its consequences. Platformization affects the production and circulation of cultural content, media ecology in terms of structural changes in contemporary society, and business models utilized by companies and other social actors that create, control, and use various platforms.

Contemporary political economy research uses theories of *digital labor* to highlight an issue of communicative power, as digital media firms "generate revenue from their power over the activity of their users" (Nixon, 2017, p. 4718). Here, the concept of an *attention economy* (Goldhaber, 1997, 2006) highlights audiences and the value of audience activities of paying attention to communication industries. The concept of audience labor comes from Smythe's (1981) *theory of the audience commodity*, which views audience activities of paying attention and making meaning as labor that is valuable to communication industries (Nixon, 2017). Research using theories of digital labor has focused on how digital platforms treat digital media as valuable labor (Andrejevic, 2007; Fuchs, 2012; Terranova, 2000), although moving audiences to the center of political economy research is still limited.

The commercialization of platform users has raised serious concerns because only a handful of platform owners dominate the global platform markets. Platforms are not only gathering information from the massively increasing number of users but also commercializing user information as a commodity, resulting in capital gains for platform owners in the West (Jin, 2015). Digital platforms, big data, and users are deeply connected, which has fundamentally changed the media ecology in the early 21st century.

Conclusion

Political economy has been ignored in several countries, including Asian and Northern European countries, regardless of its increasing role in understanding shifting media ecology in recent years. There are various elements to explain the lack of political economy research. On the one hand, social scientists in the field of communication tend to resist critical approaches because they focus on generating quantitative data instead of questioning ideological assumptions. They also tend to discount historical analyses. Their research designs tend to obscure society's macro-level power relations. On the other hand, economic elites, including media owners, are to keep their power and possessions. Analyses critical of private ownership are marginalized (Bergman, 2020, pp. 107–108).

However, political economy in the era of digital platforms has continued as the most significant theoretical and methodological framework in understanding contemporary capitalist media systems. Political economy asks people to think about several primary dimensions, such as inequality, asymmetrical power relations, and skewed ownership, which influence not only cultural content but also people's daily lives. In the early 21st century, political economy has become even more useful than in any other era because digital platforms have played a primary role in intensifying the current imbalances between the platform-haves and the platform-have-nots. Our modern capitalism relies on digital platforms as new engines for the global economy and cultures; however, the skewed structure has intensified, implying that a handful of platform owners, both domestically and globally, garner profits. The current milieu surrounding media ecology demands us to historically and systematically analyze the trend (Jin,

2018). Digital technologies, including AI, big data, and algorithms, will "continue to expand in multiple areas and continue to create struggles and contradictions between human values, judgments and corporate control and dominance" (Bilić, 2018, p. 329).

Contemporary political economy has to comprehend the complex connectivity among digital platforms owned by media giants, big data produced by user activities, and the customers as digital labor, as the capitalization process in digital platforms focuses on immaterial user activities (Jin, 2018, 2019). It does not mean that political economy gives up its analysis of traditional media; instead, what I am emphasizing is that the convergence of traditional media and new media has become a norm in the global media markets, and therefore, it is vital to analyze the power relations between digital platforms as part of the global media system, which also includes the traditional media, and the broader social milieu surrounding the continuity and change in the media and communication sector.

References

Andrejevic, M. (2007). Surveillance in the digital enclosure. *The Communication Review*, *10*(4), 295–317.

Babe, R. (2009). *Cultural studies and political economy: Toward a new integration*. Lexington Books.

Bergman, T. (2020). Extreme moderation? Critical political economy as the blindspot of Dutch journalism studies. *Democratic Communiqué*, *29*(1), 97–115.

Bilić, P. (2018). A critique of the political economy of algorithms: A brief history of Google's technological rationality. *tripleC: Communication, Capitalism & Critique*, *16*(1), 315–331.

Dyer-Witheford, N., & de Peuter, G. (2009). *Games of empire: Global capitalism and video games*. University of Minnesota Press.

Fuchs, C. (2012). Dallas Smythe today—The audience commodity, the digital labor debate, Marxist political economy and critical theory: Prolegomena to a digital labour theory of value. *tripleC: Communication, Capitalism & Critique*, *10*(2), 692–740.

Fuchs, C. (2014). *Social media: A critical introduction*. Sage.

Fuchs, C., & Mosco, V. (Eds.). (2016). *Marx and the political economy of the media: Studies in critical social sciences*. Brill.

Garnham, N. (2000). *Emancipation, the media, and modernity*. Oxford University Press.

Goldhaber, M. (1997). The attention economy and the net. *First Monday*, *2*(4). https://firstmonday.org/ojs/index.php/fm/article/view/519

Goldhaber, M. (2006). The value of openness in an attention economy. *First Monday*, *11*(6). https://doi.org/10.5210/fm.v11i6.1334

Golding, P., & Murdock, G. (1991). Culture, communications and political economy. In J. Curran & M. Gurevitch (Eds.), *Mass media and society* (pp. 15–32). Arnold.

Helmond, A. (2015). The platformization of the Web: Making Web data platform ready. *Social Media + Society*, *1*(2).

Hesmondhalgh, D. (2017). Capitalism and the media: Moral economy, well-being and capabilities. *Media, Culture & Society*, *39*(2), 202–218.

Holt, J., & Perren, A. (2019). Media industries: A decade in review. In M. Deuze & M. Prenger (Eds.), *Making media: Production, practices, and professions* (pp. 31–44). Amsterdam University Press.

Jin, D. Y. (2013). The construction of platform imperialism in the globalization era. *tripleC: Communication, Capitalism & Critique*, *11*(1), 145–172.

Jin, D. Y. (2015). *Digital platforms, imperialism and political culture*. Routledge.

Jin, D. Y. (2018). Political economy of media. In D. Cloud (Ed.), *Oxford research encyclopedia of communication*. Oxford University Press.

Jin, D. Y. (2019). Political economy of communication. In D. L. Merskin (Ed.), *The SAGE international encyclopedia of mass media and society* (pp. 1374–1375). SAGE.

Knoche, M. (2021). Capitalisation of the media industry from a political economy perspective. *tripleC: Communication, Capitalism & Critique*, *19*(2), 325–342.

Mansell, R. (2017). The mediation of hope: Communication technologies and inequality in perspective. *International Journal of Communication*, *11*, 4285–4304.

McChesney, R. (1999). *Rich media, poor democracy: Communication politics in dubious times*. The New Press.

McChesney, R. (2008). *The political economy of media: Enduring issues, emerging dilemmas*. Monthly Review Press.

Miège, B. (2019). Cultural and creative industries and the political economy of communication. In M. Deuze & M. Prenger (Eds.), *Making media: Production, practices, and professions* (pp. 73–84). Amsterdam University Press.

Mosco, V. (2009). *Political economy of communication* (2nd ed.). SAGE.

Nichols, R., & Martinez, G. (2019). Introduction. In R. Nichols & G. Martinez (Eds.), *Political economy of media industries: Global transformations and challenges* (pp. 1–6). Routledge.

Nieborg, D., Poell, T., & Deuze, M. (2019). The platformization of making media. In M. Deuze & M. Prenger (Eds.), *Making media: Production, practices, and professions* (pp. 85–96). Amsterdam University Press.

Nieborg, D. B., & Poell, T. (2018). The platformization of cultural production: Theorizing the contingent cultural commodity. *New Media & Society, 20*(11), 4275–4292.

Nixon, B. (2017). Critical communication policy research and the attention economy: From digital labor theory to digital class struggle. *International Journal of Communication, 17*, 4718–4730.

Schiller, D. (2000). *Digital capitalism*. MIT Press.

Schiller, D. (2023). *Crossed wires: The conflicted history of US telecommunications, from the post office to the internet*. Oxford University Press.

Schiller, H. (1969). *Mass communication and American empire*. Beacon.

Schiller, H. (1992). *Mass communications and American empire* (2nd ed.). Westview.

Smythe, D. W. (1981). *Dependency road: Communications, capitalism, consciousness and Canada*. Abex.

Srnicek, N. (2016). *Platform capitalism*. Polity.

Steinberg, M. (2017). Genesis of the platform concept: iMode and platform theory in Japan. *Asiascape: Digital Asia, 4*(3), 184–208.

Terranova, T. (2000). Free labor: Producing culture for the digital economy. *Social Text, 63*, 33–58.

Wasko, J. (2018). Studying political economies of communication in the twenty-first century. *Javnost–The Public, 25*(1–2), 233–239.

Wasko, J., Murdock, G., & Sousa, H. (2011). Introduction: The political economy of communications core concerns and issues. In J. Wasko, G. Murdock, & H. Sousa (Eds.), *The handbook of political economy of communications* (pp. 1–10). Wiley-Blackwell.

Winseck, D. (2011). The political economies of media and the transformation of the global media industries. In D. Winseck & D. Y. Jin (Eds.), *The political economies of media: The transformation of the global media industries* (pp. 3–48). Bloomsbury.

Winseck, D., & Jin, D. Y. (Eds.). (2011). *The political economies of media: The transformation of the global media industries*. Bloomsbury.

The Limits of Diversity and Popular Anti-Racism: The Need for Reparative Justice in the Cultural Industries

Anamik Saha

In the contemporary moment, mainstream approaches to tackling racial inequalities in media and cultural industries in the West are conducted in terms of "diversity." In these contexts, there is a recognition that cultural industries lack racial and ethnic diversity on- and off-screen. But to what extent does diversity—whether in terms of attempts at more inclusive hiring processes, employing color-blind casting, or simply ensuring that a production contains a range of people from different racialized/ethnicized backgrounds—actually attend to the entrenched nature of racism that continues to scar cultural industries and cultural production?

In this chapter, I consider the limits of the diversity approach as a form of social justice in the context of *cultural industries* (defined as industries invested in the making and selling of cultural commodities, including film, television, music publishing, and the arts). It builds on critiques of diversity that expose how diversity itself, when operationalized, is the very source of racial inequality in media. I show how diversity is the means through which the dominant culture—that is, the White, middle-class men who have historically owned and profited the most from the cultural industries—appears to accommodate the demands of minoritized groups while protecting its own status and privilege. A particular focus of this chapter is a consideration of "popular" anti-racist activism—especially as mobilized by audiences and cultural producers (those involved in the making of cultural commodities) on social media—that places a great onus on the representation and visibility of marginalized groups in the cultural industries in the name of social justice. I argue that although representation matters, treating it as the end goal will do little for racialized people who work in the media.

The chapter is divided into three parts. First, it provides an outline of diversity, its roots as formal policy, and how it is typically mobilized in cultural industries. I then highlight the limits of the diversity approach. The focus here is on what diversity *is doing* inside cultural industries but also in the context of popular anti-racist online activism. To conclude the chapter, I propose a notion of *reparative justice* as a more radical alternative to diversity. In contrast to the *soft accommodationist approach* of diversity, reparative justice demands structural change—that is, interventions focused on the level of political economy. The main purpose of the chapter is to highlight how the diversity approach is the problem itself, preventing the radical transformation of the cultural industries needed to make it, at the very least, more egalitarian.

Diversity in the Cultural Industries

Diversity is the dominant paradigm that shapes how mainstream media attempts to tackle the issue of inequalities in contemporary times. Although diversity speaks to a range of social inequalities, including in relation to class, disability, gender, and sexuality, this chapter focuses on racial and ethnic diversity in the cultural industries. It is perhaps because racial inequality feels so stark in the media that the commonsense understanding of diversity is often in relation to race.

"Diversity" normatively refers to the problem, but it also describes a type of approach. Diversity as a problem refers to the lack of people from racialized backgrounds who work in the cultural industries and who appear in media content. In an analysis of a UK workforce survey, social researchers Orien Brook, Dave O'Brien, and Mark Taylor (2020) show how little racial diversity there is across the media, with White people making up 95% of the publishing industry and 91% of the film, television, video, and radio sectors compared to 87% of the entire workforce (pp. 60–61). They also find that the percentage of racial/ethnic diversity decreases significantly at the executive level. But although these issues were once invisible, there is increasing public awareness around the problem of diversity, not least due to the media. A steady stream of industry reports published every year,[1] in addition to regular media controversies including faux pas from privileged White celebrities, has meant that the lack of diversity in the cultural industries has become popular content in itself, generating mainstream news coverage as well as intense discussion on social media, a theme I explore in the following section.

Diversity as an approach, specifically in the context of British cultural policy, stems from British Prime Minister Tony Blair's "New Labour" government and its "creative industries" policy from the early 2000s (Nwonka & Malik, 2018). In this moment, *creative industries*—conceived as any industry involving creativity, from film production to advertising to tech—were imagined as the new economic core of postindustrial Britain and, crucially, a way to address social issues and problems. Creative industries were seen to be more open and meritocratic than other economic sectors, and therefore an important site for marginalized groups to gain social, cultural, as well as economic capital (Oakley, 2004). Moreover, such industries encourage the creation of new creative hubs and cultural quarters often located in deprived inner-city areas, bringing in capital and work opportunities for the poorer migrant communities that have historically lived in these areas (Nava, 2023). In this regard, the creative industries were part of New Labour's new vision of Britain as modern, innovative, and economically prosperous. And diversity became a central tenet in creative industries policy, seen as the key driver of both economic growth and social cohesion.

New Labour's creative industries policy, and with it the emphasis on diversity, has been shaped by, as well as influenced cultural policy in a number of international contexts, including in Australia, South Korea, Jamaica, and South Africa (De Beukelaer & Spence, 2018). We have reached the point that diversity no longer just refers to a specific policy approach; instead, it has become the very language that cultural industries use to describe attempts to make media more representative of a population and, perhaps more important, more attractive to potentially lucrative international audiences. Initiatives conducted in the name of diversity include *soft forms of positive action*, including setting (nonenforceable) recruitment targets, hiring drives, and training schemes and work placements specifically for those from marginalized backgrounds. In terms of media content, media corporations privately run their own audits of the representation of diverse groups in the cultural commodities that they produce. Returning to the issue of social justice, this can feel like progress, a shift from a time when the media cared little about minority groups and whether they were being catered for or not. Although the following section complicates this account, for now I note that diversity has become the dominant paradigm for tackling racial inequalities in the cultural industries. Moreover, in contemporary times, the representation of race in media—or what Herman Gray (2016) calls

---

[1] As one of the most well-known examples, the USC Annenberg Inclusion Initiative has been producing regular reports on the state of diversity (across age, disability, gender, race, and sexuality) in American entertainment since 2007.

"race-making practices" (p. 249)—is formed according to the logics of diversity, which is having a profound effect on the media that we consume.

The Limits of Diversity as a Form of Social Justice

As alluded to previously, in recent times, academic researchers have questioned diversity policy and practices and their ability to meaningfully attend to racial inequalities inside media and cultural industries. The critique has mostly focused on the cultural industries' operationalization of diversity, which is outlined later. But in this section, I also address a less commented-upon issue—the politics of diversity as mobilized by activists, primarily on social media.

The immediate issue with diversity as an approach is that, in the United Kingdom at least, it has not led to increased participation from racialized groups (Brook et al., 2020). Whereas more policy-orientated critiques have focused on diversity initiatives and how and why they are failing, critical media and communication scholarship has drawn attention to how diversity itself—as a discourse—is the very source of racial inequality in cultural industries. This is the argument of Herman Gray (2016), who describes diversity as a "technology of power, a means of managing the very difference it expresses" (p. 242). Similarly, Clive Nwonka (2020), who has offered one of the most robust critiques of diversity in his research on UK film policy, describes diversity as containing a paradoxical quality for the way that it "represents aspirations for inclusion but also demonstrates a reluctance to take responsibility for the existing exclusion" (p. 26). The point here is that diversity is the way that the dominant culture addresses the demands of minoritized groups, but specifically in a way that maintains the dominant culture's status and privilege (Saha, 2018).

One way that diversity as discourse serves the dominant culture in this way is by changing the terms within which inequality is addressed. As the previous quote from Nwonka (2020) alludes to, the language of diversity—especially the emphasis on its economic value—in effect buries the history of racism that structures social institutions in the West, including media. In essence, the language of diversity produces a "race-blind" (Balfour, 2005, p. 802) vision of society, which in turn is blind to racism. To reiterate, addressing diversity purely in economic terms effectively removes from the agenda the issue of racism that causes the literal problem of diversity in the first instance.

This leads to the second problem with diversity: the way it is understood as a statistical problem to fix. More precisely, diversity is conceptualized—either explicitly or implicitly—in terms of attaining some sort of racial parity with the wider population. Gray (2016) critically examines the assumption around media diversity that representation is linked to the demography of the nation—an assumption that undergirds both cultural industries and academic/policy research approaches to diversity. The logic of this assumption states that, for example, if the population of Black people in a particular city is 20%, then Black journalists should make up 20% of the regional newsroom in question. The problem for Gray is that formulating diversity in this way simply entails the insertion of Black bodies in a production context, without addressing how production itself harms racialized groups and prevents them from intervening in the production of reductive racialized tropes, which is another form of racial harm felt by racialized groups more broadly. I return to this issue in the following section. For now, I flag one key theme in the critical scholarship on diversity, on how content-based diversity initiatives, such as color-blind casting in a period drama, or discreetly ensuring diversity in the lineup of contestants on a reality television show, produce a spurious post-racial vision of the world (Littler, 2017; Warner, 2015) in which an individual's racial identity is more likely to be linked to a particular lifestyle or market niche, rather than to a subject position within a historical system of domination (Gray, 2013).

Yet as much as diversity acts as a form of racial governance, it also has a threatening, destabilizing quality. After all, the emphasis on diversity within cultural industries (at times bordering on obsession) is often the direct consequence of critiques from audiences and activists over the cultural industries' institutional Whiteness (Saha & van Lente, 2022). Jo Littler (2017) describes this mobilization as a form of *popular* anti-racism. This notion features in Littler's analysis of the controversy surrounding White Hollywood actor Matt Damon on the reality television show *Project Greenlight* in which Damon interrupts, speaks over, and contradicts Black director Effie Brown, who is making a point about the importance of diversity. The specific subject of Littler's account is the subsequent mocking of Damon on social media through the hashtag #damonsplaining (a play on "#mansplaining"), which led to a flood of memes and satirical tweets. As Littler states, "The rise in popular feminist and anti-racist activisms, combined with expanding publicity of the dramatic exclusions of the media industries, provided a very fertile context for the incident to be satirized" (p. 148). In this quote, there is a reference to the earlier point on how the subject of the lack of diversity in media has become media content in itself. But of interest here is Littler reference to "popular" versions of feminist and anti-racist activism. Although it is not spelled out by Littler in this context, I define popular anti-racism as a form of activism that identifies visibility and representation in media as an important goal of social justice.

The idea of authentic racial representation as an important component of social justice is a product of the civil rights movement in the United States, and it has spread throughout other Western nations. To repeat, this is based on the acknowledgment that Western media has historically enacted symbolic violence toward racialized Others and other marginalized groups, a fact that needs to be addressed as part of anti-racist struggle (Quinn, 2012). But although it feels like common sense that the representation of minoritized groups is a matter of social justice, are there limits to an approach that, if it does not use the language of diversity directly, certainly feeds into it? At the very least, the popular anti-racism I am referring to, nearly exclusively activated on social media, puts a strong onus on the visibility of marginalized groups as well as the accuracy of their portrayal, which are the terms upon which cultural industries are held to account, and which in turn lead to the initiatives implemented in the terms of diversity. For instance, the trending of #oscarssowhite on social media in 2015, one of the most famous examples of activism that calls out racial injustice in the cultural industries, spawned similar hashtag movements in contexts beyond Hollywood and even the cultural industries (Chakravartty et al., 2018). But the question again is, To what extent does a politics based on visibility—as a facet of diversity—encourage tokenism, rather than really attend to the real structural problems of racism in the cultural industries? In the year following the #oscarssowhite controversy, the Academy awarded the Best Film Oscar to the film *Moonlight* directed by a Black director and featuring an entirely Black cast, which would be considered a victory for the anti-racist movement. But as a recent Annenberg Inclusion Initiative (2020) study finds, "there has been no meaningful increase in Black, Hispanic/Latino, or Asian characters" (p. 3) since then.

A significant part of the issue, as alluded to previously, is how this particular type of anti-racist activism unfolds nearly entirely on social media. These online discussions seemingly go on forever on Twitter feeds and comment threads, such that it is often not possible to find the instigating post. A recent example in the United Kingdom is the treatment of Meghan Markle by the British press and the extent to which it is racist or not. A clip from the BBC news debate show *Question Time* featuring an argument between reactionary White celebrity Lawrence Fox and an audience member (who it transpires is an academic) on whether Markle is the victim of racism is posted on social media, causing a flood of commentary and counter-commentary. As

Gavan Titley (2019) argues, the big tech companies that own these platforms profit from the discussion on the politics of representation precisely in this way, for how it, in effect, generates big data on the users involved, where a profile can be created on a user through their engagement, which is then sold to advertisers. What Titley calls the "debatability of racism" (p. 2)—a feature of *postracial politics* (the belief that society has overcome racism)—has taken on a commodity form in the era of platform capitalism.

My concern is that popular anti-racism in relation to media, despite its legitimate concerns that the cultural industries are a source of racial inequality in society, is falling some way short in addressing these inequalities. The terms of recognition, visibility, and accuracy upon which the cultural politics of diversity are founded, as Gray (2013) states, fail to address the (real) "struggle to rearticulate and restructure the social, economic, and cultural basis of a collective disadvantage" (p. 772). In other words, attending to race, media, and social justice demands more radical steps that transcend simplistic pushes for visibility and more accurate portrayals of racialized groups in the name of diversity. To end this chapter, I imagine some of these more radical strategies, conceptualized in the name of reparative justice.

From Diversity to Reparative Justice

To reiterate, when it comes to the ongoing racial inequalities that characterize cultural industries in the West, the problem is *not* that diversity initiatives are failing. Rather, the operationalization of diversity is the problem. Diversity as mobilized inside media is seen only as an additional extra—literally adding color to the existing makeup of an organization rather than a transformation of that organization and its work practices. As I have argued, diversity effectively smothers the language of "racism" or even just "racial inequality." I make this argument without wanting to disparage or undermine the practitioners who are working within the paradigm of diversity, equality. and inclusion, who are trying to formulate and apply more radical measures in those terms. Nonetheless, my argument is how it is the language of diversity itself that is the problem and prevents any meaningful change in media and. indeed, all other sectors in which diversity discourse is dominant.

Although my main purpose was to draw attention to the limitations of diversity as operationalized inside the cultural industries and in popular anti-racist activism, to end this chapter, I briefly discuss strategies that I argue offer a more radical approach to fixing racial inequalities in the cultural industries. In doing so, I propose a notion of *reparative justice* to be applied to media. This in turn is shaped by a *production studies approach to race* (Hesmondhalgh & Saha, 2013) that emphasizes how the industrialized form of cultural production—that is, how culture is made and sold—is the very source of racial inequalities in media. As such, the strategies outlined here are designed as structural interventions that can transform production cultures inside the cultural industries. They go beyond simplistic calls for "better representations" that can characterize the popular anti-racisms mobilized online, as described in the previous section.

The basis of the reparative justice approach to the cultural industries is the distinction between *reparation* and *reparations*. Whereas reparations refer to direct compensation, reparation is to repair (Hall, 2018). My notion of reparative justice builds on the idea of reparation as repair, for the damage caused by slavery and colonialism—including forms of symbolic violence—that continue to mark the experiences of racialized people who originate from the regions affected by this history. The idea of reparation exposes how the present—and the modern world itself—is shaped by the legacies of empire, including slavery and colonialism (Bhambra et al., 2018). Thus, as its starting point, the idea of reparative justice enables us to have a much more open conversation about racial inequality in the cultural industries and how it is part of a long history that dates back to colonialism. The fundamental idea of reparative justice is that freeing the nation from this history means owning up to and working through that history (Balfour, 2005; Kelley, 2002). Diversity discourse, on the other hand, obfuscates the historical foundation of racial inequalities in contemporary society (in that it is not interested in why and how these inequalities emerge in industries such as media) and in turn allows them to fester.

According to reparative justice, fixing racial inequalities in society demands structural change. In the context of the cultural industries, this involves dispersing concentrations of media power. Across global cultural industries, a handful of media conglomerates dominate television/streaming, film, music, and publishing. Although some racialized people have attained a measure of success inside these corporate contexts—even at times managing to widen the regime of representation—research shows how these spaces are mostly constraining for people of color in particular (for an overview of this research, see Saha, 2018, pp. 158–166). The same research demonstrates how independent forms of media (especially online) are the most fertile for marginalized communities, offering the most creative autonomy, although the overriding theme is on the difficulties in reaching mass audiences (where distribution networks are monopolized by the same big corporations) and the low rewards for labor in independent scenes, apart from a few rare instances (see Saha, 2018, pp. 147–158).

Thus, a reparative justice approach to racial inequalities in the cultural industries, as a first step, contributes to a broader media activist program which calls for more regulation that prevents media concentration (specifically horizontal and vertical forms of integration), challenging the dominance of media corporations. This strategy also involves protecting and producing a more robust and democratic/representative public service media, which are buffered from market pressures (in theory at least) and have a remit to cater for a nation's diverse communities. Although this may seem like a daunting or indeed alien task for grassroot anti-racist activists, there are campaigns such as the Media Reform Coalition in the United Kingdom that work toward this goal and that anti-racist activists can and must contribute to. Second, reparative justice entails a form of economic redress, specifically significant public funds reserved for "minority"-led media production companies to support the making and mounting of their work. Such funding should focus on helping these organizations with audience outreach initiatives. One significant form of inequality in media is how marginalized audiences are undervalued both economically and culturally and are therefore excluded from, for example, book culture, which remains focused on a core, White middle-class reader (Saha & van Lente, 2022).[2] Because the independent media I am referring to are more embedded within their communities, they are the best placed to make media that understands the needs and desires of those communities. A reparative justice program provides the material support to help them with their work.

Conclusion

The main purpose of this chapter is to highlight the limitations of diversity as a form of social justice. This mostly focused on how diversity is operationalized by the dominant culture. I have argued that it is through diversity discourse that the dominant culture maintains its status and privilege while appearing to accommodate minoritized groups. But I also included a critique

---

[2] In another example of the devaluing of marginalized audiences, Krystal Zook (1999) shows how the Fox Network initially employed a strategy of narrowcasting when it first launched to attract Black audiences (who are seen as avid consumers of entertainment) before disregarding them as the channel sought more "mainstream" (i.e., White) audiences.

of how the same discourse shapes popular anti-racist activism invested in issues of media. My argument here is that the emphasis on visibility, diversity, and accuracy fails to attend to the real nature of racism in the cultural industries. Moreover, the exclusively online nature of this activism has meant that it has taken on commodity form, where activist discourse cannot escape how big tech companies have transformed the racial identities of users into potentially lucrative brands/lifestyles/market niches. Anti-racist media activism needs to be alert to these forces, to avoid a politics that simply feeds individualized wealth accumulation.

This is where reparative justice becomes an intervention, demanding more radical structural change in contrast to the soft accommodationist policies of diversity that place limits on what marginalized groups can do and say in the cultural industries. Although my outline of practical strategies conducted through the reparative justice framework is brief, the focus here was on how such interventions need to operate at the level of political economy in a way to disperse corporate power while empowering—both materially and symbolically—the work of cultural producers from marginalized backgrounds. Moreover, as Balfour (2005) states, the notion of reparative justice creates a critical discourse that serves as a counterweight to race-blind language of diversity and incorporates acknowledgment of the past into present practices (pp. 802–803). Media can help us work through the pains of the past, which can in turn lead to heightened forms of collective flourishing *for all social groups*. Through working with the reparative justice framework, marginalized cultural producers can produce alternative narratives of nation that highlight historic injustices but also help imagine radical utopian visions of how better we can live together transnationally. In that sense, reparative justice does not work just for the benefit of historically oppressed groups but also for humanity itself.

References

Annenberg Inclusion Initiative. (2020). *Inequality in 1,300 popular films: Examining portrayals of gender, race/ethnicity, LGBTQ & disability from 2007 to 2019*. USC Annenberg Inclusion Initiative and Annenberg Foundation. https://assets.uscannenberg.org/docs/aii-inequality_1300_popular_films_09-08-2020.pdf

Balfour, L. (2005). Reparations after identity politics. *Political Theory, 33*(6), 786–811.

Bhambra, G. K., Nisancioglu, K., & Gebrial, D. (Eds.). (2018). *Decolonising the university*. Pluto Press.

Brook, O., O'Brien, D., & Taylor, M. (2020). *Culture is bad for you*. Manchester University Press.

Chakravartty, P., Kuo, R., Grubbs, V., & McIlwain, C. (2018). #CommunicationSoWhite. *Journal of Communication, 68*(2), 254–266. https://doi.org/10.1093/joc/jqy003

De Beukelaer, C., & Spence, K.-M. (2018). *Global cultural economy*. Routledge.

Gray, H. (2013). Subject(ed) to recognition. *American Quarterly, 65*(4), 771–798.

Gray, H. (2016). Precarious diversity: Representation and demography. In M. Curtin & K. Sanson (Eds.), *Precarious creativity* (pp. 241–253). University of California Press.

Hall, C. (2018). Doing reparatory history: Bringing "race" and slavery home. *Race & Class, 60*(1), 3–21.

Hesmondhalgh, D., & Saha, A. (2013). Race, ethnicity, and cultural production. *Popular Communication, 11*(3), 179–195.

Kelley, R. D. (2002). *Freedom dreams: The Black radical imagination*. Beacon.

Littler, J. (2017). *Against meritocracy: Culture, power and myths of mobility*. Routledge.

Nava, O. (2023). Multicologies? The development of multi-racial creative ecologies in East London. *International Journal of Cultural Policy, 29*(7), 911–925.

Nwonka, C. J. (2020). The new Babel: The language and practice of institutionalised diversity in the UK film industry. *Journal of British Cinema and Television, 17*(1), 24–46.

Nwonka, C. J., & Malik, S. (2018). Cultural discourses and practices of institutionalised diversity in the UK film sector: "Just get something Black made." *Sociological Review, 66*(6), 1111–1127. https://doi.org/10.1177/0038026118774183

Oakley, K. (2004). Not so cool Britannia: The role of creative industries in economic development. *International Journal of Cultural Studies, 7*(1), 67–77. https://doi.org/10.1177/1367877904040606

Quinn, E. (2012). Closing doors: Hollywood, affirmative action, and the revitalization of conservative racial politics. *Journal of American History, 99*(2), 466–491. https://doi.org/10.1093/jahist/jas302

Saha, A. (2018). *Race and the cultural industries*. Polity Press.

Saha, A., & van Lente, S. (2022). Diversity, media and racial capitalism: A case study on publishing. *Ethnic and Racial Studies, 45*(16), 216–236.

Titley, G. (2019). *Racism and media*. SAGE.

Warner, K. J. (2015). *The cultural politics of colorblind TV casting*. Routledge.

Zook, K. B. (1999). *Color by Fox: The Fox network and the revolution in Black television*. Oxford University Press.

Critical Media Effects Framework: Bridging Critical Cultural Communication with Media Effects Through Power, Intersectionality, Context, and Agency

Srividya Ramasubramanian* *and* Omotayo O. Banjo**

For about 50 years, tensions between critical cultural and social psychological approaches to studying the relationship between media and audiences has persisted, and in some cases has fueled volatile debates between scholars of these two different paradigms (Fink & Gantz, 1996, Morgan, 2007; Splichal & Mance, 2018). As critical social scientists who are trained in the media effects tradition and who study identity-related questions, we have found ourselves often caught up in methodological polarization and theoretical divides about ontological and epistemological differences that do not completely speak to our lived experiences. The multi-device, multi-platform, multiple-media environment that many media users inhabit today as digital natives means that basic conceptual definitions such as media, audience, and effects are in flux. Within the context of the evolving COVID-19 pandemic, social inequalities, rising populist fascist rhetoric, climate change emergency, rampant misinformation, and vitriolic online environments, it is important to interrogate how communication scholarship continues to stay relevant. As media landscapes become more dynamic, audiences become more complex, and sociopolitical contexts evolve rapidly, we advocate for media effects research to take a multi-perspectival approach to effectively address the most pressing research issues of today by drawing from subfields such as critical cultural communication.

Critical cultural communication and media effects scholarship are not necessarily opposing concepts and frameworks; each approach just answers different questions. Critical cultural approaches to media interrogate questions related to systemic power in media ownership, representations, and audience reception. Media effects scholarship typically uses quantitative methods to investigate the nature of media content and its impact on individual attitudes and behaviors as well as intergroup relationships. While media effects scholarship emphasizes issues such as objectivity, categorization, and generalizability, critical cultural communication focuses more on issues of power, positionality, and systemic inequalities. As Splichal and Mance (2018) state, "While critical theory and positivism are definitely opposed conceptual frameworks, critical theory and empirical research per se are not. One can combine them

---

* *Journal of Communication 70* (2021) 379–400 © The Author(s) 2021. Published by Oxford University Press on behalf of International Communication Association.

rather than endorse one of them against the other" (p. 233). The current silences, siloed thinking, and serious gaps between these subfields are detrimental to meaningfully theorizing about the new media environments, new generation of media prosumers, and new set of emerging sociopolitical challenges today. It is important for media effects theorizing to go beyond the individual to also consider how structural, institutional, and societal influences shape media experiences. Similarly, critical communication scholars could benefit from empirical, evidence-based support to help nuance theoretical mechanisms.

Almost a decade ago, Meyrowitz (2008) argued for combining critical/cultural studies and medium theory to provide a more holistic view of how media consumers interact with the media. Other scholars have used the term quantitative criticalists to describe scholars who use quantitative data to shed light on the structures and factors that lead to inequalities and injustices (McLaren, 2017; Stage & Wells, 2014). Additionally, they might "also question measures and analytic practices used in quantitative research, to ensure that they adequately represent circumstances and contexts, and do not themselves inadvertently perpetuate exclusion and hierarchy" (McLaren, 2017, p. 391). Emerging areas such as data activism and critical big data studies are examples of how empirical research could be connected with social justice in meaningful ways (Milan & van der Velden, 2016). Some examples are Data 4 Black Lives, a collective of social scientists and critical scholars that uses data sciences to bring measurable positive outcomes for Black people and the Resource Center for Minority Data at the University of Michigan that codesigns studies with communities of color.

The purpose of this article is to create the much-needed space to open up important dialogs between these two subfields to ask socially relevant research questions relating to media impacts and use multiple approaches to address them at the individual, intergroup, organizational, community, and global levels. Beyond a generic call for greater cross-area partnerships, we propose a Critical Media Effects (CME) framework as a starting point for co-creating a research roadmap for facilitating this bridging in meaningful and effective ways.

The Case for Critical Media Effects

The word "critical" means: (a) consisting of criticism, (b) exercising or involving careful judgment or judicious evaluation of, (c) relating to, or being a turning point or specially important juncture, (d) indispensable, vital, and (e) of sufficient size to sustain a chain reaction. In this essay, we use "critical" to imply all these meanings in advocating for a CME perspective: as a critique of existing literature, to bring attention to an urgent imperative for a critical turn in media effects research, and with the hope of starting a ripple effect.

Although working class women of color possibly form the majority of the world's population, much of communication scholarship has been conducted within Western, Educated, Industrialized, Rich, and Democratic (WEIRD) nations (Afifi & Cornejo, 2020; Alper et al., 2016; Henrich et al., 2010). The popular theories, canonical texts, and mainstream journal publications within media effects scholarship have historically been developed and framed within White U.S.-centric ableist heteronormative male contexts without interrogating how these choices might limit theorizing. What is considered normal within media effects scholarship could be a skewed version of reality based on limited samples and the researchers' own worldviews. By excluding non-Western or non-White perspectives, media effects scholars assume Eurocentric views as universal (which violates a significant tenet of theory building), dismiss the culturally distinctive experience of other audience members, and inadvertently participate in a form of symbolic annihilation. Even when there are attempts to go beyond the United States, media imperialism and Eurocentrism are often reinforced by centering scholarship from dominant groups in Western European nations with long histories of colonization in the Global South and discriminatory policies against minoritized groups.

Research on media effects scholarship is often examined at the individual level. In fact, media effects scholarship is often equated with media psychology today, which leads to an emphasis on the individual psyche while largely neglecting social, cultural, political, economic and other macro factors that shape media effects. Although the notion that media can have uniform, direct, and powerful effects on all viewers has largely been rejected, research on conditional media effects have focused on individual-level differences based on biological, psychological, and personality factors such as sensation-seeking, arousal, need for cognition, perspective taking, authoritarianism, and moral dispositions (Oliver, 2002). Although there is certainly merit to individual differences, media effects scholarship ought to contend with systemic, structural, and institutional inequalities, which play a role in shaping media outcomes.

Even when theories such as agenda setting, social cognitive theory, and social identity theory go beyond individual differences to include intergroup relations, they do not engage with these concepts from a critical cultural perspective by considering structural hierarchies. For instance, we note that intergroup processes within media effects scholarship often simply designate groups as "ingroups" and "outgroups" without explicitly acknowledging power relations between majority–minority groups. For example, Social Identity Theory (SIT) (Tajfel & Turner, 1979), a popular theory to study intergroup relations, posits that people, motivated to see themselves positively, evaluate themselves and the groups to which they belong more favorably than socially distant ones or out-groups. However, it does not adequately account for the role that hierarchical structure plays in motivations for an individual's need to belong and thus neglects the degree to which individuals' social location within a social system shapes media experience. Self-Categorization Theory comes close to addressing individuals as members of a social system but its emphasis is largely on cognitive grouping of identities and the circumstantial salience which prime different aspects of the social self (Turner & Reynolds, 2011).

Another concern within traditional media effects scholarship is that media patterns among majority groups are assumed to be normative and those of minoritized groups are narrowly defined as negative, abnormal, problematic, and even pathological. For instance, it is common for media content, use, and outcomes to be defined and framed as negative, violent, or excessive by researchers with little or no involvement with communities that are being studied. This gap between the researcher and the researched shapes how research problems are defined and what solutions are proposed within media effects. Even when positive and pro-social media effects such as elevation, empathy, and inspiration have been examined (Oliver & Raney, 2011), these effects have been explained within dominant mainstream groups, which leads to the question, "Positive effects for whom?" Given the power differences among minoritized and majority groups, it is crucial, then, that so-called positive media effects are inclusive and take power into consideration by asking "Who gets to feel positive about whom and why?"

Even when media effects scholarship does focus on minoritized media experiences, it does so through mono-categorical theorizing, which refers to using a single identity lens to understand, describe, and explain how identities shape experiences (Collins & Bilge, 2016; Goff & Kahn, 2013). Multiple stigmatizations and layered intersectional oppressions are not considered in understanding media outcomes. For instance, within media violence scholarship, which is arguably one of the most well-researched media topics, perpetrator–victim analysis is often limited to using gender-only or race-only identities. Intersectional erasures, even if not intentional, can have significant implications for research design, methods, and theorizing.

Critical Media Effects: Intellectual Foundations

We propose the CME framework to address some of the shortcomings outlined thus far and to facilitate a more nuanced approach to theorizing within media effects scholarship. This framework provides concrete analytical and conceptual tools on how to systematically and intentionally incorporate critical theory into media effects scholarship. It considers the most pressing socially-relevant problems of our times, how to better amplify the voices of those at the margins of society, and how media can serve as a tool for undoing systemic inequalities. It examines, validates, and affirms marginalized perspectives, including non-White, queer, feminist, postcolonial, poor, indigenous, and other minoritized ones.

In conceptualizing CME, we draw on foundational work from critical cultural scholarship, which is informed and influenced by feminist, critical race, queer, Marxist, and postcolonial approaches, to argue that media effects scholarship needs to go beyond traditional modes of theorizing to pay more attention to notions of power and structural inequities. Although communication scholars in other subareas have bridged critical theory with subfields such as health communication (Dutta, 2010, 2018), organizational communication (Mumby, 2013), technology studies (Bakardjieva & Gehl, 2017), family communication (Soliz & Phillips, 2018) and interpersonal communication (Afifi & Cornejo, 2020), the value added by this article is creating a framework specific to media effects, which has largely focused on individual-level effects using a post-positivist paradigm. Here we acknowledge the pioneering scholarship on media and identity, which has laid the groundwork for and is foundational for the framework we have proposed (Armstrong et al., 1992; Oliver, 1996).

The Critical Media Effects Framework: Roadmap, Central Pillars, and Salient Examples

The CME framework applies four interrelated concepts—power, intersectionality, context, and agency—from critical cultural communication to media effects scholarship. These concepts serve as central pillars and support structures upon which the bridging across subfields becomes possible. This is not to say that these are the only key concepts to advance CME scholarship but we believe these are the most crucial and central concepts that should be considered. **Power** addresses the hierarchical relationships and structural inequalities between dominant groups and subordinated groups that are marginalized, including within media effects scholarship. **Intersectionality** challenges mono-categorical theorizing within media effects research by acknowledging overlapping and mutually constructed intersectional identities. **Context** explores the degree to which media effects research accounts for the dynamicity of sociocultural political factors which impact the media experiences. And finally, **agency** accounts for the active role that media users can play in their media use in participatory and counter-hegemonic ways.

Below, we discuss how each pillar relates to CME, highlight salient examples and best practices (from areas such as critical/cultural studies, psychology, sociology, feminist studies, critical race theory, postcolonial studies, critical disability studies, indigenous studies, political economy, and neo-Marxism) as starting points to illustrate, broaden, and build upon existing media effects scholarship. The CME framework provides scholars with a toolkit of shared language, central concepts, and theoretical tools to converse and collaborate together.

Power and Critical Media Effects

The CME framework considers the ways in which dominant ideological structures frame users, problems, and solutions within traditional media effects. The question of how knowledge, including about media use and effects, is defined, produced, and distributed in myopic ways along asymmetric power relations across groups is at the core of examining power within CME. For example, Dutta (2010, 2018) has applied the notions of power to critical health communication by taking a culture-centered approach that analyzes structure, agency, and culture in resisting health inequalities. This approach emphasizes solidarity, reflexivity, and praxis. Similarly, the CME approach challenges the erasures of marginalized voices in the formation of research questions, methods, theories, and initiatives related to media.

Interrupting the existing structures of knowledge production within the dominant post-positivist paradigm of media effects scholarship means questioning universalist and essentialist assumptions about media users and their impacts. Critical interrogation of issues of power also allows for the cocreation of knowledge with and by media users, with an emphasis on users' agency and voice. Such theorizing turns the lens back on the assumptions of post-positivism that often ends up unintentionally reinforcing media inequalities rather than explicitly making space for social justice issues and alternative knowledge structures.

CME argues that macrolevel structural institutional dynamics and policies are just as important as microlevel individual behaviors and interpersonal dynamics in understanding the role that power plays when examining media effects. Group membership within a social system does not accurately capture oppressive societal structures which inform an individual's social experience, with implications for their cognitions, attitudes, emotions, and behaviors. For instance, Hitlin, Scott Brown, and Elder (2006) suggest that "development of a sense of racial self-categorization is inherently social and occurs within racially structured, often discriminatory interactions" (p. 1299). For example, in the context of Black women, bell hooks (2003) has argued: "subordinates in relations of power learn experientially that there is a critical gaze, one that looks to document and one that is oppositional" (p. 95).

The ontological assumptions of critical paradigms presuppose that what is structured does not exist in and of itself and is not merely determined by the individual but is shaped by systems and infrastructures that maintain status quo (Trepte & Loy, 2017). For example, Neville et al. (2000) Colorblind Racial Attitude Scale goes beyond schematic processing of racial categories to incorporate beliefs related to institutional discrimination. Within health psychology, Scheepers and Ellemers (2019) consider historical factors and structural limitations such as medical exploitation of Black people and the practice of redlining and food deserts in analyzing eating habits among various racial groups. Applying this approach to media effects, the CME framework considers the impact of power status of institutionally disenfranchised persons by connecting individual media behaviors with macrolevel systemic inequalities.

Another way in which CME scholarship incorporates power is by examining media effects through the lens of political economy, neo-Marxism and postcolonial critical perspectives (Fuchs & Mosco, 2015; Jin, 2006; Oh, 2018; Shome & Hegde, 2002). From the CME perspective, meaning construction and dominant discourses are often shaped by powerful media institutions and members of society who hold class privilege, political capital, and ideological influence (Fuchs & Mosco, 2015). Disparities in media ownership and workforce are linked to media monopolization, consolidation, and corporatization, which influence media representation, distribution, and reception processes (Castaneda et al., 2015). CME scholarship takes power structures into consideration at the global, national, and local levels by challenging "prevailing structures of domination [which] shape various discourses of resistance" (Crenshaw, 1991, p. 1243). CME amplifies the voices of communities that are marginalized within mainstream media. For example, scholars have examined media-based collective action strategies to disrupt status quo hierarchies through Arab Spring and #BlackLivesMatter

(Al-Azdee & Metzgar, 2018; Sturm & Amer, 2013). Similarly, Wabwire (2013), Pavarala (2003) and Ramasubramanian (2016) have examined the impact of media ownership on rural Kenyan, Indian, and African-American contexts respectively.

Intersectionality and Critical Media Effects

What intersectionality adds to the CME framework is the insight that factors that shape mediated experiences are coconstituted and are not mutually independent of one another (Collins & Bilge, 2016; Crenshaw, 1991). Social inequalities and power dynamics intersect such that diverse identities such as race, gender, class, sexual orientation, nationality, citizenship status, religion, and physical/mental abilities shape everyday mediated experiences in complex ways. Intersectionality as a central node of theorizing opens up important investigations about the intertwined, overlapping, and sometimes contradictory ways in which various forms of inequalities influence social hierarchies, which single-axis theorizing does not adequately account for (Bowleg, 2008; Dubrow, 2008; Goff & Kahn, 2013; Remedios & Snyder, 2018).

Rather than look at each identity in isolation, the CME framework suggests that research questions, methods, and analyses examine how multiple identities intersect in influencing mediated processes and effects (Dubrow, 2008; Else-Quest & Hyde, 2016). CME recognizes that using a race-only, gender-only, or class-only framework, for instance, only partially advances knowledge and provides an incomplete and inaccurate picture of mediated inequalities that characterize the lives of those who are simultaneously experiencing racism, sexism, class exploitation, patriarchy, homophobia, and other such oppressive systems. This is not to say that various axes of identities are equally salient, weighted equally, or additive in how they influence experiences (Bowleg, 2008; Else-Quest & Hyde, 2016).

Intersectionality is not merely asking demographic questions, just like feminist social sciences are much more than simply measuring gender or examining gender differences. Rather, intersectionality and critical approaches address various dimensions of experiences such as discrimination, stress, media access, media representation, etc. that are informed by multiple identities and power hierarchies. These factors are considered simultaneously, with the emphasis on the "and" and not the "or," in order to account for a more comprehensive understanding of complex systems of multiple oppressions and privileges (Bowleg, 2008; Remedios & Snyder, 2018). What this means is that for intersectional analyses, beyond the observed data, the media effects scholar also considers the broader structural inequalities and sociohistoric context within which the data emerge. For example, Bowleg (2008) examines observed data within sociohistoric contexts by demonstrating how social systems of racism, sexism, and homophobia are mutually constructed in shaping Black lesbians' intersectional economic inequalities.

A few studies have examined multiple identities such as LGB adolescents (Bond, 2018), colorism and gender (Dixon & Maddox, 2005), Muslim American youth (Saleem & Ramasubramanian, 2019), low-income families (Behm-Morawitz et al., 2018), socioeconomic status and race (Taylor-Clark et al., 2007), race and gender portrayals (Figueroa-Caballero et al., 2019), and ethnic marginalization of Native Americans (Kopacz & Lee Lawton, 2011). However, they do not approach it through a critical lens by engaging with intersectionality as a methodological tool or theoretical concept.

Critical social psychologists have started paving the way for incorporating issues of intersectionality into measurement, research design, and data analyses, that could serve as a possible starting point for media effects scholars to build upon (Bowleg, 2008; Dubrow, 2008; Else-Quest & Hyde, 2016; Goff & Kahn, 2013; Remedios & Snyder, 2018). For instance, Garnett et al. (2014) have used Latent Class Analysis (LCA) as an exploratory analytical tool to analyze co-occurring adverse outcomes such as weight-based bullying, homophobia, and racism without disentangling them by specific identity dimensions. Else-Quest and Hyde (2016) provide specific guidelines such as distinguishing framing identities as person variables or as stimulus variables, using within-group designs and between-group comparisons, considering conceptual equivalence and measurement invariance, and using techniques such as statistical interactions and multi-level modeling to incorporate intersectionality.

Context and Critical Media Effects

Much of the traditional media effects scholarship on context relates to examining the effects of specific media genres such as sports, news, humor, or horror. There is a need to go beyond these narrow definitions of context to consider how factors such as social, cultural, political, and technological contexts shape media effects. Medium theorists have argued for a level of analysis that emphasizes the characteristics of a specific medium, suggesting that just as the characteristics of a landscape shape the culture and develop human behavior associated with that region, the features of a particular medium draw a particular audience with specific needs or interests (Meyrowitz, 2008). Morah and Omojola's (2018), for example, examine how technological affordances of social media cultivate entrepreneurial audiences in Nigeria.

Other media effects scholars have done work on user characteristics and contextual factors (Chaffee, 1986; Katz et al., 1973; McGuire, 2004; Valkenburg & Peter, 2013). For instance, Valkenburg and Peter (2013) have proposed the differential media effects framework, which argues for more nuanced theorizing about differential effects on certain users. Similarly, Lee and Niederdeppe (2011) have contextualized cultivation effects by genre and source of information (overall versus local) on health beliefs. Such studies exemplify the need for nuanced theorizing about context to better incorporate varying needs across communities.

Building on this existing body of work, the CME approach considers environmental boundary constraints such as technological, social, political, and cultural contexts; especially in terms of how they relate to issues of power, and has varying implications for how we frame research questions and outcomes in studying media impacts within various contexts. Social scientific philosophers like Popper (2005) have argued that a goal of scientific inquiry should be to falsify (not prove) a generalizing theory in order to identify the specificity needed to examine complex phenomena. The CME perspective encourages media effects theories to be tested across multiple contexts, content types, formats, and populations, especially emphasizing historically marginalized ones, so that their generalizability, relevance, and applicability can be ascertained.

It is important to consider the social characteristics of users by incorporating the characteristics of the audience which is drawn by or avoids a particular medium. Chiu et al. (2010), for example, proposed an intersubjective approach to nonreductionist contemporary theories of psychology that argue that "social behaviors invariably take place in relational contexts and should be understood as responses to socially constructed meanings" (p. 483). The CME approach considers the social and cultural locations of content creators within media effects. It acknowledges that much of entertainment consumption, especially in a hyper-digital era, is shared and is a social experience. A few media scholars have incorporated context by studying social characteristics of media use and viewers' responses (Banjo, 2013; Banjo et al., 2017), co-viewers' gendered reactions to sexual violence in film (Tal-Or & Tsfati, 2015), social connectedness via co-viewing (Haridakis & Hanson, 2009), and social media context versus a physical viewing context (Cohen & Lancaster, 2014).

Political contexts shape how media effects researchers formulate research questions, interpret data, and draw conclusions. For example, Rodríguez et al. (2014) account for historical context and the political economy of information in citizens' media. Other scholars study the effects of political context on media directly. Cho (2011), for instance, takes a multi-level approach by examining the effect of local political information on local ad markets exemplifying the impact of community characteristics on political behaviors. Current events and political context can be used throughout all steps of the research process to generate more nuanced results. Scholars have examined representations of sociopolitically relevant groups such as immigrants (Mastro, 2019) or Muslims (Saleem & Ramasubramanian, 2019) within the broader context of discriminatory public policies against these groups. Others such as Dal Yong Jin (2006), Fuchs and Mosco (2015) and Rodríguez et al. (2014) push scholars to consider broader political economic issues such as media imperialism and neoliberal cultural politics, especially in terms of U.S. and European dominance in media environments, even as they engage with rigorous microlevel studies that test specific hypotheses in controlled settings.

Perhaps the most significant context for our field to consider is that of culture. Edward Said's (1978) important work on Orientalism challenges scholars to consider the imperialistic relationship between the West and the East and its role in how we conduct research. For example, Cho and Han's (2004) research revealed cultural differences in third person effects where greater effects emerged among individualistic samples compared to collectivistic cultures where the distance between self and other is not as great. Kim et al. (2014) find a preference for positive affect for U.S. audiences and mixed affect responses among Korean viewers, making room for new ways of theorizing media effects. Their work challenges dominant arguments in favor of trait and affective state motivations for entertainment selection by considering Buddhist inspired beliefs about hedonic pleasure among East Asian audiences. Even within a specific geographical area, subcultures can vary depending on power, status, and positionality. For instance, the cultures of Tamil-Singaporeans, Afro-Latinx Haitians, Romani-Europeans, and indigenous groups in Brazil are significantly distinct from mainstream cultures. Several non-Western media are prime candidates for studies of transportation, empathy and other emotion-oriented, affective and cognitive processing phenomena. For example, films such as *Straight Outta Compton* can be used to study nostalgia, *The Best Man Holiday* to examine interpersonal relationships or *Crazy Rich Asians* to study perceptions of romance or mood regulation. Countries such as India and Nigeria are among the biggest producers of films, those such as China, Japan, and Korea have millions of gamers, and nations like Mexico and Brazil have vast networks of television audiences whose perspectives could provide the opportunity to explore culturally relevant effects which have often been overlooked within media effects. These examples highlight the importance of situating media effects in ecologically valid ways that account for the sociocultural political contexts of individuals' media experiences.

Agency and Critical Media Effects

Building on media effects approaches such as Uses and Gratifications and selective information processing (Katz et al., 1973; McGuire, 2004; Rubin, 2009), CME emphasizes being more user focused by incorporating user agency into theories and applications of media effects. While these approaches define agency in terms of active versus passive audience based on awareness of their relationship to media, the CME approach goes beyond the active–passive binary to emphasize media users' agency to create meaning and counter the hegemonic nature of mainstream dominant media discourses from a critical cultural studies perspective (Couldry, 2004; Hall, 1980). In today's digital convergence culture of prosumption where media users are both cocreators and consumers of content, effects scholarship needs innovative ways of theorizing about user agency, especially including minoritized perspectives, by fully accounting for fandom, pleasure, participatory cultures, engagement, and agentic media use (Couldry, 2004; Jenkins & Deuze, 2008).

Without taking a technologically optimistic celebratory view of media, CME argues that dominant theorizing within media effects research tends to have focus excessively on harm, risk, and other negative effects, especially in terms of characterizing media use of minoritized groups (Alper et al., 2016; Vickery, 2017). For example, excessive media use, say the use of selfies, is framed as addictive, psychologically harmful, or narcissistic. Similarly, inoculation approaches to media literacy have been critiqued as being too prescriptive in that such interventions are often designed to "save" children from negative effects through positive role modeling without considering user-centered perspectives on media choice, use, and effects (Vickery, 2017).

The CME approach considers the hegemonic notions of what is considered high versus low culture. Media behavior of media users from marginalized groups, in particular, is examined through a deficit-based perspective of social deviance as problems to be "fixed" (Alper et al., 2016). For instance, content such as hip hop has been framed as violent or using "improper" English rather than examining the cultural context within which it emerged as a way of "talking B(l)ack." Similarly, studies of effects of erotic media content, social media consumption, reality TV, and soap operas are often assumed to be "trashy," judged as low culture or assumed to have harmful effects. The CME approach does not take an essentialist view of social differences. Difference is seen as an asset or an opportunity, and not as a problem to be fixed. It challenges what it is "normal" media use and questions if such normality is even desirable, especially if it is defined mainly from the perspective of researchers and from those in authority positions.

Although recent media effects theories include more positive effects such as inspiration and elevation (Oliver & Raney, 2011), they do not consider power relations in such theorizing. Ideas from critical disability studies (Goodley, 2013) and critical affect theory (Edbauer Rice, 2008) would readily help scholars recognize that messages about people with disabilities, for instance, overcoming everyday challenges—the supercrip narrative—might be inspirational for able-bodied persons (Bartsch et al., 2016) but could be insulting to those with disabilities. Indeed, such narratives have been referred to as inspiration porn where stories about exploited groups serve as elevation and inspiration for dominant group members in the context of disabilities[1] (Grue, 2016), poverty (Beresford, 2016), and racial/ethnic minorities (Apel, 2005).[2] CME argues that it is important to carefully examine seemingly positive portrayals such as pity and inspiration in terms of whether or not they reinforce social hierarchies (Ramasubramanian & Oliver, 2007; Ramasubramanian et al., 2020).

Centering user agency means approaching research from a space of cultural humility that allows participants the agency to cocreate knowledge and have a more active role in the research process. Inclusive language such as minoritized, enslaved populations, and overly exploited countries put the onus on those exploiting power to oppress other groups (Joseph, 2017). For example, social psychologist Carrotte et al. (2016) made sure to test their survey measures with gender and sexually diverse (GSD) participants to avoid heteronormative language that could be alienating and misrepresent some sexual experiences. Similarly, Broussard et al. (2017) worked closely with cisgender, transgender, nonbinary participants across a variety of sexual orientations to determine ways to represent gender identity accurately. CME encourages such participatory approaches to defining and measuring concepts.

CME further emphasizes examining marginalized groups within their own cultural contexts without having to compare them with dominant group norms. Only a few studies within media effects have focused on content created by and effects of mainstream media on minoritized communities (e.g., Martinez & Ramasubramanian, 2015; Saleem & Ramasubramanian, 2019). CME emphasizes minoritized users' agency to question, challenge, and subvert mainstream media by reframing content, even as mega media corporations continue to create homogenized content within neoliberal capitalist structures. Rodríguez's (2011) work, for example, formulates a theory of how media enable citizens to thrive during political unrest in Colombia and Pavarala (2003) engages with indigenous resistances through community radio.

Charting the Terrain Ahead: Implications and Future Directions

The CME framework proposed here provides a unifying framework, research toolkit, shared language, and roadmap for bridging critical cultural communication with media effects scholarship. The four central pillars of power, intersectionality, context, and agency that are elaborated upon in this framework can be applied to and extended across various mediated contexts. The salient examples, best practices, and recommendations provided here help us imagine the transformative possibilities that such collaborations, cross-area partnerships, and broad applications can offer. Beyond research and theory-building, CME also has implications for pedagogy, curriculum, hiring, promotion, mentoring, leadership and community engagement in terms of whose perspectives and experiences are privileged, how resources are allocated, and how priorities are set in terms of disciplinary directions and institutional support.

CME moves the subfield of media effects into an exciting direction by being responsive to examining, theorizing about, and addressing some of the most pressing social issues, challenges, and questions within Communication today. We envision that the next stage of CME scholarship will explore the full spectrum and range of media effects and experiences, especially minoritized perspectives. Such scholarship goes beyond a narrow focus on individual media outcomes and differences to also incorporate macrolevel questions such as media access, rights, services, representation, and policies for minoritized groups to fully participate and engage in individual and social transformation. It engages with understudied topics such as poverty, social class, racism, homelessness, transphobia, casteism, colorism, and indigeneity across various mediated contexts using critical intersectional lenses. Using an asset-based perspective, it questions implicit assumptions of what is considered "normal" in media effects, as defined from a space of privilege (such as wealth, able-bodiedness, citizenship, Whiteness, heteronormativity).

With regard to theoretical implications, the CME framework is not only applicable to studies relating to "other" cultures and to scholarship that is explicitly about identity, social justice, and discrimination. It urges media effects scholars to interrogate claims of the universal applicability, generalizability, and relevance of all media effects theories, concepts, and models. Taking, say, a color-evasive, gender-neutral, and Eurocentric approach to conceptualizing, researching and theorizing about media and its effects is not the solution. Rather, the CME approach encourages applying, studying, and testing media effects theories, including established and popular ones, across subpopulations and cultural contexts to better identify their boundaries, generalizability, robustness, applicability, and falsifiability (Popper, 2005). Replicating studies across diverse samples through intentional recruitment, cross-national collaborations, and community partnerships would increase generalizability of these existing theories. It serves as an invitation for scholars to theorize in new and inclusive ways about all types of media effects across various contexts, users, and texts.

In terms of methodological implications, CME calls to question how key variables such as social categories, identity, and media use are often defined and measured from a dominant group perspective. Practices such as cocreating conceptual definitions and pretesting research instruments with typically neglected groups could address these issues. Partnerships with community-based organizations through long-term mutually beneficial relationships can help with such participatory methods. CME research should also be open to incorporating qualitative methods such as media ethnography, examining multiple levels of analysis, and connecting individual media behaviors with structural and systemic factors. The use of multiplicative interactions, contextualization of observed data within larger sociohistorical contexts, and attention to systemic variations across subpopulations are important to consider (Bowleg, 2008; Dubrow, 2008; Else-Quest & Hyde, 2016).

With respect to inclusive sampling practices, several communication scholars have suggested practical solutions to diversify research samples in terms of geodemographic and social characteristics to capture broader user experiences and media content (Afifi & Cornejo, 2020; Soliz & Phillips, 2018). Beyond cross-cultural studies, marginalized groups can be studied on their own terms without always having to compare them to dominant group norms. Often small sample sizes and access to minoritized populations are major challenges to overcome. However, collecting data relating to minoritized groups and their experiences are important for them to feel included, respected, and heard. Through methods such as meta-analyses, combining datasets, and longitudinal data, some of the challenges of small samples can be overcome.

The CME approach seeks to bring about structural and institutional changes in media industries and media policies beyond studying individual-level effects. One way to do this is by interrogating taken-for-granted neutrality of the processes through which stories are selected, characters are created, and actors are chosen. For example, Dr. Stacy Smith's Media, Diversity, and Social Change Initiative uses empirical data to influence hiring practices across several entertainment platforms by taking media effects research beyond academe to content creators and media industries, providing opportunities to address issues of inequality in storytelling and production processes (e.g., inclusion contracts).

The CME approach actively supports alternative, community-oriented, and ethnic media initiatives from around the world through research, teaching, and advocacy efforts by working to raise awareness of what stories are being erased and silenced in mainstream media. Collaborations between activists, community leaders, and media effects scholars would strengthen evidence-based, data-driven social scientific approaches to using media for social change in socially relevant, transformative, and meaningful ways. Other examples of such community-based media initiatives are Question Bridge, Latinitas Magazine, Media Rise, Center for Scholars and Storytellers, and citizens' participatory media in India and Columbia discussed earlier (Pavarala, 2003; Ramasubramanian, 2016; Rodríguez et al., 2014). Leadership institutes, mentoring networks, and micro-financing support for alternative media can also help build capacity.

We also need to contend with structural, systemic, and institutional inequalities in conducting and publishing CME scholarship, which need to be addressed in terms of broader access to, allocation, and distribution of resources. This means working intentionally and collaboratively toward a cultural shift in terms of addressing inclusion at many different levels from research agendas to sampling techniques to theory testing to community-engaged scholarship to media activism. Doing so requires leaders working together to determine concrete benchmarks and ways to share resources for inclusive CME research, teaching, and community engagement at the disciplinary and institutional levels. Many top journals within Communication are heavily oriented toward publishing media effects research that involves multiple studies, longitudinal surveys, and complex experimental designs. However, such methodologies require resources that might not be available to scholars from marginalized communities, especially outside of the United Studies and Europe. Lab-based experimental research, for instance, involves sophisticated equipment and measurement tools, which are limited to scholars with space and funding support. Gaining access to national samples for surveys, for example, also requires funding, which may not be available to scholars from under-resourced institutions around the world. Access to knowledge in terms of journals, books, media, software, and mentorship could be barriers for scholars from underprivileged backgrounds, especially in the Global South.

Leadership in professional networks and disciplinary organizations could help alleviate these inequalities by facilitating greater collaboration across institutions, nations, and subdivisions by providing seed grants, networking opportunities, and assistance with access to data collection, publications, media texts, research materials, and equipment for those from under-resourced scholarly communities. Disciplinary leaders such as editors could be intentional about collecting author background information, having diverse editorial boards and ad-hoc reviewers, and encouraging citation of literature outside of "canonical" paradigms from non-traditional perspectives (Chakravartty et al., 2018). Communication journals and conferences could make inclusion and diversity an explicit part of their research agenda and reviewing criteria, require authors to be more intentional about justifying sampling decisions and find ways to support and reward scholarship that focuses on minoritized groups, media content, and users (Afifi & Cornejo, 2020).

The CME framework also has significant implications for teaching and curriculum development by being purposeful about diversifying who is included in conference panels, special issues of journals, textbooks, class syllabi, bibliographies, and reading lists. Universities and professional organizations need to create mechanisms for better disciplinary and institutional support for hiring, tenure, promotion, and advancement of critical media scholars through developing protocols to understand implicit biases in reviewing and feedback, developing mentoring programs, and providing support for collecting inclusive samples or for collaborating with community-based organizations as part of their research.

While championing a critical approach to studying media impacts, we are not unaware of the limitations that such an approach presents methodologically and practically in terms of research design, methods, sampling, data collection, and data analysis. We have provided some salient examples and recommendations from recent research from areas such as social psychology and health communication to start envisioning some ways to address these limitations and challenges. Through conversations and dialogs in our classrooms, at our conferences, and in our communities, and, through special issues of journals, edited books, workshops, blogs, and other outlets, the framework proposed here will be further fine-tuned, fleshed out, and firmed up. The applications, implications, limitations, and scope of the CME framework will unfold through these scholarly spaces in a dialectical manner.

In conclusion, in this article, we bridge media effects scholarship with critical cultural communication by proposing the CME framework and offer four interrelated concepts as the core pillars of this framework: power, intersectionality, context, and agency. In doing so, we hope to facilitate collaborative partnerships, productive engagement, and mutual solidarity between these two subfields. We argue for a more nuanced, intersectional, and critical approach to theorizing media effects scholarship to better reflect the diversity and dynamicity of media experiences, especially in the emerging sociopolitical landscape. We suggest that media effects scholars consider the unmitigated role of power relations, limitations of mono-categorical theorizing, and intersectional erasures in how they examine mediated experiences, impacts, and interventions. The framework considers how sociocultural and political factors impact viewers' responses, employs an asset-based approach to understanding marginalized groups' media experiences, and centers participatory, audience-created content, and alternative media. It pays attention to the ways in which dominant hegemonic structures shape media discourses and encourages media effects scholars to incorporate minoritized perspectives in cocreating knowledge, theories, and initiatives.

Notes

1 Inspiration porn is "the representation of disability as a desirable but undesired characteristic, usually by showing impairment as a visually or symbolically distinct biophysical deficit in one person, a deficit that can and must be overcome through the display of physical prowess" (Grue, 2016, p. 838).
2 Among other scholars who write on this topic, Apel (2005) draws a comparison between lynching postcards that were circulated as souvenirs by White supremacists after lynching murders of Black residents in their neighborhoods with photographs of Abu Ghraib Iraqi prisoners being tortured and humiliated being circulated as spectacles that reinforce hegemonic White American supremacy.

Acknowledgments

The authors are grateful to Mary Beth Oliver for her encouragement and guidance, to Priya Stephen and Emily Riewestahl for their research assistance, and to David Oh, the special issue editors and three reviewers for their feedback. The authors are grateful to all those on the frontlines of COVID-19, which was declared a global pandemic by WHO two days after this paper was accepted for publication. There are no financial conflicts of interest to disclose.

References

Afifi, W. A., & Cornejo, M. (2020). #CommunicationsoWEIRD: The question of sample representativeness in interpersonal communication research. In M. L. Doerfel & J. L. Gibbs (Eds.), *Building inclusiveness in organizations, institutions, and communities: Communication theory perspectives* (pp. 238–259). Routledge.

Alper, M., Katz, V. S., & Clark, L. S. (2016). Researching children, intersectionality, and diversity in the digital age. *Journal of Children and Media, 10*(1), 107–114. doi:10.1080/17482798.2015.1121886

Al-Azdee, M., & Metzgar, E. (2018). The Arab spring: Beyond media effects. *Journal of Arab & Muslim Media Research, 11*(1), 3–23. doi:10.1386/jammr.11.1.3_1

Apel, D. (2005). Torture culture: Lynching photographs and the images of Abu Ghraib. *Art Journal, 64*(2), 88–100. doi:10.1080/00043249.2005.10791174

Armstrong, G. B., Neuendorf, K. A., & Brentar, J. E. (1992). TV entertainment, news, and racial perceptions of college students. *Journal of Communication, 42*, 153–176. doi:10.1111/j.1460-2466.1992.tb00804.x

Bakardjieva, M., & Gehl, R. W. (2017). Critical approaches to communication technology—the past five years. *Annals of the International Communication Association, 41*(3–4), 213–219. doi:10.1080/23808985.2017.1374201

Bartsch, A., Oliver, M. B., Nitsch, C., & Scherr, S. (2016). Inspired by the paralympics: Effects of empathy on audience interest in para-sports and on the destigmatization of persons with disabilities. *Communication Research, 45*(4), 525–553. doi:10.1177/0093650215626984

Banjo, O. O. (2013). For us only? Examining the effect of viewing context on Black audiences' perceived influence of Black entertainment. *Race and Social Problems, 5*(4), 309–322.

Banjo, O. O., Wang, Z., Appiah, O., Brown, C., Walther-Martin, W., Tchernev, J., & Irwin, M. (2017). Experiencing racial humor with outgroups: A psychophysiological examination of co-viewing effects. *Media Psychology, 20*(4), 607–631. doi:10.1080/15213269.2016.1234396

Behm-Morawitz, E., Miller, B. M., & Lewallen, J. (2018). A model for quantitatively analyzing representations of social class in screen media. *Communication Research Reports, 35*(3), 210–221. doi:10.1080/08824096.2018.1428544

Beresford, P. (2016). Presenting welfare reform: Poverty porn, telling sad stories or achieving change? *Disability & Society, 31*(3), 421–425. doi:10.1080/09687599.2016.1173419

Bond, B. (2018). Parasocial relationships with media personae: Why they matter and how they differ among heterosexual, lesbian, gay, and bisexual adolescents. *Media Psychology, 21*(3), 457–485. doi:10.1080/15213269.2017.1416295

Bowleg, L. (2008). When Black + Lesbian + Woman ≠ Black Lesbian Woman: The methodological challenges of qualitative and quantitative intersectionality research. *Sex Roles, 59*(5–6), 312–325. doi:10.1007/s11199-008-9400-z

Broussard, K., Warner, R., & Pope, A. (2017). Too many boxes, or not enough? Preferences for how we ask about gender in cisgender, LGB, and gender-diverse samples. *Sex Roles, 78*(9), 606–624. doi:10.1007/s11199-017-0823-2

Carrotte, E. R., Vella, A. M., Bowring, A. L., Douglass, C., Hellard, M. E., & Lim, M. S. (2016). "I am yet to encounter any survey that actually reflects my life": A qualitative study of inclusivity in sexual health research. *BMC Medical Research Methodology, 16*, 86. https://doi. org/10.1186/s12874-016-0193-4

Castaneda, M., Fuentes-Bautista, M., & Baruch, F. (2015). Racial and ethnic inclusion in the digital era: Shifting discourses in communications public policy. *Journal of Social Issues, 71*(1), 139–154. doi:10.1111/josi.12101

Chaffee, S. H. (1986). Mass media and interpersonal channels: Competitive, convergent or complimentary? In G. Gumpert & R. Cathcart (Eds.), *Intermedia: Interpersonal communication in a media world, 3* (pp. 62–80). Oxford University Press.

Chakravartty, P., Kuo, R., Grubbs, V., & McIlwain, C. (2018). #CommunicationSoWhite. *Journal of Communication, 68*(2), 254–266. https://doi.org/10.1093/joc/jqy003

Chiu, C. Y., Gelfand, M. J., Yamagishi, T., Shteynberg, G., & Wan, C. (2010). Intersubjective culture: The role of intersubjective perceptions in cross-cultural research. *Perspectives on Psychological Science, 5*(4), 482–493. doi:10.1177/1745691610375562

Cho, H., & Han, M. (2004). Perceived effect of the mass media on self vs. other: A cross-cultural investigation of the third person effect hypothesis. *Journal of Asian Pacific Communication, 14*(2), 299–318. doi:10.1075/japc.14.2.06cho

Cho, J. (2011). The geography of political communication: Effects of regional variations in campaign advertising on citizen communication. *Human Communication Research, 37*(3), 434–462.

Cohen, E. L., & Lancaster, A. L. (2014). Individual differences in in-person and social media television coviewing: The role of emotional contagion, need to belong, and coviewing orientation. *Cyberpsychology, Behavior, and Social Networking, 17*(8), 512–518. doi:10.1089/cyber.2013.0484

Collins, P. H., & Bilge, S. (2016). *Intersectionality*. Wiley.

Couldry, N. (2004). Theorising media as practice. *Social Semiotics, 14*(2), 115–132. doi:10.1080/1035033042000238295

Crenshaw, K. (1991). Mapping the margins: Intersectionality, identity politics, and violence against women of color. *Stanford Law Review, 43*(6), 1241–1299.

Dixon, T. L., & Maddox, K. B. (2005). Skin tone, crime news, and social reality judgments: Priming the stereotype of the dark and dangerous Black criminal. *Journal of Applied Social Psychology, 35*(8), 1555–1570. doi:10.1111/j.1559-1816.2005.tb02184.x

Dutta, M. J. (2010). The critical cultural turn in health communication: Reflexivity, solidarity, and praxis. *Health Communication, 25*, 534–539. doi:10.1080/10410236.2010.497995

Dutta, M. J. (2018). Culture-centered approach in addressing health disparities: Communication infrastructures for subaltern voices. *Communication Methods and Measures, 12*(4), 239–259. doi:10.1080/19312458.2018.1453057

Dubrow, J. K. (2008). How can we account for intersectionality in quantitative analysis of survey data? Empirical illustration for Central and Eastern Europe. *ASK. Research & Methods,* (17), 85–100.

Edbauer Rice, J. (2008). The new "new": Making a case for critical affect studies. *Quarterly Journal of Speech, 94*(2), 200–212. doi:10.1080/00335630801975434

Else-Quest, N. M., & Hyde, J. S. (2016). Intersectionality in quantitative psychological research: II. Methods and techniques. *Psychology of Women Quarterly, 40*(3), 319–336. doi:10.1177/0361684316647953

Fink, E. J., & Gantz, W. (1996). A content analysis of three mass communication research traditions: Social science, interpretive studies, and critical analysis. *Journalism & Mass Communication Quarterly, 73*(1), 114–134. doi:10.1177/107769909607300111

Figueroa-Caballero, A., Mastro, D., & Stamps, D. (2019). An examination of the effects of mediated intragroup and intergroup interactions among Latino/a characters. *Communication Quarterly, 67*(3), 271–290. doi:10.1080/01463373.2019.1573745

Fuchs, C., & Mosco, V. (2015). *Marx and the political economy of the media*. Brill.

Garnett, B. R., Masyn, K. E., Austin, S. B., Miller, M., Williams, D. R., & Viswanath, K. (2014). The intersectionality of discrimination attributes and bullying among youth: An applied latent class analysis. *Journal of Youth and Adolescence, 43*, 1225–1239. doi:10.1007/s10964-013-0073-8

Goff, P. A., & Kahn, K. B. (2013). How psychological science impedes intersectional thinking. *DuBois Review: Social Science Research on Race, 10*(2), 365–384. doi:10.1017/S1742058X13000313

Goodley, D. (2013). Dis/entangling critical disability studies. *Disability & Society, 28*(5), 631–644. doi:10.1080/09687599.2012.717884

Grue, J. (2016). The problem with inspiration porn: A tentative definition and a provisional critique. *Disability & Society, 31*(6), 838–849. doi:10.1080/09687599.2016.1205473

Hall, S. (1980). Encoding/decoding. In S. Hall, D. Hobson, A. Lowe, & P. Willis (Eds.), *Culture, media, language*. Unwin Hyman.

Haridakis, P., & Hanson, G. (2009). Social interaction and co-viewing with YouTube: Blending mass communication reception and social connection. *Journal of Broadcasting & Electronic Media, 53*(2), 317–335. doi:10.1080/08838150902908270

Henrich, J., Heine, S. J., & Norenzayan, A. (2010). The weirdest people in the world? *Behavioral and Brain Sciences, 33*(2–3), 61–83. doi:10.1017/S0140525X0999152X

Hitlin, S., Scott Brown, J., & Elder, G. H., Jr. (2006). Racial self-categorization in adolescence: Multiracial development and social pathways. *Child Development, 77*(5), 1298–1308. doi:10.1111/j.1467-8624.2006.00935.x

Jin, D. Y. (2006). Cultural politics in Korea's contemporary films under neoliberal globalization. *Media, Culture & Society, 28*(1), 5–23. https://doi.org/10.1177/0163443706059274

Jenkins, H., & Deuze, M. (2008). Convergence culture. *Convergence: The International Journal of Research into New Media Technologies, 14*(1), 5–12. doi:10.1177/13548565 07084415

Joseph, R. (2017). What's the difference with "difference"? Equity, communication, and the politics of difference. *International Journal of Communication, 11*, 3306–3326.

Katz, E., Blumler, J. G., & Gurevitch, M. (1973). Uses and gratifications research. *Public Opinion Quarterly, 37*(4), 509–523.

Kim, J., Seo, M., Yu, H., & Neuendorf, K. (2014). Cultural differences in preference for entertainment messages that induce mixed responses of joy and sorrow. *Human Communication Research, 40*(4), 530–552. doi:10.1111/hcre.12037

Kopacz, M., & Lee Lawton, B. (2011). The YouTube Indian: Portrayals of Native Americans on a viral video site. *New Media & Society, 13*(2), 330–349. doi:10.1177/146144 4810373532

Lee, C. J., & Niederdeppe, J. (2011). Genre-specific cultivation effects: Lagged associations between overall TV viewing, local TV news viewing, and fatalistic beliefs about cancer prevention. *Communication Research, 38*(6), 731–753.

Martinez, A., & Ramasubramanian, S. (2015). Latino audiences, racial/ethnic identification, and responses to stereotypical comedy. *Mass Communication and Society, 18*(2), 209–229. doi:10.1080/15205436.2014.907427

Mastro, D. (2019). Virtual theme collection: Immigrants as minorities in the media. *Journalism & Mass Communication Quarterly, 96*(1), 31–36. doi:10.1177/1077699018824402

McLaren, L. (2017). A space for critical quantitative public health research? *Critical Public Health, 27*(4), 391–393. doi:10.1080/09581596.2017.1326214

McGuire, W. J. (2004). A perspectivist approach to theory construction. *Personality and Social Psychology Review, 8*(2), 173–182. doi:10.1207/s15327957pspr0802_11

Meyrowitz, J. (2008). Power, pleasure, patterns: Intersecting narratives of media influence. *Journal of Communication, 58*(4), 641–663. doi:10.1111/j.1460-2466.2008.00406.x

Milan, S., & Van Der Velden, L. (2016). The alternative epistemologies of data activism. *Digital Culture & Society, 2*(2), 57–74.

Morah, D. N., & Omojola, O. (2018). Social media use and entrepreneurship development in Nigeria: Lagos and Onitsha in focus. *International Journal of Advance Study and Research Work, 1*(5), 15–26. doi:10.5281/zenodo.1420101

Morgan, D. L. (2007). Paradigms lost and pragmatism regained: Methodological implications of combining qualitative and quantitative methods. *Journal of Mixed Methods Research, 1*(1), 48–76. doi:10.1177/2345678906292462

Mumby, D. K. (2013). *Organizational communication: A critical approach*. SAGE.

Neville, H. A., Lilly, R. L., Duran, G., Lee, R. M., & Browne, L. (2000). Construction and initial validation of the Color-Blind Racial Attitudes Scale (CoBRAS). *Journal of Counseling Psychology, 47*(1), 59. doi:10.1037/0022-0167.47.1.59

Oh, D. C. (2018). Racist propaganda: Discursive negotiations on YouTube of perceived anti-white racism in South Korea. *Atlantic Journal of Communication, 26*(5), 306 317. doi:10.1080/15456870.2018.1517767

Oliver, M. B. (1996). Influences of authoritarianism and portrayals of race on Caucasian viewers' responses to reality-based crime dramas. *Communication Reports, 9*(2), 141–150.

Oliver, M. B. (2002). Individual differences in media effects. In J. Bryant & D. Zillmann (Eds.), *Media effects: Advances in theory and research* (pp. 507–524). Erlbaum.

Oliver, M. B., & Raney, A. A. (2011). Entertainment as pleasurable and meaningful: Identifying hedonic and eudaimonic motivations for entertainment consumption. *Journal of Communication, 61*(5), 984–1004. https://doi.org/10.1111/j.1460-2466.2011.01585.x

Pavarala, V. (2003). Building solidarities: A case of community radio in Jharkhand. *Economic and Political Weekly, 38*(22), 2188–2197. https://www.jstor.org/stable/4413632

Popper, K. (2005). *The logic of scientific discovery.* Routledge.

Ramasubramanian, S. (2016). Racial/ethnic identity, community-oriented media initiatives, and transmedia storytelling. *The Information Society, 32*(5), 333–342. doi:10.1080/01972243.2016.1212618

Ramasubramanian, S., & Oliver, M. B. (2007). Activating and suppressing hostile and benevolent racism: Evidence for comparative stereotyping. *Media Psychology, 9*(3), 623–646.

Ramasubramanian, S., Winfield, A., & Riewestahl, E. (2020). Positive stereotypes and counter-stereotypes: Examining their effects on prejudice reduction and favorable intergroup relations. In A. Billings & S. Parrott (Eds.), *Media stereotypes: From ageism to xenophobia* (pp. 257–276). Peter Lang.

Remedios, J. D., & Snyder, S. H. (2018). Intersectional oppression: Multiple stigmatized identities and perceptions of invisibility, discrimination, and stereotyping. *Journal of Social Issues, 74*(2), 265–281. doi:10.1111/josi.12268

Rodríguez, C. (2011). *Citizens' media against armed conflict: Disrupting violence in Colombia.* University of Minnesota Press.

Rodríguez, C., Ferron, B., & Shamas, K. (2014). Four challenges in the field of alternative, radical and citizens' media research. *Media, Culture & Society, 36*(2), 150–166. doi:10.1177/0163443714523877

Rubin, A. M. (2009). Uses-and-gratifications perspective on media effects. In J. Bryant & M. B. Oliver (Eds.), *Media effects* (pp. 181–200). Routledge.

Said, E. (1978). *Orientalism.* Pantheon Books.

Saleem, M., & Ramasubramanian, S. (2019). Muslim Americans' identity management strategies in response to media stereotypes and discrimination. *Media Psychology, 22*(3), 373–393. doi:10.1080/15213269.2017.1302345

Scheepers, D., & Ellemers, N. (2019). Social identity theory. In K. Sassenbert & M. L. W. Vliek (Eds.), *Social psychology in action: Evidence-based interventions from theory to practice* (pp. 129–143). Springer.

Shome, R., & Hegde, R. S. (2002). Postcolonial approaches to communication: Charting the terrain, engaging the intersections. *Communication Theory, 12*(3), 249–270. doi:10.1111/j.1468-2885.2002.tb00269.x

Soliz, J., & Phillips, K. E. (2018). Toward a more expansive understanding of family communication: Considerations for inclusion of ethnic–racial and global diversity. *Journal of Family Communication, 18*(1), 5–12. doi:10.1080/15267431.2017.1399890

Splichal, S., & Mance, B. (2018). Paradigm(s) lost? Islands of critical media research in communication journals. *Journal of Communication, 68*(2), 399–414. doi:10.1093/joc/jqx018

Stage, F. K., & Wells, R. S. (2014). Critical quantitative inquiry in context. *New Directions for Institutional Research, 2013*(158), 1–7. doi:10.1002/ir.20041

Sturm, C., & Amer, H. (2013). The effects of (social) media on revolutions—Perspectives from Egypt and the Arab Spring. In *International Conference on Human–Computer Interaction* (pp. 352–358). Springer. doi:10.1007/978-3-642-39265-8_39

Tajfel, H., & Turner, J. C. (1979). An integrative theory of intergroup conflict. In W. G. Austin, & S. Worchel (Eds.), *The social psychology of intergroup relations* (pp. 7–24). Wiley-Blackwell.

Tal-Or, N., & Tsfati, Y. (2015). Does the co-viewing of sexual material affect rape myth acceptance? The role of the co-viewer's reactions and gender. *Communication Research, 45*(4), 577–602. doi:10.1177/0093650215595073

Taylor-Clark, K., Koh, H., & Viswanath, K. (2007). Perceptions of environmental health risks and communication barriers among low-SEP and racial/ethnic minority communities. *Journal of Health Care for the Poor and Underserved, 18*, 165–183. doi:10.1353/hpu.2007.0113

Trepte, S., & Loy, L. S. (2017). Social identity theory and self-categorization theory. In P. Rössler, C. A. Hoffner, & L. Zoonen (Eds.), *The international encyclopedia of media effects.* Wiley. doi:10.1002/9781118783764.wbieme0088

Turner, J. C., & Reynolds, K. J. (2011). Self-categorization theory. *Handbook of Theories in Social Psychology, 2*(1), 399–417.

Valkenburg, P. M., & Peter, J. (2013). The differential susceptibility to media effects model. *Journal of Communication, 63*(2), 221–243. doi:10.1111/jcom.12024

Vickery, J. (2017). *Worried about the wrong things: Youth, risk, and opportunity in the digital world.* MIT Press.

Wabwire, J. (2013). The role of community radio in development of the rural poor. *New Media and Mass Communication, 10*, 40–47.

Black Audiences and Media Resistance

David Stamps

Weitz (2001) defined resistance as an intentional act or attitude demonstrated in the proximity of influential people. Black communities are pioneers in enacting resistance, which dates back to Africans' global enslavement. Black people encompass a rich and intersectional population that includes African Americans; persons from the United States who descended from enslaved African individuals; and Black people of Haitian, Jamaican, Latin America, and other geographic and culturally distinct locations. Likewise, Black persons exist in a distinct space within the media landscape. The early work of abolitionists cemented the use of the media as a tool to educate and encourage resistance among Black communities. Black individuals have utilized multiple forms of media to promote positive cultural representation; confront racial stereotypes; and address the erasure of diverse, intersectional Black identities, each of which has constituted resistance to oppression and vilification (Stamps, 2022). Examples of media resistance include the writings of Ida B. Wells and Frederick Douglass, delivered in newsprint and pamphlets, and contemporary forms such as digital media, including Black Twitter and hashtags #BringBackOurGirls, #OscarsSoWhite, and #MeToo created by Michelle Obama, April Reign, and Tamara Burke, respectively. Black audiences' media use is a tool that uplifts advocacy efforts and, across centuries, has illustrated the Black community's commitment to resistance.

As a diverse and distinctive group, Black people have continually resisted anti-Blackness, defined as the intentional acts of vilifying, belittling, and marginalizing Black people. The use of media to aid in the resistance of anti-Blackness, which includes the creation of coalitions, the promotion of education, and the awareness and engagement in collective action (e.g., protests), is not novel. Black audiences' media use is notable because the group consumes mainstream and digital media more than other racial groups, and individuals are more active in content creation and commentary on digital media platforms, including YouTube, Twitter, and TikTok (Pew Research Center, 2021). Appropriately, scholars have demonstrated that Black audiences use media to contest marginalization and defy oppression (Brekke et al., 2021). Coleman (2013) argued that "Black audiences are taken for granted. . . . Black media audiences are subjects, agents, and constellations of community and political interests, whose social locations, relations, and identities are historically and culturally constituted" (p. vii).

Deeply Held Concepts: Intersectionality, Racial Centrality, and Counterpublics

Intersectionality (Crenshaw, 2013), racial centrality (Davis & Gandy, 1999), and counterpublics (Fraser, 1990) have contributed to the tool kits often employed by scholars to situate Black media consumers' relationship to resistance. Black individuals are not detached from the pervasive use of racial stereotypes, dog whistles, and the tokenization of Blackness in the media. However, Black audiences are acutely aware of the apparatuses and experiences that position the group to thrive despite the harmful realities (Dixon, 2001).

In its inception, *intersectionality* (Crenshaw, 2013) recognized the varied identities and subsequent subjugation that Black women faced, as racism and sexism created obstacles in a society centered on White men. Media research has adopted intersectionality and noted that identities matter within the context of media use and its impact on audiences (Ramasubramanian & Banjo, 2020). S. Williams (2021) noted that digital media had created a space for authentic and diverse images of plus-size Black women to tell their stories. Her work highlighted how Black women, poised at the intersection of race, gender, and weight, produced media narratives that amplified their day-to-day experiences and actively rejected persecution, including fat phobia. Equally noteworthy, Melissa Viviane Jefferson, also known as the Grammy Award-winning entertainer Lizzo, and self-proclaimed fat Black woman, won her first Emmy Award for outstanding competition program for *Lizzo's Watch Out for the Big Grrls*, an Amazon docuseries that focused on the same subject matter (Andrew, 2022). Empirical and anecdotal evidence has suggested that intersectional representation and resistance remain at the forefront of Black audiences and their media use (Alaoui et al., 2015).

Numerous media studies have examined *racial centrality* or the importance of racial identity among Black individuals (Brown et al., 2017; Sobande et al., 2020). This work has documented that when race matters to Black audiences, resistance is interwoven into viewers' media use and the outcomes related to the group. Maragh-Lloyd (2020) recognized that Black women, many of whom noted the prominence of their identities, exercised resistance using mediated communication to prompt resilience, advocacy, and engagement in discussions about topics related to Black liberation. Stamps (2022) explored the relationship between Black audiences' racial centrality, media consumption, and the group's consideration of collective action. Their work found a significant relationship between intentional media selectivity, specifically media that represented their group and the interests of the Black community, the importance of racial identity to Black individuals, and increased consideration of engagement in activism. These studies, although only a snapshot of the literature, help illustrate how Black audiences are not passive media consumers but, rather, are active in their media use, and their identities (e.g., race and gender) are substantial in protecting the group through resistance.

Counterpublics are enclaves where individuals who oppose mainstream or "White-focused" conventions work to destabilize exclusionary public spaces. Fraser (1990) recognized that these publics provided a retreat for marginalized communities and for resistance to be nurtured. Early examples of Black counterpublics included barbershops and churches; both places generated political discourse among Black individuals and were spaces for Black people to strategize to combat anti-Blackness (Hill, 2018). Hill (2018) coined the term *literacy counterpublics*, which recognized Black bookstores as discursive spaces that "enable community participants to reimagine the role, purpose, and function of education, schooling, and the practice of literacy itself" (p. 288). Like the brick-and-mortar spaces that supported Black communicative engagement, mediated spaces—particularly digital media platforms—have emerged as Black counterpublics (Sobande et al., 2020). Black audiences have commanded spaces to engage in advocacy, create community, and launch rally cries for Black social issues (Anderson, 2016). Scholars have recognized that mediated spaces are additional counterpublics due to the increased accessibility of the internet, the rise of social networking sites, and the digital savviness of Black media consumers (Graham & Smith, 2016). Black Twitter is Black Twitter because Black people cultivated the space and created a safe counterpublic for the group (Brock, 2012). Moreover, the role of mediated counterpublics as conducive to resistance is widespread, from the creation of hashtags that highlight social issues, including #SayHerName and #MeToo, to the emergence of digital media discourse surrounding police violence directed at Black people (Blevins et al., 2019). Scholars have denoted Black digital counterpublics, including those that exist within the blogosphere (Steele, 2018), Twitter (Brock, 2012), and within meme culture (A. Williams, 2020).

Deeply Held Theories: Social Identity Perspective, Cultivation Theory, Social Identity Gratifications, Community Cultural Wealth, Critical Media Effects, and Risk and Resilience Framework

Theoretical frameworks are applied to understand the intricate relationships between media use and Black people's attitudinal, behavioral, and cognitive responses. However, scholars have called attention to the lack of representation of Black individuals (and other non-White groups) as the media subject in these investigations (Chakravartty et al., 2018). Some primary theoretical perspectives that can center on Black audiences include cultivation and social identity/social categorization theories. The utility of these theories is appropriate, but scholars have argued that there is a resounding need to reimagine the frameworks used to recognize Black audiences' media use (Stamps, 2020). As such, I offer a brief introduction of each, and additional frameworks, including social identity gratifications, community cultural wealth, critical media effects, and the risk and resilience framework, are presented. Each theory can potentially bridge the gap between elevating Black media users and favorable outcomes related to resistance.

The *social identity perspective* (i.e., social identity/social categorization theories) focuses on how media use, particularly exposure or consumption, contributes to individual and group-based perceptions (Turner et al., 1979). The social identity perspective has postulated that people often define themselves according to their group memberships (e.g., racial group) and seek ways to uphold group identity or mitigate threats to salient identities. Although considerable individual-level variation exists regarding identity, identity often correlates to belonging. Researchers have explored the role of racial identity in Black viewers' responses to mediated depictions (Abrams & Giles, 2007; Fujioka, 2005). Much of the work has acknowledged that Black audiences' relationship to media use often aligns with support for policies that uplift Black communities, which may protect the group and increase belongingness (Fujioka, 2005). Additional research has recognized the group's attenuation of harm from consuming stereotypical Black depictions, which was related to increased collective esteem and favorable self-perceptions (Stamps, 2021a).

Cultivation theory (Gerbner et al., 1994) focuses on audiences' consuming "heavy" versus "light" media and speculates that increased or heavy viewing of certain content shapes a viewer's reality. Scholars have adopted cultivation theory and examined Black audiences' media consumption, and interestingly, results have countered claims of adverse outcomes. Ward (2004) has acknowledged that the media's impact on Black audiences is not global but may be affected by the viewer's media diet (i.e., the amount and type of media consumption) and their connection to the portrayals on-screen. Ward's work is noteworthy as they outlined nuance and depth in understanding Black audiences' media use. Ward noted that increases in consuming Black-oriented media and protective factors, such as religious identity, safeguarded Black viewers' well-being. Scholars have highlighted that increased media consumption (i.e., heavy viewing) was associated with increased esteem and a recognition of out-group (i.e., White) bias (Stamps, 2021b). Acknowledging discrimination is a documented factor that contributes to Black media consumers' commitment to resistance (Lu & Steele, 2019).

Examinations of racial groups and media remain at a crossroads, particularly regarding Black audiences and their media use. Scholars could continue focusing on White audiences' media use and their attitudes toward non-White people, yet this practice, although widely implemented, distracts from the goal of producing diverse and representative research (Chakravartty et al., 2018; Stamps, 2020). Suppose researchers focus on the global majority's media use and applicable theories that examine the experiences of this diverse and intersectional populace. In that case, individuals may better understand the relationship between diverse audiences' media use and how groups mitigate oppression and exercise resilience. Theories including social identity gratifications, community cultural wealth, critical media effects, and their relationship to Black audiences have grown. Likewise, work that utilizes the risk and resilience framework is also budding and very exciting. Here, I offer a glimpse into each framework and its application to the group.

Social identity gratifications (SIG; Harwood, 1999) propose that individuals, in addition to seeking out media for escapism and entertainment, intentionally seek media to support their social identities (e.g., racial identity). SIG aligns with the notion that individuals may use media to reaffirm their identities, increase favorable perceptions, and encourage advocacy on behalf of the group. Abrams and Giles (2007) and Stamps (2022) applied SIG to Black media users and found notable outcomes. Black individuals were intentional in their media selection. The group benefited from their media choices, including protecting esteem and promoting vitality, and in alignment with this chapter, this encouraged forms of resistance.

Yosso (2005) defined *community cultural wealth* (CCW) as an array of knowledge, skills, and abilities people of color utilize to survive and resist macro and micro oppression. Yosso argued that cultural resources, such as language and communal support, bolstered resilience and resistance to subjugation. Research has demonstrated that Black audiences prefer media that acknowledges their experiences and language styles (Maragh-Lloyd, 2020). Likewise, Black individuals who view media portrayals of their racial group have the potential to demonstrate aspirational goals, such as attending college, engaging in mentorship, and seeking emotional support (Brown et al., 2022; Stamps, 2021c). According to the CCW framework, each outcome demonstrates forms of aspirational, navigational, and resistance capital, which Yosso noted as examples of resistance. Adopting social competencies that permit Black individuals to survive and ideally thrive amid anti-Black events and circumstances matters. Media may provide the platform to launch these actions.

Critical media effects (Ramasubramanian & Banjo, 2020) build on the intersections of previously mentioned concepts, including intersectionality. Critical media effects examine marginalized and underrepresented audiences and draw attention to their experiences with the media. The critical media effects framework enables scholars to question how power and agency influence audiences' relationship to the media. Media resistance can be discussed thoroughly when scholars have the tools to interrogate relationships critically and empirically, and critical media effects are a formidable mechanism for individuals who seek to continue this work.

The *risk and resilience framework* provides a lens to understand Black audiences' efforts toward resistance (Zimmerman & Arunkumar, 1994). The risk and resilience framework articulates individuals' traits that can affect their ability to manage risk or threat and exhibit resilience. Studies that have examined Black audiences and media resistance denoted that the risk or threat was encountering discrimination or negative stereotypes in media, and attributes including high self-esteem and racial identity were buffers that promoted resilience. Tynes and associates' (2012) research found that increased racial identity and self-esteem buffered the negative health outcomes among Black audiences and provided resistance to digital media's involvement in upholding racial discrimination (Noble, 2018). Other scholars have applied the same tenets and illustrated that Black populations' media use and factors that contribute to risk reduction and resistance include religious identity (Ward, 2004), media literacy skills (Stamps, 2021a), and the increased appetite for racial justice (Blevins et al., 2019).

Deeply Held Debates: Reclaiming Our Time

An argument regarding Black audiences and media resistance is that Black people remain at the margins of scholarship, and very little is known about Black individuals' experiences outside the White gaze (Chakravartty et al., 2018; Stamps, 2020; Ward, 2004). Despite the logic for why race-related media research should shift to include diverse audiences, the argument has yet to reveal an extensive turn toward more diverse identity-based research output. Several reasons are likely to be responsible for the failed revelation. One is that the gatekeepers of academic journals continue to seek out "generalizable" samples and subject matter, both of which privilege White populations. Another reason may be that scholars are socialized to produce "attractive" research for journal editors, members of promotion and tenure boards, and members of graduate committees, many of whom are non-Black people. Last, sample populations readily available to many researchers include Western, educated, industrialized, rich, and democratic (WEIRD) populations, often excluding Black global communities (Henrich et al., 2010). Each rationale is speculative, but a text like the one you are holding should prompt different practices in conducting media research.

Other debates include the notion that the relationship between Black audiences' media use and outcomes on individuals is wholly negative. Ward (2004) has noted that Black individuals may not be susceptible to the negative influences of media. The basis of the claim is debated among scholars in social psychology, communication, Black studies, and education. Scholars have noted that Black media users employ strategies that protect self-esteem, self-perceptions, and general well-being and use media platforms to contest prejudice and discrimination (Lee, 2017; Maragh-Lloyd, 2020; Stamps, 2021a; Tynes et al., 2012). A. Williams (2020) recognized how Black meme creators used humor, satire, and strategic positioning of Blackness to disrupt White supremacy and performative racial allyship by White women. In their work, content creators engaged with digital media, specifically meme creation, as a force of resistance to endorse consequences for White people's racist actions and provide Black communities with agency. Black audiences also combat the media's one-dimensional images of Black individuals by producing multifaceted content. Arthur (2020) recognized such tactics in their exploration of Black media influencers who challenged Eurocentric negative perspectives of Black spaces and people. Arthur's work highlighted Black travel influencers who asserted, via imagery in the digital realm, the beauty of Blackness in distinct locales and among a spectrum of Black cultures. I advocate that each type of resistance allows Black people to get closer to the freedom to exist unapologetically.

Black media consumers enter the media landscape with abundant firsthand experience of Blackness and deep knowledge of Black culture. Black audiences critique and reject media images contradicting their realities and narratives (Dixon, 2001). An assumption that Black audiences are primarily subject to harmful media depictions and anti-Black narratives would be a discredit to the intelligence, tech-savviness, and range of media literacy skills that Black audiences possess (Arthur, 2020; Hill, 2018; Lu & Steele, 2018). Black people have learned to extract from the media what is beneficial and to reject what is not of value. One such example is the presence of Black-orientated media and the increased viewership of Black content, such as Marvel's *Black Panther 2: Wakanda Forever*. Anyiwo and colleagues (2018) found that Black audiences who viewed Black-orientated media promoted the strong Black women schema, which characterizes Black women as emotionally strong and independent. Black audiences are aware of the news media's demeaning portrayals; the role of entertainment media that has prompted laughable stereotypes; and the digital platforms that have urged, encouraged, or ignored racial objectification (Stamps, 2021a). Black people know better, and the Black community's resistance may lead the group closer to justice.

Conclusion

We must remain attentive to the reality that Black audiences and their resistance to anti-Blackness are a global phenomenon (Bledsoe & Wright, 2019). From the predominantly White media structures in the United States to the digital enclaves pervasive in Great Britain, Black individuals' media use can be a tool for resisting anti-Blackness everywhere (Sobande et al., 2020). Researchers have a diverse and enriched body of work to engage. Scholars can examine the role of digital media in creating counterpublics and how the impact of influencers, content creators, and media spectators provides a space for continued resistance. Researchers, including qualitative, quantitative, mixed-methods, and critical cultural scholars, may explore the relationships between Black individuals' media use and explicit acts of resistance. Resistance may include engagement in collective action, running for political office, or advocacy efforts in the form of teaching or nonprofit work. No matter the research endeavor, exploring media use and the fight for Black liberation must continue.

References

Abrams, J. R., & Giles, H. (2007). Ethnic identity gratifications selection and avoidance by African Americans: A group vitality and social identity gratifications perspective. *Media Psychology, 9*(1), 115–134. https://doi.org/10.1080/15213260709336805

Alaoui, F. Z. C., Basnet, M., Coleman, R. R. M., Chan, B. H., Charmaraman, L., Gunn, C., Harris, A., Harris, K., King, L., Lee, L., & Richer, A. (2015). *Women of color and social media multitasking: Blogs, timelines, feeds, and community.* Lexington Books.

Anderson, M. (2016, August 15). *The hashtag #BlackLivesMatter emerges: Social activism on Twitter.* Pew Research Center. https://www.pewresearch.org/internet/2016/08/15/the-hashtag-blacklivesmatter-emerges-social-activism-on-twitter

Andrew, S. (2022). *Lizzo dedicates her Emmy win to the "big grrls."* CNN. https://amp.cnn.com/cnn/2022/09/12/entertainment/lizzo-emmy-award-speech-cec/index.html

Anyiwo, N., Ward, L. M., Day Fletcher, K., & Rowley, S. (2018). Black adolescents' television usage and endorsement of mainstream gender roles and the strong Black woman schema. *Journal of Black Psychology, 44*(4), 371–397. https://doi.org/10.1177/0095798418771818

Arthur, T. O. (2020). #Catchmeinashithole: Black travel influencers and the contestation of racialized place myths. *Howard Journal of Communications, 32*(4), 382–393. http://doi.org/10.1080/10646175.2020.1819481

Bledsoe, A., & Wright, W. J. (2019). The anti-Blackness of global capital. *Environment and Planning D: Society and Space, 37*(1), 8–26. http://doi.org/10.1177/0263775818805102

Blevins, J. L., Lee, J. J., McCabe, E. E., & Edgerton, E. (2019). Tweeting for social justice in #Ferguson: Affective discourse in Twitter hashtags. *New Media & Society, 21*(7), 1636–1653. https://doi.org/10.1177/1461444819827030

Brekke, A. J., Joseph, R., & Aaftaab, N. G. (2021). "I address race because race addresses me": Women of color show receipts through digital storytelling. *Review of Communication, 21*(1), 44–57. https://doi.org/10.1080/15358593.2021.1895294

Brock, A. (2012). From the Blackhand Side: Twitter as a cultural conversation. *Journal of Broadcasting & Electronic Media, 56*(4), 529–549. https://doi.org/10.1080/08838151.2012.732147

Brown, M., Pyle, C., & Ellison, N. B. (2022). "On my head about it": College aspirations, social media participation, and community cultural wealth. *Social Media + Society, 8*(2), 1–14. http://doi.org/10.1177/20563051221091545

Brown, M., Ray, R., Summers, E., & Fraistat, N. (2017). #SayHerName: A case study of intersectional social media activism. *Ethnic and Racial Studies, 40*(11), 1831–1846. https://doi.org/10.1080/01419870.2017.1334934

Chakravartty, P., Kuo, R., Grubbs, V., & McIlwain, C. (2018). #CommunicationSoWhite. *Journal of Communication, 68*(2), 254–266. https://doi.org/10.1093/joc/jqy003

Coleman, R. M. (Ed.). (2013). *Say it loud! African American audiences, media and identity.* Routledge.

Crenshaw, K. (2013). Demarginalizing the intersection of race and sex: A Black feminist critique of antidiscrimination doctrine, feminist theory and antiracist politics. In K. Bartlett & R. Kennedy (Eds.), *Feminist legal theory: Readings in law and gender* (pp. 23–51). Routledge.

Davis, J. L., & Gandy, O. H., Jr. (1999). Racial identity and media orientation: Exploring the nature of constraint. *Journal of Black Studies, 29*(3), 367–397. https://doi.org/10.1177/002193479902900303

Dixon, T. L. (2001). Social cognition and racial stereotyping in television: Consequences for transculturalism. In V. H. Milhouse, M. K. Asante, & P. Nwosu (Eds.), *Transcultural realities: Interdisciplinary perspectives on cross-cultural relations* (pp. 215–224). SAGE.

Fraser, N. (1990). Rethinking the public sphere: A contribution to the critique of actually existing democracy. *Social Text* (25–26), 56–80. http://www.jstor.org/stable/466240

Fujioka, Y. (2005). Black media images as a perceived threat to African American ethnic identity: Coping responses, perceived public perception, and attitudes towards affirmative action. *Journal of Broadcasting & Electronic Media, 49*(4), 450–467. https://doi.org/10.1207/s15506878jobem4904_6

Gerbner, G., Gross, L., Morgan, M., & Signorielli, N. (1994). Growing up with television: The cultivation perspective. In J. Bryant & D. Zillman (Eds.), *Media effects: Advances in theory and research* (pp. 17–41). Erlbaum.

Graham, R., & Smith, S. (2016). The content of our #characters: Black Twitter as counterpublic. *Sociology of Race and Ethnicity, 2*(4), 433–449. https://doi.org/10.1177/2332649216639067

Harwood, J. (1999). Age identification, social identity gratifications, and television viewing. *Journal of Broadcasting & Electronic Media, 43*(1), 123–136. https://doi.org/10.1080/08838159909364479

Henrich, J., Heine, S. J., & Norenzayan, A. (2010). Most people are not WEIRD. *Nature, 466*(7302), Article 29. https://www.nature.com/articles/466029a

Hill, M. L. (2018). "Thank you, Black Twitter": State violence, digital counterpublics, and pedagogies of resistance. *Urban Education, 53*(2), 286–302. https://doi.org/10.1177/0042085917747124

Lee, L. A. (2017). Black Twitter: A response to bias in mainstream media. *Social Sciences, 6*(1), 1–17. http://doi.org/10.3390/socsci6010026

Lu, J. H., & Steele, C. K. (2019). "Joy is resistance": Cross-platform resilience and (re)invention of Black oral culture online. *Information, Communication & Society, 22*(6), 823–837. https://doi.org/10.1080/1369118X.2019.1575449

Maragh-Lloyd, R. (2020). A digital post-racial parity? Black women's everyday resistance and rethinking online media culture. *Communication, Culture & Critique, 13*(1), 17–35. https://doi.org/10.1093/ccc/tcz046

Noble, S. U. (2018). *Algorithms of oppression: How search engines reinforce racism.* New York University Press.

Pew Research Center. (2021, April 7). *Social media fact sheet.* https://www.pewresearch.org/internet/fact-sheet/social-media/?menuItem=2fc5fff9-9899-4317-b786-9e0b60934bcf

Ramasubramanian, S., & Banjo, O. O. (2020). Critical media effects framework: Bridging critical cultural communication and media effects through power, intersectionality, context, and agency. *Journal of Communication, 70*(3), 379–400. https://doi.org/10.1093/joc/jqaa014

Sobande, F., Fearfull, A., & Brownlie, D. (2020). Resisting media marginalisation: Black women's digital content and collectivity. *Consumption Markets & Culture, 23*(5), 413–428. http://doi.org/10.1080/10253866.2019.1571491

Stamps, D. (2020). Race and media: A critical essay acknowledging the current state of race-related media effects research and directions for future exploration. *Howard Journal of Communications, 31*(2), 121–136. https://doi.org/10.1080/10646175.2020.1714513

Stamps, D. (2021a). Media literacy as liberator: Black audiences' adoption of media literacy, news media consumption, and perceptions of self and group members. *Journal of International and Intercultural Communication, 14*(3), 240–257. http://doi.org/10.1080/17513057.2020.1789692

Stamps, D. (2021b). It's all relative: The dual role of media consumption and media literacy among Black audiences. *Southern Communication Journal, 86*(3), 231–243. http://doi.org/10.1080/1041794X.2021.1905053

Stamps, D. (2021c). B(l)ack by popular demand: An analysis of positive Black male characters in television and audiences' community cultural wealth. *Journal of Communication Inquiry, 45*(2), 97–118. http://doi.org/10.1177/0196859920924388

Stamps, D. (2022). Black audiences' identity-focused social media use, group vitality, and consideration of collective action. *Journalism and Mass Communication Quarterly, 99*(3), 660–675. http://doi.org/10.1177/10776990221104152

Steele, C. K. (2018). Black bloggers and their varied publics: The everyday politics of Black discourse online. *Television & New Media, 19*(2), 112–127. http://doi.org/10.1177/1527476417709535

Turner, J. C., Brown, R. J., & Tajfel, H. (1979). Social comparison and group interest in ingroup favouritism. *European Journal of Social Psychology, 9*(2), 187–204. https://doi.org/10.1002/ejsp.2420090207

Tynes, B. M., Umana-Taylor, A. J., Rose, C. A., Lin, J., & Anderson, C. J. (2012). Online racial discrimination and the protective function of ethnic identity and self-esteem for African American adolescents. *Developmental Psychology*, *48*(2), 343–355. http://doi.org/10.1037/a0027032

Ward, L. M. (2004). Wading through the stereotypes: Positive and negative associations between media use and Black adolescents' conceptions of self. *Developmental Psychology*, *40*(2), 284–294. http://doi.org/10.1037/0012-1649.40.2.284

Weitz, R. (2001). Women and their hair: Seeking power through resistance and accommodation. *Gender & Society*, *15*(5), 667–686. https://doi.org/10.1177/089124301015005003

Williams, A. (2020). Black memes matter: #LivingWhileBlack with Becky and Karen. *Social Media+ Society*, *6*(4), 1–14. https://doi.org/10.1177/2056305120981047

Williams, S. (2021). Watch out for the big girls: Black plus-sized content creators creating space and amplifying visibility in digital spaces. *Feminist Media Studies*, *21*(8), 1360–1370. https://doi.org/10.1080/14680777.2021.2004195

Yosso, T. J. (2005). Whose culture has capital? A critical race theory discussion of community cultural wealth. *Race Ethnicity and Education*, *8*(1), 69–91. https://doi.org/10.1080/1361332052000341006

Zimmerman, M. A., & Arunkumar, R. (1994). Resiliency research: Implications for schools and policy. *Social Policy Research*, *8*, 1–18.

CHAPTER

6

"How Do You Shift That?" Dialoguing Social Justice, Activism, and Black Joy in Media Studies

jas l. moultrie *and* Ralina L. Joseph

To joyfully uplift foundational voices in Black media studies today, the two of us—PhD student (jas) and advisor/professor (Ralina)—hosted a series of recorded dialogues[1] with luminaries we admire for their cross-genre and genre-defying scholarship in Black media and communication. Our pairings connected dyads of similarly positioned scholars in terms of time, service, and position within institutions; approaches and methodological foci; and Black media connected research. We paired the two most senior scholars of the group, media historian Jane Rhodes, who tends to "think back as well as forward," and media sociologist Herman Gray, who asks a guiding question of Black media studies, "What does Black add to [the] formulation [of Black media studies]?" We joined university leaders, John L. Jackson, Jr., a filmmaker and anthropologist, and E. Patrick Johnson, a self-described sexuality, gender, and performance studies "trickster," together in dialogue. Black horror scholar and Chief Diversity Officer, Robin Means Coleman, connected with fellow media representation scholar, Beretta E. Smith-Shomade, who calls herself an "activist" studying Black television. Finally, two pioneers of Black digital studies—Kishonna Gray, whose scholarship asks, "How are we creating and curating community?" and fellow gaming scholar André Brock, who describes himself as an "autodidactic Black information studies" scholar who is "intentionally and openly Black in [his] scholarship . . . epistemology and . . . methodology"—met for discussion. While Black studies and Black people have been under attack throughout the history of the United States, in this moment of heightened assaults,[2] centering such incisive scholarly Black voices in the service of our joy creates a radical moment of reflection within Black media studies.

Following their lead, we unapologetically center Blackness, in its fullness, as the space from which Black media studies scholars study, create, teach, and affect media. Our dialogic interviews followed the tenets of *radical listening*—deeply hearing another's story to hold questions of power (Joseph & Briscoe-Smith, 2021; Winchell et al., 2016). Radical listening, which we utilize as a form of participatory action research, amplifies disparate, discordant, and too little-heard ideas. Our research participants follow the following process:

1. Before the dialogue, they pick, choose, and add to our list of questions (Box 6.1).
2. During the dialogue, they co-facilitate their recorded conversations, choosing to focus on any (or none) of the provided questions.

---

[1] Dialogue audio clips are accessible on the University of Washington Center for Communication, Difference, and Equity's Interrupting Privilege website: http://ip.ccde.com.uw.edu/?cat=384.

[2] At the time of writing this chapter, Black studies is under attack in 18 U.S. states, including most prominently in Florida, which successfully pressured The College Board to remove virtually all critical content—including the work and any mention of E. Patrick Johnson—from its AP African American History high school class (Pendharkar, 2023).

Box 6.1 Black Media Studies and Social Justice

As a scholar of Black media studies, what are your commitments to social justice? How do you define social justice?

Are there any contradictions between being a scholar and an activist? How do you make sense of these different identities?

What other scholars, activists, artists, organizations, and people do you look to or regard as change makers?

How would you describe the current landscape of Black media practices and scholarship to a student or emerging scholar who is interested in occupying this field as a path toward change?

What possibilities for media activism lie within today's time-demanding, psychologically captivating, and increasingly internet-based media ecosystem? What limitations constrain ongoing efforts?

This racialized neoliberal regime depends on Black hypervisibility, whether through the charge of "diversity and inclusion" or via the virality of Black pain and trauma. How does this affect media's viability as a social justice tool?

Describe the ways in which Blackness instructs media today (i.e., folks behind the camera), particularly within digital media spaces?

How do we, in the everyday, sustain joy in academia? Furthermore, since joy is existence not resistance, how do you understand its relation to social justice?

How does your work contribute to/upend/reimagine the possibilities for Black media studies? Also, what is it about our narratives and stories that is so affective?

Understanding the struggle for liberation as ongoing, what technological and methodological innovations do we put our energies into? What stories and movements do we pull from the archive for guidance?

How do we utilize media, as creators and producers of scholarship, for healing, joy, and being?

3. After the dialogue, they receive the full text of their recorded dialogue to highlight and/or redact anything they want us to focus on or eliminate in our analysis.

The four dialogues from which this chapter pulls begin and end with a need for, in Rhodes' words, "a shift." This shift, as Brock notes, includes a re-interrogation of our relationships to academia and an unbridled love for Black people. The chapter celebrates this love by tending to the ways in which Black media studies scholars, in pursuit of justice and knowledge, create embodied and joyful paths in and beyond academia. Black scholars cultivate such joy in the midst of myriad forms of anti-Black racism in the academy, from daily microaggressions to the unacknowledged and disproportionate labor extracted from Black scholars (Bowden & Buie, 2021). Thus, this chapter follows three acts: Act 1, defining activism, committing to social justice, and centering Black humanity (of themselves, their communities, their research); Act 2, engaging methods for finessing boundaries; and Act 3, affirming Blackness in media and academia. We conclude with a reimagining of Black media studies as joyful practice, and a refusal to define, in the words of the late filmmaker Marlon Riggs' last documentary (1994), what "Black is . . . [and] Black ain't."

Act I: Defining Activism, Committing to Social Justice, and Centering Black Humanity

Scholars intertwined definitions of activism and social justice in distinct yet connected ways to their scholarship, administration, public engagement, and teaching; their commitments, or lack of commitment, to the terms "activism" and "social justice" varied accordingly.

In conversation with H. Gray, Rhodes laments the current online struggles for truth, information, and evidence. Thinking through the current moment in which "we're all constantly contributing to the algorithm," Rhodes notes, "a lot of American society, global society today is a sense of helplessness . . . a lot of throwing up of the hands, 'what can I do?'" as (un)willing contributors to fraught and demanding media systems. Resisting such nihilism, Rhodes offers "the activist question: How do you shift that?" She explains that shifting away from helplessness is the process of centering Black hope, of "get[ting] people to sort of have a much more sort of critical understanding that, you know, is not going to create transformation overnight, but can chip away perhaps at the most egregious parts." Such hope is tempered by the realities of anti-Blackness inside and outside the academy. In K. Gray and Brock's conversation, Brock describes one egregious part as the attempt to contain Black people not just outside the academy, but within it. Brock explains, "They want us to be a particular kind of Black person and in our doing so we end up harming ourselves." Echoing Rhodes's question, "How do you shift that?" Brock names a shift of orientation where Black academics now, post-pandemic, understand that "the work does not love us." But our spaces of care which love, respect, and uplift Black people do.[3] We argue that some spaces of care are explicitly *activist* ones, which explicitly advocate for Black scholars and Black scholarship, whereas others resist the label of "activist" while actively uplifting the *humanity* of Black scholars, communities, and research.

One scholar who details her commitments to such activism and humanity is Smith-Shomade, who expresses a desire for "justice, period of all types." For her, being a Black media studies scholar means always striving for and "achieving some sort of justice" whether that be "economic, social, [or] representational." Similarly, for Rhodes, activism is "a cause, . . . purpose or a target for what it is your knowledge should be . . . working with and towards." In other words, Smith-Shomade and Rhodes name social justice and activism as not just philosophical orientations but tangible means towards creating equitable change. Relatedly, while Jackson regards social justice as being "easy to say, but . . . hard to produce," he also shares his path of "trying to clear space for more inclusive, more equitable ways of being in the world . . . [and] pushing back against forms of exploitation and discrimination." Interestingly, Jackson also believes social justice is "often not reducible" to the work being done within the academy. Jackson explains that students are actively renegotiating this tension by "incorporating their activist . . . investments and passions into their . . . scholarship" in ways that are "radically threatening" to traditional understandings of academic work. Jackson's ongoing work to carve out a space for multimodal scholarship in the academy, "the difference [it] will . . . make if we think in images and sound, not just in words," is central here.[4]

---

[3] As we were writing this chapter, we were experiencing media coverage of yet another Black person killed at the hands of police, Tyre Nichols. Nichols was murdered by a group of majority-Black officers, which starkly reminded us, as Zora Neal Hurston famously opined, "All my skinfolk ain't kinfolk." This chapter acknowledges this reality while optimistically celebrating spaces of love for Black folks.

[4] See "Communicating Multi-Modally: Research & Expressive Culture," available at https://www.multimodal.hkbu.online.

Johnson, who is, with Jackson, leading the movement toward multimodal scholarship in media studies and communication, extends activism beyond the realm of scholarship to mentorship and community work. He defines "activism on the ground" in academic institutions—particularly for faculty of color—as the "hidden labor . . . of mentoring students of color." In addition to his generous and generative mentorship practices inside the academy, Johnson is committed to providing resources and voice to "those folks who are often forgotten." Beyond the academy, he is committed to sharing access, interrupting notions of traditional research, and redistributing wealth and resources into Black and Brown communities. Reflecting further on the role of scholars within movements for social justice, Jackson argues that in a world where change is inevitable, activism involves figuring out the "small role" we play in deterring problematic change, anticipating changes to come, and shifting "policies . . . practices, [and] cultural expectations" to increase the likelihood of changes we want. Johnson's social justice activism inside and outside the academy—representative of many of the scholars—actively creates change for minoritized people as it blurs the lines between academy and community.

Scholars toggled between articulating structures of power and the implications of those structures on Black academics in Black media studies. In their conversation, Rhodes and H. Gray highlight the former, prioritizing not the role of activists, but the role played by information and knowledge circulation. Specifically, they shift our attention away from the utility of media as tools for social justice and toward the role media plays in, as Rhodes notes, the "flow of how people understand things and enact change." As Rhodes argues in her body of work, media framing directs sentiments toward and about Blackness—often in a racist and not anti-racist formation—although savvy media actors such as, in Rhodes' research, the Black Panthers actively push back and create their own set of frames (Rhodes, 1998, 2017). Rather than continue efforts to change media industries, which are, in Rhodes' words, "never going to be receptive to the kinds of fundamental changes that we demand," both scholars emphasize the importance of our critical participation in media through activism. H. Gray, whose body of work deeply nuances questions of Black representation (Gray, 2004, 2005, 2013), describes the *activist component* as being about "not just direct encounter with industrial systems . . . but also aesthetic encounters with critiquing Blackness as a kind of static formation." Likening the challenge to current attempts to delegitimize Black studies, he argues that at stake are the ways in which we, as scholars and creatives, tell stories that create "spaces, openings, [and] push various kinds of understandings forward." Here, then, is also where possibilities for transformation lie: in the stories we tell.

The encounters H. Gray describes—even in the realm of entertainment media—should be understood as social justice, Means Coleman notes, as they are about "repair[ing] the absence of . . . marginalized voices" and "disrupting a lot of -isms and biases." Stories of *Black celebration, restoration, joy, possibility*, and *belonging*, which Means Coleman names as the cornerstones of Smith-Shomade's work, construct Means Coleman's definition of social justice. Like Johnson, both she and Smith-Shomade regard *pedagogy as activism*, "if we believe that activism is about change." In fact, she considers it one of "our most powerful tool[s]." In agreement, Smith-Shomade believes she has not done her job as a teacher if her students do not share what they learn with somebody else. Here, Smith-Shomade's philosophy embodies the African American proverb, "each one teach one," what Johnson describes as impacting Black and Brown communities both inside and outside of academia. Interestingly, whereas Means Coleman regards her scholarship within the academy as inseparable from her work as a social justice activist, Smith-Shomade gestures for us to see the split between "Beretta the activis[t]" and "Beretta the scholar." The question of scholarship itself functioning as activism has been a live debate in Black studies for decades (Marable, 2006); although being an activist is a part of her work and who she is, Smith-Shomade does not describe her scholarship as activism.

Like Smith-Shomade, Brock is not "conscientious" (the word Smith-Shomade uses) about being explicitly "activist" in his work. Both he and K. Gray highlight the centrality of Blackness in their work and push back on an "activist/m" label. Brock regards activism as a "step too far from" his intentions to build on and recover Black knowledges (Brock, 2020). Nevertheless, he, like his dialogue partner, understands the ways in which the "activist" label is applied to Black scholars, which, in K. Gray's words, happens "if we want it or we don't." Brock instead chooses to inhabit a middle space through which he "speak[s] Blackness into existence . . . in ways that are specific to our history . . . tradition and . . . joy." K. Gray considered social justice activism and the study of media and Blackness as two different projects until two key moments in 2014: the murder of Michael Brown, Jr., and the racist and sexist harassment saga known as Gamergate (K. Gray et al., 2017). It was then that she "s[a]t with some questions that didn't have answers." From there her work shifted to the structural and institutional reality that "gaming doesn't care about Black people . . . women . . . [or other] folks." Even still, she does not position herself as an activist, sharing "people think my presence is a radical act. People think our [Black scholarly] presence is a radical act. We're not radical, we're not that. I'm just existing." Lovingly, Brock interrupts to note that she received her PhD in Transformative Justice Studies, then asks, "How can you say you're not . . . an activist by training and sensibility?" K. Gray agrees, then emphasizes her desire to "expand [the] definition" of activism and "disrupt" the boundaries placed on Blackness within and outside of academia.

The scholars are aligned in their moments of *changemaking*, of searching for justice in Smith-Shomade's words, but differently oriented toward the labels "activist" and "social justice." Their changemaking happens through critical, Black media and communication studies scholarship; thoughtful, integrated mentorship of younger scholars; and collaborative, reciprocal community work. As bell hooks writes in *All About Love*, this changemaking is an expression of love as "to love well is the task in all meaningful relationships, not just romantic bonds" (2000, p. 138). A love of Black people—our students, our communities, each other—guides these scholars' work.

Act 2: Methods for Finessing Boundaries

Kishonna Gray poses the question, "Why do we have these boundaries?" while discussing the *siloed fields* of Black studies, game studies, and digital studies. She compares the systemic practice of delimiting knowledge to the boundaries imposed on Black people and shares her desire to "disrupt all that." Both she and other scholars finesse disciplinary boundaries as well as "boundaries around Blackness" through their being and refusal to stay within Black media studies.

How then are these interdisciplinary, multimodal scholars understanding Black media studies and their relationships to the field? Johnson embodies finesse as "an academic trickster because wherever you want to place me, I don't necessarily fit there." Whether as a scholar of sexuality, gender, and performance, through methodologies of ethnography, oral history and discourse analysis, or as a filmmaker and playwright, his focus is not on being positioned within Black media studies but, rather, on the modality he takes up to "interrogate a particular phenomenon" (see Johnson, 2003, 2008a, 2008b, 2010, 2018, 2019; Johnson & Jackson, 2021). Similarly, Jackson, an anthropologist of race, religion, media, identity, and academic institutions, refuses to do or be one thing. Whether locating race, place, history, class, Blackness, and, in tandem, White co-optation of Blackness, in Harlem (Jackson, 2001), illuminating the speciousness of the concept of Black "authenticity" (Jackson, 2005), or uncovering the ways in which race infiltrates our readings and understandings of the world (Jackson, 2008), Johnson's scholarship traverses academic borders and speaks beyond academia to popular audiences.

Scholars also trouble singular, staid, and controlling images of Blackness. Rephrasing the seminal question posed by cultural studies theorist Stuart Hall (1993), Jackson asks "So what is this Black of Black media studies?" He argues, "Trying to figure out what people think they mean by Black, how we understand the contemporary media and mediatized moment . . . even the idea of how we study it is up for grabs." Rather than attempt to define or delimit what constitutes Black media studies, he offers his vision of what the field is doing: "[It's] about really trying to deconstruct . . . new ways of producing representations that we think do justice in the complicated nature of people's lives, and new ways of forming intellectual and social community and conversation on issues that matter." Black media studies thus provides a look into the complexities of Black lives and provides a counternarrative to the persistent anti-Blackness in our world today.

Smith-Shomade and Means Coleman also draw our attention to the "Black" of "Black media studies." Means Coleman believes there is something "proactive about the centering of Blackness. She believes this centering—necessary for social justice—offers repair; contributes "diverse voices and perspectives to the discipline"; and, as in the #CiteBlackWomen and #BlackCitesMatter movements, fosters scholarly accountability. Although Smith-Shomade considers such centering of Blackness to be a "central part of who we are," she also believes as Black people "we are always doing and always called to do many other things that are justice related. . . . Black media studies just happens to be the venue by which we make these things manifest." Interestingly, H. Gray, urging us to recognize current conditions of knowledge and content production, believes

> the very idea that what Blackness does to media studies . . . is to insist that we think [of research, activism, and social justice] together, not separately, right? To separate them is to then kind of do violence. Both a kind of epistemological violence, but also historical violence to the work that's produced in this moment.

Blackness, H. Gray intimates, simply cannot be contained, in scholarship, in activism, in representations.

Looking back at the work that has produced this moment, Rhodes reflects:

> I remember there was a period of time when Black media studies was very much oriented towards media industries, right? That [we] were going to develop this critical apparatus that was going to change television, that was going to change, you know, the internet. And perhaps the gaze has shifted.

Rhodes speaks to critical studies of representation shifting the "gaze" beyond a "celebratory project" of media representation (Brock, 2011; K. Gray, 2020; K. Gray et al., 2018; K. Gray & Leonard, 2018; Joseph & Rhodes, 2016; Martin, 2021; Means Coleman, 2023; Smith-Shomade, 2012). One direction of expansion is a return to imagination and possibility. In his dialogue with Rhodes, H. Gray shares his appreciation of youth who are "pushing against boundaries" in creative and artistic spaces:

> They're both attacking structures, but they're [also] imagining different kinds of structures . . . elsewheres . . . and I think that's really what we've been missing in a lot of the kind of analysis of media studies, right? We've been so busy critiquing what's wrong with it and I think we want to encourage the young content makers to give us [affective] imaginations about possibility.

Holding Rhodes' question, "How do you shift that?," we imagine through Black joy, something H. Gray believes can shift our work.

Act 3: Affirming Blackness in Media and Academia

Undermining the popular notion of an academy–industry divide, Rhodes insists, "In the 21st century," the "distinction between global media and higher education [is] very little, if any." In response, H. Gray offers the urgent and "lively" challenge of understanding the ways in which we are "embedded" within the very logics we venture to study. He believes "we are in a unique position to codify . . . authorize . . . [and] circulate" understanding through the knowledges we generate and, we add, through the scholarly and mediated spaces we occupy. With love, liveliness, and joy, we now turn to affirming Blackness in media and academia.

Jackson considers academia to be a place hostile to "people who don't already have a point in." At this historical moment when many universities iterate institutional changemaking statements about diversity, equity, and inclusion (Patel, 2022), some create "points in" for Black scholars across disciplines with hires in areas such as in jas and Ralina's department, Black Studies in Communication. Reflecting specifically on the justice movements creating new Black media studies positions, K. Gray regards this push to bring Black scholars in as short-lived and believes "these should have been jobs [in] 2015." Her dialogue partner, Brock, is not surprised by the short life of institutional redress. For him, liberal inclusions of Blackness, as histories of the New Deal and Civil Rights Movement show, are always followed by a move back to "right and normal"—in other words, "a neoliberal move to privatize . . . extract from Black folk and make the policies multicultural." Brock and K. Gray remind us of the institutional factors preventing Black scholars and Black studies from creating change in official academic spaces. Our activisms and recoveries necessarily have to flow in and out of academia.

Rhodes also calls for increased collaboration beyond the academy and across borders, age, and media by returning to the guiding question, "How do we shift that?" She promotes a shift toward writing not for academics but, rather, for "some collective of folks for whom it matters." Such *collectivity* means we can be Black in expansive, multifaceted, and intersectional ways. In our research, in our connections to communities, and in what we choose to bring to universities. Brock again expands upon this third signal:

> we want to represent ourselves in ways that are not pathological or deviant. . . . [Our institutions] don't want us to be too Black. They want us to be Black enough in ways that they can apprehend us for lack of a better word. . . . They want us to be a particular kind of Black person and in our doing so we end up harming ourselves.

Seemingly responding to Brock's idea in his dialogue with Johnson, Jackson reflects on the journey of

> trying to figure out how to be in the Academy, but [do] it in a way that's much more holistic. That doesn't demand that [we] bracket out key fundamental parts of [our]selves and [our] investments in the world to do the job of being a scholar. . . . If we can figure out a way to do that well, not only will we hail different kinds of students to this place, but they'll actually be healthier while they're here, right?

He regards this shift away from "business as usual" as another form of activism, and his dialogue partner embodies this by choosing, in Johnson's words, to enter academic spaces with his "whole self, meaning [his] working class background . . . public school educated background . . . Blackness . . . [and] queerness." *Tricksterism*, Johnson argues, is a form of activism in which you can "weasel your way into being at a meeting where an important decision is being made." Fundamentally, these scholars seek the possibility Brock offers of "keep[ing] moving [past and through anti-Blackness] in order to find spaces that hopefully will sustain us."

Means Coleman speaks to the ways Black people "keep moving"—or continue to not let appropriation or exploitation of Blackness stop us—through the power of Black Twitter:

> We know they're going to snatch our stuff, meme it, try to do it . . . and before it goes out we have already rescripted, moved on [to] the next thing. And that isn't unique to Twitter. We have always done that because that's what Black vernacular is. . . . Black speech is about moving on because we know that you like the culture, and you're going to grab it, and we're going to keep it moving.

She considers Black Twitter to be a "whole, full, authentic" Black space and, like other forms of Black culture, does "not just mimic or respond to culture, but creates [it]." Similarly, Brock points to social media as a place where we, knowing there are "no innocent infrastructures," "still carve out space" to "be ourselves in really productive, life affirming, giving ways." Means Coleman also points to her own area of academic expertise, Black horror (Means Coleman, 2023), as another space for sustaining Black life. Horror "interrogates" moments of anti-Blackness by letting them "play out on the big screen and entertainment so we don't have to, ideally."

Further affirming the disruptive and space-making powers of Blackness, Smith-Shomade shares:

> When you're talking about where Black folks are present in great numbers, you're already talking about some disruption [going on] . . . people [today] are having different kinds of conversations. They're centering Black life and Black concerns in ways that we just haven't had done prior, and it's emboldened makers and creators, and hopefully everybody else . . . to move beyond our own respectability politics somewhat and to take this up.

She points specifically to "new platforms" as spaces that "allow for a certain kind of freedom, and a certain kind of emboldened activist enterprise that we haven't seen." Both she and Means Coleman speak to the contributions of Black-owned media, including press coverage of Black stories that, in Smith-Shomade's words, "would never have been brought to light."

Conclusion: Black ~~Activism~~Joy in the Everyday

> The question that underwrites all of these questions is, kind of, what does Black add to [the] formulation [of Black media studies], right, as a kind of social formation, as a kind of intellectual enterprise, as a kind of research project, right? Have we kind of exhausted [the] salience of what Blackness qualifies in that or are we just getting started after . . . several generations? But now we have a critical mass of students and faculties and meetings and papers and journals, and so it strikes me as an interesting moment to kind of think about, you know, the question of activism, the question of research, and the question of media studies in in the moment that we're in.
>
> —*Herman Gray*

We hope this chapter responds to H. Gray's challenge of understanding how we are implicated in what we study. We strived to answer Means Coleman's invitation to "think about Blackness as whole and full" by tending to the scholars themselves studying Blackness and media. No, as Brock warns, the "work does not love us," but our collectives and communities do. Love from and for them guides our pursuits of justice and understanding. Even the painful understanding, from bearing witness to the state-sanctioned killing of Tyre Nichols, that anti-Blackness can be embodied by any one of us. Loving Blackness is a joyful exercise, one sheltering our being through the work. We prioritize Black joy because, as Brock notes,

[It] is not simply about resisting oppression. It's about building the resources necessary to make it to the next day with your spirit as intact as possible. And that's not really resistance, that's living . . . not joy as resistance but more joy as living, Black living.

The experience of listening to these foundational scholars was incredibly joyful, and we committed to doing justice to their offerings by storying our time together. As Gray tells it, "If we don't have joy as our basic premise . . . these institutions will eat us up," and as Smith-Shomade makes plain,

These stories are always about telling us something about ourselves. . . . And sometimes we don't even care what y'all are doing, this what we doing, and this what we're celebrating. This is how we're moving and understanding ourselves. . . . As creators and as scholars it is important that we are always mindful of all the ways in which our humanity shows up, and we move into the how I got over because . . . we all get tired of the trauma of it all.

We feel an urgency to create justice with/in our Black communities. But there is not one way Black media studies and communication create and talk about justice. We are struck by the range and depth of responses to questions on activism and social justice, and by the connection between their and our understanding of Blackness as everything and nothing, as always "shap[ing] and be[ing] shaped by experiences" (Oliver, 2013). There is no singular way to define activism or social justice, just as there is no one way to be Black or to hold Blackness. Our commitments, positionings, and methods are as vast as the interests, constraints, and opportunities that brought us here. Like Johnson, we refuse to "believe that [we] can't make a difference in [historically White academic] spaces." We hold on to Brock's comment that "all of us in some ways have made an impact on how people understand Blackness in particular, and the digital, and the world." Whether as scholars, activists, artists, or media critics; through researching, filmmaking, gaming, and teaching; for career advancement, justice, liberation, and sake of understanding; or all and none of the above, we are creating space for, by, and with Black people. These collective efforts reflect, yet still do not define, activism and social justice for Black media and communication studies. This chapter contributes one offering to the collection.

References

Bowden, A. K., & Buie, C. R. (2021). Anti-Black racism in academia and what you can do about it. *Nature Reviews Materials, 6*, 760–761.

Brock, A. (2011). When keeping it real goes wrong: Resident Evil 5, racial representation, and gamers. *Games and Culture, 6*(5), 429–452.

Brock, A. (2020). *Distributed blackness: African American cybercultures.* New York University Press.

Gray, H. (2004). *Watching race, television, and the sign of Blackness* (2nd ed.). University of Minnesota Press.

Gray, H. (2005). *Cultural moves: Culture, identity and the politics of representation.* University of California Press.

Gray, H. (2013). Race, media, and the cultivation of concern. *Communication and Critical/Cultural Studies, 10*(2–3), 253–258. https://doi.org/10.1080/14791420.2013.821641

Gray, K. (2020). *Intersectional tech: Black users in digital gaming.* LSU Press.

Gray, K., Buyukozturk, B., & Hill, Z. G. (2017). Blurring the boundaries: Using Gamergate to examine "real" and symbolic violence against women in contemporary gaming culture. *Sociology Compass, 11*(3), Article e12458. https://doi.org/10.1111/soc4.12458

Gray, K., & Leonard, D. J. (Eds.). (2018). *Woke gaming: Digital challenges to oppression and social justice.* University of Washington Press.

Gray, K., Voorhees, G., & Vossen, E. (Eds.). (2018). *Feminism in play.* Palgrave Macmillan.

Hall, S. (1993). What is this "Black" in Black popular culture? *Social Justice, 20*(1–2), 104–114.

hooks, b. (2000). *All about love: New visions.* Harper.

Jackson, J. L. Jr. (2001). *Harlemworld : Doing race and class in contemporary Black America.* University of Chicago Press.

Jackson, J. L., Jr. (2005). *Real Black: Adventures in racial sincerity*. University of Chicago Press.

Jackson, J. L., Jr. (2008). *Racial paranoia: The unintended consequences of political correctness*. Basic Books.

Johnson, E. P. (2003). *Appropriating Blackness: Performance and the politics of authenticity*. Duke University Press.

Johnson, E. P. (2008a). *Sweet tea: Black gay men of the south—An oral history*. University of North Carolina Press.

Johnson, E. P. (2008b). *Pouring tea: Black gay men of the south tell their tales* [Stage reading].

Johnson, E. P. (2010). *Sweet tea—The play* [Play].

Johnson, E. P. (2018). *Black. Queer. Southern. Women: An oral history*. University of North Carolina Press.

Johnson, E. P. (2019). *Honeypot: Black southern women who love women*. Duke University Press.

Johnson, E. P., & Jackson, J. L., Jr. (2021). *Making sweet tea* [Documentary film].

Joseph, R. L., & Briscoe-Smith, A. (2021). *Generation mixed goes to school: Radically listening to multiracial kids*. Teachers College Press.

Joseph, R. L, & Rhodes, J. (2016). African American representation and the politics of respectability. *Souls, 18*(2–4), 187–191.

Marable, M. (2006). *Living Black history: How reimagining the African American past can remake America's racial future*. Basic Books.

Martin, A. L., Jr. (2021). *The generic closet: Black gayness and the Black-cast sitcom*. Indiana University Press.

Means Coleman, R. R. (2023). *Horror noire: A history of Black American horror from the 1890s to present* (2nd ed.). Routledge.

Oliver, V. C. (2013). *Radical presence Black performance in contemporary art*. Contemporary Arts Museum Houston. https://issuu.com/thecamh/docs/2012_radical_presence

Patel, L. (2022). *No study without struggle: Confronting settler colonialism in higher education*. Beacon Press.

Pendharkar, E. (2023, January 24). Florida's ban on AP African American studies, explained. *Education Week*. https://www.edweek.org/teaching-learning/floridas-ban-on-ap-african-american-studies-explained/2023/01

Rhodes, J. (1998). *Mary Ann Shadd Cary: The Black press and protest in the nineteenth century*. Indiana University Press.

Rhodes, J. (2017). *Framing the Black Panthers: The spectacular rise of a Black Power icon* (2nd ed.). University of Illinois Press.

Smith-Shomade, B. E. (2012). *Watching while Black—Centering the television of Black audiences*. Rutgers University Press.

Winchell, M., Kress, T. M., & Tobin, K. (2016). Teaching/learning radical listening: Joe's legacy among three generations of practitioners. In M. F. Angello & W. M. Reyonlds (Eds.), *Practicing critical pedagogy: The influences of Joe L. Kincheloe* (pp. 99–112). Springer.

CHAPTER 7

Latine Media Studies: From Near Omission to Radical Intersectionality

Angharad N. Valdivia

Latine[1] media studies is a growing field with maturing scholarship that represents the fruit borne by the promise of cumulative knowledge from at least four stages of scholarship and enriches communication and media studies, both historically and contemporarily. As with any recent field of study, scholarship arises from previously existing cognate disciplines and interdisciplines, following paradigm shifts and questions that cannot be answered by previous theories (Kuhn, 2012). This chapter begins with a brief review of the stages of inclusion of Latine in mainstream media and then presents a historical overview of the field of Latine media studies via a four-stage assessment, exploring both the institutionalization of the field and the stages of scholarship. The stages are not mutually exclusive. Whereas in the first two stages of research, much of the scholarship drew on cognate fields, by the third and fourth stages, our field had a robust quantity and quality of scholarship and scholars who work within communication and media studies. The four stages follow a familiar path of near omission; peripheral inclusion; steps toward institutionalization and maturation of scholars; and a present that is rich in hybrid, intersectional, and transnational scholarship. Latine media studies is no longer a promise but, rather, a full-blown reality. Thus, as a growing area of study, it contributes to social justice via diversified production (ideally but not always done by Latine), increased and progressive representations, and creating spaces for audience identification and sometimes activism.

Before proceeding, I mention the great heterogeneity within this ethnic category. Although in the United States the most numerous element within *Latinidad* is Mexican American, there is also a long-standing presence of Puerto Rican communities—in addition to the colonized islands of Puerto Rico. Alongside the many waves of Cuban migration, and more recent flows from throughout the Americas, the term *Latine* is an inclusive effort to group this wide-ranging group of populations with varied sexualities and identifications for the purposes of understanding the production, representation, and audiences that include Latine and the resulting academic research that endeavors to account for and analyze our inclusion.

In mainstream media production and representation, omission was never complete because the visibility and meaning of ethnicity have to be accomplished via a reference to an *other*, even if an absent or implicit other. Marginalized populations sign in through absence, our implicit presence a backdrop against which theories of purity and practices perpetuating homogeneity can be inscribed. The near omission period of Latine led to inclusion via symbolic annihilation, such as Eva Longoria in *Desperate Housewives* being the only Latina (and person of color) in an ensemble cast of four, three of whom are White women. *Symbolic annihilation* refers to the underrepresentation and further marginalization or sensationalization of

---

[1] I use this term to refer to gender neutral designation of Latina/o/x people. When a particular gender is specifically mentioned, I use either *Latina* for women or *Latino* for men.

women or, in this case, people of color (Tuchman, 1978).[2] As another strategy of differential inclusion, sidekicks such as Miranda Sanchez/LaLaine in *Lizzie McGuire* perform a degree of presence and representation yet foreground the White main character or protagonist. Diverse ensemble casts complement strategies of differential inclusion, illustrated by light and ambiguous ethnics such as in *Barney* or by the addition of a classic spitfire, such as Sofia Vergara in *Modern Family*, a show that touts its inclusivity via Sofia and a gay married couple despite its stereotypical representation of these three characters. An occasional television show or a movie populated mostly by Latine stands out as an exception to the rule, such as *The George Lopez Show* and *Stuck in the Middle*, the former sometimes exploring Latine-specific issues and the latter largely proceeding with a nearly imperceptible amount of Latinidad (Leon-Boys & Valdivia, 2021). Latine are currently sprinkled throughout a range of mainstream media, performing continuous tropes and some rupture roles, which go against the grain of colonizing narratives (Hall, 2003; Hammer, 2017).

Similarly, one can map academic research along stages, finding overlap between them. In this chapter, I outline the above listed four stages of Latine media studies. From the first stage of near omission of the study of Latine, scholars began developing a complex area of studies. In the second stage, an occasional tokenistic mention—for instance, "a special box in chapter eight "minorities," conference panel usually scheduled early in the morning of the Sunday of a conference, or a special issue of a journal—although not of a major journal" (Valdivia, 2018, pp. 101–102)—announced the presence of an emerging scholarship. In the third stage, communication journals allowed for a "special issue" on Latinos (e.g., *Communication Review*, 2004, Vol. 7, Issue 2), and later Latino Studies journals published a special issue on the media (e.g., *Latino Studies*, 2011, Vol. 9, Issue 2–3). Within Latino studies, media studies research is not given full respect, with history, sociology, and literature scholars often writing about the media with minimal, if any, reference to media studies research. Moreover, publication expansion included acceptance in some journals, presses willing to include this research (e.g., University of Arizona Press, New York University Press, and University of Texas Press), and eventually book series in either Latina/o studies (Rutgers University Press) or critical Latina/o media studies (University of Florida Press) opened a space for the circulation of Latina media studies.

The drive toward institutionalization of Latina/o/x studies and the expansion of scholarship within communication and media studies within the third stage proved fertile ground for the creation of the fourth stage of scholars, many of whom were able to take a full set of courses on ethnic and Latina/o/x studies. Whereas the "Bronze race" metaphor of the first stage (Fregoso, 1993) referred to a middle ground of brown-ness, the contemporary fourth stage within Latine media studies extends into a complex and hybrid understanding of issues of race within the field, such as the expansion into *AfroLatinidades* and *Latina/o/x Indigeneities*, which include a self-introspection of anti-Blackness within Latinidad and the field of Latine media studies (Contreras, 2023). Although issues of gender arose at the end of the first stage, by the fourth stage the field was enriched by scholars of queer and trans identities as well as the rich literature on girls studies and the hypervisibilization of mediated quinceañeras. Nonetheless, the four stages are not mutually exclusive, and internal critiques remain a healthy warning to keep expanding the register of the meaning of Latinidad within mainstream media and the study of Latinidad within our field.

---

[2] Tuchman's research originally applied to women—White women to be exact. However, this finding has been extended to the one woman of color in an ensemble cast of otherwise White women. It has also been extended to the one person of color in an ensemble cast for advertising, and so on.

Before proceeding to the stages, I single out some enduring tropes and concepts we find in Latine media studies. Harking back to Hall (2003), cultural scholars track the vast range of continuities and the much smaller, if any, ruptures as we study mainstream media. Scholars such as Clark (1969) identified stages of representation based on paradigms available in the 1960s, and my proposed stages build on that foundation and also draw on the expanded theoretical and methodological approaches advanced by interdisciplinary and intersectional scholarship. Throughout the stages, after near omission, we find continuous symbolic annihilation, the myth of discovery, the flattening of difference, and the eternal foreigner tropes. As a rupture, in the latter two stages we begin to witness the appearance of an acknowledgment of hybridity—in racial, cultural, sexuality, and national origin terms. Whereas the first two stages were more or less ensconced within the U.S. national imaginary, by the latter two stages scholars examined the inevitable transnationally of population and cultural flows.

First Stage: Near Omission of Latine Within Media Studies

Latine media studies research predates the acknowledgment of the presence of this population category and area as an intellectual subfield. That first wave of scholars, roughly published until the late 1990s, developed Latina/o media studies research on their own, within departments of English/literature/cinema studies, history, or sociology yet focusing on communication and media (Aparicio, 1998; Fregoso, 1993; Rodriguez, 1997). Informed by a combination of a wide range of continental intellectuals, including Marx, Foucault, and Gramsci, as well as U.S. humanities scholars such as Gloria Anzaldúa and Renato Rosaldo, this first wave seeded the ground for an interdisciplinary field. Latina feminist media scholars built on scholarship by and about African American women (Bobo, 1995), Latin American women (Mattelart, 1986), and transnational feminist scholars (Shohat & Stam, 1994), germinating a transnational and intersectional field of study. These early studies on Chicano film (Fregoso, 1993), ways of understanding the presence of Latine in film and television (Rodriguez, 1997), and salsa (Aparicio, 1998) demonstrated great breadth of methods, theories, media, and research locations as well as a focus on different groups of Latine—Mexican American, Puerto Rican, and the range of Latinidades.

Second Stage: Peripheral Inclusion of Latine Media Studies

The second stage, dating roughly up to 2009, expanded the research of first-stage scholars. Scholars not only published on Latine media studies but also taught and recruited scholars so as to move beyond being the only person in a faculty specializing in this field. Seeding the field with the utopian goal of creating a new generation of the professoriate included the goal of bolstering Latine media scholars both in departments of communications and in freestanding departments of Latinx studies:

> In this second stage the special Latino studies issue of *The Communication Review* (2004, 7:2) included canonical essays in Latina media studies: "Brain, Brow and Booty" (Molina-Guzmán and Valdivia) and "The Gender of Latinidad: Latinas Speak About Hispanic Television" (Rojas), the former setting out an anti-essentialist mapping of the complicated terrain of gender, media and Latinidad and the latter addressing the gap in research of Latinas as audiences. (Valdivia, 2018, p. 102)

Scholars continue to research representational tropes documenting the finding of symbolic annihilation both qualitatively and quantitatively (e.g., Mastro & Stern, 2003; Merskin, 2007). An overflowing, standing-room-only panel on Latina media studies at the Latin American

Studies Association (LASA) 2006 conference held in Puerto Rico led to the edited volume *Latina/o Communications Studies Today* (Valdivia, 2008). By the end of the first decade of the millennium, which had begun with the U.S. census announcement that Latina/os were the most numerous minority in the United States, research in Latine media studies transitioned from emerging to institutionalized status.

Third Stage: Institutionalization of Latine Media Studies

The third stage yielded a generation of scholars drawing on an established subfield, acknowledging heterogeneity, working toward self-reflexivity, and collaborating with other subfields (Cepeda, 2016). This third stage overflows with diversity, creativity, and complexity. This generation of scholars has taken courses in the fields of ethnic studies, gender studies, and, if fortunate, Latine media studies. In addition, scholars present their research in interest groups and divisions such as Ethnicity and Race in Communication of the International Communication Association, the Latina Latino Communication Studies division and La Raza Caucus both at NCA (National Communication Association), and the Latinx/a/o Caucus at SCMS (Society for Cinema and Media Studies), to name a few of the major organizations. Moreover, both Latino studies and LASA (Latin American Studies Association) have divisions for Latinx studies in which Latine media scholars present. Major university presses, such as Rutgers University Press, have entire series, including *Latinidad: Transnational Cultures in the United States*, in which scholars can publish their book-length monographs.

Scholarship explores blurred boundaries, queer spaces, hybridities, ambiguities, multiple national identities, and cross-ethnic identifications and alliances (Molina-Guzmán & Cacho, 2013). Analyses extend the Latina/o space across global borders as scholars explore a large range of media, platforms, and genres. Scholars explore production issues (Casillas, 2014; Castañeda, 2012), audiences (Báez, 2021), and Latina stars, in relation to a long history of presence clouded through assimilationist narratives, such as *Latina/o Stars in Their Eyes* (Beltrán, 2009), *Musical ImagiNation* focusing on Shakira (Cepeda, 2010), and *Selenidad* singling out Selena (Paredez, 2009). Single-authored books such as Isabel Molina-Guzmán's *Dangerous Curves* (2010) coexist with inclusive edited collections such as *From Bananas to Buttocks* (Mendible, 2007) and *The Routledge Companion to Latina/o Media* (Casillas & Cepeda, 2017). The former is grounded in feminist theory and the latter represents a wide range of Latine media scholars.

Fourth Stage: Toward Radical Intersectionality Within Latine Media Studies

The fourth generation of scholars bears out the promise of intersectional, transnational, hybrid, gender-focused, and multimedia paradigm coming of age. Scholars explore issues of citational justice, the political economy of labor and production, youth and children, internal racism within the field and within media production of Latinidad, and the expansion into queer and trans inclusion. Scholars find that the trope of the eternal foreigner status of U.S. Latine endures, such as Disney's so-called first Latina Princess whose hot mess of locations and signifiers span Latin America but mostly Mexico in a brilliant display of the flattening of difference (Leon-Boys, 2023). Disney either represents Latin America, such as in *Encanto* (2021), or prefers light and ambiguous Latine characters (Valdivia, 2020). Dating back to Dávila's research in 2001 and up to the present, mainstream media authorizes and legitimates Latin Americans as authentic Latina/o producers and actors. U.S. Latina/o cultural creators and performers continue to struggle against this sidelining current. In an exceptional convergence of themes, Diaz (2021) reveals the fissures behind the symbiotic and exploitative relationship between celebrity culture, Latino labor, and White female journalism. This group of scholars combines political economy, cultural studies, gender studies, and Latine media studies seamlessly and urgently.

Addressing exclusionary practices in the production and circulation of scholarship, taking to task our dominant culture colleagues, scholars are calling out the politics of erasure, which reproduce the tedious narrative of U.S. White exceptionalism and have material effects for scholars of color. If our research is not referenced, we will not be hired, tenured, and/or promoted (Mejia, 2020; Washington, 2017): "If you do not recognize our work nor our experiences as legitimate, you are a part of the problem because your willful ignorance is erasing our existence" (Mejia, 2020, p. 361). Citational justice affects all emergent fields of study.

In addition, research on Latine youth takes center stage. For example, Boffone and Herrera (2022) "explore the diverse ways that contemporary mainstream film, theatre, and young adult literature invoke, construct, and interpret adolescent Latinidad" (p. 25). Likewise, Pérez (2021) takes the trope of the ingenue, "which typically casts young white women as one-dimensional subordinates to male leads and passive subjects of the male gaze" and infuses it with analytical lenses of race, sexuality, and adultification. Mazzarella (2020) foregrounds Emma González in a larger study about girls and moral panic, which teases out the celebrification of an inadvertent trauma-driven teen gun control activist. The expanding research on youth, including the work on quinceañeras, examines their assertion of gender fluidity and their efforts to valorize and visibilize their experiences in a mainstream popular culture that tends to marginalize and demonize them (González, 2019; Valdivia et al., 2022–2023). Whereas research on children and media seldom focuses on Latine and research on Latine youth seldom focuses on young children, Leon-Boys (2023) addresses both gaps in her book-length study of the circuit of culture of *Elena of Avalor*.

Latinx studies as a field is beginning to come to terms with the internal racism within Latinidad. Within Latine media studies, scholars point out the near erasure of Blackness and Indigeneity by media and by scholars (Hernandez, 2020; Jiménez Román & Flores, 2009; Molina-Guzmán, 2021; Salas-Pujols, 2022). For example, the AfroChicanx Digital Archives project on Instagram foregrounds the unacknowledged presence of AfroMexicans, including some who took part in the Underground Railroad to Mexico (Contreras, 2023). Public intellectuals and scholars are confronting the racism within Latine studies and communities. Contributory nations to Latinidad bring racism with them because Latin America is not inclusive of its Black or Indigenous populations. In that vein, Báez (2021) examines the legible and illegible representational labor that artists Amara La Negra and Yalitza Aparicio perform, not just in their music and movies but also in their interventional activism when they disrupt the symbolic racial order of mainstream media and Latine culture. As such, Báez's research represents the state of the art on issues of Indigeneity and Blackness as they form part of Latine media culture and Latine media studies. Studies of AfroLatinidad illustrate the transnational circulation of artists and culture (Henson, 2023; Reighan, 2022).

Acknowledgment of the hybridity of Latinidad and its internal discriminations pervades much of the research in this fourth stage. Hybridity originally was deployed ideologically to assert superiority of "White" Europeans versus the peoples they colonized, as well as against any of the mixed races in the colonies. Contemporary scholars find hybridity in population, culture, and blood. Understanding hybrid outcomes, especially in popular cultures, is imperative in a historical moment of immense mobility, more so for culture than for people. Hybridity as a concept can be used to assert the presence of an imagined/undocumented purity, or it can be used to acknowledge that we are mixed people living in lands of mixture; the latter proves most generative for Latine media studies. Applying hybridity to the study of Latinidad, the state or process of becoming a U.S. Latina/o/x, has proven to be immensely fruitful. Post-1492, the Americas were invaded by settler colonialists from all of Europe and have been the site of involuntary enslavement of people from Africa and Asia. Before 1492, the Americas experienced the arrival of Nordic and African travelers, and within the Americas there was migration. There is no purity in the Americas, Europe, Asia, or Africa. The two principal colonizers, Spain and Portugal, headed to the Americas following a period of nearly eight centuries of Moorish occupation, an African presence that resulted in extensive racial mixing. Furthermore, as the Spanish kings enacted their national project, consolidated through the Christian religion, they expelled both Jewish and Muslim populations, many of whom headed to the Americas. The Spanish asserted that they represented Whiteness, and that fiction endures today and partly fuels the discourses that render U.S. Latinas/os/x eternally foreign in the United States and inauthentic in relation to Latin Americans.

Hybridity as a concept enables the study of the construction and deployment of Latinidad, and it illuminates the impossibility of purity and the radical hybridity of Latinas/os/x, our culture, and our population (Valdivia, 2020). As such, hybridity opens the door to the study of ethnicities in relation (Shohat & Stam, 1994) and to consider the hybridity that prevails across all ethnic categories (e.g., Ocampo, 2016; Washington, 2017). Nonetheless, Latinas/os/x as a visible category in mainstream media remain "stuck in the middle," between Blackness and Whiteness, a move that attempts to fix all three ethnic categories outside of hybridity and within an essential purity (Leon-Boys & Valdivia, 2021). Mainstream media uses Latinidad to expand its gendered and racialized audiences by deploying a light hybrid visibility, light enough not to be noticed by general (read White) audiences yet including some signifiers that might appeal to ethnic and Latine audiences. The ambiguity might be read as Latina/o/x by some or Indian by others or Filipina by others or Native American by others or Italian by others, etc. The expansion of the ethnic register has both national and global aims for transnational media conglomerates, none of which can afford to function within a limited nation space.

Finally, some media about Latine and Latine media scholars foreground queerness and queer subjectivities. Even in mediated quinceañeras, shows such as Starz's *Vida*, HBO's *15: A Quinceañera Story*, Netflix's *The Beauty and the Baker*, and the rebooted *One Day at a Time* visibilized queerness (Valdivia et al., 2022–2023). Zecena (2022) provides an elegant analysis that brings audience and Latine media studies together to exemplify the work of fourth-stage scholars.

Conclusion

This chapter outlined four stages of Latine media studies from the 1990s to the present. As the visibility of the Latine population grows by fits and starts in mainstream media, scholars have sought to track this uneven presence of the United States' most numerous minority. Latine media studies has grown and expanded since the mid-1980s when scholars published research on what was then an ethnic category called "Hispanics." Augmented acknowledgment of the in-between "brown" group, located metaphorically between Blackness and Whiteness, has increased to an understanding of a heterogeneous ethnic group whose makeup runs the gamut of the racial spectrum—from Black to White and everything in between, including Asian-nesses, Indigeneities, etc.—with multiple national origins, diversity of sexuality and religion, political complexity, and unending potential for creativity across ever increasing media platforms drawing on centuries-old traditions from throughout the world.

In production, representation, and audiences, Latine form an indisputable component of mainstream media, which by mid-2023 had splintered into multiple platforms and segmented audiences. Continuities include the eternal foreigner trope and flattening of difference across Latinidades. Ruptures include expansion into queer and trans visibilities as well as not only acknowledgment of Latine Blackness but also a critique of the racism within Latine communities and within Latine studies. So-called social media[3] occupies the attention and creativity of Latine youth. Latine stars Rita Moreno and Jennifer Lopez enjoy enduring long careers lasting seven and four decades, respectively. The 2020 Super Bowl featured two Latinas, Shakira and Jennifer Lopez, simultaneously visibilizing Latinidad, flattening difference, and underscoring the fact that one Latina is not enough for the Super Bowl halftime.

Regardless of the increased presence and economic contribution of Latine, mainstream media continues to deploy the "eternal outsider" trope. Producing the rebooted *West Side Story*, Steven Spielberg consulted with Puerto Ricans at the University of Puerto Rico, whereas New York City was the location and provided the narrative for the movie. *Black Panther: Wakanda Forever* (2022) integrated Indigeneity into the narrative but did so by reiterating the eternal outsider trope—how much more outside can one be than under water—and the Meso-American specificity, which located the origin of the Talokan tribe in Mexico: inclusion through exclusion.

Migration remains a major theme in the news and public rhetoric (Chávez, 2021; Flores, 2020), as well as in fictional entertainment fare such as *The Lion King, Black Panther: Wakanda Forever*, the rebooted *Party of Five*, etc. Indeed, mainstream media continues to represent Latine in terms of fear and desire: the constructed fear of the migrant and the desire for the sexualized Latina. However, there is much more going on, with healthy expansion into the politics of race and Indigeneity, acknowledgment of the hybridity of Latinidad, and inclusion of a range of sexualities. Scholars have constructed a robust field whose findings apply to our discipline at large. Implicitly and explicitly, the research and the institutionalization of a field contribute to a project of social justice: Inclusionary scholarship and an inclusive academy are crucial components of social justice.

References

Aparicio, F. R. (1998). *Listening to salsa: Gender, Latin popular music, and Puerto Rican cultures*. Wesleyan University Press.

Báez, J. (2021). "I know I can't wait to see my name in lights": Nickelodeon's Taina and Latina television history. *Feminist Media Histories, 7*(4), 7–26.

Beltrán, M. C. (2009). *Latina/o stars in their eyes: The making and meanings of film and TV stardom*. University of Illinois Press.

Bobo, J. (1995). *Black women as cultural readers*. Columbia University Press.

Boffone, T., & Herrera, C. (2022). *Latinx teens: U.S. popular culture on the page, stage, and screen*. University of Arizona Press.

Casillas, I., & Cepeda, M. E. (Eds.). (2017). *The Routledge companion to Latina/o media studies*. Routledge.

Castañeda, M. (2012). Feeling good while buying goods: Promoting commodity activism to Latina consumers. In R. Mukherjee & S. Banet-Weiser (Eds.), *Commodity activism* (pp. 273–291). New York University Press.

Cepeda, M. E. (2010). *Musical ImagiNation: U.S-Colombian identity and the Latin music boom*. New York University Press.

Cepeda, M. E. (2016). Beyond "filling in the gap": The state and status of Latina/o feminist media studies. *Feminist Media Studies, 16*(2), 344–360.

Chávez, C. (2021). *The sound of exclusion: NPR and the Latinx public*. University of Arizona Press.

Clark, C. C. (1969). Television and social control: Some observations on the portrayals of ethnic minorities. *Television Quarterly, 8*, 18–22.

Contreras, R. (2023, May 3). *New project explores lives of Afro Mexicans in the U.S.* Axios. https://www.axios.com/2023/05/02/afro-mexicans-history-university-of-new-mexico

Dávila, A. (2001). *Latinos Inc.: The marketing and making of a people*. University of California Press.

---

[3] Media studies scholars know that all media is social; therefore, "social media" is a misnomer, which nonetheless has gained widespread currency.

Flores, L. A. (2020). *Deportable and disposable: Public rhetoric and the making of the "illegal" immigrant*. The Pennsylvania State University Press.

Fregoso, R. (1993). *The Bronze screen. Chicana and Chicano film culture*. University of Minnesota Press.

González, R. V. (2019). *Quinceañera style: Social belonging and Latinx consumer identities*. University of Texas Press.

Hall, S. (2003). *Cultural studies and the centre: Some problematics and problems*. In *Culture, media, language* (pp. 12–45). Routledge.

Hammer, R. (2017). Epistemic ruptures: History, practice, and the anticolonial imagination. In T. Barkawi & G. Lawson (Eds.), *International origins of social and political theory* (pp. 153–180). Emerald. doi:10.1108/S0198-871920170000032010

Henson, B. (2023). *Emergent quilombos: Black life and hip hop in Brazil*. University of Texas Press.

Hernandez, J. (2020). *Aesthetics of excess: The art and politics of Black and Latina embodiment*. Duke University Press.

Jiménez Román, M., & Flores, J. (2009). *The Afro-Latin@ reader: History and culture in the United States*. Duke University Press.

Kuhn, T. (2012). *The structure of scientific revolutions* (4th ed.). University of Chicago Press.

Leon-Boys, D. (2021). Disney's specific and ambiguous princess. *Girlhood Studies*, 14(2), 29–45.

Leon-Boys, D. (2023). *Elena, princesa of the periphery: Disney's flexible Latina girl*. Rutgers University Press.

Leon-Boys, D., & Valdivia, A. N. (2021). The location of U.S. Latinidad: Stuck in the middle, Disney, and the in-between ethnicity. *Journal of Children and Media*, 15(2), 218–232.

Mastro, D. E., & Stern, S. R. (2003). Representations of race in television commercials: A content analysis of prime-time advertising. *Journal of Broadcasting & Electronic Media*, 47(4), 638–647.

Mattelart, M. (1986). *Women, media, crisis: Femininity and disorder*. Comedia.

Mazzarella, S. (2020). *Girls, moral panic and news media: Troublesome bodies*. Routledge.

Mejia, R. (2020). Forum introduction: Communication and the politics of survival. *Communication and Critical/Cultural Studies*, 17(4), 360–368.

Mendible, M. (2007). *From bananas to buttocks: The Latina body in popular film and culture*. University of Texas Press.

Molina-Guzman, I. (2010). *Dangerous curves: Latina bodies in the media*. New York University Press.

Molina-Guzmán, I. (2021, November 16). The blurring binaries of Black/Latinidad in U.S. popular culture. *Flow*. https://www.flowjournal.org/2021/11/blurring-binaries-black-latinidad

Molina-Guzmán, I., & Cacho, L. M. (2013). Historically mapping contemporary intersectional feminist media studies. In C. Carter, L. Steiner, & L. McLaughlin (Eds.), *The Routledge companion to media & gender* (pp. 71–80). Taylor and Francis.

Ocampo, A. C. (2016). *The Latinos of Asia: How Filipino Americans break the rules of race*. Stanford University Press.

Paredez, D. (2009). *Selenidad: Selena, Latinos, and the performance of memory*. Duke University Press.

Pérez, S. M. (2021, October 8). Queen of the neighborhood: Monse Finnie mobilizes and defies the ingenue trope in Netflix's *On My Block*. *Flow*. https://www.flowjournal.org/2021/10/queen-of-the-neighborhood

Reighan, G. (2022). *Visualizing Black lives: Ownership and control in Afro-Brazilian media*. University of Illinois Press.

Rodriguez, C. E. (Ed.). (1997). *Latin looks: Images of Latinas and Latinos in the US media*. Westview Press.

Salas-Pujols, J. (2022). "It's about the way I'm treated": Afro-Latina Black identity development in the third space. *Youth & Society*, 54(4), 593–610. https://doi.org/10.1177/0044118X20982314

Shohat, E., & Stam, R. (1994). *Unthinking Eurocentrism: Multiculturalism and the media*. Routledge.

Tuchman, G. (1978). The symbolic annihilation of women by the mass media. In G. Tuchman, A. Kaplan Daniels, & J. Benit (Eds.), *Hearth and home: Images of women in the mass media* (pp. 3–38). Oxford University Press.

Valdivia, A. N. (2008). *Latina/o communication studies today*. Peter Lang.

Valdivia, A. N. (2018). Latina media studies. *Feminist Media Histories*, 4(2), 101–106.

Valdivia, A. N. (2020). *The gender of Latinidad: Uses and abuses of hybridity*. Blackwell.

Valdivia, A. N., Perez, S., & Herrera, Z. (2022–2023). *A dream quinceañera! Latina girlhood in mainstream media*. Smithsonian Voices in conjunction with the Latinx Girlhood Exhibit. Smithsonian Museum (National Museum of the American Latino).

Washington, M. S. (2017). *Blasian invasion: Mixed-race blacks and Asians in the celebrity industrial complex*. University Press of Mississippi.

Zecena, R. E. (2022). Messy queer familias: Negotiating desire, pleasure and melancholia in vida. *Queer Studies in Media & Popular Culture*, 7(1), 69–81.

CHAPTER 8 — Queer of Color Approaches to Critical Cultural Media Studies

Keisuke Kimura *and* Shinsuke Eguchi

The LGBTQ+ people's movement advocating for equality and human rights is gaining visibility while backlashes against it are increasing. Under the current political landscape surrounding LGBTQ+ people throughout the world, queer of color approaches that centralize often invisible connections between queerness and race as an analytical method for studying media practices and social justice are particularly useful. Queer of color critique emerged as a U.S.-based critical discourse within academia and activism in the 1990s in response to the sociopolitical and cultural climate (Ferguson, 2004; LeMaster & Tristano, 2023). For example, liberation movements such as feminist and civil rights movements, Black Power, and movements in Chicana/o, Asian American, and Native American communities have advanced critical discourses about racial issues and social justice in the United States. Building on women of color feminism and queer studies, queer of color critique unfolds the hypocrisy and contradiction of the neoliberal state of anti-racist and anti-colonial agenda governed by Western and White supremacy that have further produced marginality and oppression of queer and people of color in the United States and beyond (Ferguson, 2004). By centralizing the invisible connections between queerness and race, queer of color approaches disrupt colonial structures of neoliberalism that legitimize violence against queer people of color and challenge White-/Western-centric views about racial knowledge, subjectivities, and experiences in relation to queerness (Brockenbrough, 2015; Ferguson, 2004).

In addition to their genealogical development, queer of color approaches in media studies both celebrate queer visibility and challenge the contemporary landscape of media and social justice that continuously overlook the material realities of LGBTQ+ people of color. U.S.-based media have historically focused on White, cisgender, male, and heteronormative narratives (Lee, 2018; LeMaster & Tristano, 2023). Increased media representations of LGBTQ+ people are crucial in countering the historical continuum of heteronormative structures of society and advocating for more inclusive space for gender and sexual minorities. However, mainstream queer representations continue to (re)center White, cisgender, male, and middle-/upper-class subjectivity and knowledge production (Eguchi et al., 2018; Lee, 2018). In this way, queer of color approaches in media studies attend to the intersectional politics of racial capitalism and queerness in media scape through deconstructing imbalanced systems and practices of power, such as cisheteronormativity, White supremacy, and neoliberalism.

Specifically, queer of color approaches politicize, historicize, and contextualize racialized queerness as non-normative identities, performances, and politics to deconstruct and reconstruct taken-for-granted conditions, structures, and relations of power. Simultaneously, queer of color approaches value historically saturated and culturally specific ways of knowing about interactions and processes, institutions, and systems that have emerged from the experiences of queer people of color, mirroring the simultaneous operations of differences (e.g., race, gender, sexuality, class, nation, and the body). Accordingly, queer of color approaches often conceptualize queerness as an *impossible possibility*, suggesting how the present moment normalized by the existing White cisheteronormative patriarchal capitalist supremacy surveils, disciplines, and controls queerness (e.g., Chambers-Letson, 2018; Keeling, 2019; Muñoz, 2009). Hence, centering intersectional knowledge as the referring points, scholars who deploy queer of color approaches question and critique normalized media practices that produce content imbued with situated meanings.

In this chapter, we redirect our attention to map out a brief synopsis of existing critical cultural media scholarship that engages with queer of color approaches. We summarize our synopsis into the following three areas of inquiry: media industry, media representation, and media use and resistances. The first section pays attention to the queer of color scholarship, interrogating the production and distribution of media as a cultural industry. The second section showcases how scholars examine media representations of queer people of color. Last, the third section highlights how technology serves as an alternative platform of popular culture, materializing the experiences of queer people of color. By reviewing these three specific areas of inquiry, the overall goal of this chapter is to reevaluate the significance of queer of color approaches in the study of media and social justice. In the following section, we showcase the first area of critical cultural media scholarship—media industry.

Queer of Color Approaches to Media Industry

We understand the *industry* as a broad term in critical cultural media studies, including both individual and organizational layers of content distributors (e.g., representations, narratives, advertisements, and more) that are created, produced, distributed, packaged/licensed, and sold on media platforms (Christian, 2020). As Ferguson (2004) suggests, queer of color critique is an analytical framework that "extends women of color feminism by investigating how intersecting racial, gender, and sexual practices antagonize and/or conspire with the normative investments of nation-states and capital" (p. 4). Thus, queer of color critique is a powerful framework for resisting and disrupting the dominant systems of the media industry to include historically marginalized voices, narratives, and perspectives (Brockenbrough, 2015; Ferguson, 2004). Questioning the politics of differences organizing the industry's climates, scholars have illustrated the problematic concept of *diversity* in media production, marketing, and distribution (Christian, 2020; Ng, 2013; Puar, 2007; Tiffe, 2013).

A few corporations working with dominant ideologies to attract a mass audience have been controlling the production and distribution of the cable industry (Hall, 2005; Horkheimer & Adorno, 2012). The profit-making–driven nature of the media industry silenced, ignored, and misrepresented the voices and stories of LGBTQ+ people in general and LGBTQ+ people of color in particular (Christian, 2020; Martin, 2018; Ng, 2013; Rodriguez, 2023). However, with the emergence of the internet, the rapid development of broadcasting media platforms such as streaming services and social networking sites has expanded the array of distributors, allowing individual content creators to construct and/or deconstruct the systems of the media industry through specific narratives (Christian, 2020). Still, the climate of the broadcasting system has not changed as imbalanced power relations continue to marginalize LGBTQ+ people (Fischer, 2018; Ng, 2013). The media industry persists in its control over the production, distribution, and consumption of content. For example, the industrial practices of homonormativity are persistent. Theorized by Duggan (2002), *homonormativity* refers to a "new neoliberal sexual politics" that is subjected to "the possibility of a demobilized gay constituency and a privatized, depoliticized gay culture anchored in domesticity and consumption" (p. 179). It is a neoliberal project that incorporates gay cultures for the purpose of profit-making.

Rodriguez (2023) highlights the media industry's uncritical celebration of LGBTQ+ visibility and inclusion in the digital space. YouTube, a U.S.-based video-sharing platform under Google, has become a major platform for LGBTQ+ representations and expressions. However, he argues that specific LGBTQ+ content is strategically selected and commodified for the benefit of YouTube/Google's branding of a socially liberal and progressive agenda through LGBTQ+ inclusion and diversity (Christian, 2020). This aligns with Puar's (2007) concept of *homonationalism*, which highlights the Whiteness of queer identities and bodies that are strategically depoliticized and incorporated to sustain the imperialist dominance of the U.S. nation-state and capital.

Rodriguez (2023) elaborates on YouTube's vague guidelines for nudity, sexual content, and adult content that regulate what content is ad-friendly or not, which ultimately determines whether it is profitable or not. Specifically, content related to transness and transgender identities—even if they are educational materials that meet YouTube's exception policy—is often removed or deleted by YouTube's algorithm and deemed controversial. Moreover, he explains how the narratives of LGBTQ+ characters/people of color are often belittled as side stories and desexualized as they are excluded as potential romantic/sexual partners in mainstream media representations. In this way, LGBTQ+ texts are censored and policed in producing noncontroversial sexual content to expand commercial partnerships and viewership. Fischer (2018) also reminds us that the increased representations of transgender identities do not equal the improved condition of living for trans people and the LGBTQ+ community at large. Industrial discriminatory practices of profit-making that are working with homonationalism continue to marginalize LGBTQ+ people in the digital media space (Rodriguez, 2023).

With the increased LGBTQ+ visibility in the media industry production, scholars claim the significance of intersectionality in the processes of production and distribution of LGBTQ+ content. Christian (2020) examines the possibility of creating values for historically marginalized and excluded communities' narratives in TV programming through the scale of production and reception. Specifically, he examines the value of intersectionality in industrial contexts in order to disrupt and restructure the exclusionary system and practices against LGBTQ+ communities. Intersectionality is a powerful analytical tool grounded in Black feminist thought, elucidating multiple intersecting vectors of identities such as race, gender, sexuality, class, and more that co-constitute experiences of historically marginalized individuals and/or communities (Collins, 2000; Crenshaw, 1991). While acknowledging the transgressive shifts of diversifying LGBTQ+ representations in Hollywood production, Christian emphasizes the pitfall of commodifying cultural identities as the market in digital spaces amplifies misrepresentation, stereotypes, and the dominant matrix of power that exploits LGBTQ+ individuals and communities (see also Ng, 2013). The disparities of the legacy media era are being replicated by distributors, who prioritize larger audiences over smaller ones, using the value of *diversity* as a rhetorical strategy for attracting "buzz" and awards (Christian, 2020). Mainstream media often targets audiences who are socially liberal and politically progressive in order to secure popularity and make profits through the commodification of LGBTQ+ identities in the market. With the current climate of situating LGBTQ+ identities as the market, Christian envisions the industry's incorporation of intersectionality in platforms driven by algorithms for developing programs and marketing strategies that can attract a wider spectrum of audiences and increase commercial success for streaming channels (see also Christian et al., 2020). This is where Christian emphasizes the possibility of carefully attending to intersecting politics of race, gender, sexuality, and class in developing algorithms for the industry's distribution and marketing models.

Simultaneously, Martin (2020) reminds us that industry-based critical analysis in media studies still lacks careful engagement with intersectionality as queer of color subjectivities are continuously produced and distributed by and for the dominant market and reception. Specifically, he asserts how scholars in queer production studies often lack the axis of race in their analysis of queer media production (see also Martin, 2018). Queer of color representations and expressions have been increasing in the media industry, yet they are significantly overlooked as a site of inquiry through the realm of industry, production, and structural practices (Christian, 2020; Rodriguez, 2023).

Hegemonic practices of the media industry marginalize LGBTQ+ people through the production, distribution, and consumption of content while favoring the White, cisgender, male, middle class, and able-bodied. Working with homonormativity and homonationalism, production practices and the socially liberal consumption of queer content provide mass audiences with an illusionary embodiment of diversity and inclusion. Thus, we contend that queer of color approaches to the media industry offer valuable contributions to critical cultural media studies because they disrupt existing systems of profit-making in cultural production and marketing strategies that perpetually marginalize queer of color subjectivities and positionalities. In the following section, we move on to the second area of inquiry—media representation.

Queer of Color Approaches to Media Representation

Because representations matter, concerns for representations matter (Gray, 2013). For historically marginalized subjects and groups such as LGBTQ+ people of color who have been underrepresented in the media, gaining visibility through intersectional representations of who they are, what they do, and how they make sense of what they do implicates the progressive shaping of politics through activism and social movements (Christian, 2020). However, the ways media produce, commodify, and distribute underrepresentations of LGBTQ+ people of color often point to the current political economy of media that strategically capitalize diversity and multiculturalism for profit-making. Doing so ultimately maintains ongoing histories of social inequality and injustice. Media practices of producing content almost always mirror the normalized, majoritarian codes of ideas, values, and beliefs rooted in the existing White cisheteronormative patriarchal capitalist supremacy (Nishime, 2011; Squires & Brouwer, 2002). However, the historically saturated and culturally specific representations of LGBTQ+ people of color that may possibly challenge the unequal relations of power are also emerging from multiple media platforms. Accordingly, scholars have paid attention to complex, contradictory, and dynamic ways in which LGBTQ+ people of color are underrepresented in the media. While the legacy cable networks' corporate system that grants power to small numbers of executives to make decisions has struggled to dismantle production and distribution inequalities related to representations of cultural diversity (Christian, 2020), they have been producing some representations of LGBTQ+ people of color for their profit-making needs in the past two decades.

The cable television network owned by Paramount Global, VH1, produces and distributes a popular, well-known reality television series *Love & Hip Hop Hollywood* (LHHH) featuring a number of figures associated with the hip hop music industry in Los Angeles. LHHH's season 2 ran from September 7, 2015, to November 23, 2015, featuring the story of a Black cisgender male rap artist Miles "Siir Brock [SIC]" coming out. The season specifically centers on Miles' romantic relationship with another cast member who is a Black cisgender male rapper/producer/model/activist Milan Christopher Brown. According to Eguchi et al. (2018), the season opens with Miles and Milan in bed, where they are both unclothed and share a kiss. The scene is followed by diary sessions of both Miles and Milan. Here, Miles reveals that he will tell his girlfriend

Amber about his same-sex relationship with Milan. However, this season opener challenging the anti-queer landscape of the hip hop industry where rappers rarely disclose their sexual fluidities gradually shifts to a homonormative narrative in which Miles wants to come out of the closet throughout the season. Here, the representation of coming out is strategically framed as a healthy choice for Miles to discover who he truly is. As McCune (2014) reminds, the paradigm of coming out reifies the liberal, progressive logic of exceptional individualism and sexual freedom through which people are easily assumed to be able to queer beyond ongoing histories of structural constraints such as racism, sexism, and classism. The closet paradigm that signifies a conservative space of sexual backwardness discounts how some queer people of color, especially those coming from racialized and classed communities, do not subscribe to such an individualistic sexual paradigm working with the supremacy of Whiteness. Still, the queer romantic representation of a Black man loving another Black man is extremely rare in the cable networks and their prime reality series. Hence, LHHH's season 2 representing Miles' coming out story is a moment of transgression that represents impossible possibilities of Black queerness constrained by the existing White cisheteronormative patriarchal capitalist supremacy (Eguchi et al., 2018). LHHH season 2 is important from queer of color approaches to media and social justice.

Another example comes from the reality competition series *RuPaul's Drag Race*, produced by World of Wonder. The cable channel Logo TV, owned by Paramount Media Network, distributed the series between 2009 and 2016. VH1 then distributed the series between 2017 and 2022. In 2023, MTV became the distributor of the series. Speaking with the emerging field of queer intercultural communication (Chávez, 2013; Eguchi, 2021) that examines intersections between gender and sexuality, cultural differences, and globalization, LeMaster and Tristano (2023) pay attention to one of the Asian American drag queen contestants Gia Gunn, who first appeared in 2014's season 6. Centering trans of color criticism, LeMaster and Tristano together showcase the strategically nuanced way in which Gia produces the embodied performance of being an Asian trans femme through Orientalized transmisogyny. Specifically, Gia's intersectional performance of race, gender, and trans queerness ambiguously troubles both the controlling image of being a "good transgender person" created in and through White womanhood and stereotypical assumptions associated with gay and Asian people (LeMaster & Tristano, 2023). Overall, media makers capitalize the logic of Orientalism supporting the feminization of Asia and Asian people to accent Gia's trans queer performance imitating Whiteness of womanhood. Doing so strategically produces a *transmisogynistic* mode of becoming and being an Asian trans femme subject. Consequently, Gia's racialized gender represents an ongoing interplay of contradictory tensions between White womanhood and gay Asian male stereotypes producing the Asian American trans femme formation that troubles the popular cultural imaginations of what being Asian and Asian American means. Hence, Gia's intersectional performance of race, gender, and trans femme queerness that emerged from *RuPaul's Drag Race* points to a brief moment of de-/reconstruction of the existing White cisheteronormative patriarchal capitalist supremacy (LeMaster & Tristano, 2023). Again, Gia is an embodied text of racialized trans queerness that is quite significant for studies on media and social justice.

By paying attention to the two examples described above, we have showcased queer of color approaches to examine how media representations of LGBTQ+ people of color illuminate impossible possibilities. Although there are more media and social justice scholarships that draw queer of color approaches to representations, we note that the scholarships tend to be U.S.-centric because queer of color approaches (e.g., Cohen, 1997; Ferguson, 2004; Johnson, 2001; Muñoz, 2009) originally emerged from the U.S. academic knowledge productions. However, queer of color approaches are undeniably making an impact on global, transcultural studies on media representations of LGBTQ+ people of color (Chávez, 2013; Eguchi, 2021). Hence, queer of color approaches have the potential to make an international contribution to critical cultural media studies. Next, we turn our attention to media use and resistances.

Queer of Color Approaches to Media Use and Resistances

Technology has been serving as a dominant platform of popular culture that allows LGBTQ+ people of color to materialize and share their lived and embodied experiences in ways that were previously impossible (Bennett, 2003; Keeling, 2014; Mitra & Gajjala, 2008; Ng, 2013). LGBTQ+ people of color have been able to create and distribute digital media content through social media; Web-based platforms; and other digital technologies, such as TikTok, Instagram, Twitter, YouTube, video games, blogs, and more. Keeling (2014) highlights the intersections between queerness and technology in envisioning how technology shapes, alters, and transgresses the ways of understanding systems of gender and sexuality and intersecting politics of identity. Keeling showcases the possibilities of what she calls "Queer OS," an operating system that is designed to disrupt "common senses"—heteronormative structures of society that (re)produce violence, oppression, domination, and marginalization—and to imagine uncommon and/or unpredictable relationships between identity and digital space. Rodriguez (2018) highlights the possibilities of digital space that further incites fluidity of gender and sexuality because internet users (e.g., websites, social media, games, blogs, and more) can create a computer-generated identity that is not necessarily tied to the physical body. But simultaneously, scholars emphasize how users' gender and sexual identities affect the users' participation and experiences in digital spaces, perpetuating dominant structures of power (Pullen, 2010; Thompson, 2014; Wakeford, 1997).

Mitra and Gajjala (2008) bridge the gaps between queer theory and South Asian studies through their queer of color critique of Indian *digital diasporas*. They examine queer blogging in India, which has become an essential site for queer people in India to establish relationalities, share experiences, and challenge heteronormative systems of gender and sexuality that criminalize queer sexual practices. However, they also address the dilemma of how individualization of online participation delinks the users from community-based resources and support that are critical in navigating online and offline spaces. Importantly, their analysis elucidates the Western-centric notions and practices of gender and sexuality that are locally translated or adopted in South Asian contexts.

Concerning another digital platform of technology and popular culture, Chang (2015) explores queer relationships represented in mainstream video games such as *FrontierVille* (currently *The Pioneer of Trail*) and *World of Warcraft*. He underscores the erasure and/or marginalization of queer relationalities and stories (i.e., "straightwashing") in the gaming industry by analyzing character design, romantic desire, and story development in relation to race, gender, and sexuality. Although both games are referred to as "inherently queer" and gender and sexuality systems are seemingly fluid and customizable, Chang stresses that these gamic spaces provided by American game developers reinforce White superiority and heteronormative assumptions about romantic relationships that fail to disrupt stereotypes, stigma, and essentialized narrative of queer identities (Chess, 2016; Nakamura, 2012). Chang's arguments underscore the neoliberal logic of diversity and inclusivity of LGBTQ+ identity.

Ng (2013) examines the concept of a *post-gay era* with the media phenomenon of "gay-streaming" through the analysis of Logo, a U.S.-based network channel. She challenges the logic of a post-gay era which claims that because LGBTQ+ people are well-integrated in mainstream media, they therefore no longer face marginalization and discrimination. In popular culture examples such as TV shows and films, including LGBTQ+ characters, narratives, and relationalities in mainstream media and streaming services has become more prevalent than ever, which illuminates the possibility of inclusion and diversity for LGBTQ+ representations and expressions. However, Ng contends that the U.S. popular culture production uses homonormativity as strategic rhetoric of concealing real-life struggles and challenges pertaining to LGBTQ+ people. She acknowledges the increased representations of queer characters, stories, and personalities on the legacy cable networks and streaming services in the past two decades that have been contributing to LGBTQ+ visibility. But simultaneously, she asserts that "the discourses around gaystreaming also feed into construction of homonormativity that are enabled by the concomitant marginalization of other queer bodies and practices" (p. 270). Thus, Ng reminds the celebration of LGBTQ+ visibility is undergirded by the strategic inclusion and exploitation of LGBTQ+ people of color identities for advancing the U.S. neoliberal project.

Conclusion

Mapping out the brief synopsis of existing critical cultural media scholarship about areas such as media industry, media representation, and media use and resistances, we reiterate that queer of color approaches are imperative for disturbing and restructuring the profit-making nature of mass media that disproportionately marginalizes LGBTQ+ people. Our reviews of scholarships highlight how the U.S./Western hegemonic practices of media production working with homonormativity and homonationalism reproduce a neoliberal logic of inclusion and diversity that commodifies LGBTQ+ identities as the market and excludes LGBTQ+ people of color. Moreover, we envision the potential of queer of color approaches that further unsettle White, U.S./Western superiority and centricity in critical cultural media studies as scholars are bringing international and transcultural perspectives into the politics of LGBTQ+ people of color (Chávez, 2013; Eguchi, 2021; Mitra & Gajjala, 2008). Continuously unpacking the complex and nuanced experiences of LGBTQ+ identities in national and global contexts, an intersectional perspective is also essential for better making sense of how race, gender, sexuality, class, nation, the body, and other vectors of identities intersect and shape the lived experiences of LGBTQ+ individuals and communities through mass media (Christian, 2020; Martin, 2020).

References

Bennett, W. L. (2003). New media power: The internet and global activism. In N. Couldry & J. Curran (Eds.), *Contesting media power* (pp. 17–38). Rowman & Littlefield.

Brockenbrough, E. (2015). Queer of color agency in educational contexts: Analytic frameworks from a queer of color critique. *Educational Studies, 51*(1), 28–44. https://doi.org/10.1080/00131946.2014.979929

Chambers-Letson, J. (2018). *After the party: A manifesto for queer of color life.* New York University Press.

Chang, E. Y. (2015). Love is in the air: Queer (im)possibility and straightwashing in *FrontierVille* and *World of Warcraft. QED: A Journal in GLBTQ Worldmaking, 2*(2), 6–31. https://doi.org/10.14321/qed.2.2.0006

Chávez, K. R. (2013). Pushing boundaries: Queer intercultural communication. *Journal of International and Intercultural Communication, 6*(2), 83–95. https://doi.org/10.1080/17513057.2013.777506

Chess, S. (2016). The queer case of video games: Orgasms, heteronormativity, and video game narrative. *Critical Studies in Media Communication, 33*(1), 84–94. https://doi.org/10.1080/15295036.2015.1129066

Christian, A. J. (2020). Beyond branding: The value of intersectionality on streaming TV channels. *Television & New Media, 21*(5), 457–474. https://doi.org/10.1177/1527476419852241

Christian, A. J., Day, F., Díaz, M., & Peterson-Salahuddin, C. (2020). Platforming intersectionality: Networked solidarity and the limits of corporate social media. *Social Media + Society, 6*(3), 1–12. https://doi.org/10.1177/2056305120933301

Cohen, C. J. (1997). Punks, bulldaggers, and welfare queens: The real radical potential of queer politics? GLQ: *A Journal of Lesbian and Gay Studies, 3*(4), 437–465. https://doi.org/10.1215/10642684-3-4-437

Collins, P. H. (2000). *Black feminist thought: Knowledge, consciousness, and the politics of empowerment.* Routledge. https://doi.org/10.4324/9780203900055

Crenshaw, K. (1991). Mapping the margins: Intersectionality, identity politics, and violence against women of color. *Stanford Law Review, 43*(6), 1241–1299. https://doi.org/10.2307/1229039

Duggan, L. (2002). The new homonormativity: The sexual politics of neoliberalism. In R. Castronovo & D. Nelson (Eds.), *Materializing democracy: Toward a revitalized cultural politics* (pp. 175–194). Duke University Press.

Eguchi, S. (2021). On the horizon: Desiring global queer and trans* studies in international and intercultural communication. *Journal of International and Intercultural Communication, 14*(4), 275–283. https://doi.org/10.1080/17513057.2021.1967684

Eguchi, S., Files-Thompson, N., & Calafell, B. M. (2018). Queer (of color) aesthetics: Fleeting moments of transgression in VH1's *Love & Hip-Hop: Hollywood Season 2*. *Critical Studies in Media Communication, 35*(2), 180–193. https://doi.org/10.1080/15295036.2017.1385822

Ferguson, R. (2004). *Aberrations in black: Toward a queer of color critique*. University of Minnesota Press.

Fischer, M. (2018). Queer and feminist approaches to transgender media studies. In D. Harp, J. Loke, & I. Bachmann (Eds.), *Feminist approaches to media theory and research* (pp. 93–107). Palgrave Macmillan. https://doi.org/10.1007/978-3-319-90838-0

Gray, H. (2013). Race, media, and the cultivation of concern. *Communication and Critical/Cultural Studies, 10*(2–3), 253–258. https://doi.org/10.1080/14791420.2013.821641

Hall, S. (2005). The rediscovery of "ideology": Return of the repressed in media studies. In T. Bennett, J. Curran, M. Gurevitch, & J. Wollacott (Eds.), *Culture, society, and the media* (pp. 52–86). Routledge. https://doi.org/10.4324/9780203978092

Horkheimer, M., & Adorno, T. W. (2012). The culture industry: Enlightenment as mass deception. In B. Ollman & K. B. Anderson (Eds.), *Karl Marx* (pp. 405–425). Routledge. https://doi.org/10.4324/9781315251196

Johnson, E. P. (2001). "Quare" studies or (almost) everything I know about queer studies I learned from my grandmother. *Text and Performance Quarterly, 21*(1), 1–25. https://doi.org/10.1080/10462930128119

Keeling, K. (2014). Queer OS. *Cinema Journal, 53*(2), 152–157. https://doi.org/10.1353/cj.2014.0004

Keeling, K. (2019). *Queer times, Black futures*. New York University Press.

Lee, B. (2018). Pop out! Mass media and popular culture. In M. J. Murphy & B. Bjorngaard (Eds.), *Living out loud: An introduction to LGBTQ history, society, and culture* (pp. 249–288). Routledge. https://doi.org/10.4324/9781315640228

LeMaster, L., & Tristano, M., Jr. (2023). Performing (Asian American trans) femme on *RuPaul's Drag Race*: Dis/orienting racialized gender, or, performing trans femme of color, regardless. *Journal of International and Intercultural Communication, 16*(1), 1–18. https://doi.org/10.1080/17513057.2021.1955143

Martin, A. L., Jr. (2018). Introduction: What is queer production studies/why is queer production studies? *Journal of Film and Video, 70*(3–4), 3–7. https://www.jstor.org/stable/10.5406/jfilmvideo.70.3-4.0003

Martin, A. L., Jr. (2020). For scholars . . . When studying the queer of color image alone isn't enough. *Communication and Critical/Cultural Studies, 17*(1), 69–74. https://doi.org/10.1080/14791420.2020.1723797

McCune, J. Q., Jr. (2014). *Sexual discretion: Black masculinity and the politics of passing*. University of Chicago Press.

Mitra, R., & Gajjala, R. (2008). Queer blogging in Indian digital diasporas: A dialogic encounter. *Journal of Communication Inquiry, 32*(4), 400–423. https://doi.org/10.1177/0196859908321003

Muñoz, J. E. (2009). *Cruising utopia: The then and there of queer futurity*. New York University Press.

Nakamura, L. (2012). Queer female of color: The highest difficulty setting there is? Gaming rhetoric as gender capital. *Ada: A Journal of Gender, New Media, & Technology, 1*. https://doi.org/10.7264/N37P8W9V

Ng, E. (2013). A "post-gay" era? Media gaystreaming, homonormativity, and the politics of LGBT integration. *Communication, Culture & Critique, 6*(12), 258–283. https://doi.org/10.1111/cccr.12013

Nishime, L. (2011). Aliens: Narrating U.S. global identity through transnational adoption and interracial marriage in *Battlestar Galactica*. *Critical Studies in Media Communication, 28*(5), 450–465. https://doi.org/10.1080/15295036.2010.518620

Puar, J. (2007). *Terrorist assemblages: Homonationalism in queer times*. Duke University Press.

Pullen, C. (2010). Introduction. In C. Pullen & M. Cooper (Eds.), *LGBT identity and online new media* (pp. 1–13). Routledge. https://doi.org/10.4324/9780203855430

Rodriguez, J. A. (2018). Lesbian, gay, bisexual, transgender, and queer media: Key narratives, future directions. *Sociology Compass, 13*(4), 1–10. https://doi.org/10.1111/soc4.12675

Rodriguez, J. A. (2023). LGBTQ incorporated: YouTube and the management of diversity. *Journal of Homosexuality, 70*(9), 1807–1828. https://doi.org/10.1080/00918369.2022.2042664

Squires, C., & Brouwer, D. (2002). In/discernible bodies: The politics of passing in dominant and marginal media. *Critical Studies in Media Communication, 19*(3), 283–310. https://doi.org/10.1080/07393180216566

Thompson, N. J. A. (2014). Queer/ing game space: Sexual play in the World of Warcraft. *Media Fields Journal, 8*(8), 1–12. http://mediafieldsjournal.org/queering-game-space

Tiffe, R. (2013). *Original Plumbing*: Performing gender variance through relational self-determination. *Liminalities: A Journal of Performance Studies, 9*(4), 1–19. https://scholarworks.merrimack.edu/com_facpub/1

Wakeford, N. (1997). Cyberqueer. In A. Medhurst & S. Munt (Eds.), *Lesbian and gay studies: A critical introduction* (pp. 20–38). Cassell.

Queer and Transgender Media Studies

Erique Zhang *and* Thomas J Billard

Media activists have long believed in the power of representation and visibility as tools for social justice (Billard, 2024b; Gross, 2001). The media advocacy organization GLAAD, for example, publishes annual reports that document numbers of queer and transgender characters on television, while the annual International Day of Transgender Visibility relies on the assumption that seeing trans people will promote greater acceptance of trans people. Scholars of queer and trans media, however, critically interrogate this assumption, asking how representation works, what it does, and whether it has been an effective strategy in the fight for LGBTQ+ (lesbian, gay, bisexual, transgender, queer, and other related communities) rights. Moreover, scholars challenge the centrality of representation in media studies as new and emerging technologies complicate the contemporary media landscape, turning instead to deeper questions about media's impacts on LGBTQ+ communities. The proliferation of queer and trans media studies in recent decades speaks to the complexities of cultural production in an increasingly mediated, networked, and politicized world.

In this chapter, we offer an overview of research in queer and trans media studies and its relation to queer politics and social justice. We begin by briefly tracing the development of queer and trans theory, teasing out central questions in and divergences between the two related fields. We then discuss how scholars apply queer and trans theory to the study of media, starting with the issue of representation before turning to other questions about technology and media infrastructures. We argue that queer and trans media scholars must use diverse methods, drawing not only from humanistic inquiry but also from the social sciences, to gain a more holistic understanding of media. To that end, we explore how communication scholars and other social scientists use empirical methods to extend queer and trans media studies beyond representation to ask questions about production, reception, and political economy. Finally, we conclude by offering future research directions, focusing on the rise of digital and other emerging technologies and their relation to social justice.

Queer and Trans Theory

In 1990, feminist scholar Teresa de Lauretis organized a conference at the University of California, Santa Cruz, dedicated to gay and lesbian theory. The work presented at the conference was published in a 1991 special issue of the journal *differences* titled "Queer Theory: Lesbian and Gay Studies." In the introduction to the special issue, de Lauretis (1991) explains,

> The project of the conference was based on the speculative premise that homosexuality is . . . no longer to be seen either as merely transgressive or deviant vis-a-vis a proper, natural sexuality (i.e., institutionalized reproductive sexuality), according to the older, pathological model, or as just another, optional "life-style," according to the model of contemporary North American pluralism. (p. iii)

Rather, she argues, *sexualities* must be understood as "social and cultural forms in their own right" (p. iii). The development of "queer theory," then, was meant to shift gay and lesbian studies toward a critical interrogation of the sociocultural emergence of queer (sub)cultures and practices and their divergences from dominant (hetero)sexual culture.

Queer theory has often been described in terms of *dismantling, denaturalizing,* and *deconstructing* ideologies about gender and sexuality as dichotomous and natural (Hammers, 2016). Queer theory takes as a central tenet the idea that gender and sexuality are not natural categories but, rather, socially constructed ones, formed in relation and opposition to dominant cultural forms of heterosexuality. Judith Butler (1990), for example, argues that gender is not an inherent biological fact of the body but is produced and reproduced through social acts, which then inscribe gender onto bodies. Their theory of gender performativity has remained influential to queer theorists as a way to explain the social formation of gender.

This interest in denaturalization places heavy focus on *heteronormativity*, the idea that dominant heterosexual culture is assumed to be the norm. *Queerness* represents a threat to the stability of heteronormativity by revealing the production of gender and sexuality to be culturally contextual and not biologically natural. As an alternative to "gay and lesbian," identity labels that queer theorists assert have been subsumed into mainstream liberal politics, queer identity is often envisioned to be more radical and subversive, being concerned with anti-normativity rather than assimilation.

Scholars of race, however, have made important interventions into queer theory by critiquing its unmarked Whiteness. Queer of color critique posits that race, gender, and sexuality are interlocking forms of social stratification that all rely on the logics of capitalism and (re)productivity that construct the "deviant" body as one that does not perform proper productive labor (Ferguson, 2003). Meanwhile, Cathy Cohen (1997) questions the radical potential of queer politics because of its continued reliance on a binaristic division of people into "queer" and "not queer." In doing so, she argues, the queer movement excludes other marginalized groups deemed not queer, such as Black heterosexuals, whose racialized genders and sexualities have nonetheless been pathologized as non-normative by hegemonic society. She calls instead for a more expansive approach to liberatory politics that sees people of all marginalized statuses as working in solidarity. (For a more detailed discussion of queer of color critique and its relation to media studies, see Chapter 8.)

Emerging as a cognizable field well over a decade after queer theory, *transgender studies* has been described by trans studies pioneer Susan Stryker (2004) as "queer theory's evil twin" (p. 212). By this, Stryker means that trans studies traces similar intellectual lineages to queer theory (a point some scholars debate; see Billard et al., 2022), while diverging from queer theory's political investments where it concerns "identity, embodiment, and desire" (p. 214). In particular, trans studies has worked to resist the gravitational pull of queer theory, which attempts to subsume trans studies as a mere extension of sexual analysis into the domain of gender (Chu & Harsin Drager, 2019; Keegan, 2020a, 2020b).

As trans theorist Cáel M. Keegan (2020b) argues, queer theory's investment in deconstructing the binary gender system in an effort to "unravel heteronormativity" (p. 387) puts it fundamentally at odds with trans studies' insistence that gender is, in fact, an important site of identity and difference. Whereas queer theorists often maintain that trans identity is "some 'ultimate form' of queerness that manifests literally the metaphor of gender transgression" (Billard et al., 2020, p. 4500) or, conversely, "an anti-queer impulse toward binary conformity" (Billard & Zhang, 2022, p. 195), trans studies resists such characterization. Trans studies insists upon the validity of binary gender identification at the same time that it insists that a binary model of gender insufficiently accounts for the infinite possibilities of gendered experience—an experience shaped in no small part by race, culture, and history (Billard & Nesfield, 2021; Snorton, 2017). As such, trans studies is not (necessarily) invested in the end of gender for the purposes of sexual liberation but is, rather, invested in the opening up of gender for the purposes of gender liberation.

Queer and Trans Media Analysis

Given that queer theory emerged during an era when network television was in its heyday, it may come as little surprise that queer theorists have long been interested in media and other cultural texts as sites for excavating meaning around gender and sexuality. As Michael Warner (1991) notes, queer theory looks to mass culture to "show in ever more telling detail how pervasive the issues of lesbian and gay struggles have been in modern culture, and how various they have been over time" (p. 5). Film and media have been particularly fruitful areas for queer theorists to analyze how ideologies about gender and sexuality are produced and communicated to broader publics, as well as how queer and trans communities use media to produce anti-hegemonic texts that resist heteronormativity.

Early research in the subfield of queer and trans media studies was often interested in the representational power of media, looking largely at questions of visibility and "positive" versus "negative" representation. Larry Gross' (2001) landmark book *Up from Invisibility*, for example, traces the history of the gay rights movement and its relationship with media representation. The title foregrounds (in)visibility, and indeed, Gross writes that the book is "about the emergence of lesbian and gay Americans from the shadows of invisibility" (p. xiii). This work is emblematic of queer media scholars' interest in interrogating the role of positive representation in improving public opinion about LGBTQ+ communities.

Later work by queer and trans media scholars has complicated this assumption, however, showing how positive representations can still uphold normative ideas about race, gender, and sexuality. Keegan (2022) argues that "good" media representation relies on "*assimilative strategies*," fitting queer and trans people into heteronormative logics rather than contesting them (p. 27, italics added). Erique Zhang's (2023b) research on trans representation in fashion media, for example, suggests that trans women's identities are legitimized largely based on whether they conform to restrictive ideals of White, cisgender female beauty. Alongside work by Julian Kevon Glover (2016) and Emily Skidmore (2011), this research underscores how *transnormativity* in media privileges trans people who fit into dominant ideals of Whiteness, class, and heteronormativity.

Other queer and trans media scholars are concerned less with mainstream *representation*, turning instead to media *produced by* queer and trans subcultures to understand how these groups resist dominant heteronormative culture. José Esteban Muñoz's (1999) research focuses on figures whose work challenges hegemonic ideas about race, gender, and sexuality, such as artist Jean-Michel Basquiat, filmmaker Richard Fung, and drag performer Vaginal Creme Davis. LaVelle Ridley (2019) and Moya Bailey (2021) similarly explore how independently-produced media, such as the film *Tangerine* and the Web series *Skye's the Limit*, open up new possibilities for portraying Black queer and trans life. This scholarship reveals how those who are doubly marginalized within the LGBTQ+ community, especially queer people of color, continue to face erasure and invisibility in mainstream queer media and how they use media and cultural production as tools to challenge dominant queer culture.

The rise of digital media has allowed for a collapse of the division between producer and consumer, raising important questions about self-representation. The video-sharing platform YouTube, which was instrumental in popularizing participatory digital media since the mid-2000s, has been particularly well-studied. Researchers underscore how queer and trans digital content creators negotiate expectations about authenticity with the demands of being public figures, critically examining how notions of self-representation are predicated on larger social contexts (Homant & Sender, 2019; Zhang, 2023a). Moreover, research on digital media provides for a richer understanding of the potential of media activism to build community and further social justice causes by combatting dominant stereotypes about queer and trans people (Billard, 2024b; Miller, 2019; Raun, 2016).

In this section, we provided a brief overview of how communication and media scholars have approached the topic of queer and trans representation. However, as the field of queer and trans media studies grows, it continues to move beyond simply debating whether representation is good or bad, instead asking what media representation does and how queer communities can use media for their own purposes (Billard & Zhang, 2022). These issues are complicated by emerging digital media technologies and platforms, which blur the lines between media producers, users, and consumers. In the following section, we give selected examples of research that explore the impact of digital media technologies on queer and trans communities, politics, and activism.

Digital and Emerging Media Technologies

In the previous section, we focused primarily on research on legacy media (e.g., print, film, and television), before shifting to digital media studies. Communication and media scholars have increasingly turned their attention to digital and emerging media technologies to understand their impacts on society. The ubiquity of these technologies has transformed how individuals interact with media, complicating traditional distinctions between media producers and users and giving rise to new social issues. In this section, we highlight research on selected digital media technologies—video game studies and digital art, dating apps and sexual racism, and mis- and disinformation studies—to trace how queer and trans media scholars grapple with the effects of emerging technologies on LGBTQ+ populations.

Kara Keeling (2014) uses the operating system as a metaphor in naming her concept of QueerOS, an analytic framework that understands media technologies as complex systems involving various actors, interfaces, and affordances (see also Barnett et al., 2016). Bo Ruberg's (2019, 2022) foundational work in queer and trans video game studies exemplifies how scholars apply such frameworks to digital technologies. While Ruberg excavates histories of queer and trans representation in video games, they also call for media scholars to move beyond representation to examine topics such as how queer audiences and users experience media and how queer media producers might use digital media technologies to recontextualize and transform them. Whit Pow (2021) takes up this call in their work on queer artist Jamie Faye Fenton's *Digital TV Dinner*, a piece of digital art that utilizes video game technologies to intentionally create glitches. Like Keeling and her concept of QueerOS, Pow takes glitches as a metaphor for trans experience, describing Fenton's work as "beyond the binaries and boundaries of computational rule sets" (p. 200).

Like video games, mobile apps have also become a popular topic of research for media and communication scholars. Several researchers have taken a particular interest in dating apps, asking how platforms like Grindr and Tinder have transformed how queer individuals seek out romantic and sexual partners. At the same time, these apps have come under fire for exacerbating existing issues of racism, transphobia, and sizeism in LGBTQ+ communities. C. Winter Han (2021) and Apryl Williams (2024), for example, argue that dating apps reproduce sexual racism even among LGBTQ+ users, while failing to protect those who embody multiple axes of marginalization, such as queer and trans people of color. Other researchers are interested in how users choose to represent themselves on dating apps, such as when and how trans users choose to disclose their trans status to potential partners (Fernandez & Birnholtz, 2019). This research shows how even seemingly innocuous media technologies such as dating apps can have deleterious impacts on marginalized communities.

In our increasingly networked media ecology, the issue of mis- and disinformation has become particularly pressing for communication scholars. (Although the two terms are often conflated in popular discourse, Rachel Kuo and Alice Marwick [2021] define disinformation as "false or misleading information intentionally spread for profit, to create harm, or to advance political or ideological goals" [p. 1]; misinformation is not intentionally spread to cause harm.) Disinformation is often associated with right-wing activist groups that use digital platforms such as Twitter, Facebook, and podcasts to spread false and harmful information about groups they seek to suppress. As Ruth Pearce et al. (2020) and TJ Billard (2023, 2024a) argue, disinformation is a powerful tool used by groups of anti-trans activists known as gender critical feminists or trans-exclusionary radical feminists (TERFs) to demonize trans people and influence politicians to roll back protections for trans communities. Disinformation further reveals how distinctions between legacy media and new media are often porous and indiscrete: TERFs take advantage of both established media outlets such as newspapers and digital platforms such as social media to spread their views. As TERFs gain increasing prominence in the political landscape, communication scholars must grapple with the complex effects that media technologies have on queer and trans communities.

Media and communication scholars must take a holistic approach to the study of media if they are to fully understand the contemporary media landscape and its impacts on marginalized communities. This imperative extends beyond just what types of media scholars choose to research, taking into consideration the very methods that scholars use. Although much research in queer and trans media studies has relied on humanistic methods, such as literary and textual analysis, the expansiveness of the questions that scholars tackle requires a diversity of methodologies. These methods have been informed by scholars trained in social scientific fields, such as cultural sociology and communication studies, whose empirical methods complement the humanistic ones that have been traditional to media studies. In the next section, we explore some of these methodological approaches.

Methods in Queer and Trans Media Studies

To be overly simplistic, media studies can be loosely divided into three primary areas and sites of inquiry: representation/text, reception/audience, and production/industry. As we detailed previously, many foundational studies in queer and trans media studies were focused on representational analysis, often using textual analytic methods rooted in literary and film theory. These methods engage with the content of media, asking how images and texts produce discourses about trans and queer communities. However, given the complexity of today's media systems and infrastructures, scholars have increasingly looked to social scientific methods to answer questions about reception and production. We have previously called for queer and trans media scholars to use sociology of culture frameworks in order to move beyond representation to understand more deeply how queer and trans people themselves think about media, its production, and its meaning (Billard & Zhang, 2022). In this section, we give some examples of queer trans and media scholarship that use empirical methods.

Stuart Hall (1980) challenged the once-popular paradigm of media studies that believed that media directly influence audiences' beliefs and behaviors, instead proposing a decoding/encoding model in which audiences become active participants in interpreting media texts.

According to Hall, media have *encoded* ideological meanings that audiences then *decode*, actively interpreting, negotiating, and even outright opposing the encoded meanings. This conception of audiences as active participants is central to the subfield of reception studies, which seeks to understand how audiences make sense of media. Andre Cavalcante's (2018) work exemplifies the application of reception studies methods in queer and trans media studies. He uses ethnographic and interviewing methods, speaking directly with trans audiences to study not just how they consume media but also how they use digital media technologies, such as mobile apps and Web forums. In line with social and digital media studies, this work complicates the traditional division between producer and consumer to highlight the active role that audiences play in creating meaning through media.

Meanwhile, production scholars look behind the scenes to study the political economic forces behind media production. Katherine Sender's (2004) work on gay advertising, for example, shows how media corporations make business decisions around how to represent queerness to mainstream audiences in ways that depoliticize queer communities. Meanwhile, Aymar Jèan Christian's (2018) research focuses on the experiences of queer media producers of color and the challenges they face working in both legacy and digital media industries. Christian's research helps us understand how media producers from marginalized backgrounds, such as queer people of color, learn to navigate corporate structures and cultural gatekeepers (Christian & Peterson-Salahuddin, 2023). His academic scholarship is supplemented by his community-based research project Open TV (OTV), a platform that supports queer producers of color in developing and distributing their media productions. His work with OTV draws on participatory methods, allowing him to study how independent artists use digital media platforms to bypass legacy media gatekeepers and to tell more complex and less mainstream stories (Christian et al., 2020).

Beyond representation, production, and reception, scholars of queer and trans media also use a variety of social scientific methods to explore larger sociopolitical contexts. Sarah Jackson, Moya Bailey, and Brooke Foucault Welles (2018) employ discourse analysis and network analysis to trace how trans women of color's digital activism spreads through online spaces. Toby Beauchamp's (2019) and Mia Fischer's (2019) research bridges trans media studies with surveillance and technology studies, exploring how the U.S. security state limits trans people's freedom, even internationally. These studies use diverse methods, including computational methods, digital and traditional ethnography, and archival research, to answer complex questions about digital media, emerging technologies, and queer and trans politics.

As these examples show, the broad field of queer and trans media studies can take wildly divergent shapes. Early work often used textual analysis to critique media representation, asking how portrayals of queer and trans people communicate ideas about gender and sexuality. As communication scholars increasingly enter the field, they have brought with them social scientific, participatory, and computational methods, shifting the focus on representation to think more deeply about media systems, infrastructures, and technologies. This research complicates our understanding of queer and trans representation by asking how media are shaped by actors, institutions, and economies. This work also aligns with communication studies' interest in issues such as political economy, oppositional media, and media activism, and it exemplifies how scholars apply queer and trans theory to empirical questions in order to identify and find solutions for real-world social problems.

Conclusion and Future Directions

In this chapter, we offered a brief overview of queer and trans theory and their application to media and communication studies. We highlighted key questions and debates in the subfields of queer and trans media studies, particularly around representation, production, and reception, and laid out various methodological approaches and analytical frameworks for the study of queer and trans media. We assert that as the field continues to grow, scholars must make use of diverse methods, drawing from both humanistic and social scientific traditions, to understand more fully the impact of media on society and queer and trans social justice. We conclude this chapter by briefly recommending future directions for queer and trans media studies, focusing on digital and emerging technologies.

If queer and trans media scholars are to further a social justice-oriented mission, they must engage with deeper questions about media and society. Although analyses of media representation are certainly useful in understanding how ideologies about queer communities are produced and disseminated, these studies do not fully capture the complexity of media systems and politics. Scholars will need to explore the institutions behind media as well as how media shapes social consciousness. Digital media and other emerging technologies must also be central to the growth of queer and trans media studies, given how omnipresent these technologies are in contemporary life.

Media and communication scholars have argued that digital media technologies are never ideologically neutral but, rather, are shaped by social contexts, biases, and politics (Broussard, 2023; Noble, 2018). As digital technologies become more ingrained in social life, scholars must grapple with media's relationship with queer and trans politics and social justice. Emerging questions in queer and trans media studies include the role of mis- and disinformation in influencing the public's attitudes and political beliefs (Billard, 2023, 2024a); the linkages between media technologies and international technologies of surveillance (Beauchamp, 2019; Fischer, 2019); and the problematics of algorithmic bias, artificial intelligence, and machine learning (Scheuerman et al., 2021). These and other research questions underscore the need for queer and trans media scholars to take a holistic and interdisciplinary approach in order to tackle the complex social issues that plague LGBTQ+ communities in an increasingly digitized and globally connected world.

References

Bailey, M. (2021). *Misogynoir transformed: Black women's digital resistance*. New York University Press.

Barnett, F., Blas, Z., Cárdenas, M., Gaboury, J., Johnson, J. M., & Rhee, M. (2016). QueerOS: A user's manual. In M. K. Gold & L. F. Klein (Eds.), *Debates in the digital humanities 2016*. University of Minnesota Press. http://dhdebates.gc.cuny.edu/debates/text/56

Beauchamp, T. (2019). *Going stealth: Transgender politics and U.S. surveillance practices*. Duke University Press.

Billard, T. J. (2023). "Gender critical" discourse as disinformation: Unpacking TERF strategies of political communication. *Women's Studies in Communication*, *46*(2), 235–243.

Billard, T. J. (2024a). The politics of transgender health misinformation. *Political Communication*, *41*(2), 344–352.

Billard, T. J. (2024b). *Voices for transgender equality: Making change in the networked public sphere*. Oxford University Press.

Billard, T. J., Abbott, T. B., Haimson, O. L., Whipple, K. N., Whitestone, S. B., & Zhang, E. (2020). Rethinking (and retheorizing) transgender media representation: A roundtable discussion. *International Journal of Communication*, *14*, 4494–4507.

Billard, T. J., Everhart, A. R., & Zhang, E. (2022). Whither trans studies? On fields, post-disciplines, and the need for an applied transgender studies. *Bulletin of Applied Transgender Studies*, *1*(1–2), 1–18. http://doi.org/10.57814/pe84-4348

Billard, T. J., & Nesfield, S. (2021). (Re)making "transgender" identities in global media and popular culture. In J. M. Ryan (Ed.), *Trans lives in a globalizing world: Rights, identities, and politics* (pp. 66–89). Routledge.

Billard, T. J., & Zhang, E. (2022). Toward a transgender critique of media representation. *JCMS: Journal of Cinema and Media Studies*, *61*(2), 194–199. https://doi.org/10.1353/cj.2022.0005

Broussard, M. (2023). *More than a glitch: Confronting race, gender, and ability bias in tech*. MIT Press.

Butler, J. (1990). *Gender trouble: Feminism and the subversion of identity*. Routledge.

Cavalcante, A. (2018). *Struggling for ordinary: Media and transgender belonging in everyday life.* New York University Press.

Christian, A. J. (2018). *Open TV: Innovation beyond Hollywood and the rise of Web television.* New York University Press.

Christian, A. J., Day, F., Díaz, M., & Peterson-Salahuddin, C. (2020). Platforming intersectionality: Networked solidarity and the limits of corporate social media. *Social Media + Society, 6*(3). https://doi.org/10.1177/20563 05120933301

Christian, A. J., & Peterson-Salahuddin, C. (2023). Rage against the streaming studio system: Worker resistance to Hollywood's networked era. *Information, Communication & Society, 26*(5), 923–940. https://doi.org/10.1080/1369118X.2023.2166363

Chu, A. L., & Harsin Drager, E. (2019). After trans studies. *TSQ: Transgender Studies Quarterly, 6*(1), 103–116. https://doi.org/10.1215/23289252-7253524

Cohen, C. J. (1997). Punks, bulldaggers, and welfare queens: The radical potential of queer politics? *GLQ: A Journal of Lesbian and Gay Studies, 3*, 437–465.

de Lauretis, T. (1991). Queer theory: Lesbian and gay sexualities: An Introduction. *Differences, 3*(2), iii–xviii. https://doi.org/10.1215/10407391-3-2-iii

Ferguson, R. A. (2003). *Aberrations in black: Toward a queer of color critique.* University of Minnesota Press.

Fernandez, J. R., & Birnholtz, J. (2019). "I don't want them to not know": Investigating decisions to disclose transgender identity on dating platforms. *Proceedings of the ACM on Human–Computer Interaction, 3*(CSCW), 1–21. https://doi.org/10.1145/3359328

Fischer, M. (2019). *Terrorizing gender: Transgender visibility and the surveillance practices of the U.S. security state.* University of Nebraska Press.

Glover, J. K.. (2016). Redefining realness? On Janet Mock, Laverne Cox, Ts Madison, and the representation of transgender women of color in media. *Souls, 18*(2–4), 338–357. https://doi.org/10.1080/10999949.2016.1230824

Gross, L. (2001). *Up from invisibility: Lesbians, gay men, and the media in America.* Columbia University Press.

Hall, S. (1980). Encoding/decoding. In S. Hall, D. Hobson, A. Lowe, & P. Willis (Eds.), *Culture, media, language: Working papers in cultural studies, 1972–79* (pp. 117–127). Routledge.

Hammers, C. J. (2016). Queer. In A. E. Goldberg (Ed.), *The SAGE encyclopedia of LGBTQ studies* (pp. 906–908). SAGE.

Han, C. W. (2021). *Racial erotics: Gay men of color, sexual racism, and the politics of desire.* University of Washington Press.

Homant, E., & Sender, K. (2019). Queer immaterial labor in beauty videos by LGBTQ-identified YouTubers. *International Journal of Communication, 13*, 5386–5404.

Jackson, S. J., Bailey, M., & Foucault Welles, B. (2018). #GirlsLikeUs: Trans advocacy and community building online. *New Media & Society, 20*(5), 1868–1888. https://doi.org/10.1177/1461444817709276

Keegan, C. M. (2020a). Against queer theory. *TSQ: Transgender Studies Quarterly, 7*(3), 349–353. https://doi.org/10.1215/23289252-8552978

Keegan, C. M. (2020b). Getting disciplined: What's trans* about queer studies now? *Journal of Homosexuality, 67*(3), 384–397. https://doi.org/10.1080/00918369.2018.1530885

Keegan, C. M. (2022). On the necessity of bad trans objects. *Film Quarterly, 75*(3), 26–37. https://doi.org/10.1525/fq.2022.75.3.26

Keeling, K. (2014). Queer OS. *Cinema Journal, 53*(2), 152–157. https://doi.org/10.1353/cj.2014.0004

Kuo, R., & Marwick, A. (2021). Critical disinformation studies: History, power, and politics. *Harvard Kennedy School Misinformation Review, 2*(4). https://doi.org/10.37016/mr-2020-76

Miller, J. F. (2019). YouTube as a site of counternarratives to transnormativity. *Journal of Homosexuality, 66*(6), 815–837. https://doi.org/10.1080/00918369.2018.1484629

Muñoz, J. E. (1999). *Disidentifications: Queers of color and the performance of politics.* University of Minnesota Press.

Noble, S. U. (2018). *Algorithms of oppression: How search engines enforce racism.* New York University Press.

Pearce, R., Erikainen, S., & Vincent, B. (2020). TERF wars: An introduction. *The Sociological Review, 68*(4), 3–24. https://doi.org/10.1177/0038026120934713

Pow, W. (2021). A trans historiography of glitches and errors. *Feminist Media Histories, 7*(1), 197–230. https://doi.org/10.1525/fmh.2021.7.1.197

Raun, T. (2016). *Out online: Trans self-representation and community building on YouTube.* Routledge.

Ridley, L. (2019). Imagining otherly: Performing possible Black trans futures in *Tangerine. TSQ: Transgender Studies Quarterly, 6*(4), 481–490. https://doi.org/10.1215/23289252-7771653

Ruberg, B. (2019). *Video games have always been queer.* New York University Press.

Ruberg, B. (2022). Trans game studies. *JCMS: Journal of Cinema and Media Studies, 61*(2), 200–205. https://doi.org/10.1353/cj.2022.0006

Scheuerman, M. K., Pape, M., & Hanna, A. (2021). Auto-essentialization: Gender in automated facial analysis as extended colonial project. *Big Data & Society*, *8*(2). https://doi.org/10.1177/20539517211053712

Sender, K. (2004). *Business, not politics: The making of the gay market*. Columbia University Press.

Skidmore, E. (2011). Constructing the "good transsexual": Christine Jorgensen, Whiteness, and heteronormativity in the mid-twentieth-century press. *Feminist Studies*, *37*(2): 270–300.

Snorton, C. R. (2017). *Black on both sides: A racial history of trans identity*. University of Minnesota Press.

Warner, M. (1991). Introduction: Fear of a queer planet. *Social Text*, *29*, 3–17.

Williams, A. (2024). *Not my type: Automating sexual racism in online dating*. Stanford University Press.

Zhang, E. (2023a). "I don't just want to look female; I want to be beautiful": Theorizing passing as labor in the transition vlogs of Gigi Gorgeous and Natalie Wynn. *Feminist Media Studies*, *23*(4), 1376–1391. https://doi.org/10.1080/14680777.2022.2041687

Zhang, E. (2023b). "She is as feminine as my mother, as my sister, as my biologically female friends": On the promise and limits of transgender visibility in fashion media. *Communication, Culture and Critique*, *16*(1), 25–32. https://doi.org/10.1093/ccc/tcac043

Digital Religion and the Negotiation of Gender/Sex Norms

Ruth Tsuria

This chapter outlines the various ways religious communities have been using the internet to negotiate feminist issues. A comprehensive review of the literature in this field shows the complexities of digital religion: how anonymity might enable minority voices and perspectives to be heard; and participatory culture might "cancel" these alternative voices by strengthening traditionally religious, and even fundamental, approaches to gender and sexual norms.

Although the data discussed in this chapter are mostly derived from existing literature, and thus the chapter can be considered an extended literature review, I have done my best, when possible, to add some empirical examples. In terms of methodology, I took a double approach: In relation to the empirical examples, I combined digital observations with selective internet uses. This included information gathered from active religious informants, information gained from scholarly works, and active searches on Google browser for software and applications dedicated to users who identify as religious. The extended literature review methodology was based on Rocca's (2010) interdisciplinary literature review. The chapter examines these sources especially while paying attention to digital divides, polarizations, and the processes of power and normalization as they take place in online communities.

The chapter is divided into five sections. First, an overview of the relationship between religion and sexuality more broadly is presented, followed by a review of religion and sexuality in traditional media. Then, a dialectic approach is offered with an overview of digital media as a liberating force, contrasted by a view of digital media as a tool for enforcing traditional sexual norms in three areas of study: LGBTQIA+, female sexuality, and heteronormative behaviors. The next section of the chapter deconstructs this dualistic approach by providing a more complex model that argues for theorizing digital media as a Foucauldian discourse, where power and resistance are in constant play. The chapter combines an extended literature review with insight from a 6-year-long research project. These various sources will examine issues related to gender and sexuality in five major world religions (Islam, Christianity, Hinduism, Buddhism, and Judaism). Through the chapter, we can see how the internet plays a double and complicated role regarding feminist issues and concepts.

Short History of Digital Religion and the Negotiation of Gender/Sex

As a prelude to this chapter, a brief review of the scholarship of digital religion and its relationship to feminist issues is needed. First, digital religion studies explore the "evolution of religious practices online which are linked to online and offline contexts simultaneously" (Campbell, p. 1). That is, from the mid-1990s onwards, scholars of digital religion have examined how religious institutions and individuals use digital media; how digital media becomes a space for the development of new religious movements; and how religious norms, rituals, institutions, and concepts are negotiated via communication technologies (Campbell & Tsuria, 2021).

Most recently, scholars of digital religion have focused on exploring the daily religious use of digital technology—for example, studying religious iTune applications (Wagner, 2012), religious games or religious symbolism in video games (de Wildt & Aupers, 2020), or religious internet memes (Bellar et al., 2013). As can be seen from these examples, more nuanced attention is being given to the specific medium, its affordances, and how it is used by religious individuals. This current wave also displays an array of intersectional studies, which combine the study of digital religion with questions of race, ethnicity, nationality, sexuality, and gender.

In terms of understanding gender and sexuality within the sphere of digital religion, most studies focused on that intersection tend to highlight the online uses of feminist women from religious traditions (see Peterson, 2022). However, as Mia Lövheim argues, "Gender is . . . a fundamental source for structuring identities, traditions, values and rituals within religious traditions" (p. 2). Therefore, more attention paid toward this interaction would benefit our general understanding of current religious trends as well as digital media uses.

Scholars, like myself, who examine digital religion and gender/sex tend to be informed from the long tradition of feminist studies, and specifically cyber-feminism. Cyber feminists such as Sadie Plant have argued that feminist progress and technological progress can be viewed as interconnected (Plant, 1997). However, the reality of power in digital media is complicated, and digital media is used in both feminist and nonfeminist ways. According to Anne Balsamo (1996), "Technologies of the body not only manipulate alterity, but also reproduce it. Sexual differences are both the input and the output of the technological production of the gendered bodies" (p. 159). In other words, Balsamo states that technology is created in-line with current social norms regarding gender, and therefore technology is used to replicate and enforce those norms. It is the work of cyber-feminists to untangle the relationship between technology and society, understand media as a force that influences society's understanding of gender and sexual norms, and explore which power structures are in play and how they impact notions of gender and sex. Based on this understanding of digital religion and cyber-feminism, the rest of the chapter examines specific studies related to the intersection between religion, gender/sex, and digital media. The next section begins this exploration by investigating digital religious media in relation to queer identities.

LGBTQIA+ Representation and Negotiation

Whereas traditional religious media tends to support religious ideology, the internet, because of its participatory qualities, allows for the empowerment of alternative voices (Campbell, 2010). This is apparent in the case of queer identities and religious organizations. For religious LGBTQIA+ individuals, who live in more religiously traditional societies that reject their identities, digital media is an important source of information (Burke, 2014). For example, Burke shows that online resources provide an avenue for Christians to explore a variety of sexual "awakenings": "Evangelicals use the internet to shape, interpret and make meaning of sex in ways different than what is presented in popular evangelical literature" (p. 17). In addition to using digital media for support and community, religious LGBTQIA+ individuals use digital media to question and negotiate the religious norms in their community that relate to their identities.

One prominent avenue of this negotiation happens on social media. In Taylor et al.'s (2014) study of Christian youth in the United Kingdom, they found that social media plays a pivotal role in understanding and communicating one's identity. Taylor et al. suggest that for these participants, their religious and sexual identities were not "separate and divergent paths" but, rather, two parts of one's identity that "mutually and complexly construct one another" (p. 1139). Participants use digital media to create a space for themselves that might have been at odds with the religious organization or with perceived notions of LGBTQIA+ identity. Taylor et al. show

how those who occupy both identities as religious and queer use digital media to communicate this "mixed" identity: "In order to truly publicly live through potentially conflicting identities, this must be reflected by the online embodiment in Facebook" (p. 1145). Thus, social media becomes the arena not only for coming out but also for negotiating one's religious identity.

Similarly, Mokhtar et al. (2019) examined the role of social media for LGBTQIA+ individuals in Malaysia. According to Mokhtar et al., "In Malaysia, LGBT is considered to be a taboo subject, due to strict Islamic practices and laws" (p. 78). Combining interviews and online social media observations, these researchers found that LGBTQIA+ individuals in Malaysia have a "strong relationship with social media" (p. 79). Many of Mokhtar et al.'s informants noted feeling isolated in their immediate surroundings but that social media offer a space in which they can connect with others, share experiences, and "find people like them" (p. 80). Users also employed social media to advocate for the acceptance of LGBTQIA+ individuals in the broader religious society.

In religious societies, social media is used by minorities to suggest alternative perspectives and negotiate religious sexual norms. Naturally, negotiating one's religious and queer identity online tends to bleed over to different forms of activism. For example, the Tumblr page Queer Ummah: A Visibility Project works to make LGBTQIA+ Muslims visible. As the page self-describes, "LGBTQ+ Muslims exist. And some of them are ready for you to listen."[1] Indeed, according to a recent study, this page and other digital activist efforts have resulted in higher visibility for queer Muslims (Tellawi et al., 2020). In summary, queer religious users have been able to employ digital media to voice their concerns, form communities, and negotiate their identity—both inside the religious community and external to it. Unlike traditional religious media, which either erases queer identities or persecutes it (Perry & Snawder, 2016; Yi et al., 2017), digital media allows, through its participatory affordances, LGBTQIA+ religious users to articulate their identity through their own words.

In opposition to the previously described uses of digital media to promote sexual freedom, there are also ways in which digital media is used to enforce traditional religious approaches to sexuality/gender. Although digital media is an important outlet for LGBTQIA+ individuals, it is also being used by religious individuals to combat nontraditional sexuality. Anti-LGBTQIA+ content online has proven to be an issue because it can incite online (or offline) hate speech and even online/offline hate crimes against queer individuals.[2] Many hate groups use social media and other digital media avenues to spread anti-LGBTQIA+ content. In some cases, these groups are directly tied to religious traditions. For example, the Faithful World Baptist Church (based in the United States) has been identified as a hate group by the Southern Poverty Law Center. Its website declares as a doctrine statement that "homosexuality is a sin and an abomination which God punishes with the death penalty."[3] Similarly, Żuk and Żuk (2020) show how Catholic-inspired homophobia and anti-gender narratives are popular in Polish social media. They explain that

> the atmosphere of fear, moral indignation and propaganda against "the other" strengthen the right-wing authoritarianism that appeals to nationalism, [and] conservative values. . . . For the image of the enemy to be effectively internalized, this creation must take place on many levels. . . . The anti-gender discourse was . . . present in various communication channels (Church messages, PiS's political narrative, YouTube, conservative journalists' discourse, slogans at street demonstrations). (p. 585)

---

[1] https://queerummah.tumblr.com.
[2] http://www.galop.org.uk/what-is-online-anti-lgbt-hate-speech-and-hate-crime.
[3] http://www.faithfulwordbaptist.org/page6.html.

Using social media is an important avenue for religious anti-LGBTQIA+ campaigning because it positions these opinions as popular, and not only hierarchical. This phenomenon is further theorized by Tom Boellstorff (2020) as "digital heterosexism." In his review of the anti-LGBTQIA+ movement in Indonesia, he claims that "online media are key" (p. 8) in promoting populist and exclusionary opinions. Boellstorff shows how anti-LGBTQIA+ sentiments were mediated online and then translated into real government decisions—for example, by banning Grindr and other LGBTQIA+-related web applications. In that sense, for Indonesia, "digital spaces were becoming construed as part of the national imagined community" (p. 15)—spaces in which the larger community can dictate correct sexual behavior.

Religious anti-LGBTQIA+ sentiments can be promoted through a combination of authority and participation, specifically on social media. According to Weng (2015), media-savvy Islamic preachers use social media in a form known as "online *dakwah*." Online *dakwah* can promote an anti-LGBTQIA+ attitude, using the logics of digital culture to disseminate traditional approaches to sexuality (Weng, 2015). An example is the anti-LGBTQIA+ social media campaign Wear White, a combined effort of Christian and Muslim participants in Singapore. According to Han (2018), the Wear White campaign was launched on Facebook in 2014 as a reaction to the Pink Dot Pride Parade. The campaign's goal was to "send a message to LGBTQIA+ activists that there is a conservative majority in Singapore who will push back and will not allow them to promote their homosexual lifestyle and liberal ideologies" (Han, 2018, p. 44). The use of social media was especially powerful because it allowed both Christian and Muslim individuals to participate simply by using the hashtag #wearwhite. The campaign included photos, videos, arguments, and simple visuals—all various communication tactics that feel natural to the social media environment. In that way, this campaign exemplifies how social media and social media logics can be used against liberal values, and specifically by religious individuals to disseminate anti-LGBTQIA+ messages. A similar tension between uses of digital media to resist or support religious traditional notions of gender/sex can be noted in regard to female sexuality, which is explored in the next section.

Understanding Female Sexuality

Like LGBTQIA+ individuals, women have been overlooked or oppressed in most religious traditions (Stopler, 2003). This oppression happens in religious institutional leadership (from which women are usually banned); the performance of household chores and child-raising (work that tends to be viewed as a woman's responsibility); and the bedroom, where female sexuality is often ignored, disregarded, or suppressed. Whereas many religious traditions also dictate and suppress male sexuality (e.g., by banning masturbation), female sexuality tends to be transparent in religious traditions. Because most religions were created and maintained by male leadership, it is not surprising that they neglect a focus on female sexual needs. With the advent of digital media, religious women's voices are heard and have become part of the public debates within their religious communities.

For example, the Israeli–Jewish website Kipa.co.il, in association with Yahel Center, created an online video series explicitly about intimacy and challenging existing sexual norms in the Orthodox community. The rationale for the video series was that the Orthodox society needs to be able to discuss intimacy in a "clean" way. Although the majority of the users' reactions to this video series were negative (Tsuria, 2017), some users supported this effort and praised this groundbreaking content. This online video content was especially unique in its focus on female sexuality, meditated by female leaders. The videos feature women talking about sexuality and *Halacha* (Jewish religious law), not only having their voices heard but also de facto acting as teachers and religious authorities. Digital media seems to allow female leadership to flourish, which then increases the visibility of female needs. For example, according to Tomalin et al. (2015), "In recent years . . . Buddhist women's social movement activity has been conducted digitally through websites, Facebook pages, and Twitter accounts. . . . Buddhist women globally make use of a wider range of Web-based opportunities" (pp. 12–13). These digital opportunities have allowed Buddhist nuns and female leaders to become more visible, and in turn, they began highlighting women's needs, including their sexuality. Amma Thanasanti, a female spiritual teacher, wrote the following on the popular webpage Alliance for Bhikkhunis:[4]

> I see a pathway forward; a pathway that helps us create life out of the ash. This pathway integrates the masculine and feminine—solar and lunar aspects of ourselves. . . . This pathway encompasses our sexuality, basic needs, power needs, and capacity for empathy.

While recognizing the difference between males and females, religious feminists on digital media utilize this platform to increase female leadership and discuss taboo issues such as female sexuality. It is worth noting that these religious feminist attempts still tend to be binary in their discussion of gender and lack inclusion of nonconfirming genders.

Defending female sexuality is not just about making it visible to religious societies, as portrayed by the above two examples. Digital media can also be used to literally defend the right of women to have a more "liberated" sexuality. This was the case with the Pink Chaddi social media campaign in India (Chattopadhyay, 2011). According to Chattopadhyay, following an attack of a few women in a nightclub by a few male members of the Hindu right-wing party in 2009, a female journalist started a Facebook group called Consortium of Pub-Going, Loose and Forward Women (later known as Pink Chaddi). The Facebook group, which started as a joke, soon became a hub for activism against Hindutva—a Hindu movement that promotes, among other things, a gendered and sexist extremism. The Hindutva movement in India "draws on images of women as ideal mothers, chaste wives, and compliant daughters. Not surprisingly, these notions are grounded on the idea of virtue being the precondition of women's entry into the public sphere of nation-building" (p. 65). Therefore, removing the control around female sexuality is an important avenue for this ideological struggle. Using digital media, women and feminists from throughout the world joined this struggle. As Chattopadhyay explains, "Online media and Web services provide the space and tools for advocacy, where the personal can become political" (p. 64). Females' personal choices—how to dress, drink, or interact—were defended and women's freedoms advocated for in this online campaign. In these ways, digital media allows women in religious societies to discuss, enact, and protect their sexual needs and freedoms.

Although many online sources are used to empower women to ask and speak about their sexuality, digital media is also used by women and men alike to urge a more traditional approach to female bodies. For example, even in the case of the Pink Chaddi, discussed previously, digital media also worked as an enforcer of "modesty." The Vishva Hindu Parishad, the organization whose members attacked the women at the bar that led to the online Pink Chaddi campaign, is an example of a traditional, extremist religious organization that uses digital media to oppress women (Chattopadhyay, 2011).

Another potent example is how religious digital media portrays female masturbation as a sin. A major aspect of the sexual liberation movement was recognizing female sexual needs, including masturbation. This recognition allows women to engage with sexuality more fully

---

[4] https://www.bhikkhuni.net/news_2017.

and in a healthier way and feel less abused or objectified. Women who masturbate also enjoy higher self-esteem and greater marital and sexual satisfaction (Hurlbert & Whittaker, 1991). In other words, it allows them to be a subject in the sexual act, not just an object. Although most religious traditions have no explicit language against female masturbation (probably because female sexuality was largely dismissed), contemporary religious texts online tend to object to it (Tsuria, 2020). For example, an article on the Today's Christian Woman website suggests that masturbation is a complicated topic and that "if in doubt, don't do it."[5] Covenant Eyes, a Christian website with a goal to "equip people with tools . . . in the fight against internet temptation,"[6] dedicates an entire section to female masturbation. The website suggests that "if you're a woman who has struggled with any sort of lustful sin habit, including masturbation, you're not alone. Millions of Christian women (single and married) are facing similar temptations every day."[7] Through this type of discourse, female masturbation—and female sexuality—is framed as sinful and problematic. In these various examples, we see again how digital religious media is used to both combat religious traditional notions of female sexuality and enforce them. The next section highlights this tension regarding general heteronormative behaviors, including dating and marriage.

Religious Heterosexual Norms Online

Another avenue in which digital media is used as an emancipating force is dating in religious communities. In many traditional religious societies, young unmarried people are strictly observed by family members and their love lives are restricted in various ways. Online dating, however, has allowed a shift in dating habits within religious communities. As a result, there is a growing number of religiously specific dating websites and apps, which allow for users to date digitally but still within the boundaries of their religious tradition and community (Richardson et al., 2020). For example, within the religious Jewish community, there seems to be a growing acceptance of online dating and dating applications (Cohen & Tsuria, 2019). In general, the use of digital media is not encouraged in Orthodox religious Judaism. However, according to Cohen and Tsuria (2019), leaders in even the more conservative denominations tend to permit using online dating. Because the goal of marriage is so important in this religious tradition, using even unsupervised means, such as online dating, is approved (Cohen & Tsuria, 2019).

Although it might be approved by religious leaders, online dating does challenge the traditional norms of pre-matrimonial relationships in religious communities. Most notably, it increases individual agency in the process (Rochadiat et al., 2018). Rochadiat and colleagues interviewed 16 Muslim American women who self-identified as "moderate Muslims." Using digital media tools for dating, these women reported an increased sense of personal agency. It seems that online dating allows women more control in the process of dating. However, the women do not simply abandon traditional/religious dating norms. Instead, they engage in a delicate and complicated act of balancing new technology and agency with traditional norms—for example, keeping their families involved in the dating process (p. 1635). Although technology can support a greater individual agency, a person's religious values also play a meaningful part in how they use the technology.

In other words, research should note how religious users bring their set of religious concepts and behavior to online dating, and in turn, these concepts shape the use of the

---

[5] https://www.todayschristianwoman.com/articles/2014/may/masturbation-is-it-always-sin.html.

[6] https://www.covenanteyes.com/about-covenant-eyes/corporate-history.

[7] https://www.covenanteyes.com/2017/04/19/women-masturbation-talking-openly.

technology. Many religious dating websites do not function with the same logic as secular websites. On religious dating websites, one might find categories such as level of religious observance (Coehn & Tsuria, 2019) or a stronger emphasis on marriage and limiting dating or sexual "hookups" (Naji Bajnaid & Elyas, 2017). In general, religious dating websites offer religious-valued avenues for dating. Although these websites adhere to religious values, they still allow users higher agency and privacy in comparison with traditional religious dating.

Digital media is also used implicitly to police heterosexual norms within religious communities. This mostly happens through normalizing discourse (Tsuria, 2016). According to Tsuria, digital media use within communities can work as a site of push-and-pull, of negotiation of norms. However, often, those already empowered—for example, religious leaders—tend to have a stronger pull. The participatory uses of technology are then applied to show support for traditional norms and leadership, not resistance to it. Examining Jewish questions and answers (Q&A) on sexuality, Tsuria (2016) provides various examples in which the Q&A serves as a regulatory tool. For instance, when a young woman discloses to a rabbi that she is forming a friendship with a man, the rabbi advises against a friendship that is not intended on marriage, explaining that "for a girl to be close friends with a guy and want it not to go any further, is like eating donuts and not wanting to gain weight" (p. 6).

Digital media, and specifically religious web platforms, is used to educate and regulate traditional religious norms. Another stark example is Christian efforts in the United States against online pornography and the general encouragement toward modesty and premarital celibacy. Although many of such efforts occur offline, there are also growing online efforts. One should keep in mind that the root of such efforts tends to be a religious adherence to avoid masturbation and to maintain purity. The increased accessibility to the internet and also the increase in pornographic material online have led Christian religious leaders to declare that "pornography may be the greatest area of immorality inflicted on and pursued by Generation Z" (White, 2017, p. 60). This is true for Christians in the United States as well as in the Global South. Examining the issue for Pentecostal Christians in Democratic Republic of the Congo, Pype (2013) writes that "Pentecostals deem that Christian households, and the Christian community at large are endangered by this new technology." To combat this "danger," several churches created online resources to help individuals avoid consuming pornography. Many Christian websites have articles and advice regarding the topic. For example, Cru.com, an interdenominational Christian parachurch organization, has articles such as "How I Overcame My Porn Addiction."[8] The discourse on such websites strengthens the more traditional norms of sexuality, which view sexuality as sacred to heterosexual marriage alone, and discourages premarital sexual intimacy or masturbation.

Digital media is used to maintain traditions on the path to heterosexual marriage. Although the previous examples discussed the autonomy and agency given to individuals through online dating, online dating also reinforces religious traditional views of marriage. Many religious dating websites and applications only allow for heterosexual relations (Cohen & Tsuria, 2020). Another interesting example is the issue of caste in Hindu dating. Caste is a cultural–religious construct that is preserved through the religious Hindu tradition. On various Hindu digital dating platforms, caste is usually a major profile category one must self-describe (Titzmann, 2019). Thus, as Titzmann argues, digital media "emphasize[s] caste as an

---

[8] https://www.cru.org/us/en/how-to-know-god/my-story-a-life-changed/how-i-overcame-my-porn-addiction.html.

important social criterion to be considered in matchmaking" (p. 35). Through these design choices, digital dating platforms uphold religious, traditional, heteronormative assumptions.

Digital media also provides space for more extremist ideologies—for example, the "red-pill" and the "manosphere." The manosphere is a collection of male-oriented blogs, social media sites, and discussion forums that reject feminism and instead promote a strong sense of masculinity and even misogyny. Although most users who lead the manosphere are self-proclaimed atheists, many of the ideas they promote are traditional religious gender divisions (women should stay at home, women should serve men, etc.), dressed in a scientific rhetoric. Recently, one of the leaders of this online community announced his commitment to Eastern Orthodox Christianity. According to *The Washington Post* journalist Tara Burton, this story is "representative of a broader trend within far-right Internet-based groups: Some of their members come to embrace a highly conservative, traditionalist version of Christianity as a bulwark against what they see as the decadent, liberal modern world."[9] Fundamental groups from other religions—such as the Vishva Hindu Parishad (a Hindu right-wing organization), discussed above—also use digital media to promote an extremely heteronormative traditional approach to masculinity.

These case studies demonstrate how digital media is used by religious individuals and organizations to promote conservative views of sexuality—views that oppose LGBTQIA+ identities, ban masturbation, uphold traditional family gendered relations, and encourage traditional approaches to female sexuality. At the same time, the review also discussed case studies in which digital media is used to allow female voices, promote a conjoined queer and religious identity, and debate liberal approaches to gender and sex within religious communities. The next section makes sense of these two opposing directions.

Digital Media, Religion, and Sexuality: A "Space" of Their Own

The internet, although communicated via binary code, is not a binary space. It is composed of a spectrum of human lived experience. This is also true for religious uses of digital media. Whereas some use digital media to resist traditional gendered norms, others use it to strengthen existing religious sexual behaviors. Even more complex are uses that are not declaratively liberal or conservative, such as using a Hindu dating app or shopping online for modest swimwear. But uniting these various online communication behaviors is the fact they are created by religious people for religious people.

Unlike mass media, which tends to be secular, or traditional religious media, which tends to be produced by religious leaders and organizations, religious digital media provides an opportunity for individuals and communities to negotiate their own norms. It is a media through which religious communities can (more) openly discuss their theology, ideology, identity, practices, and worldviews. Through digital media, different voices in each religious community can be heard—those of leaders and laypeople, different genders, different sexual orientations, etc. That does not mean all voices are equal and are weighed the same: A tweet from @Pontifex might mean more to more people than a tweet from @ChurchToo. But it does mean that religious cultural norms—in this case, sexual norms—are debated online. Digital media, unlike other forms of media, is not just a tool for representation. It becomes a tool for introspection and emic dialogue—by emic, I mean internal to the community. It can also be thought of as a site of struggle in a Foucauldian sense—that is, a space where norms

---

[9] https://www.washingtonpost.com/outlook/a-notorious-pickup-artist-found-god-lots-of-angry-white-radicals-do/2019/05/30/8f009d24-8237-11e9-9a67-a687ca99fb3d_story.html.

are created, negotiated, resisted, and policed through the discursive practices of various community members (Tsuria, 2017, 2020).

Conclusion

This chapter provided various examples of the intersection of digital media and sexuality from world religions. The chapter offered case studies from Christianity in Congo, Islam in Malaysia, Hinduism in India, Buddhism in Bhutan, and Judaism in the United States, to name a few. But throughout the various locations and traditions, what connects these cases is that they all exemplify how religious individuals are using media for their own needs—using it as a "space of their own," to paraphrase Virginia Woolf, to negotiate and make sense of gender/sex relations, identities, and norms.

References

Balsamo, A. (1996). *Technologies of the gendered body: Reading cyborg women*. Duke University Press.

Bellar, W., Campbell, H. A., Cho, K. J., Terry, A. J., Tsuria, R., Yadlin-Segal, A., & Ziemer, J. A. (2013). Reading religion in internet memes. *Journal of Religion, Media and Digital Culture, 2*, 1–39.

Boellstorff, T. (2020). Om toleran Om: Four Indonesian reflections on digital heterosexism. *Media, Culture & Society, 42*(1), 7–24.

Burke, K. (2014). What makes a man: Gender and sexual boundaries on evangelical Christian sexuality websites. *Sexualities, 17*(1–2), 3–22.

Campbell, H. A. (2010). Religious authority and the blogosphere. *Journal of Computer-Mediated Communication, 15*(2), 251–276.

Campbell, H. A. (2013). Digital religion: Understanding religious practice in new media worlds. Routledge.

Campbell, H. A., & Tsuria, R. (2021). *Digital religion: Understanding religious practice in digital media*. Routledge.

Chattopadhyay, S. (2011). Online activism for a heterogeneous time: The Pink Chaddi campaign and the social media in India. *Building and Strengthening Communities and Social Networks, 27*(2), 63–67.

Cohen, Y., & Tsuria, R. (2019). A match made in the clouds: Jews, rabbis and online dating sites. In A. Hetsroni & M. Tuncez (Eds.), *Internet-infused romantic interactions and dating practices* (pp. 177–190). Institute of Network Cultures.

de Wildt, L., & Aupers, S. (2020). Pop theology: Forum discussions on religion in videogames. *Information, Communication & Society, 23*(10), 1444–1462.

Han, S. (2018). Wear white: The mediatized politics of religious anti-LGBT activism in Singapore. *Nordic Journal of Religion and Society, 31*(1), 41–57.

Hurlbert, D. F., & Whittaker, K. E. (1991). The role of masturbation in marital and sexual satisfaction: A comparative study of female masturbators and nonmasturbators. *Journal of Sex Education and Therapy, 17*(4), 272–282.

Lövheim, Mia, ed. (2013). *Media, religion and gender: Key issues and new challenges*. Routledge.

Mokhtar, M. F., Sukeri, W. A. E. D. W., & Abd Latiff, Z. (2019). Social media roles in spreading LGBT movements in Malaysia. *Asian Journal of Media and Communication, 3*(2), 77–82.

Naji Bajnaid, A., & Elyas, T. (2017). Exploring the phenomena of online dating platforms versus Saudi traditional spouse courtship in the 21st century. *Digest of Middle East Studies, 26*(1), 74–96.

Perry, S. L., & Snawder, K. J. (2016). Longitudinal effects of religious media on opposition to same-sex marriage. *Sexuality & Culture, 20*, 785–804.

Peterson, K. M. (2022). *Unruly souls: The digital activism of Muslim and Christian feminists*. Rutgers University Press.

Plant, S. (1997). *Zeroes + ones: Digital women + the new technoculture*. Doubleday.

Pype, K. (2013). *Cursing the mobile phone: Pentecostal understandings of urban sociality, sexuality and social media in contemporary Kinshasa*. https://ssrn.com/abstract=2253735

Richardson, M., Cannon, S., Teichert, L., Vance, A., Kramer, I., Barter, M., King, J., & Callahan, C. (2020). Religion-focused dating apps: A Q methodology study on the uses of mutual. *Telematics and Informatics, 55*, Article 101448.

Rocca, K. A. (2010). Student participation in the college classroom: An extended multidisciplinary literature review. *Communication Education, 59*(2), 185–213.

Rochadiat, A. M., Tong, S. T., & Novak, J. M. (2018). Online dating and courtship among Muslim American women: Negotiating technology, religious identity, and culture. *New Media & Society, 20*(4), 1618–1639.

Stopler, G. (2003). Countenancing the oppression of women: How liberals tolerate religious and cultural practices that discriminate against women. *Columbia Journal of Gender & Law, 12*, 154–221.

Taylor, Y., Falconer, E., & Snowdon, R. (2014). Queer youth, Facebook and faith: Facebook methodologies and online identities. *New Media & Society, 16*(7), 1138–1153. https://doi.org/10.1177/1461444814544000

Tellawi, G., Khanpour, S., & Rider, G. N. (2020). Navigating (queer) sexuality in Islam. *Current Sexual Health Reports, 12*(4), 329–334. https://doi.org/10.1007/s11930-020-00290-4

Titzmann, F. M. (2019). Hindu religious identification in India's online matrimonial market. In X. Zeiler (Ed.), *Digital Hinduism* (pp. 35–50). Routledge.

Tomalin, E., Starkey, C., & Halafoff, A. (2015). Cyber sisters: Buddhist women's online activism and practice. *Annual Review of the Sociology of Religion, 6*, 11–33.

Tsuria, R. (2016). Jewish Q&A online and the regulation of sexuality: Using Foucault to read technology. *Social Media + Society, 2*(3). https://doi.org/10.1177/2056305116662176

Tsuria, R. (2017). *New media in the Jewish bedroom: Exploring religious Jewish online discourse concerning gender and sexuality* [Doctoral dissertation]. Texas A&M University. http://works.bepress.com/ruth-tsuria/4

Tsuria, R. (2020). The discourse of practice: Online Q&A as normalizing gender and sexual behaviors. *International Journal of Communication, 14*, 3595–3613.

Wagner, R. (2012). You are what you install: Religious authenticity and identity in mobile apps. In Campbell, H. A. (Ed.), *Digital religion: Understanding religious practice in new media worlds* (pp. 199–207). Routledge.

Weng, H. W. (2015). Dakwah 2.0: Digital Dakwah, street Dakwah and cyber-urban activism among Chinese Muslims in Malaysia and Indonesia. In N. C. Schneider & C. Richter (Eds.), *New media configurations and socio-cultural dynamics in Asia and the Arab world* (pp. 198–221). Nomos Verlagsgesellschaft.

White, J. E. (2017). *Meet Generation Z: Understanding and reaching the new post-Christian world.* Baker Book House.

Yi, J., Jung, G., & Phillips, J. (2017). Evangelical Christian discourse in South Korea on the LGBT: The politics of cross-border learning. *Society, 54*, 29–33.

Żuk, P., & Żuk P. (2020). "Murderers of the unborn" and "sexual degenerates": Analysis of the "anti-gender" discourse of the Catholic Church and the nationalist right in Poland. *Critical Discourse Studies, 17*(5), 566–588. doi:10.1080/17405904.2019.1676808

Critical Disability Media Studies

Katie Ellis *and* Jessica Keeley

Although people with disability are the largest minority group in the world, comprising almost 20% of the population, disability is most often considered a medical problem requiring a medical solution. Yet, disability cannot be resolved exclusively through medical means. This chapter aims to put disability on the agenda for media and social justice research by demonstrating the ways disability is socially and culturally constructed and sustained across a number of social institutions.

The origins of disability studies as an academic discipline can be traced back to UK disability activist efforts of the 1960s and 1970s (Oliver, 1990). As Vic Finkelstein (1975) explains,

> Disabled people have begun to organise for their emancipation and joined the growing numbers of groups struggling against social discrimination. We are taking a deeper look at ourselves, at the way we are treated and at what is meant by disability. (p. 31)

Key to Finkelstein's activist efforts was the assertion that disability was a result of social discrimination—specifically the stigma attached to disabled people's bodies. Drawing on these insights, in this chapter we argue that people with disability are an important group to include to gain a comprehensive overview of media and social justice. Despite increasing recognition that people with disability experience social discrimination, media representation often continues to locate disability in the body. People with disability have typically been represented in the media in three ways: as an object of pity, a source of inspiration, or a punishment for wrongdoing.

We begin this chapter with a brief overview of two main approaches to disability—the medical and social models of disability—before moving on to a brief explanation of the reciprocal influence of culture, the media, and disability. We bring into dialogue research and conceptualizations of disability, media, and culture focusing on the work of Rosemarie Garland-Thomson and Tom Shakespeare in particular. This theoretical synthesis allows us to draw attention to the role of media representation in the experience of disability as a complex interaction of medical, personal, social, and political forces. In the second part of the chapter, we interrogate the impacts that media representation has had on people with disability within the justice system. We draw on research demonstrating the ways media discourses are reproduced unproblematically by judges, lawyers, and juries. The chapter concludes with reflections about the damaging effects of media representations that suggest people with disability are inherently burdensome and without value.

Models of Disability

Disability is often thought of as a medical problem that can be solved through medical intervention. Within critical disability studies, this is recognized as one approach to disability and is often described as the "medical model of disability" (Ellis & Goggin, 2015; Kafer, 2013).

The medical model of disability focuses on bodies, diseases, diagnoses, and cures (Grue, 2015). As Conrad (2007) explains, "Medical ideologies, interventions and therapies have reset and controlled the borders of acceptable behavior, bodies and states of being" (p. 13). Through *medicalization*, the normal is transformed into the pathological. The study of medicalization allows a focus on "the creation, promotion and application of medical categories (and treatments and solutions) to human problems and events" (Conrad, 2007, p. 13). This medicalization of disability has obscured the ways disability is constructed by social factors. In addition to the medical model, some theorists refer to this approach to disability as the individual or personal tragedy model because the problem of disability is considered a tragedy and located within the individual's body to solve. When the individual, medical, and tragedy aspects of disability are focused on, it leaves little room to consider disability as related to anything other than the body. As a result, social justice aspects are minimized.

In 1980, the World Health Organization defined *disability* in health terms in the *International Classification of Impairments, Disabilities, and Handicaps* as follows: "In the context of health experience, a disability is any restriction or lack (resulting from an impairment) of ability to perform an activity in the manner or within the range considered normal for a human being" (World Health Organization, 1980, p. 143). Although the medical model is often referred to in disability studies, it is difficult to find a definition of this model that does not emphasize critique or identify its limitations. Indeed, by the time the World Health Organization had articulated the medical model of disability in the *International Classification of Impairments, Disabilities, and Handicaps*, disability scholars and activists had already established the tools required to critique it (Grue, 2015, p. 52). The medical model of disability therefore might be more usefully considered as a descriptive term used for the way bodily limitations are made comprehensible to medical institutions than a cohesive theoretical framework.

The *social model of disability* is a direct response to the medicalization of disability and seeks to expose the ways disability is created by social factors such as inaccessible environments and negative attitudes toward people with impairments (Oliver, 1996). The social model of disability separates socially created disablement from impairment, which is recognized as existing within the body. This model examines the socially created barriers people with disability must navigate. Michael Oliver (1996) identified the separation of disability and impairment as a key feature of the social model of disability:

> We define impairment as lacking part of or all of a limb, or having a defective limb, organ or mechanism of the body; and disability as the disadvantage or restriction of activity caused by a contemporary social organization which takes no or little account of people who have physical impairments and thus excludes them from participation in the mainstream of social activities. Physical disability is therefore a particular form of social oppression. (p. 22)

This separation of disability and the body was a conceptually powerful point from which to progress social justice understandings of disability. Yet, as Tom Shakespeare (1994) explains, it also had the unfortunate side effect of neglecting a consideration of the impacts of impairment and, by extension, the role of cultural representation in social disablement.

Disability in Culture and Media

Disability is culturally defined in opposition to an *imagined normal body* (Davis, 1995; Garland-Thomson, 1997). We begin our analysis of disability in media and culture with two influential conceptualizations of disability and culture. First, in 1994, UK disability theorist Tom Shakespeare observed a lack of attention paid to the role of culture within the social model of disability. To redress this omission, Shakespeare drew on the work of U.S.-based disability theorists who had already been discussing the role of culture and media representation (Gartner & Joe, 1987; Kriegal, 1987; Longmore, 1987). Drawing on a number of feminist and disability theorists, Shakespeare (1994) demonstrated the ways people with disability are objectified and othered:

> Disabled people are scapegoats. It is not just that disabled people are different, expensive, inconvenient, or odd: It is that they represent a threat—either, as Douglas suggests, to order, or, to the self-conception of western human beings, who, since the Enlightenment, have viewed themselves as perfectible, as all-knowing, as god-like: able, over and above all other beings, to conquer the limitations of their nature through the victories of their culture. (p. 298)

Second, Rosemarie Garland-Thomson's 1997 conceptualization of *the normate and extraordinary body* offers an important theorization of the position of people with disability in culture and the role of culture in perpetuating discrimination against this group. For Garland-Thomson, the normate is "the constructed identity of those who, by way of the bodily configurations and cultural capital they assume, can step into a position of authority and wield the power it grants them" (p. xii). The extraordinary body, by comparison, is the normates' opposite, the disabled body appearing in culture and literature, constructed as an outsider (Garland-Thomson, 1997).

Later, theorists such as Sharon Snyder and David Mitchell (2006) observed that disability is everywhere in culture. Snyder and Mitchell argued that the social and cultural meanings attached to disability imagery act as a narrative prosthesis to support and hold narratives together: "As a character-making trope in the writer's arsenal, as a social category of deviance, as a symbolic vehicle for meaning-making and cultural critique, and as an option in the narrative negotiation of disabled subjectivity" (p. 1).

With reference to news media, theorists such as John Clogston and Beth Haller observe the ways disability is leveraged as a framing technique (Clogston, 1994; Ellis & Goggin, 2015; Haller, 1995).

Reciprocal Influence of Disability and the Media

The relationship between media representations and public perceptions is reciprocal: They influence each other, perpetuating social ideas and attitudes (Fairclough, 1995). The media's framing of people with disability is broadly criticized as portraying inaccurate and harmful representations of those so labeled (Ellis, 2019; Haller et al., 2012). The media's influence on public perceptions is problematic because social barriers can restrict interactions between people with and without disability, resulting in the media being the primary source of information about people with disability for some (Haller et al., 2012). In the absence of contradictory references, inaccurate and harmful media representations can become socially accepted "truths" that are disseminated and perpetuated. The media have the power to educate and mobilize the community around important social problems (Huck et al., 2009). However, issues that affect the lives of people with disability are generally underrepresented in the media, limiting opportunities to create change (Devotta et al., 2013).

One way that people with disability are discredited in the media is through infantilizing discourses. *Infantilization* works to demean people with disability and does not acknowledge or respect the individual's life and experiences (Shakespeare et al., 1996). Renwick et al. (2014) found that people with developmental and intellectual disability were infantilized in cinema depictions of occupational participation. Film characters with disability were shown to take part in child-like tasks in a child-like manner, in contrast to those completed by characters without disability. Similar belittling messages are evident in sentencing remarks from cases in which parents have killed their children with disability that overemphasize toileting support needs and the use of incontinence wear (i.e., nappies; Sullivan, 2017). Infantilizing messages reinforce the idea that people with disability are abnormal and burdensome (Renwick et al., 2014; Sullivan, 2017). The media degrades and discredits people with disability in various ways that impact public perceptions and consequently outcomes for people with disability in criminal justice settings.

The Media's Impact on Criminal Justice Outcomes for People with Disability

In this part of the chapter, we turn to a case study exploration of how media representations of people with disability are reproduced in social justice settings focusing on criminal justice contexts, drawing primarily on examples and literature from Australia. The interplay between media portrayals and public perceptions is examined with specific reference to Australian news media. Furthermore, we discuss the effect of these perceptions within criminal justice settings and the detrimental outcomes for people with disability. In line with Shakespeare's (1994) arguments introduced previously, throughout this analysis we demonstrate the importance of bringing both impairment and representation into social model analyses of disability in culture.

The media's influence on public perception can impact notions of credibility and competency of people with disability. Within the context of sexual abuse, people with intellectual disability have reported experiences of not being believed and of being considered incapable of providing an accurate witness account (Fraser-Barbour et al., 2018; Phasha, 2009). Furthermore, witness reports by children with intellectual disability tend to be considered less accurate than those made by children without disability (D. Brown & Lewis, 2013). These findings suggest that the public tends to consider people with disability as having little credibility and competency, which has detrimental outcomes in criminal justice settings.

People with disability are also discredited in child protection news media narratives. The Australian news media frame "good" parenting in relation to care and skill within the context of child protection (Fraser & Llewellyn, 2015). However, parents with disability are constructed in terms of deficits and as absent, passive, pitiable, and dangerous (Fraser & Llewellyn, 2015). Many parents with intellectual disability have their children removed from their custody (LaLiberte et al., 2017), and these negative messages may be a contributing factor. Furthermore, research demonstrates that some children have been removed exclusively because of the parents' intellectual disability without any investigation (Lightfoot & DeZelar, 2016). Narratives such as these devalue and distance people with disability from parents without disability and traditional parenting roles (Fraser & Llewellyn, 2015). Media constructions within Paralympic reporting have also found representations that degrade and distance people with disability through tragic and dangerous depiction of those so labeled (Maika & Danylchuk, 2016).

Australia news articles about disability support pensions have increased in volume and in content, suggesting fraudulent behaviors in recent years (Martin et al., 2022). This escalation corresponds with welfare reform and the constriction of disability support pension eligibility criteria. Similar narratives have been portrayed by the media in the United Kingdom (Briant et al., 2013). Martin et al. (2022) argue that the welfare reform subjected people with disability to public skepticism that was perpetuated by the media. A consequence of this narrative is that people with disability are portrayed as dishonest and unworthy. Outcomes within criminal justice contexts may be negatively affected by the dissemination of negative stereotypes that belittle and devalue people with disability. An example of a detrimental outcome is lenient sentences for perpetrators who kill people with disability. This leniency has been demonstrated in sentencing outcomes for four parents who were tried for murdering their adult children with disability in the United Kingdom, with only one being required to serve a short amount of jail time (5 years) (H. Brown, 2012). Disability activists have condemned such outcomes, arguing that they devalue people with disability and assume a limited quality of life (H. Brown, 2012).

Lenient sentencing may also reflect the public's reduced empathy for people with disability. In a mock jury study from the United States, participants assigned equivalent verdicts and responsibility to fathers who allegedly murdered their infants with and without disability (Bottoms et al., 2011). A lack of value for the lives (and deaths) of people with disability was demonstrated when the father of the infant with disability was given a significantly shorter sentences and assigned less mental health problems. This suggests that the murder of an infant with disability is considered more justifiable (i.e., less necessary to rationalize behavior with mental health problems) and that it deserves less punishment (i.e., shorter sentence). In 2014, Australian disability activist Stella Young wrote that the public are "a little less horrified" when discovering a murder victim has a disability (para. 6). Both this statement and the literature suggest that the public empathize less and feel more dissimilar to people with disability compared to people without (Bottoms et al., 2011).

In addition, Young (2014) criticized news media narratives that describe murderers as having "snapped" under the burden of the victim's disability. This discourse is highly problematic because it implies that all people with disability are inherently burdensome, privileges the experience of the perpetrator without disability, and shifts responsibility toward the victim with disability. In contrast, news media reports on the murders of people without disability are not constructed in this way (H. Brown, 2012). Comparable narratives are evident in sentencing remarks from cases in which family carers murdered people with disability. Analyses of these comments in cases from the United Kingdom and Australia have found examples that also include the "snap" narrative (H. Brown, 2012; Sullivan, 2017). Family carers are described as suffering under the overwhelming weight of burden of people with disability, whose lives are portrayed as not worth living (H. Brown, 2012; Sullivan, 2017). Sullivan argues that sentencing remarks such as these suggest that "disability incites violence" (p. 417). These comments and remarks considered with reference to Young's observations about the media and culture demonstrate the continuing importance of Haller's (1995, 2010) observations about media framing.

Conclusion

This chapter sought to center disability within the context of media and social justice. We presented the theoretical and social history that underpins the current representation of people with disability in the media. Furthermore, we discussed how those representations affect public perceptions and, in turn, outcomes in criminal justice settings. Opportunities for people with disability to access justice are restricted because of negative public perceptions disseminated and perpetuated in the media. Harmful portrayals are demonstrated in the media, devaluing the lives and deaths of people with disability. These narratives are reflected in criminal justice settings and contrast with representations of people without disability. More research is needed to understand how media representations impact outcomes for people with disability in criminal justice settings in order to improve outcomes for those so labeled.

References

Bottoms, B. L., Kalder, A. K., Stevenson, M. C., Oudekerk, B. A., Wiley, T. R., & Perona, A. (2011). Gender differences in jurors' perceptions of infanticide involving disabled and non-disabled infant victims. *Child Abuse and Neglect, 35*(2), 127–141. https://doi.org/10.1016/j.chiabu.2010.10.004

Briant, E., Watson, N., & Philo, G. (2013). Reporting disability in the age of austerity: The changing face of media representation of disability and disabled people in the United Kingdom and the creation of new "folk devils." *Disability & Society, 28*(6), 874–889. https://doi.org/10.1080/09687599.2013.813837

Brown, D. A., & Lewis, C. N. (2013). Competence is in the eye of the beholder: Perceptions of intellectually disabled child witnesses. *International Journal of Disability, Development and Education, 60*(1), 3–17. https://doi.org/10.1080/1034912X.2013.757132

Brown, H. (2012). Not only a crime but a tragedy [. . .] exploring the murder of adults with disabilities by their parents. *Journal of Adult Protection, 14*, 6–21. https://doi.org/10.1108/14668201211200763

Clogston, J. (1994). Disability coverage in American newspapers. In J. A. Nelson (Ed.), *The disabled, the media, and the information age* (pp. 45–57). Greenwood Press.

Conrad, P. (2007). *The medicalization of society: On the transformation of human conditions into treatable disorders.* Johns Hopkins University Press.

Davis, L. (1995). *Enforcing normalcy: Disability, deafness, and the body.* Verso.

Devotta, K., Wilton, R., & Yiannakoulias, N. (2013). Representations of disability in the Canadian news media: A decade of change? *Disability and Rehabilitation, 35*, 1859–1868. https://doi.org/10.3109/09638288.2012.760658

Ellis, K. (2019). *Disability and digital television cultures: Representation, access, and reception.* Routledge. https://doi.org/10.4324/9781315755663

Ellis, K., & Goggin, G. (2015). *Disability and the media.* Palgrave Macmillan.

Fairclough, N. (1995). *Media discourse.* Arnold.

Finkelstein, V. (1975). To deny or not to deny disability. *Magic Carpet, 27*(1), 31–38.

Fraser, V., & Llewellyn, G. (2015). Good, bad or absent: Discourses of parents with disabilities in Australian news media. *Journal of Applied Research in Intellectual Disabilities, 28*, 319–329. http://doi.org/10.1111/jar.12142

Fraser-Barbour, E. F., Crocker, R., & Walker, R. (2018). Barriers and facilitators in supporting people with intellectual disability to report sexual violence: Perspectives of Australian disability and mainstream support providers. *Journal of Adult Protection, 20*(1), 5–16. https://doi.org/10.1108/JAP-08-2017-0031

Garland-Thomson, R. (1997). *Extraordinary bodies: Figuring physical disability in American culture and literature.* Columbia University Press.

Gartner, A., & Joe, T. (Eds.). (1987). *Images of the disabled, disabling images.* Praeger.

Grue, J. (2015). *Disability and discourse analysis.* Farnham: Routledge. https://doi.org/10.4324/9781315577302

Haller, B. (1995). Rethinking models of media representation of disability. *Disability Studies Quarterly, 15*(2), 26–30.

Haller, B. A. (2010). *Representing disability in an ableist world: Essays on mass media.* Louisville: The Avocado Press.

Haller, B., Rioux, M., Dinca-Panaitescu, M., Laing, A., Vostermans, J., & Hearn, P. (2012). The place of news media analysis within Canadian disability studies. *Canadian Journal of Disability Studies, 1*(2), 43–74. http://doi.org/10.15353/cjds.v1i2.42

Huck, I., Quiring, O., & Brosius, H. (2009). Perceptual phenomena in the agenda setting process. *International Journal of Public Opinion Research, 21*, 139–164. http://doi.org/10.1093/ijpor/edp019

Kafer, A. (2013). *Feminist, queer, crip.* Indiana University Press.

Kriegal, L. (1987). The cripple in literature. In A. Gartner & T. Joe (Eds.), *Images of the disabled, disabling images* (pp. 31–46). Praeger.

LaLiberte, T., Piescher, K., Mickelson, N., & Lee, M. H. (2017). Child protection services and parents with intellectual and developmental disabilities. *Journal of Applied Research in Intellectual Disabilities, 30*(3), 521–532. https://doi.org/10.1111/jar.12323

Lightfoot, E., & DeZelar, S. (2016). The experiences and outcomes of children in foster care who were removed because of a parental disability. *Children and Youth Services Review, 62*, 22–28. https://doi.org/10.1016/j.childyouth.2015.11.029

Longmore, P. (1987). Screening stereotypes: Images of disabled people in television and motion pictures. In A. Gartner & T. Joe (Eds.), *Images of the disabled, disabling images* (pp. 65–78). Praeger.

Maika, M., & Danylchuk, K. (2016). Representing Paralympians: The "other" athletes in Canadian print media coverage of London 2012. *International Journal of the History of Sport, 33*(4), 401–417. https://doi.org/10.1080/09523367.2016.1160061

Martin, S., Schofield, T., & Butterworth, P. (2022). News media representations of people receiving income support and the production of stigma power: An empirical analysis of reporting on two Australian welfare payments. *Critical Social Policy, 42*(4), 648–670. https://doi.org/10.1177/02610183211073945

Oliver, M. (1990). *The individual and social models of disability*. Joint workshop of the Living Options Group and the research unit of the Royal College of Physicians on people with established locomotor disabilities in hospitals. https://disability-studies.leeds.ac.uk/wp-content/uploads/sites/40/library/Oliver-in-soc-dis.pdf

Oliver, M. (1996). *Understanding disability: From theory to practice*. Macmillan.

Phasha, N. (2009). Responses to situations of sexual abuse involving teenagers with intellectual disability. *Sexuality and Disability, 27*, 187–203. https://doi.org/10.1007/s11195-009-9134-z

Renwick, R., Schormans, A. F., & Shore, D. (2014). Hollywood takes on intellectual/developmental disability: Cinematic representations of occupational participation. *Occupation, Participation and Health, 34*, 20–31. https://doi.org/10.3928/15394492-20131118-01

Shakespeare, T. (1994). Cultural representation of disabled people: Dustbins for disavowal? *Disability & Society, 9*(3), 283–299.

Shakespeare, T., Gillespie-Sells, K., & Davies, D. (1996). *The sexual politics of disability*. Cassell.

Snyder, S., & Mitchell, D. (2006). *Cultural locations of disability*. University of Chicago Press.

Sullivan, F. (2017). Not just language: An analysis of discursive constructions of disability in sentencing remarks. *Continuum Journal of Media and Cultural Studies, 31*, 411–421. https://doi.org/10.1080/10304312.2016.1275143

World Health Organization. (1980). *International classification of impairments, disabilities, and handicaps*. https://apps.who.int/iris/bitstream/handle/10665/41003/9241541261_eng.pdf

Young, S. (2014, September 16). *Disability and murder: Victim blaming at its very worst*. ABC News. https://www.abc.net.au/news/2014-09-16/young-victim-blaming-at-its-very-worst/5745346

Methods and Meaning-Making

Critical Discourse Analysis

Marissa Joanna Doshi

I was a few months postpartum and scrolling through my Instagram feed when I noticed that my feed had changed drastically since giving birth: Posts and stories about popular culture had been replaced with posts and stories about tummy time for infants, formula and chestfeeding advice, and ads for postpartum recovery fashion. Clearly, my late-night searches had cued the social media's algorithms about what was on my mind at the time, and I was now being shown content that was seemingly aligned with my interests. Except of course, in addition to connecting me with resources and ideas that mattered to me, I was also being inducted into the norms and expectations of "intensive mothering" (Hays, 1996). As a feminist scholar of digital culture, it was fascinating to observe how my interactions with digital platforms were not only shaping my media diet but also inflecting my offline interactions and self-understanding of this new-to-me social identity of "mother."

I offer this anecdote to illustrate how we often are (or should be) critically engaged with cultural texts. Not only do we consume content but also, often, we can think through the content we consume, begin to identify patterns in media content, and then reflect on how those patterns are showing up in other contexts, such as interpersonal relationships, policy decisions, etc. That is, mindful engagement with media allows us to articulate the broader ideas and values shaping and dominating our society and communities. In short, we can and likely do conduct a version of "critical discourse analysis" in our everyday lives.

This anecdote is not meant to suggest that critical discourse analysis is an atheoretical or haphazard method. Rather, I think it is helpful to demystify the process of conducting critical discourse analysis and emphasize that the process has been systematized over time. Although researchers conducting critical discourse analysis have to account for aspects such as sampling and engagement with prior scholarly conversations, this methodology has the potential to democratize knowledge generation and remains a valuable tool for anyone interested in being an informed and active participant of their communities (Farrelly, 2019). Moreover, as researchers, it is a reminder to be open to novel ways of knowing that deviate from postpostivist assumptions about rigor and validity in research design. For those interested in social justice, imagining liberatory futures, and identifying the dynamics of privilege, oppression, and survival, critical discourse analysis remains a valuable tool because its explicit goal is making visible the ways in which power infuses interactions, identities, and institutions (Martínez Guillem & Toula, 2018).

It is my hope that by the end of this chapter, readers not only understand how to conduct critical discourse analysis but also begin to think of ways in which this research methodology can be further expanded or modified to achieve the goals of social justice and liberation.

To that end, this chapter begins with a brief overview of definitions and terms, and then it presents a short overview of the history of critical discourse analysis. Next, I tackle the steps involved in conducting a critical discourse analysis and supplement that discussion with case studies that illustrate the value and process of conducting critical discourse analysis of digital culture.

Definitions and Terms

It is perhaps useful to clarify what the term *discourse* means. Today, scholars who use critical discourse analysis with the explicit purpose of advancing social justice often draw on Stuart Hall's and/or Michel Foucault's definitions of discourse. Both theorists were concerned with the operation of power in society, and thus, they understand discourse in fairly similar ways even while emphasizing different aspects in their definitions. Hall (1992), for example, uses discourse to emphasize the role of language in signifying and re(presenting) social and material realities. Rather than focusing on the literal or denotative meaning of individual words or sentences, Hall uses discourse to reference the idea that meanings about reality are created through language. That is, the focus is on the connotative potential and power of language. Thus, for Hall, the term discourse is valuable for showing the power-laden connections between language and social reality. In other words, he emphasizes that language is not neutral but, rather, a vehicle for ideology.

Foucault (1972), similar to Hall, understands discourse as "productive"—that is, as a force shaping social realities, and not necessarily in a negative way. Specifically, for Foucault (1972), discourse refers to the power-laden interactions between knowledge systems, language, and behaviors. Thus, like Hall, Foucault (1972) acknowledges that discourse is a site of struggle over meaning and representation and that it evolves over time and context. Foucauldian ideas of discourse can be useful for researchers trying to understand how knowledge is constituted with relations of power—that is, how knowledge is produced and comes to be understood as authoritative and how it circulates (Foucault, 1978).

For researchers interested in issues of social justice, both these formulations of discourse provide a conceptual basis for articulating how and why social inequalities persist as well as how they became naturalized through language and knowledge systems even while helping these researchers identify how language and knowledge systems can be reconstituted toward emancipatory ends.

History and Evolution of Critical Discourse Analysis

Today, critical discourse analysis is an interdisciplinary method often used by scholars from diverse disciplines in the humanities, arts, and social sciences. The method, as we understand it today, evolved from discourse analysis in approximately the 1980s after scholars who were interested in unpacking social inequalities began noting that discourse analysis (and a closely related method, conversation analysis), with its emphasis (at the time) on units of language, was inadequate for understanding language as a motivated social practice. In response, scholars such as Norman Fairclough, Teun A. van Dijk, Theo van Leeuwen, and Ruth Wodak began developing and popularizing approaches to discourse analysis that were explicitly "critical."

At this juncture, it is perhaps useful to clarify how colloquial uses of "critical" differ from the ways in which it is typically used in scholarship. Everyday uses of the term critical usually refer to something negative or something of great importance. In contrast, scholars use critical to refer to a process of considered, complex contemplation or analysis of a text, practice, or phenomenon in order to arrive at understandings that move us beyond superficial and literal interpretations or observations. Increasingly, critical approaches are used to imply a focused interest in power and related concepts such as ideology and hegemony, which in the Western academy are concepts that can be traced back to the Frankfurt School (for a detailed discussion of how "critical" is understood within the critical paradigm of social science and humanities research, see Breeze, 2011). In the context of critical discourse analysis, Fairclough (1996) distinguishes it from non-critical discourse analysis by emphasizing that the critical discourse analysis' end goal goes beyond description to include interpretations and explanations of how texts and social order are connected.

Within this formulation, *critical discourse analysis* is a method for examining how discourses are constructed and constrained by operations of power such as hegemony and ideology. Importantly, critical discourse analysis explains how social identities, social relations, and worldviews are not neutral or "common sense." To achieve critical analysis of a discourse, Wodak, for example, suggests analyzing discourses within their social and historical contexts (Wodak & Meyers, 2009). van Dijk's (1994) approach to critical discourse analysis, which explores how media discourses shape public opinion, for example, emphasizes macro-level mechanisms such as framing and stereotyping. Furthermore, his approach includes a consideration of the role of cognition in processing and circulating discourses. For those seeking an in-depth yet accessible account of the history of critical discourse analysis, I recommend reading "Critical Discourse Analysis: History, Agenda, Theory, and Methodology" by Wodak and Meyer (2009).

As with any history, the one presented in this chapter is partial. The theorists referenced in this section were chosen because theirs are the names often referenced in contemporary studies (published in English) that use critical discourse analysis; most historical accounts of the method also reference them. As such, I acknowledge that this historical account, which is grounded in hegemonic publishing practices, does not challenge current citational politics. Indeed, an example of scholarship that takes a critical approach to discourse analysis that predates the specific formulations of critical discourse analysis popularized by the theorists mentioned above is Edward Said's (1979) work on Orientalism (grounded in a Foucauldian definition of discourse). In his germinal book, Said shows how conceiving the "Orient" as exotic, uncivilized, and ahistorical is a motivated discourse that is constructed and perpetuated by the West in order to justify past and present colonizing endeavors.

Today, the methods of critical discourse analysis continue to be reviewed, refined, and deployed to further larger projects of decolonization and liberation (Ahmed, 2021; Macedo, 2023). For example, critical discourse analysis is often used to study non-Western discourses as well as to study how the West has wielded discursive control over the non-West by probing phenomena such as neoliberalism, neocolonialism, heteronormativity, and queer worldmaking in addition to other subaltern or marginalized knowledge systems (Asante, 2020; Chun, 2017; Golnaraghi & Daghar, 2017; Kinefuchi & Cruz, 2015). Scholars from the Global South, such as Viviene Resende (2010), have presented sustained and energetic critiques of the coloniality of critical discourse analysis that results when contextual factors and local knowledge systems are not engaged with in a rigorous manner. Thus, Macedo (2023) suggests integrating Afroperspectives when studying race/racism in Brazil in order to analyze the coloniality of contemporary racial dynamics. Similarly, Shivaprasad's (2020) analysis of Indian stand-up comedy routines, which revealed how these routines reify upper-caste dominance, shows the importance of attending to caste when conducting critical discourse analysis in Indian contexts. In addition, contemporary studies have expanded their objects of analysis from studying language to include a variety of texts, including visual analysis (Rose, 2022), with multimodal analysis becoming increasingly popular. Examples of such studies include analysis of texts produced by subcultures and fandoms and analysis of social media posts and artifacts such as hashtags (see Boling, 2020; Gong, 2016; Rens, 2021).

In the context of the study of digital culture from a critical perspective, an important, influential development is critical technocultural discourse analysis (CTDA). André Brock (2018), who developed the method, describes it as a multimodal analytic technique for the investigation of Internet and digital phenomena, artifacts, and culture. It integrates an analysis of the technological artifact and user discourse, framed by cultural theory, to unpack semiotic and material connections between form, function, belief, and meaning of information and communication technologies (ICTs). CTDA requires the incorporation of critical theory—critical race, feminism, queer theory, and so on—to incorporate the epistemological standpoint of underserved ICT users so as to avoid deficit-based models of underrepresented populations' technology use. (p. 1012)

Thus, central to CTDA is a critical analysis of not only online content but also the medium and technologies used to produce and circulate the content, with particular attention paid to the sense-making processes of minority users.

In summary, "critical discourse analysis has moved towards more explicit dialogue between social theory and practice, richer contextualization, greater interdisciplinarity and greater attention to the multimodality of discourse" (van Leeuwen, 2009, p. 292).

Conducting Critical Discourse Analysis

Although the specifics of conducting critical discourse analysis might differ depending on which theorist's approach is foregrounded, in general, critical discourse analysis starts with researchers identifying objects of analysis (often referred to as texts) and then moving from description to interpretation and, finally, a discussion of implications. However, although most critical discourse analysis relies on extant texts, the phase of "data collection" is not well-defined—that is, there is no defined end point for data collection, so data collection and analysis might proceed in an iterative manner. Furthermore, a researcher with an a priori expertise in the specific context of interest can benefit from such expertise because it allows them to competently select an appropriate corpus of texts for analysis. That is, they might be better able to identify texts as "typical" or "atypical," "representative" or "unusual," "dominant" or "marginal," which are criteria usually used to define the boundaries of the data set (corpus of texts being studied) given that understanding power dynamics is the overarching goal of this method. In addition, although most researchers use a corpus of texts, some studies might be conducted with a single text.

The process of conducting the analysis is usually abductive (Wodak & Meyers, 2009). Some researchers might start from an inductive approach by identifying a corpus of texts that seem interesting and begin analyzing the texts without a specific theoretical framework guiding the analysis. They might recognize theoretical insights during the analysis process and then move toward a more deductive approach in which the emergent theoretical perspectives then guide the rest of the analysis. Alternatively, some researchers might start from a deductive approach by identifying theoretical concepts or processes of interest and look for how they operate in a chosen corpus of texts. They might then modify their theoretical focus to account for ideas emerging from their analysis. In practice, most researchers start somewhere in the middle, with analysis being simultaneously guided by existing theoretical interests while main-taining an openness to additional themes or ideas that present themselves during the analysis.

A key stage during analysis is immersion within the texts. This involves not only close read-ing (and rereading) or engagement with the text but also immersion in the context grounding the texts, such as understanding how culture, history, politics, economics, as well as user social identities and the affordances of a medium are manifest in the form and context of the texts being analyzed (Brock, 2018; Wodak & Meyers, 2009). It is this deep, sustained attention to context that allows researchers to articulate and identify how power is operating and thus fulfill the "critical" impetus of this method of analysis. Importantly, another dimension of such immersion is making interpretations based on not only what is clearly visible or present in the texts but also interrogating absences or silences in the texts. Questioning what is presented as normative or common sense, identifying which perspectives are highlighted and which are sidelined, and connecting interpretations to larger contextual factors are all part of the analysis (Stokes, 2013).

Finally, at all times, researchers need to be aware of how their own identities, goals, and contexts are shaping their analysis. Although not all published studies articulate the positionality of researchers (such an explicit articulation is more common in studies of empirical qualitative research), it is important for researchers to have an awareness, at the very least, of how their analysis benefits or is limited by their own social realities. Such an awareness helps researchers ground their interpretations, opens opportunities for deep interpretations, and prevents overgeneralizations. Wodak and Meyer (2009) clarify that

> although there is no consistent CDA [critical discourse analysis] methodology, some features are
> common to most CDA approaches: (1) They are problem-oriented and not focused on specific
> linguistic items, yet linguistic expertise is obligatory for the selection of the items relevant to specific
> research objectives; (2) theory as well as methodology is eclectic, both of which are integrated as far
> as is helpful to understand the social problems under investigation. (p. 31)

Case Studies

Now that we understand how critical discourse analysis has evolved and how it is conducted, it is time to explore in detail how it is being used by researchers to further the goals of social justice. By unpacking two case studies that examine digital culture, one which uses Fairclough's (2003) approach to critical discourse analysis and one that uses Brock's (2018) formulation of CTDA, I hope readers gain additional insights into how this methodology can be applied in their own projects.

Case Study 1

A powerfully persuasive example of the value of critical discourse analysis for studying how gender norms are being reshaped is Peng's (2021) study about the gendered dimensions of the discourse of neoliberalism in China. Specifically, Peng tries to demonstrate how neoliberalism has shaped ideas about manhood by analyzing WeChat posts by Mimeng, a key yet controversial opinion leader.

Peng (2021) provides readers with both a rationale for the criteria for selection of texts used in the analysis and specifics about the number of texts used. Peng clarifies that because these posts comprise only one-fifth of Mimeng's posts, this critical discourse analysis uses a "snapshot" approach. This approach is justified as follows: "The sample size is small but salient, because these posts comprise the entire archive of Mimeng's content specifically tackling issues of gender relations in China" (p. 121). The author's transparency about sampling is refreshing and empowering to researchers who might be under the impression that valuable critical discourse analysis requires large data sets. As this study shows, rather than focusing on the size of the data set in isolation, sampling should focus on creating a data set in size and content that is best suited to answer one's research question.

Next, Peng (2021) provides an in-depth description of and reasoning for using Fairclough's (2003) method of critical discourse analysis. This explanation is particularly useful given that there are multiple ways in which critical discourse analysis can be conducted. Not only does this section allow readers to understand why this formulation of critical discourse analysis was used in Peng's study but also the details provided can help them think through if Fairclough's method might work for their own studies.

Deep contextual understanding is demonstrated through the literature review wherein the author summarizes relevant contextual and theoretical concepts such as neoliberal feminism, the specifics of neoliberalism in China, especially as it relates to Chinese neoliberal feminism, contemporary iterations of patriarchy in China, and Chinese masculinities. These concepts and ideas ground the interpretations articulated in the analysis section to give readers clear insights into how neoliberal feminism is shaping masculine ideals. Insights such as "Mimeng juxtaposes feministic terms and neoliberal rationale to brand herself as 'feminist' while embedding patriarchal values within her 'feminist' discourse" (p. 123) are made by providing excerpts from the text and then linking the ideas in the texts to larger operations of power, such as gender and economic hierarchies.

In addition, the linguistic expertise of the researcher is evident in their analysis and is deployed to deepen their analysis. For example, Peng (2021) draws on their knowledge of Chinese grammar and syntax in their texts to argue that "Mimeng's engaging communicative style is constituted by her strategic use of a second-person pronoun" (p. 122).

By using critical discourse analysis, Peng (2021) reveals the strategic ways in which key opinion leaders use feminist language to perpetuate patriarchy. In addition, the study can also be used as a template for conducting critical discourse analysis using a fairly small set of social media posts.

Case Study 2

Apryl Williams' (2020) study focuses on a specific genre of memes called "BBQ Becky" and "Karen" memes that were created in response to offline incidents of harassment and surveillance of Black people by White women in public spaces in the United States. Williams' article stands out for its incisive integration of critical race theory with CTDA. Her analysis of popular digital artifacts, memes, challenges the simplistic understanding of memes as trivial by demonstrating the role that memes play in constructing anti-racist discourses. Importantly, in line with CTDA's foundational requirements, her study prioritizes the epistemic contributions and viewpoints of marginalized users by using critical race theory to analyze the artifacts.

Williams (2020) lays the foundation for her analysis by first providing a clear context for the emergence of BBQ Becky and Karen memes. As part of this contextualization process, she includes a clear rationale for why these memes are significant to Black people despite being trivialized by non-Black populations. Thus, she clearly positions her corpus of texts as racialized and, therefore, useful for studying issues central to social justice.

Next, Williams (2020) draws on critical race theory to ground her analysis by providing a gendered account of White supremacy that connects White women's current acts of racial surveillance with historical acts of surveillance. Finally, she also shows how memes are powerful sources of humor as well as racialized and political commentary.

In terms of applying CTDA, Williams (2020) provides details about data collection from Twitter. She explains in detail how tweets were collected, sorted, and selected. This careful explanation provides transparency about the process while helping readers clearly understand criteria used by the author for inclusion or exclusion from analysis. Furthermore, she explains,

CTDA is not designed to derive representative, generalizable notions based on data. CTDA focuses on understanding discourse as a whole. I have provided an overview of tweet volume so readers can better understand the context in which memes are situated. (p. 6)

This explanation helps readers understand why the corpus of tweets chosen is relevant even if not generalizable. Ethics should be a key consideration of any research that situates itself within the critical paradigm. Although most institutional review boards consider tweets and digital artifacts as part of the public archive, Williams (2020) goes beyond this minimum standard by explaining how she was mindful of the privacy of users.

In her analysis, in line with CTDA's framework, Williams (2020) focuses on not only the content of memes but also how the structure of Twitter intersects with the development and circulation of this particular anti-racist discourse. Throughout the analysis, Williams offers a rich, theoretical context for her conclusions. By putting visual evidence from memes in conversation with concepts from critical race theory, such as racial surveillance, White tears, racial ignorance and discomfort, and Whiteness-informed civility, the author helps readers understand these memes as part of an expression of agency in the face of a long history of racial violence that is ongoing. In the context of this chapter, this case study provides a template for readers looking to understand how CTDA can be used. It also demonstrates that critical analysis of discourse has both descriptive and analytic potential.

Conclusion

Advancing social justice is an explicit goal of critical discourse analysis. As this chapter has discussed, it achieves this goal by drawing interpretations and providing explanations about how power operates and by paying attention to language and a variety of texts and modalities. Thus, one of the strengths of this method is its explanatory power. It is particularly useful for understanding how subject positions intersect with contextual factors and providing arguments about the material and strategic impacts of discourse, particularly as it pertains to the creation or perpetuation of social inequalities. Depending on the object of analysis, critical discourse analysis is also useful for articulating how social actors use discourse as a route to emancipation or survival.

However, the method has been critiqued for reinscribing the very power relations it attempts to rectify. That is because the method privileges the analytic perspective of researchers instead of participants/communities and because researchers often fail to clarify their positionality (Billig, 2008), critical discourse analysis can maintain epistemic inequality. Scholars such as Bernadette Calafell (2014), Kent Ono (2011), and Ono and John Sloop (1995) have provided a sustained criticism of discourse analyses that claim to be "critical" even while ignoring the embodied dimensions of rhetoric and rhetorical actors. Finally, critical discourse analysis has been critiqued for using unsystematic approaches in data collection and analysis, as well as failing to articulate sense-making processes clearly and transparently, particularly the move from interpretation to explanation (Stubbs, 1997; Verschueren, 2001; Widdowson, 1996). These criticisms remain crucial driving forces for keeping critical discourse analysis relevant and improving methodological clarity. Importantly, power relations are not static; consequently, the methods we use to study them need to keep evolving in order to remain useful. Even as studies using traditional approaches to critical discourse analysis proliferate, critical scholars should remain mindful of the criticisms outlined above and use these criticisms to create and develop nuanced approaches for conducting discourse analysis.

References

Ahmed, Y. (2021). Political discourse analysis: A decolonial approach. *Critical Discourse Studies*, *18*(1), 139–155.

Asante, G. A. (2020). Anti-LGBT violence and the ambivalent (colonial) discourses of Ghanaian Pentecostalist–Charismatic church leaders. *Howard Journal of Communications*, *31*(1), 20–34.

Billig, M. (2008). The language of critical discourse analysis: The case of nominalization. *Discourse & Society*, *19*(6), 783–800.

Boling, K. S. (2020). #ShePersisted, Mitch: A memetic critical discourse analysis on an attempted Instagram feminist revolution. *Feminist Media Studies, 20*(7), 966–982.

Breeze, R. (2011). Critical discourse analysis and its critics. *Pragmatics, 21*(4), 493–525.

Brock, A. (2018). Critical technocultural discourse analysis. *New Media & Society, 20*(3), 1012–1030.

Calafell, B. M. (2014). Performance: Keeping rhetoric honest. *Text and Performance Quarterly, 34*(1), 115–117.

Chun, C. W. (2017). Neoliberalism, globalization and critical discourse studies. In J. Flowerdew & J. Richardson (Eds.), *The Routledge handbook of critical discourse studies* (pp. 421–433). Routledge.

Fairclough, N. (1996). Rhetoric and critical discourse analysis: A reply to Titus Ensink and Christoph Sauer. *Current Issues in Language & Society, 3*(3), 286–289.

Fairclough, N. (2003). *Analysing discourse: Textual analysis for social research*. Routledge.

Farrelly, M. (2019). Critical discourse analysis. In P. Atkinson, S. Delamont, A. Cernat, J. W. Sakshaug, & R. A. Williams (Eds.), *SAGE research methods: Foundations*. SAGE. https://doi.org/10.4135/9781526421036815631

Foucault, M. (1972). *The archaeology of knowledge and the discourse of language*. VintageBooks.

Foucault, M. (1978). *The history of sexuality: An introduction*. Vintage Books.

Golnaraghi, G., & Daghar, S. (2017). Feminism in the third space: Critical discourse analysis of Mipsterz women and grassroots activism. In A. Pullen, N. Harding, & M. Phillips (Eds.), *Feminists and queer theorists debate the future of critical management studies* (pp. 103–127). Emerald.

Gong, Y. (2016). Online discourse of masculinities in transnational football fandom: Chinese Arsenal fans' talk around "gaofushuai" and "diaosi." *Discourse & Society, 27*(1), 20–37.

Hall, S. (1992). The West and the rest: Discourse and power. In S. Hall & B. Gieben (Eds.), *Formations of modernity* (pp. 275–331). Polity Press.

Hays, S. (1996). *The cultural contradictions of motherhood*. Yale University Press.

Kinefuchi, E., & Cruz, G. (2015). The Mexicans in the news: Representation of Mexican immigrants in the internet news media. *Howard Journal of Communications, 26*(4), 333–351.

Macedo, L. B. (2023). Intersecting Afroperspective thinking and critical discourse analysis: Possibilities to decolonize discursive studies. In S. M. de Barros & V. Resende (Eds.), *Coloniality in discourse studies* (pp. 52–65). Routledge.

Martínez Guillem, S., & Toula, C. M. (2018). Critical discourse studies and/in communication: Theories, methodologies, and pedagogies at the intersections. *Review of Communication, 18*(3), 140–157.

Ono, K. A. (2011). Critical: A finer edge. *Communication and Critical/Cultural Studies, 8*(1), 93–96.

Ono, K. A., & Sloop, J. M. (1995). The critique of vernacular discourse. *Communication Monographs, 62*(1), 19–46.

Peng, A. Y. (2021). Neoliberal feminism, gender relations, and a feminized male ideal in China: A critical discourse analysis of Mimeng's WeChat posts. *Feminist Media Studies, 21*(1), 115–131.

Rens, S. E. (2021). Women's empowerment, agency and self-determination in Afrobeats music videos: A multimodal critical discourse analysis. *Frontiers in Sociology, 6*. https://doi.org/10.3389/fsoc.2021.646899

Resende, V. M. (2010). Between the European legacy and critical daring: Epistemological reflections for critical discourse analysis. *Journal of Multicultural Discourses, 5*, 193–212.

Rose, G. (2022). *Visual methodologies: An introduction to researching with visual materials*. SAGE.

Said, E. W. (1979). *Orientalism*. Vintage Books.

Shivaprasad, M. (2020). Humour and the margins: Stand-up comedy and caste in India. *IAFOR Journal of Media, Communication & Film, 7*(1). https://doi.org/10.22492/ijmcf.7.1.02

Stokes, J. (2013). Researching texts. In J. Stokes (Ed.), *How to do media and cultural studies* (pp. 118–169). SAGE.

Stubbs, M. (1997). Whorf's children: Critical comments on critical discourse analysis. In A. Ryan & A. Wray (Eds.), *Evolving models of language* (pp. 100–116). Multilingual Matters.

van Dijk, Teun A. (1994). Critical discourse analysis. *Discourse & Society, 5*(4), 435–436.

van Leeuwen, T. (2009). Critical discourse analysis. In J. Renkema (Ed.), *Discourse, of course: An overview of research in discourse studies* (pp. 277–292). John Benjamins Publishing Company.

Verschueren, J. (2001). Predicaments of criticism. *Critique of Anthropology, 21*(1), 59–81.

Widdowson, H. (1996). Reply to Fairclough: Discourse and interpretation: Conjectures and refutations. *Language and Literature, 5*(1), 57–69.

Williams, A. (2020). Black memes matter: #LivingWhileBlack with Becky and Karen. *Social Media + Society, 6*(4). doi:2056305120981047

Wodak, R., & Meyer, M. (2009). Critical discourse analysis: History, agenda, theory, and methodology. In R. Wodak & M. Meyer (Eds.), *Methods for critical discourse analysis* (pp. 1–22). SAGE.

Data Justice: The Role of Data in Media and Social Justice

Srividya Ramasubramanian, Shannon Burth, *and* Minnie McMillian

In this chapter, we elaborate on data's role in shaping media and social justice work. We use data justice and quantitative criticalism to examine how empirical quantitative data can serve social justice goals within media studies. Drawing on our experiences within the CODE^SHIFT research lab (Collaboratory for Data Equity, Social Healing, Inclusive Futures, and Transformation), this chapter helps orient those committed to media and social justice to mindful quantitative data principles and practices. Even when media and social justice scholarship is not community-oriented, one can still center issues of ethics, equity, inclusion, and social justice in their work on media. For instance, inclusive sampling techniques help ensure that surveys are more reflective of individuals typically marginalized within research. In addition, making data more accessible, transparent, and legible to policymakers and community leaders is another pathway toward data justice. Throughout this chapter, we present more ethical considerations for doing media and social justice work.

The chapter reviews the central tenets of quantitative criticalism; provides guidelines for greater inclusion in various stages of the research process, from formulating questions to disseminating the research; and elaborates on the CODE^SHIFT model, which offers a step-by-step framework on the role of data in community-engaged media interventions. The chapter also provides recommendations for media practitioners, policymakers, and public scholars on critical approaches toward data for the advancement of social justice within the realm of media.

Significance of Data Justice to Media Scholar–Activism

Data justice calls us to critically include the voices of communities most negatively impacted by social justice issues. In scholarship that sits at the nexus of media and social justice, data play a significant role in every stage of the social transformation process. Communities that are marginalized and oppressed through interlocking systems such as patriarchy, heteronormativity, White supremacy, ableism, capitalism, and colonialism are often erased, trivialized, or misrepresented within data systems. Similar to other forms of capital, data capital is also a contentious space where data collection, sharing, and use are influenced by political, economic, and other socioeconomic factors. In an increasingly datafied world, "media" no longer refers to just legacy media such as television or newspapers. Instead, it is about integrated data networks including the platform economy, machine learning, smart technologies, artificial intelligence, and automated systems. Analogous to how land, oil, minerals, and other physical resources have been excavated and exploited, data too are being mined and extracted. Within this larger context of how "development" is being associated with technologies that rely on incomplete and lopsided data largely for the benefit of corporations and profit, we ask how data can serve the larger greater good, especially those who are otherwise historically marginalized.

Drawing on prior datafication scholarship (Goldkind et al., 2021; Heeks & Shekhar, 2019; Taylor, 2017; Taylor et al., 2020), we highlight the role of data in the emerging context of new media technologies and social justice. It is crucial for media practitioners, educators, activists, scholars, and policymakers to understand how data are being (mis)used for surveillance, oppression, and maintaining the status quo. We use quantitative criticism as an anchoring approach to guide those doing research on media and social justice while using empirical quantitative data. In every stage of the research process—from forming research questions to sharing study findings—we need to consider how we use data to identify the problem, gather the data, frame the solutions, and share our findings in ways that can benefit those marginalized within their communities.

Quantitative Criticalism and Social Justice

Quantitative criticalism functions to expose injustices and inequalities, while using quantitative research methods. With the tools associated with quantitative research, such as surveys and experiments, quantitative criticalists pursue research questions to reveal structures of power that create and perpetuate inequalities (Stage & Wells, 2014). Quantitative methods can be used to critique distributions of power and privilege in society, wherein data become a tool for increasing legitimacy and providing a rationale for policy change (Scharrer & Ramasubramanian, 2021). Qualitative methods seek to amplify voices and experiences and expand on the reductive outcomes often associated with numbers by humanizing and contextualizing media experiences as opposed to quantitative research, which, from a post-positivist standpoint, focuses on objectivity and generalizability (Denzin, 1994; Guba & Lincoln, 1994). However, quantitative criticalism opposes this distinction, emphasizing the power that numbers can have for social justice research.

Numbers and statistical analysis persuade many people, as findings from quantitative research are often perceived as reliable, relatively unbiased, and verifiable (Allen & Preiss, 1997; Hughes & Cohen, 2012). With this in mind, we are reminded that trust in data can help illuminate lived experiences and create a powerful argument and rationale for social change (Ponterotto et al., 2013; Scharrer & Ramasubramanian, 2021). Quantitative critical scholarship can also be used as a counterpart to qualitative findings, enhancing or supporting findings (McLaren, 2017).

Although quantitative researchers have the tools to conduct social justice research, there is a responsibility to think carefully and critically about the implications of such work. Data can be used with negative intent just as easily as they can be used to improve our communities. When used improperly or with the wrong purpose, data can support or perpetuate racism, sexism, classism, and ableism, as well as negative stereotypes and phobias associated with minoritized groups (Scharrer & Ramasubramanian, 2021). Therefore, quantitative scholarship must also critically question measures and practices (McLaren, 2017). In the next section, we discuss and give nuance to these important methodological considerations.

Inclusive Data Practices for Media Research on Social Justice

Social media for today's social justice issues can be likened to what television was for the civil rights movement of the 1950s and 1960s. The connection between media and social issues has been influential through its capability to generate awareness and increase civic engagement. Furthermore, this relationship has been well documented in media and other social science research. For example, prior media and social justice research investigated the Black Lives Matter movement (Blevins et al., 2019; Chang et al., 2022) and #StopAsianHate (Lee & Jang, 2023; Xie et al., 2023). In addition, media researchers have examined LGBTQ issues. Some studies have explored social media as an outreach for LGBTQ youth (Ciszek, 2017), the exclusion of LGBTQ people of color during media coverage of a mass shooting (Meyer, 2020;

Ramirez et al., 2018), and the importance of online communities for transgender individuals (Cavalcante, 2016; Fischer, 2016). Evidence from these studies demonstrated that (a) media plays a substantial role in calling attention to a myriad of social justice issues, (b) online media provides supportive communities for individuals impacted by marginalized identities, and (c) media research provides contexts into how this is influencing the lives of these individuals.

With media being a ubiquitous part of our lives, media scholars have the opportunity to investigate how this is contributing to the progression of societal issues. Furthermore, it is imperative during these investigations to use inclusive strategies to thoroughly conduct research related to social justice issues, especially if it concerns those from historically marginalized communities. Therefore, the purpose of this section is to provide considerations for conducting media research on social justice, mainly inclusive practices.

Designing the Research Study

At the research question development stage, the researcher has collected adequate background information to determine their focus area (e.g., mass incarceration, women's rights, housing crisis, etc.) and the purpose of the project. In addition, the researcher has defined and operationalized the concepts of interest. For example, suppose the purpose of a study was to examine media narratives related to the maternal mortality crisis in the United States. In that case, the researcher has collected background information about the issue and who it affects and has identified the type of media they will explore. Furthermore, when posing the research questions for the project, one crucial part of promoting inclusivity is ensuring inclusive language and accurate labels. For instance, using the maternal mortality crisis as an example, when developing inclusive research questions, the researcher must use accurate labels by focusing on the group disproportionately affected by the issue (e.g., Black women and Black birthing people). Including "Black women" and "Black birthing people," the researcher recognizes and ensures the experiences of those who can become pregnant but do not identify as a woman.

When developing inclusive research questions, another consideration is determining the appropriate theoretical framework to guide the project. One prominent theory that incorporates the complexity of multiple marginalized identities and can be helpful in media research and social justice is intersectionality. *Intersectionality theory* is defined as how "systems of power and oppression co-construct each other to create complex and unique forms of systemic harm and injustice" (Coles & Pasek, 2020, p. 315). Specifically, conflict and exclusion levels can arise within social justice movements when the focus concerns a single axis of identity (Crenshaw, 1991). One prominent example described in research and scholarship is the invisibility of Black women within feminist and anti-racist movements. This exclusion leads to the lack of representation and acknowledgment of some of the unique oppression that Black women face (Collins, 2000). Therefore, when considering research questions for a study related to social justice issues, one approach could use an intersectional lens to guide the research.

Within media studies, the critical media effects framework (CME; Ramasubramanian & Banjo, 2020) can be used to guide critically conscious research. This theoretical framework bridges traditional media effects scholarship with critical cultural studies approaches, both dominant paradigms within media studies. By bringing these two siloed approaches into conversation with one another, the CME framework allows media researchers to combine critical theory with empirical quantitative data. This makes space, within hegemonic social scientific approaches and media effects theorizing, to incorporate critical consciousness, intersectionality, power, context, and agency. Reexamining the maternal mortality example, a researcher could use the CME approach to understand how the media addresses the factors contributing to those disparaging maternal mortality rates. For instance, a researcher could determine that the media focuses on the rates of maternal mortality without discussing the attributing factors that exist, such as racial bias within health care or inequitable access and treatment.

Data Collection

At this stage of the study design, choosing the appropriate measures is essential. Scharrer and Ramasubramanian (2021) have emphasized the importance of using measurement in quantitative research to ensure scientific and ethical soundness. One argument, as discussed by Scharrer and Ramasubramanian, describes how researchers face a difficult challenge when determining a measure to use; the challenge arises with the expectations that researchers are inherently knowledgeable and should be aware of all possible outcomes associated with such measures. One criticism of social science measurements of constructs is that most were developed using large samples of White and middle-class populations (Afifi & Cornejo, 2020); therefore, one way to promote inclusive measurement practices is by including valid and reliable measurements for the group or individuals of interest (Knight et al., 2009), mainly if they do not fall within the White and middle-class populations. This could be done by verifying whether the measure accurately reflects or conveys a different meaning within certain groups of people. Take, for another example, the numerous scales measuring discrimination. Some measures cover general discrimination across various racial and ethnic groups (e.g., Perceived Discrimination Scale; Williams et al., 1997), whereas other measures were developed to consider the unique and multiple ways discrimination manifests within certain social groups. Within research, sometimes researchers face challenges when considering a measurement for a study. One is a reliable and valid measure for a study. Sometimes researchers may need to modify an existing measure or develop additional questions related to the construct of interest. In addition to modifying measurements within a study, researchers could also adjust their data collection strategy. This could include increasing accessibility by offering translation for participants, using large text, or providing an optional pen-and-paper method. Measurements are essential for research, especially quantitative. Still, when considering a measure to use, researchers should ensure that the measure can apply to their group of interest and that the language within the measure does not inadvertently suggest biases toward a group of people.

Sampling Techniques

Media researchers focusing on social justice aim to amplify the voices and experiences of those oppressed by systems to make tangible change. Yet, their voices are often excluded from study samples; therefore, researchers must take further initiative to ensure they are acknowledged and represented. Marginalized groups are often difficult to reach in terms of having the time and resources to participate in research. Taking a culturally inclusive approach, sensitive to the needs and goals of participants, is essential. The main aspect of sampling involves building trust and rapport with those within the research process. Often, one is stepping into a research study in which previous researchers have simply parachuted themselves into the community, collected data through stories or attitudes, and then never given back to the community. Because of such harm caused by the scientific community in the past, researchers working on social justice issues have to first spend time building rapport with the community before expecting participants to readily volunteer information that is useful to the researchers. Building rapport with communities is an important part of the CODE^SHIFT model, which we discuss in greater detail later.

Scharrer and Ramasubramanian (2021) recognize that it might not always be possible to include data from difficult-to-reach groups. Therefore, they describe using research strategies such as oversampling or weighting when the researcher has exhausted other means to include marginalized voices. Researchers oversample their studies by purposely selecting more participants from a certain group. Using this method ensures that some groups, which usually are underrepresented, are not overlooked. The other method, weighting, is a process during data analysis that places values on smaller groups more and less on those overrepresented. Altogether, these two processes can help bring inclusivity in sampling techniques to inform research with various social groups.

Dissemination of Findings

An essential phase of the research process is the ability to communicate the results across audiences and platforms. For social justice–centered media research, dissemination is a necessary process that helps increase awareness and promote societal change on an issue. It is also about making research findings accessible and meaningful to the groups that helped shape it.

Traditionally, researchers disseminate their studies through academic channels (e.g., books or academic journals), conferences, and professional workshops. When possible, researchers should seek to publish their studies in open-access journals. These journals remove the barrier between academia and the public by providing free access to articles. Currently, many published journal articles are behind paywalls, and people are charged to get full access to the literature (Resnick & Belluz, 2019). As a response, more inclusive data practices have emerged, including dissemination beyond the academic spaces (Scharrer & Ramasubramanian, 2021). Other responses include spin-off journals that are freely accessible (Resnick & Bellus, 2019) and communicating research on less formal platforms such as social media and blogs (Mollett et al., 2017).

In addition, with the ubiquitous nature of social media, researchers could disseminate their research to a wider audience on these platforms. Most recently, scholars have begun publicly posting or linking their published papers on social media platforms to engage with the public. Other academics have also used strategies such as blogging or submitting op-ed pieces to online news platforms to discuss their research and call attention to the issues they address within their studies. By communicating their research findings beyond academia, scholars are breaking away from the exclusion that happens when publishing in journals that are not accessible to the public. These strategies help community members, policymakers, or public officials become aware of the impact of issues within their communities. Furthermore, by increasing recognition, researchers plant the seed to start the process of change.

Another way in which researchers doing social justice scholarship can make their work more inclusive is to avoid jargon and find ways to make their work accessible. This could mean translating research findings into multiple languages and making them available across various media formats, platforms, and modalities. Whether it is the Associated Press, the Association for Internet Researchers, or the American Psychological Association, there are several guidelines provided by publishing and research organizations about how to be mindful and inclusive in the type of language used in surveys, questionnaires, research papers, and newspaper articles. For instance, the use of pronouns, correct spellings of names, and culturally inclusive ways of addressing people within a community are important considerations to demonstrate honor and respect for participants.

Data Justice and Community-Engaged Communication Scholarship

To incorporate data justice and inclusionary practices into social justice research, we next highlight the CODE^SHIFT model. This model incorporates several considerations described in the previous section while also developing a cyclical framework for sustainable, long-term change. This model is built on a culture-centered approach (CCA; Dutta, 2008), which emphasizes building a communication infrastructure within communities to establish long-term social transformation (Dutta, 2021). Although data-driven, CCA is a social justice–oriented theory. In practice, a culture-centered approach reframes data as voices from the community and redefines community ownership. Culture-centered interventions also make the distinction between community-*based* and community-*engaged* research. The former suggests that a community is being researched, whereas the latter centers the community members as active participants in the research process. In the case of community-engaged research, community members define the scope of the project and the goals of the data as well as make sense of the data (Dutta, 2007). By using the CODE^SHIFT model, researchers can build feedback mechanisms with the communities they research (Ramasubramanian & Dutta, 2024).

The CODE^SHIFT model presents four overlapping categories wherein data justice is a goal, tool, and organizing strategy for addressing inequalities. Data justice is also prominent within each stage of this process. As researchers, we reframe who is designing and leading processes. Similar to disability justice, research and transformation-based practices should center those most impacted in leadership positions to find strategies of resistance (Sins Invalid, 2019). These four categories are presented as a cycle with steps, yet community-engaged research is complex and dynamic, resulting in constant overlap. With community voices and experiences as data, this model is represented as (a) identifying pressing social issues, (b) bridging for cross-sector coalitions and partnerships, (c) organizing collective impact activities, and (d) sustaining through capacity-building and social transformation (Ramasubramanian & Dutta, 2024; Scharrer & Ramasubramanian, 2021).

In the first step, identifying pressing social issues, researchers map out sociocultural contexts and histories to understand the root of community difficulties and inequalities. At this stage, researchers are defining the scope of their study and what questions they might explore. As mentioned previously, the researcher collects ample background information; this can be done through systematic content analysis or more casually through conversations with community members. Background research can and should inform the creation of codebooks or survey measures. Also, it might reveal a more culturally sensitive practice for collecting demographic data.

Past research, such as that by Scharrer, Ramasubramanian, and Banjo (2022), used content analysis to reveal that various media underrepresented minoritized social groups proportionate to the actual U.S. population. A study such as this one can reveal misrepresentation, lack of representation, or complete invisibility of a minoritized group. Similarly, quantitative researchers might use methods such as bibliometric analysis to examine large sets of data (scholarly research), determine the current state of the research, and identify communities that are not being researched (Paré et al., 2015). Ultimately, at this point, researchers begin to map the needs of a community or the issues the members might be facing.

The next stage of the CODE^SHIFT model is bridging for cross-sector coalitions and partnerships. Building coalitions and long-term relationships with members of the community aligns with community-engaged research, a core principle of CCA. Building rapport with the communities emphasizes active listening, particularly to groups that are most impacted, marginalized, or silenced. It is at this point that sampling practices should be carefully considered. To avoid harmful practices, such as parachuting into a community, building community rapport is crucial. This step presents an opportunity for quantitative researchers to consider mixed methods.

In line with a quantitative criticalist approach, using mixed methods leverages the strengths of numerical findings and the benefits of rich qualitative data. Qualitative findings can provide robust perspectives from community members, wherein researchers can build relationships with those who are experiencing injustices (Mertens, 2007, 2013). The utilization of both qualitative and quantitative methods can also support data triangulation. By collecting data with complementary methods, such as in-depth interviews and surveys, data triangulation can help researchers include multiple perspectives or present longitudinal data (Scharrer & Ramasubramanian, 2021). With the CODE^SHIFT model in mind, mixed-methods research and triangulation can achieve long-term relationships with community members.

The next step in the CODE^SHIFT model is to organize collective impact activities. This is presented as the third stage because it is informed by the prior two stages. After gathering stories and perspectives from community members and building coalitions, researchers are in a position to brainstorm solutions and concrete steps to achieve them. Researchers will test their ideas for change and then share the outcomes with the community. Organizing activities such as workshops and incubation programs can provide data to prove efficacy and rationale for resources needed. With regard to intentionality, at this stage, researchers must rely on the feedback mechanism that is built in the previous two stages. Careful dissemination practices, such as presenting findings in an accessible and easy-to-understand manner, are crucial. Effective dissemination can lead to open and honest feedback from the community.

Familiar quantitative methods, such as experiments, can be integrated into this stage. Using field experiments, for instance, researchers can test what they have learned from the community members and explore the relationships between injustices and experiences (variables). Therefore, with this method, a collective impact idea can be tested systematically. Quantitatively, feedback can be in the form of pre- and post-testing data. Yet, as the previous stage suggests, feedback may take a more qualitative form such as interviews or focus groups that follow the experiment.

The fourth stage of the CODE^SHIFT model emphasizes sustaining long-term impact through policy change and building communication infrastructure. After identifying problems, building relationships, and testing small ideas, a researcher has enough to publish a study or share their findings at a conference. After the findings have been disseminated, the CODE^SHIFT model encourages sustaining relationships with communities by mobilizing funds and initiatives for change or policy change.

Data Justice for Media Practitioners, Public Scholars, and Policymakers

Data justice is accomplished when we create meaningful connections during the research process. More clearly, from community members to policymakers and media practitioners, building a pathway that includes everyone is necessary. Those within academic institutions engage in data justice in numerous ways. Scharrer and Ramasubramanian (2021) distinguished several types of social justice research applied in academic institutions. However, we focus on translational research, engaged scholarship, and policy research. For instance, translational researchers engage in accessible and relevant academic research for the non-academic audience (Tracy, 2002). Translational researchers understand that historically, research institutions have consistently and purposefully excluded non-academics by restricting access through the overuse of jargon or journal paywalls. Engaged scholars are also interested in relevant research by combining theory and practice for practitioners and the community. Last, researchers can also use their academic expertise to address societal problems, known as conducting policy research (Scharrer & Ramasubramanian, 2021).

Because researchers are experts in their field, providing their knowledge to journalists and news platforms is imperative, especially if their research advances social justice issues. One way researchers can be more inclusive in their interactions with news media is to discuss their studies in a way that the public can easily comprehend. This includes eliminating technical words and using real-world examples to explain complex theories or data points. Previously, we discussed several methods to communicate research findings, such as blogs, social media platforms, or op-eds. Communicating research knowledge to policymakers takes similar forms; these include policy briefs, reports, executive briefs, or one-pagers. For example, executive briefs are a type of policy writing piece that involves using research findings to discuss the issue and can generate either a call to action or some potential outcomes (Scharrer & Ramasubramanian, 2021). These formats are necessary because policymakers may use research findings to help guide or frame their focus issue. More clearly, media researchers are just one of the pieces that can help policymakers initiate substantial change.

Conclusion

In this chapter, we champion for social justice–oriented media researchers, activists, scholars, and educators to consider quantitative empirical research as a tool for advancing social justice. We offer quantitative criticalism and data justice as frameworks to guide them through important considerations in various stages of research design, implementation, and dissemination. To bring about the long-term policy changes and social transformation that media scholars, activists, and policymakers committed to social justice seek, it is becoming increasingly important to understand how data are shaping problem definition, collective impact, and systemic change processes. Within the larger context of emerging media technologies, datafication of society, monopolization of platforms, and artificial intelligence, we urge social justice–oriented media scholars, practitioners, and researchers to pay greater attention to data literacies.

References

Afifi, W. A., & Cornejo, M. (2020). #CommSoWEIRD: The question of sample representativeness in interpersonal communication research. In M. L. Doerfel & J. L. Gibbs (Eds.), *Organizing inclusion: Moving diversity from demographics to communication processes* (pp. 238–259). Routledge.

Allen, M., & Preiss, R. W. (1997). Comparing the persuasiveness of narrative and statistical evidence using meta-analysis. *Communication Research Reports, 14*(2), 125–131.

Blevins, J. L., Lee, J. J., McCabe, E. E., & Edgerton, E. (2019). Tweeting for social justice in #Ferguson: Affective discourse in Twitter hashtags. *New Media & Society, 21*(7), 1636–1653.

Cavalcante, A. (2016). "I did it all online": Transgender identity and the management of everyday life. *Critical Studies in Media Communication, 33*(1), 109–122.

Chang, H. H., Richardson, A., & Ferrara, E. (2022). #JusticeforGeorgeFloyd: How Instagram facilitated the 2020 Black Lives Matter protests. *PLoS One, 17*(12), Article e0277864.

Ciszek, E. L. (2017). Advocacy communication and social identity: An exploration of social media outreach. *Journal of Homosexuality, 64*(14), 1993–2010.

Coles, S. M., & Pasek, J. (2020). Intersectional invisibility revisited: How group prototypes lead to the erasure and exclusion of Black women. *Translational Issues in Psychological Science, 6*(4), 314–324.

Collins, P. H. (2000). *Black feminist thought: Knowledge, consciousness, and the politics of empowerment* (2nd ed.). Routledge.

Crenshaw, K. (1991). Mapping the margins: Intersectionality, identity politics, and violence against women of color. *Stanford Law Review, 43*(6), 1241–1299. https://doi.org/10.2307/1229039

Denzin, N. K. (1994). The art and politics of interpretation. In N. K. Denzin & Y. S. Lincoln (Eds.), *Handbook of qualitative research* (pp. 500–515). SAGE.

Dutta, M. (2007). Communicating about culture and health: Theorizing culture-centered and cultural sensitivity approaches. *Communication Theory, 17*(3), 304–328. https://doi.org/10.1111/j.1468-2885.2007.00297.x

Dutta, M. (2008). *Communicating health: A culture-centered approach*. Polity Press.

Dutta, M. (2021). Culture-centered approach to digital health communication: Sustaining health, addressing inequalities, transforming structures. *Catalan Journal of Communication & Cultural Studies, 13*(2), 311–319. https://doi.org/10.1386/cjcs_00056_7

Fischer, M. (2016). #Free_CeCe: The material convergence of social media activism. *Feminist Media Studies, 16*(5), 755–771.

Goldkind, L., Wolf, L., & LaMendola, W. (2021). Data justice: Social work and a more just future. *Journal of Community Practice*, *29*(3), 237–256. https://doi.org/10.1080/10705422.2021.1984354

Guba, E. G., & Lincoln, Y. S. (1994). Competing paradigms in qualitative research. In N. K. Denzin & Y. S. Lincoln (Eds.), *Handbook of qualitative research* (pp. 105–117). SAGE.

Heeks, R., & Shekhar, S. (2019). Datification, development and marginalised urban communities: An applied data justice framework. *Information, Communication & Society*, *22*(7), 992–1011. https://doi.org/10.1080/13691 18X.2019.1599039

Hughes, C., & Cohen, R. L. (Eds.). (2012). *Feminism counts*. Routledge.

Knight, G. P., Roosa, M. W., & Umaña-Taylor, A. J. (2009). Measurement and measurement equivalence issues. In G. P. Knight, M. W. Roosa, & A. J. Umaña-Taylor (Eds.), *Studying ethnic minority and economically disadvantaged populations: Methodological challenges and best practices* (pp. 97–134). American Psychological Association.

Lee, C. S., & Jang, A. (2023). Questing for justice on Twitter: Topic modeling of #StopAsianHate discourses in the wake of Atlanta shooting. *Crime & Delinquency*, *69*(13–14), 2874–2900.

McLaren, L. (2017). A space for critical quantitative public health research? *Critical Public Health*, *27*(4), 391–393.

Mertens, D. M. (2007). Transformative paradigm. *Journal of Mixed Methods Research*, *1*(3), 212–225. https://doi.org/10.1177/1558689807302811

Mertens, D. M. (2013). Emerging advances in mixed method research: Addressing social justice. *Journal of Mixed Method Research*, *7*(3), 215–218. https://doi.org/10.1177/1558689813493994

Meyer, D. (2020). An intersectional analysis of LGBTQ online media coverage of the Pulse nightclub shooting victims. *Journal of Homosexuality*, *67*(10), 1343–1366.

Mollett, A., Brumley, C., Gilson, C., & Williams, S. (2017). *Communicating your research with social media: A practical guide to using blogs, podcasts, data visualizations, and video*. SAGE.

Paré, G., Trudel, M., Jaana, M., & Kitsiou, S. (2015). Synthesizing information systems knowledge: A typology of literature reviews. *Information & Management*, *52*, 183–199. http://dx.doi.org/10.1016/j.im.2014.08.008

Ponterotto, J. G., Matthew, J. T., & Raughley, B. (2013). The value of mixed methods designs to social justice research in counseling and psychology. *Journal for Social Action in Counseling and Psychology*, *5*(2), 42–68.

Ramasubramanian, S., & Banjo, O. O. (2020). Critical media effects framework: Bridging critical cultural communication and media effects through power, intersectionality, context, and agency. *Journal of Communication*, *70*(3), 379–400. https://doi.org/10.1093/joc/jqaa014

Ramasubramanian, S., & Dutta, M. J. (2024). The CODE^SHIFT model: A data justice framework for collective impact and social transformation. *Human Communication Research*, *50*(2), 173–183.

Ramirez, J. L., Gonzalez, K. A., & Galupo, M. P. (2018). "Invisible during my own crisis": Responses of LGBT people of color to the Orlando shooting. *Journal of Homosexuality*, *65*(5), 579–599.

Resnick, B., & Belluz, J. (2019, July 10). *The war to free science: How librarians, pirates, and funders are liberating the world's academic research from paywalls*. Vox. www.vox.com/the-highlight/2019/6/3/18271538/open-access-elsev ier-california-sci-hub-academic-paywalls

Scharrer, E., & Ramasubramanian, S. (2021). *Quantitative research methods in communication: The power of numbers for social justice*. Routledge.

Scharrer, E., Ramasubramanian, S., & Banjo, O. (2022). Media, diversity, and representation in the US: A review of the quantitative research literature on media content and effects. *Journal of Broadcasting & Electronic Media*, *66*(4), 723–749. https://doi.org/10.1080/08838151.2022.2138890

Sins Invalid. (2019). *Skin, tooth, and bone: The basis of movement is our people: A disability justice primer* (2nd ed.). Self-published. https://www.flipcause.com/secure/reward_step2/OTMxNQ==/65827

Stage, F., & Wells, R. (2014). *Critical quantitative inquiry in context. New directions for institutional research*. Jossey-Bass.

Taylor, L. (2017). What is data justice? The case for connecting digital rights and freedoms globally. *Big Data & Society*, *4*(2). https://doi.org/10.1177/2053951717736335

Taylor, L., Sharma, G., Martin, A., & Jameson, S. (Eds.). (2020). *Data justice and COVID-19: Global perspectives*. Meatspace Press. https://meatspacepress.com/go/data-justice-and-covid-19-internet-archive

Tracy, S. J. (2002). Altered practice ↔ altered stories ↔ altered lives: Three considerations for translating organizational communication scholarship into practice. *Management Communication Quarterly*, *16*(1), 85–91.

Williams, D. R., Yu, Y., Jackson, J. S., & Anderson, N. B. (1997). Racial differences in physical and mental health: Socio-economic status, stress and discrimination. *Journal of Health Psychology*, *2*(3), 335–351.

Xie, C., Liu, P., & Cheng, Y. (2023). Praxis, hashtag activism, and social justice: A content analysis of #StopAsianHate narratives. *Asian Journal of Communication*, *33*(2), 121–137.

CHAPTER 14

Justice Informatics, Justice for Us All: Liberation from Techno-Ideology

Tanya Loughead *and* Jasmina Tacheva

At 2:30 p.m. on Saturday, May 14, 2022, less than a mile away from our university, Canisius University, in Buffalo, New York, a White man stormed into a grocery store in a predominantly Black neighborhood and killed 10 people, most of whom were Black. The 18-year-old shooter's manifesto and gruesome actions unequivocally make this hate crime an act of domestic terrorism motivated by White supremacy. His terrorist ideology did not occur in a vacuum, nor was the location accidental: He traveled for hours with the specific intention of striking an area with a high concentration of Black residents and meticulously documented the steps of his plan on digital platforms whose far-right extremist subcommunities he called "home." It is precisely the digital space he inhabited that is, according to an investigative report commissioned by New York State Attorney General Letitia James, responsible for the White supremacist mass murderer's radicalization (Office of the New York State Attorney General Letitia James, 2022, p. 23). His manifesto is replete with posts suggesting "that the White race is dying out, that Blacks are disproportionately killing Whites," and that "memes have done more for the ethnonationalist movement than any manifesto" (p. 23). It is digital artifacts such as these that constitute the shooter's road to radicalization on anonymous anything-goes forums such as 4chan and Reddit (p. 24).

This digital-disinformation-to-hate pipeline is not unique to just the Buffalo mass shooting: The Australian terrorist who killed 51 people at two mosques in Christchurch was radicalized by YouTube videos (Shead, 2020). Hate-filled anti-2SLGBTIAQ+ online material was cited as a leading factor in the radicalization of the domestic terrorist who killed 49 in an Orlando, Florida, nightclub in 2016 (Council on Foreign Relations, 2016). Philosopher Christa Hodapp (2017) argues that online chat groups have long been a space for disappointed, angry, and entitled men to gather to complain about women and plot their revenge upon them:

> In 2018, a rented cargo van plowed through pedestrians along a 1.5-mile stretch of Toronto's bustling Yonge Street, running through red lights and onto sidewalks. Ten people were killed in the attack. Police arrested the driver, [a man] accused of 26 charges of first-degree and attempted murder. (Ling, 2020)

A message posted to the killer's Facebook page shortly before the attack began read, "The Incel Rebellion has already begun!" In the same online post, he refers to "Supreme Gentleman Elliot Rodger"—a male misogynist terrorist who killed 6 and injured 14 people to punish women for rejecting him. As Hodapp (2017) argues, such incels and "men's rights" groups operate and grow as a movement—defining their voice, vocabulary, and methods—predominantly online.[1] We should also bear in mind that nearly all mass shooters and terrorists are men,

---

[1] The term *incels* refers to involuntarily celebate men—heterosexual men who, because they perceive women to have too much power, eschew relationships with women. They are related to and sometimes a subsection of MRAs or "men's rights associations," which believe that it is men, not women, who are the oppressed and beleaguered sex.

and therefore, to understand violence, the notion of masculinity itself must be investigated (Martin & Bowman, 2021). Although certainly frustration, pain, and suffering exist across demographics, there is no other demographic—across race, religion, ethnicity, or caste—that is more responsible for mass death than men. Any analysis of violence (online or offline) must begin with this fact.

Because online spaces can be echo chambers that discourage broad and critical thinking, they can perpetuate and intensify long-standing systems of racial and gender violence. Therefore, they must be studied as thoroughly as other aspects of our social world. Philosophers pave the way for this research by perpetually questioning deep-seated foundational beliefs that lead to unexamined structural inequities. This work is being done not only within the academy but also by a growing number of activists and coalitions. Nonetheless, with the rise of ubiquitous connectivity, digital media poses unprecedented challenges to traditional critical analysis. For example, because most online content is powered by opaque proprietary algorithmic systems—what has come to be known as "the black box society" (Pasquale, 2015)—it may become difficult for organizers and critical researchers to thoroughly investigate and combat the digital ecosystems that exacerbate oppression.

In this chapter, we analyze and suggest a path forward from this problem using the lens of philosophy and critical theory applied to the field of social informatics, which is commonly defined as "the interdisciplinary study of the design, uses and consequences of information and communication technologies that takes into account their interaction with institutional and cultural contexts" (Kling, 2007, p. 217). We call our approach *justice informatics*, and, with full awareness of the rapid shifts and changes in technology, scholarship, and organizing, we make no claim to offer an exhaustive definition of what this field might encompass; rather, we issue a series of principles and practices that would advance justice in informatics. This foundation for justice informatics allows us to evaluate the justice potential of existing digital work. It enables us to see, for example, that the presence of racist, sexist, homophobic, casteist, or xenophobic content in digital spaces is not by chance; rather, it is the result of a lucrative weaponized capitalist digital–industrial complex. Focused on justice, we require collective movements both online and on the ground to analyze our world and offer sustained resistance to this totalizing digital regime.

The regime of the digital recognizes no limits and is equally potent in ostensibly democratic "developed" countries and "developing" nations enveloped by neoliberalism or state-controlled means of material and knowledge production: from the use of biometric mass surveillance to track Uyghur people in China to the surveillance of period tracker apps to criminalize abortion in the United States. A justice informatics framework therefore argues that to fully grasp the insidious dimensions of this digital–industrial complex, scholars, media theorists, humanists, activists, and virtually anyone using digital media must critically engage digital space as part of "racial capitalism, heteropatriarchy, internationalism, and transphobia" (Davis et al., 2022, p. 2) to understand and withstand the extent of its harms.

Committing to a justice informatics framework allows us to (a) identify interlocking oppressive systems that the digital perpetuates and intensifies, (b) comprehend the ideological foundations of our societies, and (c) develop tools and tactics for collective liberation. The sections that follow define and explain each of these three justice informatics principles using Herbert Marcuse's (1941) concept of terroristic technocracy, our concept of techno-ideology, and the liberatory methods of abolition and feminism that Angela Davis (2016) envisions and practices.

Technology as Terroristic Technocracy Rather Than a Sociotechnical System

Albeit serving seemingly very different functions, Amazon Prime's same-day delivery, Facebook's scroll, Uber's instant ride option, and the knowledge graphs accompanying Google Search are all expressions of the same combination of "utmost expediency with utmost convenience" afforded by technology that Marcuse (1941, p. 419) observed long before the rise of the internet. Marcuse's warnings about technology are echoed by contemporary data studies scholar–activists such as Simone Brown and Ruha Benjamin. They argue that cutting-edge artificial intelligence (AI) technologies like the ones powering Big Tech perpetuate and intensify centuries-old racist, colonial, sexist, homophobic, xenophobic, and ableist oppressions (Benjamin, 2019; Browne, 2015).

Marcuse (1941) conceptualized technology as a "rational," "all-embracing" "apparatus" "saving time and energy, removing waste, adapting all means to the end, anticipating consequences, sustaining calculability and security," and, most important, as much more than the hardware and software infrastructure making real-time information exchange possible (p. 419). Specifically, he defines technology as "business, technics, human needs and nature . . . welded together into one rational and expedient mechanism" (p. 419). In addition to emphasizing the role of nature in the ecosystem of technology, the Marcusean view underscores the co-constitutive relationship between sociality and technology: Society determines the work machines do but is also, in turn, determined by this work in a perpetual cycle. This cycle does not simply bring more convenience and expediency to the existing social fabric; rather, through the "power" of "production and distribution," it engenders a new form of thinking that Marcuse interchangeably calls "technological attitude" and "technological rationality" (p. 422).

Under the spell of this new kind of rationality, Marcuse (1941) argues that "the free economic subject" has developed "into the object of large-scale organization and coordination, and individual achievement has been transformed into standardized efficiency" (p. 417). Thus, states Marcuse, the work of the worker "supplements the machine process rather than makes use of it" (p. 418). The logic of this technological rationality whose fetishization of efficiency has brought about a system of "terroristic technocracy" (p. 437) extends beyond technology workers and beyond the 1940s into today's digital economy.

Grounding justice informatics in the Marcusean view of technology enables critical scholars and organizers to transcend the traditional social informatics paradigm according to which technology is *sociotechnical*, comprising the "interactions between people, organizations, institutions, and a range of technologies in rather intricate heterogeneous arrangements in which what is 'social' and what is 'technical' cannot be readily isolated in practice" (Lamb et al., 2000). Although useful for band-aid reforms, this paradigm lacks long-term transformative potential because it takes the *system* in which "people," "organizations," "institutions," and "technologies" operate for granted and never critically examines it. Because our system is never named and interrogated in such analyses, it remains unchallenged, despite decades of organizing and scholarly work demonstrating that justice is only possible if we dismantle the current system and envision a different mode of *relationality* (Simpson, 2014). Marcuse's (1941) concept of terroristic technocracy, on the other hand, both names and challenges oppressive systems, revealing the destructive extent to which they are internalized by anyone caught up in them. Terroristic technocracy, however, is not limited by the technological attitude. With the increasing dominance of the internet and AI, we argue that terroristic technocracy relies on a basis of deeply entrenched beliefs and practices. We deem this basis *techno-ideology* to emphasize its powerful and largely unconscious character; these practices carry on in normative society without much thought as to how, why, and who or what they serve.[2]

The Digital as Techno-Ideology

In the regime of "surveillance capitalism" (Zuboff, 2019), we have been promised global connectedness, real-time communication, continuous news coverage, and instant gratification. These promises come at a cost: rather than independent decision-makers, we, just like the machine workers in Marcuse's (1941) example, are nothing more than a supplement to the machine process, a sentiment captured by the adage that "if something is free, you are the product," in the context of ostensibly *free* services such as Facebook and Instagram.

And yet, despite the growing volume of critical work that challenges the harms of technological rationality and uncovers the atrocities perpetrated by Big Tech giants such as Meta (Kantayya, 2020), the terroristic technocracy Marcuse (1941) foresaw is well and thriving. In fact, it has, more than other geopolitical factors, come to define reality. Marcuse's conceptualization of technological rationality helps illuminate this development, but even its prescience falls short of capturing the intensity with which the architects of Big Tech's terroristic technocracy believe in technology's power to be the ultimate arbiter of truth and success.

The belief that beyond solving straightforward engineering problems, technology can also solve the most complex social issues, such as poverty, racism, and violence, has come to be known as *technosolutionism* (Morozov, 2013). And yet, more than believing in the power of the technological apparatus, the enormous investments of capital, labor, research, natural resources, human lives, and affect associated with settler–colonial desires such as colonizing Mars or recolonizing the African continent through AI infrastructure signify a robust and pernicious system of beliefs transcending technology. Since at least the early 1900s, philosophers have raised an eyebrow at the supposed "neutrality" or "objectivity" of the sciences.[3] More recently, critical data scholars have begun to question the neutrality of technology in similar ways.[4] Yet, we argue that justice informatics should go a step further and understand the cult of technological progress as a pervasive *ideology*—one we deem techno-ideology. In addition to seeing through the feigned neutrality and objectivity of technology, techno-ideology affords us the triple-jeopardy[5] intersectional conceptualization of the digital as a set of deep-seated unexamined beliefs produced not only by terroristic technocracy's technological attitude, technosolutionism, and surveillance but also by the confluence of many interlocking systems, such as capitalism, racism, patriarchy, colonialism, and ableism.

There are several interconnected beliefs that characterize techno-ideology, and more will undoubtedly emerge. One such belief is the inflated sense of self-importance associated with digital work, particularly AI algorithms, which is perceived as somehow superior to other work and frequently leads to a "god-like" complex among data capitalists. Another is the belief that expediency, convenience, and efficiency are necessary and sufficient markers of quality and progress—a belief critiqued by Marcuse (1941), as well as by recent critical analyses of Taylorism and Fordism from critical data studies researchers and whistleblower computer

---

[2] We have in mind the work of philosophers such as Louis Althusser (1972) on the concept of "ideology."

[3] See, for instance, Edmund Husserl's 1936 (1970 in English) work. Husserl believes that the phenomenological method will help us question the narrowness of Enlightenment science that he thinks is responsible for the violent "crisis" in Europe.

[4] See especially Ruha Benjamin's and Safya Noble's work.

[5] We refer to Third World Women's Alliance's (1971) urge to move beyond the intersection of race and gender and critically interrogate capitalism as well, as Davis et al. (2022, p. 4) remind us.

scientists.[6] Building on Enlightenment-era scientism, digital technology, especially AI, is supposed to save humanity (well, not all humans, right?) and shape its future—a future that is, judging by tech hype, extraterrestrial and thus appears to absolve us from the responsibility to fight climate catastrophe and the mass extinction of species on this planet. A further hallmark of techno-ideology is the belief in individualist notions of "negative freedom," which views questions of ethics and justice as obstacles to "progress" and invites us to "move fast and break things" (Facebook's slogan), ignoring laws, social norms, and criticism. This mentality leads to a dangerous convergence between the extreme right and extreme tech: The same neo-authoritarian demeanor exhibited by Donald Trump can be clearly seen in Elon Musk's actions after his Twitter takeover, such as the amplification of "anti-woke" propaganda and the censorship of critical voices.

By perpetuating beliefs such as data being "abstract," "raw," "objective," or "the new oil" rather than coming from people, freely available online to be "grabbed" and "mined" by analytical "mercenaries" to produce "objective," "unbiased," and "accurate" models relying on "infallible" math and promising ways to find the right candidates for a job or stop crimes before they occur, techno-ideology proves itself to be the culmination of neoliberal, racial, patriarchal, colonial, ableist, and speciesist logic—the very opposite of a concern for justice. With this toxic cyber-masculinity recipe, it is only natural that social media algorithmic content curation continues stoking hatred and mass shootings. What can be done to stop this?

Reservoirs of Hope

As with most social–political issues, justice informatics urges us to learn to analyze and deepen questions rather than narrowly focus on "solutions." Thinking is not ontologically prior to action; thinking *is* action and must be undertaken continuously and coexistent with all other actions. Angela Davis' abolition feminism is particularly helpful in this regard. The question for justice informatics organizers and scholars cannot be "What can corporations or governments do in order to regulate online space and the use of digital information?" Current governments—including Republican, Democrat, American, European, Indian, Chinese, and so on—are thoroughly neoliberal. At best, they might prosecute some of the worst individual, online cases of threats, violence, hate, violations of privacy, or use of information to willingly harm. But we should not count on them to do even that.

Similarly, when discussing the Trayvon Martin case, Davis (2016) maintains that whether George Zimmerman was or was not found guilty, the movement must focus on thinking and analyzing structural racism collectively. Individual prosecution does very little to fight the structural problem of racism. "It is a mistake to assume that these issues can be resolved on an individual level"—"a mistake to assume that all we have to do is guarantee the prosecution of the cop who killed Michael Brown"; rather, we need "consciousness of the structural character of violence" (p. 15).

---

[6] In the early 20th century, Henry Ford's assembly-line production and Frederick W. Taylor's "scientific management" led to a class and power divide between poorly compensated workers and the affluent managerial class, who oversaw their work in factories and believed them to be expendable. Kate Crawford, in her 2021 book *The Atlas of AI*, connects those historic shifts in industrial capitalism to modern Big Tech's oppressive labor conditions and its prioritization of perceived efficiency over human dignity. She suggests that these industries are the latest iteration of Ford and Taylor's principles. Recently, whistleblower computer scientist Timnit Gebru and philosopher Émile Torres (2024) coined the term TESCREAL (transhumanism, extropianism, singularitarianism, cosmism, rationalism, effective altruism, and longtermism) to expose the pervasive misogynist, racist, colonialist, and capitalist origins of the belief system that undergirds contemporary advancements in AI.

Problems are not individual, and neither are solutions. Therefore, the question must be reformulated as "What kinds of lives do we collectively want to live? How can we talk about this? How can we think, strategize, and build movements for this?" In our thinking, we must be actively anti-capitalist, anti-racist, feminist, and global in perspective. For instance, Davis (2016) offers as an example that in South Africa, the head of police is a Black woman: "Many of the positions of leadership from which Black people were totally excluded during apartheid are now occupied by Black people," "yet, it doesn't matter that a Black woman heads the national police" because the "technology, the regimes, the targets are still the same" (pp. 17–18). When thinking about the problems of the digital, following Davis' example, we cannot focus on individuals as the only problem (Musk, Gates, etc.) any more than we can seek heroes as the solution.

In her work during the past decade as part of the Black Lives Matter movement, Davis has repeatedly emphasized that we need to stop focusing on heroes and saviors (particularly "powerful male individuals") and focus on the everyday people who build and sustain movements. She rejects turning Martin Luther King, Jr., or Malcolm X into "savior" figures just as she resists it when people deem *her* that. We know that "Lincoln did not free the slaves" but, rather, thousands of enslaved people started a movement wherein they freed themselves (Davis, 2016, p. 69). Lincoln followed their movement. Likewise, the bus boycott was not formed or led by King—he was asked to speak in solidarity with them after the movement had already been formed. It was a movement of majority Black women domestic workers. "Even though we may not know the names of all of those women," we should "acknowledge their collective accomplishment" (p. 67). As we read it, then, Davis has at least two problems with this typical depiction of history as the succession of individual actors: (a) It is simply not true (as she illustrates throughout her work), and (b) "it is essential to resist the depiction of history as the work of heroic individuals in order for people today to recognize their potential agency as part of an ever-expanding community of struggle" (p. 2).

In fact, what we need to struggle against terroristic technocracy and techno-ideology as organizers, critical theorists of technology, and its users is—by now considered an old-fashioned word—*consciousness-raising*. We need "broad consciousness" of the "work that will be required to build a better world" (Davis, 2016, p. 84). Key to this consciousness-raising is thinking carefully through the different ways that oppression exists. "The question of how to bring movements together is also a question of the kind of language one uses and the consciousness one tries to impart" (p. 21). The type of consciousness we, along with Davis, advocate for is distinctly abolitionist: it aims to envision and work towards a "world free of xenophobia and racism," of "homophobia and transphobia," "punishment of incarceration," where life necessities are not "subject to the demands of capitalist profit" and "where everyone learns to respect the environment and all of the creatures, human and nonhuman like, with whom we cohabit our world" (pp. 75–76).

We see little hope in government or market regulation of the digital. The digital has one rule: profit and power. We know that historically, law is a weak tool (at best) for fighting capitalist injustice. Our tool of choice is consciousness-raising. Just as the digital is not a neutral tool but, rather, serves neoliberal capitalism through techno-ideology, consciousness-raising is also not a neutral tool—it serves *collective liberation*. The goal of consciousness-raising is that ordinary people adopt a critical stance in the way they perceive their relationship to reality and in collective consciousness to begin to imagine new worlds and "find reservoirs of hope and optimism" (Davis, 2016, pp. 49, 67).

Conclusion

Through the integration of critical theory, media studies, and social informatics, this chapter offers a way of conceptualizing the scholar–activist work of analyzing and educating about digital content. We call this approach *justice informatics* and outline three of its core principles: (a) naming the interlocking oppressive systems the digital perpetuates and intensifies—terroristic technocracy; (b) understanding the digital's ideological grounding in techno-ideology; and (c) developing tools and tactics for collective liberation through consciousness-raising and abolition feminism. Although there are many approaches to justice in the digital sphere, we should be cautious about applying the provisional label of "justice informatics" to them. For example, in the tech world, appeals to "fairness," "transparency," and "AI safety" proliferate but ultimately fail to produce substantive change because they work in tandem with, not against, techno-ideology. Similarly, while calls for "data justice" or "decolonizing data science" are more critical, they are ultimately doomed to failure because although they aim to advance marginalized communities, they fall short of naming and challenging the root cause of the problem: global racial colonial heteropatriarchal capitalism. To truly center justice, we must envision the digital to be otherwise—Indigenous rather than settler–colonial, collective rather than individualistic and alienating, not-for-profit and open-source rather than proprietary and profit-driven, anti-racist and anti-casteist rather than racializing and racist, queer and feminist rather than heteropatriarchal. A living archive of justice informatics collectives and projects is available at bit.ly/justiceinfo.

References

Althusser, L. (1972). Ideology and ideological state apparatuses: Notes towards an investigation. https://www.marxists.org/reference/archive/althusser/1970/ideology.htm

Benjamin, R. (2019). *Race after technology: Abolitionist tools for the new Jim Code.* Polity Press.

Browne, S. (2015). *Dark matters: On the surveillance of blackness.* Duke University Press.

Council on Foreign Relations. (2016, June 16). *The Orlando massacre and the conundrum of online radicalization.* Digital and Cyberspace Policy Program.

Crawford, K. (2021). *The atlas of AI: Power, politics, and the planetary costs of artificial intelligence.* Yale University Press.

Davis, A. Y. (2016). *Freedom is a constant struggle: Ferguson, Palestine, and the foundations of a movement.* Haymarket Books.

Davis, A. Y., Dent, G., Meiners, E. R., & Richie, B. E. (2022). *Abolition. Feminism. Now.* Haymarket Books.

Gebru, T., & Torres, É. P. (2024). The TESCREAL bundle: Eugenics and the promise of utopia through artificial general intelligence. *First Monday, 29*(4). https://doi.org/10.5210/fm.v29i4.13636

Hodapp, C. (2017). *Men's rights, gender, and social media.* Rowman & Littlefield.

Husserl, E. (1970). *The crisis of European sciences and transcendental phenomenology.* Northwestern University Press. (Original work published 1936)

Kantayya, S. (2020). *Coded bias.* 7th Empire Media.

Kling, R. (2007). What is social informatics and why does it matter? *The Information Society, 23*(4), 205–220.

Lamb, R., Sawyer, S., & Kling, R. (2000). A social informatics perspective on socio-technical networks. *AMCIS 2000 Proceedings*, Article 1. https://aisel.aisnet.org/amcis2000/1

Ling, J. (2020, June 2). *Incels are radicalized and dangerous. But are they terrorists?* Foreign Policy. https://foreignpolicy.com/2020/06/02/incels-toronto-attack-terrorism-ideological-violence

Marcuse, H. (1941). Some social implications of modern technology. *Zeitschrift für Sozialforschung, 9*(3), 414–439.

Martin, M., & Bowman, E. (2021, March 27). *Why nearly all mass shooters are men.* NPR. https://www.npr.org/2021/03/27/981803154/why-nearly-all-mass-shooters-are-men

Morozov, E. (2013). *To save everything, click here: The folly of technological solutionism.* Public Affairs.

Office of the New York State Attorney General Letitia James. (2022, October 18). *Investigative report on the role of online platforms in the tragic mass shooting in Buffalo on May 14, 2022.* https://www.documentcloud.org/documents/23167059-buffaloshooting-onlineplatformsreport

Pasquale, F. (2015). *The black box society: The secret algorithms that control money and information.* Harvard University Press.

Shead, S. (2020, December 8). *YouTube radicalized the Christchurch shooter, New Zealand report concludes.* CNBC. https://www.cnbc.com/2020/12/08/youtube-radicalized-christchurch-shooter-new-zealand-report-finds.html

Simpson, A. (2014). *Mohawk interruptus: Political life across the borders of settler states.* Duke University Press.

Zuboff, S. (2019). *The age of surveillance capitalism: The fight for a human future at the new frontier of power.* Profile Books.

Researching Closed Fields: What We Can Learn from Analyzing So-Called Constrained, Inaccessible, and Invisible Media Contexts

Hanan Badr

Defining Closed Fields of Study

Why do we need to rethink doing research in media and communication studies? Our discipline is unevenly marked by structural and cultural imbalances that shape the knowledge produced and circulated. Several factors affect how we make sense of the data and phenomena around us: Scholars' geopolitical location, socialization, biographies, visibility, access, networks, and publishing venues shape the knowledge we produce. Scholarship from non-Western contexts remains marginalized in multiple ways in terms of who gets to speak and be heard. Geography and gender dynamics favor years of accumulated knowledge produced by White masculinity most predominantly in Western, Anglophone research locations (Chakravartty et al., 2018; Demeter & Goyanes, 2021; Ekdale et al., 2022; Freelon et al., 2023). The centers of knowledge production in communication studies in the Northern metropoles perpetuate fundamental inequalities in material infrastructures and symbolic capital of knowledge production (Dutta, 2020). Entire research, linguistic, and geopolitical terrains and research traditions remain invisible and inaccessible, especially if operating in a non-English–dominated arena such as Latin American, Arab, or even French and Spanish academic work (Averbeck-Lietz, 2012). In addition, global border regimes disadvantage Global South scholars, limiting their mobility for conferences or data collection, further marginalizing their positions in academia.

Hostility of closed research environments toward scholars is another factor that perpetuates academic inequalities. In an ideal world, producing critical knowledge should not lead to safety concerns for researchers, yet reality shows otherwise. The problem for the field is that we cannot inspire people to study hostile or closed fields if (a) they do not want to pursue these areas of study, (b) they do not have the competency to work in unpredictable research environments that require a minimum of regional and linguistic expertise, (c) they do not want to take the risk, or (d) their countries or institutions do not materially support this research either directly through travel or cooperation restrictions or indirectly through uneven funding and grant calls. Can we blame scholars if they do not feel inspired to research faraway closed contexts with a higher threshold of required skills and that may be hazardous?

Acknowledging the difficulties in studying media and justice in closed research environments regardless of the official government type is a crucial starting point. This chapter intentionally uses the term "closed contexts" (Koch, 2013a) rather than authoritarian regime. "Closed" is broader and includes a wider umbrella of constrained settings. It also overcomes the normative liberal–illiberal binary along a one-dimensional conception of power and subjects' agency that is eroding (Koch, 2013a, pp. 390–391). In times of global authoritarian backsliding, nuancing research dilemmas and practices beyond the one-dimensional linear spectrum of liberal versus illiberal practices benefits social sciences because it helps scholars navigate different levels of closure as illiberal techniques exist even in formal democracies (see Hintz & Milan, 2018; Mohammad & Sidaway, 2013). Evidence shows limits of academic freedom worldwide, where even democracies in the European Union have closures and restrictions on issues such as LGBTQ rights or pro-Palestinian solidarity.

Applying Closed Fields to the Arab Media Contexts

Can media and communication studies in its current form adequately explain the Arab media realities? Researching non-Western contexts such as the Arab media raises questions on suitability of importing communication theories that have developed in different geographic contexts (Hafez, 2013; Kraidy, 2012). Social theories are meant to detect regularities and patterns to make sense of what is out in the social world. But theory-building is a social construct and therefore tends to reflect global and epistemic power structures (Natter, 2022). Using research paradigms and methods originating in the Enlightenment-inspired classic empiricist positivism to find out a universal and objective truth does not do justice to researching communication phenomena outside Western polities (Wang, 2014). Research design and methodology derive from a liberal understanding of subjectivity and polity (Koch, 2013b, p. 413). This raises questions on origins of theory abstraction and limitations on its transfer—questions on how and why theories travel, how they evolve across contexts, and the politics of deciding who/what constitutes a theorist/theory (Bilgin, 2021).

Two examples illustrate the limitations of imported concepts. The first is how the analysis of the Arab media landscape by Kraidy (2012, p. 198) shows the limits of Hallin and Mancini's media systems typology. Studying the Saudi Lebanese regional cross-border media connections in labor and capital flows revealed a unique dimension of "transnational parallelism" referring to two interdependent processes that take place in different national geographies. The second example of limitations of imported concepts is how the concept of "media accountability" has been applied to Arab contexts. Pies (2022) notes the epistemic challenges to finding meaningful answers to explain media–society relations in closed contexts as the concept of accountability developed in liberal traditions and connected media freedom with the absence of state intervention (Scott et al., 2023, p. 89).

Although there are challenges in applying such non-Western concepts to specific cultural contexts, we cannot afford to dismiss closed research ontologies. Researching closed media contexts is risky but not impossible. This chapter makes the case that a categorical dismissal is not productive for media and communication studies because it is important to research closed contexts for several reasons. From a purely self-serving utilitarian logic, limited research is better under closed circumstances than no research at all, even under conditions of uncertainty. Researching closed contexts enhances our discipline because it expands the empirical and theoretical base of knowledge. Studying media and social justice in closed Arab contexts strengthens comparative media systems and global communication. Neglecting how to research non-Western contexts is an epistemic flaw—that is, imbalances in the way we view the world—that prevents "viable communication studies" (Richter, 2016, p. 95). By showing the possibilities of producing meaningful and valid knowledge—that could deviate from mainstream methods—despite the challenging closed contexts, the chapter contributes to overcoming the epistemic exclusion of geographic fields.

Research methods still reflect the discipline's positivist, largely American and Eurocentric beginnings that favored policy and administrative research over critical research traditions (Meyen, 2020). For example, academic relevance for studying closed contexts is justified through the lens of securitization and othering paradigms, amplifying the threats in issues and actors underscoring the policy research orientation of communication studies, such as studies of the Arab Spring, terrorism, migration, or the Cold War.

This means that researching closed media contexts requires a delicate balance between complete dismissal and an unprepared deep dive: Dismissing closed media contexts entirely is not an option because it risks losing potential innovative insights so that the discipline is predictable and less diverse (Ustad Figenschou, 2010). But pretending that we can study closed contexts without preparation or caution is short-sighted and not safe (Glasius et al., 2018). Performing research in global media contexts according to practices developed in open contexts can be tricky: They evolved in stable, safe, formalized, and accessible research realities that do not necessarily fit the research ontologies that can be more constrained or simply have different logics, where researchers must balance multiple principles such as do no harm, not arousing suspicions by the government and security bodies, and handling safety threats such as bureaucratic hurdles, shadowing, interrogations, and deportations (Gentile, 2013).

Little has been written about communication research in closed media fields, Unlike the extensive discussions and best-practice guidelines in disciplines such as political science, anthropology, geography, and area studies.[1] Researching closed contexts is a step toward an "engaged communication scholarship" that centers "theories, methods and practices to work with and for oppressed, marginalized and under-resourced groups and communities" (Carragee & Frey, 2016, p. 3975). This chapter engages with the growing body of literature in the de-Westernization debate in communication studies. During the past four decades, scholars have repeatedly called for a critical scrutiny of power, capital, and flows to open the field toward a cosmopolitan discipline (Chakkravarrty et al., 2018; Ganter & Badr, 2022; Mellado et al., 2020; Thussu, 2022; Waisbord & Mellado, 2014). Cosmopolitan communication studies gained trajectory in recent years and means bringing different epistemic perspectives into the field to decenter it.

Slow and gradual adjustments can be seen: We have witnessed a diversification of editorial boards (Tandoc et al., 2020), "mindful inclusion" (Rao, 2019), and a call to diversify political communication (Gagrčin & Butkowski, 2023). Innovating the criteria for research quality is overdue. Scholars at the annual conference of the International Communication Association (ICA23) critically discussed reviewing practices to make them more inclusive. This includes openness to data from repressive fields that can be unstructured, anonymized, or limited, which at the same time attests to the researcher's ability to gain trust, a "fragile and valuable commodity" (Glasius et al., 2018). Another example is moving away from mainstream methods that center objectivity and dismiss the validity of subjective feelings during research. In closed media contexts, "bad feelings" such as sadness, frustration, or confusion can raise important and critical questions about structural, institutional, and disciplinary conditions that do not feel right during field research (Moussawi & Puri, 2022, p. 76) or that have a mental health impact on scholars and research participants (Glasius et al., 2018).

Reality of Researching Closed Media Contexts

Can there be ethical and safe social scientific research in closed contexts? This section reconstructs the constrained, inaccessible, and invisible research situations among macrostructures of unpredictability, poverty, and corruption in closed contexts. It does not offer a best practice guideline but, rather, draws on two decades of research expertise in Egypt as a local and

---

[1] References in Middle East studies include the Project on Middle East Political Science (2014), Glasius et al. (2018), and Grimm et al. (2020).

external researcher. Inspired by bell hooks' "oppositional gaze" (1999), this chapter applies a feminist decolonial lens to produce knowledge about closed contexts. Because "looking is power" (hooks, 1999, p. 308), investigating closed contexts and constructing knowledge about them empowers the scholars. Power holders can view this as a possible challenge that needs to be silenced. Here, I elaborate on what is meant by constrained, inaccessible, and invisible research contexts. I use Arab media systems to illustrate these terms with examples.

Constrained

Although research in closed contexts is usually not eventful and control includes bureaucratic hurdles, restricting access, shadowing, and subtle or overt intimidation (Glasius et al., 2018), the rare brutal cases involving detainment, torture, and even murder have long-term silencing consequences (Anderson, 2016). In constrained contexts, social science and humanities are conflated with espionage so that social scientists are considered potential state security hazards and citizens' distrust leads to reporting of other citizens (Fahmy, 2022). Interviewing in a public place can lead to the scholars' arrest. For example, a self-proclaimed patriotic bystander reported an Egyptian journalist and *Le Monde* diplomatique editor in chief when she overheard them in a Cairene café. The situation led to a brief detainment and interrogation by the Egyptian police (Finn, 2015). Legitimate safety concerns and ethical principles in increasingly closed fields lead to a "serious reversal" of research into outdated "Orientalist practices" where writing *about* the region without field research is considered (Fahmy, 2022).

Unpredictable factors influence the quality of research, especially if the researcher is not attuned to the surroundings, does not speak the language, or does not have a safe and trusted network. For example, interrogations by security officers can be indirect pressure to illicit bribery or to control the data (Gentile, 2013). Another factor of unpredictability is that cultural and social values in human interactions limit the research outcome if they affect the data collection process. In Arab fields, the desire to appease scholars or give desirable results influences audience's responses, thus affecting the quality and truthfulness of data (Douai, 2010).

Research in closed contexts does not have deterministic outcomes. Recent critical scholarship recognizes the interactive dynamics between scholars' and research participants' positionalities, viewing the latter as research collaborators in the research process (Connor et al., 2018). Research participants have an active agency in the research and data collection process that can facilitate the research process (Schulz, 2021) or hinder and block the data collection. Empirical evidence suggests that gender and positionality intersect in nuanced ways depending on the society, social strata, and geographic location. So, it might be difficult for a male Arab researcher to invite a female participant to a public space in a conservative setting because it may be "somewhat associated with 'loose,' unwanted behavior, or mere lack of social desirability" (Douai, 2010, p. 85). On the other hand, ambivalences occur: Privilege gives access to local high-profile "spokespersons" despite the assumed constrained gender dynamics (Glasius et al., 2018). Access to political and media elites was easier for Western female researchers because the interviewees were more willing to talk to Western women, as they recognize their status and capital compared to local researchers, yet occasional experiences of sexism and harassment required creative and professional ways to maneuver the negative experiences (Schwedler, 2006; Ustad Figenschou, 2010).

Inaccessible

How can scholars gain research access in closed contexts under potentially repressive conditions? Power, archives, and access to knowledge are closely intertwined. The politics of archiving reflects what the people in a position to collect and document data deem worthy: Who tells the story? Does the knowledge belong to the state or to the people? What voices set the narrative? Doing Arab media research is particularly difficult because media archives are rare, costly, and politicized in practices of collection and availability. Archives are "centers of interpretations that require epistemological and ethical credibility" (El Shakry, 2015, p. 925). Media materials from the Arab uprisings are limited because those from several short-lived media initiatives that thrived in the free post-revolutionary years were not collected at all. In addition, destruction of archives in the Arab region as a result of conflicts, wars, or upheavals makes researching certain time periods difficult. Most Libyan newspaper archives have been destroyed; even in the largest Middle East collection at the Library of Congress, Arab media archives are selective. Another example of lost material is the Egyptian Muslim Brotherhood–affiliated newspaper *Horreya and Adala* (*Freedom and Justice*), which was not publicly archived, making researching an important phase of a vibrant public sphere in Egypt difficult. Nonexisting archives raise analytical and conceptual barriers to comparative media work, as the firsthand experience in a German Research Council-funded project comparing North Africa and Eastern Europe showed: The presence of U.S. backed-up archives of Radio Free Europe during the Cold War indicated how uneven archives can be.

Not only is finding the media corpora in libraries difficult but also locating the relevant archives themselves is part of a tedious fieldwork and attests to unequal power (El-Hibri & Askari, 2023). Scholars working with archives in Arab closed contexts speak of "adventures in the archives" (Fahmy, 2021) to draw attention to the precarity of conducting academic research in Egypt. In addition to language skills and cultural sensitivity, orality and formality prevail in closed contexts. Often, researchers only get access to otherwise nondocumented or unknown idiosyncratic archives through personal connections. Attaining access to archives and social science fieldwork is difficult and usually securitized through formal and legal requirements to obtain a security clearance or a research permit by the Egyptian Central Agency for Public Mobilization and Statistics (CAPMAS), a technical hurdle that makes research more difficult for foreign researchers in Egypt. Challenging and time-consuming research realities disfavor the region and propel a dislocation of archives outside the region, centralizing power in the Western centers of knowledge production.

In Arab academic environments marked by informality, low resources, and limited access to public knowledge, the legal conceptualization of accessibility to material has a different meaning. Researchers share publications in open homemade repositories to show solidarity, even if it raises legal issues with intellectual property. For example, when an Egyptian media lecturer passed away, his Google Drive of PDF books was made widely available as a *Sadaqat* (a religious term in Islam meaning charity), which was not viewed as a legal violation but as an act of generosity.

But there does not always have to be a bleak tendency toward "postcolonial melancholia" (El Shakry, 2015): Evidence shows a possible trend beyond pessimistic determinism when the political elite invokes legal and structural changes that open the fields and archives for scholars. In postrevolutionary Tunisia, a new law provided citizens access to information (Campagna & Filippinye, 2016). Recently, Gulf Cooperation Council countries have also invested in archives, realizing their interpretative and epistemological power to document and frame a national narrative (see El-Hibri & Askari, 2023).

Invisible

Countering mainstream scholarship shaped by power means developing theories from the margins—for example, deconstructing orientalist narratives in the Arab media contexts. Practicing a scholarly gaze in closed contexts needs to capture the subtle and invisible phenomena: How can we research subtle activist forms that operate everyday "art of presence" (Bayat, 2012) without safe options of open protests with no political cost for dissent? Scholarly analysis also needs to recognize and uncover patterns. However, this requires time and tranquility, which are not present in turbulent contexts. Finding one's scholarly voice during times of disruption is a methodological dilemma: Researchers need time to digest, regenerate, and grasp the events in transitional times, which often requires emotional labor, especially if the field is not a foreign field but, rather, home as a "site of research" (Moussawi & Puri, 2022, p. 77).

Invisibility also affects academic knowledge production: Due to repression and surveillance, scholars use self-censorship and technocratic, vague, and boring language as techniques of survival (Badr & Richter, 2022; Glasius et al., 2018, p. 49). Self-silencing includes "internalized orientalism," a concept building on Edward Said's work, which means internalizing perceptions of oneself as inferior and having nothing to contribute (Alahmed, 2020). Examples of self-silencing include graduate students' self-doubt with regard to employing their own authentic knowledge, language, and cultural skills, and hesitancy to cite literature from their region, especially from the Global South or other marginalized communities. In digitally networked public spheres, invisibility of fields refers to the impossibility of archiving closed groups on Signal or WhatsApp and short-term media initiatives, such as Facebook pages, which are sold and change names and thus are, in a way, lost knowledge.

Ways Forward for Doing Research in Closed Media Contexts

How do we study closed contexts? The chapter concludes with three suggestions that reflect on a range of practical and theoretical issues when designing and conducting research in unpredictable terrains.

Nuancing Research Practice to Balance Means Versus Ends

We can sketch four different scenarios that juxtapose ethics, safety, and pragmatics in difficult contexts, which map out researchers' repertoire of agency to navigate the field and counter constrained conditions, restricted access, and invisibility.

Scenario A follows "clean" ethics that advance honest communication, formalized processes, and professional transparency, which might elicit data that is less in quantity and quality. In closed contexts, with repressive and securitized politics, this type of research might not be possible, or data may not be accessible.

Scenario B is the radical opposite: data at any price. Questionable ethics are used to secure access to the field, such as bribery, deception, or manipulation—research practices that are never endorsed, even though it is sometimes a hushed practice. Examples include unregistered and undocumented ways of getting access to archival materials that border ethical boundaries.

Scenario C, adhering to tradecraft skills, is a middle ground pursuing self-protective tactics that do not violate ethics to balance outcome and integrity. This calls for reflexive research practice beyond the strict medico-scientific approaches (Hammett et al., 2022). In this scenario, scholars need ethical risk management and case-by-case evaluation, expertise for navigating the field, intercultural and linguistic skills, and an enhanced cultural attunement to the surrounding. Strategies include the use of survival language, technocratic labels (Badr & Richter, 2022; Koch, 2013b), evasive interview techniques to avoid interruption and expulsion from the field (Ustad Figenschou, 2010), securing consent in verbal instead of written form, accepting anonymity to avoid frightening participants, or creative solutions to counter bureaucratic and administrative hurdles to protect data collection (Anderson, 2016).

In scenario D, delegating vital research steps to local scholars is a widely accepted practice, yet it raises a whole different set of issues regarding safety, intellectual property, and levels of inclusive collaboration in international projects (Faciolince, 2019; Project on Middle East Political Science, 2014). "Academic sightseeing" and data mining reduced local researchers to native informants (Abaza, 2011). The uneven distribution of academic capital leads to a hierarchy of knowledge production. Research on the Arab uprisings is a good example. Apart from the short-lived scholarly attention inspired by modernist democratization paradigms, research quickly subsided and converted into the securitization paradigm, reflecting unequal research terrains and funding according to higher education policies from the donor countries. The keyword "Arab Spring" was often used as a "buzzword" instead of true engagement with the phenomenon on the ground (Richter & Badr, 2018).

Cross-Disciplinary Fertilization

The field of media and communication studies have much to learn from area studies, especially from Arab and Middle East studies. Communication studies is a latecomer compared to other social sciences. Therefore, debating potential junctions between area studies and media and communication studies is still budding. The latter will benefit if it accepts Arab and Middle East media studies as a legible and legitimate infusion to expand the "narrow data base from the Global South" (Richter, 2016). Arab media research contributed to advancing the communication research agenda and coining new terms, for example, by theorizing the role of social media and activism. Adding empirical work from underresearched regions means overcoming barriers and limitations on our knowledge about media systems and embracing the "possibility of actively different locales, sites, situations for theory, without facile universalism or over-general totalizing" (Bilgin, 2021, p. 250). Terms coined in the West circulate more visibly into scholarship even if they do not conform to the local realities and self-assigned labels, such as "Arab Spring." Labels coined in the Global South rarely travel to the Global North, even when they accurately use self-ascribed local phenomena, such as "electronic committees" and "digital flies" in the Arab region to describe online trolls, unlike their Western equivalents.

Therefore, a "dire need" (Hafez, 2013) to integrate Arab studies into communication studies exists to advance communication studies through emic culture-sensitive theoretical contributions that account for the nuanced historicized complexities and meaningful interpretations (Kozman, 2021, p. 241). Developing a scholarly "double identity" bringing area studies expertise and the theoretical and methodological toolbox from communication studies counters the "oversimplification, sterility and lack of concrete knowledge" on the regional media contexts (Richter, 2016, pp. 97, 100).

Letting Diasporic Scholars Speak?

A third possible way to produce meaningful research in closed contexts is to highlight the role of diasporic scholars as knowledge producers with a unique positionality. They can bridge the local–international scholars' gap, have the "double vision" in terms of DuBois (2018), and can navigate the power asymmetries. The question is, can the exile speak? Historical and empirical evidence shows the importance of exiled scholarship that maintains the critical distance, cultural skills, affinity, and independent position outside the constrained contexts. Diasporic scholars combine insider and outsider privilege in making their countries of origin legible fields. This bears risks of tokenization and confinement to an exotic research agenda if not embraced by the discipline.

Much literature has laid the ground rules for safety and best practice strategies for external or non-resident researchers who travel into the field and then return home. Less has been written about local researchers who live and do research in the closed fields and how it affects their daily lives and careers. Diasporic researchers can wear both hats, enabling them a wider margin of maneuvering the closed contexts. However, repressive systems often also abuse and harass them, as multiple cases show (Fahmy, 2022).

Conclusion: Toward a More Inclusive Future in Communication Research

Researching closed fields enhances the knowledge production in communication studies. In addition to the normative inclusive approach, this young discipline has much to learn from researching closed contexts to overcome the inequalities in theoretical concepts, methods, and data. This chapter detailed how doing research in closed contexts is not impossible but operates under different realities of doing research. Constrained fields, inaccessible data or archives, and invisible phenomena with difficulties to linger the scholarly gaze for knowledge production affect how we do meaningful and ethical research. Dismissing closed regions does not advance knowledge production, especially if it provides a nuanced and contextualized knowledge. Difficulties in finding and identifying relevant archives add to the invisibility of the closed contexts. We need to rethink why our curricula do not empower authenticity or encourage future generations to cultivate their valuable access to original data and fields.

To study closed contexts, we need innovative approaches and nuanced qualitative methods on the ground. There is not much within the power of individual academics to change macrostructures of power inequalities such as global mobility, economy, and freedom of expression. But within the scholarly agency, this chapter suggests multiple ways to develop future theory building, expand an agenda, and critique check (Ganter & Badr, 2022; Mellado et al., 2020). Drawing on field research experience in Arab contexts, primarily Egypt, centering power asymmetries in knowledge production, researchers' gaze, and positionality, the chapter discussed three ways forward to navigate closed contexts while balancing safety and ethics, as a reflective process, not a guidelines approach. Nuancing the research practices and changing the academic culture in accepting nontraditional methods in difficult research contexts is a start. This means we need to develop new criteria to evaluate the quality of research—criteria of excellence that acknowledge and honor the intellectual and emotional labor of doing research in closed contexts. The chapter also calls for the strong need for a cross-disciplinary fertilization to enable epistemic expansion through the subfield of Arab media studies. Finally, capitalizing on their unique position, enabling diasporic scholars to navigate research in closed contexts, and allowing them to speak beyond a tokenized form of knowledge production can strengthen the knowledge toward a more inclusive future in communication studies.

Acknowledgments

I thank Daniel Baker, University of Cardiff, for his valuable feedback on earlier drafts of this chapter, as well as Deborah Fleischmann, Paris London University of Salzburg, for her editorial assistance.

References

Abaza, M. (2011, September 27). Academic tourists sight-seeing the Arab Spring. *Jadaliyya*. https://www.jadaliyya.com/Details/24454

Alahmed, A. (2020). Internalized Orientalism: Toward a postcolonial media theory and de-Westernizing communication research from the Global South. *Communication Theory*, *30*(4), 407–428. https://doi.org/10.1093/ct/qtz037

Anderson, L. (2016, August 17). Academic freedom in a globalized world. *Science & Diplomacy*. https://www.sciencediplomacy.org/perspective/2016/academic-freedom-in-a-globalized-world

Averbeck-Lietz, S. (2012). French and Latin American perspectives on mediation and mediatization: A lecture note from Germany. *Empedocles*, *3*(2), 177–195.

Badr, H. (2022). "Beware of terrorists, spies and chaos!": Stabilization techniques from the Arab uprisings. In N. Ribeiro & C. Schwarzenegger (Eds.), *Media and the dissemination of fear* (pp. 221–246). Palgrave Macmillan. https://doi.org/10.1007/978-3-030-84989-4_11

Badr, H., & Richter, C. (2022). Teaching journalism in Egypt: Captured between control and transformation. In D. Garrisi & X. Kuang (Eds.), *Journalism pedagogy in transitional countries* (pp. 91–109). Palgrave Macmillan.

Bayat, A. (2012). *Life as politics: How ordinary people change the Middle East* (2nd ed.). Stanford University Press.

Bilgin, P. (2021). On the "Does theory travel?" question: Traveling with Edward Said. In Z. G. Capan, F. dos Reis, & M. Grasten (Eds.), *The politics of translation in international relations* (pp. 245–255). Palgrave Macmillan. https://doi.org/10.1007/978-3-030-56886-3_13

Campagna, J., & Filippinye, E. (2016, September 27). *Tunisia's new right to information law needs people power to work*. Open Society Foundations. https://www.opensocietyfoundations.org/voices/tunisia-s-new-right-information-law-needs-people-power-work

Carragee, K. M., & Frey, L. R. (2016). Communication activism research: Engaged communication scholarship for social justice. *International Journal of Communication, 10*, 3975–3999. https://ijoc.org/index.php/ijoc/article/viewFile/6004/1750

Chakravartty, P., Kuo, R., Grubbs, V., & McIlwain, C. (2018). #CommunicationSoWhite. *Journal of Communication, 68*(2), 254–266. https://doi.org/10.1093/joc/jqy003

Connor, J., Copland, S., & Owen, J. (2018). The infantilized researcher and research subject: Ethics, consent and risk. *Qualitative Research, 18*(4), 400–415. https://doi.org/10.1177/1468794117730686

Demeter, M., & Goyanes, M. (2021). A world-systemic analysis of knowledge production in international communication and media studies: The epistemic hierarchy of research approaches. *Journal of International Communication, 27*(1), 38–58. https://doi.org/10.1080/13216597.2020.1817121

Douai, A. (2010). Media research in the Arab world and the audience challenge: Lessons from the field. *Journal of Arab & Muslim Media Research, 3*(1–2), 77–88.

DuBois, W. E. B. (2018). *The souls of Black folk* (10th ed.). Penguin.

Dutta, M. J. (2020). Whiteness, internationalization, and erasure: Decolonizing futures from the Global South. *Communication and Critical/Cultural Studies, 17*(2), 228–235. doi:10.1080/14791420.2020.1770825

Ekdale, B., Biddle, K., Tully, M., Asuman, M., & Rinaldi, A. (2022). Global disparities in knowledge production within journalism studies: Are special issues the answer? *Journalism Studies, 23*(15), 1942–1961. https://doi.org/10.1080/1461670X.2022.2123846

El-Hibri, H., & Askari, K. (2023). Documents, archives, absence: Current challenges and insights from media research in the Middle East and beyond. In J. F. Khalil, G. Khiabany, T. Guaaybess, & B. Yesil (Eds.), *The handbook of media and culture in the Middle East* (pp. 147–161). Wiley. https://doi.org/10.1002/9781119637134.ch14

El Shakry, O. (2015). "History without documents": The vexed archives of decolonization in the Middle East. *American Historical Review, 120*(3), 920–934. https://doi.org/10.1093/ahr/120.3.920

Faciolince, M. (2019, August 20). *The "local" researcher—merely a data collector?* https://frompoverty.oxfam.org.uk/the-local-researcher-merely-a-data-collector

Fahmy, K. (2021, February 2). *Adventures in the archives* [Video]. YouTube. https://www.youtube.com/watch?embeds_referring_euri=https%3A%2F%2Fkhaledfahmy.org%2F&source_ve_path=Mjg2NjQsMTY0NTA2&feature=emb_share&v=RjP6c7Cvtdo

Fahmy, K. (2022, January 16). *The perils of conducting academic research in Sisi's Egypt*. https://khaledfahmy.org/en/2022/01/16/the-perils-of-conducting-academic-research-in-sisis-egypt

Finn, T. (2015, February 13). *In Egypt, where café chatter can get you arrested*. Middle East Eye. https://www.middleeasteye.net/news/egypt-where-cafe-chatter-can-get-you-arrested-0

Freelon, D., Pruden, M., Eddy, K., & Kou, R. (2023). Inequities of race, place, and gender among the communication citation elite, 2000–2019. *Journal of Communication, 73*(4), 356–367. https://doi.org/10.1093/joc/jqad002

Gagrčin, E., & Butkowski, C. (2023). Out of sight, out of mind? Qualitative methods in political communication research. *Political Communication Report, 2023*(27). http://dx.doi.org/10.17169/refubium-39042

Ganter, S. A., & Badr, H. (Eds.). (2022). *Media governance. A cosmopolitan critique*. Palgrave Macmillan. https://doi.org/10.1007/978-3-031-05020-6

Gentile, M. (2013). Meeting the "organs": The tacit dilemma of field research in authoritarian states. *Area, 45*(4), 426–432. http://www.jstor.org/stable/24029921

Glasius, M., de Lange, M., Bartman, J., Dalmasso, E., Lv, A., Sordi, D., Michaelsen, M., & Ruijgrok, K. (2018). *Research, ethics and risk in the authoritarian field*. Palgrave Macmillan.

Grimm, J., Koehler, K., Lust, E. M., Saliba, I., & Schierenbeck, I. (Eds.) (2020). *Safer field research in the social sciences: A guide to human and digital security in hostile environments*. SAGE.

Hafez, K. (2013). The methodology trap: Why media and communication studies are not really international. *Communications: The European Journal of Communication Research, 38*(3), 323–329. https://doi.org/10.1515/commun-2013-0019

Hallin, D., & Mancini, P. (2004). *Comparing media systems*. Cambridge University Press.

Hammett, D., Jackson, L., & Bramley, R. (2022). Beyond "do no harm"? On the need for a dynamic approach to research ethics. *Area*, *54*(4), 582–590. https://doi.org/10.1111/area.12795

Hintz, A., & Milan, S. (2018). Through a glass, darkly: Everyday acts of authoritarianism in the liberal West. *International Journal of Communication*, *12*, 3939–3959.

hooks, b. (1999). The oppositional gaze: Black female spectators. In *Feminist film theory: A reader* (pp. 307–320). Edinburgh University Press. https://doi.org/10.1515/9781474473224-033

Koch, N. (2013a). Introduction—Field methods in "closed contexts": Undertaking research in authoritarian states and places. *Area*, *45*(4), 390–395. http://www.jstor.org/stable/24029916

Koch, N. (2013b). Technologising the opinion: Focus groups, performance and free speech. *Area*, *45*(4), 411–418. http://www.jstor.org/stable/24029919

Kozman, C. (2021). Reconceptualizing Arab media research: Moving from centrism toward inclusiveness and balance. *Journalism & Mass Communication Quarterly*, *98*(1), 241–262. https://doi.org/10.1177/1077699020942924

Kraidy, M. (2012). The rise of transnational media systems: Implications of pan-Arab media for comparative research. In D. Hallin & P. Mancini (Eds.), *Comparing media systems beyond the Western world* (pp. 177–200). Cambridge University Press. doi:10.1017/CBO9781139005098.011

Mellado, C., Georgiou, M., & Nah, S. (2020). Advancing journalism and communication research: New concepts, theories, and pathways. *Journalism & Mass Communication Quarterly*, *97*(2), 333–342.

Meyen, M. (2020). The social-scientific sources of media and communication research. In K. B. Jensen (Ed.), *A handbook of media and communication research* (3rd ed., pp. 54–69). Routledge. https://www.taylorfrancis.com/chapters/edit/10.4324/9781138492905-4/social-scientific-sources-media-communication-research-michael-meyen?context=ubx&refId=ca2ff11f-8858-4699-92fa-aadc2e42db84

Mohammad, R., & Sidaway, J. D. (2013). Fieldwork amid geographies of openness and closure. *Area*, *45*(4), 433–435. http://www.jstor.org/stable/24029922

Moussawi, G., & Puri, J. (2022). "Bad feelings": Reflections on research, disciplines, and critical methodologies. In K. Davis & J. Irvine (Eds.), *Silences, neglected feelings, and blind-spots in research practice* (pp. 75–90). Routledge. https://doi.org/10.4324/9781003208563-8

Natter, K. (2022). Theories on the move. In *The politics of immigration beyond liberal states: Morocco and Tunisia in comparative perspective* (pp. 20–43). Cambridge University Press. https://doi.org/10.1017/9781009262668.002

Pies, J. (2022). Media accountability in a non-democratic context: Conceptual challenges and adaptations. In S. A. Ganter &H. Badr (Eds.), *Media governance* (pp. 81–100). Palgrave Macmillan. https://doi.org/10.1007/978-3-031-05020-6_5

Project on Middle East Political Science. (2014, July 2). *The ethics of research in the Middle East.* http://pomeps.org/wp-content/uploads/2014/07/POMEPS_Studies_8_Ethics.pdf

Rao, S. (2019). Commentary: Inclusion and a discipline. *Digital Journalism*, *7*(5), 698–703. https://doi.org/10.1080/21670811.2019.1634482

Richter, C. (2016). Area studies: Regional studien in der Kommunikationswissenschaft. In S. Averbeck-Lietz & M. Meyen (Eds.), *Handbuch nicht standardisierte Methoden in der Kommunikationswissenschaft* (pp. 95–108). Springer. https://doi.org/10.1007/978-3-658-01656-2_26

Richter, C., & Badr, H. (2018). Communication studies in transformation: Self-reflections on an evolving discipline in times of change. In F. Kohstall, C. Richter, S. Dhouib, & F. Kastner (Eds.), *Academia in transformation: Scholars facing the Arab uprisings* (pp. 143–160). Nomos.

Schulz, P. (2021). Recognizing research participants' fluid positionalities in (post-)conflict zones. *Qualitative Research*, *21*(4), 550–567. https://doi.org/10.1177/1468794120904882

Schwedler, J. (2006). The third gender: Western female researchers in the Middle East. *PS: Political Science & Politics*, *39*(3), 425–428. https://doi.org/10.1017/S104909650606077X

Scott, M., Bunce, M., Myers, M., & Fernandez, M. C. (2023). Whose media freedom is being defended? Norm contestation in international media freedom campaigns. *Journal of Communication*, *73*(2), 87–100.

Tandoc, E., Jr., Hess, K., Eldridge, S., II, & Westlund, O. (2020). Diversifying diversity in digital journalism studies: Reflexive research, reviewing and publishing. *Digital Journalism*, *8*(3), 301–309. https://doi.org/10.1080/21670811.2020.1738949

Thussu, D. K. (2022). De-colonizing global news-flows: A historical perspective. *Journalism Studies*, *23*(13), 1578–1592. https://doi.org/10.1080/1461670X.2022.2083007

Ustad Figenschou, T. (2010). A voice for the voiceless? A quantitative content analysis of Al-Jazeera English's flagship news. *Global Media and Communication*, *6*(1), 85–107. https://doi.org/10.1177/1742766510362023

Waisbord, S., & Mellado, C. (2014). De-Westernizing communication studies: A reassessment. *Communication Theory*, *24*(4), 361–372. https://doi.org/10.1111/comt.12044

Wang, G. (2014). Culture, paradigm, and communication theory: A matter of boundary or commensurability? *Communication Theory*, *24*(4), 373–393. https://doi.org/10.1111/comt.12045

Digital Archives and Unexpected Crossings: A Data Feminist Approach to Transnational Feminist Media Studies and Social Media Activism

Ololade Faniyi *and* Radhika Gajjala

If a woman faced imprisonment, exclusion from an educational institution, or even loss of life due to her choice of wearing or not wearing hijab, many of us would first hear about it through social media. We would then embark on an online exploration, clicking on numerous related links in search of a clearer understanding. These links would often lead us to platforms such as Instagram, Twitter, or Facebook. We would scrutinize the information, questioning if it could be misinformation or propaganda from an unknown source. To verify the authenticity, we would turn to legacy media websites, reminiscing about the material experience of holding a newspaper as we placed our trust in websites displaying familiar logos. Convinced of the event's occurrence, we would return to Instagram, Twitter, or Facebook to dig further into threads and comments. As we multitasked or procrastinated on work emails, we would venture further through hashtags and retweet links, encountering conflicting opinions, trolls, and advertisers capitalizing on the trending hashtag. We would discover distinct clusters of interactions within niche communities, each with their own perspectives on the issue. Immersed in our filter bubbles or entering spaces of intense contention, we would experience unexpected encounters. As researchers, we would eventually set aside our cup of coffee and document our findings, scrolling through our screens as we begin to consider the implications of what we witnessed unfolding in real time across transnational digital publics.

In this case, as communications researchers interested in how events from the Global South become visible through algorithmic publics and how counterpublics are being formed by users, members of our research team—Research Lab for Situated Data Analytics, Digital Humanities, Digital Archiving and Data Feminism—began a flurry of email exchanges, text messages, and WhatsApp conversations. With each of us attempting to make sense of what was happening, we are implicitly informed by our own sociocultural and generational backgrounds as many of us had personal experiences in the geographical locations being "tweeted" and "instagrammed" about. Several of the clusters of communication we encountered on social media connect in the big social media data space to create a visual battlefield of contestations and debates. What sorts of discursive contestations and nuances emerge around the "hijab" in such mediated environments? Employing our preferred methods of data collection, some of us frantically captured screenshots from Instagram, while others hastily set up data visualization software on their laptops to locate and download relevant messages using specific keywords and hashtags. Meanwhile, a few among us turned to the Twitter application programming interface (API) downloader to retrieve historical data, driven by a curiosity to understand when this news had originally burst forth on the platform.

In our quest to understand what was happening—how the stories were being told, why they were being told, and the practices made possible or impossible because of the features of each social media platform—we became a haphazard group of accidental hashtag archivists. As highlighted by Dencik (2019), the performative power of data plays a crucial role in explaining the profound impact of datafication on the transformation of both our social fabric and academic culture. This process of archiving social media data requires curating and contextualizing what emerges in digital publics. As Conley (2021) argues, "communication technologies transform, interfaces disappear, meaning constructed through social media use changes" (p. 755). These accidental archives are derived and mapped through situated human (researcher) recognition, where smaller sets of data begin to make sense through contextual understandings and research offline. However, nestled within big social data, they also become "uncertain archives," characterized by ambiguity, errors, and vulnerabilities (Thylstrup et al., 2021). Therefore, beyond the descriptive part of Twitter text lies a critical data gap that holds contextual significance.

Unveiling Nuances Through Combining Quantitative and Qualitative Approaches in Social Media Data Analysis

Often, the data collected in response to trending hashtags contain very few actual texts, and the significance of these data sets arise from the number of retweets they receive. Thus, the algorithmic infrastructure that makes visible a particular topic via select hashtags operates on the basis of quantification. The greater the number of retweets and likes, the higher the likelihood that the topic will reach a broader audience within the social media platform. Indeed, other factors influence content visibility on each platform, such as a user's follower count, the accounts they follow, or their verification status as a "blue tick" user. However, the text itself is not always highly nuanced, so an interpretive approach focused only on examining the text may not produce an understanding of what is happening on the platform.

We can observe the existence of polarized views on various topics, identify instances of right-wing propaganda, and recognize the contribution of social media platform content to the spread of hatred. We might also note that protestors are mobilizing the use of social media. However, the textual content itself is not thick enough to provide the context of detail without the researcher doing additional research that goes beyond the platform being examined. Likewise, examining the data purely through the quantitative analytic tools available for scraping masses of big data tells us very little. For instance, when we scraped the data on #hijab for 60 days using Netlytic.org or spent a few hours over several days using the open-source software Gephi, the statistical features mainly gave us a descriptive overview of the number of connected clusters of users and "betweenness centrality"—the influence of users in propagating hashtags or conversations across clusters. These details make no sense unless we look closely at the textual data.

Adopting either a qualitative textual approach or a purely quantitative approach, while providing a glimpse into the descriptive aspects of the data, failed to yield a nuanced understanding. However, combining these analytical approaches with background research and contextual understanding of the larger events that prompted the social media posts proved more productive. We began to see how social media influencers contributed to creating visibility for particular kinds of content through specific practices aimed at jostling the platform algorithms to enhance visibility. Regardless of what side of the debate the person tweeting is on, they adopt the same practices to enhance their content's visibility. These practices are shaped by a marketing logic because social media platforms (e.g., Twitter and Meta Platforms) are situated in this logic (Burgess & Bruns, 2015).

Our contribution in this chapter, therefore, is to point to the interesting practices within Twitter that yield unexpected or unique information and transnational visibility for local issues—accidental archives perhaps—connecting through some highly visible hashtags. Approaching what we see online as enmeshed in everyday praxis while also structured through algorithmic and offline hierarchies of governmentality and access to technology, we argue that to understand the implications of the multiplicity of crisscrossing communicative exchanges online, we must take both a macro and a micro look at the data sets. As low-resourced social science and humanities researchers in a mid-level university trying to do this work, our team comprised a small group of graduate students and a faculty member adopting a self-styled "do-it-yourself" approach. We negotiated access to computational software and computer space, among other things, which compelled us to work with smaller subsets of the extensive data available through our academic researcher and developer access to Twitter API tools.[1] Our goal was to try to get a deep look at sections of the data, leveraging privileged sociocultural context and praxis of technology use. As highlighted by Ruppert et al. (2017), the "emergence and transformation of professional practices such as data science, data journalism . . . and data analysis" (p. 1) are intricately linked to the reconfiguration of power dynamics and knowledge production in the accumulation of public and private data.

Therefore, we started our spontaneous archiving of Twitter data around the hashtag "hijab" following two events: the ban on hijabs in a school in Karnataka, India, and the killing of an Iranian woman, Mahsa Amini, by all accounts, over the "incorrect" wearing of the hijab in Iran. Although this chapter represents part of a larger investigation into the hashtagification of "hijab" that we started in 2022, it deviates from examining those specific events. During the data analysis process, one of our collaborators (the first author of this chapter), a young Nigerian woman and feminist activist currently pursuing a doctorate degree in Atlanta, Georgia, after obtaining her Master of Arts degree in northwest Ohio, identified tweet clusters that resonated with her sociocultural background. As a result, this chapter discusses these select data clusters around the Nigerian context, while other clusters are being examined and written about by co-authors in other essays (Gajjala et al., 2024). In the following sections, we describe the Nigerian context, discuss the methods employed, and present the emerging themes from analyzing the data and practices of relevant Twitter users.

The Nigerian Context

In December 2017, a law school graduate, Amasa Firdaus, was denied her call to bar, a legal ceremony that signifies a lawyer's qualifications to represent another in court, because she was wearing a hijab beneath her lawyer wig—a headpiece made from horsehair worn by barristers in Nigeria and other Commonwealth countries during formal events and court proceedings. This sparked a series of conversations in digital "anxious" publics and traditional media about the right of Muslim women lawyers to choose and express their religious values, including the right to wear their hijab to their call to bar ceremony. In Nigeria, social ideologies encompass a diverse combination of Africanist/traditional, Eurocentric, and Arabic legacies and influences that vary across different regions, and the country reflects a normative framework shaped by an interplay of religion, culture, and colonial ethics. The 2015 report from the Pew Research Center reveals that 50% of Nigerians are Muslim, 48.1% are Christians of varying denominations, and 1.9% are either traditional African religious or unspecified (Hackett et al., 2015). #EndDiscriminationAgainstHijab soon emerged in response to Firdaus' denial to the call to bar, causing a series of religion-centered conversations in which Muslim men and women and others with non-Muslim beliefs debated on Firdaus' resistance despite how much she had to lose.

---

[1] Since July 2023, the Twitter academic developer account and API tools has been restricted and monetized, as the platform, under its new leadership became X. Our engagement in this chapter predates the Elon X takeover, so we stick to the description that is faithful to that context.

Firdaus was eventually called to bar in 2018 after the Body of Benchers passed a resolution that stopped the discrimination of hijabi lawyers and approved their wearing of the hijab at the call to the bar ceremony. Since 2018, every call to bar has led to the mention of Firdaus' name on Nigerian Twitter, with new hijabi lawyers thanking her for her victorious struggle against their discrimination. Here, we explore not just how this resistance played out in digital publics in December 2017 but also the context collapse that emerged as users made connections to Iran and the resilience of Rosa Parks. Although this is a relatively small data set within the multitude of transmissions in big online data sets, what makes this Nigerian hijabi struggle important for our feminist intersectional small data research is how users from Global South contexts engage hashtags to produce visibility for their protests and connect these messages with clusters online, despite geographical location. In addition, they also connect their activism to crossings beyond their context as stories that give them strength and educated hope for an equitable future.

Method: Analyzing Digital Archives with a Data Feminist Approach

Approaching the comparatively small sets of collected archives as feminist researchers required us to attempt to unravel contextual specificities in layers. This process also required us to examine practices of Twitter use as material practices within the "habitus" (Bourdieu, 1995) that is Twitter. Rather than treating the social media platform as a flat surface of discursive texts, images, and shared links or the algorithmic infrastructure as a flat hierarchy implicitly and intentionally coded, we center our experience working to retool computational tools for social media research from a critical humanities lens (Gajjala et al., 2024). We first discuss the human collaboration process and then describe how we worked with computational tools to examine "small social data." Finally, we use one example from a recent research project to discuss how we worked together to arrive at evidence-based yet self-reflective and critically engaged conclusions.

For this project, we started with two sets of spontaneously collected data engaging the affordances of Python scripts in Google Colab, Netlytic, DiscoverText, Gephi, and ATLAS.ti to scrape Twitter data. We collected data using the keyword and hashtag "hijab' in February 2022, when we heard of the hijab ban in Karnataka, India, and later in September 2022, when Mahsa Amini was killed in Iran. The data, gathered through our Twitter API access, revealed to us the dynamic, shifting nature of content in Twitter publics. While examining these sets of spontaneously collected data in 2022, we noted different contexts in which the keyword or hashtag "hijab" was deployed. We also noted that a strategy for ensuring visibility for different contexts was to piggyback on already existing highly visible hashtags from other contexts, making cultural crossings shaped by ideologies that manifest in various encounters and use of digital networks by users. As established, this chapter, taken from a larger investigation around the hashtagification of "hijab" in 2022, examines specifically the case highlighted from Nigeria.

As mentioned previously, our methods are mixed as we adopt close feminist reading and data analytics tools for networked data scraping and visualization. As data feminist or feminist digital humanities scholars, we acknowledge the digital labor of activists engaging with hashtags to produce visibility for their resistance against state and non-state oppressors (Faniyi et al., 2023). We must, however, note here that our approach does not credit the mediatization of the work of activists to the digital networks without acknowledging the offline groundwork or cultural specificity that made them feminist/political subjects in the first place. In fact, our work is rooted in an awareness of the ways in which social media platforms, which have been rightfully criticized for operating on racist and extractive logic (Benjamin, 2019; Noble,

2018), continue to privilege certain dominant voices while depending on the emotional labor and community management of activists and women from marginalized backgrounds who might find the "freedom" to express their feelings on these platforms inspiring.

However, we nonetheless acknowledge that social networks and data collecting sites such as Twitter give us access to a material archive of the work done and curated by activists' agential capabilities. As Florini (2019) argues, Twitter "commonly serves as a content aggregator and bridge between multiple platforms" (p. 70). Therefore, as the offline activist effort feeds into the digital production of visibility, we use computational tools to filter and visualize these data. With the "bigness" of data typical of digital networks, our approach centers small parts of this larger data by amplifying resistance from whisper networks and counterpublics that might often seem minute in comparison to other big data sets online but are no less subversive in exemplifying intentional or unlikely activists pushing against the oppressive status quo. As a team, we have explored these manifestations across several Global South contexts, including India, Nigeria, Iran, and Afghanistan, in interrogating hashtag activisms such as #womenofshaheenbagh, #sayhernamennigeria, and #hijab. Our approach to undertaking feminist intersectional small data research engages big data tools in our attempt to intentionally center voices from the margins in context. For instance, the hashtag movement #sayhernamenigeria had a frequency of 74,059 mentions after one year since its emergence in April 2019, compared to the millions of hashtags in larger transnational movements. However, what small data sets such as #sayhernamenigeria and big data sets such as #sayhername and #BLM reflect across contexts is citizen-led resistance against police brutality with critical intersectional nuances.

By pushing against the grain of generalization or flattening typical with work on big data sets online, our approach prioritizes activists as co-authors of the discourses they create in line with the precedent of scholars such as D'Ignazio and Klein (2020) and Jackson et al. (2020). Our work centers the principles of data feminism, as coined by D'Ignazio and Klein, as "a way of thinking about data, both their uses and their limits, that is informed by direct experience, by a commitment to action, and by intersectional feminist thought" (p. 9). In this way, our data feminist perspective refers to our application of feminist intersectional principles to our mixed methods quantitative and close feminist reading approaches, as well as, more often than not, in-depth interviews that place human, contextual, and historical specificity in otherwise taxonomical machine-to-machine communication.

Members of our team have varied experiences working in data analytics and feminist activism; some of us have been imbricated as participants/observers in the workings of activist communities online. Before the formal construction of digital humanities as a field, our work had established us as accidental hashtag archivists who curated the repertoire and archive of feminists/women in overt or subtle protest against the matrices of oppression, countering the "big"-ness of computational data with careful multiple locationally situated analysis.

In this chapter, our process details how our work examining digital archives on Muslim women's resistance against the state and oppressive systems established us as (accidental) hashtag archivists creating contexts from the evidence of their activism. Because a fraction of our data is not historical—that is, we did not collect it live but, rather, after a period of active affective transmissions online—we used a Python script to collect data on the peak period of #EndDsicriminationAgainstHijab from December 14, 2017, to December 16, 2017, revealing that the hashtag was used 5,977 times within that period. Our Python script ran once for 15 minutes, and we got the data into formats as a .json file and node and edges data in .csv. We converted the .json file for reading convenience into .csv, and these data relayed users' tweet text, ids, locations, mentions, and accompanying image URLs, among others. Despite this ease of access offered by our computational tools, the human agency and feminist practices still came to the fore as we worked through the data manually to filter deleted tweets or tweets from users whose identities must be protected from unwarranted hypervisibility.

While we acknowledge the threats to user privacy and security that can result from unethical use of Twitter data, we situate our research on the knowledge that just as this access and data can be extractive and exploitative, it nonetheless offers a solution to inequalities and oppression. Data is power, and even more so, visibility and archiving are important for activism and resistance. Our Python script networked this hashtag into nodes and edges—that is, the people in the network and the connections between them. We imported these into Gephi, the network visualization tool that allowed us to closely read smaller chunks of data and filter as needed. We referred to our converted .csv Twitter data set file as we looked through our previewed visualizations to locate original tweet text and connections between users and their mentions. Our close feminist intersectional reading was thus the basis of our analysis as we interpreted from the information revealed by the nodes and clusters what field of possibilities and affordances digital networks offered voices from Nigeria and the Global South.

#EndDiscriminationAgainstHijab: Deliberate Connections Between Historical Contexts of Muslim Women's Activism

Our attention was drawn to context collapse in this data set, exemplified by the blurring of distinct contexts when various sociopolitical and cultural backgrounds collide in online conversations. This phenomenon, potentially leading to misunderstandings and oversimplification, became evident through a specific tweet interaction involving users @hauwa_ojeifo, @adlexy, and @oduolates (Figure 16.1). By examining the deliberate connections made between

Figure 16.1 Context collapse blurring contexts and meanings of Muslim women.

different historical contexts of Muslim women's activism, we argue for the crucial understanding of specific sociopolitical nuances within which struggles for agency and freedom unfold, while debasing universalizing tendencies that overlook contextual factors in discussions on Muslim women's agency.

The original tweet by user @hauwa_ojeifo had praised the Amasa Firdaus in appreciation of the several hijabi lawyers called to bar in 2022. User @adlexy responded by connecting to the ongoing Iranian revolution and hashtag activism #mahsamini. Mahsa Amini, a 22-year-old Iranian woman, was detained on September 13, 2022, because she was not wearing her hijab properly. She later died, reportedly at the hands of Iran's religious morality police. Her death provoked one of the largest demonstrations in Iran since 2009, with female protesters cutting their hair or removing their hijabs publicly as an act of defiance of Iranian regulation of women's bodies and appearance. It also reopened discussions about the hijab as a choice and the regulation of (Muslim) women's attire. Drawing from the insights of scholars such as Abu-Lughod (2013), Mahmood (2005), and Razack (2008), user @adlexy's insinuation that hijabi lawyers in Nigeria needed help and saving due to the struggle against the hijab in Iran directly reflects the Orientalist discourses prevalent in Western perspectives, which portray veiled Muslim women as victims in need of rescue, solely highlighting religion while flattening the mutually occurring poverty, colonial violence, and political authoritarianism. Abu-Lughod's work, particularly her book *Do Muslim Women Need Saving?*, challenges such Western assumptions and vocabulary and calls for a critical examination of power dynamics affecting Muslim women's lives. Mahmood's book, *Politics of Piety*, also emphasizes veiled Muslim women's moral agency and subjectivity, as she questioned the Western liberal portrayal of veiled women as victims. Just as Razack's *Casting Out* explores how the construction of veiled Muslim women as threats in the context of national security reinforces colonial power structures.

In response to @adlexy's insinuation, user @oduolates asserts that the situations in Iran and Nigeria represent opposite instances of women fighting for their right to choose. This tweet aligns with these critical arguments highlighting the importance of understanding the diverse contexts, power dynamics, and agency within hijab struggles. In Iran, the hijab is enforced by its government and morality police, but in Nigeria, it is a choice, and Muslim women lawyers are defending their choice to wear it to their call to bar, amidst the tensions and complexities of representation. On the one hand, the image of the female lawyer would typically spark conversations on the need for empowerment and policies that allow women to pursue careers just like men. On the other hand, this pride in the female lawyers called to bar that connects strangers on the internet is disrupted by the symbiotic interactions of Islamophobia and radicalization (Abbas, 2019) that, counter to the celebration of women's agency, replicate the discrimination of Muslim hijabi lawyers.

We used Gephi to visualize the #EndDiscriminationAgainstHijab data set in a network graph, which, based on our assigned filtering and statistics, revealed the users and keywords with the highest degrees. The graph shown in Figure 16.2 depicts a cluster of nodes representing Twitter users, hashtags, keywords, and other metadata with high centralities in the #EndDiscriminationAgainstHijab network. The nodes are connected by edges indicating the frequency and strength of interactions between the metadata. The nodes and edges have distinct colors showing the different clusters of users online in conversation with one another.

The phenomenon of context collapse often manifests in nonlinear ways, either through users' deliberate connections or through the interventions of other users engaging the tweet.

Figure 16.2 Visualization of the #enddiscriminationagainsthijab network between December 14 and 16, 2017, generated through Gephi. Nodes are sized by degree—that is, the number of times retweeted and mentioned.

Figure 16.3 shows how @ogundamisi connects Firdaus' resistance to Rosa Parks, an American civil rights activist remembered for the Montgomery bus boycott after she refused to give up her seat on a bus in Montgomery, Alabama, in favor of a White passenger. In response, another user asks, "What does Rosa Park have to do with this?" and @ogundamisi responds, "a lot, defying the norm, challenging the norm so society can reflect and adjust. Got it now," accompanying this tweet with an eye-roll gif. In many ways, this tweet connects to a deliberate legacy of activism similar to Firdaus. Furthermore, this example of context collapse highlights the unique information yielding from highly visible networks and showcases an unprecedented situation of Firdaus among a legacy of activists who courageously defend their dignity and right to freedom and choice, even when these are from distinct historical contexts.

Conclusion

In this chapter, we explored #EndDiscriminationAgainstHijab by extracting it from the broader data that form digital archives on hijab resistance. We noted how our journey through the archives led us to this unexpected local cluster of meaning-making amid the larger

Káyòdé Ògúndámisí 🎗️✅
@ogundamisi
...

#EndDiscriminationAgainstHijab in Nigeria. Like Rosa
Park in America. The brave lady started a
conversation and it is worth looking into by the
Nigerian Law School. Regulations are not static. Don't
let your bias and fear of the unknown becloud your
sense of justice.

11:31 AM · Dec 15, 2017

515 Retweets   22 Quote Tweets   293 Likes

Figure 16.3 @ogundamisinario of context collapse emerging #Enddiscriminationagainsthijab with Rosa Parks'
activism.

transnational debates around the hijab. We highlighted how our data feminist approach and
close attention to small clusters of data bring out nuances that need to be engaged by transnational feminist media studies scholars. This chapter draws on our spontaneous archiving
of Twitter data (since 2022) on the #hijab with a close look at the contextual implications in
Nigeria that we accidentally encountered because we did not enter the platform with prede-
termined expectations of what we would find. Examining tweet clusters that connect with the
sociopolitical implications in Nigeria, we highlighted events that sparked a context collapse as
Twitter users deliberately connected ideologically distinct hijab struggles in Iran and Nigeria,
and further connected Amada Firdaus' resistance to Rosa Parks' activism. However, although
we have curated situated sections of the data, we make no claims that we have a general overarching understanding of all contexts in which this hashtag was deployed.

As Dencik (2019) argues, there is an ongoing challenge of comprehending how diverse
actors utilize and are influenced by data in their understanding and actions regarding social
and political issues. For instance, in the case of Iran, not all activists and social media influencers agree on the issue of hijab as choice, whereas in the case of the Indian context, the hijab
issue takes on other complex and contextual directions. Overall, we emphasize the critical
importance and interesting practices within networked conversations on Twitter that yield
unexpected or unique information and transnational visibility for local issues, linking via
highly visible hashtags and fostering powerful crossings that transcend geopolitical borders.
With this chapter, we aim to provide readers with a deeper understanding of the complexities

surrounding the tweet interactions, urging critical thinking about context, power structures, and agency in the context of transnational feminist media studies and social media activism.

References

Abbas, T. (2019). *Islamophobia and radicalisation: A vicious cycle*. Oxford University Press.

Abu-Lughod, L. (2013). *Do Muslim women need saving?* Harvard University Press. https://www.jstor.org/stable/j.ctt6wpmnc

Benjamin, R. (2019). *Race after technology: Abolitionist tools for the New Jim Code*. Wiley.

Bourdieu, P. (1995). Structures, habitus, practices. In J. Faubion (Ed.), *Rethinking the subject* (pp. 31–45). Routledge.

Burgess, J., & Bruns, A. (2015). Easy data, hard data: The politics and pragmatics of Twitter research after the computational turn. In G. Langlois, J. Redden, & G. Elmer (Eds.), *Compromised data: From social media to big data* (pp. 93–111). Bloomsbury.

Dencik, L. (2019). Situating practices in datafication: From above and below. In H. Stephansen & E. Treré (Eds.), *Citizen media and practice: Currents, connections, challenges* (pp. 243–255). Routledge.

D'Ignazio, C., & Klein, L. F. (2020). *Data feminism*. MIT Press.

Faniyi, O., Nduka-Nwosu, A., & Gajjala, R. (2023). #SayHerNameNigeria: Nigerian feminists resist police sexual violence on women's bodies. In B. Wiens, M. MacArthur, S. MacDonald, & M. Radzikowska (Eds.), *Stories of feminist protest and resistance: Digital performative assemblies* (pp. 51–66). Lexington Press.

Florini, S. (2019). *Beyond hashtags: Racial politics and Black digital networks*. New York University Press.

Gajjala, R., Faniyi, O., Rahut, D., Edwards, E., & Ford, S. (2024). Get the hammer out! Breaking computational tools for feminist, intersectional "small data" research. *Journal of Digital Social Research, 6*(2), 9–26.

Hackett, C., Connor, P., Stonawski, M., Skirbekk, V., Potančoková, M., & Abel, G. (2015). *The future of world religions: Population growth projections, 2010-2050*. Pew Research Center.

Jackson, S. J., Bailey, M., & Welles, B. F. (2020). *#HashtagActivism: Networks of race and gender justice*. MIT Press.

Mahmood, S. (2005). *Politics of piety: The Islamic revival and the feminist subject*. Princeton University Press.

Noble, S. U. (2018). *Algorithms of oppression: How search engines reinforce racism*. New York University Press.

Razack, S. H. (2008). *Casting out: The eviction of Muslims from Western law and politics*. University of Toronto Press. https://www.jstor.org/stable/10.3138/9781442687554

Ruppert, E., Isin, E., & Bigo, D. (2017). Data politics. *Big Data & Society, 4*(2). https://doi.org/10.1177/2053951717717749

Thylstrup, N. B., Agostinho, D., Ring, A., D'Ignazio, C., & Veel, K. (2021). *Uncertain archives: Critical keywords for big data*. MIT Press.

Resistance and Revisioning

Mediated Socioeconomic Injustice: Representations of Poor and Working-Class People in Mainstream Media

Charisse L'Pree Corsbie-Massay

Socioeconomic class is the complex position of an individual in an economic social hierarchy. It includes both objective indicators of socioeconomic status (e.g., income, education, or career) and the aggregated social expectations associated with different classes or levels in the social hierarchy (e.g., poor, working class, middle class, upper class, or elite). According to daily per capita income in 2020,[1] approximately half (51%) of the global population is considered to be low income, 10% poor, 17% middle income, 15% upper middle income, and 7% high income (Kochhar, 2021). In the United States, for example, it is generally estimated that approximately 30% of the population is in the lower income classes, 50% in the middle class, and 20% in the upper classes (Martin, 2017).

Classism is the individual and institutional belief systems and practices that assign value to people according to their socioeconomic ranking (Corsbie-Massay, 2023). Classism includes associations regarding (i.e., stereotypes), attitudes toward (i.e., prejudice), and behaviors/actions taken based on (i.e., discrimination) socioeconomic class. It operates in both directions (i.e., valorizing the wealthy and demonizing the poor), thus exacerbating *economic inequality*—the divide between the amount of resources held by those in the top income bracket and those held by the lowest income bracket, including property and investments. Although negative stereotypes about the upper classes are prevalent (e.g., evil billionaire), upper classes hold disproportionate power and resources compared to their representation in the population. In 2022, the top 10% of global earners held 76% of global wealth, whereas the bottom 50% held 2% of global wealth (Chancel et al., 2022). Therefore, stereotypes and prejudices against the lower classes have a unique impact on these groups because those in power make decisions that impact the lives and livelihoods of those in the lower classes.[2]

In the United States, the opportunity for socioeconomic advancement has become an institutionalized ideology commonly referred to as the *American Dream* or the belief that with enough hard work, anyone can excel in the United States due to a unique conflagration of opportunity, democracy, and capitalism. But the American Dream and the aspiration for socioeconomic advancement are not restricted to the United States. Class membership can change over time, and narrative tropes across cultures and generations feature stories of

---

[1] The income groups are defined as follows: The poor live on $2 or less daily, low income on $2.01–$10, middle income on $10.01–$20, upper-middle income on $20.01–$50, and high income on more than $50; figures expressed in 2011 purchasing power parities in 2011 prices. https://www.pewresearch.org/global/interactives/global-population-by-income

[2] In the United States, people in poverty have limited access to education and health care, as well as limited access to quality food, air, and water. Lower income Americans have a shorter life span (Chetty et al., 2016), and deaths attributable to social factors are comparable to deaths from heart attacks and stroke (Galea et al., 2011).

socioeconomic advancement that romanticize wealth and the wealthy (e.g., rags to riches or marrying a prince) and demonize poverty and those who are poor. This rhetoric has manifested in a series of archetypes about poverty and poor people that is reiterated and reinforced through media.

This chapter describes three media archetypes of people in different socioeconomic classes featuring examples from advertising, journalism, and entertainment before addressing what this means for social justice in the 21st century. Socioeconomic class is much more complicated than a simple binary divide, but Antony Manstead's 2018 analysis of the psychology of socioeconomic class aggregates class into lower/working and middle/upper to address phenomena in both the United States and Europe, for which different terms are deployed to discuss those at the bottom and the top of the socioeconomic hierarchy. Therefore, I refer to the plural lower classes to indicate those at (or perceived to be at) the bottom of the socioeconomic hierarchy (e.g., poor or working class), and I refer to the plural upper classes to indicate those at (or perceived to be at) the top of the socioeconomic hierarchy (e.g., upper-middle class, elite, or 1%) throughout the chapter.

Lower Classes Are Scary

The term "underclass" was originally understood as an objective phenomenon and used as an objective term to describe people who were at the bottom 5–10% of the socioeconomic hierarchy. But the term has evolved into a discriminatory word that activates prejudicial constructs (Gans, 2007). The term underclass in the United States has become a trait characteristic instead of a flexible state characteristic. Although anyone can be part of the underclass, the underclass is taken to mean a *certain* type of person, often uneducated, unintelligent, and racially coded as Black or Brown.

Stereotypes of working and lower classes as dangerous are millennia old. According to Marcus Aurelius (121–180 AD), "Poverty is the mother of crime," synonymizing those who lack resources as criminals. In the United States, these mediated stereotypes are replicated in part due to the fact that participating in the media industry requires wealth and Americans of middle and upper classes disproportionately comprise this industry (Gold, 2013; Wilby, 2008; Williamson, 2020), ensuring a circular mechanism of class representation: People in the middle and upper classes have limited real-world interaction with people of lower classes and rely on media messages for information about this group, and then they create messages that are rooted in this limited knowledge (Butsch, 2003). Furthermore, these stereotypes are profitable when targeting upper-income audiences that are desirable to marketers. Media content focuses on middle- and upper-class narratives and audiences because they are considered a more desirable target audience (Deery, 2017).

In doing so, the media frames the lower classes as something to fear, an existential horror that is the worst thing to happen to "respectable people" and "polite society" (i.e., people in the middle and upper classes; McGrath, 2005). Although poor people are largely absent from news coverage (Iyengar, 1990), journalism about poverty focuses on the misery and neglect experienced by those in the lower classes, specifically that "the poor constitute a separate society living in urban slums or rural decay" (Rose & Baumgartner, 2013, p. 29), along with the dangers of living in slums and the economic and physical barriers that cause people to be poor. This narrative of pity and decay is also present in photography and documentary content in which images of the urban working classes (e.g., *How the Other Half Lives: Studies Among Tenements of New York* by Jacob Riis, 1890/2022) and rural agricultural poor (e.g., *Harvest of Shame* hosted by Edward R. Murrow, 1960) are constructed to elicit sympathy, ensuring that the visual representation of the lower classes can be exploited for corporate profit and philanthropy.

Representing impoverished neighborhoods or life in the slums is also a common subject in movies and film, especially since the release of the critically acclaimed *City of God* (2002), but one that frequently involves appropriating and sensationalizing stories for entertainment and artistic value (Deery, 2017; Linke, 2012). Internationally, impoverished neighborhoods—favelas in Brazil (Levy, 2021); the Kibera neighborhood outside Nairobi, Kenya (Ekdale, 2014); and those in India (Dyson, 2012) and the Philippines (Ong, 2015), among others—have been homogenized as a dangerous place that is culturally distant, frightening, and perpetually threatening middle- and upper-class communities (Macek, 2016; Rosler, 1989).

"Nightmare" (Emirates, 2015)

In 2015, the Dubai-based airline Emirates launched a $20 million global campaign with American actress Jennifer Aniston that encapsulated this fear. In the 60-second spot titled "Nightmare," Aniston, clad in a white bathrobe, looks around a darkened airplane cabin confused. She approaches the flight attendants and asks for the showers. The attendants tell her that there are no showers, but they can offer her hot towels and bags of peanuts. When Aniston protests, claiming that Emirates planes have showers, the attendants laugh at her. Aniston becomes confused as the attendants' laughter becomes more maniacal and the scene turns into a distorted nightmare. Aniston collapses and wakes up in a luxurious first-class sleeper cabin with a relieved sigh. The scene then cuts to the dressed Aniston recounting the nightmare to a bartender in the lounge of an Emirates plane.

The spot demonstrates the terror associated with falling in the socioeconomic hierarchy; for Aniston, a popular and acclaimed actress with an international following, a life without extremely luxurious air travel is distressing. Engaging with flight attendants who do not hang on to your every word in a hotel-like lounge thousands of feet in the air is horrifying. Traveling in economy or coach—widely considered to be the average flying experience of the middle classes—is a nightmare.

The spot was immediately met with sharp criticism. Commenters online called it "elitist," "snobby," and made middle-class audiences feel "poor," which was in itself terrifying for those who identify as middle-class. According to a tweet, "a first class flight from New York to Dubai on Emirates would cost over $25,000 round trip," three times the global media income.[3] Emirates defended the ad, stating that the ad had received a positive response and that "passengers choose the airlines on which they fly" (McCarthy, 2015). This reply to the criticisms demonstrates the power that this narrative has from a corporate perspective: It resonates with wealthy elite consumers internationally, the target audience to which Emirates caters.

A year later, Emirates released a second ad titled "Co-Pilot," in which Aniston befriends a child who appears to be lost in first class. The child tells Aniston that they dream of being a pilot before the two walk back to economy class to the child's parents. Aniston changes seats with the child's mother, demonstrating that although first class on Emirates is very luxurious, flying economy is also very comfortable. The sequel was largely ignored by audiences in the United States, and most of the coverage was neutral to pleasant, with many sampling the language of the Emirates press release. The spot was framed as "adorable" and "heartwarming," as Aniston appeared approachable and friendly, embracing the dreams of a literal lower-class child and elevating the experiences of the child's mother in a subtle upper-class savior trope (discussed later in this chapter). As of the writing of this chapter, both of the videos are marked

---

[3] In 2015, $25,000 was one-half of the median income in the United States. The media annual income in the United Arab Emirates in 2015 was also $25,000 (https://www.ceicdata.com).

as "private" on Emirates platforms, although the press releases are still available via https://www.emirates.com.

Working Classes Are Lazy

There is a long-standing stereotype that people from lower classes are lazy and unintelligent. This stereotype is built on and perpetuates an extended segregation of socioeconomic classes in geography, education, occupation, culture, and more. Historically, people in the lower classes were forced to serve the upper classes, performing group agrarian labor, domestic labor, or skilled labors (e.g., construction and tailoring) that were deemed undesirable by the upper classes. Although the age of discovery and colonization promised a new world in which people could be free from their historical socioeconomic tethers, this class divide continued in the colonies. Those who could afford to establish a space for themselves and bring their family over from the Old World were able to create the means to survive and thrive, whereas those without resources were ultimately dependent on those who did.

At the same time, the ideology of the American Dream states that those who work hard are rewarded with socioeconomic advancement; similarly, the converse (i.e., those who are rewarded have worked hard), inverse (i.e., those who do not work hard are not rewarded), and contrapositive (i.e., those who are not rewarded have not worked hard) are also taken to be true. If the world is fair and people get what they deserve, then people fail to succeed because of their own inaction or inherent character flaws, not because of institutional structures. Greater belief in a just world is correlated with blaming the poor (Harper et al., 1990).

In entertainment messages, working- and lower-class characters have been presented as buffoonish and socially inept. Over seven decades of American sitcoms, the White working-class man has been framed as a "buffoon," who is incapable of maintaining any control over his household or his life—a point evident in his often overweight physique and laziness—and is framed as a clown for the audience's amusement (Butsch, 2017); this archetype includes Ralph Kramden from *The Honeymooners* (1955), Archie Bunker from *All in the Family* (1970–1979), Al Bundy from *Married with Children* (1987–1997), and Frank Gallagher from *Shameless* (2011–2021). Unscripted shows such as reality programs and daytime talk shows were more likely to feature people from lower classes than primetime content, but these individuals were more likely to be shown languishing in dysfunctional relationships, suffering from addiction, or participating in the illicit drug trade (Grindstaff, 2008).

This phenomenon was amplified by a shift in news coverage of poverty through the latter half of the 20th century. Whereas almost all (more than 90%) of the stories about poverty in the 1960s featured structural frames—the vast majority (more than 70%) discussed the misery and neglect faced by those in poverty—by the 1980s, structural frames dropped to 60%, replaced by individual frames that posited people in poverty as lazy (Rose & Baumgartner, 2013). At the start of the 21st century, more than half of the news stories about poverty framed individuals living at or below the poverty line as lazy. This emphasis on individual frames over structural frames (e.g., the isolation and ghettoization of urban slums and rural decay previously described) impacts policy through collective attitudes: The "tone of media coverage was a significant predictor of government spending on the poor" (Rose & Baumgartner, 2013, p. 41).

News Coverage of the 2021 Labor Shortage

In the summer of 2021, return to economic normality after the COVID-19 vaccine became widely available, but it was found that workers were not returning to jobs in previously anticipated numbers. Many news outlets investigated this social phenomenon, unpacking the experiences of American workers in the wake of the pandemic, which illuminated issues regarding a living wage, lack of universal health care, and an overall desire for a greater quality of life and better workplace value (Parker & Horowitz, 2022).

However, many outlets continued to frame ongoing unemployment issues as the individual moral failings of service workers. Articles about people in upper classes who chose to avoid returning to white-collar jobs described it as a "Great Resignation," where people refused to accept the pre-pandemic expectations of the workplace now that work from home had become the norm. But discourse regarding employees in service jobs such as food service and retail continued to feature accusations of laziness and a supposedly "entitled" unwillingness to literally service others. During this period of anxiety, many articles featured quotes from exasperated restaurant owners blaming government benefits that they believed incentivized people to stay home (Barone, 2021).

One article in *Business Insider* (Dean, 2021) on staffing shortages led with multiple quotes from restaurant owners decrying the laziness of workers before mentioning the perspective of said workers. One restaurant owner in Oregon expressed frustration with workers who had extended gaps in their work history (Allison, 2021):

> My fear is that folks took an 18-month break and they were on the couch the whole time and now they're forced to go back into the labor market and it "sucks" and they "just want to get paid" and I fear they're not going to want to do the actual physical job of working.

This sentiment that workers would just stay home and collect benefits were echoed in California (e.g., "I feel like most folks now want to stay home and take advantage of that unemployment and continue to collect without working" [Dean, 2021]) and from the governor of Iowa: "Now that our businesses and schools have reopened, these payments are discouraging people from returning to work" (Cohen & Ember, 2021).

Stories throughout the world featured this sentiment (Figure 17.1), including Canada (e.g., "People are not coming back to work. . . . The CRB [COVID-19 Canada Recovery Benefit] is killing us"; Leitner , 2021) and Australia ("I just don't get why people don't want to work here; there is so much that those towns can give, yet they are often so underrated by city people"; Harris, 2021). However, newspapers outside the United States were more likely to recognize the complexity of returning to work beyond simple laziness. These articles acknowledged workers' desire for better treatment, better wages, better health care, and more. In Zimbabwe, the Rural Teachers Union president stated, "No one wants to work for this government which is underpaying (its workers)" (Muromo, 2021).

Upper Classes Save

The stereotypical understanding of lower classes as rife with character flaws and a scary threat to upper classes persists because of a systematic segregation of socioeconomic classes. A form of *aversive discrimination* (Dovidio & Gaertner, 2004), upper classes retain negative evaluations of lower classes *because* they avoid interactions with these groups to resolve this conflict between egalitarian values and prejudice. Enter the narrative trope of the upper-class savior: a character who uses their socioeconomic privilege and resources to improve the lives of people in the lower classes. In doing so, the upper-class savior becomes morally better than others from the upper classes, and the savior is redeemed for their disproportionate retention of and access to resources.

This upper-class savior can be considered a variation of the *White savior trope*, where a White character's "innate sense of justice drives . . . racial cooperation, nonwhite uplift, and

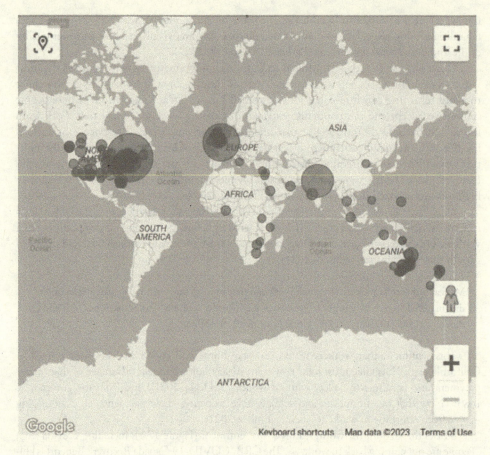

Figure 17.1 "Nobody wants to work": Visualization of news articles featuring this adage and derivatives, June 2021 to June 2022.

white redemption"[4] (Hughey, 2014, p. 7). White savior narratives abound, and they include everything from American classic literature such as *To Kill a Mockingbird* (Lee, 1960) to modern films such as *The Help* (2011) and *Green Book* (2018). The White savior story often draws on class-based disparities given the connection of race and socioeconomic status in the United States. Independent of race (but frequently incorporating race), the upper-class savior possesses an innate sense of justice, leading them to cooperate with and socioeconomically uplift people in the lower classes. Like the White savior story, these narratives laud the development of the upper-class character and minimize the existing institutional conditions.

The trope of the upper-class savior often objectifies and flattens the experiences of those in the lower classes, making their existence and issues fit neatly into the collective imagination and the entertainment of middle and upper classes. The term "poverty porn" emerged widely[5]

---

[4] Thereby maintaining and repairing "the most dangerous myth of race—a tale of normal and natural white paternalism" (Hughey, 2014, p. 7).

[5] There are other instances of the phrase "poverty porn" used before 2008 to describe the phenomenon (Phoca, 2002; Van Toorn, 2004).

in the wake of Danny Boyle's film *Slumdog Millionaire* (2009), which was simultaneously critiqued for its representation of poverty and lower classes in India and critically acclaimed, winning Oscar for Best Director and Best Picture. Poverty porn refers to the voyeuristic appeal of gazing upon the misery and neglect of those in lower classes, and it has been investigated through the lens of journalism, nongovernmental organization advertising, and entertainment. At the same time, the study of slum tourism or "activities undertaken by people of wealth, social standing, or education in urban specs inhabited by the poor" (Koven, 2004, p. 9) has been updated to consider the role of mass media; movies and television programs allow for virtual poverty tourism or being immersed in the environment of poverty without putting oneself at risk (Dyson, 2012; Selinger & Outterson, 2010), and social media rewards individuals via engagement (e.g., views, likes, and comments) for sharing their user-generated poverty porn as a slum tourist (Crapolicchio et al., 2022; Von Schuckmann, et al., 2018).

From Pretty Woman (1990) to Parasite (2019)

The films *Pretty Woman* (1990) and *Parasite* (2019) were produced decades and continents apart, but they both approach the narrative of the upper-class savior from the perspective of the marginalized lower classes. This approach allows the audience to embody the perspective of lower classes while reinforcing that one can only be saved by the upper classes.

Pretty Woman tells the story of Vivian (played by Julia Roberts), a sex worker who is picked up by Edward (played by Richard Gere), a wealthy businessman who is spending the week in Los Angeles. Over the course of the week, she learns to fit into upper-class society by buying a new wardrobe with Edward's money and taking etiquette lessons with the manager of the high-end hotel in which Edward resides. Following their separation at the end of the film, Edward arrives in a white limousine (a metaphoric horse) at Vivian's tenement apartment as her Prince Charming to save her from her old life.

Parasite tells the story of the Kims, a family of four living in a slum basement apartment in Seoul, South Korea, trying to make ends meet. A friend of the family invites the son to take over English tutoring for the wealthy Park family, after which the family quickly schemes to take over all the domestic roles in the house (e.g., tutor, driver, and housekeeper). The Kim family fantasizes about their own socioeconomic advancement made possible by the Parks, until they are confronted by a couple who have been residing in the sub-basement of the Parks house and are forced to flee after a series of very unfortunate events.

In both films, the upper-class life is something to which one should aspire but from which lower classes are systematically shut out. The characters are defined by their socioeconomic class: Vivian and the Kims live in cramped quarters surrounded by poverty, whereas Edward and the Parks reside in spacious homes with seemingly infinite space per capita. This disparity is underscored in parallel iconic shots of Vivian and Ki-jung; these young women from lower classes luxuriate in a bath while enjoying media content (portable music in *Pretty Woman* and a mounted television in *Parasite*), providing concrete visual representations of wealth and socioeconomic advancement (Figure 17.2).

The opportunity for these women to lounge in these upper-class settings is only made possible by an upper-class savior who lifts these women out of their lower-class life and defends them against the classism of others. In *Pretty Woman*, Edward accepts Vivian despite her occupation and defends her honor against his lawyer, thus redeeming the "obscene" wealth he acquired as a venture capitalist. In *Parasite*, Yeon-gyo's "simple" desire to take care of her family makes the Kims' ascent possible, especially as she defends their class-based transgressions to the sensibility of her classist husband, including their subway smell (i.e., "like boiling rags").

Figure 17.2 Bubble baths are classy: Parallel frames from *Pretty Woman* (1990) and *Parasite* (2019) showcase women in the lower classes sampling the life of luxury.

In both films, the lower-class characters perform for the satisfaction of their upper-class saviors—and the audience—demonstrating that their value in the world of the upper classes is synonymous with their humanity. In *Pretty Woman*, the audience wants Vivian to live the Cinderella story, advancing from prostitution to penthouse because of her savior Edward. In *Parasite*, the audience roots for the Kims to get out of the infested semi-basement, uprooting the lives of the other characters from lower classes (i.e., the original driver and housekeeper) but continuing to ensure the safety and comfort of their (unknowing) upper-class saviors. This is also a form of classism, wherein we recognize and agree that those without resources do not have value, and they must learn to behave as if they have resources in order to attain value.

All Classes Matter: Changing Representation of Socioeconomic Classes with Digital and Social Media

Digital and social media technologies have disrupted the discourse related to socioeconomic class by enabling user-generated content and reducing barriers from concept to distribution. Users without access to the media industry can use low-cost recording devices and editing tools to create their own content and share this content widely via social media sites, inviting engagement and amplification from a global audience. Historically marginalized people across social categories have used these technologies to share messages that would not have been distributed in the 20th-century legacy broadcast model, thus contributing to public discourse despite systematic disenfranchisement.

Users share content via these technologies that disrupt the rhetoric of lower and working classes, including images and messages that demonstrate the skillful work undertaken by people considered lower class (e.g., United Farm Workers [2019] sharing video of a person deftly picking and bundling radishes: "This incredibly skilled worker earns $1.86 per 60 bundles of radishes . . . and has the method down to a science") and injustices faced by those employed in service jobs,[6] such as customers verbally berating or physically attacking workers, as well as trends in the absurdity of classism via memes (Old Economy Steve meme [Corsbie-Massay, 2023]) and content aggregation ("A Brief History of Nobody Wants to Work Anymore" [Paul Fairie, 2022]). This kind of hegemonically disruptive content is less likely to be embraced by mainstream legacy media that prioritizes large audiences with disposable income (Corsbie-Massay, 2019; Corsbie-Massay et al., 2022).

Furthermore, digital technology fosters "virtual communities," affinity spaces where users with similar interests can share and connect with others across space and sometimes time

---

[6] During the pandemic, instances of workplace violence increased. From March 2021 to August 2021, more than half (57%) of workplace violence events occurred in retail and food service (Marsh et al., 2022).

(Gee, 2005). These opportunities to connect and collaborate independent of traditional or legacy media outlets such as newspapers, radio, and television also allow users to coordinate to promote and achieve real-world change. These movements include the MeToo movement launched in 2006 on Myspace by Tarana Burke and amplified in 2017 on Twitter with the hashtag #metoo;[7] the Arab Spring movement in 2011, where protests across a dozen countries in North Africa and the Middle East resulted in the topping of rulers in Tunisia, Libya, and Egypt, among others; and the Black Lives Matter movement launched in 2014 after the acquittal of the man who killed Trayvon Martin in Florida and amplified after the police killing of George Floyd in Minnesota. These movements recognized the role of socioeconomic injustice as an intersectional factor, whereas the 2011 Occupy Wall Street protest launched in New York City and which spread to almost 80 countries worldwide actively focused on institutional classism.

Occupy Wall Street (2011)

Inspired by the Arab Spring protests earlier in 2011, *Adbusters*, an anti-consumerist Canadian-based magazine, distributed a poster for its July edition that featured the hashtag #occupywallstreet and plans for a Wall Street protest on September 17, 2011. In the weeks leading up to the protest, organizational gatherings received social media (and police) attention, and phrases such as "We are the 99%" were shared widely (Conover et al., 2013; Lalinde et al., 2012). On the day of the event, protesters connected and coordinated in real time via social media sites to congregate in Zuccotti Park, approximately five blocks north of the iconic Charging Bull statue in downtown Manhattan. Over the next 2 months, thousands of people occupied the park in a demonstration against financial greed and corruption. The protest spread to cities throughout the United States (Bowers, 2011) and more than 80 countries worldwide (Weisenthal, 2011), establishing a pattern of using social media to share information more than promotion (Theocharis et al., 2015).

The Occupy protests revealed how many people were impacted by socioeconomic injustice—people who in earlier iterations of the media environment may have been led to believe that they were alone in their struggles or that they were solely individually responsible for any failure to advance socioeconomically. Through the lens of media representation, the sheer number of protests and diversity of people engaging in the protests worldwide fostered community and ensured that the issue was visible. Digital and social media technologies allowed them to take hold of their own presentation, an essential precursor to greater representation (Maragh-Lloyd & Corsbie-Massay, 2022).

However, as the protests gained the attention of mainstream media outlets, the narrative of the movement was adapted to fit into the *protest paradigm*, a phenomenon wherein news coverage frames protests in a manner so as to support the status quo and disparage protesters (McLeod & Detender, 1999; Shoemaker, 1984), often through elevating trivialization of the protesters, marginalizing their goals, denying the effectiveness of their methods, and exaggerating the threats of the movement to mainstream society (Gitlin, 1980). This strategy has been repeated in protests by a wide variety of marginalized social groups, but it has a unique impact on those experiencing socioeconomic injustices, who have been historically trivialized as buffoonish (Butsch, 2017) and ineffective (Ess & Burke, 2022), and who have been historically

---

[7] In addition to the MeToo movement, the voices of women in restaurants and hospitality industries were also amplified, revealing intersectional issues of class and gender (as well as race and ethnicity) with respect to workplace safety.

framed as a criminal and threatening respectable middle-class communities (Macek, 2016; Rosler, 1989).

Multiple content analyses investigating the coverage of the Occupy protests demonstrate the presence of these phenomena. In analysis of *The New York Times* and *USA Today*, frames of lawlessness were present in approximately half of articles in the 4 months following the original occupation, more than one-third (37%) of articles mentioned the visual spectacle of the protesters (e.g., young age, funny dress, or immature appearance; twice as likely to appear in *The New York Times* compared to *USA Today*), and one-fourth of articles emphasized the negative impact of the protest to mainstream Americans (Xu, 2013). Similarly, articles in the *Wall Street Journal* were framed so as to "reaffirm the influence of the ruling class" (Douai & Wu, 2014, p. 157). Several studies also revealed the representation in legacy broadcast media differed from the overall tone in social media coverage, which was markedly more varied and considerate in its representation of the movement's goals, participants, and accomplishments (Cissel, 2012; DeLuca et al., 2012).

Conclusion

The socioeconomic tropes described in this chapter were present in public discourse and narratives long before the 20th-century electronic media environment, and they have continued into the 21st century. Framing those living at or below the poverty line as something to be feared, dismissing the work ethic of the literal working class, and promoting positive philanthropic stories of the wealthy dehumanize those at the bottom of the socioeconomic hierarchy while valorizing those at the top. In doing so, these media tropes ensure that socioeconomic stereotypes are maintained individually and institutionally. Media content that disrupts these tropes and makes visible the diversity of humanity within these socioeconomic stratifications is essential for productive policymaking that ensures the dignity of people throughout the world (Rose & Baumgartner, 2013).

Furthermore, social media is a catalyst for grassroots social change, but it is not always a force for progressive change. The tendency of mainstream media to frame socioeconomic movements in a manner that perpetuates preexisting socioeconomic hegemony reveals that media alone will not save us from historic and present discrimination. Scholars and activists who target all forms of injustice must consider the complicated dimension of socioeconomic injustice and how stereotypes against lower classes have been normalized through media messages, including actively disrupting addressing socioeconomic stereotypes and issues of access. "Although we frequently talk about the marginalization of race, gender, and sexuality, the oppression of those groups is often operationalized through systematic economic disadvantage" (Corsbie-Massay, 2023, p. 32), making socioeconomic class foundational to any discussion of social injustice (e.g., Black Lives Matter and the racial wealth gap, disparities in resources and justice regarding MeToo, and disability activism and health care).

Scholars and activists have a responsibility to connect the threads of historic injustices to showcase the current complexity of discrimination as well as the struggles in achieving equality and justice. Affecting change involves crafting wide-reaching and effective messages that break through the din, draw attention to but do not replicate socioeconomic injustice, and encourage a critical mass of the audience to consider classism differently. The first step in this process is to be aware of individual and institutional tendencies toward classism and to question the effectiveness of these approaches both in the short term (e.g., popularity of specific content) and the long term (e.g., policies and practices that maintain institutional classism).

References

Allison, M. (2021, September 12). Restaurant owners in Portland see spike in applications as federal jobless benefits end. KTVL10. Retrieved June 5, 2024, from https://ktvl.com/news/restaurant-owners-in-portland-see-spike-in-applications-as-federal-jobless-benefits-end

Barone, E. (2021, June 29). This should be a boom time for restaurants. But owners—and the few workers remaining—are struggling. *TIME*. Retrieved June 12, 2023, from https://time.com/6076710/restaurants-labor-shortage

Bowers, C. (2011, October 14). Occupy Wall Street: List and map of over 200 U.S. solidarity events and Facebook pages. *Daily Kos*. Retrieved June 12, 2023, from https://www.dailykos.com/stories/2011/10/4/1022722/-

Butsch, R. (2003). Ralph, Fred, Archie, and Homer: Why television keeps re-creating the White male working-class buffoon. In G. Dines & J. Humez (Eds.), *Gender, race, and class in media: A text-reader* (pp. 575–585). SAGE.

Butsch, R. (2017). Class and gender through seven decades of American television sitcoms. In J. Deery & A. Press (Eds.), *Media and class* (pp. 38–52). Routledge.

Chancel, L., Piketty, T., Saez, E., & Zucman, G. (Eds.). (2022). *World inequality report 2022*. Harvard University Press.

Chetty, R., Stepner, M., Abraham, S., Lin, S., Scuderi, B., Turner, N., Bergeron, A., & Cutler, D. (2016). The association between income and life expectancy in the United States, 2001–2014. *Journal of the American Medical Association, 315*(16), 1750–1766. https://doi.org/10.1001%2Fjama.2016.4226

Cissel, M. (2012). Media framing: A comparative content analysis on mainstream and alternative news coverage of Occupy Wall Street. *Elon Journal of Undergraduate Research in Communications, 3*(1), 67–77.

Cohen, P., & Ember, S. (2021, June 5). Federal unemployment aid is now a political lightning rod. *The New York Times*. Retrieved June 12, 2023, from https://www.nytimes.com/2021/06/05/business/economy/unemployment-benefits-cutoff.html

Conover, M. D., Ferrara, E., Menczer, F., & Flammini, A. (2013). The digital evolution of Occupy Wall Street. *PLoS One, 8*(5), Article e64679. https://doi.org/10.1371/journal.pone.0064679

Corsbie-Massay, C. L. (2020). *20th century media and the American psyche: A strange love*. Routledge.

Corsbie-Massay, C. L. (2023). *Diversity and satire: Laughing at processes of marginalization*. Wiley.

Corsbie-Massay, C. L., Riley, B. K., & Soraia de Carvalho, R. (2022). Examinations of the unprofitability of authentic Blackness: Insights from Black media professionals. *Journal of Applied Communication Research, 50*(3), 327–343. https://doi.org/10.1080/00909882.2022.2083433

Crapolicchio, E., Sarrica, M., Rega, I., Norton, L. S., & Vezzali, L. (2022). Social representations and images of slum tourism: Effects on stereotyping. *International Journal of Intercultural Relations, 90*, 97–107. https://doi.org/10.1016/j.ijintrel.2022.08.002

Dean, G. (2021, September 15). A Portland restaurant owner said job applications are up 50% since unemployment benefits ended, but other restaurants say they're still scrambling to find workers. *Business Insider*. Retrieved June 12, 2023, from https://www.businessinsider.com/labor-shortage-fpuc-unemployment-benefits-portland-restaurant-job-applications-employment-2021-9

Deery, J. (2017). TV screening: The entertainment value of poverty and wealth. In J. Deery & A. Press (Eds.), *Media and class* (pp. 53–67). Routledge.

DeLuca, K. M., Lawson, S., & Sun, Y. (2012). Occupy Wall Street on the public screens of social media: The many framings of the birth of a protest movement. *Communication, Culture & Critique, 5*(4), 483–509.

Douai, A., & Wu, T. (2014). News as business: The global financial crisis and Occupy movement in the *Wall Street Journal*. *Journal of International Communication, 20*(2), 148–167. https://doi.org/10.1080/13216597.2014.948033

Dovidio, J. F., & Gaertner, S. L. (2004). Aversive racism. *Advances in Experimental Social Psychology, 36*, 1–52. https://doi.org/10.1016/S0065-2601(04)36001-6

Dyson, P. (2012). Slum tourism: Representing and interpreting "reality" in Dharavi, Mumbai. *Tourism Geographies, 14*(2), 254–274. https://doi.org/10.1080/14616688.2011.609900

Ekdale, B. (2014). Slum discourse, media representations and *maisha mtaani* in Kibera, Kenya. *Ecquid Novi: African Journalism Studies, 35*(1), 92–108. https://doi.org/10.1080/02560054.2014.886277

Ess, M., & Burke, S. E. (2022). Class attitudes and the American work ethic: Praise for the hardworking poor and derogation of the lazy rich. *Journal of Experimental Social Psychology, 100*, Article 104301. https://doi.org/10.1016/j.jesp.2022.104301

Fairie, P. [@paulisci]. (2022 Jul 19). *A brief history of nobody wants to work anymore* [Tweet]. Twitter. https://twitter.com/paulisci/status/1549527748950892544

Galea, S., Tracy, M., Hoggatt, K. J., DiMaggio, C., & Karpati, A. (2011). Estimated deaths attributable to social factors in the United States. *American Journal of Public Health, 101*(8), 1456–1465. https://doi.org/10.2105%2FAJPH.2010.300086

Gans, H. (2007). Deconstructing the underclass. In P. S. Rothenberg (Ed.), *Race, class, and gender in the United States: An integrated study* (pp. 102–108). Worth.

Gee, J. P. (2005). Semiotic social spaces and affinity spaces. In D. Barton & K. Tusting (Eds.), *Beyond communities of practice: Language power and social context* (pp. 214–232). Cambridge University Press.

Gitlin, T. (1980). *The whole world is watching: Mass media and the making and unmaking of the new left*. University of California Press.

Gold, R. (2013, July 9). Newsroom diversity: A casualty of journalism's financial crisis. *The Atlantic*. Retrieved June 12, 2023, from https://www.theatlantic.com/national/archive/2013/07/newsroom-diversity-a-casualty-of-journalisms-financial-crisis/277622

Grindstaff, L. (2008). *The money shot: Trash, class, and the making of TV talk shows*. University of Chicago Press.

Harper, D. J., Wagstaff, G. F., Newton, J. T., & Harrison, K. R. (1990). Lay causal perceptions of Third World poverty and the just world theory. *Social Behavior and Personality, 18*(2), 235–238. https://psycnet.apa.org/doi/10.2224/sbp.1990.18.2.235

Harris, C. (2021, August 12). Cummings GP loving fresh EP start. *Stock Journal*. https://www.stockjournal.com.au/story/7385641/cummins-gp-loving-fresh-ep-start

Hughey, M. (2014). *The white savior film: Content, critics, and consumption*. Temple University Press.

Iyengar, S. (1990). Framing responsibility for political issues: The case of poverty. *Political Behavior, 12*, 19–40. https://doi.org/10.1007/BF00992330

Kochhar, R. (2021). *The pandemic stalls growth in the global middle class, pushes poverty up sharply: Methodology*. Pew Research Center. Retrieved June 12, 2023, from https://www.pewresearch.org/global/2021/03/18/global-middle-class-2021-methodology

Koven, S. (2004). *Slumming: Sexual and social politics in Victorian London*. Princeton University Press.

Lalinde, J., Sacks, R., Guiducci, M., Nicholas, E., & Chafkin, M. (2012, January 10). Revolution Number 99. *Vanity Fair*. https://www.vanityfair.com/news/2012/02/occupy-wall-street-201202

Leitner, R. (2021, August 30). Stoney Creek Chamber backs vaccine passports. *Stoney Creek News*. https://www.thespec.com/news/stoney-creek-chamber-backs-vaccine-passports/article_9a089e59-d21f-5aa9-8452-771b4e3b19a8.html

Levy, H. (2021). Surveying research on favelas and the media: Emphases and absences in decades of critical exploration. *Popular Communication, 19*(4), 251–265. https://doi.org/10.1080/15405702.2020.1841195

Linke, U. (2012). Mobile imaginaries, portable signs: Global consumption and representations of slum life. *Tourism Geographies, 14*, 294–319. https://doi.org/10.1080/14616688.2012.633218

Macek, S. (2016). Gritty urban realism as ideology: The Wire and the televisual representation of the "inner city." In K. Wilhite (Ed.), *The city since 9/11: Literature, film, television* (pp. 229–243). Fairleigh Dickinson University Press.

Manstead, A. S. (2018). The psychology of social class: How socioeconomic status impacts thought, feelings, and behaviour. *British Journal of Social Psychology, 57*(2), 267–291. https://doi.org/10.1111/bjso.12251

Maragh-Lloyd, R., & Corsbie-Massay, C. L. P. (2022). Embodying resistance: Understanding identity in a globalized digital future through the lens of mixed and multiracial Caribbeans. *Journal of International and Intercultural Communication, 15*(3), 235–255. https://doi.org/10.1080/17513057.2021.1940243

Marsh, S. M., Rocheleau, C. M., Carbone, E. G., Hartley, D., Reichard, A. A., & Tiesman, H. M. (2022). Occurrences of workplace violence related to the COVID-19 pandemic, United States, March 2020 to August 2021. *International Journal of Environmental Research and Public Health, 19*(21), Article 14387. https://doi.org/10.3390%2Fijerph192114387

Martin, E. (2017, June 30). *70% of Americans consider themselves middle class—but only 50% are*. CNBC. Retrieved June 12, 2023, from https://www.cnbc.com/2017/06/30/70-percent-of-americans-consider-themselves-middle-class-but-only-50-percent-are.html

McCarthy, S. (2015, November 5). *Emirates defends "snobbiest ad ever" featuring Jennifer Aniston*. FOX News. Retrieved June 12, 2023, from https://www.foxnews.com/travel/emirates-defends-snobbiest-ad-ever-featuring-jennifer-aniston

McGrath, C. (2005, June 8). In fiction, a long history of fixation on the social gap. *The New York Times*. Retrieved June 12, 2023, from https://www.nytimes.com/2005/06/08/us/class/in-fiction-a-long-history-of-fixation-on-the-social-gap.html

McLeod, D. M., & Detenber, B. H. (1999). Framing effects of television news coverage of social protest. *Journal of Communication, 49*(3), 3–23. https://doi.org/10.1111/j.1460-2466.1999.tb02802.x

Muromo, C. (2021, October 19). Govt changes tack on vaccination. *NewsDay*. https://www.newsday.co.zw/slider/article/21893/govt-changes-tack-on-vaccination

Murrow, E. R. (Host.). (1960, November 25). *Harvest of shame*. CBS.

Ong, J. C. (2015). *The poverty of television: The mediation of suffering in class-divided Philippines*. Anthem Press.

Parker, K., & Horowitzh, J. E. (2022, March 9). *Majority of workers who quit a job in 2021 cite low pay, no opportunities for advancement, feeling disrespected*. Pew Research Center. Retrieved June 12, 2023, from https://www.pewresearch.org/short-reads/2022/03/09/majority-of-workers-who-quit-a-job-in-2021-cite-low-pay-no-opportunities-for-advancement-feeling-disrespected

Riis, J. (2022). *How the other half lives: Studies among the tenements of New York*. Scribner. (Original work published 1890)

Rose, M., & Baumgartner, F. R. (2013). Framing the poor: Media coverage and US poverty policy, 1960–2008. *Policy Studies Journal, 41*(1), 22–53. https://doi.org/10.1111/psj.12001

Rosler, M. (1989). In, around, and afterthoughts (on documentary photography). In R. Bolton (Ed.), *The contest of meaning: Critical histories of photography* (pp. 303–342). MIT Press.

Selinger, E., & Outterson, K. (2010). The ethics of poverty tourism. *Environmental Philosophy, 7*(2), 93–114. http://www.jstor.org/stable/26168044

Shoemaker, P. J. (1984). Media treatment of deviant political groups. *Journalism Quarterly, 61*(1), 66–82. https://doi.org/10.1177/107769908406100109

Theocharis, Y., Lowe, W., Van Deth, J. W., & García-Albacete, G. (2015). Using Twitter to mobilize protest action: Online mobilization patterns and action repertoires in the Occupy Wall Street, Indignados, and Aganaktismenoi movements. *Information, Communication & Society, 18*(2), 202–220. https://doi.org/10.1080/1369118X.2014.948035

United Farm Workers. [@UFWupdates]. (2019, November 27). *This incredibly skilled worker earns $1.86 per 60 bundles of radishes. She's done this work for the same employer for more than a decade and has the method down to a science. #WeFeedYou #ThankAFarmworker* [Video attached] [Tweet]. Twitter. https://twitter.com/UFWupdates/status/1199825583485509632

Von Schuckmann, J., Barros, L. S., Dias, R. S., & Andrade, E. B. (2018). From slum tourism to smiley selfies: The role of social identity strength in the consumption of morally ambiguous experiences. *Journal of Consumer Psychology, 28*(2), 192–210. https://doi.org/10.1002/jcpy.1016

Weisenthal, J. (2011, October 15). It's getting massive, as hundreds of Occupy Wall Street protests are happening all around the world today. *Insider*. Retrieved June 12, 2023, from https://www.businessinsider.com/october-15-occupy-protests-all-around-the-world-today-2011-10

Wilby, P. (2008, April 7). A job for the wealthy and connected. *The Guardian*. Retrieved June 12, 2023, from https://www.theguardian.com/media/2008/apr/07/pressandpublishing4

Williamson, H. (2020, July 10). Journalism has a class problem, too. *Foreign Policy*. Retrieved June 12, 2023, from https://foreignpolicy.com/2020/07/10/class-race-media-journalism-interns

Xu, K. (2013). Framing occupy Wall Street: A content analysis of *The New York Times* and *USA Today*. *International Journal of Communication, 7*, Article 21. https://ijoc.org/index.php/ijoc/article/view/2089

Challenging Caste Hierarchies in Tamil Cinema

Swarnavel Eswaran

A Brief Introduction to Caste

Caste has parallels with race regarding the inhumanity of oppression, segregation, violence, and inequity. But they are also different in many ways, including their vastly different history. Caste is also complex because it is intricately intertwined with the Hindu religion. Dr. Babasaheb Ambedkar, the preeminent intellectual regarding the challenging of the caste system in India, resisted and challenged caste through his philosophy of "educate, agitate, and organize" in his objective of annihilating caste (Ambedkar, 1944/1979). According to him,

> Caste System is not merely a division of labourers which is quite different from division of labour—
> it is a hierarchy in which the divisions of labourers are graded one above the other. . . . Social and
> individual efficiency requires us to develop the capacity of an individual to the point of competency
> to choose and to make his own career. This principle is violated in the Caste System in so far
> as it involves an attempt to appoint tasks to individuals in advance, selected not on the basis of
> trained original capacities, but on that of the social status of the parents. . . . [The c]aste System
> is positively pernicious. Industry is never static. It undergoes rapid and abrupt changes. With
> such changes an individual must be free to change his occupation. Now the Caste System will
> not allow Hindus to take to occupations where they are wanted if they do not belong to them by
> heredity. . . . The division of labour brought about by the Caste System is not a division based on
> choice. Individual sentiment, individual preference has no place in it. It is based on the dogma of
> predestination. (p.75)

Ambedkar draws attention to the dogma of *Manusmiriti* (Laws of Manu), a *dharmashastra* or a legal text of Hinduism, dating back to the period from 200 BCE to 300 CE. Arguably, exemplifying the most regressive of all human thinking, ***Manusmiriti***, the primordial doctrine of the caste system and the Aryan society of its times, considered the Brahmins to be at the top of the caste and social hierarchy, having "exclusive privileges, and the other castes were assigned duties necessary for their protection and preservation" (Sawant, 2020). The next in line, "the Kshatriyas were to protect and defend the land, the Vaishyas were to produce food by tilling the land and tending the animals and plants [as well as trading] in the produce, and the Shudras were to serve as menials" for all the above castes (Sawant, 2020). The most glaring instance of social injustice is how it condemns Shudras to serve the other castes. Even the Kshatriyas and Vaishyas could learn but not teach. Nonetheless, the apologists would defend it by saying that it determined "'varna' based on 'talents, jobs, and abilities rather than birth'" (Goswami, 2022). But the reality is different, and varna-based Hindu society led Dalits ("untouchables" in the past) to be rendered outside the caste hierarchy as outcastes. As Ambedkar notes, caste-driven non-inclusivity and intolerance are also central to Hindu scriptures. Mahatma Gandhi used the label Harijans (the children/people of Hari/God) to coopt them into the mainstream. But he was criticized for his condescending attempts to solve the issue of discrimination within the Hindu religious fold, which was the problem in the first place, with its patriarchal and casteist epics and mythologies.

Cinema and Inclusivity

Cinema as a cultural industry in India had to appeal to the masses and keep its box office rolling to survive. Despite *class-related hierarchy*, as typified by the difference in ticket prices in India regarding the distance from the screen and the quality of the seats, cinema could not enforce segregation inside cinema halls as seen outside in society at large. The production, distribution, and exhibition were almost entirely in the hands of the upper castes and the wealthy. The upper caste hegemony, therefore, is ubiquitous not only in the privileging of caste regarding cast and crew but also in the choice of genres such as the mythological, particularly in the 1930s after the arrival of sound (Baskaran, 2008). Nonetheless, the narratives themselves were not monolithic because they had to cater to the masses and their perceived interests/preoccupations, as reflected by the sociocultural milieu of the period. Although the politics had to be covert to escape the (then British) censor board, it often created ruptures in narrative continuity, throwing open spaces for the creativity of the directors through song picturizations, as detailed by Lalitha Gopalan (2002).

It is important to note here the critical differences in the trajectory of popular Hindi cinema, often (wrongly) perceived as India's national cinema at the exclusion of many of its regional cinemas, notably the equally enormous Tamil and Telegu cinema industries in terms of the numbers and robustness of the sector. However, Hindi cinema may be more extensive regarding box office returns due to its larger spoken territory within India and the diasporic advantage. Although Indian films are made in more than 20 languages, most are made in Hindi, closely followed by Tamil and Telugu. In addition, there are other prolific movie industries, such as Malayalam, Bengali, Kannada, Marathi, Punjabi, and Bhojpuri, to name a few. In early Hindi cinema, films such as *Achhut Kanya* (*The Untouchable Maiden*, 1936) and *Achhut* (*Untouchable*, 1940) made their intention clear in addressing caste oppression as the central theme. More important, caste was in the subtext of many films in the *mythological genre*, the dominant genre of early Indian cinema. However, in catering to a supposedly national audience, Gandhian anti-British and pro-independence imperatives were predominant, as exemplified in films such as *Kismet* (*Destiny*, 1943), which were released during the Quit India movement. " '*Door Hato ae* Duniya Walon *Hindustan Hamara hai*/Move away outsiders, India is ours,' the song from the film was directly speaking to the Indian masses. For the *Kismet* song, arrest warrants were issued against Kavi Pradeep and composer Anil Biswas" (Vittal, 2008).

One could even see *Bhakt Vidur* (1921), a pivotal character from the epic *Mahabharata*, sporting a topi symbolic of the Congress party. In addition, the Gandhian *charka* (spinning wheel), symbolizing nationalism, "led the film to be banned" (Vittal, 2008). But the (women spinning the) *charka* was ubiquitous in song sequences that provided a way to escape the censor. However, Tamil cinema's interventions juxtaposing pro-independence or Gandhian themes with the critique of caste and progressive objectives were often more complex and creative. One reason could be they were less on the radar of the British administrators because of the local Congress ministry's leniency, particularly from 1937 to 1939, than their Hindi counterparts. Nevertheless, the Tamil filmmakers were very inventive (Baskaran, 2008, 2013).

Caste and Early Tamil Cinema

As Theodore S. Baskaran (2009), the preeminent historian of Tamil cinema, informs us, before Indian independence in 1947, there were significant Tamil films that engaged with caste, oppression, and prejudice. The anti-caste appeal of those films lay in the way they invoked the popular Indian leader Mahatma Gandhi and his call for equality and the upliftment of *Harijans*—the children of Hari, one of the many names of the famous Hindu god Vishnu that Gandhi gave to replace the inhumane *acchut* or the untouchable. However, the oppressed community, who suffered because of the caste system, challenged and rejected the label Harijan that reinforced Hindu hegemony, the religion that is at the source of the discrimination, and adopted the name *Dalit*, meaning broken or scattered, which is rebellious and challenging in its spirit. Such Harijan upliftment ideology, mainly in films produced and directed by the members of the upper caste, often had social themes such as widow remarriage or the hazards of alcoholism along with the anti-caste agenda.

For instance, the iconic Gandhian film in Tamil, *Thyagabhoomi* (1939), the early film discussed in this chapter whose print is available, made a plea for allowing the Harijans into temples, just like its predecessor *Desamunnetram* (*Uplift/Progress of the Nation*, 1938) (Guy, 2011). As Baskaran (2008, 2009) notes, because a predominantly Brahmin cast and crew made *Thyagabhoomi*, including the writer Kalki and the director K. Subramanyam, their gesture toward equity seemed authentic, as it seemed to come from the guilt of their hierarchical caste privilege, the main reason why Dalits were at the bottom of the caste system and thus left out to suffer. Nonetheless, Dalits are brought into the temple in *Thyagabhoomi* to save them from the devastating cyclone.

Later films *Thyagi* (*Martyr*, 1947)—revolving around the lives of a Dalit girl barred from drawing water from a well and a Gandhian protagonist, the "foreign returned," another familiar trope, son of a wealthy landlord—and *Jeeva Jyothi* (*Flame of Life*, 1947) had scenes of Dalits entering the temple, the theme's popularity indicating the desire of the ordinary people who frequented theaters and who came from across the spectrum of class and caste even though the reality outside was different with regard to segregation and caste oppression. Director K. Subramanyam adopted a Prem Chand story for his subsequent film, *Seva Sadanam* (1939; Figure 18.1), which focused on reforming prostitutes through the narrative of a suffering wife whose abusive husband threw her out. However, the anti-caste Gandhian impulse of

Figure 18.1 Still from *Seva Sadanam* (1939). Courtesy Stills Gnanam.

the director has its root in the earlier *Balayogini* (*Girl Saint*, 1936), which is a critique of the hypocrisy and double standard of the Brahmin priest(s) (Govindan, 2002).

These examples are not the only instances of social or social-themed films with a progressive streak regarding caste discrimination and oppression. Social issue–driven films such as *Harijana Singham* (*Lion Among Harijans*, 1938) juxtaposed caste identity with nationalism, whereas mythological films such as (*Bhakta*) *Nandanar* (1935 and 1942), *Thayumanavar* (1936), and *Sri Ramanujar* (1938) addressed caste in myriad ways (Baskaran, 1996)—for example, through the life of the protagonist born in the Dalit community (*Nandanar*); through their philosophy of monism without discrimination (*Thayumanavar*); or by an act of inclusivity—in the case of *Ramanujar*, through his act of preaching in the open the holy mantra, what was prescribed as a secret to be passed on to chosen Brahmins and denied to others. The subsequent *Bhakta Gowri* (1941), although not a mythological film, puts its female protagonist Gowri at the center in a narrative that focuses on the union of the violently split believers of Shiva and Vishnu, its subplot revolving around the inclusivity of Harijans. *Sathi Murali* (1941) combined the mythological with the social in framing the narrative through Narada, the puranic musician, and bringing the love between the low-caste man (Seenu) and the high-caste woman (Murali) to a closure by resolving the conflicts through the intervention of Krishna. The iconic temple entry, signifying the erasure of caste boundaries or hierarchies and, more important, untouchability, predicated on unscientific purity, marked the critical sequences in most of these films. Nonetheless, the socials and the mythological genre were popular and produced by the upper castes with an eye on the market for progressive narratives, particularly among the urban middle-class audiences. Caste was commodified and has to be considered in the context of the popularity of Gandhi and his anti-British and pro-independent imperatives and, by extension, his vision for an equal and just society after independence within the idea of a secular Hindu society/nation. (But as Ambedkar has argued, a casteless Hindu society is an oxymoron, an impossibility [http://www.ambedkar.org]).

As genre specialist Rick Altman (1999) has noted, apart from the investment in the specificity of the *semantic* (visual iconography) and the *syntactic* (the narrative structure), the *pragmatic* (the response of the audiences as could be inferred through reviews in magazines, trade journals, and fan clubs) is equally significant in determining film productions. For instance, the Brahmin and the Dalit (Harijan) are visually differentiated by their wealth and poverty through costumes and the milieu where they live. The syntactic aspect of the narrative is in the benevolence of the upper caste Brahmin who enables the upward/spatial mobility of the Dalit, who is denied agency, by allowing the temple entry. The pragmatism of making such films lay in the box office success of such Gandhian social films that appealed to patriotism and equity. However, the relatively more popular mythological tempts K. Subramanyam to make *Bhakta Chetha* (*Devotee Chetha*, 1940), in which an "untouchable" protagonist Chetha from the cobbler community is ostracized by his Brahmin counterpart and barred from entering the temple of Vishnu. But as fate would have it, the Brahmin's son falls in love with the Dalit's daughter, who, although shocked, initially accepts it as God's design. The Brahmin orders Chetha to make a thousand footwear by the morning or he will be beheaded. Miraculously, the required number is ready by the morning. The haughty Brahmin relents and accepts the devotion of Chetha and his beautiful daughter as the bride for his son. *Bhakta Chetha* is, therefore, regressive in relying on divine intervention and the benevolence of a Brahmin for the inclusion of a Dalit and his daughter. It is not the toil of the Dalit that helps him but, rather, his unwavering faith in a Brahminical God, thus entrenching the caste hierarchy.

Dravidian Movement and Tamil Cinema

Although caste was addressed in subtle ways in most Tamil films of the 1930s, in the crucial decade after the arrival of sound, generally, the hierarchy of caste was reinforced by positing the people from the higher castes, particularly Brahmins, as capable of giving up their status and being benevolent in accepting a Dalit into their home or community. The only intervention, one could argue, was in images such as people across castes entering the temple or drawing water from the common village well, challenging the idea of purity and untouchability—for instance, when people walk together, protesting for Indian independence and against the British, in a film such as *Harijana Singham*. The hierarchy and superiority of the Brahmin, pervasive in the Tamil films of the 1930s and most of the 1940s, were challenged and subverted only after independence. However, as we have seen, there were exceptions, such as *Balayogini*.

E. V. Ramasamy, known by his sobriquet as *Periyar* (the respected or elder one), was the foundational social reformer who not only gave voice to the equality and emancipation of women in the 1930s but also was a rationalist who challenged and undermined religion and caste as irrational and inhumane. Periyar was the founder of *Dravida Kazhagam* (DK; Federation of Dravidians) in 1944 and fought for equality and self-respect for women and people across castes. Because Periyar was trenchant in his critique of the establishment and uncompromising in his stance against religion and Brahmin/higher caste dominance, he was not in favor of contesting in elections as he did not want to dilute or compromise his goals (Subramanian, 2011). Therefore, in 1949, some of his protégées, the young ideologues, split from his party to form the *Dravida Munnetra Kazhagam* (DMK; Federation for the Progress of Dravidians). They agreed with Periyar in questioning caste hierarchy and blind faith and equity regarding gender; they also wanted to be inclusive to reach a larger Tamil audience in their investment in electoral politics and to change the caste-ridden society (Pandian, 1991). Tamil mainstream cinema provided the space they needed to address audiences and challenge caste oppression through the figure of the cunning and hypocritical priest.

Figure 18.2 Still from *Parasakthi* (1952). Courtesy Stills Gnanam.

In addition, the enunciatory potential of cinema, where a character could be used to address the audiences inside and outside the frame and a voice thus owned given to issues they were invested in, attracted them. For instance, Dravidian cinema's critically acclaimed inaugural films, such as *Velaikkari* (*Maid Servant*, 1949) and the iconic *Parasakthi* (*Goddess*, 1952; Figure 18.2), featured court scenes during the climax. Those scenes allowed the protagonist as a defendant to make a case against the established norms of caste hierarchy and class divide by addressing the judge and the audiences within the diegesis and, more important, to audiences/masses outside. Cinema could also be argued to be waiting for such artists to explore its potential. The two predominant Dravidian ideologues who were instrumental in challenging caste hierarchy and significant influence behind the corpus of films labeled "Dravidian cinema" were the founder of the DMK, Annadurai, and his lieutenant, M. Karunanidhi; both were invested in writing for plays and cinema. In addition, they also went on to become Chief Ministers of the state. Annadurai names the caste of one of the main characters in his screenplay for *Ore Iravu* (*One Night*, 1951) as Thevar, but the narrative does not engage with caste, unlike the seminal screenplays for *Velaikkari* and *Sorgavaasal* (*Gates of Heaven*, 1954).

Velaikkari created shock waves when it was released, mainly because of the disdain with which it treats the holy space of the sanctum sanctorum of the Kaali temple when the protagonist Anandan (K. R. Ramasamy), dismayed at her silence for not heeding his pleas regarding justice, directly questions the deity and throws down the sacred objects meant for the puja/ prayers, letting loose his pent-up anger:

> Your devotee has arrived late, missing the time of the Puja. Are you wondering why? . . . How could you reduce me to this state? . . . How could you bless a guy whose machination and deceit led to the ruin of my family? Is it just? He [Vedachalam] ruined a lot of families. He killed my innocent father; how could you protect him? (Translated by the author)

If we accept Ambedkar and Periyar's critique about the intricate ties of the Hindu religion with the caste system, then this sequence was seminal in critiquing religion as protecting the elites/higher castes. The despondent Anandan is unsuccessfully trying to avenge his father's death, who committed suicide due to his inability to repay the loans and the humiliation he suffered at the hands of the scheming lender/landlord Vedachalam (D. N. Balasubramaniam). However, Vedachalam is marked as a Mudaliyar and Anandan, a Pillai, both higher castes, next only to the Brahmins in the hierarchy. But the challenge to caste hierarchy is in the form of a fraud Yogi Hariharadas, whom Murthy, the good-hearted son of Vedalacham (who, against his father's diktats, is in love with their servant's daughter), encounters when he lands at the ashram to seek shelter and solace on wrongly believing his beloved is dead. On knowing the Brahmin Yogi's true colors, when Murthy encounters him, there is a tussle, and the godman dies. Nonetheless, keeping with the requirements for success at the box office, the film ends on a happy note when Anandan is successful in making Vedachalam mend his ways and in uniting Murthy with his lover (Eswaran & Thirunavukkarasu, 2020).

Parasakthi takes the discourse of undermining Brahmanical hegemony further by including a critical sequence in which the protagonist, Kalyani (Sriranjani), is molested within the sanctum sanctorum of the Parasakthi temple. She arrives at the temple as the last abode after a series of unfortunate events, including the deaths of her husband and father in quick succession. She is then left alone to fend for herself and her infant son, predicated on the inhumane Tamil society, chiefly marked by the masculinity of depraved men who at every opportunity try to take advantage of a young, destitute widow with a child to care for. Although *Parasakthi*, as the iconic film of the Dravidian movement and cinema, is famous for its politics, particularly its critique of the Congress rule during the Madras presidency and the policies of its highly religious Chief Minister, Chakravarthy Rajagopalachari, it is equally known for its portrayal of the dark, cruel, lascivious priest who cunningly targets the helpless Kalyani (Pandian, 1991). It is finally left for her brother Gunasekaran (Sivaji Ganesan) and, similar to *Velaikkari*, there is a court scene in which he addresses the characters inside the diegesis, such as the judge, and the audiences outside, lending voice to the ideology of the DMK regarding social justice. Gunasekaran defends his action of attacking the Brahmin priest and says, "I caused chaos in the temple . . . since the temple must not become a shelter for savages. I attacked the priest, not because he is a believer, but to rebuke his façade of faith" (translated by the author). Thus, caste hierarchy is destabilized by rendering the priest as a lowly figure, and the benevolent Brahmin figure of the 1930s cinema is deconstructed by pointing to his deviousness and salaciousness. Nonetheless, faith and the temple space are left unblemished in DMK's imperatives for appealing to a larger audience, marking the difference with Periyar's uncompromising ideology (Eswaran, 2021). The Dravidian ideologues, such as Karunanidhi, Murasoli Maaran, A. K. Velan, and Aasai Thambi, wrote for films in the 1950s and 1960s. However, after the DMK came to power in 1967, their focus shifted to politics.

The 1970s saw Tamil cinema moving out of studios, shooting outdoors, and experimenting with village-based subjects within the mainstream. For example, in *Uthirippookkal* (*Strewn Flowers*, 1979), the narrative revolved around a misogynistic anti-hero (Eswaran, 2012). Although the caste of the characters was marked in rare instances by occupation, such as the barber, challenging caste hierarchy was generally not a major preoccupation, unlike engaging with the relative realism of the village milieu. One reason could be, as noted by Ambedkar in his speech in November 1948: "What is a village but a sink of localism, a den of ignorance, narrow-mindedness, and communalism?" As Dalit intellectual/activist Stalin Rajangam (2016) notes, the 1980s were a regressive period in Tamil cinema when caste hierarchy and pride were mostly reinforced through films. Similarly, films such as *Thevar Magan* (directed by Bharathan, 1992), *Chinna Gounder* (directed by R. V. Udaya Kumar, 1991), or *Nattamai* (directed by K. S. Ravikumar, 1994) continued the trend by portraying servants and farm workers as dispensable bonded laborers to their higher caste landlords and employers. In addition, the Dalit identity of the characters represented as a mass was erased to glorify the patriarchy, masculinity, and caste of the protagonist.

Contemporary Dalit Cinema and the Subversion of Caste

The most remarkable intervention in the history of Indian cinema was the arrival of the Dalit icon Pa. Ranjith, who broke the erstwhile trend by clearly marking his main characters, particularly the protagonist and his family, as Dalits. Although from the times of folklore-inspired *Madurai Veeran* (1956) and *Kathavarayan* (1958), Dalit protagonists were present, the later disclosure of divine/upper caste origins undermined their identity. *Kaadhal* (*Love*, 2004) by Balaji Shakthivel, the contemporary master of realism, rendered its protagonist Murugan as a Dalit who falls in love with a higher caste girl (Aishwarya), but he is denied agency as he is violently beaten up and then forced to beat the mercy of the higher caste husband of his lover in the end. Ranjith, however, celebrates the Dalit milieu, whether the protagonist and friends come from the suburbs (*Attakathi* [*Cardboard Knife*], 2012) or the city (*Madras*, 2014). Eswaran (2022; Figure 18.3) states,

> Unlike in Hindi, where a film like *Article 15* (2019) still needs a non-Dalit protagonist to speak on behalf, Ranjith's protagonists and their milieu are marked as Dalit. Nevertheless, by drenching the contested wall, the center of his narrative in *Madras* (2014), with the blue color of the Republican Party of Babasaheb Ambedkar, Ranjith unequivocally questions the erasure of the vibrant Dalit

Figure 18.3 Still from *Kaala* (2018). Courtesy Stills Gnanam.

presence through the overwhelming ubiquity of black, red, and the white [symbolizing the Dravidian parties] from the 1960s onwards in Tamil society/cinema. [However,] the traces of the Dravidian cinema is visible in Ranjith's characterization of the religious and "white" antagonist Nana Patekar, as opposed to the "black" protagonist Rajnikanth in *Kaala* (2018), wherein the Hindu religious agenda of the right (BJP) and the anti-"Madrasi" rhetoric of the local party (Shiv Sena) are effectively juxtaposed.

Equally significant is the contribution of Mari Selvaraj, who, through his films based in Tirunelveli—*Pariyerum Perumal* (*Horse-Mounting Deity*, 2018) and *Karnan* (2021)—not only has challenged the (northern) Madurai genre/formula films such as *Virumandi* (2004), *Paruthiveeran* (2007), and *Subramanyapuram* (2008), in which the Thevar community's martial masculinity and caste pride are privileged, but also has posited them as the antagonists to recover the erased voices of the Dalit community and their unsung heroes of the past (Damodaran & Gorringe, 2017; Krishnan, 2008; Leonard, 2015). Whereas Vetrimaaran's *Asuran* (*Demon*, 2019), based on the preeminent Tamil (Dalit) writer Poomani's novel *Vekkai* (*Heat*, 2012), is an equally significant intervention in positing the vulnerable predicament of Dalits and the casteist violence that is thrust on them in the deep south, Mari's *Karnan* foregrounds the active participation of the state machinery in connivance with the higher caste in violently and inhumanely repressing and tyrannizing the Dalits. From the local, Ranjith's *Kabali* (2016) takes us across borders to discuss and interrogate caste in Malaysia with its Dalit protagonist (Ram Manoharan, 2021), whereas *Kaala* (2018) examines both casteist and religious oppression at the national level in Mumbai.

Conclusion

From the 1930s onward, Tamil cinema in India had engaged with caste, with mythological and social genre films challenging the status quo of the unquestioned caste system. Initially, however, the Brahmin, the symbol of the caste hierarchy as an enforcer through rituals, was posited as benevolent in accepting the outcaste Dalits into the fold. Later, in the late 1940s and 1950s, Dravidian cinema emerged, which, in its critique of the caste system, undermined the priest figure. Nonetheless, other intermediate (higher) castes were generally not held to account, and the Dalits were erased. Tamil Dalit cinema of the past two decades questions the willful absence of Dalits, foregrounds their voices and recovers their erased history and challenges, and subverts the caste hierarchy/system.

Addressing the caste system and oppression in a narrative with a Dalit character(s) is not recent in Indian cinema, as exemplified by the Bengali master Satyajit Ray's *Ashani Sanket* (*Distant Thunder*, 1973) and *Sadgati* (*Salvation*, 1981). But as serious films in the art cinema category, their circulation is limited. Even when screened on television, their audiences are generally middle-class/upper castes. Pa. Ranjith's intervention, like that of Nagaraj Manjule (*Fandry* [*Pig*; 2013] and *Sairat* [*Wild*; 2016]), is to reach a vast audience through mainstream cinema to provoke a discussion. Nevertheless, films such as *Kabali* and *Kaala* are criticized for foregrounding Dalit masculinity. Therefore, Dalit cinema anticipates women filmmakers from oppressed castes will narrate their stories at the intersection of caste and gender. It is heartening that Pa. Ranjith's Neelam Productions has co-produced a documentary, *B. R. Ambedkar: Now and Then* (2023), directed by Jyoti Nisha. Similarly, his Casteless Collective has created a space for many talented musicians across caste and gender. The future of Dalit cinema thus holds promise.

References

Altman, R. (1999). *Film/genre*. British Film Institute.

Ambedkar, B. R. (1979). Annihilation of caste: With a reply to Mahatma Gandhi. In *Dr. Babasaheb Ambedkar, writings and speeches, Vol. 1*. Government of Maharashtra. (Original work published 1944)

Baskaran, T. S. (1996). *The eye of the serpent: An introduction to Tamil cinema*. EastWest Books.

Baskaran, T. S. (2008). Encountering a new art: Writers response to cinema in Tamil Nadu. In V. Selvaraj (Ed.), *Tamil cinema: The cultural politics of India's other film industry* (pp. 111–123). Routledge.

Baskaran, T. S. (2009). *History through the lens: Perspectives on south Indian cinema*. BlackSwan.

Baskaran, T. S. (2013). *The serpent's egg* [ebook]. Tranquebar Press.

Damodaran, K., & Gorringe, H. (2017, June). *Madurai formula films: Caste pride and politics in Tamil cinema*. South Asia Multidisciplinary Academic Journal.

Eswaran, S. (2012). The 1970s Tamil cinema and the post-classical turn. *South Asian Popular Culture, 10*(1), 77–89.

Eswaran, S. (2021, January 4). *Periyar, Dravidian ideologues, and Tamil cinema*. The Periyar Project. Retrieved January 11, 2023, from https://theperiyarproject.com/tag/swarnavel-eswaran

Eswaran, S. (2022, May 19). "Indian" cinema and Dravida Nadu. *Outlook India*. Retrieved January 15, 2023, from https://www.outlookindia.com/art-entertainment/-indian-cinema-and-dravida-nadu-magazine-197524

Eswaran, S., & Thirunavukkarasu, P. (Eds.). (2020). *Tamil cinema vimarsanangal (1931–1960)* [Tamil cinema reviews (1931–1960)]. Nizhal.

Gopalan, L. (2002). *Cinema of interruptions: Action genres in contemporary Indian cinema*. British Film Institute.

Goswami, G. (2022, June 24). Past and prejudice: Manusmriti is neither anti-Dalit, nor pro-Brahmin. *Firstpost*. https://www.firstpost.com/opinion/past-and-prejudice-manusmriti-is-neither-anti-dalit-nor-pro-brahmin-10830251.html

Govindan, K. (2002). *Tamil thirappadangalil saathimatha bethangal* [Caste and religious discrimination in Tamil cinema]. Kumaran.

Guy, R. (2011, December 17). Blast from the past: Desa Munnetram (1938). *The Hindu*. Retrieved January 15, 2023, from https://www.thehindu.com/features/cinema/Blast-from-the-past-Desa-Munnetram-1938/article13430576.ece

Krishnan, R. (2008). Imaginary geographies: The makings of the "South" in contemporary Tamil cinema. In S. Velayutham (Ed.), *Tamil cinema: The cultural politics of India's other film industry* (pp. 139–152). Routledge.

Leonard, D. (2015). Spectacle spaces: Production of caste in recent Tamil films. *South Asian Popular Culture, 13*(2), 155–173. doi:10.1080/14746689.2015.1088499

Pandian, M. S. S. (1991). Parasakthi: Life and times of a DMK film. *Economic and Political Weekly, 26*(11–12), 759–770. http://www.jstor.org/stable/4397433

Rajangam, S. (2016). *Tamil cinema: Punaivil iyangum samugam* [Tamil cinema: Narratives drive society]. Pragnai Pathippagam.

Ram Manoharan, K. (2021). Being Dalit, being Tamil: The politics of Kabali and Kaala. In S. Velayutham & V. Devadas (Eds.), *Tamil cinema of the twenty-first century: Caste, gender, and technology* (pp. 52–65). Routledge.

Sawant, P. B. (2020, November 16). The Manusmriti and a divided nation. *The Wire*. Retrieved January 15, 2023, from https://thewire.in/caste/manusmriti-history-discrimination-constitution

Subramanian, N. (2011). *Ethnicity and populist mobilization: Political parties, citizens and democracy in South India.* Oxford University Press.

Vittal, B. (2018, August 21). On Indian cinema and patriotism. *The Hindu*. Retrieved January 15, 2023, from https://www.thehindu.com/entertainment/movies/cinema-indian-independence-patriotic-cinema/article24744170.ece

CHAPTER

19

Media Representations, Incarceration, and Social Justice

Adam Key

Per the World Prison Population List, as of 2015 there were more than 10.35 million prisoners worldwide (Walmsley, 2016). Despite the plethora of nations and conditions these millions of prisoners are kept in, one situation remains true throughout: They are only permitted to be consumers and subjects of media, but never producers of it. As such, prisoners are in a unique position as a minoritized group with little or no control over their mediated portrayal. This results in beliefs garnered from media consumption about prisoners that lend themselves in service of the messaging of the powerful rather than the powerless. This chapter explores those messages, the biases they produce, and how scholars can work to resist them.

The Western public has been fascinated with prison media since the turn of the 20th century. Beginning with the *The Great Train Robbery* in 1903 and *The Big House* in 1930, prisons became regular settings for Hollywood (Surette, 1998). Following the release of *Scar Face* in 1932, the film industry was met with a significant demand for prison-based movies that became mainstays at theaters from the 1940s until the present day (Bailey & Hale, 1998). As home television ownership expanded in the 1950s, families were able to view all manner of prison- and criminal-themed programming (Snauffer, 2006). By the 1960s, one in every four primetime television shows centered on crime, a trend that continued for decades (Surette, 2007). By the 1990s, prisoners, and prisons, joined crime as one of the most popular television themes (Cecil, 2015). This repeated exposure to criminal and prison media, then, shapes the general public's view of prisons and prisoners and leads them to make false assumptions about both.

Although these misconceptions could be benign if they had minimal impact, the reality is far more nefarious. The mediated representations of prisons and prisoners shape the public imaginary of them and bias the public against them. It is this bias that empowered conservative social media firebrand Candace Owens to claim that George Floyd, a Black man whose murder by a police officer captured on video resulted in global protest, could not be a hero nor a martyr because he was a criminal (Owens, 2020). This bias also undergirded Texas Governor Greg Abbott's executive order banning the release of any prisoner during the height of the COVID-19 pandemic with a current or past conviction for a violent crime, effectively sentencing dozens of incarcerated men and women to death by disease (Abbott, 2020). This same bias led the U.S. Congress to ban the use of Pell grants, federal aid provided to low-income students, for incarcerated learners in 1994, shuttering all but roughly a dozen prison college programs (Key, 2021). This bias, its effects, and how media scholars can help educate and produce against them are the subject of this chapter.

Defining Prison

Imprisonment consists primarily of two factors: involuntary confinement and the latter status being the result of the presumed violation of laws. Brown (2014) noted that globally, those experiencing confinement include "prisoners, refugees, internally displaced persons, detainees, irregular migrants, and a host of other invisible actors caught beyond recognition and representation" and are housed in "disparate sites as prison systems; migrant detention centers; border, conflict, and disaster zones; factories and maquiladoras; new war prisons; and refugee and concentration camps" (p. 177). Although Brown makes an argument that all groups within the list experience carceral conditions in that they are confined and "share restricted rights and weaker claims to citizenship" (p. 177), there are necessary distinctions between the groups. Brown noted, "Few sociologists, for instance, have identified refugee populations dislocated by environmental disaster and political conflict as penal subjects" (p. 178). Instead, "humanitarian discourses have predominated, defining refugees as victims" (p. 178). Whether the victim definition is helpful or not to refugees and other involuntarily confined persons who have not been convicted of crimes, the same attitude does not apply to prisoners. They are rarely perceived as victims in the public consciousness; rather, they are viewed as victimizers.

As expounded upon later in this chapter, there exists a significant social bias against prisoners, one that is distinct from the biases against groups such as refugees and migrants. Although a racial majority, for example, might fear that groups of migrants may disrupt their cultural dominance, that is distinct from the fear of prisoners as violent and irredeemable savages. A member of one such group is likely to tell a migrant to go back to their home country but believe prisoners deserve to be locked up away from society. Similar distinctions exist between prisoners and those confined to mental health institutions and for the same reason. A person involuntarily confined to a mental health institution, while often stereotyped as potentially violent in media (McGinty et al., 2016), is defined by the same humanitarian discourses as a person in need of medical help. The reason for these disparate reactions is the second element of imprisonment: a result of a presumed violation of the law. The social backing of the law empowers a sense of moral superiority in the unincarcerated to judge prisoners in ways they do not judge those with mental health issues or migrants. Although much could and should be written about the mediated portrayal of other confined groups, given the distinctions, it is important to understand the effects of mediated depictions of prisoners, which is the subject of this chapter.

Mediated Images of Prisons and Prisoners

Although media can be defined in numerous ways, this chapter focuses primarily on fictional media programming, including film and television, reality television, and documentaries. Furthermore, prisoner media is specifically used here as the above listed programming that uses prisoners as subjects and prisons as a primary setting. This differs from crime media, which includes the commission, policing, and prosecution of crime.

Media consumers "use knowledge they obtain from the media to construct a picture of the world, an image of reality on which they base their actions" (Surette, 2007, p. 1). In most cases, this image is tempered with a person's individual experience with members of the group portrayed. For example, a viewer who sees racist stereotypes of Black, Indigenous, and people of color (BIPOC) on television will likely have BIPOC friends and co-workers who do not meet these bigoted standards. At minimum, this is likely to cause some degree of cognitive dissonance in which the viewer realizes that media presents an imperfect image of reality. Unfortunately, the same phenomenon is less likely for viewers of media containing prisoner stereotypes. "Prisons purposefully exist, in both location and design, in a manner which hides them, and their occupants, from the public eye" (Key, 2021, p. 40). Because most media viewers lack access to prisons and prisoners, both in desire and ability, their mediated images are never confronted with reality. Instead, the mediated image of prison becomes the only image, thus forming the viewers' reality of how prisons and prisoners are. This type of media exposure "can leave the recipient of such information feeling that they are appropriately informed about the reality of the prison, and with little or no desire to challenge such evidence" (Ridley, 2014, p. 18). As Wilson (2003) stated, "Ultimately when we present an image of prison, we shape the public's expectation about what prison is like, and what happens inside; of who prisoners are and what they have done" (p. 28).

Compared to other minoritized groups, there is an admitted and unfortunate lack of scholarship concerning the mediated images of prisoners (O'Sullivan, 2001). Here, I draw on three primary published analyses of prisoner media. What all three are united on is that the portrayal of prisoners is resoundingly negative. In the first article, Cheliotis (2010) notes the dichotomy of how prisons and prisoners are shown: "Prisons are most usually typecast either as dark institutions of perpetual horror and virulent vandalism or idyllic holiday camps offering in-cell television and gourmet cuisine on the back of taxpayers," whereas prisoners "are portrayed as degenerate beasts beyond redemption or undeserving layabouts" (p. 175). The image of the prisoner as a layabout in a holiday camp is echoed in water cooler conversations in which people complain that prisoners have access to cable television, as if that is a luxury only available to the upper class. The more common—and damaging—stereotype, however, is that prisoners are irredeemably violent savages deserving of maltreatment. Rapping (2003) found this to be especially true in his analysis of the television show *Oz*, which revealed that the program "presents a vision of hell on earth in which inmates are so depraved and vicious that no sane person could possibly think they should ever again be let loose upon society" (p. 81). Nellis (2013) notes that the same portrayal holds true even for science fiction and fantasy programming, arguing they taught viewers that "prisons of the future will be hellish places, and . . . there will surely be villains bad enough to justify their existence" (p. 223).

Prisoners are consistently portrayed violently. Llinares (2015) argued that the viewing of such programs "satisfies an almost primordial desire to view punishment as fundamental to the exercising of power" (p. 211). In order to be worthy of punishment, prisoners must be vile and dangerous and, most notably, fundamentally different from the viewing public. Imagining prisoners as villains props up the societal division of the "civilized and the savage" because in order for the viewers to consider themselves civilized, there must be savages to compare themselves to (Sarat, 2002, p. 82). Mediated images, therefore, serve the fundamental need of audiences to feel that they are good and moral members of society, especially compared with criminals. The effect of this is to make invisible the inequities within the entirety of the criminal justice system that serve the powerful and punish the powerless within society. If these films are to be believed, low-income and BIPOC people are serving time in higher numbers because of individual moral failings rather than systemic bias.

In addition to making the audience feel better about themselves, prisoners are portrayed as dangerous for a second and more troubling reason: to make audiences afraid. Since World War II, criminal- and prison-based films have become increasingly violent (Surette, 1998). These violent portrayals play on the viewers' "fears by overstating the danger of criminal victimization, targeting weak and marginalized swathes of the population, criticizing the authorities for laxity, calling for more and harsher punitive measures, and blocking or neutralizing the imagery of human suffering thereby caused" (Cheliotis, 2010, p. 178). The effect of this is that viewers become "determined to keep themselves safe in what they perceived as a social landscape filled with mass murderers run amok, with teenage 'superpredators,' and with murder and mayhem around every corner" (Rapping, 2003, p. 73). Unlike other genres, such as horror, that scare viewers by design, criminal and prisoner media lead to real fears by claiming to be based in reality. Approximately half of all prisoner films claim to be based on a true story, and television channels and streaming services are littered with so-called reality television programs based in prisons (Rafter, 2006). "The viewing public is largely unaware of the production processes of such media and are largely unable to determine which elements are fictitious and which are based in reality" (Key, 2021, p. 46). Intriguingly, Van den Bulck and Vandebosch (2003) found that even prisoners themselves were influenced by such programs. Their work showed incoming inmates who had viewed this type of media were led to "expect that the majority of inmates would be convicted of very serious crimes, that the experienced inmates would subject newcomers to an initiation ritual and that rape and violence were part of the daily fare of prison life" (p. 108).

Streaming Toward the Same Destination
One might hope that the advent of streaming media, with its plethora of options and perspectives, might yield a more humanitarian view of prisoners. Unfortunately, our work found more of the same. In the spring and summer of 2020, we coded 35 hours of prison programming from Netflix and Amazon Prime Video. During January 2020, we reviewed Netflix, Hulu, and Amazon Prime Video to identify all prison media. At the time, Hulu had no prison media, although *For Life* did debut during the time of review. All films were included and episodes of shows were randomly selected to comprise 35 hours of programming. The sample of shows included *Jailbirds*; *First and Last*; *Girls Incarcerated*; *I Am a Killer*; *The Inmate*; *Orange Is the New Black*; *Behind Bars: America's Toughest Jails*; *Behind Bars: Rookie Year*; *Lifers Behind Bars*; *They Call Us Monsters*; *Inside Supermax*; and *Hope Dealers*. Seven were reality television programs, three were documentaries, and two were fictional programs. We coded for antisocial and negative behaviors in the following categories: violence, disrespect of authority, cursing, displays of anger/aggression, and illegal activities/rulebreaking. This revealed 444 different instances, equating to 12.68 per hour or one per every 4 minutes and 43 seconds. Our findings are detailed in Table 19.1, with the most common behaviors coded being verbal aggression and violence.

Common plotlines revolved around verbal aggression and violence, usually with the former precipitating the latter. Prisoners also regularly engaged in antisocial behavior such as screaming and cursing. Most of this, however, was directed at fellow prisoners rather than guards. Although there was certainly disrespect to authority shown, conflicts with guards were minimal and were typically resolved quickly if not violently. The disproportionate lack of issues with guards and the filming of illegal activities seem to support the notion that prisons control production. That is, the final product produced prisoners as violent and angry, whereas the guards were good at their jobs and minimized lawbreaking. Even on a streaming platform that arguably does not rely on the same stereotypes as broadcast, media companies continue to put new prison wine in old prison wineskins.

The dual functions of prisoner media—to make the audience feel civilized and afraid of the allegedly savage prisoners—work in conjunction to create a systemic bias against prisoners. I label this phenomenon *convictism*. In the next section, I explain convictist bias and the effects of current prison media.

The Frame of Convictism
Exposure to various forms of media can create internal biases within viewers who normalize certain behaviors and groups while treating others as deviant. Media consumption can bias viewers regarding sex and gender, race, sexual orientation, class, and a number of other social categories. This also includes bias against prisoners, also known as convictism. "Convictism is the belief that those without criminal convictions are wholly superior—intellectually, morally,

Table 19.1 Analysis of Prisoner Media Portrayals

Television Program	No. of Instances				
	Violence	Verbal Aggression	Disrespect to Authority	Antisocial Behavior	Illegal Activities
Behind Bars: America's Toughest Jails	6	9	10	8	6
Behind Bars: Rookie Year	8	13	12	11	4
First and Last	3	9	10	7	5
Girls Incarcerated	6	28	12	32	4
Hope Dealers	0	0	0	0	0
I Am a Killer	26	0	0	0	11
Inside Supermax	7	5	1	1	2
Jailbirds	14	20	1	20	8
Lifers Behind Bars	18	1	1	2	7
Orange Is the New Black	10	39	0	8	0
The Inmate	14	15	3	13	0
They Call Us Monsters	8	3	1	2	0
Total	120	142	51	104	47

and socially—to those with criminal convictions" (Key, 2021, p. 57). I first wrote about the phenomenon in my book, *The Rhetoric of Resistance to Prison Education: How the War on Crime Became the War on Criminals* (Key, 2021). It functions on the same lines as other discriminatory systems, such as racism, sexism, and homophobia. In all these forms of systemic discrimination, the minoritized group forms the savage foil to the civilized majority. Unlike most other forms of bigotry, it focuses on behavior more than an immutable characteristic. The notable exception to this is classism, in which poverty is believed to be the result of moral failings (and the uneducated belief that sexual orientation is somehow a choice). Unlike classism, however, the convictist bias is seemingly permanent. Whereas someone in a lower economic class might work or luck their way into a higher one, the stain of criminal conviction is permanent in the public imaginary. Explaining convictism further, I wrote,

> It is rooted in a rhetorical positioning of us vs. them, where we are the deserving heroes and they the unworthy villains. Since we have not been convicted of a crime, we believe that anyone who has possesses a reprobate mind and a criminal personality. After all, we've all been tempted to break the law on occasion, but we resisted the urge, so why can't they? The answer must be because we are morally superior to them, not that their choices fundamentally differed from our own. (p. 57)

In developing the theory, I drew on the works of anti-racist scholars Feagin, Entman, and Rojecki. Feagin is most known for his work on the White racial frame (Feagin, 2010). Feagin's work demonstrates that major media present images through this frame in a way that normalizes and, in turn, makes invisible Whiteness and its effects. That is, to view Western media is to watch through a White point of view. The frame minimizes the effects of systemic racism and largely pretends racial inequities are a thing of the past. Instead, it quietly props up White success as the result of hard work and attributes BIPOC struggles to cultural deficiencies.

The frame is pervasive to the point that it is "so institutionalized that all major media outlets operate out of some version of it" (Feagin, 2010, p. 141). Entman and Rojecki further expand the nuanced understanding of the mechanics of racism in their book, *The Black Image in the White Mind* (Entman & Rojecki, 2001). In this text, they problematize the idea of a binary between being racist and not racist. Instead, they promote the Spectrum of White Racial Sentiment to better explain the degrees of racism. Rather than racist and non-racist, they use Comity, Ambivalence, Animosity, and Racism. I added a fifth category between Comity and Ambivalence based on Paulo Freire's (1970) notion of false charity as "any attempt to 'soften' the power of the oppressor in deference to the weakness of the oppressed almost always manifests itself in the form of false generosity" (p. 26). Table 19.2, based on Entman and Rojecki's spectrum, details levels of animus toward prisoners in four distinct areas:

> Negative Homogeneity dealt with how much people believed behavior was the result of the individual or the [incarcerated] group. Structural Impediments concerned whether people believed discrimination was prevalent and, in the case of the [Convictism] category, necessary. Conflicting Group Interests examined whether people thought [convicted and unconvicted] groups political interests were aligned or mutually exclusive. Finally, Emotional Responses consider the valence and intensity of emotional feelings related to [prisoner] issues. (Key, 2021, pp. 67–68)

Arguably, most unconvicted people in the United States fall into either the Animosity or Convictism categories, attitudes largely conceived through media exposure. Whereas Feagin (2010) argued for the existence of the White racial frame, my research indicates the presence of a similar anti-prisoner frame. According to Munro-Bjorklund (1991), "Public attitudes toward criminals in general, the types of people who are or should be incarcerated, and prison conditions that should be tolerated become evident through the treatment of criminal characters in film" (pp. 56–57). Essentially, the public views prisoners as savages who, without intervention of state authorities, are rewarded for their misdeeds with holiday resort-like stays and luxury amenities such as edible food and basic cable. Instead, the state authorities, who as unconvicted are morally superior to prisoners, are a necessary force to fight against their savagery. As Mathiesen (1995) stated, "In the whole range of media, the prison is simply not recognised as a fiasco, but as a necessary if not always fully successful method of reaching its purported goals" (p. 144). Rather than a necessary evil, the mistreatment of the convicted by the state is viewed as a welcome good.

Within this framing of prisoners as evil and prisons as good, the public becomes emboldened to demand "tough on crime" policies from their elected representatives. As such, the "portrayal of crime and justice in the media has been forwarded as also influencing the public agenda for justice by sensitizing the public to particular issues" (Surette, 1984, p. 5). These include policies such as mandatory minimum sentencing, three-strikes laws, depriving both current and former prisoners of the right to vote, removing eligibility for Pell grants for prison college programs, and laws prohibiting former prisoners from living in certain areas or working in certain professions. The effect of these so-called tough on crime policies is to actually increase the crime rate (Key, 2021). The American public, however, remains unbothered by this because the proliferation of convictist media means "citizens of the United States hate criminals far more than they hate crime itself" (Key, 2021, p. 4).

Challenging Convictist Media

Given the prevalence of convictist media and the public's lack of access, what can social justice–minded scholars do to challenge it? To challenge media, new and better media is necessary. First, scholars can help produce and promote prisoner-authored media in the form of films

Table 19.2 Scale of Convictual Sentiment

Dimension	Sentiment				
	Comity	False Charity	Ambivalence	Animosity	Convictism
Negative homogeneity	Individual prisoners and non-prisoners vary widely in traits.	Prisoners tend to display more negative traits than non-prisoners, but they have no control over them.	Prisoners tend to display slightly more negative traits than non-prisoners.	Prisoners, on the whole, possess many more negative traits than non-prisoners.	Prisoners are inherently evil and possess negative traits by nature.
Structural impediments	Discrimination is widely prevalent, leading to unequal opportunity and high recidivism.	Discrimination is prevalent and should be stopped because prisoners are incapable of helping themselves.	Discrimination may occur occasionally, but it is not a major issue.	Discrimination no longer happens; any negative treatment is justice for the crimes prisoners committed.	Discrimination is fundamentally necessary because prisoners are evil, and society needs to be protected from them.
Conflicting group interests	The interests of prisoners and non-prisoners are the same; cooperation is fundamentally necessary for society.	Non-prisoners should make decisions for prisoners because they are incapable of making good choices.	Interests of prisoners occasionally conflict with non-prisoner interests and should be overruled when they conflict.	Helping prisoners means hurting non-prisoners; cooperation means non-prisoners lose in a zero-sum game.	Prisoner interests are in destroying society and are extremely dangerous to non-prisoners.
Emotional responses	Low intensity; positive or neutral feelings	High intensity; positive feelings about saving prisoners from themselves	Moderate intensity; varies between positive and negative	Moderate intensity; largely negative toward prisoners	High intensity; extremely negative toward prisoners

and podcasts. This is not to say that every scholar should become a producer of media, but those who can should, and those who cannot product it should promote the media by sharing it in their classes and other avenues.

In their analysis of prison-based reality programming, Cecil (2007) noted that in addition to the typical dubious authenticity of reality television, prison programs had a unique problem. In order to be granted continual access to prisons and prisoners, production companies had to make a product that was acceptable to the prison system. The prison system is historically resistant to allow filming by outside groups and maintains complete and unfettered control over who is and is not allowed access (Turnbo, 1992). If prisoners are shown humanely or the system is shown in a negative light, the warden can simply pull the plug on production, citing some vague security risk. In addition, production companies have to sell their product to a public already primed by media exposure to be convictist. Media that humanizes prisoners is "taken as a sign of indifference to the suffering of those who have been harmed by others and of lack of common sense in the face of obvious social dangers" (Rhodes, 2004, p. 6). As a result, "the editing process results in countless hours of film on the cutting-room floor, thus creating a highly edited version of prison life" (Cecil, 2007, p. 208).

Scholars, however, are in a better position than production companies to alleviate concerns. First, we are more likely to produce a documentary or podcast than a television series. An offending documentary will likely be completed before earning a warden's ire, and podcast interviews can be done over the phone, which has far less regulation than bringing cameras into prison units. Second, they are not beholden to the pitfalls of profitability. Whereas a production company makes a film or series as a means to make money, faculty are employed independently of their media productions. As such, we can focus on making a truer representation even if it does not sell well.

Faculty can become documentarians or podcast hosts relatively affordably given the access provided by current technology. In the past, producing media was a prohibitively expensive endeavor. Currently, there exist numerous free or affordable audio and video editing software options, and cameras continue to become cheaper. As of this writing, Anchor hosts podcasts free of charge, and Amazon Prime Video takes independent productions. The tools to humanize prisoners are now at our fingertips and, in many cases, on our phones.

Although I imagine most reading this chapter are scholars of media effects and analysis, rather than production, I leave with one final question: Who better than us, who understand the effects of media, to produce better and more humanizing content? Scholars have unique sets of skills garnered from our profession. We are able to research, to summarize, to create, to critically unmask infrastructure, to uncover hidden truths. As media scholars in particular, we have particularized knowledge about what media does and what it can do. We have also learned the power of collaboration and invention. This could mean partnering with film faculty or students, creating capstone courses to help develop this kind of media, or simply downloading the Anchor app to provide scholarly insight as a one-person podcast. Whatever we do, it produces more humanizing media to be consumed.

Conclusion and Future Directions

There is a distinct need for more analysis of prison and prisoner media. As noted in this chapter, there is a considerable lack of scholarship on the subject. Although there is certainly substantial scholarship published relating to tertiarily connected topics such as media and crime, media and mental health patients, and others, there is an admitted lack of analysis of media specifically dealing with prisoners and prisons. Within this gap is a scarcity of intersectional research on prison media. Although there are a few articles dealing with the depiction of women in prison, most are about men or about prisoners in general. Research should be done examining the interaction between the mediated portrayals of prisoners and gender, race, sexual orientation, and class.

Given the constraints preventing prisoners from producing their own counter-media, it is crucial that media scholars take up the call. Having served as the prisoner advocate for the institutional review board at a top-ranked Western university for the better part of a decade, I am well aware of the hurdles involved for universities and prison systems to access prisoners for human subjects research. Furthermore, I am keenly familiar that most media scholars are not themselves media producers. However, as someone who taught more than 1,000 prisoners over 8 years, I am also cognizant of their ability to make do with what limited tools they have at their disposal to create what they need. We should do the same. Social justice requires action, often outside our comfort zones. Prisoners cannot produce media on their own, so they are counting on you to do it.

References

Abbott, G. (2020). *Executive Order GA-13 relating to detention in county and municipal jails during the COVID-19 disaster*. https://gov.texas.gov/uploads/files/press/EO-GA-13_jails_and_bail_for_COVID-19_IMAGE_03-29-2020.pdf

Bailey, F. Y., & Hale, D. C. (Eds.). (1998). *Popular culture, crime, and justice*. Wadsworth.

Brown, M. (2014). Visual criminology and carceral studies: Counter-images in the carceral age. *Theoretical Criminology, 18*(2), 176–197.

Cecil, D. K. (2007). Looking beyond caged heat: Media images of women in prison. *Feminist Criminology, 2*(4), 304–326.

Cecil, D. K. (2015). *Prison life in popular culture: From* The Big House *to* Orange Is the New Black. Rienner.

Cheliotis, L. K. (2010). The ambivalent consequences of visibility: Crime and prisons in the mass media. *Crime, Media, Culture, 6*(2), 169–184.

Entman, R. M., & Rojecki, A. (2001). *The Black image in the White mind: Media and race in America*. Wiley.

Feagin, J. R. (2010). *The White racial frame: Centuries of racial framing and counter-framing*. Routledge.

Freire, P. (1970). *Pedagogy of the oppressed*. Continuum.

Key, A. (2021). *The rhetoric of resistance to prison education: How the "war on crime" became the "war on criminals."* Routledge.

Llinares, D. (2015). Punishing bodies: British prison film and the spectacle of masculinity. *Journal of British Cinema and Television, 12*(2), 207–228.

Mathiesen, T. (1995). Driving forces behind prison growth: The mass media. *Nordisk Tidsskrift for Kriminalvidenskab, 83*(2), 133–143.

McGinty, E. E., Kennedy-Hendricks, A., Choksy, S., & Barry, C. L. (2016). Trends in news media coverage of mental illness in the United States: 1995–2014. *Health Affairs, 35*(6), 1121–1129.

Munro-Bjorklund, V. (1991). Popular cultural images of criminals and prisoners since Attica. *Social Justice, 18*(3), 48–70.

Nellis, M. (2013). Future punishment in American science fiction films. In P. Mason (Ed.), *Captured by the media* (pp. 210–228). Willan.

O'Sullivan, S. (2001). Representations of prison in nineties Hollywood cinema: From *Con Air* to *The Shawshank Redemption. Howard Journal of Crime and Justice, 40*(4), 317–334.

Owens, C. (2020). *Confession: #GeorgeFloyd is neither a martyr or a hero. But I hope his family gets justice.* Twitter. https://twitter.com/RealCandaceO/status/1268280610818101248

Rafter, N. H. (2006). *Shots in the mirror: Crime films and society*. Oxford University Press.

Rapping, E. (2003). *Law and justice as seen on TV*. New York University Press.

Rhodes, L. A. (2004). *Total confinement: Madness and reason in the maximum security prison* (Vol. 7). University of California Press.

Ridley, L. (2014). No substitute for the real thing: The impact of prison-based work experience on students' thinking about imprisonment. *Howard Journal of Crime and Justice, 53*(1), 16–30.

Sarat, A. (2002). *When the state kills: Capital punishment and the American condition*. Princeton University Press.

Snauffer, D. (2006). *Crime television*. Greenwood.

Surette, R. (1984). *Justice and the media: Issues and research*. U.S. Department of Justice, Office of Justice Programs.

Surette, R. (1998). Some unpopular thoughts about popular culture. In F. Y. Bailey & D. C. Hale (Eds.), *Popular culture, crime, and justice* (pp. xiv–xxiv). Wadsworth.

Surette, R. (2007). *Media, crime and criminal justice: Images, realities and policies*. Wadsworth.

Turnbo, C. (1992). News at eleven. *Federal Prisons Journal, 3*, 47–50.

Van den Bulck, J., & Vandebosch, H. (2003). When the viewer goes to prison: Learning fact from watching fiction. A qualitative cultivation study. *Poetics, 31*(2), 103–116.

Walmsley, R. (2016). *World prison population list*. Institute for Criminal Policy Research.

Wilson, D. B. (2003). Lights, camera, action. *Prison Report, 60*(1), 27–29.

CHAPTER

20

Heroes of the Border: Using Counternarratives to Break Border Stereotypes and Create Superhero Narratives

Anthony R. Ramirez

When people hear the words "comic book," most think of characters such as Superman, Batman, Spider-Man, Wonder Woman, and Iron Man. It would be safe to assume that most people would not think of Latine immigrants who are superheroes.[1] Most of the time, Latine immigrants are seen as threats and other negative stereotypes due to political rhetoric and media representations. Aldama and Gonzalez (2019) mention how the border-crossing narrative is often portrayed in a dramatic and politically timely way. They argue that border crossing is a common trope found in Latine media because it is a profitable one for many studios. Many of the stigmas and stereotypes against immigrants from the southwest U.S.–Mexico border still linger throughout examples of U.S. media and popular culture, including within comic books. In this chapter, I use Latina/o critical communication theory to analyze counternarratives featured in the comic books *El Peso Hero* (Rodriguez, 2016, 2019a) and *Home* (Anta, 2021), centered on the southern U.S. border, and analyze representation and their contribution to the larger conversation of popular culture, comics, and border studies. The authors of both books use their comic books as a platform to discuss various social justice efforts related to immigrants and the U.S.–Mexico border. All of which are counternarratives that resist the stereotypical and often negative depictions of immigrants and people of the U.S.–Mexico border.

The first comic series I focus on comprises two independent titles from Rio Bravo Comics titled *El Peso Hero: Border Stories* and *El Peso Hero: Borderland*, both written by Hector Rodriguez III. *El Peso Hero* are "one-shot" single stories that tell the narrative of a Mexican superhero. El Peso Hero helps Mexican immigrants and undocumented children who are facing various challenges, such as crossing the border, being held in detention facilities, and dealing with the border patrol or customs agents. The second comic series that I discuss, *Home*, written by Julio Anta and published by Image Comics, focuses on Juan and his mother, Mercedes, who are seeking asylum at the U.S. border. Juan is separated from Mercedes, and upon discovering he has superhuman abilities, he escapes the custody of the border patrol. According to the U.S. Census Bureau (2020), there are 60.6 million Latine people in the United States. The southern border of the United States is a persistent topic in news media and in politics. Media representations focus on issues such as immigration, migrants, drug smuggling, and human trafficking. In 2016, political tensions between the United States and Mexico heightened when then U.S. President Donald Trump constantly mocked Mexican

---

[1] Throughout this chapter, I use the term Latine to be inclusive toward those who identify as nonbinary or gender neutral within Latin American cultures and communities. In addition, the term is also inclusive toward language grammar because it can be used with English and Spanish.

immigrants with hateful rhetoric. A significant point of Donald Trump's political campaign promised to build a physical wall between the United States and Mexico. This rhetoric fueled problematic racial stereotypes about southwest immigrants as people who deplete the United States of its resources, "steal" jobs from White Americans, erode national U.S. culture, serve as drug dealers, and are criminals. Words such as "alien" and "illegal" are often used to describe them (Nadler & Voyles, 2020).

Theory of Resistance

In this chapter, I use Latina/o critical communication theory (LatComm) as my theoretical approach. LatComm as a theoretical approach for this study provides a better structure for communication scholars who want to analyze race within media and popular culture critically. The five tenets of LatComm are (a) centralize the Chicana/o and Latina/o experience, (b) deploy decolonizing methodological approaches, (c) acknowledge and address the racism faced by Latina/o communities, (d) resist literacy-colorblind language and rhetoric toward Latinas/os, and (e) promote a social justice dimension (Anguiano & Castaneda, 2014). Each of these tenets allows for communication scholars to expand on the underrepresented scholarship that critically analyzes Latine experiences and communities, as well as racial and social prejudice toward Latine people within mass media. This approach allows for communication scholars to use communication-related practices in relation to social, cultural, and political questions regarding the Latine community. I explore and textually analyze popular culture, specifically Latine and U.S.–Mexico border representation in comic books, by using LatComm.

According to Suna (2018, p. 32), the producers of entertainment formats must be considered as gatekeepers because they decide which cultural references are to be adapted and reinterpreted for audiences. This also applies to Latine comic book storytellers because they provide a representational point of view that is more complex in comparison to the stereotypical portrayals found in media (Alemán, 2017). Moreover, Latine people are subjects of "controlling images" in media, which they constantly challenge in order to create a definitive space for themselves (Vasquez, 2010). These controlling images are powerful because they can be both positive and negative in terms of creating and maintaining race, class, and gender oppression (Collins, 2008). By using LatComm, this chapter examines elements of racist depictions and stereotypes that Latine individuals along the U.S.–Mexico border face, including discriminatory rhetoric claiming that people from south of the U.S. border are drug dealers and rapists. Although it is unfortunate that these forms of representation do appear in some of the comic books analyzed, it is also important to note that these negative depictions were not the only forms of Latine representation that were included within the artifacts analyzed. Authors such as Hector Gonzalez III and Julio Anta use counternarratives to showcase complex and diverse forms of representation of Latine individuals along the U.S.–Mexico border and create Latine immigrant superheroes who help fellow migrants or Latine individuals within the borderlands.

Findings

Setting the Stage: Using Political Rhetoric to Discuss the Border

The introduction of *Home* begins with narration of a statement from U.S. Attorney General William Barr issuing a zero-tolerance policy that would prevent immigrants from entering into the United States. Within the statement, Trump calls immigrants "cold-blooded criminals," "rapists," and individuals who bring drugs and crime into the United States. In addition, the policy states that children would be separated from their families. These sentiments are felt throughout *Home* as the zero-tolerance policy is brought up multiple times in the first issue and as Juan escapes to save his mother and goes to Houston, Texas, with his aunt. *El Peso*

Hero: Borderlands features Trump as he is being briefed about El Peso Hero's break into an immigration detention center. Later, Trump orders his associates to get El Peso Hero dead or alive and send him to the Guantanamo Bay detention camp. The U.S.–Mexico border and immigration is a popular topic within political spheres, so it make senses that politicians and political issues appear in these comic books.

Using Counternarratives: Latine Immigrants as Superheroes

In the comic books *Home* and *El Peso Hero*, migrants and Latine are the main characters and are viewed as superheroes, thus presenting a counternarrative not typically found within comic book storylines. Critical race theory comprises various principles, including the social construction of race and the idea of storytelling and counter-storytelling (Crenshaw et al., 1995; Delgado et al., 2012; Solorzano & Yosso, 2001). Delgado (1989) constructed counter-storytelling as a method to tell the stories and experiences of those who are marginalized in society and as a tool for analyzing and challenging the stories of those in power and hegemonic members of society. Alemán (2017) discusses how counter-storytelling can be viewed in two ways: as a group of presumptions, preconceived wisdoms, or cultural understandings by the predominant race in their discussions of race; or as a fictional narrative that centers the experiences of minoritized communities and individuals in order to reduce the validity of assumptions and myths, especially ones held by the predominant race. However, the comic book creators of *Home* and *El Peso Hero* both include counternarrative approaches within their comic book stories because they include Latine immigrants as superheroes. *Home* focuses on Juan, a young migrant who faces multiple traumatic situations, including anxiety from being in a detention center, being separated by his mother, and further anxiety from escaping the immigration facility, which slowly triggers his powers. In the story, the audience learns that Juan's father, who passed away, had powers and it runs on that side of the family, as his cousins also have superpowers. *Home*'s author, Julio Anta, uses *familismo* (familism) in an interesting way as family is the connector, both genetically and situationally, that leads Juan to have his powers. *El Peso Hero*'s title character is a Superman-like hero from Northern Mexico who speaks in Spanish. *El Peso Hero*'s author and creator, Hector Rodriguez, III (2019b), states that he created the character because he wanted to feel culturally connected to a character. El Peso Hero is a character who leads with empathy, sympathy, and *respeto* (respect) as he saves migrant children and families who are facing militants, U.S. Immigration and Customs Enforcement (ICE), and other difficult situations that migrants face. Both characters are significant and important because they are underrepresented characters who have leading roles in a way that other comic books have not presented—the immigrant front and center as the hero. Popular culture scholar, Maurico Espinoza (2016), states, "Mainstream comic book publishers—who had for decades excluded minorities from the exceedingly white and masculine realm of superheroism—created a few Latino/a superheroes during the next two decades, but they generally played minor roles and relied on stereotypes" (p. 181). In addition, these authors, characters, and narratives also resist the stereotypical portrayals of immigrants in the media.

To further this conversation of counternarratives, all three stories take place at the U.S.–Mexico border, which is not common because most comic book stories are located in large cities such as New York City or fictional metropolitan areas such as Gotham or Metropolis. Both characters face various dilemmas along the border, including racial discrimination and divide, migrating to search of a better life, and separating from their families. El Peso Hero and Juan both focus on helping the people at the border, whether it is their own families, migrants, or the community they serve; both characters make a positive impact and create a positive form of representation of being a hero to those who are marginalized.

La Familia es Importante—Familismo

In the comic books analyzed, familismo plays an important role within the origin story of each character. Familismo or familism is a core Latine cultural value that has been discussed by many scholars in a variety of ways (Ayon et al., 2010; Calzada et al., 2012; Ruiz & Ransford, 2012; Steidel & Contreras, 2003). Most of these scholars state that familismo is a collectivistic trait, or cultural value, of Latine people because the Latine population tends to be group-oriented. According to Carter et al. (2008), Latine people are characterized as interdependent, collectivistic, and family-oriented compared to White Americans, who are viewed as independent, individualistic, and self-focused (p. 7). In addition, Carter et al. explain that Latine "values of interdependence prioritize family, unity, honor, and loyalty over individual needs and goals" and cultural values extend beyond just family to other relationships such as friends and other networks beyond relatives (p. 7).

From the very start of *Home,* familismo is a key signifier that is strongly tied to the narrative of the story. The protagonist, Juan, is learning to cope with his powers, in addition to coping with being in a new environment and being separated from his mother. His aunt becomes his superhero mentor and guide throughout the story, which again ties everything back to familismo and the connection of family. Family is a recurring theme in each of the five issues of *Home* as it becomes the connection or narrative thread of each of these issues. Familismo is a common cultural value in Latine media, and *Home* continues this trend as Juan and his family play a major part in the story and in how he obtains his superpowers.

El Peso Hero showcases familismo through various segments with his grandparents. His signature "PH" belt buckle is given to Ignacio (the real name of El Peso Hero) by his grandfather after Ignacio gets detained by border patrol agents. Although Ignacio gets his powers from a mystical crystal and curandera, the sentimental value of the belt buckle holds high esteem to Ignacio, who wears the buckle proudly throughout the comic series. In addition, *El Peso Hero* displays familismo through other characters, such as the migrants whom the title character saves. *El Peso Hero* and *Home* illustrate familismo through their narrative of migrants crossing through dangerous terrains together with their families. As mentioned previously, although families become separated, as in *El Peso Hero* comic stories, in a more positive aspect of the stories they reunite.

Using Language as a Cultural Signifier to Enforce the Counternarratives

Throughout the comic books, language is a key counternarrative tool and an important cultural signifier of Latine and border representation. Language is important to highlight and analyze because it is not only an important part of the culture but also an important part of highlighting the lived realities of those who are not commonly represented within comic books and other forms of popular culture. The makeup of the people at the border is significant because most Latine people from the border are bilingual, mainly speaking Spanish and English. Border scholar Gloria Anzaldúa (1987) describes how there are various languages within the Latine/Chicanx culture, including Chicano Spanish. According to Anzaldúa, Chicano Spanish is a border tongue that developed naturally and is a living language (p. 79). People on the border needed a language they could connect to that incorporates both Spanish and English.

Although most comic books are written in English, both *El Peso Hero* and *Home* include Spanish in some capacity. Characters who are Latine, especially in mainstream comic books, speak mainly in English. In *Home*, whenever Juan and his mother speak, the language is in red text, signifying that they are speaking in Spanish. On the other hand, *El Peso Hero* uses both English and Spanish throughout the narrative. Rodriguez wanted to include a title character and superhero who only spoke in Spanish, thus furthering the counternarrative approach to his storytelling. Rodriguez (2019b) states that he did this because he believed that "it is important for [El Peso Hero] not to lose his culture, language, and self."

Both titles are independent titles that do not follow the mainstream structures or rules, thus furthering their establishment as counternarratives within comic book lore. Within comic book spheres, most mainstream comic books are written in English and are written mainly as superhero stories that have to follow a history and structure for their characters. Again, it is worth noting that comic books from independent publishers allow their authors more creative freedom with their storytelling and character development.

Law Enforcement: Villains of the Border

In most media depictions, law enforcement is meant to be the protagonist or hero, yet in these stories, the narrative is flipped as they become the villains. Border law enforcement such as immigration enforcement, ICE agents, and Border Patrol agents are some of the key villains in these stories. It is important to note that although the characters in these comic books are fictional, there is some reality and truth to these representations. In September 2021, various members of the U.S. Border Patrol were caught wielding cords and allegedly using whips on Haitian migrants who were at an encampment site under a bridge on the U.S.–Mexico border around Del Rio, Texas, and Ciudad Acuna, Mexico ("US Officials to Probe Whip-Like Cords Used Against Migrants," 2021). This sparked an outrage with many people over social media calling for the U.S. government to defund the Border Patrol after witnessing the mistreatment of these migrants.

El Peso Hero features the title character facing supervillains, but many of the stories feature El Peso Hero going against banditos, migrant smugglers, and border law enforcement. In various stories of *El Peso Hero*, El Peso Hero battles these characters along the U.S.–Mexico border and in immigration facilities. One issue in particular focuses on El Peso Hero saving various migrants who are on *La Beastia* (The Beast), the train migrants sneak onto and use to travel into the United States, from organized crime groups and gangs. Here, El Peso Hero is reminiscent of Superman with his feats of strength lifting vehicles and also being empathic and kind toward the migrants, even helping them cross rivers and treacherous terrain. Crime groups and gangs such as these are common on the Mexico side of the border.

Another issue of *El Peso Hero* features ICE agents invading a young girl's home and detaining her father for deportation. The story then transitions to an immigration center in Uvalde, Texas, where El Peso Hero saves young migrant children who are in the facility. Another example of using counternarrative villains within *El Peso Hero* is the inclusion of former U.S. President Donald Trump as an antagonist. It is completely justifiable that a hero such as El Peso Hero is needed within these immigration camps because many of them are often crowded and the living conditions are poor.

As previously mentioned, *Home* features Juan and his family battling ICE and other immigration and law enforcement officials as they try to capture him and return him to an immigration facility. Throughout the five issues, law enforcement and immigration officials are a looming threat, using violent and hostile means to "terminate the threat," as one of the officers states. Juan and his family retaliate by using their powers in a defensive manner rather than attacking the immigration and law enforcement officials. The final pages of the graphic novel feature the Governor of Texas and Mayor of Houston (both fictitious versions) saying that they stand with Juan and his family, as they both support immigrant families, and that the families have nothing to worry about. Juan's cousins are hesitant about this situation because they believe something does not feel right and that they should not trust the government.

Conclusion

It is important to emphasize that although there are Latinx superheroes who exist within the larger scope of comic books and graphic novels, the characters discussed in this chapter are unique because they resist popular narratives and stereotypical tropes seen throughout media and popular culture. It is not common for characters such as El Peso Hero and Juan, who are Latine and live in or are from a border area, and in some cases migrants to be superheroes and lead characters in a comic book. Nor is it common in other examples of popular culture or media. The creators of these comic book characters center the Latine experience in their stories and use counternarratives to break stereotypes and common representations of Latine individuals from the U.S.–Mexico border and make these characters into superheroes. The authors use their characters to advance issues of social justice, to further center Latine identity and representation using cultural signifiers such as language and familismo, and to showcase the strength of immigrants. It is with great hope that in the future there will be comic book creators who continue to write, illustrate, and focus on stories and issues concerning the U.S.– Mexico border. Also, it is hoped that these future Latine representations will be presented in a positive manner and in a not so violent and demeaning tone, such as the ones depicted in other forms of media and popular culture.

Representation in media, including comic books and graphic novels, matters. The Latine community wants to see their stories told in a variety of formats, including comic books (Barbosa, 2018). Not only should media representation of the Latine community grow but also the stigma many news outlets and politicians have created surrounding Latine immigrants needs to change. It is understandable that politicians on both sides of the border must support and implement immigration policies, but these regulations need to be helpful and safe for people on both sides of the border. By analyzing comic books that focus on the U.S.–Mexico border and center around Latine representation, I discussed how many of the comic books include complex forms of representation of Latine immigrants, including intersectional identities such as being immigrant superheroes. A further practical implication that this chapter presents is that comic book and popular culture enthusiasts can gain a new perspective on the U.S.–Mexico border. The U.S.–Mexico border is a topic that is rarely covered and discussed in comic books, especially mainstream comic books. Many comic books and graphic novels are independent titles (non-Marvel Comics or DC Comics) that are not typically available in comic book stores and are only available at comic conventions, on independent publishers' websites, or through online comic readers such as Amazon's Comixology. Comic books can include complex and diverse characters and powerful narratives that can teach audiences about diverse representation, inclusion of people of color, and the fight for equitable rights and representation within popular culture.

References

Aldama, F. L. (2017). *Latinx superheroes in mainstream comics*. University of Arizona Press.

Aldama, F. L., & Gonzalez, C. (2019). *Reel Latinxs*. University of Arizona Press.

Alemán, S. M. (2017). A critical race counterstory: Chicana/o subjectivities vs. journalism objectivity. *Journal of Culture and Education*, 16(1).

Anguiano, C., & Castaneda, M. (2014). Forging a path: Past and present scope of critical race theory and Latina/ o critical race theory in communication studies. *Review of Communication*, 14(2), 107–124. http://dx.doi.org/10.1080/15358593.2014.951954

Anta, J. (2021). *Home*. Image Comics.

Anzaldúa, G. (1987). *Borderlands/La Frontera: The new mestiza* (4th ed.). Aunt Lute Books.

Ayon, C., Marsiglia, F. F., & Bermudez-Parsai, M. (2010). Latino family mental health: Exploring the role of discrimination and familismo. *Journal of Community Psychology, 38*(6), 742–756.

Barbosa, B. (2018, April 13). The need for Latino superheroes. ComicBook Debate. https://comicbookdebate.com/2018/04/13/the-need-for-latino-superheroes/

Calzada, E. J., Tamis-LeMonda, C. S., & Yoshikawa, H. (2012). *Familismo* in Mexican and Dominican families from low-income, urban communities. *Journal of Family Issues, 34*(12), 1696–1724. https://doi.org/10.1177/01925 13X12460218

Collins, P. H. (2008). *Black feminist thought: Knowledge, consciousness, and the politics of empowerment.* Routledge.

Crenshaw, K., Gotanda, N., Peller, G., & Thomas, K. (Eds.). (1995). *Critical race theory: The key writings that formed the movement.* New Press.

Delgado, R. (1989). Storytelling for oppositionists and others: A plea for narrative legal storytelling. *Michigan Law Review, 87*(8), 2411–2441.

Delgado, R., Stefancic, J., & Liendo, E. (2012). *Critical race theory: An introduction* (2nd ed.). New York University Press.

Espinoza, M. (2016). The alien is here to stay: Otherness, anti-assimilation, and empowerment in Latino/a superhero comics. In F. L. Aldama & C. Gonzalez (Eds.), *Graphic borders: Latino comic books past, present, and future* (pp. 181–202). University of Texas Press.

Nadler, J. T., & Voyles, E. C. (2020). *Stereotypes: The incidence and impacts of bias.* Praeger.

Rodriguez, H., III. (2016). *El Peso Hero: Border stories* (Vol. 1). Rio Bravo Comics.

Rodriguez, H., III. (2019a). *El Peso Hero: Borderland.* Rio Bravo Comics.

Rodriguez, H., III. (2019b, April 4). *El Peso Hero protects both sides of the border—From a comic book panel.* The World. https://theworld.org/stories/2019-04-04/el-peso-hero-protects-both-sides-border-comic-book-panel

Ruiz, M. E., & Ransford, H. E. (2012). Latino elders reframing familismo: Implications for health and caregiving support. *Journal of Cultural Diversity, 19*(2), 50–57.

Solorzano, D. G., & Yosso, T. J. (2001). Critical race and LatCrit theory and method: Counter-storytelling. *International Journal of Qualitative Studies in Education, 14*(4), 471–495.

Steidel, A. G. L., & Contreras, J. M. (2003). A new familism scale for use with Latino populations. *Hispanic Journal of Behavioral Sciences, 25*(3), 312–330. https://doi.org/10.1177/0739986303256912

Suna, L. (2018). Negotiating belonging as cultural proximity in the process of adapting global reality TV formats. *Media and Communication, 6*(3), 30–39. https://doi.org/10.17645/mac.v6i3.1502

U.S. Census Bureau. (2020, August 11). *Hispanic heritage month* 2020. https://www.census.gov/newsroom/facts-for-features/2020/hispanic-heritage-month.html

US officials to probe whip-like cords used against migrants. (2021, September 21). Al Jazeera. https://www.aljazeera.com/news/2021/9/21/us-officials-to-probe-whip-like-cords-used-against-migrants?utm_campaign=later-linkin bio-aljazeeraenglish&utm_content=later-2075 9715&utm_medium=social&utm_source=linkin.bio

Vasquez, J. M. (2010). Blurred borders for some but not "others": Racialization, "flexible ethnicity," gender, and third-generation Mexican American identity. *Sociological Perspectives, 53*(1), 45–71. https://doi.org/10.1525/sop.2010.53.1.45

Media Creation and Consumption as Activism Among African Transnational and Diasporic Communities

Omotayo O. Banjo *and* Tomide Oloruntobi

Until recently, entertainment studies have primarily privileged racial constructs when inquiring about or unpacking audience responses. In the United States, for example, scholars have primarily differentiated between Black, White, Asian, and non-White Hispanic, when these racial categories do not adequately reflect the myriad of audiences that the media industry and scholars have access to. In addition to mixed-race or biracial audiences, immigrants and their children are another important audience group that should be given consideration as multiculturalism in the United States rises. According to Ward and Batalova (2023) of the Migration Policy Institute immigrants make up 13.7% of the population in the United States. Furthermore, children of foreign-born U.S. citizens make up approximately 12% of the U.S. population and their children comprise up to 75% of the population. Following Mexico, China, and India, approximately 6% of immigrants come from various African countries, which is of particular interest to us.

These shifts in the U.S. population have also given rise to the production of transnational media content (Matsaganis et al., 2011), thereby impacting the ways in which immigrants as transnationals and their children as diasporans interact with this media content. Although scholars have examined entertainment needs and ethnic media use (Alakija, 2016; Ramasubramanian, 2016) among immigrants and their children, there has been little or no research on audiences of African descent. And although it is beneficial to examine the motivations for seeking out ethnic programming, the concept of engagement has been limited to consumption. It seems media researchers have not sufficiently accounted for these shifts toward transnationalism and its implications for how we measure such identities and examine its interaction with media content. We contend that an examination of these evolving cultural productions will yield valuable insight to the ways in which immigrants and their children assert their power. We consider how these positionalities use their power both in creation and in audience engagement. Furthermore, we expand audience engagement beyond cognitive and affective interactions to *affective investments*—using one's resources to support and maintain the transnational flow of these cultural productions. We argue that both the work of creation and audiences' investive responses are acts of social justice worthy of scholarly attention.

This chapter centers the discussion of content creation and audience engagement among immigrants and their children on the current wave of Nigerian cultural production in film, television, and music. First, we delineate points of distinctions and overlap between the positionalities we seek to center: immigrants, second generation, transnational, and diaspora. Second, focusing on African transnationals, we discuss how these positionalities integrate to create entertainment that complicates and disrupts static racial understandings and speaks to Blackness globally, which we conceptualize as *Black fusion*. Last, we argue that our explorations of these communities should supersede content and audience responses on the basis of enjoyment but also include creative agency and creative participation within a global economy.

Migrations, Movement, and Mobility: Explicating Diasporic and Transnational Identities

The delineation of identities marked by migration, placement, and belonging is complex, especially within global capitalist structures that impact not only the flow of commerce but also communities. To begin, a conversation about transnational identities cannot start without the story of an immigrant—an individual who relocates, whether of their own volition, by force, or due to diverse global migration push–pull factors, to a different country. An immigrant is not native to the land in which they reside, and within a global capitalist market whereby movement and labor are interrelated, they may be or may become products of transnationalism. Basch et al. (1994) stated that "transnationalism refers to the processes by which immigrants forge and sustain multi-stranded social relations that link together their societies of origin and settlement" (p. 6). Moreover, these communities are often outcomes of global market growth, globalization, and movements of jobs and opportunities outside of their ancestral lands.

Depending on one's definition, this group of immigrants is somewhat distinct from historic movements of communities that constitute diasporas. Anthropologists have generally argued that *diaspora* is a *historical* phenomenon composed of groups who have dispersed from an original homeland to which they have a connection as well as the collective community (Clifford, 1994; Owen, 2015). Whereas the term originally referred to communities of people who have been exiled, Safran (1991) critiqued in the 1990s that the term was becoming a "metaphoric designation" for communities of people who have been dispersed by other means (i.e., expatriate, refugee, etc.). Contemporary contemplations of the term argue that diasporic communities may also include the progeny, the beginning of a new generation of transnational identities that evolve into hybrid identities. Zeleza (2009) categorizes these groups as new diasporas who are "more fully socialized into the experiences and identities of the historic diaspora" (p. 42) and negotiate their identities within the contextual, constructed, and multi-consciousness identities informed by their diasporic and transnational ties and affective investments. Similar to transnationals, they may have maintained strong connections to their home country and culture, even though they may be living in a host country. While acknowledging that diasporic communities are the resonance of transnational movement over time, Georgiou (2005) also identifies the shifts in contemporary understandings of diaspora, stating that "diaspora is a contested concept—having at times implied ethnic homogeneity and identity essentialism—in debates around globalization, transnationalism, and mediation, the diaspora has been re-appropriated to recognize heterogeneity and diversity, transformation and difference" (p. 17). In other words, although each has its own history or narrative about how they came to be, which has an impact on how they connect or disconnect from their ancestral lands, each also presents an opportunity to explore issues such as hybridity, dual/multi-consciousness, or identity negotiation that may be at play during the creation and reception process of entertainment consumption.

In this chapter, we center audiences who have connections to more than one country and culture. Specifically, we focus on African transnational creatives and audiences as subjects, receivers, and consumers of transnational media productions. Our exploration is contextualized by the current global flow of Afrobeatz music; the integration between the Nigerian film industry and streaming sites such as Netflix; as well as the intentional fusion of Nigerian aesthetics in film, music, and television in diasporic contexts. For the purpose of this exploration, we offer simple definitions of transnational and diasporic audiences. *Transnational audiences* are individuals or communities that maintain connections and relationships across national borders but do not necessarily identify with a specific diaspora. They may have multiple residences, citizenship, or business interests in different countries. Transnational audiences are often mobile and have a global perspective, which allows them to navigate and participate in multiple cultural contexts. *Diasporic audiences*, on the other hand, are individuals or communities that are generations removed from the first generation of immigrants. This category ranges from historic dispersions (American Blacks) to second-generation Americans of African descent, who also largely support and benefit from these transnational cultural productions. Acknowledging the complexity of these concepts, we use them here to denote identities and cultural perspectives that maintain affiliative connections and continue to make *effective investments* to a home that is different from their current space/place of residence (Okpewho, 2009; Zeleza, 2009). Our discussion begins with a brief review of Nigerian transnational entertainment.

Transnational Flow of Nigeria's Media Product

Nigeria's film industry has long held the record of being the second highest film producer in the world, followed by Hollywood (United States) and preceding Bollywood (India). Note that though there are other film industries on the continent of Africa, including Swahiwood (Tanzania), Ghollywood (Ghana), Kinauganda (Uganda), and South Africa's film industry, Nollywood has yielded a wider distribution of film and television. Much of this reputation is in large part due to the direct-to-video content creation practiced by Nigerian creatives. Moreover, this practice affords accessibility to transnational and diasporic audiences overseas. In addition, although there are several music industries on the African continent, with artists from Senegal, Egypt, Ghana, and the Congo, Nigeria's music industry is hailed as the largest, having dominated the African music industry for more than a decade (Emokpae, 2018). Together, Nigeria's creative industries comprise up to 5.2% of the country's gross domestic product (Okoeguale, 2022). When considering Nigeria's populous, Nigerians comprise most of the population of African immigrants in the United States (Kenin & Fuller, 2022). Given these trends and our own positionalities as Nigerian transnationals and diasporan, it is without question that we should explore this flow and its potential impact on Nigerian transnational and diasporic audiences.

Adejunmobi (2014) refers to Nigeria's storytelling industry as a "minor transnational practice," pointing to a broken infrastructure that historically has relied and at times continues to rely on informal distributions (i.e., piracy and direct-to-video). Currently, a significant percentage of Nigerian films are viewed by transnational and diasporic audiences in what she calls "affinitive transnationalism." We consider these affinity politics as enhancing transformative possibilities that mobilize the Nigerian/African product within global capital flow. At the same time, they foster pushback to constructs and structures that aim to stifle the African story. These are intangible social justice concerns that transnational media products provide in enhancing the aesthetics, stories, experiences, and popular cultures capable of bridging the structural gap and techno-social inequities between the margin and its centers.

Adejunmobi (2014) argues that what makes Nigerian transnational film profitable is the extent to which the content resonates with audiences who are longing for "home" and thus, she claims, the films are best when they are produced in Nigeria. However, the boundaries of the provided definition exclude the possibilities and potential value of entertainment produced for and by transnationals. This exclusion is dismissive to the communities that help maintain its flow, and this perspective neglects the intangible impact of cultural proximity. *Cultural proximity theory* invites us to inquire about the extent to which Nigerian transnational media content offers aesthetics, values, and messages that resonate with culturally dispersed audiences, including American Blacks. Yoon (2017) specifically argues that the affordances of new communication technologies allow for a *cultural translation* that overrides linguistic barriers. In line with Mallapragada's (2006) claim about the production of Indian American content, we contend that the technological processes through which African transnational media content is produced and distributed invite diasporans and transnationals alike to reconsider the boundaries of "home."

Cultural proximity aids in our understanding of how dispersed audiences not only engage with transnational content but also find a sense of place. This interpretation inspires reflection on how transnationals are motivated by their affinity and identity needs, as well as how diasporic audiences may be motivated by a need to belong. With consideration for low-narrative art forms such as music, Yoon (2017) highlights the affective dimensions of cultural products, suggesting they facilitate these cultural affinities and affiliative connections often disrupted by displacement. As Mallapragada (2006) notes, the tension between identity and belonging is sharply informed by "migration, mobility, dislocation and relocation" (p. 208).

Whereas some contend Nigeria's film industry lacks identity and coherent philosophy, thus propagating negative imagery of Africa, Okoeguale (2022) suggests that Nigeria's music industry "serve[s] as a vehicle for the promotion of Nigerian cultural heritage" (p. 84). Although the music has evolved over time through traditional forms such as juju, fuji, and Fela's Afrobeat music to more contemporary styles such as Afrobeats, Okoeguale describes contemporary Nigerian music as largely influenced by the West. The current trend toward collaboration with American artists such as Chris Brown, Beyoncé, Drake, Future, and Coldplay is an indication of the global success of the music industry.

Previous scholars, such as Schiller (1993), expressed concern regarding the Westernization of global media productions; however, scholars such as Ang (1990) questioned the validity of *cultural imperialism*, arguing for the multiple unanticipated ways global social actors negotiate global intrusion. Specifically, Ang suggested that "social groups inside and between nations [will find] informal ways to construct their own collective identities within the boundaries of the system that limits and binds us all" (p. 255). Moreover, in addressing the subjects of glocalization, Kraidy (2005) and Asante et al. (2016) have argued for the diverse ways in which global–local interactions can produce and disrupt imperial and oppressive regimes of power. We contend that these local–global interactions are beneficial in affirming the Black imagination, revitalizing global Blackness and cultures, and disrupting negative significations of what it means to be African and Black. In addition, these collaborations and local–global media engagements serve as transformative resources in a climate infested with distortion of Black/African histories, (mis)representations, anti-Blackness, and promotion of mainstream hegemonic consumption and fandom politics. In this instance, media and representational politics of historically silenced groups are paradigmatic vessels for collective memorialization and affinities.

Similar to the popularization of Jamaica's reggae music, Okoli and Atelhe (2018) contend that the global success of African music is due to its ability to resonate with the identity and values of Africans throughout the world. The authors suggest that African music takes a globalized approach, adapting to local environments instead of being taken over by Western influence. In particular, African pop music "utilizes the platform and opportunities offered by globalization to promote and project African contents through their songs and performances" (Okoli & Atelhe, 2018, pp. 49–50). The current wave of Nigerian music artists is significant to the identities of not only African migrants but also Black Americans. Salm (2010) explains that Afro-pop music "link[s] the past to present, merging African and non-African styles, and highlighting artists who reside in multiple localities and manage a mosaic of cultural resources in the age of globalization" (p. 1328). As we explore the global impacts of Nigerian transnational media on transnational and diasporic audiences, we may also consider the potential of such media to connect those displaced without choice and those displaced by choice. In so doing, it is probable that the transnational flow of Nigerian media not only serves the needs of transnationals but also serves as a cultural bridge for diasporans, including descendants of enslaved Africans. Next, we discuss the pattern, potential, and promise of transnational African media to cultivate a Black diasporic imagination that yields insight into how media scholars can newly explore identity effects.

Black Fusion: Examining Black Diasporic Imagination and Cultural Bridging

Throughout the course of history, tensions have existed between African Americans or Blacks and African immigrants. There are multiple perspectives on the contributions of this intraracial conflict, but many scholars believe historical racial discrimination and its impact on Black Americans' self-understanding as well as resource allocation, stereotyping, and microaggressions are significant factors (Dapherede Otusanya & Castle Bell, 2018; Okonofua, 2013). Scholars contend that these tensions present communication barriers between Blacks and African immigrants (Whittington et al., 2021). Moreover, some believe that such intraracial tensions are produced by and benefit White supremacy. Nonetheless, African immigrants and Black Americans have developed deep connections through language, cultural practices, and the arts. In addition, the recent transnational flow of African-produced content and its resonance and popularity among Black Americans serve as an opportunity to explore how the creative works of transnationals and diasporans might disrupt the intended benefits of historical intraracial tension.

The past decade or so of arts and entertainment has seen exponential growth in production by African transnationals and/or children of African immigrants. Luvvie Ajayi, for example, came to the United States by age 5 and became an author, speaker, and podcast host. Actors such as Lupita Nyong'o (Kenya), Daniel Kaluyaa (Uganda), or Danai Gurira (Zimbabwe) and singers such as The Weeknd (Ethiopian Canadian), Jidenna (Nigerian American), Amaarae (Ghanaian American), or Vic Mensa (Ghanaian America) are examples of a shift away from monolithic conceptions of Blackness to a hybrid or global one. We argue that such positionality invites creatives to use their platforms to cultivate a new construction of Blackness, one that allows for members within the diaspora to find representations closer to home while also reconceptualizing home. Moreover, we argue that the recent creative collaborations between Black Americans and African immigrants nurture a hope for cultural bridging, connections that are worthy of scholarly attention. Such collaborative commitments create a kind of Black fusion that reconceptualizes Blackness not necessarily through a futuristic lens but, rather, as a holistic and dynamic Black diasporic imagination. We implore media scholars to examine the emergence of Black diasporic texts especially as it relates to the agentic power and potential of the media to counter White supremacists' racial logics and transform Blackness into something much more nuanced, complex, and honorable. We contend that creative projects by Black transnationals and American Blacks work together to interrogate Blackness, hold it as sacred, and employ hybridity strategically to foster a Black diasporic imagination that invites transnational and diasporic audiences to invest in ways that supersede mere consumption, moving them into active and affiliative investments.

Blackness Interrogated and Unbound

In CBS's *Bob Hearts Abishola* (*BHA*), created by British Nigerian Gina Yashere and Chuck Lorre, Abishola, the main character, is portrayed within the complex intersections of race, gender, belonging, transnational ties, and transcultural relational demands that help flesh out her character. This show, one of its kind in representing African migrant lives in America, enables a critique of intraracial tensions in global Black diasporic communities (Frederick et al., 2021). Aside from (re)producing racial Black–White binaries that center the cultural differences in America among these two composite communities, it misses an opportunity to holistically explore the nuances of racial stereotypical scripts that are played out by African migrants as demonstrated in previous work on intraracial tensions among Black communities: African, African American, and the Caribbeans (Asante et al., 2016; Dapherede Otusanya & Castle Bell, 2018; Jackson & Cothran, 2016; Oloruntobi, 2023). However, *BHA* provides a unique approach to how we can rethink notions of Blackness globally within the evolving global Black movement that distills conventional ideas of home. It also provides the context for media scholars to explore the nuances of *postcoloniality* and how transnational bodies may, subconsciously, enhance sustainability of coloniality against the desires and anti/decolonial struggles of Black diasporic communities. *BHA*, then, animates ideas of Blackness as it is a contested identity in global identity frameworks.

Shows such as *BHA* reveal that Blackness is an open, expansive, and flexible yet complex identity that draws from different historical logics and frameworks of identity. As Asante et al. (2016) and Oloruntobi (2023) note, many Africans found that they became Blacks as soon as they left their continental home. Ochonu (2019) also critiqued the nuances of *colonial mentality* as facilitating racist interactions among Africans. Ochonu emphasizes that "colonial signs have persisted in the African postcolonial public space, shaping elite aspirational cultures and marking social distinctions that are with the language of class and culture" (p. 3). In *BHA*, Abishola's parental choices animate the disguised distinctions that activate racist difference-marking in her son Dele's social activations and ideations of race. Through the Black American character of Gloria, Abishola's stereotypical beliefs were perpetuated, making Nigerianness more desirable at the expense of Blackness. The implication, therefore, is that Black/African transnational media representations hold the possibilities of portraying and critiquing conventional experiences but also critique inherent misrepresentation to speak with diasporic communities rather than against. In their critique of *Black Panther*, Asante and Pindi (2020) note the representations and identifications of/with Blackness "do not inevitably connote the same meaning between Africans in the diaspora and those in continental Africa" (p. 221). Black diaspora is a complex terrain on arrival (Madison, 2005).

For the characters in *BHA*, home is flexible, not fragile. Fragility in this sense becomes a pushback at essentialist definitions of the diasporic and transnational identities in migration studies in which critiques of home as physical place, time, and immobile are troubled. As such, the home is mobile, has no fixed meaning, and goes beyond ideas/notions of authenticity. Rather than thinking of diaspora from a nostalgic sense of place, we think of the new possibilities it creates in cultural and media studies and ideas of Black identities through notions of Black diasporic imagination. In Raupach's (2012) definition, the diasporic imagination involves the use of cultural elements, which encourages bonding and collectivism across the communities within the diaspora that challenges White racial superiority. We extend this to say that the notion of Black diasporic imagination calibrates the liberatory power of imagination brought to light through the articulation, representation, calibration, and politics of home and Blackness in the multiple diasporic contests through which Black lives are experienced.

Perhaps a more glaring illustration of these possibilities was the box-office success of Marvel's *Black Panther* films. *Black Panther* (2018) and *Black Panther: Wakanda Forever* (2022) present enriching narratives of culture, heritage, and attend to group-image/vitality through the superhero film genre. By reenacting existing/real experiences in Nigeria (i.e., Boko Haram kidnapping in the opening scene) to remind us of the complexities of the Black experience, the Black imagination becomes a tool for (dis)connecting with the Black diasporas with its multidimensional implications. Emphasizing the complexities of connection and disconnection made possible by the Black diasporic imagination, *Black Panther* scales beyond the space of its creation to the intricate identity questions it introduces, negotiations, and critiques. Although the movies emphasize the heterogeneous nature of Black identity, *Black Panther* depoliticizes, in no small measure, the nuances of Black American lives that *Black Panther: Wakanda Forever* attempts to reconcile.

Fusing the Sacred

In HBO's *Lovecraft Country*, an African American man travels across the United States looking for his father during the Jim Crow era. On his journey, audiences are introduced to the practice of *incantations*—a form of spiritual magic inherited in the family by an enslaved person. Whereas incantations within a Black context are generally viewed as barbaric, in the series, the African orientation to "incantation" is used as a dialogic tool to flesh out identity frameworks in race-related American television shows. Our analysis centers around the mobilizations of word-based magic that is similar both in textual construction and in cultural performances of power in Nollywood and African genealogy: The spoken word is a sacred tool that invokes terrestrial powers that enforce natural power order capable of shaping human realities and/or creating alternate realities. This is the bane of incantation as used in *Lovecraft Country*. From a transnational diasporic perspective, the show provides context for us to examine how local film features can be layered into diasporic cultural materials that in turn produce an effective recalibration of being diasporic and transnational. The show demonstrates the power of words as sacred, magical, and implicated in the natural order of life and spirituality. With incantation, symbolic apparatuses that connect with local filmic experimentations and genres are created to animate their uniqueness, prestige, and sense of cultural identity. When incantation becomes a tool for establishing social affiliation wherein Blackness is cast as a global phenomenon that connects people within an order, it inadvertently projects a communion that is facilitated through racial similarity, bond, and association.

We also see the implementation of African spirituality in Beyoncé's *Black Is King* (2020) album. Citing Lewis (2008), Smith and Coleman (2022) note the centrality of spirituality as "the technology element of Afrofuturism because spirituality facilitates communication with higher powers. . . . Spirituality is defined as a consciousness, lifestyle, and discourse that privileges spirit as a primary attribute of self that determines health and wellbeing" (p. 249). Thus, spirituality as "conduit of communication" (Smith & Coleman, 2022, p. 249) engineers a connection that binds people from within/out to animate its cohesive possibility. The Black/African histories, with their inherent complexities and layers, remind us of stories of vitality, hope, despair, heritages of loss and growth, liberation, and struggles and what they facilitate in the future and possibilities the Black life can imagine. From the title, lyrics, to sequences, each song in *Black Is King*—"Balance," "Bigger," "Find Your Way Back," "Brown Skin Girl," "Black Parade," among others—bears these messages that hold the transformative power of spiritualizing and rethinking the Black self. Here, we refer to the affective significance of the collaborations, the vitality, and, more fundamentally, the pride with which these works were rendered. For a group that has consistently been casted within certain master narratives both individually and collectively, such collaborative celebration and connection is taking on revitalizing identity impulse.

Black as Hybrid

Through the characters T'Challa and N'Jadaka (Killmonger), the problems of essentialism and immutability of identity are troubled in both *Black Panther* movies. Killmonger was not recognized as one of Wakanda because of his outsideness/Americanness. His anti-hero character was born out of sheer interest in ensuring that Black lives matter globally, which was possible through democratization of access to Wakanda resources. Although his vision bears an underlying good will, his approach was put to test and questioned by the end of the movie. With *Black Panther: Wakanda Forever*, however, we see that the Black experience and approach to it can be multidimensional yet productive when harnessed. Shuri eventually understood this, which helped unlock and promote peaceful coexistence with the Wakanda underwater neighbor. Citing Bhabha (1999), Canagarajah and Silberstein (2012) believe that "hybridity should be treated as a strategy and not a stable state or end product" (p. 83). Although hybridity in its postcolonial context is not readily without critiques, here we view hybridity as cultural and an individuated strategy through the synergistic and co-optative framework that mobilizes the characters of Queen Ramonda, Shuri, and Namor. Shuri's hybrid approach becomes the unifying tool within that brings the Black diasporic imagination to life—where initially place-bound approaches to identity are diffused. These are facilitated by her embodiment of the pains, triumphs, and complexities of the Wakanda past and present. The disconnection it creates is not only attended to in the movie's sequel but also problematized further as the only son of T'Challa also experiences, early on, the nuances of migration in a fast-growing globalized world. The implication here is the transcendent nature of the closures and openness that Killmonger's character brings to Wakanda, where the diaspora can coexist beyond limits of essentialist approaches to identity.

Black Panther is also celebrated for its cultural fusion with many different African cultural artifacts. Deploying the notion of Black fusion in media and culture, we see that the uniqueness of *Black Panther*'s portrayal of cultural artifacts, including music, fashion, art, resources, and beauty, is not restricted within a nation-bound cultural essentialism but, rather, defies essentialist ideas of the Black life. In other words, it does not simplify the complicated nature of the Black experience in local spaces. Yet, it provides a space for us to celebrate the uniqueness of these cultures without reducing it to essentialist approaches to and perception of culture and identity. In contextualizing this further, the Blackness becomes a unifying space where collective identity is politicized and negotiated, and the diaspora/transnational becomes a space for recalibrating the nuances of belonging, authenticity, and vitality. The Black Lives Matter movement, through the diasporic imagination that acknowledges the uniqueness of Black experiences in different contexts and because of its unifying tendency, calls to question the many tension-generating intraracial politics that constitute global Black identity. Overall, *Black Panther* successfully adds a context for us to understand and critique Blackness as both local and global politics that the media facilitates its negotiation. It not only provides the affective context for engaging the Black past, in all its imperfection, but also the beauty, resilience, and possibilities for connection that helps us to re-imagine Blackness. Also, it reminds us of the potentials of differential negotiation and the much needed dialogue that Black communities must have to engage with one another and understand the sociohistorical, political, and economic factors influencing their negotiations and performance of Blackness in diverse contexts, facilitating mutual understanding while enhancing group dialogue and change among these groups.

Affiliative Connections and Affective Investments: Exploring Audience Responses

Although extensive work has been done on affect in cultural studies, media studies, and psychology, it is essential to extend discourses around affect into the contexts of Black diasporic media. Scholars can examine involvement from the perspectives of the affective energies that calibrated them and that they calibrate. The implication here is that while contemporary Black media is centering the Black narrative, Black experiences and being both local and global, we look at affect from the perspective of tangible and intangible investments that audiences make in facilitating the dissemination and promotion of cultural materials in diasporic/transnational contexts. Affective investments capture the transnational/diasporic labor of audiences that accumulates into (a) global acceptances of cultural products, (b) perceptual changes that accumulate over time, (c) intentional efforts to balance algorithmic injustices deriving from audience engagement counts, and (d) translocal mobilizations that produce tangible and intangible capital in global media and entertainment.

In elaborating the above, (transnational) affective investments create accumulations that negate the hegemonic centering of global capital that is produced and concentrated in the so-called First World. Through diasporan's and transnational effective investments in the Black diasporic imagination, we see a resistance to White supremacy. Also, the evolving nature of algorithmic listening includes feeding the system data that are facilitated by user engagement (number of listens/views, dislikes and likes, shares, etc.). Ongoing global technological inequities that include internet inaccessibility affect artists and producers alike because their primary communities are perhaps operating in the *download cultures* and not *streaming cultures* (whereas the former download once and listen repeatedly offline, the latter stream and feed the algorithm data that generate platform referrals and algorithmic suggestions). In this case, transnational investments manifest as intentional efforts to promote these cultural materials. The audience becomes a channel of mainstreaming artistic products whose unpopularity is the result of global marginalizations and affective frameworks that match discourses around contexts of production with quality and content of production. Audience engagement, therefore, becomes intangible social justice work in which audiences use entertainment choices as investments for redirecting notions of being African, for instance, in the West.

Audience engagement and investment also appear in the global advocacy of Black people throughout the world. Not only might scholars investigate how audiences participate in this industrial narrative shift as well as activist consumption but also they can examine how these shifts enhance Blackness as a global identity/phenomenon. In the context of #ENDSARS in Nigeria, for instance, the protest garnered global participation, including from American Blacks, that elicited global concerns about police brutality in Nigeria and other sub-Saharan African countries (Ekoh & George, 2021). Similarly, many Nigerians in Nigeria protested the death of George Floyd (Okri, 2021). The implication is that contemporary media provides the avenue for us to discursively engage the commonality, vitality, and essence of the Black experience in their commonalities and dissimilarities. These artistic collaborations have provide the resources to leap across the line, know more about other Black communities, familiarize with the commonalities these communities share, and learn to understand the dissimilarities. Our goal, ultimately, is to encourage conversations about difference as it is created and negotiated within diverse Black communities, highlighting the need for us to embrace and celebrate difference to enhance group cohesion, mutual respect, and vitality. Scholars can explore the complexities of these cultural products not only in terms of what work still lies ahead but also in terms of how audiences are receiving, promoting, and actively participating in the distribution and mainstreaming of identity-based media.

Conclusion

We make the case about the openness, flexibility, complexity, and hybridity of Blackness as an identity construct that invites scholars to reconsider how we explore representation and audience responses. Decades ago, social and scholarly understandings of Blackness were reduced to stereotypical tropes and monoliths within the boundaries of the United States. However, we argue that media centering transnational stories, pushing beyond the boundaries of the West to African ancestral lands, and creative collective collaborations offer media scholars an opportunity to engage with new and global articulations of Blackness. We contend that transnational and diasporic creatives actively use media platforms to resist and disrupt racial ideals. The current transnational flow requires us to question why Black Hollywood is looking to represent and/or fuse African culture, music, instruments, and fashion in its work. It is important to understand that the Black narrative is not a place-bound narrative r(e)construction but, rather, a holistic overhaul that de-essentializes hegemonic construction of Blackness as a global identity marker.

We also invite scholars to engage, critically, the diverse ways in which (ongoing) colonialism and the postcolonial nature of continental Africans (and their media representations) affect Black diasporic discourses. This invitation is in lieu of Nollywood, among other African media industries. There is a need for critical cross-functional engagement that facilitates global-mindedness and resists stereotypical reproduction of hegemonic narratives of Black histories, experiences, and cultures. African cultures are not place-bound, much like Blackness. This authenticity-defying perspective animates the decolonial vision that we believe will mobilize conceptions of Blackness in totality. Hence, we invite scholars and media producers alike to center the perspective that decoloniality is social activism which, when centered in media production, reception, and analyses, will help us understand the complexities of Blackness, culture, and interrelationships and tensions that exist in understanding Black diasporas. Nollywood, in reference to diverse other continental African media industries, cannot continue to reproduce hegemonic narratives of Blackness. This must be addressed as a structural, social, and critical representation problem with a decolonial mindset.

Last, media effects scholars may explore the psychosocial impact of such narratives on Blacks' group vitality and belonging. One might ask what is the relationship between consumption of African transnational media content and how Black audiences perceive Blackness, and thus themselves and their commitments to supporting these products. In addition, we may want to reconsider our measures of Blackness and account for hybrid identities. Such developments reveal insights into how hybrid identities negotiate and engage their entertainment experience, leaving room for newer theoretical developments regarding involvement, appreciation, and selective exposure. Moreover, we extend audience responses beyond these factors to active investments of energy, time, resources, and community to sustain the success and flow of these products. Taking a critical media effects perspective, we must also interrogate effects of power on the degree of impact. For example, although there is increased awareness of African transnational products, the West still dominates storytelling. There are still structural issues that constitute new and ongoing barriers for transnational creatives. We ask, how might these realities interact with the potential of these works to do good for Black audiences? Moreover, inequity in pay across African media systems continues to have a major impact on what is produced. Scholars must engage these concerns as sociocultural, economic, and system issues.

References

Adejunmobi, M. (2014). Evolving Nollywood templates for minor transnational film. *Black Camera: An International Film Journal, 5*(2), 74–94.

Alakija, O. B. (2016). Mediating home in diaspora: Identity construction of first and second generation Nigerian immigrants in Peckham, London [Doctoral dissertation]. University of Leicester.

Ang, I. (1990). Culture and communication: Towards an ethnographic critique of media consumption in the transnational media system. *European Journal of Communication, 5*(2), 239–260.

Asante, G., Sekimoto, S., & Brown, C. (2016). Becoming "Black": Exploring the racialized experiences of African immigrants in the United States. *Howard Journal of Communications, 27*(4), 367–384. http://dx.doi.org/10.1080/10646175.2016.1206047

Asante, G. A., & Pindi, G. N. (2020). (Re)imagining African futures: Wakanda and the politics of transnational Blackness. *Review of Communication, 20*(3), 220–228. https://doi.org/10.1080/15358593.2020.1778072

Basch, L., Schiller, N. G., & Blanc, C. S. (1994). *Nations unbound: Transnational projects, postcolonial predicaments and deterritorialized nation-states.* Routledge.

Canagarajah, S., & Silberstein, S. (2012). Diaspora identities and language. *Journal of Language, Identity, & Education, 11*(2), 81–84. https://doi.org/10.1080/15348458.2012.667296

Clifford, J. (1994). Diasporas. *Cultural Anthropology, 9*(3), 302–338.

Dapherede Otusanya, A., & Castle Bell, G. (2018). "I thought I'd have more trouble with White people!": Exploring racial microaggressions between West African immigrants and African Americans. *Qualitative Research Reports in Communication, 19*(1), 44–50. https://doi.org/10.1080/17459435.2018.1468808

Ekoh, P. C., & George, E. O. (2021). The role of digital technology in the EndSars protest in Nigeria during COVID-19 pandemic. *Journal of Human Rights and Social Work, 6*(2), 161–162.

Emokpae, M. E. (2018). *The role of collective management organizations in the evolution of the Nigerian music industry.* SSRN. http://dx.doi.org/10.2139/ssrn.3179727

Frederick, N., Banjo, O. O., & Nwachukwu, E. (2021). Immigrants make America great: A textual analysis of Bob Hearts Abishola. In O. O. Banjo (Ed.), *Immigrant generations, media representations, and audiences* (pp. 111–133). Palgrave.

Georgiou, M. (2005). Diasporic media across Europe: Multicultural societies and the universalism–particularism continuum. *Journal of Ethnic and Migration Studies, 31*(3), 481–498.

Jackson, J. V., & Cothran, M. E. (2016). Black versus Black: The relationships among African, African American, and African Caribbean persons. *Journal of Black Studies, 33*(5), 576–604. https://doi.org/10.1177/0021934703033005003

Kenin, J., & Fuller, J. (2022, February 20). *1 in 10 Black people in the U.S. are migrants. Here's what's driving that shift.* NPR. https://www.npr.org/2022/02/20/1080667639/1-in-10-black-people-in-the-u-s-are-migrants-heres-whats-driving-that-shift%20Show%20less

Kraidy, M. M. (2005). *Hybridity, or the cultural logic of globalization.* Temple University Press.

Madison, D. S. (2005). *Critical ethnography: Methods, ethics, and performance.* SAGE.

Mallapragada, M. (2006). Home, homeland, homepage: Belonging and the Indian-American Web. *New Media & Society, 8*(2), 207–227.

Matsaganis, M. D., Katz, V. S., & Ball-Rokeach, S. J. (2011). *Understanding ethnic media: Producers, consumers, and societies.* SAGE.

Ochonu, M. E. (2019). Looking for race: Pigmented pasts and colonial mentality in "non racial" Africa. In P. Essed, K. Farquharson, K. Pillay, & E. J. White (Eds.), *Relating worlds of racism* (pp. 3–37). Palgrave Macmillan. https://doi.org/10.1007/978-3-319-78990-3_1

Okoeguale, A. (2022). Nature of Nigerian creative economy: A review of the Nigerian film and music industry. *Journal of African Films and Diaspora Studies, 5*(4), 77–99.

Okoli, A. C., & Atelhe, A. G. (2018). Globalization and "Africanization" of contemporary pop music: Implications for history and theory. *Covenant University Journal of Politics and International Affairs, 6*(2).

Okonofua, B. A. (2013). "I am Blacker than you": Theorizing conflict between African immigrants and African Americans in the United States. *Sage Open, 3*(3), Article 2158244013499162.

Okpewho, I. (2009). Introduction: Can we "go home again"? In I. Okpewho & N. Nzegwu (Eds.), *The new diaspora* (pp. 3–30). Indiana University Press.

Okri, B. (2021). "I can't breathe": Why George Floyd's words reverberate around the world. *Journal of Transnational American Studies, 12*(1).

Oloruntobi, T. (2023). Revisiting cross-cultural adaptation: An embodied approach. *Journal of International and Intercultural Communication*, *16*(4), 283–299. https://doi.org/10.1080/17513057.2022.2120207

Owen, J. (2015). Transnationalism as process, diaspora as condition. *Journal of Social Development in Africa*, *30*(1), 31–48.

Ramasubramanian, S. (2016). Racial/ethnic identity, community-oriented media initiatives, and transmedia storytelling. *The Information Society*, *32*(5), 333–342.

Raupach, K. (2012). "Black magic" and diasporic imagination. *Current Objectives of Postgraduate American Studies*, *3*. https://doi.org/10.5283/copas.67

Safran, W. (1991). Diasporas in modern societies: Myths of homeland and return. *Diaspora: A Journal of Transnational Studies*, *1*(1), 83–99.

Salm, S. J. (2010). Globalization and West African music. *History Compass*, *8*(12), 1328–1339.

Schiller, H. I. (1993). Transnational media: Creating consumers worldwide. *Journal of International Affairs*, *47*, 47–58.

Smith, C., & Coleman, L. S. (2022). Ancestor is king: The role of Afrofuturism in Beyoncé's *Black Is King*. *Critical Studies in Media Communication*, *39*(4), 247–259. https://doi.org/10.1080/15295036.2022.2038386

Ward, N., & Batalova, J. (2023). *Frequently requested statistics on immigrants and immigration in the United States.* Retrieved from Migration Policy Institute on June 10, 2023. https://www.migrationpolicy.org/article/frequently-requested-statistics-immigrants-and-immigration-united-states#:~:text=In%202021%2C%20immigrants%20comprised%2013.6,share%20they%20comprised%20in%202019

Whittington, E. Y., Castle Bell, G., & Dapherede Otusanya, A. (2021). Exploring discursive challenges between African Americans and African-born US immigrants from the standpoint of African Americans. *Southern Communication Journal*, *86*(1), 71–83.

Yoon, K. (2017). Korean wave cultural translation of K-pop among Asian Canadian fans. *International Journal of Communication*, *11*(17), 2350–2366.

Zeleza, P. (2009). Africa and its diasporas: Remembering South America. *Research in African Literature*, *40*(4), 142–164. https://doi.org/10.2979/ral.2009.40.4.142

Subaltern Digital Cultures: Precarious Migrants on TikTok

Elisha Lim, Satveer Kaur-Gill, *and* Krittiya Kantachote

To rephrase Gayatri Spivak's (1998) classic question, Can the subaltern TikTok? This chapter discusses some considerations for studying subaltern access and use of TikTok. Using the case study of migrant domestic workers in Singapore and their TikTok use, this chapter responds to the sometimes taken-for-granted preconception of social media for "social justice," typically assumed by social media studies and particularly influencer studies, that users are individuated subjects of *social capital* or, as Spivak argues, a "naturally articulate subject of oppression" (p. 288). This chapter recognizes subaltern digital cultures, specifically migrant domestic workers in Singapore who create content, build a following, engage in comment threads, and develop influence (Chee, 2023) while living in conditions of unfree indenture, stigmatization, and "soft violence" (Parreñas & Kantachote, 2021). The experience of unfree indenture denies these users' human rights, free speech, personal privacy, legal recourse, or any other requirements for building or retaining social capital. The fact that they are aspiring influencers nonetheless challenges the assumptions of platform studies around notions such as content creator, entrepreneur, privacy "rights," the requisites of "authenticity," as provincialized Euro-Western pretexts of liberal social capital. In particular, this chapter builds on the seeming paradox of unfree TikTok users to open up opportunities for contemplating the meaning and limitations of social justice in media studies.

Abidin (2020) highlights that TikTok is unique as a platform for social justice content in that "while social justice pursuits may sometimes involve sophisticated persuasion and the organization of mass rallies and displays (Bogle, 2019), in other instances, this takes on the guise of meme-making, trend-setting, virality-seeking, or public-shaming" (p. 84). The latter, specifically meme-making and public shaming of poor employment and living conditions, are practices reflected by some precarious migrants on the platform (Chee, 2023; Kaur-Gill, 2023; Jaramillo-Dent et al., 2022). However, as Spivak (1998) surmises, "The subject of exploitation cannot know and speak the text of female exploitation, even if the absurdity of the nonrepresenting intellectual making space for her to speak is achieved. The woman is doubly in shadow" (p. 288). This chapter discusses how historic cultural conditions, discursive media practices, platform business models, and the nonrepresenting intellectual definitions of a "user" limit discussions of social justice on social media platforms such as TikTok.

We begin by challenging assumptions around "users," "creatives," and "cultural producers" in established influencer studies. Then, we contextualize the structural conditions of the host countries that contribute to the precarity and subalternity of migrant domestic workers in Singapore, tracing local media representation and employer discourse surrounding domestic workers and their digital surveillance and regulation in the host country. We proceed to discuss the affordances and limitations of TikTok and how they shape any user's behavior to align with the platform's advertising goals. Finally, the chapter concludes by recognizing that migrant domestic workers' platform use is limited by platform agendas and digital (im)mobility.

Who Is, or Is Not, a Social Media "User"?

Influencer studies and platform studies typically focus on "content creators" with privileged social capital and access. Equity-based discussions about content creation focus on economic inequalities created by monopolistic corporate platforms around gender, sexuality, race, and ethnicity in the face of a rise in hate speech and disinformation and an undemocratic social sphere cultural producers within the creative industries–"for example, journalists, musicians, authors" (Poell et al., 2022, p. 6). These studies focus on the problem of an uneven creative playing field, where platform governance, technology, distribution, marketing, and monetization unfairly privilege platform interests over the rights of cultural producers. However, what about content creators who do not have access to a level playing field or even human "rights"?

The goal of a democratic, level playing field in a democratic social sphere draws on Jurgen Habermas' 1991 conception of the "bourgeois democratic public sphere," in which private individuals can agitate for equal access in order to contest their political roles. However, Habermas' public sphere has been challenged by feminist cultural theorists since Nancy Fraser's (1994) article, "Rethinking the Public Sphere: A Contribution to the Critique of Actually Existing Democracy," in which she asserts that culture is not just shaped by privileged equal access of private individuals with professional industry jobs. Culture is also shaped by counterpublics and counterdiscourse, "members of subordinated social groups—women, workers, peoples of color, and gays and lesbians" (p. 67). This "subaltern counterpublic" (p. 67) is not *outside* cultural production but, rather, essential to cultural production. Marxist feminists assert that these groups must not be excluded from economic analysis because they are essential frontline workers whose labor empowers capitalist operations (Bhattacharyya, 2018; Gimenez, 2019). Intersectional social media scholars focus on these counterpublics as important subversive social margins that expose oppressive social norms. Tufekci (2018) observes how, during the Arab Spring uprising of 2010, Facebook algorithms pushed activists to tailor their protests and "gear towards feel-good content (that gets 'likes') along with quarrelsome, extreme claims (which tend to generate comments?)" (p. 161).

Some scholars push the question of democratic public spheres even further by examining groups that are more oppressed than Fraser's (1994) subaltern counterpublic. For example, Abigail Rabindran (2023) shows how, even on social media, Dalit discourse is excluded by a hegemonic English-speaking caste (see also Thakur, 2020). Dalits are marginalized in the lowest position of the Indian caste system, making up a large proportion of low-paid labor, such as sanitation, factory, and leather work. This essential frontline work keeps industries operating— including creative industries in the globalized economy (Sur, 2020). In other words, Dalits are not *outside* of cultural production but, rather, essential to cultural production. Similarly, migrant domestic workers are essential to cultural production, conducting child care, cooking, and cleaning while having limited freedoms, which then enables middle-class households to function in First-World countries and frees up the independence, productivity, leisure time, and self-expression of their employers.

Affordances and Limitations of TikTok

This section discusses the behind-the-scenes forces that limit the public sphere of social media, specifically TikTok. These forces mold TikTok into a nonpublic, privatized, commercial sphere that is not shaped by democratic ideals, social norms, or even popularity. Instead, this section shows how TikTok, like all corporate social media platforms, is algorithmically choreographed by the platform's market agenda, advertising rules, and revenue model in order to generate clear, targetable niche markets. This agenda limits the prospects of social justice and is especially stark in its limitations of subaltern creative expression.

TikTok is a short mobile video platform owned by Chinese company ByteDance, and it has distinguished itself from its major competitors by offering personalized videos based on previous views, likes, and shares. Algorithms guide content, selectively feeding the "for you" page based on the user's profile and interest (Apple, n.d.).

Ads Manager is a behind-the-scenes interface that is useful for understanding the forces that shape platform content. Although Ads Manager is a back-end, advertiser-facing interface, its tagging system determines what users need to do to be visible on its front-end interfaces. Ads Manager works because it merges the values of advertisers, end-users, and developers. In other words, Ads Manager user data classifications determine ads, but they also determine the content recommended by algorithms. Machine learning captures user interests in order to predict the content that is most relevant and meaningful for each user. According to the TikTok Manager pop-out box, "Interests are defined by data on long-term user engagement with in-app content," and this engagement determines how users are classified for Detailed Targeting.

In other words, users are shown videos that align with their interests *as detailed advertising targets*. The videos that are the most visible on the platform are those that guide, flag, or serve target advertising. This virtuous cycle shapes user behavior to align with the platform's advertising goals. Algorithm scholar Rob Kitchin (2014) explains that algorithms shape behavior and turn our attention away from capta surveillance (he uses "capta" in place of "data") to capta classification, which powerfully shapes user behavior:

> Unlike traditional forms of surveillance that seek to self-discipline, new forms of surveillance seek to produce objectified individuals where the vast amount of capta harvested about them is used to classify, sort, and differentially treat them, and actively shapes their behavior. (p. 86)

On social media, algorithmic classifying, sorting, and differentiation offer attention and positive feedback as strong social incentives for aligning user behavior in line with platform norms. Platform affordances such as video and audio editability features allow users to mimic, remix, and blend content (Abidin, 2020; Zulli & Zulli, 2022), appealing to migrant demographic groups who can now participate in produsage (Bruns, 2008) by culturally customizing content tailored to their audiences (Kaur-Gill, 2023).

Thus, social media users who seek visibility change their behavior in pursuit of *algorithmic legibility*. To become more legible to advertising algorithms, users embody consistent, predictable, commercially targetable performance of identity, interests, and demographics (Lim, 2021). Political content is forbidden on TikTok, where the most sensitive "special ad categories" are limited to "housing," "employment," and "credit;" unlike Meta, for example, where advertisers must declare yet are allowed to advertise "social issues" (e.g., the economy or civil and social rights). Furthermore, whereas social media platforms such as Instagram and Facebook tailor to millions of drilled down specific customer tastes, TikTok Ads Manager serves broad interests, and TikTok "producers" (Bruns, 2008) must appeal to its vague, sweeping 28 categories of "kinds of creators": Comedy, Drama, Talent, Relationship, Motivation & Advice, Daily Life, Society, Family, Animal, Fashion & Beauty, DIY & Life Hacks, Homes & Garden, Art, Oddly Satisfying, Food & Beverage, Travel, Game, Sport, Fitness & Health, Transportation & Vehicle, Occupation, Transition (Photo or Film Taking Techniques), Lip-Sync, Random Shoot, Acg Content (Cosplay or Comics), Outdoor Activities & Nature, Tech and Education, and Pop Culture (Figure 22.1).

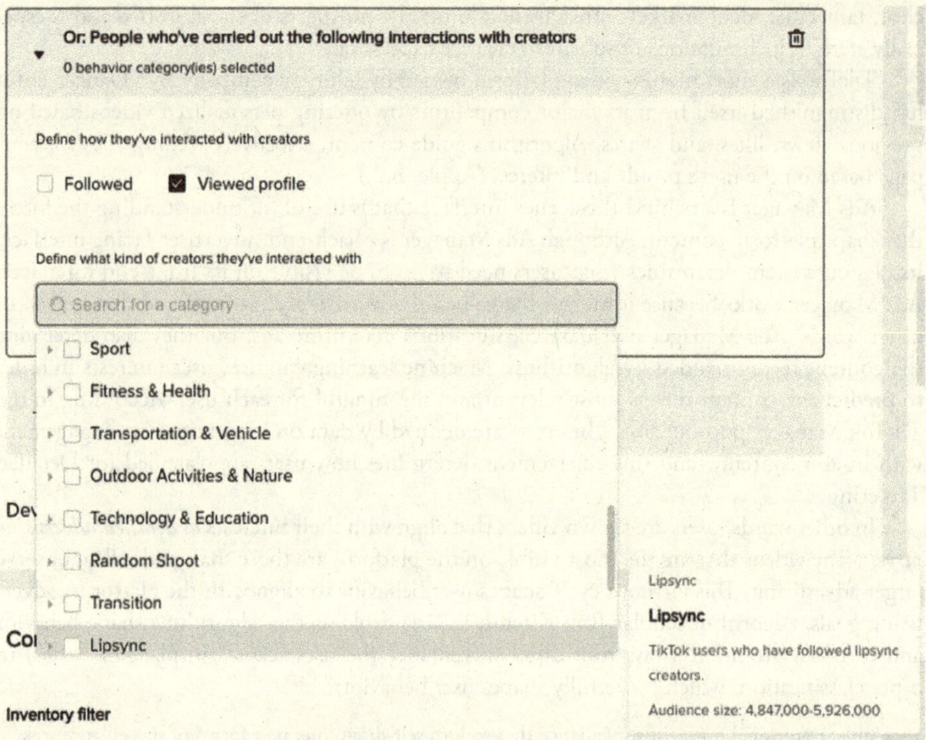

Figure 22.1 December 18, 2022, screenshot of TikTok Ads Manager, f Tfine what kind of creators they classes sampling t."

The key to TikTok's competitive recommendations may be that its *recommender algorithms* promote general and broad tastes within the archetypical 28 interests, leading users beyond their "friends-of-friends" to a sense of greater discovery and originality as long as they stay within the same umbrella of 28 interests. This broad tailoring allows domestic workers, like any users, to gain visibility on TikTok: (a) TikTok users do not require large friend networks in order to have their content recommended; (b) in order to harness algorithmic traction, content cannot touch on the political, economy, or civil or social rights issues; and (c) content must consistently appeal to one of the broad 28 categories.

However, these so-called advantages limit migrant domestic workers' content to marketable behavior that exacerbates the very neoliberal restrictions they face. TikTok flexibly deploys neoliberal command through what Ong (2006) calls "self-animation" and "self-government" so that some populations can optimize for "efficiency and competitiveness in turbulent market conditions" and accept their limited life chances (p. 6). Foreign domestic workers' self-animation is limited to content that produces TikTok's viral content and advertising niches (Lim et al., 2022). Their self-government creates a small window of opportunity to communicate, share stories, feel a sense of creative leadership, and even aspire to sponsorships—willingly optimizing for even greater competitiveness in an unfree, unjust system of limited life chances. TikTok capitalizes on the affective modulation of domestic workers' self-authored labels such as "hardworking," "sexy," "desirable," or "morally proper," producing new market circulation and value for the platform, consistently appealing to broad

TikTok advertising categories and rigidly regulated to a limited form that avoids "political, economy, civil or social rights issues."

Platform scholars attend to the fact that social justice rhetoric is limited and curated by social media's neoliberal business models (Noble, 2018; Tufekci, 2018). In particular, critical data studies take up Deleuze's (1994) theory of the "control society" to argue that social media platform business models and ad-driven metrics shape human behavior:

> In the relation between a representation and an action (reproduction of the Same) (Deleuze, 1994, p. 22), the computer-based learning encounter inherits a tendency toward reproduction rather than heterogeneity. . . . It is timely to think about the specific ontologies, or modeled worlds, required by these computer-based processes. (Sellar & Thompson, 2016, p. 492)

The computer-based learning encounter drives the "reproduction" of the market as a model world. Movements that gain social media traction are those that fulfill market ontologies by flagging potential target customers (Lim, 2021). For this reason, social justice advocacy has little chance of success unless it aligns with the agendas of commercial and state interests. Platform-dependent hashtags export ideologies of liberal rights-as-property. Worse, they perpetuate the imperialist subject constitution of privileged social capital.

As aspiring influencers, migrant domestic workers on TikTok would have little chance of sustaining platform influence if they attempted to draw attention to their real conditions of exploitation or social justice causes. Like all aspiring influencers, they must align their content with the most marketable material. Next, we discuss how these commercialized expressions of personhood are further limited by these workers embedded within employment conditions of soft violence, limited internet access, and stigmatizing media discourse.

Overview of Precarious Migrant Domestic Workers

The exclusion and expulsion of migrant domestic workers as peripheral subjects for exploitation in high-income economies such as Singapore, Hong Kong, Qatar, and United Arab Emirates have been extensively critiqued by migration scholars (Catedral, 2022; Fernandez, 2018; Kandilige et al., 2022; Kaur-Gill et al., 2023; Pande, 2013; Pandi, 2023; Parreñas, 2015), including their digital activity (Chee, 2023; Kaur-Gill, 2023). Key threads on domestic work, migrants, and precarity include calls to change hiring policies and employment protections for migrant workers hired through systems of indenture. These changes include macro- and meso-level changes to policies that perpetuate extreme neoliberal management practices anchored in authoritarian techniques of control, such as surveillance, deportability, and exclusion from civil society organizing (Bal, 2015; Dutta, 2020; Dutta & Kaur-Gill, 2018). In the micro-context, domestic workers have limited communicative spaces and platforms to challenge their conditions and advocate against poor work conditions.

In the field of migration studies, domestic work in Singapore performed by migrant workers has been described as "unfree indenture" because of their diminished control over their labor (Parreñas, 2021). This system creates a subsequent position of unequal dependency on their employers (Parreñas, 2021). In Singapore, this unequal dependency is aggravated by the uneven power the state grants employers over the lives of these subaltern women the moment they arrive as migrant workers in the host country. Subaltern communities are excluded from dominant development ideologies, narratives, and the norms of civility in society. They face "raced, classed, gendered subjectivities" (Dutta, 2018, p. 89) that systemically erase them from civil society organizing and participation, materially relegating them to the margins of society.

The policy practices for hiring migrant domestic workers include temporary, single sponsorship visas, medical surveillance, practices of indenture, employer-guided hiring and deportability, perpetuating conditions of indenture, servitude, erasure, and displacement in host countries (Kaur-Gill & Dutta, 2023). Furthermore, the illegality of unionizing and civil society participation for migrant workers excludes their voices from advocating for better health and occupational conditions (Yeoh et al., 2020). These intersecting exploitations make domestic workers subalterns in the host country.

In Singapore, domestic workers face systemic marginalization, including not being covered by the Employment Act, leaving them vulnerable to employer exploitation. The exploitative conditions have been conceptualized by Parreñas et al. (2021) as conditions of being unfree through practices of indenture: unfree because of the hiring policies for migrant domestic workers that tie them to a single sponsor and unfree by the nature of the constraining hiring nexus involved in keeping migrant workers in the margins of the host country. These contexts also create conditions in which employers engage in soft violence with limited repercussions.

Discourse on Domestic Workers

Discourses on domestic workers in the Singaporean media and popular culture have stigmatized migrant domestic workers as subjects for surveillance. Stigmatization through discourse plays out through the use of stereotypes. The "promiscuous" domestic worker is one such example (Lim & Paul, 2021), a stereotype associated with workers regulating their mobility and, therefore, a product of state policies aimed at regulating the bodies of domestic workers in specific ways. As of 1987, domestic workers in Singapore are subjected to mandatory biannual examinations to test for pregnancy and sexually transmitted infections. If a domestic worker becomes pregnant, they have to be immediately repatriated. These mandatory examinations are one of the only points of health access for domestic workers that are mandatory and out of the control of their employers. From 2010 onwards, employers no longer lose their $5,000 Singapore dollars' security bond (Ministry of Manpower, 2009). The public has been found to remain limitedly aware of these changes (Platt, 2015).

This worsened when a new regime of sexual surveillance started in 2013 when all Singaporean employers became legally required to give their domestic workers a mandatory weekly day off. Before that, domestic workers had no guaranteed day off. This law generated an outpouring of anxiety. In the same week, a media frenzy over the murder–suicide of a Filipina domestic worker and her Bangladeshi migrant construction worker boyfriend dominated the news headlines ("Foreign Love Turns Fatal in Singapore," 2012). The same week also featured the front-page headline, "Weekly Day Off for Domestic Workers" with the subheadline "Where Will Your Maid Go?" accompanied by a photograph of a domestic worker in the arms of a foreign construction worker ("Weekly Day Off," 2012). Platt (2015) shows that in the wake of these new laws, employers used typically stigmatizing stereotypes referencing "the mischief and ghastly behavior in which these servants will indulge on their off days" (p. 131) or that they "get some extra money from their lovers by having sex with them" (p. 143) to resist the day off regulation.

The same attitudes dominated throughout the COVID-19 pandemic. The Humanitarian Organization for Migration Economics (HOME), widespread abuse, overwork, and surveillance of domestic workers in Singapore who were now confined to their employers' homes due to COVID-19 lockdown policies. Kaur-Gill's (2020) study discussed how the mistreatment of foreign construction workers was highlighted during the pandemic; these are men who arrive from impoverished communities in the Global South, hired to work in construction in similarly indentured labor. However, Kaur Gill et al. (2021) found that the civil rights of domestic workers who are women were not discussed and attributed instead to neoliberal narratives of individual employer–employee relationships, state benevolence, and management responsibilities. These narratives do not support human rights but, rather, cast domestic workers as unequal subjects or, worse, as employer property in the eyes of the Singaporean media and law.

For example, a May 2020 Singaporean state advisory allowed employers to keep domestic workers at home to prevent the spread of the virus, even on their single weekday off, while family members were allowed to move freely (Kaur-Gill et al., 2021). This resulted in employers taking advantage of this rule to make domestic workers work on their day off but for no pay (Lay, 2021). When this issue was reported in Singapore media outlets *The Straits Times* and *Mothership*, their official posts received long comment threads with multiple opinions narrating the ideology of an unmanageable servant class, such as the following comment:

> There are some employers like me who give 3hrs rest time everyday on top of her rest day each month. And my helper still can complain & grumble. And most importantly she uses her phone like us whenever she wants. (Comment thread following article by Lay, 2021)

In these comments, a structured workday is not a right but, rather, a privilege extended to what is viewed as a subordinate class of workers. In this context of *hyper(in)visibility*, coined by Johnson and Boylorn (2015) to refer to representations as orchestrated by the powerful, social media acts as a "critical space of possibility" (p. 6). Subaltern workers using TikTok for visibility on the platform through high-traffic profiles and followers is a resistive feature to the hyper(in)visibility of their lives in the host country.

Soft Violence, Smartphones, and TikTok

Parreñas et al. (2021) elucidate how domestic workers in Singapore depend on their employers for legal status, which contributes to the precarity of domestic workers. Employers engage in soft violence. Although employers recognize domestic workers as human and relieve these workers of unequal dependency and servitude via adequate food, decent accommodation, decent breaks, and communication, employers amplify domestic workers' servitude through practices such as imposing curfews, withholding salaries, and restricting mobile phone usage (Parreñas et al., 2021; Parreñas & Kantachote, 2021). This highlights the temporal and scalar magnitudes of domestic workers' precarity during employment (Chacko & Price, 2021).

According to the Ministry of Manpower (2015), 98.2% of domestic workers have cellular phones. Access to cellular phones by domestic workers can be used as a tool to understand domestic workers' employment conditions. A cellular phone is crucial because it alleviates the isolated nature of domestic workers' work and allows them to connect to the outside world. Furthermore, it is essential to maintain ties with family and friends in the origin country (Madianou & Miller, 2011; Parreñas & Kantachote, 2021).

Parreñas and Kantachote (2021) found that most employers do not bar domestic workers from access to cellular phones, but some employers do. Cheros, a 37-year-old Filipina domestic worker, shared how she had difficulty communicating with her family in the Philippines:

> For two years, I did not have a day off, and for two years, I did not have a handy phone. So I would just write letters to the Philippines once in a while or sometimes I will ask my employer if I can call the Philippines and they can just charge me the bill when it comes. So I will call sometimes. That was very expensive. (p. 155)

In addition to struggling to maintain transnational ties with family back home, not allowing migrant domestic workers access to a cellular phone also limits the workers' ability to use various internet platforms and social media, such as Facebook, TikTok, and Instagram. These platforms contain valuable information that can help migrant workers express their identity and navigate their lives, such as worker rights and social justice (Abidin, 2020; Kaur-Gill, 2023; Ueno & Belanger, 2019).

Nevertheless, this is not to say that migrant domestic workers have unlimited freedom to express themselves on TikTok. In Crenshaw's (1991, 2017) work on oppression and marginalization, intersectionality is emphasized as experiences and lives that cannot be considered separate identities of class, gender, and race. Instead, those identities overlap and intersect, depending on the context and situation. This is also the case for migrant domestic workers. Their social identity as women from a lower social status and ethnic, national, race, and gender identities are intentionally erased from mainstream audiences. Furthermore, because migrant domestic workers are known to depend on their employers for legal residency (Parreñas et al., 2021), some employers use their status to act as legal guardians in screening the types of content that the workers can create on TikTok. The workers' cellular phone usage is also often limited to after work hours. This potentially means that domestic workers may be delayed in receiving the latest news regarding their working conditions and/or other relevant issues.

Digital (Im)Mobility and Social Justice

With the smartphones of domestic workers embedded in constraining employment conditions, we examine critically how domestic workers use TikTok for social justice via self-actualization and community building. It is important to recognize that multiple gatekeepers are in operation in the regulation of migrant domestic workers and their social media use. In addition to Singapore's context of segregation of domestic workers, social media adds to these restrictions by starkly stripping identity politics hashtagging down to a market-ready representational optics aligned with the commercial agendas of corporate and state regulations. Leung (2020) critiques the current limitations of the digital divide literature as failing to recognize the complexity of the digital mobilities of migrants that goes beyond infrastructural challenges and simplistic assumptions of digital literacy as inclusion and exclusion. Whereas Leung's (2020) analysis addresses refugees and the digital divide, our research adds to the author's argument on the complexities of citizen and noncitizen in shaping and exclusion and temporariness in the host country. These factors are key threads for understanding migrants' use of social media applications such as TikTok. Fundamentally, the pervasive fear of surveillance and threats, and the regulations and limitations of the platform, influences how they use and produce content on social media in (im)mobile ways. Wallis (2018) notably references another layer of gatekeeping in the communicative empowerment of domestic workers through nongovernmental organizations that perpetuate a top-down rather than a bottom-up engagement with social media activism.

The multiple limitations faced by subaltern social media users offer an opportunity to interrogate broader discussion on social media and the real possibilities of using TikTok to facilitate social justice. The affordances of an application as enabling mobilities of subaltern groups must engage the sociopolitical context of migrant (im)mobilities. Precarious migrant workers' smartphone use operates within a context of surveillance, threats, and employer guidelines. Employer guidelines include giving the worker access to a Wi-Fi service at home and phone confiscation. Nevertheless, these users are aspiring influencers—which offers a productive way to revise the unexamined liberal definitions that limit current studies of platforms, content creators, influencers, and users. TikTok users who seek visibility and positive feedback must adapt to its standards, rules, and norms.

TikTok's rigid self-government cannot contest the neoliberal state of precarity and unfree indenture. However, amid hyper(in)visibility, a lack of human rights, and conditions of soft violence such as regulated phone use, domestic worker TikTok content that asserts identities such as "hardworking," "sexy," "desirable," or "morally proper" can be seen as a subversive form of self-authorship. Subaltern migrants are agentically but subversively documenting spaces to posture alternative ways of micro-resistance that might be captured through standard definitions of social justice activism. These are significant moments of visibility ruptures amid the narrow spaces for platforming voice.

Domestic workers who are TikTok users generate popular accounts whose visibility, attention, and desirability can be considered in this context as radical social justice. Chee's (2023) study of domestic workers in the Gulf who use TikTok identifies their content as stories of counterconduct, where they recognize how they are controlled and regulated, responding to their subjugation through resistive strategies. Through humor and play, Chee examines how domestic workers resist by making visible their private work conditions in public ways.

Conclusion and Future Directions

This chapter breaks down the various intersections of oppression—economic, social, and commercial—that interact to limit TikTok participation for social justice by migrant domestic workers, a subaltern group residing in an illiberal host country. From their subjugation through indentured practices of hire to how the platform is structured for capitalistic intent, the migrant domestic worker is embedded in multiple systems of marginalization that restrict the opportunity for social media participation, particularly for social justice intent. Thus, a techno-optimistic reading of social media platforms for marginalized groups remains unresponsive to the tiers of structural oppression that migrant domestic workers navigate as lived experience. Future research on social media for social justice among groups facing subalternity must engage in critically documenting the limits in their production of subversive content. Asking domestic workers what they cannot produce on social media, the ways in which they cannot participate on the platform (Zapata, 2018), and what filtering decisions factor into their content production are important insights to critically engaging the literature on digital literacy and social media empowerment for failing to factor in the account of the broader implications of structural oppression as limiting social justice activism on social media by subaltern groups.

References

Abidin, C. (2020). Mapping internet celebrity on TikTok: Exploring attention economies and visibility labours. *Cultural Science Journal*, *12*(1), 77–103.

Apple. (n.d.). *App Store preview: TikTok*. https://apps.apple.com/us/app/tiktok/id835599320

Bal, S. C. (2015). Dealing with deportability: Deportation laws and the political personhood of temporary migrant workers in Singapore. *Asian Journal of Law and Society*, *2*(2), 267–284.

Bhattacharyya, G. (2018). *Rethinking racial capitalism: Questions of reproduction and survival*. Rowman & Littlefield.

Bruns, A. (2008). *Blogs, Wikipedia, Second Life, and beyond: From production to produsage* (Vol. 45). Peter Lang.

Catedral, L. (2022). (Re)chronotopizing the pandemic: Migrant domestic workers' calls for social change. *Language, Culture and Society*, *4*(2), 136–161.

Chacko, E., & Price, M. (2021). (Un)settled sojourners in cities: The scalar and temporal dimensions of migrant precarity. *Journal of Ethnic and Migration Studies*, *47*(20), 4597–4614.

Chee, L. (2023). Play and counter-conduct: Migrant domestic workers on TikTok. *Global Society*, *37*(4), 593–617.

Crenshaw, K. (1991). Mapping the margins: Intersectionality, identity politics, and violence against women of color. *Stanford Law Review*, *43*(6), 1241–1299.

Crenshaw, K. (2017). *On intersectionality: Essential writings*. New Press.

Deleuze, G. (1994). *Difference and repetition*. Columbia University Press.

Dutta, M. J. (2018). Culturally centering social change communication: Subaltern critiques of, resistance to, and reimagination of development. *Journal of Multicultural Discourses*, *13*(2), 87–104.

Dutta, M. J. (2020). COVID-19, authoritarian neoliberalism, and precarious migrant work in Singapore: Structural violence and communicative inequality. *Frontiers in Communication*, *5*, Article 58.

Dutta, M. J., & Kaur-Gill, S. (2018). Precarities of migrant work in Singapore: Migration, (im)mobility, and neoliberal governmentality. *International Journal of Communication*, 12, 4066–4084.

Fernandez, B. (2018). Health inequities faced by Ethiopian migrant domestic workers in Lebanon. *Health & Place*, *50*, 154–161.

Foreign love turns fatal in Singapore. (2012, March 9). *The New Paper*.

Fraser, N. (1994). Rethinking the public sphere: A contribution to the critique of actually existing democracy. In H. A. Giroux & P. McLaren (Eds.), *Between borders* (pp. 74–98). Routledge.

Gimenez, M. E. (2019). Capitalist social reproduction. In M. Vidal, T. Smith, T. Rotta, & P. Prew (Eds.), *The Oxford handbook of Karl Marx*. Oxford University Press.

Habermas, J. (1991). *The structural transformation of the public sphere: An inquiry into a category of bourgeois society*. MIT press.

Jaramillo-Dent, D., Contreras-Pulido, P., & Pérez-Rodríguez, A. (2022). Immigrant influencers on TikTok: Diverse microcelebrity profiles and algorithmic (in)visibility. *Media and Communication*, *10*(1).

Johnson, A., & Boylorn, R. M. (2015). Digital media and the politics of intersectional queer hyper/in/visibility in between women. *Liminalities*, *11*(1).

Kandilige, L., Teye, J. K., Setrana, M., & Badasu, D. M. (2023). 'They'd beat us with whatever is available to them': Exploitation and abuse of Ghanaian domestic workers in the Middle East. *International Migration, 61*(4), 240–256.

Kaur-Gill, S. (2020). The COVID-19 pandemic and outbreak inequality: Mainstream reporting of Singapore's migrant workers in the margins. *Frontiers in Communication, 5*.

Kaur-Gill, S. (2023). The cultural customization of TikTok: Subaltern migrant workers and their digital cultures. *Media International Australia*, *186*(1), 29–47.

Kaur-Gill, S., & Dutta, M. J. (2023). The COVID-19 pandemic and precarious migrants: An outbreak of inequality. In S. Kaur-Gill & M. J. Dutta (Eds.), *Migrants and the COVID-19 pandemic: Communication, inequality, and transformation* (pp. 1–25). Palgrave Macmillan.

Kaur-Gill, S., Pandi, A. R., & Dutta, M. J. (2021). Singapore's national discourse on foreign domestic workers: Exploring perceptions of the margins. *Journalism*, *22*(12), 2991–3012.

Kitchin, R. (2014). *The data revolution: Big data, open data, data infrastructures and their consequences*. SAGE.

Lay, B. (2021, May 29). Some domestic workers in S'pore made to work on off days for no pay when they can't go out this Phase 2 (Heightened Alert). *Mothership*. https://mothership.sg/2021/05/maids-work-off-days-phase-2-heightened-alert

Leung, L. (2020). *Digital divides*. SAGE.

Lim, E. (2021). Personal identity economics: Facebook and the distortion of identity politics. *Social Media+ Society*, *7*(2). https://doi.org/10.1177/20563051211017492

Lim, E., Kantachote, K., Suwana, F., & Kaur-Gill, S. (2022, June 1-2). *Glocalization in Southeast Asia: the Advantages and Limitations of Platform-Dependent Activism*. [Conference Presentation] Global Perspectives on Platforms and Cultural Production. University of Amsterdam.

Lim, N., & Paul, A. M. (2021). Stigma on a spectrum: Differentiated stigmatization of migrant domestic workers' romantic relationships in Singapore. *Gender, Place & Culture*, *28*(1), 22–44.

Madianou, M., & Daniel, M. (2011). Mobile phone parenting: Reconfiguring relationships between Filipina migrant mothers and their left-behind children. *New Media & Society*, *13*(3), 457–470.

Ministry of Manpower. (2009, September 25). *Obligations of employers of foreign workers tweaked* [Press release]. https://www.mom.gov.sg/newsroom/press-releases/2009/obligations-of-employers-of-foreign-workers-tweaked Privacy

Ministry of Manpower. (2015). *Foreign Domestic Worker Study 2015: Report on findings*. https://www.mom.gov.sg/~/media/mom/documents/statistics-publications/fdw-study-2015.pdf

Noble, S. U. (2018). Algorithms of oppression. In *Algorithms of oppression: How search engines reinforce racism* (pp. 171–182). New York University Press.

Pande, A. (2013). "The paper that you have in your hand is my freedom": Migrant and the sponsorship (Kafala) system in Lebanon. *International Migration Review*, *47*(2), .

Pandi, R. A. (2023). *Indonesian domestic workers in Malaysia during the COVID-19 pandemic*. In S. Kaur-Gill & M. J. Dutta (Eds.), *Migrants and the COVID-19 pandemic: Communication, inequality, and transformation* (pp. 131–148). Palgrave Macmillan.

Parreñas, R. (2015). *Servants of globalization* (2nd ed.). Stanford University Press.

Parreñas, R. S., & Kantachote, K. (2021). Negotiating indenture: Migrant domestic work and temporary labor migration in Singapore. In C. S. Ramirez, S. M. Falcon, J. Poblete, S. C. McKay, & F. A. Schaeffer (Eds.), *Precarity and belonging* (pp. 145–160). Rutgers University Press.

Parreñas, R. S., Kantachote, K., & Silvey, R. (2021). Soft violence: Migrant domestic worker precarity and the management of unfree labour in Singapore. *Journal of Ethnic and Migration Studies, 47*(20), 4671–4687.

Platt, M. (2015). Foreign domestic workers in Singapore: Historical and contemporary reflections on the colonial politics of intimacy. In V. K. Haskins & C. Lowrie (Eds.), *Colonization and domestic service: Historical and contemporary perspectives* (pp. 131–147). Routledge.

Poell, T., Nieborg, D. B., & Duffy, B. E. (2022). *Platforms and cultural production*. Wiley.

Rabindran, A. S. (2023). The subaltern Dalit counterpublic: Implications for a social media age. *Contemporary Voice of Dalit, 15*(2), 248–252.

Sellar, S., & Thompson, G. (2016). The becoming-statistic: Information ontologies and computerized adaptive testing in education. *Cultural Studies ↔ Critical Methodologies, 16*(5), 491–501.

Sur, P. (2020). Under India's caste system, Dalits are considered untouchable. The coronavirus is intensifying that slur. *CNN*, April 16. https://www.google.com/amp/s/amp.cnn.com/cnn/2020/04/15/asia/india-coronavirus-lower-castes-hnk-intl

Thakur, A. K. (2020). New media and the Dalit counter-public sphere. *Television & New Media, 21*(4), 360–375.

Tufekci, Z. (2018). How social media took us from Tahrir Square to Donald Trump. MIT Technology Review, *14*, 18.

Ueno, K., & Belanger, D. (2019). in Singapore. *Tokyo Women's Christian University Annals of Sociology, 7*, .

Wallis, C. (2018). Domestic workers and the affective dimensions of communicative empowerment. *Communication Culture & Critique, 11*(2), 213–230.

Weekly day off for domestic workers. (2012, March 12). *The New Paper*.

Yeoh, B. S., Goh, C., & Wee, K. (2020). Social protection for migrant domestic workers in Singapore: International conventions, the law, and civil society action. *American Behavioral Scientist, 64*(6), 841–858.

Zapata, D. B. (2018). Social change methodologies. In M. J. Dutta & D. B. Zapata (Eds.), *Communicating for social change: Meaning, power, and resistance* (p. 173). Palgrave Macmillan.

Zulli, D., & Zulli, D. J. (2022). Extending the internet meme: Conceptualizing technological mimesis and imitation publics on the TikTok platform. *New Media & Society, 24*(8), 1872–1890.

Media and Mental Health Interventions Among Migrants: Addressing the Disparities

Rukhsana Ahmed *and* Seulgi Park

The use of media for public health promotion is well-documented (Institute of Medicine, 2002; World Health Organization [WHO], 2022). Particularly, there has been an increased use of digital technologies such as social media for health purposes, including among migrant groups. Nonetheless, there is a lack of use of these media platforms for promoting migrant health (Ahmed, 2023; Goldsmith et al., 2022; Hong et al., 2021). Media- and technology-based interventions, which involve the delivery of interventions predominantly via "computer-based and Web-based interventions, text messaging, interactive voice recognition, smartphone apps, and emerging technologies" (Tofighi et al., 2018, p. 2), are considered promising approaches to mental health promotion for migrants (Abtahi et al., 2023; El-Haj-Mohamad et al., 2022). However, the efficacy of these digital interventions has yet to be accurately measured; accordingly, further research is deemed necessary to evaluate the effectiveness of using media- and technology-based interventions for addressing the mental health needs of migrants (Abtahi et al., 2023; Alegría et al., 2021; El-Haj-Mohamad et al., 2022; Kruzan et al., 2022).

Worldwide, there are approximately 1 billion migrants, including international migrants (281 million), internally displaced (48 million), refugees (26.4 million), and asylum seekers (4.1 million) (WHO, n.d.). This high-need population is at greater risk of facing a wide variety of health issues, including mental health disorders. In this chapter, we use the term *migrant* as defined by the International Organization for Migration (Sironi et al., 2019) for its comprehensive treatment of different categories of people such as migrant workers, immigrants, and refugees:

> An umbrella term, not defined under international law, reflecting the common lay understanding of a person who moves away from his or her place of usual residence, whether within a country or across an international border, temporarily or permanently, and for a variety of reasons.

Migrants are an understudied and underserved population group who are disproportionately affected by higher risk for mental illness. In this chapter, we review and synthesize the findings from media- and technology-based mental health interventions on migrant populations. Considering that migrants are faced with additional stressors stemming from migration and that they have barriers to seek mental health care, media- and technology-based interventions have great potential for improving the mental health of migrants. However, the empirical evidence is limited to date, with a need for additional rigorous studies, especially with migrant groups, to further build the evidence base.

Migration often entails multiple stressors, such as language and culture differences, homesickness, discrimination, and economic hardships, that can affect the mental health of migrants over time after settling in a new country (Dow, 2011). Migrant groups are more likely to experience higher rates of post-traumatic stress disorder (PTSD), anxiety, and depressive disorders because of their exposure to emotional and psychological trauma during all stages of the migration process: pre-migration, migration, and post-migration (WHO, 2021). This higher burden of mental health disorders is further heightened by disparities in access to and utilization of mental health care among migrants (Chiarenza et al., 2019; Gadermann et al., 2022), especially during the COVID-19 pandemic (Parenteau et al., 2023). Mental health disparities in access to and utilization of mental health services already exist across race, economic status, and immigration status in the United States (Derr, 2016; Sarría-Santamera et al., 2016), and these may have been exacerbated by blame and stigma for a certain racial or ethnic group fueled by the COVID-19 pandemic (Croucher et al., 2020).

One promising solution to mental health disparities is the utilization of technology and media, especially new media, for interventions. Migrants' access to and use of media and information and communication technology (ICT) have been studied as a way to promote integration, especially in recent years (Karimi et al., 2022). Studies found that social media allow migrants to maintain their identity and networking in the host country (Smets, 2018). In addition to these social support and networking aspects, migrants also use new media and technology as an important source of health information (Pottie et al., 2020). For example, one review found that migrants relied on social media such as WeChat and WhatsApp for important and fast-evolving health information, such as COVID-19 vaccine information (Goldsmith et al., 2022). Scholars have argued that ICT and media can be effective tools for improving the mental health of migrants (Bock et al., 2020).

Although there is limited evidence on interventions to address mental health problems among migrants in general, there is a relative lack of research particularly on the role of media and technology interventions to improve mental health of migrants. This lack of evidence makes it difficult to ensure mental health needs are met by delivering appropriate, effective, and safe care for these marginalized groups. Accordingly, this chapter performs a systematic review of recent literature to (a) summarize evidence on media- and technology-based mental health interventions for migrant groups and (b) provide evidence-informed recommendations to use new media as a tool to eliminate mental health disparities among migrants. Here, our focus is on media- and technology-based mental health interventions, including interventions delivered through media or technology such as Web pages, mobile apps, video calls, and text messages.

Review of the Literature on Migrants, Mental Health, and Media Interventions

For this systematic review, we performed a literature search in four databases: PubMed, CINAHL Plus, PsycInfo, and Web of Science. The keyword combinations were "migrant or immigrant" AND "mental health, mental illness, mental disorder, mental disease, mental problem, psychol* health, psychol* illness, or psycho* disorder" AND "media, technology, web, internet, online, or digital" AND "intervention." We limited the search to peer-reviewed journal articles published in English. We also excluded review articles, editorials, commentaries, or study protocols. The reviewed articles included randomized clinical trials (RCTs); non-randomized experimental studies; evaluations for feasibility, development, acceptability, or implementation of interventions; or descriptive studies. From 694 articles identified from the electronic searches, 21 articles were selected as the final pool of this review after screening based on the titles and abstracts. In order to be included in this review, studies needed to have mental health interventions that are based on mass media (e.g., television or radio), new media (e.g., social media), or technology (e.g., Web pages on the internet or mobile apps) targeted for migrants. The search and screening process is illustrated in Figure 23.1.

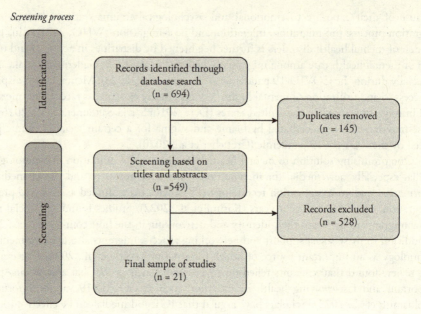

Screening process

Identification

Records identified through database search (n = 694)

Duplicates removed (n = 145)

Screening

Screening based on titles and abstracts (n =549)

Records excluded (n = 528)

Final sample of studies (n = 21)

Figure 23.1 Screening process.

Key information such as intervention types, target populations, target mental health issue, effect size, and summary of results was extracted from the final pool of the studies to allow for identification of common categories and comparison of the results. The 21 studies were independently reviewed by the two researchers. The data in this review were synthesized using Popay et al.'s (2006) narrative synthesis approach, allowing the researchers to combine the results from studies with different research designs.

Overall, there was a small number of articles that met the inclusion criteria of this systematic review, indicating the lack of media- and technology-based interventions for mental health of immigrants and refugees. A total of 21 articles were reviewed, which included 6 RCTs; 10 articles about intervention evaluation studies such as feasibility, implementation, or acceptability evaluation of interventions (Burchert et al., 2019; Eylem et al., 2021; Heilemann et al., 2017; Liem et al., 2022; Lindegaard et al., 2022; Lindegaard, Kashoush, et al., 2021; Nygren et al., 2018; Ornelas et al., 2022; Sabri et al., 2021; Shala et al., 2020); 4 articles about pilot or exploratory experiments for preliminary effectiveness of an intervention (García et al., 2019; Lindegaard, Seaton, et al., 2021; Orang et al., 2023; Reich et al., 2021); and 1 article that was based on a survey about a hypothetical intervention to assess factors related to the willingness to use the intervention (Hall et al., 2018).

Although the search was not limited to any set period of time, the publication years of the reviewed articles clearly show emerging scholarship in this area: 86% of the reviewed articles (*n* = 18) were published between 2018 and 2022, and 72% (*n* = 13) of these were published between 2020 and 2022. This could reflect that media- and especially technology-based interventions are more novel approaches to mental health promotion for migrants. In terms of methodology, quantitative studies accounted for more than half (57%, *n* = 12), whereas mixed-methods studies accounted for one-third of the reviewed pool (33%, *n* = 7). Only 2 studies employed qualitative methodology such as focus-group discussions or in-depth interviews.

Many studies targeted immigrants (n = 15), whereas a smaller number of studies targeted refugees (n = 6). For some interventions, subgroups of immigrants were defined by using language groups such as Arabic, Farsi, Dari, or Tamil (Lindegaard et al., 2022; Lindegaard, Kashoush, et al., 2021; Lindegaard, Seaton, et al., 2021, Nickerson et al., 2020). Other interventions targeted immigrants or refugees with certain national backgrounds, such as Greek- or Italian-born immigrants, Filipino workers, or Turkish immigrants (Eylem et al., 2021; Hall et al., 2018; Ince et al., 2013; Kiropoulos et al., 2011), or broader racial/ethnic backgrounds such as Black immigrant women or Latina women (Ornelas et al., 2022; Sabri et al., 2021). A few studies did not distinguish subgroups of immigrants or refugees but, rather, described their participants as immigrants or refugees from various backgrounds (García et al., 2019; Orang et al., 2023). In terms of geographical locations, most of the studies were based in European countries such as Germany, Sweden, or Switzerland (n = 13), whereas a few were in other regions (3 in the United States, 2 in Australia, 1 in Lebanon, and 2 in China).

Types of Media-Based Mental Health Interventions for Migrants

Many interventions were designed to address mental health issues including depression, anxiety, perceived stress or post-traumatic stress, insomnia, quality of life or subjective well-being, stigma, and self-efficacy of seeking help. Among these, depression and anxiety were the most frequently targeted mental health issues in the reviewed articles. Depression or depressive symptoms were measured as a primary outcome by the Patient Health Questionnaire–9, the Beck Depression Inventory–II, or the Center for Epidemiologic Studies Depression Scale. Anxiety was measured in many studies as a primary or secondary outcome by using the General Anxiety Disorder–7. Post-traumatic stress was measured by the Posttraumatic Diagnostic Scale for DSM-5, the Impact of Event Scale–Revised, or the PTSD Checklist for DSM-5. Perceived stress was measured by the Perceived Stress Scale (PSS 10 or PSS 14).

Interventions included internet-based cognitive–behavioral therapy (ICBT) delivered through websites or mobile apps, a multilingual online website, text messages, or storytelling-based therapy. ICBT was most often used as a mental health intervention for immigrants and refugees (Burchert et al., 2019; Cuijpers et al., 2022; Eylem et al., 2021; Liem et al., 2022; Lindegaard et al., 2022; Lindegaard, Kashoush, et al., 2021; Lindegaard, Seaton, et al., 2021; Nygren et al., 2018, 2019; Shala et al., 2020). Three of the studies adapted Step-by-Step, a Web-based mental health intervention developed by WHO, for their target population (Burchert et al., 2019; Cuijpers et al., 2022; Shala et al., 2020). Step-by-Step was designed as a modular intervention consisting of five story sessions to deliver educational narratives and interactive exercises on CBT techniques such as behavioral activation, psychoeducation, stress management, increasing social support, and relapse prevention (Carswell et al., 2018). Three of the studies that employed Step-by-Step adapted the narratives and fictional characters to tailor to cultural orientations of the target population (Burchert et al., 2019; Cuijpers et al., 2022; Shala et al., 2020).

Other ICBT interventions used similar approaches in that they had modular sessions of written or video narratives and interactive exercises. For example, Lindegaard et al. (Lindegaard et al., 2022; Lindegaard, Kashoush, et al., 2021; Lindegaard, Seaton, et al., 2021) used the design of the self-help material developed by Nygren et al. (2018, 2019) and adapted it to the guided intervention format. Interventions in both research groups were based on sessions presenting CBT principles and exercises for mental health issues such as depression, anxiety, post-traumatic stress, and insomnia. Although interventions commonly included written materials (e.g., Lindegaard et al., 2022; Lindegaard, Kashoush, et al., 2021), interactive media components such as video presentations (Heilmann et al., 2017; Nygren et al., 2018, 2019) or games and exercises (Röhr et al., 2021) were also often used as part of the interventions.

Whereas the above interventions were designed to be delivered mainly through online or mobile platforms, some other interventions were reliant on face-to-face components such as therapy sessions with counselors (García et al., 2019; Ornelas et al., 2022; Orang et al., 2023). In García et al. (2019), face-to-face therapy was provided to both intervention and control groups, and the intervention group received four daily text messages from an automatic system during the intervention period. Orang et al. (2023) also provided face-to-face therapy sessions of value-based counseling (VBC) to migrants and refugees while outcomes were compared depending on the modality of delivery. The intervention group received VBC through an online platform for video-chat calls with a certified counselor accessed on a computer, tablet, or smartphone, whereas the control group received VBC in person. Last, Ornelas et al. (2022) compared intervention outcomes depending on the online and in-person delivery of intervention because they had to adapt their intervention originally designed for in-person delivery to online Zoom sessions due to the COVID-19 pandemic.

Effectiveness of Media-Based Interventions in Improving Migrant Mental Health Disparities

Most RCTs (n = 6) had mobile (n = 2) or Web-based interventions (n = 4) for a relatively short intervention period (intervention ranging from 1 hour to 8 weeks and follow-up assessment at 1 week to 11 months). Five RCTs were based on a modular online program of evidence-based techniques such as CBT[1], mindfulness, or psychoeducation (Cuijpers et al., 2022; Ince et al., 2013; Nickerson et al., 2020; Nygren, 2019; Röhr et al., 2021), whereas 1 RCT was conducted on a multicultural online information on depression (MIDonline; Kiropoulos et al., 2011).

Overall, the interventions were effective in improving mental health of immigrants or refugees, with moderate to large effect sizes. For depression, effect sizes (Cohen's d) of the interventions ranged from 0.48 to 1.27 (Cuijpers et al., 2022; Ince et al., 2013; Nygren et al., 2019). Online-based intervention was also effective in reducing self-stigma for PTSD and help-seeking compared to the wait-listed control group (Nickerson et al., 2020). However, one RCT reported no significant group differences in PTSD symptoms between the group of Syrian refugees who accessed a CBT-based self-help smartphone app and the control group who accessed psychoeducation reading materials for 4 weeks (Röhr et al., 2021).

Challenges and Limitations in Designing and Implementing Media-Based Mental Health Interventions for Migrants

Some common issues related to feasibility, development, and implementation of interventions targeting immigrants or refugees were discussed in the reviewed articles. One such issue was the difficulty in recruiting and consequent small sample sizes. Although some studies conducted power analysis for significant between-group effects and were able to obtain a sufficient sample size (e.g., Cuijpers et al., 2022; Nygren et al., 2019; Nickerson et al., 2020; Kiropoulos et al., 2011), other studies commonly mentioned difficulty in recruiting the eligible sample for their studies (Eylem et al., 2021; Ince et al., 2013; Lindegaard et al., 2022; Lindegaard,

---

[1] Cognitive–behavioral therapy is the most common method of psychotherapy, combining the two forms of therapy—cognitive therapy and behavioral therapy. Based on the principle that a person's thoughts, feelings, and behavior are interconnected, CBT aims for treatment by changing the way the person thinks or their thought patterns and developing coping strategies.

Kashoush, et al., 2021). Difficulty in recruitment often limited statistical analysis or resulted in underpowered findings (Ince et al., 2013; Nickerson et al., 2020).

Because the interventions were internet-based or mobile-based, attrition and nonadherence were generally high in the reviewed articles. Attrition was as high as 62% in one study (Ince et al., 2013). Nygren et al. (2019) reported attrition rates of 20% in the treatment group and 28% for the whole sample, which, according to a meta-analysis, are similar to those of other ICBT interventions (Fernandez et al., 2015). Studies often accounted for high attrition in recruiting their sample, which makes it all the more important to recruit as a large a sample as possible.

In general, studies often used some type of guide for the intervention, which ranged from regular feedback of trained psychologists or untrained "coaches" to phone calls, text message reminders, or even computerized algorithms for automatic feedback. One study that used the self-management approach without guidance or support reported no significant differences between the treatment and control groups in their primary and secondary outcomes, such as post-traumatic stress, anxiety, or somatic symptoms (Röhr et al., 2021).

Many studies reported that they conducted cultural adaptation of their intervention. The most common way to adapt the intervention was to translate the material into the language used by the target population and adapt the content of the intervention to represent cultural backgrounds. For example, ICBT interventions with fictional narratives and characters were adapted by using cultural cases or examples (Eylem et al., 2021; Ince et al., 2013). A few studies reported deep structure cultural adaptation by incorporating cultural beliefs or values (Reich et al., 2021; Shala et al., 2020). However, in most cases, cultural adaptation was limited to the surface structure such as linguistic adaptation or the use of cultural cases and examples.

Despite the many benefits of technology-based interventions, attrition of these interventions has been an issue regardless of target conditions (Linardon & Fuller-Tyszkiewicz, 2020; Meyerowitz-Katz et al., 2020). Moreover, attrition in mental health care interventions has been particularly high compared to that in interventions in other medical fields (Mitchell & Selmes, 2007). RCTs reviewed in this chapter also reported overall high attrition rates, thus highlighting the need for effective strategies to address this issue (e.g., Ince et al., 2013; Nygren et al., 2019). One of the ways to reduce attrition rates is to employ guided interventions (Baumeister et al., 2014). Research shows that mobile-based interventions involving community health workers (CHWs) are effective, although the cultural relevance of interventions and training CHWs present challenges (Early et al., 2019). CHWs can potentially serve as guides to technology- and media-based interventions and thus reduce attrition and contribute to culturally relevant interventions.

Considerations for Future Research on Media-Based Interventions for Migrant Mental Health

As found in past systematic reviews of internet- or new media-based mental health interventions (Kruzan et al., 2022; Rathbone & Prescott, 2017), this systematic review found that technology- and media-based interventions were generally effective for improving mental health of migrants. RCTs reported overall significant improvement of mental health outcomes, and pilot or preliminary intervention studies also reported generally positive results. Studies on the development or implementation of mental health interventions for this population provided valuable insights and directions for future research.

Although internet- and mobile-based interventions have great potential for the prevention and treatment of mental health disorders, the efficacy of these interventions for mental health promotion across different population groups remains less known (Mor et al., 2021; Sander et al., 2016). This lack of evidence has important implications for the digital divide that disproportionately affects marginalized groups (e.g., women, older adults, and ethnic minorities) and causes inequality in access to technology and related skills (Hardy et al., 2022). The reviewed studies provided valuable insights into this issue. Some studies mentioned technical barriers such as inconsistent signal reception, having to rely on free Wi-Fi spots for connectivity, and not owning a private device but sharing it with family members (García et al., 2019; Liem et al., 2022). A closer examination of the usage patterns of mobile or internet devices among the target migrant group, especially in the context of private and potentially taboo topic such as mental health, should precede the implementation of interventions to address any potential inequalities for this marginalized group.

In addition to technical barriers, studies recognized barriers stemming from the lack of mental health literacy or digital literacy (Burchert et al., 2019; Eylem et al., 2021; Liem et al., 2022; Nygren et al., 2018). However, mental health literacy or digital literacy was rarely incorporated as a variable in these studies. Nor did the studies explicitly discuss how they addressed the issue of low mental health literacy or digital literacy. Kiropoulos and colleagues (2011) were the only researchers who measured mental health literacy of the sample in their study. Future research should incorporate mental health literacy or digital health literacy in the design of interventions in order to maximize their effectiveness.

Past research underscored cultural adaptation of internet-based or mobile-based interventions as a promising approach to increase their acceptance and effectiveness (Spanhel et al., 2021). Yet, there is a dearth of evidence on the cultural adaptation of these interventions (Shala et al., 2020) and limited guidelines for culturally adapting them (Spanhel et al., 2021). An encouraging finding was that most reviewed studies reported using focus group interviews with the target population or community advisory boards for cultural adaptation of their interventions (e.g., Heilmann et al., 2017; Lindegaard, Kashoush, et al., 2021; Nygren et al., 2018; Röhr et al., 2021; Sabri et al., 2021; Shala et al., 2020). The article by Shala et al. (2020) specifically focused on cultural adaptation of an intervention, reporting surface level as well as deep structure level topics for adaptation based on survey and focus group discussion results, whereas many others included cultural adaptation as part of feasibility testing or development of an intervention. The use of focus group interviews or community advisory boards is consistent with what previous research recommends for not only cultural adaptation but also ensuring research ethics and the safety of the participants (Mugenyi et al., 2021; Spanhel et al., 2021). However, some qualitative findings revealed that cultural adaptation (e.g., the use of culturally appropriate cases in the intervention) should be approached carefully (Eylem et al., 2021). If not well designed, cultural references can contribute to attrition or nonadherence because participants may believe that the intervention is not relevant to them (Lindegaard, Seaton, et al., 2021; Eylem et al., 2021). When an intervention is designed to target a language group (e.g., Arabic speaking or Spanish speaking) whose members are from diverse countries, this makes it even more difficult to implement cultural adaptations (Lindegaard, Kashoush, et al., 2021; Lindegaard, Seaton, et al., 2021; Nygren et al., 2018). Future research should carefully consider the trade-off between making an intervention relevant to a specific language group (e.g., Levantine Arabic for Syrian refugees [Burchert et al., 2019]) and designing an intervention accessible for more participants (e.g., aiming for Arabic translation that can be recognizable by a wide range of participants from different backgrounds [Lindegaard, Kashoush, et al., 2021]).

Conclusion

Evidence-based, rigorously evaluated, culturally competent interventions can effectively address migrant mental health needs. The findings suggest that media- and technology-based mental health interventions are effective for improving a range of migrant mental health outcomes and improving mental health disparities among migrant groups. Partnerships are important: Health care practitioners and service providers serving migrant groups in diverse settings can help implement culturally tailored, internet- and mobile-based mental health interventions to achieve health equity and social justice for migrants. Migrants with mental illnesses come from diverse backgrounds and cultures. They have unique and complex mental health needs and thus may not experience improvement in outcomes by a single intervention at the same intensity level. Nevertheless, internet- and mobile-based mental health interventions can be used across various settings, such as health care and social service organizations serving migrants. These interventions can also benefit migrant groups which are not seeking services and can help practitioners provide more culturally informed services. With proper attention to attrition and cultural adaptation, media- and technology-based interventions can greatly contribute to improving the mental health of migrants and reducing disparities among them. Particularly, we advocate for co-designing these interventions, involving the intended user population—in this case, members of migrant groups. Planning and implementing media- and technology-based mental health interventions together can help eliminate oppressive structural barriers associated with the larger social context of mental health care delivery and facilitate digital access for these populations to achieve social justice in mental health care (Hynie et al., 2023).

References

Abtahi, Z., Potocky, M., Eizadyar, Z., Burke, S. L., & Fava, N. M. (2023). Digital interventions for the mental health and well-being of international migrants: A systematic review. *Research on Social Work Practice, 33*(5), 518–529. https://doi.org/10.1177/10497315221118854

Ahmed, R. (2023). Social media: Migrant health (invited). In E. Y. Ho, C. L. Bylund, J. C. M. van Weert, I. Basnyat, N. Bol, & M. Dean (Eds.), *The international encyclopedia of health communication*. Wileyhttps://doi.org/10.1002/9781119678816.iehc0633

Alegría, M., Yip, T., Marks, A., Juang, L., Cohen, L., & Cuervo-Torello, F. (2021). Editorial: Improving mental health for immigrant populations. *Frontiers in Psychiatry, 12*, Article 785137. https://doi.org/10.3389/fpsyt.2021.785137

Baumeister, H., Reichler, L., Munzinger, M., & Lin, J. (2014). The impact of guidance on internet-based mental health interventions: A systematic review. *Internet Interventions, 1*(4), 205–215. https://doi.org/10.1016/j.invent.2014.08.003

Bock, J. G., Haque, Z., & McMahon, K. A. (2020). Displaced and dismayed: How ICTs are helping refugees and migrants, and how we can do better. *Information Technology for Development, 26*(4), 670–691. https://doi.org/10.1080/02681102.2020.1727827

Burchert, S., Alkneme, M. S., Bird, M., Carswell, K., Cuijpers, P., Hansen, P., Heim, E., Harper Shehadeh, M., Sijbrandij, M., Van't Hof, E., & Knaevelsrud, C. (2019). User-centered app adaptation of a low-intensity e-mental health intervention for Syrian refugees. *Frontiers in Psychiatry, 9*, Article 663. https://doi.org/10.3389/fpsyt.2018.00663

Carswell, K., Harper-Shehadeh, M., Watts, S., Van't Hof, E., Abi Ramia, J., Heim, E., Wenger, A., & van Ommeren, M. (2018). Step-by-Step: A new WHO digital mental health intervention for depression. *mHealth, 4*, Article 34. https://doi.org/10.21037/mhealth.2018.08.01

Chiarenza, A., Dauvrin, M., Chiesa, V., Baatout, S., & Verrept, H. (2019). Supporting access to healthcare for refugees and migrants in European countries under particular migratory pressure. *BMC Health Services Research, 19*(1), Article 513. https://doi.org/10.1186/s12913-019-4353-1

Croucher, S. M., Nguyen, T., & Rahmani, D. (2020). Prejudice toward Asian Americans in the Covid-19 pandemic: The effects of social media use in the United States. *Frontiers in Communication, 5*, Article 39. https://doi.org/10.3389/fcomm.2020.00039

Cuijpers, P., Heim, E., Abi Ramia, J., Burchert, S., Carswell, K., Cornelisz, I., Knaevelsrud, C., Noun, P., van Klaveren, C., Van't Hof, E., Zoghbi, E., van Ommeren, M., & El Chammay, R. (2022). Effects of a WHO-guided digital health intervention for depression in Syrian refugees in Lebanon: A randomized controlled trial. *PLoS Medicine*, *19*(6), Article e1004025. https://doi.org/10.1371/journal.pmed.1004025

Derr, A. S. (2016). Mental health service use among immigrants in the United States: A systematic review. *Psychiatric Services*, *67*(3), 265–274. https://doi.org/10.1176/appi.ps.201500004

Dow. H. D. (2011). An overview of stressors faced by immigrants and refugees: A guide for mental health practitioners. *Home Health Care Management & Practice*, *23*(3), 210–217. https://doi.org/10.1177/1084822310390878

Early, J., Gonzalez, C., Gordon-Dseagu, V., & Robles-Calderon, L. (2019). Use of mobile health (mHealth) technologies and interventions among community health workers globally: A scoping review. *Health Promotion Practice*, *20*(6), 805–817. https://doi.org/10.1177/1524839919855391

El-Haj-Mohamad, R., Nohr, L., Niemeyer, H., Böttche, M., & Knaevelsrud, C. (2022). Smartphone-delivered mental health care interventions for refugees: A systematic review of the literature. *Global Mental Health*, *10*, Article e6. https://doi.org/10.1017/gmh.2022.61

Eylem, O., van Straten, A., de Wit, L., Rathod, S., Bhui, K., & Kerkhof, A. J. F. M. (2021). Reducing suicidal ideation among Turkish migrants in the Netherlands and in the UK: The feasibility of a randomised controlled trial of a guided online intervention. *Pilot and Feasibility Studies*, *7*(1), Article 30. https://doi.org/10.1186/s40814-021-00772-9

Fernandez, E., Salem, D., Swift, J. K., & Ramtahal, N. (2015). Meta-analysis of dropout from cognitive behavioral therapy: Magnitude, timing, and moderators. *Journal of Consulting and Clinical Psychology*, *83*(6), 1108–1122. https://doi.org/10.1037/ccp0000044

Gadermann, A. M., Petteni, M. G., Janus, M., Puyat, J. H., Guhn, M., & Georgiades, K. (2022). Prevalence of mental health disorders among immigrant, refugee, and nonimmigrant children and youth in British Columbia, Canada. *JAMA Network Open*, *5*(2), Article e2144934. https://doi.org/10.1001/jamanetworkopen.2021.44934

García, Y., Ferrás, C., Rocha, Á., & Aguilera, A. (2019). Exploratory study of psychosocial therapies with text messages to mobile phones in groups of vulnerable immigrant women. *Journal of Medical Systems*, *43*(8), Article 277. https://doi.org/10.1007/s10916-019-1393-3

Goldsmith, L. P., Rowland-Pomp, M., Hanson, K., Deal, A., Crawshaw, A. F., Hayward, S. E., Knights, F., Carter, J., Ahmad, A., Razai, M., Vandrevala, T., & Hargreaves, S. (2022). Use of social media platforms by migrant and ethnic minority populations during the COVID-19 pandemic: A systematic review. *BMJ Open*, *12*(11), Article e061896. https://doi.org/10.1136/bmjopen-2022-061896

Hall, B. J., Shi, W., Garabiles, M. R., & Chan, E. W. W. (2018). Correlates of expected eMental Health intervention uptake among Filipino domestic workers in China. *Global Mental Health*, *5*, Article e33. https://doi.org/10.1017/gmh.2018.25

Hardy, A., Ward, T., Emsley, R., Greenwood, K., Freeman, D., Fowler, D., Kuipers, E., Bebbington, P., & Garety, P. (2022). Bridging the digital divide in psychological therapies: Observational study of engagement with the SlowMo mobile app for paranoia in psychosis. *JMIR Human Factors*, *9*(3), Article e29725. https://doi.org/10.2196/29725

Heilemann, M. V., Soderlund, P. D., Kehoe, P., & Brecht, M. L. (2017). A transmedia storytelling intervention with interactive elements to benefit Latinas' mental health: Feasibility, acceptability, and efficacy. *JMIR Mental Health*, *4*(4), Article e47. https://doi.org/10.2196/mental.8571

Hong, Y. A., Juon, H. S., & Chou, W. S. (2021). Social media apps used by immigrants in the United States: Challenges and opportunities for public health research and practice. *mHealth*, *7*, Article 52. https://doi.org/10.21037/mhealth-20-133

Hynie, M., Oda, A., Calaresu, M., Kuo, B. C. H., Ives, N., Jaimes, A., Bokore, N., Beukeboom, C., Ahmad, F., Arya, N., Samuel, R., Farooqui, S., Palmer-Dyer, J.-L., & McKenzie, K. (2023). Access to virtual mental healthcare and support for refugee and immigrant groups: A scoping review. *Journal of Immigrant and Minority Health*, *25*, 1171–1195. https://doi.org/10.1007/s10903-023-01521-1

Ince, B. U., Cuijpers, P., van 't Hof, E., van Ballegooijen, W., Christensen, H., & Riper, H. (2013). Internet-based, culturally sensitive, problem-solving therapy for Turkish migrants with depression: Randomized controlled trial. *Journal of Medical Internet Research*, *15*(10), Article e227. https://doi.org/10.2196/jmir.2853

Institute of Medicine, Committee on Assuring the Health of the Public in the 21st Century. (2002). *The future of the public's health in the 21st century*. National Academies Press. https://www.ncbi.nlm.nih.gov/books/NBK221224

Karimi, M., Costa, G., & Concilio, G. (2022). Innovative ICT based solutions and (im)migrants integration. *Social Sciences*, *11*(6), Article 244. https://doi.org/10.3390/socsci11060244

Kiropoulos, L. A., Griffiths, K. M., & Blashki, G. (2011). Effects of a multilingual information website intervention on the levels of depression literacy and depression-related stigma in Greek-born and Italian-born immigrants living in Australia: A randomized controlled trial. *Journal of Medical Internet Research, 13*(2), Article e34. https://doi.org/10.2196/jmir.1527

Kruzan, K. P., Williams, K. D., Meyerhoff, J., Yoo, D. W., O'Dwyer, L. C., De Choudhury, M., & Mohr, D. C. (2022). Social media-based interventions for adolescent and young adult mental health: A scoping review. *Internet Interventions, 30*, Article 100578. https://doi.org/10.1016/j.invent.2022.100578

Liem, A., Pakingan, K. A., Garabiles, M. R., Sit, H. F., Burchert, S., Lam, A. I. F., & Hall, B. J. (2022). Evaluating the implementation of a mental health app for overseas Filipino workers in Macao China: A mixed-methods study of stakeholders' perspectives. *Frontiers in Psychiatry, 13*, Article 836156. https://doi.org/10.3389/fpsyt.2022.836156

Linardon, J., & Fuller-Tyszkiewicz, M. (2020). Attrition and adherence in smartphone-delivered interventions for mental health problems: A systematic and meta-analytic review. *Journal of Consulting and Clinical Psychology, 88*(1), 1–13. https://doi.org/10.1037/ccp0000459

Lindegaard, T., Kashoush, F., Holm, S., Halaj, A., Berg, M., & Andersson, G. (2021). Experiences of internet-based cognitive behavioural therapy for depression and anxiety among Arabic-speaking individuals in Sweden: A qualitative study. *BMC Psychiatry, 21*(1), Article 288. https://doi.org/10.1186/s12888-021-03297-w

Lindegaard, T., Seaton, F., Halaj, A., Berg, M., Kashoush, F., Barchini, R., Ludvigsson, M., Sarkohi, A., & Andersson, G. (2021). Internet-based cognitive behavioural therapy for depression and anxiety among Arabic-speaking individuals in Sweden: A pilot randomized controlled trial. *Cognitive Behaviour Therapy, 50*(1), 47–66. https://doi.org/10.1080/16506073.2020.1771414

Lindegaard, T., Wasteson, E., Demetry, Y., Andersson, G., Richards, D., & Shahnavaz, S. (2022). Investigating the potential of a novel internet-based cognitive behavioural intervention for Dari and Farsi speaking refugee youth: A feasibility study. *Internet Interventions, 28*, Article 100533. https://doi.org/10.1016/j.invent.2022.100533

Meyerowitz-Katz, G., Ravi, S., Arnolda, L., Feng, X., Maberly, G., & Astell-Burt, T. (2020). Rates of attrition and dropout in app-based interventions for chronic disease: Systematic review and meta-analysis. *Journal of Medical Internet Research, 22*(9), Article e20283. https://doi.org/10.2196/20283

Mitchell, A. J., & Selmes, T. (2007). Why don't patients attend their appointments? Maintaining engagement with psychiatric services. *Advances in Psychiatric Treatment, 13*(6), 423–434. https://doi:10.1192/apt.bp.106.003202

Mor, S., Grimaldos, J., Tur, C., Miguel, C., Cuijpers, P., Botella, C., & Quero, S. (2021). Internet- and mobile-based interventions for the treatment of specific phobia: A systematic review and preliminary meta-analysis. *Internet Interventions, 26*, Article 100462. https://doi.org/10.1016/j.invent.2021.100462

Mugenyi, L., Mijumbi, A., Nanfuka, M., Agaba, C., Kaliba, F., Semakula, I. S., Nazziwa, W. B., & Ochieng, J. (2021). Capacity of community advisory boards for effective engagement in clinical research: A mixed methods study. *BMC Medical Ethics, 22*(1), Article 165. https://doi.org/10.1186/s12910-021-00733-0

Nickerson, A., Byrow, Y., Pajak, R., McMahon, T., Bryant, R. A., Christensen, H., & Liddell, B. J. (2020). "Tell Your Story": A randomized controlled trial of an online intervention to reduce mental health stigma and increase help-seeking in refugee men with posttraumatic stress. *Psychological Medicine, 50*(5), 781–792. https://doi.org/10.1017/S0033291719000606.

Nygren, T., Berg, M., Sarkohi, A., & Andersson, G. (2018). Development of an internet-based cognitive behavioral therapy self-help program for Arabic-speaking immigrants: Mixed-methods study. *JMIR Research Protocols, 7*(12), Article e11872. https://doi.org/10.2196/11872

Nygren, T., Brohede, D., Koshnaw, K., Osman, S. S., Johansson, R., & Andersson, G. (2019). Internet-based treatment of depressive symptoms in a Kurdish population: A randomized controlled trial. *Journal of Clinical Psychology, 75*(6), 985–998. https://doi.org/10.1002/jclp.22753

Orang, M., Missmahl, I., Gardisi, M., & Kluge, U. (2023) Internet-delivered value based counseling (VBC) aimed at the reduction of post-migration psychosocial stress: A pilot study, *Journal of Technology in Human Services, 41*(1), 23–42. https://doi.org/10.1080/15228835.2022.2156973

Ornelas, I. J., Perez, G., Maurer, S., Gonzalez, S., Childs, V., Price, C., Nelson, A. K., Perez Solorio, S. A., Tran, A., & Rao, D. (2022). Amigas Latinas Motivando el Alma: In-person and online delivery of an intervention to promote mental health among Latina immigrant women. *Journal of Integrative and Complementary Medicine, 28*(10), 821–829. https://doi.org/10.1089/jicm.2022.0491

Parenteau, A. M., Boyer, C. J., Campos, L. J., Carranza, A. F., Deer, L. K., Hartman, D. T., Bidwell, J. T., & Hostinar, C. E. (2023). A review of mental health disparities during COVID-19: Evidence, mechanisms, and policy recommendations for promoting societal resilience. *Development and Psychopathology, 35*(4), 1821–1842. https://doi.org/10.1017/S0954579422000499

Popay, J., Roberts, H., Sowden, A., Petticrew, M., Arai, L., Rodgers, M., Britten, N., Roen, K., & Duffy, S. (2006). *Guidance on the conduct of narrative synthesis in systematic reviews: A product from the ESRC Methods Programme.* Lancaster University.

Pottie, K., Ratnayake, A., Ahmed, R., Veronis, L., & Alghazali, I. (2020). How refugee youth use social media: What does this mean for improving their health and welfare? *Journal of Public Health Policy, 41,* 268–278. https://doi.org/10.1057/s41271-020-00231-4

Rathbone, A. L., & Prescott, J. (2017). The use of mobile apps and SMS messaging as physical and mental health interventions: Systematic review. *Journal of Medical Internet Research, 19*(8), Article e295. https://doi.org/10.2196/jmir.7740

Reich, H., Zürn, D., & Mewes, R. (2021). Engaging Turkish immigrants in psychotherapy: Development and proof-of-concept study of a culture-tailored, Web-based intervention. *Clinical Psychology in Europe, 3*(4), Article e5583. https://doi.org/10.32872/cpe.5583

Röhr, S., Jung, F. U., Pabst, A., Grochtdreis, T., Dams, J., Nagl, M., Renner, A., Hoffmann, R., König, H. H., Kersting, A., & Riedel-Heller, S. G. (2021). A self-help app for Syrian refugees with posttraumatic stress (Sanadak): Randomized controlled trial. *JMIR mHealth and uHealth, 9*(1), Article e24807. https://doi.org/10.2196/24807

Sabri, B., Vroegindewey, A., & Hagos, M. (2021). Development, feasibility, acceptability and preliminary evaluation of the internet and mobile phone-based BSHAPE intervention for Immigrant survivors of cumulative trauma. *Contemporary Clinical Trials, 110,* Article 106591. https://doi.org/10.1016/j.cct.2021.106591

Sander, L., Rausch, L., & Baumeister, H. (2016). Effectiveness of internet-based interventions for the prevention of mental disorders: A systematic review and meta-analysis. *JMIR Mental Health, 3*(3), Article e38. https://doi.org/10.2196/mental.6061

Sarría-Santamera, A., Hijas-Gómez, A. I., Carmona, R., & Gimeno-Feliú, L. A. (2016). A systematic review of the use of health services by immigrants and native populations. *Public Health Reviews, 37*(1), Article 28. https://doi.org/10.1186/s40985-016-0042-3

Shala, M., Morina, N., Burchert, S., Cerga-Pashoja, A., Knaevelsrud, C., Maercker, A., & Heim, E. (2020). Cultural adaptation of *Hap-pas-Hapi,* an internet and mobile-based intervention for the treatment of psychological distress among Albanian migrants in Switzerland and Germany. *Internet Interventions, 21,* Article 100339. https://doi.org/10.1016/j.invent.2020.100339

Sironi, A., Bauloz, C., & Emmanuel, M. (Eds.). (2019). *International Migration Law No. 34: Glossary on migration.* International Organization for Migration. https://publications.iom.int/books/international-migration-law-nde g34-glossary-migration

Smets, K. (2018). The way Syrian refugees in Turkey use media: Understanding "connected refugees" through a non-media-centric and local approach. *Communications, 43*(1), 113–123. https://doi.org/10.1515/commun-2017-0041

Spanhel, K., Balci, S., Feldhahn, F., Bengel, J., Baumeister, H., & Sander, L. B. (2021). Cultural adaptation of internet- and mobile-based interventions for mental disorders: A systematic review. *NPJ Digital Medicine, 4*(1), Article 128. https://doi.org/10.1038/s41746-021-00498-1

Tofighi, B., Abrantes, A., & Stein, M. D. (2018). The role of technology-based interventions for substance use disorders in primary care: A review of the literature. *Medical Clinics of North America, 102*(4), 715–731. https://doi.org/10.1016/j.mcna.2018.02.011

Ventevogel, P., Pereira, X., Verghis, S., & Silove, D. (2019). Mental health of refugees. In P. A. Allotey & D. Reidpath (Eds.), *The health of refugees: Public health perspectives from crisis to settlement* (2nd ed., pp. 106–127). Oxford University Press.

World Health Organization. (n.d.). *Refugee and migrant health.* https://www.who.int/health-topics/refugee-and-migrant-health#tab=tab_1

World Health Organization. (2021, August 31). *Mental health and forced displacement.* https://www.who.int/news-room/fact-sheets/detail/mental-health-and-forced-displacement

World Health Organization. (2022, September 30). *The role of media in supporting health.* https://www.who.int/tools/your-life-your-health/a-healthy-world/people-s-roles/the-role-of-media-in-supporting-health

Health Media Activism: Latin American Organizing in Response to Feminicides

Leandra Hinojosa Hernández

In late January 2020, Isabel Cabanillas de la Torre, a Mexican artist and women's rights activist, was found murdered in Ciudad Juárez. Cabanillas de la Torre's death has been characterized by many as a feminicide, given that she was an outspoken activist who worked tirelessly to advocate on behalf of women's rights throughout Mexico. Angelita Baeyens, the program director of advocacy and litigation at the Robert F. Kennedy Human Rights organization, described Cabanillas de la Torre's death as a blow to "the movement of courageous women activists, many of them mothers, sisters and friends of victims of femicide in Mexico" (Gamboa et al., 2020, para. 4). Bayens also noted that Cabanillas de la Torre's death "exposes the danger in which human rights defenders working to combat violence operate" (Gamboa et al., 2020, para. 6).[1]

The murder of Cabanillas de la Torre is a grievous loss linked to the murder of other activists and women throughout Mexico, an act that immediately prompted protests to call attention to senseless violence against women and the country's lack of responsibility or action to bring justice to friends, family members, and communities. Nelly Ornelas, a member of the anti-domestic violence organization Love Is Not Violence, said, "Since the authorities are indifferent, lazy, the men think that they can keep killing women. So the feminists, we are going to keep going out until they learn to respect us" (Guthrie, 2020). Moreover, the National Institute of Women and the Chihuahuan Institute of Women stated, "The crime against Isabel represents an attack on activism, which for months has been harassed and assaulted by those who try to silence the legitimate right of women to demonstrate, to demand a life free of violence" (Gamboa et al., 2020).

Similarly, in December 2019, a Chilean protest song about victim shaming and rape culture "became a viral anthem for feminists around the world" (McGowan, 2019). Written by Lastesis, a Chilean feminist group, the song was titled "Un Violador en Tu Camino" ("A Rapist in Your Path"). It was first performed in Chile in response to social unrest and later spread across Latin America to Spain, France, and the United Kingdom. The song was also utilized to inspire protests and anti-feminicide mass organizing. According to McGowan, the song is "based on the work of the Argentinian theorist Rita Segato, who argues that sexual violence is a political problem, not a moral one." Moreover, McGowan describes the larger implications of the song's lyrics in a violence context:

> The lyrics describe how institutions—the police, the judiciary and political power structures— uphold systematic violations of women's rights: "The rapist is you/ It's the cops/ The judges/ The

---

[1] Although the terms "femicide" and "feminicidio" are often utilized interchangeably in academic scholarship, I utilize the term feminicidio to center its origin in Latin American feminist scholarship and in the Spanish language. If the term femicide is used in a direct quote or by the authors, however, I use that term to honor their scholarship.

state/ The president." Another section repudiates the many ways that women are blamed for falling victim to sexual violence ("And it's not my fault / nor where I was / nor what I wore") before concluding: "The rapist is you."

The spirit and choreography of "Un Violador en Tu Camino" are a response to the crisis in which security forces throughout the country have faced allegations of torture, rape, and shooting to kill. I utilize this case here as a contemporary representation of the larger anti-violence and anti-rape activism that has gained traction and momentum, as women throughout Latin America and beyond are speaking out and organizing against violence, rape, torture, and human rights violations. One factor that has facilitated transnational anti-violence and anti-femicide activist organizing is digital interactivity and hashtag feminism, as activists have utilized social media to join forces and organize efforts across borders and oceans. In this chapter, I examine Latina/o/x and Latin American perspectives on health activism in the mass media through the lens of digital interactivity, logics of connective action, and community resistance to femicides and violence against women.

Gender Violence and Feminicides: A Global Public Health Concern

Representation of feminicides, and by extension, activism to end feminicides, is a health communication and media studies case study linked to larger concerns of power and Whiteness in the communication discipline more broadly. Critical health communication and media studies scholars have long advocated for research that deliberately rethinks power imbalances, centers marginalized populations, and recognizes the significance of health and media case studies that impact queer communities and communities of color (Cepeda, 2016; Cooke-Jackson, Rubinsky, et al., 2021; Cooke-Jackson, Spieldenner, et al., 2021; Dutta, 2020; Hernández & De Los Santos Upton, 2018, 2019, 2021; Molina & Cacho, 2014; Sastry et al., 2021). The domination of Whiteness in communication studies spaces has contributed to several problematic outcomes for people of color, particularly concerning the symbolic annihilation of people of color in the mass media and the implication that violence against people of color is less important than violence against White people.

For example, as an outdoor enthusiast and scholar of health communication, journalism, and gender violence, I tracked the death of Gabby Petito closely. Petito's case highlights the aforementioned discrepancies present in news coverage of violence against women. In August 2021, Petito was killed by her fiancé when they were traveling together exploring the outdoors across the United States. She disappeared in late August 2021, and her case continues to inspire news articles tracking her disappearance, the case against her fiancé, and other case details. Her case also inspired several authors to critique various news outlets' coverage of violence against women and their continued reliance on "missing White woman syndrome," a phenomenon that describes how the mass media and law enforcement tend to hyperfocus on White victims at the expense of other missing and murdered individuals, particularly those who are Black, Indigenous, and people of color (Rosner, 2021). In other words, missing White woman syndrome is a "hunger for stories about victims who look like Petito, to the exclusion of all others" (Rosner, 2021, para. 1).

Ultimately, the domination of Whiteness (and ensuing concerns of racism and exclusionary practices) in health communication and media studies spaces results in additional issues, such as racial/ethnic health disparities (Cooke-Jackson, Spieldenner, et al., 2021; Hernández, 2023) and problematic representations of communities of color in the mass media (particularly crime and violence news) (Dixon et al., 2019; Hernández & De Los Santos Upton, 2018; Mastro, 2019; Slakoff, 2020). The health communication subfield has also long struggled with disciplinary origins that overfocus on health interventions and underfocus on health activism (see Sastry et al., 2021; Zoller & Kline, 2008); as such, scholars have advocated for more perspectives that center culture, activism, and community empowerment (Dutta, 2007; Sastry et al., 2021). Thus, scholars have asserted that intersectionality is strongly needed in both critical health communication and feminist media studies spaces (Cepeda, 2016; Hernández & De Los Santos Upton, 2019; Valdivia, 2021), and this study of gender violence against women and anti-violence community activism contributes to this larger genealogy.

Gender violence, specifically violence against women, is a global public health concern—a "shadow epidemic" that has become more concerning in the light of the COVID-19 pandemic (UN Women, n.d.). Globally, before COVID-19, one in three women experienced physical or sexual violence. After COVID-19, gender violence concerns have intensified, particularly with increases in calls to domestic violence shelters and the diverting of gender violence aid to assist with COVID-19 efforts (UN Women, n.d.). Furthermore, according to UN Women (2017), among the 25 countries with the highest rates of feminicide in the world, 14 countries are in Latin America and the Caribbean, with Mexico often described as one of the most dangerous countries in the world.

Several factors have contributed to disproportionately increasing rates of feminicide throughout Latin America. In Mexico, in particular, spikes in feminicides made national and international headlines in the 1990s when several women who worked as maquiladoras were murdered in Cuidad Juárez. Later, Ciudad Juárez was ranked as the most violent city in the world outside of a war zone from 2009 to 2011, with several images proliferating the mass media: "visions of beheadings, carjackings, child assassins, abandoned houses, extortion, informal settlements made of scavenged materials, the bodies of raped and murdered women dumped in public spaces, and narco culture" (Driver, 2015, p. xii). According to reports from 1985 to 2014, there were 47,178 women killed in Mexico due to their gender; moreover, statistics on the number of femicides that occur in Mexico continue to increase with each passing year (Gamboa et al., 2020).

Within the context of gender violence are several types of violence, such as femicide, feminicide, and reproductive femicide. Diana Russell, a feminist advocate and sociologist, introduced the term femicide in public discourse in the mid-1970s when testifying about violence against women at the International Tribunal on Crimes Against Women. Later, in the 1990s, Russell and Radford operationalized the term as "the misogynistic killing of women by men" (Russell, 2011). In the early 2000s, Russell and Radford revised the term as the killing of females by males because they are female, thus highlighting the gendered nature of the violence committed against women and the purpose and motives underlying such violent acts (Russell, 2021). The introduction and evolution of the term are significant because they highlight the uneven power relations and the driving force of male power and domination over women (Hernández & De Los Santos Upton, 2018).

Although Russell and Radford's contributions have been significant to feminist theory and activism in American and international contexts, Mexican and Latin American feminists have utilized the term feminicide (or feminicidio) to signify violence against women in particular Latin American contexts at the intersections of cultural, national, and gender politics. The term feminicide (or feminicidio), first coined by Mexican feminists Julia Monárrez and Marcela Lagarde, centralizes the experiences of Mexican (and Latin American) women and expands femicide, "a gender-specific word for homicide," to include the killing of women *based on their gender*, "the murder of women because of their sexuality, reproductive features, and social status or success" (Estévez, 2016, para. 17). In other words, according to Fregoso and Bejarano (2010), the term feminicide disrupts "essentialist notions of female identity that equate gender and biological sex and looks instead to the gendered nature of practices and behaviors, along with the performance of gender norms" (p. 3). The term feminicide "shift[s] the analytic focus to how gender norms, inequities, and power relationships increase women's vulnerability to violence" (Fregoso & Bejarano, 2010, p. 4). It also strengthens Latin American cultural and political connections, "as feminicide is a direct English translation of the Spanish term feminicidio and provides the space for a transborder, transcultural, translocational focus" (Hernández & De Los Santos Upton, 2018, p. 71).

The term feminicide has also inspired the creation of other terms, such as *reproductive feminicide*, an act of gendered violence against women on the reproductive spectrum, spanning from a structural limitation of reproductive options to the murdering of women because of their reproductive capabilities (Hernández & De Los Santos Upton, 2019). From a health activism perspective, feminicidios are a significant health concern because of the intertwined relationships among sexism, patriarchy, misogyny, and violence that result in the murder of women solely because of their gender. In response to feminicidios throughout Latin America, activists have organized across state and country lines to challenge gender violence, assert their agency, and envision new futures for women.

Digital Organizing and Logics of Connective Action

Two concepts that are fundamental to health activist organizing in the wake of gender violence are digital interactivity and logics of connective action. Although it has largely been used to discuss interactivity between companies and consumers or between consumers and television programming, *interactivity* is a term that has been widely utilized in new media research and has promise for its role in activist contexts as well. The term interactivity highlights the ways in which individuals have engaged with computer-mediated communication in multiple contexts. As Dewdney and Ride (2006) describe, interactivity is a foundational term when thinking about the "radical newness of digital media" for two reasons: (a) New technologies and modalities of interaction create new ways of thinking and action for the human mind, and (b) it creates a new set of communication tools that empowers the relationship between authors and audiences and creates new freedoms of expression (or in this case, freedoms of action and organizing).

Another significant concept in the context of health activism is logics of connective action. As social movement and technology scholars have explained, the creation of social media and other digital technologies has led to the creation of technology-enabled networking (Livingston & Asmolov, 2010) wherein mediated communication processes are fundamental building blocks in structuring organizational actions and connective action. Moreover, such digital technologies enable "increasing coordination of action by organizations and individuals using digital media to create networks, structure activities, and communicate their views directly to the world" (Bennett & Segerberg, 2012, p. 749). Bennett and Segerberg built upon the term *logic of collective action*, which emphasizes efforts to galvanize individuals to contribute to the public good, to create the term *connective action*, which consists of networks that are individualized, technologically organized, and recognize digital media as the fundamental organizing agent. Building upon Benkler's (2006) research, Bennett and Segerberg explain that participation is self-motivated, as participation in relation to a common good or common cause is initiated by a self-motivated effort to share posts, engage with digital media, and more.

For the purposes of this chapter, digital interactivity and connective action help explain the ways in which social movements such as Ni Una Menos have gained and maintained momentum in both physical and digital organizing spaces (Hernández & Munz, 2023). The movement known as *Ni Una Menos* originated in Argentina and grew into an international movement that combats violence against women in Latin America. The original movement was founded by a collective of journalists, writers, communicators, organizers, and community members with similar interests in anti-violence advocacy and communicating their messages to the masses (Bedrosian, 2022). Ni Una Menos' name came from a 1995 phrase from the Mexican activist and poet Susana Chávez Castillo, "Ni una muerta más," which refers to the Ciudad Juárez femicides from the 1990s. Chávez Castillo was later assassinated in 2011, and her phrase became "el símbolo de la lucha" moving forward (#NiUnaMenos, 2015). Its origin story has roots in the 2015 murder of Chiara Páez, a 14-year-old Argentinian girl who was murdered by her boyfriend, 16-year-old Manuel Mansilla, when she was 8 weeks pregnant. Páez was discovered under the patio of her boyfriend's family home, and reports suggest that he murdered her after discovering she was pregnant. He was later charged with aggravated murder, forced abortion, and femicide.

Páez's murder inspired the first Ni Una Menos (Not One Less/Not One More) march against gender violence and was a pivotal case in the origins of the movement, although movement organizers have also noted that the movement's genealogy includes the Mothers of the Plaza de Mayo, the mothers of victims of the Argentinian dictatorship in the late 1970s. The movement held its first-ever women's mass strike in Argentina in October 2016 in response to the murder of 16-year-old Lucía Pérez. She was found drugged, raped, and impaled in Mar del Plata, and the ensuing protest utilized the hashtag #MiércolesNegro (Black Wednesday) to signify this moment. This strike gained traction both nationally and internationally, with similar demonstrations occurring during the same time frame in Mexico, Paraguay, Bolivia, El Salvador, Guatemala, and Brazil, to name a few.

Ni Una Menos has utilized a combination of physical presence and digital assemblies to construct a new "political discourse and practice" (Palmeiro, 2020, p. 1). As Mason-Deese (2020) has explained, Ni Una Menos has created "feminist assemblies, working groups, and conversations [that] proliferate in digital and physical spaces, producing new feminist encounters and creating a sense of solidarity among women and other 'dissident identities'" (p. 1). Historically, many social movements pre-social media and pre-digital interactivity utilized more traditional, physical, space-bound modalities of organizing. However, with the creation of new digital technologies, Ni Una Menos has combined several organizing strategies—marches, protests, strikes, and transnational coalition building efforts—with digital strategies such as tweets, hashtags, and reposts to garner more support for its efforts and involve more individuals in activist efforts throughout the world. In the wake of evolving technologies, Ni Una Menos transitioned from hashtags and other social media functions to the

> coordinated involvement of millions of women through the sharing of personal stories and violence testimonios on social media, the use of SMS technologies to connect across regional lines, the use of technologic alliance-building to coordinate with the mass media, and the ultimate "weaving of webs." (Hernández & Munz, 2023, p. 207)

From a personal motivation perspective, social media allowed organizers, activists, and supporters of Ni Una Mas to express their individual stories of violence and survivorship and join others in larger collective efforts (Mason-Deese, 2020). Moreover, through collective decision-making, the movement decided on hashtags such as #NiUnaMas, #NiUnaMenos, #YoParo, #InternacionalFeminista, #JuntasSomosInfinitas, #NotOneWomanLess, and #NosotrasParamos to guide its technologic efforts (Mason-Deese, 2020), which later resulted in the publicizing of micro- and macro-level issues surrounding violence against women. Ultimately, through digital interactivity, Ni Una Menos gained traction and international momentum through its coordinated digital assembly-gathering, its conjoining of individual experiences or testimonios with larger collective stories, and its ability to enact transformative justice to combat violence against women (Fuentes, 2019; Hernández & Munz, 2023).

Concluding Thoughts: Anti-Feminicide Activism and Digital Technologies

As this chapter has illustrated, social movements such as Ni Una Menos have utilized digital interactivity, logics of connective action, and other social media components to create, sustain, and transform transitional efforts to combat violence against women. By utilizing social media to connect individual women to the larger collective, Ni Una Menos has connected survivors and activists from throughout the world to share stories, organize, and change the landscape of how police organizations and cultural forces shape violence against women. Much of the research to date has focused on hashtags and social media outlets such as Twitter and Facebook. However, future research should explore the use and function of other social media outlets, such as TikTok, in contributing to larger anti-violence digital assemblies. For example, what new possibilities and technologic opportunities can the app TikTok provide supporters and organizers? Are new ethical concerns present with the use of the app's functions? Once researchers are able to answer these questions, we will have a more coherent picture of the ways in which Ni Una Menos activists engage with social media to achieve justice-related goals.

References

Bedrosian, A. (2022). How# NiUnaMenos used discourse and digital media to reach the masses in Argentina. *Latin American Research Review, 57*(1), 100–116.

Benkler, Y. (2006). *The wealth of networks: How social production transforms markets and freedom.* Yale University Press.

Bennett, W. L., & Segerberg, A. (2012). The logic of connective action. *Information, Communication & Society, 15*(5), 739–768.

Cepeda, M. E. (2016). Beyond "filling in the gap": The state and status of Latina/o feminist media studies. *Feminist Media Studies, 16*(2), 344–360.

Conley, T. (2021). A sign of the times: Hashtag feminism as a conceptual framework. In S. Macdonald, B. I. Wiens, M. Macarthur, & M. Radzikowska (Eds.), *Networked feminisms: Activist assemblies and digital practices* (pp. 21–47). Lexington Books.

Cooke-Jackson, A., Rubinski, V., Spieldenner, A., Hudak, N., Gunning, J. N., & Aragon, A. (2021). Researching marginalized populations in intimate health communication: Observations from the field. In A Cooke-Jackson & V. Rubinsky (Eds.), *Communicating intimate health* (pp. 227–249). Lexington Books.

Cooke-Jackson, A., Spieldenner, A., Hudak, N., & Ben, C. (2021). Rethinking imbalances of power through health communication: Challenges for scholars, practitioners, and activists. In T. L. Thompson & N. Grant Harrington (Eds.), *The Routledge handbook of health communication* (3rd ed., pp. 522–537). Routledge.

Dewdney, A., & Ride, P. (2006). *The new media handbook.* Routledge.

Dixon, T. L., Weeks, K. R., & Smith, M. A. (2019). Media constructions of culture, race, and ethnicity. In *Oxford research encyclopedia of communication.* Oxford University Press. https://doi.org/10.1093/acrefore/9780190228 613.013.502

Driver, A. (2015). *More or less dead: Feminicide, haunting, and the ethics of representation in Mexico.* University of Arizona Press.

Dutta, M. J. (2007). Communicating about culture and health: Theorizing culture-centered and cultural sensitivity approaches. *Communication Theory, 17*(3), 304–328.

Dutta, M. J. (2020). Whiteness, internationalization, and erasure: Decolonizing futures from the Global South. *Communication and Critical/Cultural Studies, 17*(2), 228–235.

Estévez, A. (2016). Latin American women's problem: We keep getting murdered. *The Conversation.* https://theconve rsation.com/latin-american-womens-problem-we-keep-getting-murdered-67351

Fregoso, R., & Bejarano, C. (2010). Introduction: A cartography of feminicide in the Américas. In R. Fregoso & C. Bejarano (Eds.), *Terrorizing women: Feminicide in the Américas* (pp. 1–42). Duke University Press.

Fuentes, M. A. (2019). #NiUnaMenos (#NotOneWomanLess): Hashtag performativity, memory, and direct action against gender violence in Argentina. In A. G. Altinay, M. J. Contreras, M. Hirsch, J. Howard, B. Karaca, & A. Solomon (Eds.), *Women mobilizing memory* (pp. 172–191). Columbia University Press.

Gamboa, S., Shen-Berro, J., Flores Guzmán, K., & Abdelkader, R. (2020, January 24). *Shooting death of young woman activist returns spotlight to "femicides" in Juarez and Mexico*. NBC News. https://www.nbcnews.com/news/latino/shooting-death-young-woman-activist-returns-spotlight-femicides-juarez-mexico-n1120811

Guthrie, A. (2020, January 25). *Mexican women protest murders of activists, target monuments*. ABC News. https://apnews.com/international-news-general-news-97fb23c7552cc493e6cd61605c4ea804

Hernández, L. H. (2023). Health disparities: Latinx. In E. Y. Ho, C. L. Bylund, J. C. M. Van Weert, I. Basnyat, N. Bol, & M. Dean (Eds.), *The international encyclopedia of health communication*. Wiley. https://doi.org/10.1002/9781119678816.iehc0834

Hernández, L. H., & De Los Santos Upton, S. (2018). *Challenging reproductive control and gendered violence in the Américas: Intersectionality, power, and struggles for rights*. Lexington Books.

Hernández, L. H., & De Los Santos Upton, S. (2019). Critical health communication methods at the U.S.–Mexico border: Violence against migrant women and the role of health activism. *Frontiers in Communication, 4*, Article 34.

Hernández, L. H., & De Los Santos Upton, S. (2021). Migrant gender violence, reproductive health, and the intersections of reproductive justice and health communication. In A. Cooke-Jackson & V. Rubinsky (Eds.), *Communicating intimate health* (pp. 201–209). Lexington Books.

Hernández, L. H., & Munz, S. M. (2023). Leaderless rebellions: An analysis of digital feminist anti-violence activism. In A. Wallace & R. Luttrell (Eds.), *Social media activism: Repression, resistance, rebellion, and reform*. Routledge.

Livingston, S., & Asmolov, G. (2010). Networks and the future of foreign affairs reporting. *Journalism Studies, 11*(5), 745–760.

Mason-Deese, L. (2020). Not one woman less: From hashtag to strike. *Spheres: Journal for Digital Cultures, 6*, 1–15.

Mastro, D. (2019). Virtual theme collection: Immigrants as minorities in the media. *Journalism & Mass Communication Quarterly, 96*(1), 31–36.

McGowan, C. (2019, December 6). Chilean anti-rape anthem becomes international feminist phenomenon. *The Guardian*. https://www.theguardian.com/world/2019/dec/06/chilean-anti-rape-anthem-becomes-international-feminist-phenomenon

Molina, I., & Cacho, L. M. (2014). Historically mapping contemporary intersectional feminist media studies. In C. Carter, L. Steiner, & L. McLaughlin (Eds.), *The Routledge companion to media and gender* (pp. 71–80). Routledge.

#NiUnaMenos: ¿Quién fue la autora de la consigna que une a miles contra la violencia de género? (June 3, 2015), *Minuto Uno*. https://www.minutouno.com/sociedad/niunamenos/quien-fue-la-autora-la-consigna-que-une-miles-contra-la-violencia-genero-n365815

Palmeiro, C. (2020, March 12). Ni Una Menos and the politics of translation. *Spheres: Journal for Digital Cultures*. https://spheres-journal.org/contribution/ni-una-menos-and-the-politics-of-translation

Rosner, H. (2021, October 8). The long American history of "missing white woman syndrome." *The New Yorker*. https://www.newyorker.com/news/q-and-a/the-long-american-history-of-missing-white-woman-syndrome

Russell, D. E. H. (2011, December). *The origin and importance of the term femicide*. http://www.dianarussell.com/origin_of_femicide.html

Russell, D. E. H. (2021). My years campaigning for the term "femicide." *Dignity: A Journal of Analysis of Exploitation and Violence, 6*(5), 1–5.

Sastry, S., Zoller, H. M., & Basu, A. (2021, January 25). Editorial: Doing critical health communication: A forum on methods. *Frontiers in Communication, 5*. https://doi.org/10.3389/fcomm.2020.637579

Slakoff, D. C. (2020). The representation of women and girls of color in United States crime news. *Sociology Compass, 14*(1), Article e12741.

UN Women. (n.d.). *The shadow pandemic: Violence against women during COVID-19*. https://www.unwomen.org/en/news/in-focus/in-focus-gender-equality-in-covid-19-response/violence-against-women-during-covid-19

UN Women. (2017, February 15). *Take five: Fighting femicide in Latin America*. https://www.unwomen.org/en/news/stories/2017/2/take-five-adriana-quinones-femicide-in-latin-america

Zoller, H. M., & Kline, K. N. (2008). Theoretical contributions of interpretive and critical research in health communication. *Annals of the International Communication Association, 32*(1), 89–135.

CHAPTER
25

Using Artificial Intelligence to Address Health Disparities: Challenges and Solutions

Kelly Merrill Jr.

Advancements in technologies have continued to transform the health care industry (Viswanath & Kreuter, 2007). Indeed, scholars have acknowledged that various technologies can help address *health disparities* (Gibbons et al., 2011), which are systematic differences in health that are experienced by historically marginalized communities (Braveman et al., 2011). Currently, many patients have increased access to health care and improved health care delivery because of the technologies they have access to. For example, patient portals allow patients to interact with their health care providers, and electronic medical records house personal health-related data in a secure, online space. These technologies, among others, have been instrumental in promoting health equity among vulnerable populations who have encountered barriers to obtaining adequate health care. Although there are many technologies that have been used to address health disparities, one such approach has focused on the use of artificial intelligence (AI).

Artificial intelligence refers to the processes in which a system mimics human intelligence to accomplish a variety of tasks (Copeland, 2020). In fact, AI can mimic human intelligence in various ways, such as demonstrating an ability to reason, make decisions, generalize, and learn from prior experiences. AI is also referred to as machine intelligence (Rong et al., 2020). As such, AI technologies encompass various fields, including machine learning and robotics.

The adoption of AI in the health care industry includes using the tool for diagnosing patients, performing surgeries, monitoring patients, conversing with patients, enhancing patient independence, assisting with patient mobility, and conducting health-related tasks with patients (LaRosa & Danks, 2018). Furthermore, AI in health is manifested in many ways, such as conversational agents, robots, telemedicine, diagnosis predictor tools, algorithms, and even facial recognition. For example, Jess the Robot, as featured in *The Robot Will See You Now*, is a health care robot powered by an AI system (Figure 25.1; Fulford, 2017). Other examples include virtual health assistants, robot-assisted surgery, and customer service chatbots.

The adoption of AI in health can be attributed to several reasons. First, the health care industry is in high demand, as life expectancy continues to rise and the global population continues to grow (World Health Organization, 2020). Many suggest that AI, along with various other health technologies, can assist with this ever-increasing demand (Spatharou et al., 2020). AI also has the potential to lessen human error. By automating various processes that have been previously overseen by a human, AI can work in an efficient and effective manner to accurately report observations. Similarly, AI can lessen physician fatigue by completing simple, routine tasks and freeing up time for physicians so that they can spend more time with their patients (Yu et al., 2018). For example, AI technologies can remind patients to take their medication at a specific time, or they can alert a diabetic patient about their low levels of blood sugar.

Figure 25.1 Jess the Robot as featured in *The Robot Will See You Now* (Fulford, 2017).

Another benefit of adopting AI in the health care industry is the reduced costs of health care and its increased accessibility through telemedicine services.

AI can also increase the quality of care provided by health care providers. This is made possible by AI's ability to generate substantial amounts of patient-generated health data (PGHD). PGHD can then be used by health care providers to better understand their patients. Furthermore, AI can learn from these large amounts of PGHD and offer more accurate and specific recommendations for future health care visits. AI also has the ability to assist health care providers with medical recommendations and decisions (Long et al., 2017). Indeed, recommendations provided by AI are generally on par with those provided by a certified health care provider (Esteva et al., 2017). Finally, AI can reach populations that have not previously had access to health care and resources (Jackson et al., 2021). Ultimately, these benefits suggest that AI can improve the efficiency of the health care industry.

Addressing Concerns Regarding the Use of Artificial Intelligence in Health

Although AI provides many benefits to the health care industry, there are several concerns regarding the use of AI in health, which can further exacerbate health disparities. This section focuses on issues of accessibility, usability, algorithmic bias, privacy, and trust. Recommendations, including increasing accessibility and usability of AI in health and developing fair and just AI systems, are provided throughout. Following these recommendations will ensure that AI used for health can benefit all individuals.

Accessibility and Usability

As AI continues to penetrate the health care industry, it is important to note that not everyone has access to the benefits this technology provides. The *digital divide* refers to the disparity in access to and use of technologies and is largely experienced by historically marginalized communities (Medero et al., 2022). Scholars generally study the effects of the digital divide on two levels (Hargittai, 2001). The first level is concerned with ownership, availability, affordability, and maintenance of technologies (Gonzales, 2016; Van Deursen & Van Dijk, 2019). Indeed, many advanced AI technologies are costly, and some health care organizations may have difficulty obtaining access to them. In the United States, many hospitals in rural areas and in lower-income areas have less funding compared to hospitals in more urban areas or higher-income areas. Furthermore, private hospitals are able to afford more modern equipment due to their high patient fees. Although public hospitals may have access to modern equipment, their equipment is often overused and damaged (Astran, 2021). Beyond the United States, many countries lack the funding to afford advanced technologies such as AI (Frost & Reich, 2009). Without funding to support these endeavors, many people in these countries are unable to reap the benefits of AI used for health. Thus, to address these first-level digital divide disparities, governments throughout the world need to prioritize digital health funding and ensure that it is equitably distributed across health care facilities. In doing so, digital health technologies can help address some of the health disparities that exist today by providing health care access to individuals who have historically had difficulty obtaining it (Jackson et al., 2021).

The second level of the digital divide focuses on the skills and knowledge that are necessary to use technologies (Büchi et al., 2016; Hargittai, 2001). To illustrate, someone may be able to obtain a social robot used for health but may have difficulty operating it. Thus, varying levels of digital health literacy among patients present unique challenges for those interested in using AI for health. *Digital health literacy* is "the ability to appraise health information from electronic sources and apply the knowledge gained to addressing or solving a health-related problem" (Smith & Magnani, 2019, p. 280). As such, those interested in using AI for health-related reasons have to leverage not only their health literacy but also their technological literacy. Indeed, digital health literacy and the use of digital health technologies tend to be lower for older individuals, racial and ethnic minorities, and individuals with lower levels of educational attainment (Gordon & Hornbrook, 2016; Smith & Magnani, 2019). To address this second-level digital disparity, increasing digital health literacy among potential users of AI for health, especially among minority and underserved populations, should be prioritized. Some suggestions include using simple language in health messages, creating education and awareness programs, and implementing evidence-based interventions. When given the tools to understand how to appraise health information from AI used for health, minority and underserved populations can better leverage the benefits that are provided by these technologies. Indeed, health literacy and technological literacy are positively related to health outcomes such as quality of life and engaging in healthy behaviors (Neter & Brainin, 2019).

Algorithmic Bias

Another concern regarding the use of AI in health is *algorithmic bias* (Nelson, 2019), which occurs when machine learning produces an error that is systematically wrong. AI in the form of machine learning is commonly used in health care because algorithms are often used to assess a patient's risk of developing certain conditions, detect abnormalities in a patient's records, and develop individualized treatment plans. Thus, errors that result from this process can subsequently affect the treatment, recommendations, and care the patient receives (Matheny et al., 2019).

Although it is inaccurate, algorithmic bias is a product of the data provided to an AI system. AI is trained with historical data, or data that are based on past observations. As such, it is likely that the data may reflect previous biased decisions and deeply rooted inequities that negatively affect certain groups of people. If gone unnoticed, AI will continue to make decisions that are rooted in historical patterns of discrimination and will perpetuate health disparities among vulnerable populations. Algorithmic bias may also exist due to structural barriers, which result in limited access to data of particular populations. For example, the lack of health-related data from individuals living in some areas of the Appalachian region of the United States may be due to the limited number of health care providers and facilities. Without these data, AI cannot gain a representative understanding of health-related issues specific to this population, resulting in decisions or recommendations that do not have the specific population's best interests in mind (Ibrahim et al., 2021).

Indeed, empirical evidence demonstrates that AI does not always provide accurate predictions of health-related outcomes across various identities, including age, gender, race, ethnicity, and socioeconomic status (Chen et al., 2019). For example, Seyyed-Kalantari et al. (2021) found that AI-based models are more likely to underdiagnose patients if they are of underserved populations, which included women, racial and ethnic minorities, those with Medicaid, and those that identify with intersectional subgroups. Similarly, many algorithms trained to detect skin cancer are provided with images of fair-skinned individuals, which makes it difficult for the algorithm to assess whether someone with a darker skin tone has skin cancer (Adamson & Smith, 2018). This algorithmic bias then affects the recommendations for those with darker skin tones, ultimately impacting their overall health. Thus, certain groups of people are at a disadvantage when using AI designed for health.

Several actions can be taken to avoid algorithmic bias that further perpetuates health disparities and inequities. First, we must develop bias-aware AI that treats all people fairly (Agarwal et al., 2023). In doing so, we must consider the differential needs that various groups of people have when training an AI for health. Failure to do so could potentially lead to health recommendations and decisions that may only benefit certain groups of people. Second, considering that AI relies on the availability of data to train its algorithm (Yu et al., 2018), it is important for future developers to verify that their AI is trained on data that are representative of the population of interest. Thus, collecting additional data, especially among underrepresented and minority patients, can assist with making the data more representative. Third, it is crucial for AI developers to be from diverse backgrounds as well, reflecting various social identities (Matheny et al., 2019). Diverse AI developers can help keep their community's interests in mind, which can improve the effectiveness of their AI technology. By taking these steps, we can work toward creating AI that is socially responsible and does not discriminate based on any social identity.

Privacy and Trust

Privacy concerns are other issues that may affect the adoption of AI designed for health (Shi et al., 2021). Patients are particularly reserved about their private health information. As such, it is likely that patients may not want AI to collect some, or all, of their health-related data. Failure to collect comprehensive patient data could cause concerns because large quantities of patient data are needed to ensure AI algorithms are accurate. For example, if an AI algorithm is only allowed to collect live patient data, then the subsequent recommendation provided by the AI system will not account for potentially relevant information, such as a patient's health history of diabetes.

Patients may also be concerned about who will have access to their health-related data. Many advanced health technologies, such as AI used for health, are owned and created by large technology companies, including Google, Apple, Microsoft, Meta, and IBM. Indeed, many of these companies have previously used patient data for their own benefit (e.g., creating new health-related technologies) and have not handled the data with care or regard (Murdoch,

2021). In 2019, Meta (formerly Facebook) used AI technology to collect mental health information from its users without their consent (Goggin, 2019). Similarly, DeepMind, an AI company owned by Google, recently faced a class action lawsuit for providing discounted use of a smartphone application in exchange for health data from the National Health Service in the United Kingdom (Lomas, 2023). Given the reoccurring history of malpractice related to patient health data, many patients may be hesitant to interact with an AI designed for health. Further, data security and data breaches may be a concern that many patients have when using AI for health. Without proper systems in place to protect the large amounts of PGHD that AI may collect, patients may be hesitant to use AI.

To address these ethical concerns, patients must be reassured that the health-related data collected by an AI will be private and will not be accessed by unwanted parties. Furthermore, AI should only collect data that are absolutely necessary, and the data should only be shared with providers that need the information to make decisions and recommendations regarding the patient's health. This recommendation ensures that AI is not collecting additional data that could be used for other means. Privacy laws can also be enacted to protect patients and their health-related data (Matheny et al., 2019). These laws can restrict the sharing of health-related data, as well as halt the collection of identifiable characteristics without proper informed consent.

A trust-related issue regarding the use of AI in health concerns is known as the "black box" problem. The *black box problem* refers to the idea that the inputs and outputs of a system are accessible, but the internal workings or the implementation of these decisions are opaque or not accessible (Murdoch, 2021). That is, an AI diagnosis predictor tool can analyze patient data and provide a surgical recommendation for the patient, but information regarding how the AI tool came to that conclusion will be unavailable. Without knowledge of the implementation process, it may be difficult to discern whether the AI tool arrived at its decisions and recommendations based on an appropriate analysis or whether systematic bias was at play. Ultimately, these concerns will affect whether patients are comfortable with using AI designed for health.

Avoiding the black box problem can be accomplished in several ways. First, users of AI designed for health care should be provided a terms of use, or a disclaimer, that clearly outlines the function of the AI system, as well as the data that will be collected. If the data collected are to be used for other means, the patient should be well-informed of these intentions. Furthermore, AI's decision-making processes should be accessible and routinely examined. Health care providers using AI must be held accountable for ensuring that it provides accurate results. Thus, those using AI for health should conduct routine audits of their systems as a means of evaluating the performance of their AI tools. In addition, having access to these decision-making processes can help health care providers understand how the AI tool came to its conclusions and can also allow health care providers to assess whether the conclusions are biased. Indeed, researchers are developing AI that can be interpretable, which will be key to adopting AI in health and ensuring that many individuals can trust AI in health settings (Ahmad et al., 2018).

Implementation of these recommendations can assist with addressing privacy concerns related to the use of AI in health and can ultimately lead to increased trust in these AI systems. Fostering trust is particularly important because it is a key factor that contributes to the adoption of these technologies (Shi et al., 2021). Furthermore, increased interactions with AI are positively associated with positive attitudes about AI (Sutherland et al., 2019). Thus, patients will grow to trust AI after repeated use, especially if AI consistently put the patient's needs first.

Conclusion

Artificial intelligence designed for health has great potential to benefit many individuals. However, it is important to ensure that these advanced technologies are accessible and designed in a manner that prioritizes fairness, privacy, trust, and transparency. Indeed, several scholars highlight the important role of AI being used as a complement to the current approach to health (Chen et al., 2019; Matheny, 2019; Nelson, 2019); that is, we should not replace health care providers with AI. Instead, we should identify places where processes can be automated and completed by AI, allowing health care providers to spend more time with their patients. In doing so, we can leverage the use of AI to improve the health care industry.

References

Adamson, A. S., & Smith, A. (2018). Machine learning and health care disparities in dermatology. *JAMA Dermatology*, *154*(11), 1247–1248. https://doi.org/10.1001/jamadermatol.2018.2348

Agarwal, R., Bjarnadottir, M., Rhue, L., Dugas, M., Crowley, K., Clark, J., & Gao, G. (2023). Addressing algorithmic bias and the perpetuation of health inequities: An AI bias aware framework. *Health Policy and Technology*, *12*(1), Article 100702. https://doi.org/10.1016/j.hlpt.2022.100702

Ahmad, M. A., Eckert, C., & Teredesai, A. (2018, August). Interpretable machine learning in healthcare. In *Proceedings of the 2018 ACM International Conference on Bioinformatics, Computational Biology, and Health Informatics* (pp. 559–560). Association for Computing Machinery. https://doi.org/10.1145/3233547.3233667

Astran, J. (2021, May 14). *Compare and contrast features of public and private hospitals.* HealthMed.org. https://health med.org/compare-and-contrast-features-of-public-and-private-hospitals

Braveman, P. A., Kumanyika, S., Fielding, J., LaVeist, T., Borrell, L. N., Manderscheid, R., & Troutman, A. (2011). Health disparities and health equity: The issue is justice. *American Journal of Public Health*, *101*(Suppl. 1), S149–S155. https://doi.org/10.2105/AJPH.2010.300062

Büchi, M., Just, N., & Latzer, M. (2016). Modeling the second-level digital divide: A five-country study of social differences in internet use. *New Media & Society*, *18*(11), 2703–2722. https://doi.org/10.1177/1461444815604154

Chen, I. Y., Szolovits, P., & Ghassemi, M. (2019). Can AI help reduce disparities in general medical and mental health care? *AMA Journal of Ethics*, *21*(2), 167–179. https://doi.org/10.1001/amajethics.2019.167

Copeland, B. J. (2020). *Artificial intelligence.* Encyclopedia Britannica.

Esteva, A., Kuprel, B., Novoa, R. A., Ko, J., Swetter, S. M., Blau, H. M., & Thrun, S. (2017). Dermatologist-level classification of skin cancer with deep neural networks. *Nature*, *542*(7639), 115–118. https://doi.org/10.1038/nature21056

Frost, L. J., & Reich, M. R. (2009). Creating access to health technologies in poor countries. *Health Affairs*, *28*(4), 962–973. https://doi.org/10.1377/hlthaff.28.4.962

Fulford, T. (Director). (2017). *The robot will see you now* [Film]. Double Act Productions/Channel 4 Television Corporation.

Gibbons, M. C., Fleisher, L., Slamon, R. E., Bass, S., Kandadai, V., & Beck, J. R. (2011). Exploring the potential of Web 2.0 to address health disparities. *Journal of Health Communication*, *16*, 77–89. https://doi.org/10.1080/10810730.2011.596916

Goggin, B. (2019). Inside Facebook's suicide algorithm: Here's how the company uses artificial intelligence to predict your mental state from your posts. *Business Insider*. https://www.businessinsider.com/facebook-is-using-ai-to-try-to-predict-if-youre-suicidal-2018-12

Gonzales, A. (2016). The contemporary US digital divide: From initial access to technology maintenance. *Information, Communication & Society*, *19*(2), 234–248. https://doi.org/10.1080/1369118X.2015.1050438

Gordon, N. P., & Hornbrook, M. C. (2016). Differences in access to and preferences for using patient portals and other eHealth technologies based on race, ethnicity, and age: A database and survey study of seniors in a large health plan. *Journal of Medical Internet Research*, *18*(3), Article e5105. https://doi.org/10.2196/jmir.5105

Hargittai, E. (2001). Second-level digital divide: Mapping differences in people's online skills. *arXiv*, Article cs/0109068. https://doi.org/10.48550/arXiv.cs/0109068

Ibrahim, H., Liu, X., Zariffa, N., Morris, A. D., & Denniston, A. K. (2021). Health data poverty: An assailable barrier to equitable digital health care. *Lancet Digital Health*, *3*(4), e260–e265. https://doi.org/10.1016/S2589-7500(20)30317-4

Jackson, D. N., Trivedi, N., & Baur, C. (2021). Re-prioritizing digital health and health literacy in *Healthy People 2030* to affect health equity. *Health Communication*, *36*(10), 1155–1162. https://doi.org/10.1080/10410236.2020.1748828

LaRosa, E., & Danks, D. (2018, December). Impacts on trust of healthcare AI. In *Proceedings of the 2018 AAAI/ACM Conference on AI, Ethics, and Society* (pp. 210–215). Association for the Advancement of Artificial Intelligence and Association for Computing Machinery. https://doi.org/10.1145/3278721.3278771

Lomas, N. (2023, May 19). UK court tosses class-action style health data misuse claim against Google DeepMind. *TechCrunch*. https://techcrunch.com/2023/05/19/uk-court-tosses-class-action-style-health-data-misuse-claim-against-google-deepmind

Long, E., Lin, H., Liu, Z., Wu, X., Wang, L., Jiang, J., An, Y., Lin, Z., Li, X., Chen, J., Li, J., Cao, Q., Wang, D., Liu, X., Chen, W., & Liu, Y. (2017). An artificial intelligence platform for the multihospital collaborative management of congenital cataracts. *Nature Biomedical Engineering, 1*(2), 1–8. https://doi.org/10.1038/s41551-016-0024

Matheny, M., Israni, S. T., Ahmed, M., & Whicher, D. (2019). *Artificial intelligence in health care: The hope, the hype, the promise, the peril.* National Academy of Medicine.

Medero, K., Merrill Jr, K., & Ross, M. Q. (2022). Modeling access across the digital divide for intersectional groups seeking Web-based health information: National survey. *Journal of Medical Internet Research, 24*(3), Article e32678. https://doi.org/10.2196/32678

Murdoch, B. (2021). Privacy and artificial intelligence: Challenges for protecting health information in a new era. *BMC Medical Ethics, 22*(1), Article 122. https://doi.org/10.1186/s12910-021-00687-3

Nelson, G. S. (2019). Bias in artificial intelligence. *North Carolina Medical Journal, 80*(4), 220–222.

Neter, E., & Brainin, E. (2019). Association between health literacy, eHealth literacy, and health outcomes among patients with long-term conditions. *European Psychologist, 24*(1). https://doi.org/10.1027/1016-9040/a000350

Rong, G., Mendez, A., Assi, E. B., Zhao, B., & Sawan, M. (2020). Artificial intelligence in healthcare: Review and prediction case studies. *Engineering, 6*(3), 291–301. https://doi.org/10.1016/j.eng.2019.08.015

Seyyed-Kalantari, L., Zhang, H., McDermott, M., Chen, I. Y., & Ghassemi, M. (2021). Underdiagnosis bias of artificial intelligence algorithms applied to chest radiographs in under-served patient populations. *Nature Medicine, 27*(12), 2176–2182. https://doi.org/10.1038/s41591-021-01595-0

Shi, S., Gong, Y., & Gursoy, D. (2021). Antecedents of trust and adoption intention toward artificially intelligent recommendation systems in travel planning: A heuristic–systematic model. *Journal of Travel Research, 60*(8), 1714–1734. https://doi.org/10.1177/0047287520966395

Smith, B., & Magnani, J. W. (2019). New technologies, new disparities: The intersection of electronic health and digital health literacy. *International Journal of Cardiology, 292*, 280–282. https://doi.org/10.1016/j.ijcard.2019.05.066

Spatharou, A., Hieronimus, S., & Jenkins, J. (2020, March 10). *Transforming healthcare with AI: The impact on the workforce and organizations.* McKinsey & Company. https://www.mckinsey.com/industries/healthcare-systems-and-services/our-insights/transforming-healthcare-with-ai

Sutherland, C. J., Ahn, B. K., Brown, B., Lim, J., Johanson, D. L., Broadbent, E., MacDonald, B., & Ahn, H. S. (2019, May). The doctor will see you now: Could a robot be a medical receptionist? In *2019 International Conference on Robotics and Automation (ICRA)* (pp. 4310–4316). Institute of Electrical and Electronics Engineers. https://doi.org/10.1109/ICRA.2019.8794439

Van Deursen, A. J., & Van Dijk, J. A. (2019). The first-level digital divide shifts from inequalities in physical access to inequalities in material access. *New Media & Society, 21*(2), 354–375. https://doi.org/10.1177/1461444481 8797082

Viswanath, K., & Kreuter, M. W. (2007). Health disparities, communication inequalities, and eHealth. *American Journal of Preventive Medicine, 32*(5), S131–S133. https://doi.org/10.1016/j.amepre.2007.02.012

World Health Organization. (2020). *Life expectancy and healthy life expectancy.* https://www.who.int/data/gho/data/themes/mortality-and-global-health-estimates/ghe-life-expectancy-and-healthy-life-expectancy

Yu, K. H., Beam, A. L., & Kohane, I. S. (2018). Artificial intelligence in healthcare. *Nature Biomedical Engineering, 2*(10), 719–731. https://doi.org/10.1038/s41551-018-0305-z

Pedagogies of Resistance: Social Movements and the Construction of Communicative Knowledge in Brazil

Paola Sartoretto

Colonial Legacy, Insurgency, and Counterhegemonic Communication

The history of Brazil in the 20th century is marked by the inheritance of colonization and slavery even though the country had become a republic and abolished slavery in the previous century. By the mid-1900s, Brazil was an essentially rural country, and formerly enslaved populations still lived in slavery-like conditions with limited access to salaried jobs, housing, and education. The country's once numerous originary peoples had been reduced due to systematic killing and diseases spread in contact with urban, predominantly White, populations. Policies that aimed to colonize remote areas in the country, inhabited by rural populations usually composed of Indigenous groups and former enslaved communities, were characterized by a developmentalist Eurocentric agenda that aimed to "civilize" these groups by stripping them of their collective identities and cultures to be turned into a mass of disciplined workers in the new industries and agricultural production. In addition, a White working and middle class was forming in cities and rural areas that was composed of, among other groups, European immigrants (notable Italian and German) brought to Brazil to replace enslaved Africans in the plantations and, admittedly, to "whiten" the darker population, as Brazilian cultural anthropologist Lilia Schwarcz (1999, see Chapter 2) explains.

The myth of a racial democracy based on the work of Brazilian sociologist Gilberto Freyre (1933/1946) served to justify policies to incorporate the formerly enslaved populations into the workforce and engineer societies modeled on European standards and costumes (Guimarães, 2001). Policies to establish workers' rights and universal education also contributed to creating a class society that largely relegated former enslaved Black communities, traditional rural communities living off the forests and by the riverbanks, and Indigenous peoples to exclusion. A more progressive government took power in 1961, with president Janio Quadros, and started a series of structural reforms to respond to the demands of unions. Social movements suffered a backlash from conservative sectors of society that, backed by the military, ousted president João Goulart in 1964.

Progressive governments that took power in Latin America during the second half of the 20th century were viewed as a threat to the United States' economic and political dominance in the Americas. During the 1960s, the United States exerted systematic cultural and political influence in Latin America and orchestrated, in collaboration with local elites, coups in several Latin American countries, including Chile, Uruguay, Argentina, Paraguay, and Brazil (Klein, 2007). In this process, democratically elected governments were overthrown and replaced with civil–military dictatorships. Brazil was under civil–military authoritarian rule between 1964 and 1985. Organized collectives working to grant equal rights for many marginalized groups, such as women, rural workers, Black communities, and Indigenous communities, were very active in Brazil, as in other countries, during that time (e.g., student associations in the United

States, France, and Italy and anti-colonial mobilizations in Africa and India). During the civil–military dictatorship, these groups and individuals were persecuted and criminalized, which forced them to go underground. One of the most used measures by these governments to neutralize opposition was to censor and control communication, including journalism and cultural production such as cinema, music, and theater.

The systematic and structural racialization of the Brazilian population that segregated even when formally proclaiming a racial democracy—in contrast to objective segregation policies implemented in countries such as the United States and South Africa—has consistently been met by organized opposition that is articulated through communication and media. Indigenous, rural, and Black movements, among others, have not only constituted their own media and communicative practices but also continuously create and circulate knowledge about these practices. In this Chapter, I discuss two characteristics of this counterhegemonic mobilization in Brazil from the second half of the 20th century: the articulation of marginalized groups who claim specific group rights and the constitution of a popular public communication ecology (Tacchi, 2009) composed of organizations, media, practices, and rituals. These groups engage both in communication practices and in the reproduction of such practices, constituting pedagogies of resistance centered around communicative processes.

In January 2023, a new government took power with the installation of Indigenous leader Sonia Guajajara as Minister of Indigenous People and anti-racism activist Anielli Franco—sister of Mariele Franco, Rio the Janeiro's local councilor brutally murdered in 2018 allegedly by organized crime members—as Minister of Racial Equality. Black law scholar Silvio Almeida was nominated Minister of Human Rights and Citizenship. These individuals from minority groups occupying high-ranking government offices, in areas that reflect the political action of the groups in which they belong, are at least nominal evidence of the political relevance achieved by communities at the margins. These marginalized communities have actively projected their collective voices to step into a position where they have the possibility to intervene in decisive instances of power (Sodré, 2005, p. 11). These three ministries, which did not exist during Jair Bolsonaro's term in office, were established through the political struggle of Indigenous, racial, gender, and class minorities that made a historical move from the margins to the center of power. This level of representation would not be possible without long-term and systematic communicative processes and praxis that becomes knowledge and is the substance of resistant pedagogies. Against this historical background, the discussion in this chapter highlights the need for media and communication studies to develop a more inclusive outlook to understand such marginalized practices, moving beyond the dominant Western paradigms of media production, content analysis, and transmission of information.

Counterhegemonic Community Communication

Brazilian sociologist Maria da Glória Gohn (2007, p. 13) defines *social movement* as collective actions with a sociopolitical and cultural character that make it possible for people to organize and express their demands. The terms *collective, organize,* and *express* are key to understanding the importance of communication and media for social movements. Collective action, as opposed to individual action, means that people must discuss and negotiate what unites them—a common identity or a common problem such as discrimination; discussion and negotiation are communicative practices. For this reason, social movements can be considered collective actors because they are composed of many individuals with shared views about constructing a different reality through their actions. Once the collective is created around common aspects that will generate demands—for instance, anti-discrimination laws or demarcation of land for Indigenous peoples—these demands must be expressed through organized action, including communication practices through media. In Brazil, the Indigenous organizations published their first newspaper, *Porantim*, in 1979, during the dictatorship. The newspaper was a way to express collective demands and construct an Indigenous collective. Similarly, the Brazilian Landless Workers Movement (MST) has published a bulletin, which turned into a newspaper, since 1981, also during the dictatorship.

When marginalized groups become an organized collective and express their demands, they engage in a cultural process that generates practices such as protests, demonstrations, assemblies, and meetings, which in turn construct alternatives to alter reality. Italian philosopher Antonio Gramsci defined *hegemony* as the ability of a group to claim and dictate its conceptions of reality as "objective truth" (1971, pp. 445–446). However, these conceptions of reality are always negotiated, particularly when they negatively affect other groups, and communication, conceived as social interaction (see Craig, 1999; Waisbord, 2019), is the social fabric by which hegemony is exercised and contested.

In addition to collective actors, marginalized social movements in Brazil also constitute communities able to endure over time through the reproduction of practices and modes of interaction. A sociological understanding of *community* focuses on the organic character of community relations and the sense of mutual dependence that underpins individual relations, as opposed to the mechanical associations and symbolic character of a society (Tönnies, 1887/ 2001, p. 17). It can be argued that through communication, these marginalized groups construct communitarian relations of mutual solidarity which transcend the instrumental collective formation that has the objective to achieve collective demands, such as gender and racial equality.

For these social movements, planned and structured communication such as institution of designated communication task forces, institutionalization of meetings and assemblies, and creation of movement media; serves both to articulate collective demands and to construct a counterhegemonic alternative. Communication in these is considered *praxis* (Freire, 1967/ 2019), a process through which practice and theory mutually inform each other to change reality and develop new knowledge. While engaging in communicative practices by doing certain things—for example, producing content and organizing protests—these collectives are also producing and circulating counterhegemonic knowledge and views about reality.

Communication and Political Participation: Non-Western Perspectives

Two concepts in particular offer valuable nuance to understand the relation between communication and political participation from a non-Western, collective perspective: conscious appropriation of media (Sartoretto, 2015) and critical dissonance (Suzina, 2019). *Conscious appropriation of media* is a collective process through which marginalized groups engage with media technologies with an awareness of the limitations of technologies and their deceptive aspects as discussed by, for example, Couldry (2010) and Dean (2009). Conscious appropriation analytically addresses processes that complexify usage of media technologies, adding to these processes the agency of a collective subject (see Sartoretto, 2015. p. 192). This kind of technological appropriation is grounded on rationales about the relation between communication, media technologies, and political change and generates collective meta-knowledge about media among marginalized groups that is constantly circulated, educating new generations of community communicators (see Sartoretto & Custódio, 2019, pp. 66–67). An example of conscious appropriation is the engagement with social networking sites, which is often a subject of discussion and critique and is met with ambivalence by organized social movements and other collective actors (Sartoretto, 2015, pp. 207–213; Sartoretto & Custódio, 2019). Members of youth organizations in urban peripheries and in the MST, both in Brazil, show an acute awareness of the disadvantages of using social media, such as algorithmic bias and surveillance, but recognize the benefits of using platforms such as Facebook to reach a broader audience and create strategies to circumvent surveillance and mitigate algorithmic bias.

Whereas conscious appropriation explains communicative processes in relation to media technologies, *critical dissonance* (Suzina, 2019) defines how the substance and processes of social movement communication construct political imaginaries of change. Suzina (2019) explains that critical dissonance is a process in which marginalized groups engage in order to effect social change by negotiating hegemonic views of reality. Suzina further argues that the appropriation of media channels and logics aims for more than achieving freedom of expression (in the terms discussed by Dean, 2009). The goal is to "interfere in shared meanings that orient the interpretation of the world and the organization of societies" (Suzina 2019, p. 157). The idea of Brazil as a "racial democracy," mentioned above, is a clear example of an hegemonic view of reality that has been contested by the Brazilian Black movement at least since the 1970s. Currently, there is a mainstream consensus in Brazil about the persistence of racial discrimination and its effects on society that has led to affirmative action such as a quota system for racialized students in higher education institutions.

This process of changing material reality through altering understandings of reality relates to Freire's (1967/2019) idea of "world reading" as a critical reflexive practice supported by the ability to read and write. World reading is thus the conscious appropriation of the ancient communication technologies of reading and writing. Consider, for instance, how popular communicator and scholar Gizele Martins (2019) explains the role of community media in the struggle against military intervention in Rio de Janeiro's *favelas*, the slum marginalized areas that are home to a predominantly racialized population affected by segregation and state negligence. Martin argues that the production of community media is motivated by a will to construct and reconstruct local memory of the communities and report the damage caused by state powers to these communities from their own perspective (p.109). *Community media* in the favelas, particularly during the period leading up to the 2016 Olympics in Rio de Janeiro, mobilized collectively to prevent damage by the state and the police to their communities, and they constructed critical dissonance in and through their media channels. Community communication as a set of practices and structures (Peruzzo, 2022) can be understood as further development of world reading to understand and change the world through understanding and changing media and communication structures and logics.

Communication and the Pedagogy of Resistance

As briefly explained above, the history of Brazil and its society is marked by a continuum of oppression, exclusion, and inequality. From colonization and the slave trade in the 16th century to the civil–military dictatorship in the 20th century and the emergence of the extreme right, culminating with Jair Bolsonaro's presidential term from 2019 to 2022, in the 21st century. *Intersectional oppression* combining the axes of race, class, ethnicity, and gender has, through time, materialized in processes such as slavery, structural racism (Almeida, 2019), widespread gender-based violence (Fórum de Segurança Pública, 2022, p. 14), systematic killing of originary Indigenous peoples, wealth inequality, and urban segregation.

Marginalization in Brazil is thus intersectional. It cuts across and combines different symbolic minorities who are, in fact, the majority of the Brazilian population. In this sense, Sodré (2005, p. 11) explains that a contemporary notion of minority is conditioned by the possibility of agency in the deliberative instances of power. Consider, for instance, favela dwellers in Rio de Janeiro, who face racial segregation, class oppression, state violence, and urban segregation. It is a telling tale that in preparation for the Olympics in 2016, the Rio the Janeiro municipality built a wall along the road that connects the international airport to the city, conveniently shielding Favela da Maré from the sight of visitors arriving to the city for the Olympic games. The wall thus becomes a material symbol of marginalization through invisibility and urban segregation. Not only was the favela hidden away and rendered invisible but also the understanding of favela dwellers about the wall was dismissed by politicians and, to a certain extent, by established media. Although Rio de Janeiro's Tourism Secretary denied the allegations that the wall was built to hide the favela, dwellers of Favela da Maré used their media channels to criticize the wall (creating critical dissonance), which they called the "wall of shame."

The "wall of shame" anecdote illustrates how intersectionally marginalized groups in Brazil have constructed themselves as political actors who continuously reclaim their agency and visibility in public discourse and political processes through communication. Likewise, Indigenous and Black collectives have carved a communicative environment through conscious appropriation of technologies that are used to create critical dissonance and achieve (in the long term) political and social change. Against this backdrop, I argue that the political process of collective resistance to marginalization is underpinned by the formation of a resistant communicative environment with established practices built on the consciousness of oppression (cf. Freire, 1967/2019), with an understanding that social change is dependent on, albeit not exclusively, visibility. Marginalized actors in Brazil have learned that public discourse, materialized in the media, is historically exclusionary and partially renounces participation in something like an idealized liberal public sphere (Habermas, 1962/1992) that includes a variety of political positions.

The connecting thread among these groups is their inability to access, discursively and materially, political and social rights that are constitutionally granted in Brazil. *Discursive accessibility* means the ability to define and express demands and be heard as an interlocutor, and *material accessibility* means the actual fulfillment of rights to, for instance, education, language, housing, and so on. Similarly, Sodré (2005, pp. 13–14) argues that minorities share four basic characteristics:

Sociolegal vulnerability: It is more difficult for marginalized groups to assess rights and to demand these rights, such as housing.
Identity in formation: Marginalized groups need to construct themselves as a collective sharing an identity, such as rural workers, Black, and Indigenous.
Counterhegemonic struggle: Marginalized groups need to counter dominant views of reality as objective truth.
Discursive strategies: Marginalized groups need to collectively engage in communicative practices that are continuously reproduced.

Moreover, demanding rights to the establishment of a collective voice to represent identities in formation, for these groups in Brazil, requires more than the type of social mobilization described and analyzed in mainstream Western sociology that explains how identity is used as an umbrella to claim special rights or how the liberal state becomes an object of claims posed by collective actors. The intersectional nature of marginalization means that these collectives construct and reproduce counterhegemonic ideas of reality that they act to materialize—for instance, different modes of land ownership and more egalitarian racial relations. As these ideas become reality through social change by means of political action, they are projected into the future; therefore, this process is called *prefiguration*—collectively imagining how society could be different. The prefiguration of a collective future is the object of the pedagogy of resistance as a collective learning process among these organized collective actors.

This means that in these cases communication is pedagogical in its substance and structure. Through the process of conscious appropriation, minority groups as collectives and individuals construct a *communicative ecology* (Tacchi, 2009) consisting of media outlets, creative communities, social media profiles, communication initiatives, and interventions that construct critical dissonance. This can be illustrated by the MST view on communication as "informative and formative" in the sense that it is a way to transmit information but also a process to form subjects (collective and individual) in the praxis of collective resistance. Among minority and marginalized groups, communication has become a subject of specific knowledge, extrapolating the sphere of practice and experience. Black, Indigenous, rural workers, and urban unhoused do not only engage in production of content, media practices, and direct action with instrumental purposes but also produce and circulate knowledge about these practices. This knowledge becomes the substance of pedagogic and educational practices (see Dewey, 1938/2008). See, for instance, the booklet, "Homeless Worker Movement in Brazil and the Struggle for Digital Sovereignty,"[1] in which the movement outlines its views on collective data production and digital politics.

Resistant Communication Pedagogies: Moving Forward

The examples described above illustrate how marginalized groups in Brazil become protagonists of communication processes through conscious appropriation of media. These groups further construct and circulate knowledge and practices oriented toward media and communication—what I call resistant communication pedagogies. Indigenous, Black, rural, and peripheric communities thus become protagonists and agents of political change through communicative processes, in stark opposition to views of the Other as passive, underdeveloped, and the object of so-called modernization projects. The experiences and knowledge constructed by different minority groups in and through communication, seen through a historical and decolonial lens, are evidence of how these communities establish themselves as collective political actors through communication mobilized in resistant pedagogies.

Community communication can and should be understood beyond the flattening perspective of Western mainstream communication theories that explain media production and transmission of information. Mexican communications scholar Claudia Magallanes-Blanco (2022) argues that "coloniality makes the perspective of the Other invisible by rewriting it in relation to the dominant colonial matrix, giving rise to the coloniality of representations" (p. 268). We can identify this logic in media and communication studies that usually confine community communication, particularly practices and knowledges stemming from the Global South, as a marginal field of situated conceptualizations with little relevance and credence outside their locales of production. Referring to Indigenous communication, for instance, Magallanes-Blanco (2022) contends that it cannot be understood as "a mechanism for transmitting information" or "media input" but, rather, as a "substantive part of community life" (p. 269). This substantive character of communication as a process of sociability and collective construction is what needs to be understood and conceptualized from a decolonial perspective to understand how marginalized groups become the protagonists of communicative processes that aim to change reality. Subfields that have emerged and developed in Brazil and Latin America in the past decades, such as popular communication, folk communication, and community communication, should be analyzed from the outset as a legitimate expression of social and political processes engendered by minoritized communities. Acknowledging community

---

[1] https://nucleodetecnologia.com.br/docs/Cartilha-MTSTec-ENG.pdf.

communication as a resistant pedagogy means viewing it as a substantive part of community life in a multipolar global media landscape, as proposed by Magallanes-Blanco. Within this perspective, an important research challenge will be to understand political engagement through activism and its communicative elements not as a side activity exercised separately from other realms of life but, rather, as a constitutive element of social experience.

References

Almeida, S. (2019). *Racismo estrutural* [Structural racism; in Portuguese]. Pólen Produção Editorial LTDA.

Couldry, N. (2010). *Why voice matters: Culture and politics after neoliberalism.* SAGE.

Craig, R. T. (1999). Communication theory as a field. *Communication Theory, 9*(2), 119–161.

Dean, J. (2009). *Democracy and other neoliberal fantasies.* Duke University Press.

Dewey, J. (2008). *Experience and education.* Free Press. (Original work published 1938)

Freire, P. (2019). *Pedagogy of the oppressed* (M. Bergman & D. Macedo, Trans.). Bloomsbury. (Original work published 1967)

Freyre, G. (1946). *The masters and the slaves: A study in the development of Brazilian civilization* (S. Putnam, Trans.). Knopf. (Original work published 1933)

Gohn, M. D. G. (2007). *Movimentos sociais no início do século XXI: Antigos e novos atores sociais* [Social movements in early XXI century: Old and new social actors; in Portuguese]. Ed. Vozes.

Gramsci, A. (1971). Selections from the prison notebooks (Q. Hoare & G. N. Smith, Trans.). *International Publishers.*

Guimarães, A. S. A. (2001). A questão racial na política brasileira (os últimos quinze anos) [The racial question in Brazilian politics (the last fifteen years); in Portuguese]. *Tempo Social, 13,* 121–142.

Habermas, J. (1992). *The structural transformation of the public sphere: An inquiry into a category of bourgeois society.* Polity Press. (Original work published 1962)

Klein, N. (2007). *The shock doctrine: The rise of disaster capitalism.* Macmillan.

Magallanes-Blanco, C. (2022). Media and communication studies: What is there to decolonize? *Communication Theory, 32*(2), 267–272.

Martins, G. (2019). *Militarização e censura: A luta por liberdade de expressão na Favela da Maré* [Militarization and censorship: The struggle for freedom of expression at Favela da Maré; in Portuguese]. Núcleo Piratininga de Comunicação.

Peruzzo, C. M. K. (2022). Culturas populares na folkcomunicação e na comunicação popular, comunitária e alternativa: Da decodificação mediática à resistência política [Popular cultures in folk-communication and popular, community and alternative communication: From media decodification to political resistance; in Portuguese]. *Revista Internacional de Folkcomunicação, 20*(44), 174–203.

Sartoretto, P. (2015). Voices from the margins: People, media, and the struggle for land in Brazil [Doctoral dissertation]. Karlstad University.

Sartoretto, P., & Custódio, L. (2019). The production of knowledge in Brazilian social movement families. *Journal of Alternative and Community Media, 4*(2), 60–73.

Schwarcz, L. M. (1999). *The spectacle of the races: Scientists, institutions, and the race question in Brazil, 1870–1930.* Hill & Wang.

Sodré, M. (2005). Por um conceito de minoria [For a conceptualization of minority]. In R. Paiva & A. Barbalho (Eds.), *Comunicação e cultura das minorias* [Minorities' communication and culture; in Portuguese] (pp. 11–14). Editora Paulus.

Suzina, A. C. (2019). Dissonância crítica e solidária: A contribuição das mídias populares ao processo de mudança social [Critical and solidarian dissonance: The contribution of popular media to the process of social change; in Portuguese]. *Chasqui: Revista Latinoamericana de Comunicación, 140,* 147–162.

Tacchi, J., Foth, M., & Hearn, G. (2009). Action research practices and media for development. *International Journal of Education and Development Using ICT, 5*(2), 32–48.

Tönnies, F. (2001). *Community and society* (J. Harris & M. Hollis, Trans.). Cambridge University Press. (Original work published 1987)

Waisbord, S. (2019). *Communication: A post-discipline.* Wiley.

Emboldening Democratic Pedagogies About Media and Justice Through Critical Media Literacy and Peer Teaching

Andrea Gambino *and* Jeff Share

In the United States, *media literacy* has typically focused on building students' competencies to "access, analyze, evaluate, create, and act using all forms of communication" (National Association for Media Literacy Education, n.d., para. 1). Although these skills are essential building blocks for critical thinking, they do not include an engagement with ideology and systems of power or a critical disposition to question the political nature of education and to address social and environmental justice (Funk et al., 2016). For too long, media literacy in the United States has prioritized competencies that continue the social reproductive functions of traditional schooling instead of developing transformative pedagogies to challenge the dominant narratives and empower students to question oppressive ideologies (Higdon et al., 2021). In the past decade, the literature about media literacy has been addressing more issues of social, racial, and climate justice (Cubbage, 2022; De Abreu, 2022; Mihailidis et al., 2021; Ramasubramanian et al., 2021). However, there is still a dominant neoliberal approach to media education in the United States that has focused on protecting children from "inappropriate" content to more recently calling for "resiliency" as defense against fake news and disinformation. Although learning to recognize false information is a start, there is a more foundational need for critical analysis that empowers students to question and create alternative media that challenges oppressive systems, structures, and ideologies.

At the University of California, Los Angeles, we have been teaching *critical media literacy* since 2011 to master's level/pre-service teachers in our teacher education program (Share et al., 2019) and more recently to undergraduate students in the new major in Education and Social Transformation. Basing critical media literacy on cultural studies (Durham & Kellner, 2002; Hammer & Kellner, 2009) and critical pedagogy (Darder et al., 2003; Kincheloe, 2007), we designed our critical media literacy courses to address intersectional issues of racism, sexism, classism, and other systems of oppression and environmental injustice (Collins, 2000; Crenshaw, 1989; Kellner & Share, 2007; López, 2021). Through critical analysis and alternative media production, critical media literacy empowers students to challenge the myths that education is not political and media can be objective (Share & Gambino, 2022). This is an inquiry process that aims to critically question the relationships between media and audiences, information and power (Kellner & Share, 2019). In this chapter, we discuss how we implemented critical media literacy and peer teaching with undergraduate students during the COVID-19 pandemic.

Critical Media Literacy

Critical media literacy is a transformative pedagogy that has evolved from critical researchers in the 20th century at the Frankfurt Institute for Social Research and the Centre for Contemporary Cultural Studies at the University of Birmingham, as well as incorporating concepts of semiotics, postmodernism, multiculturalism, and feminism (Kellner, 1995). More recently, critical media literacy has been influenced by fields of study that are currently under attack in the United States, such as queer studies, ethnic studies, intersectionality, and critical race theory (Cubbage, 2022; Yosso, 2020). Another development in critical media literacy can be seen in the pioneering work by Antonio López (2021) in *ecomedia literacy* that has brought a focus to the ways media frame the narrative about environmental justice and the climate crisis.

Critical media literacy includes three pedagogical dimensions (Share & Gambino, 2022). The first involves a *critical awareness* about systems, structures, and ideologies that reproduce hierarchies of power and knowledge concerning race, gender, class, sexuality, and other forms of identity and environmental justice, as well as general understandings about how media and communication function. The second dimension engages the *skills* to critically think and question media representations and biases; deconstruct and reconstruct media texts; and use a variety of media to access, analyze, evaluate, create, and act. The third dimension involves developing a *disposition* for empathy, critical consciousness, and empowerment to take action to challenge and transform society to be more socially and environmentally just. This third dimension is based on Freire's (2010) notion of *conscientização*, a revolutionary critical consciousness that involves perception as well as action against oppression. These three dimensions of critical media literacy pedagogy are supported through an inquiry process and framework with six conceptual understandings and questions (Table 27.1).

The critical media literacy framework provides guidance for educators to use the conceptual understandings to plan and facilitate their teaching and for students to use the questions to make meaning of the media texts they analyze and create. This framework is a tool for inquiry that can be applied in many ways. One strategy that we implemented during the pandemic was peer teaching as a form of democratic pedagogy. By empowering students to co-design their learning with us, they chose "generative themes" (representations and cultural codes relevant to their lives) to develop lessons about social and environmental justice (Freire & Macedo, 1987; Morrell et al., 2013). This freedom to choose their generative themes was supported by the course curriculum that covered intersecting topics such as racism, White supremacy, microaggressions, colorism, sexism, patriarchy, Eurocentric beauty standards, homophobia, transphobia, classism, ownership of media, surveillance capitalism, social media, algorithmic bias, overconsumption, environmental injustice, extractivism, colonialism, greenwashing, disinformation, ideology, different epistemologies, as well as positive uses of media for social movements, artivism, culture jamming, ad busting, community journalism, sharing diverse perspectives, and promoting justice.

Peer Teaching

Peer-to-peer instruction can be a useful pedagogical strategy to increase interactive, student-centered, and democratic pedagogies as opposed to solely incorporating lecture-based models in post-secondary education. Although there is not a single method for peer-to-peer teaching (Dawson et al., 2014), Stigmar (2016) defines a *peer tutor* as a student who has prior content knowledge and "operates as a complement and active partner with university teachers in

Table 27.1 Critical Media Literacy Framework

Conceptual Understandings	Guiding Questions
1. Social constructivism All information is co-constructed by individuals and/or groups of people who make choices within social contexts.	*Who* are all the possible people who made choices that helped create this text?
2. Languages/semiotics Each medium has its own language with specific grammar and semantics.	*How* was this text constructed and delivered/accessed?
3. Audience/positionality Individuals and groups understand media messages similarly and/or differently depending on multiple contextual factors.	*How* could this text be understood differently?
4. Politics of representation Media messages and the medium through which they travel always have a bias and support and/or challenge dominant hierarchies of power, privilege, and pleasure.	*What* values, points of view, and ideologies are represented or missing from this text or influenced by the medium?
5. Production/institutions All media texts have a purpose (often commercial or governmental) that is shaped by the creators and/or systems within which they operate.	*Why* was this text created and/or shared?
6. Social and environmental justice Media culture is a terrain of struggle that perpetuates or challenges positive and/or negative ideas about people, groups, and issues; it is never neutral.	*Whom* does this text advantage and/or disadvantage?

Kellner and Share (2019, p. 8).

the process of learning and teaching" (p. 124). Cornwall (1980) observed that peer teachers' mutual identity as students creates the potential to improve information transmission, which can enhance students' understanding of content knowledge (Bath et al., 2004). When peer instruction is integrated in higher education settings, it is frequently used as a pedagogical tool to provide formative feedback to the instructor and gauge students' attainment or misunderstanding of subject matter (Fagen et al., 2002).

However, two systematic literature reviews about peer instruction in higher education identified that peer teaching can do more than just improve information transmission or assessments. They assert that peer instruction can also expand learner agency, motivation, critical thinking, collaboration, as well as increase metacognitive and communication competencies (Dawson et al., 2014; Stigmar, 2016). Peer teaching can also enhance students' sense of belonging, leadership skills, and reception of others' perspectives, which can build stronger classroom communities (Stigmar, 2016). Assinder (1991) identified six key factors for successful peer teaching: (a) incorporating subject matter connected with and relevant to students' lives, (b) providing goal-oriented tasks that elicit a range of skills, (c) co-developing curriculum and pedagogies with students, (d) engaging in learning processes through collaborative small groups, (e) facilitating iterative full-class and individual student feedback on learning tasks, and (f) demonstrating knowledge through peer teaching presentations.

Building from Assinder's (1991) list, we found the following five elements useful to improve peer teaching with critical media literacy: (a) cultivating a caring community and developing interpersonal relationships through continual dialogue; (b) valuing students' lived experiences, creativity, passions, and leadership skills; (c) providing frequent peer teacher instructional design meetings with iterative feedback; (d) affording ample class time to integrate peer-led lessons; and (e) eliciting critical reflection about the learning process from peer teachers, student participants, and instructors. Given the scarce literature on peer teaching in higher education and the desire to address social justice in media literacy education, we describe our experiences integrating peer teaching with critical media literacy.

Teaching Critical Media Literacy Online

During winter 2021, one year into the COVID-19 pandemic, we were teaching critical media literacy remotely to undergraduate students. We were struggling to create a sense of community in an online environment in the midst of lockdowns, protests, and an insurrection. So much was unknown in these times before the vaccine: students were losing friends and family members, mental health was a daily concern, and yet school continued.

We are a teaching team composed of a lecturer who taught elementary school before teaching in higher education (JS) and a doctoral student who taught middle/high school and worked as a teaching assistant in numerous university courses (AG). We shared a desire to disrupt the traditional hierarchy in the classroom and create a more democratic space for students to learn and teach *with* us. We also shared a similar journey from teaching to teacher training and a mutual interest in putting critical theory into classroom practice. Our students came from a variety of cultural backgrounds and academic disciplines.

Following in the legacy of John Dewey and Paulo Freire, we wanted to create an environment with active hands-on learning and critical problem-posing pedagogy, rather than the traditional "banking model of education" (Freire, 2010, p. 72) that prioritizes lecture, memorization, and testing. Dewey's (1938) inquiry-based learning methods reposition all classroom members as teachers and learners guided by their intellectual curiosity. The teacher serves as a facilitator, partnering with students in an inquiry process of research, discovery, synthesis, and sharing. Dewey suggests that the pursuit of new knowledge through active investigations can fortify critical thinking and problem-solving skills that can contribute to a participatory democracy. Freire's (2010) critical pedagogy builds onto this pragmatic vision with problem-posing pedagogy that requires dialogue between students and teachers, learning and teaching each other to name the systems and conditions of oppression that infringe on democracy. This dialogical process occurs through *praxis*, uniting critical reflection and action for social transformation. These ideas became the basis for our partnership to co-create, co-plan, and co-teach courses grounded in democratic pedagogies.

The initial critical media literacy class we taught together was the first time all courses at our university were required to be online; therefore, we had freedom to redesign and shape the course to respond to the current events and our students' needs. Before COVID-19, both of us had taught critical media literacy numerous times with students from kindergarten to higher education. Those practical experiences were a driving force for how we structured the class to be more interactive and participative than typical university courses. We scaffolded learning through multiple and varied student groupings so that everyone had opportunities to work with different students and get to know each other.

Building a sense of community that was supportive, emotionally and intellectually, was a priority throughout the course. We began each class with social–emotional check-ins, followed by short lectures, discussions, and activities in order for students to work in small groups to create media projects as often as possible. A key aspect of critical media literacy pedagogy involves analyzing and creating media with the intention of deepening the learning process through collaborative production (Morrell et al., 2013). Jenkins (2006) asserts that media education should help students "to think of themselves as cultural producers and participants and not simply as consumers, critical or otherwise" (p. 259). Our students created movies and digital stories, took pictures, designed posters, produced ads, remixed memes, and shared their work with the whole class online. Students also maintained their own digital portfolios with Google Slides, allowing us an asynchronous space to provide individualized feedback. After each activity, we engaged in collaborative metacognitive reflection by debriefing the learning process.

The first 2 weeks of the quarter began with both of us meeting for 15 minutes online with each of the 40 students. We asked them about why they were taking the class, what they were hoping to learn, and what they wanted us to know about them. We also gave each student time to ask any questions they had about the course or us. We took copious notes during these meetings and met regularly to discuss the students and the course. These entrance interviews served a powerful role in building community and learning about students' interests, concerns, and funds of knowledge (Moll, 2019). Our notes became valuable resources that we revisited throughout the quarter and even later in other classes. This was important information to help us adapt our curriculum and design the course to be more culturally relevant for students (Ladson-Billings, 2021). These individual meetings became an important opportunity for connecting and building relationships with students, as well as disrupting power hierarchies.

There were several students who had taken other classes with JS previously and were strong advocates for social and environmental justice. They expressed a desire to learn more about teaching and sharing what they had learned in previous classes. We met with these students online after class to discuss their interests and explore possibilities for how we could support them in designing a lesson to teach their peers. This turned into weekly meetings with a committed group of eight students who were passionate about creating a lesson and teaching critical media literacy and ecomedia literacy.

We began the weekly meetings with everyone sharing about themselves, and then we stepped back to encourage them to lead the discussions. We guided the students to create a lesson that included analysis and production. The peer teachers wanted to create an experience that was meaningful to the other students and decided to survey the class about which environmental justice topics they wanted to explore. This provided the feedback to structure their lesson around biophilia (love of nature) and environmental racism.

Students were tasked with determining how to engage their peers in an interactive media-making activity. They were inspired by a poem written by one of their peers during the previous environmental justice course, and they noticed how much their classmates enjoyed using photography. Combining these interests, they designed a digital poem activity in which students would create photographs and write poetry to accompany the images. One week before their class session, they invited their peers to take pictures of their relationships with nature and show how environmental racism impacts their communities. Those photographs were uploaded to a collaborative website for everyone to see each other's images.

On the day of the peer teaching, the student who wrote the poem that inspired this lesson read her poem to the whole class. Next, the student leaders explained the lesson and provided the instructions for the activity. They divided the class into four groups, with two of them facilitating each group. In breakout rooms, the groups discussed their photographs while the peer teachers guided the discussions and took notes. In an article the peer teachers wrote later, they explain how this process

> allowed for the rest of the class to put themselves in the speaker's shoes when listening to the context connected to each picture. Hearing each other's personal narratives and background stories was crucial for creating the poems together. This also gave us an opportunity to gain trust with one another and create a tight-knit community, something that most of us had not experienced before. (Ojeda et al., 2024, p. 114)

In the four groups, the peer teachers led the discussion and process for choosing the photographs and creating the poems. They used the notes of what students said about their own pictures as the first draft of the stanzas, then collaboratively wordsmithed the lines to combine images with words. The final stage of the process involved each person recording themselves reading their own lines and then sending their audio file to the peer teachers. The images and recordings were gathered after class for the peer teachers to assemble into four digital poems—two about biophilia and two about environmental racism (one of the digital poems is available at https://tinyurl.com/avc9t4a5).

Although everyone was focused on creating digital poems, we emphasized that education should prioritize the learning process over the final product. The peer teachers took this to heart and spent considerable time designing the activity to include everyone's voices and offer a meaningful learning experience. Modeling positive teamwork, they gave many affirmations and accolades to their peers throughout the lesson. After reflecting about the process, they wrote,

> When we started the activity and had the students share their photographs, we realized that the learning environment didn't feel like the one we were accustomed to. Instead, we were all collaborators and allies in our shared educational space. Although the task of the group may have been to create a poem in tandem with the images, our main priority was ensuring that we could learn from each other and the different perspectives we shared. (Ojeda et al., 2024, p. 113)

At the end of that quarter, we met again individually with each of the 40 students for a 15-minute online exit interview to learn about their experiences in the class. During these meetings, many students expressed how much they enjoyed the peer teaching lesson. When asked about what was her biggest takeaway from the class, one student replied,

> Hands down the environmental justice lesson. We got to collaborate in a way I haven't done in any other class, we switched between focusing on talking about the images we took, to then building poems and using voice-overs to make a video. Our peers really made this possible. I loved this lesson so much. Now, I want to think about how to educate kids about climate justice to get them to really care about it. (Personal communication, March 14, 2021)

Teaching Critical Media Literacy in Person

After seeing the powerful learning that occurred for the peer teachers who went through the process of creating the lesson and teaching it, as well as for the students on the receiving end of the learning experience, we decided to do this again in the next class we taught together. The second class was an introductory course in the fall of 2021 that focused more on critical media literacy pedagogy in kindergarten through Grade 12 (K–12) classrooms, rather than the previous class that had delved deeper into media systems and politics of representation. This was the first time we were back in person since the pandemic began, and students were excited about engaging with each other, even though we were social distancing and wearing masks.

Four students in this class who had taken the course with us previously volunteered to create a lesson they would teach to their peers. We met with them weekly for a month to explore examples of student-created media and discuss academic goals and practical logistics. We facilitated the discussions and tried not to dominate the space, supporting their decision-making process. The peer teachers noticed that their classmates liked hands-on experiences, so they designed the final class of the quarter for students to collaboratively create digital stories.

Recognizing how much time is necessary for meaningful media production, the peer teachers streamlined the process by recording a tutorial to explain their instructions and demonstrate the technical skills for creating a digital story. They also produced examples to model expectations and created a handout with instructions, including optional topics.

Unlike the previous peer teaching, this time the entire class was divided into six random groups without a peer teacher member. The four peer teachers took on support roles based on their strengths (technical skills, script writing, visual storytelling, and connecting to the critical media literacy framework). Once the groups received their initial instructions and moved to different spaces in the building, the peer teachers moved between groups. They used a group text to coordinate their support, strategically sending the person or supplies as needed.

The six student groups had the autonomy to create their digital stories about any topic that was covered in the class, using their own physical or digital drawings, original script, sound effects, and voiceover narration. Although they had creative freedom to develop their topic, they were guided to create short visual stories with only three to six images. Students drew or selected their pictures, wrote their scripts, and then recorded their voices on top of the illustrations (Figure 27.1). This culminating activity provided an opportunity for everyone to collaboratively express their ideas in creative ways to critically reflect and apply their learning about the issues that concerned them most. The media that students created also became a form of authentic assessment of their learning, as demonstrated in their digital stories representing environmental issues, challenging disinformation, exposing Eurocentric beauty standards, and questioning surveillance and data mining.

As the concluding phase of this lesson, everyone presented their digital stories and debriefed the process they went through to create them. The four peer teachers facilitated

Figure 27.1 Digital story about influencers and beauty standards created by students in Introduction to Critical Media Literacy, Fall 2021. This digital story can be seen and heard at https://tinyurl.com/ye2bynbr.

group dialogue and metacognitive reflection that highlighted the learning gained through the process. This final class was more than just a celebration of the final products; it was also a powerful example of student leadership. Too often in education, the final product of student-created work is overvalued at the detriment of the learning process. The peer teachers not only demonstrated their understanding of process over product but also skillfully helped their peers name it.

Teaching Critical Media Literacy in a Hybrid Format

Responding to equity and access concerns from students, we incorporated a hybrid-learning model (in-person and online) to support students and their families who were at high risk for the effects of COVID-19 or dealing with mental health issues related to the trauma of the pandemic. During our individual online entrance interviews, former students began asking if they could co-teach one session, like the peer teachers they had seen previously. It was exciting to hear the students asking for this and seeing their desire to step up and lead the class. None of the students had done this before, and for many of them, this required stepping outside their comfort zone. This was a turning point for us; no longer were we the ones asking them to volunteer—now they were asking us.

We began the process early in the quarter, meeting online with the peer teachers to assist them in planning their lesson. Five students volunteered and quickly decided that they wanted to have the class create TikTok videos about environmental justice. They focused on the genre of TikTok as memes rather than movies and created examples using current trending templates. They designed their lesson to begin by teaching production skills for creating a TikTok, and they curated resources with critical media texts about environmental justice.

This course yielded new challenges amidst a COVID-19 surge, causing temporary campus closures and periods of in-person, remote, and hybrid learning. The peer teachers were intentional about ensuring that their lesson was accessible for all students' learning needs. For example, the peer teachers consulted with us and their classmates about how to adapt their instruction to bring remote and in-person learners together strategically. They organized in-person volunteers from each group to assist with Zooming or FaceTiming their remote colleagues while ensuring that all members could participate meaningfully and felt welcome.

The peer teachers' focus on centering student learning led them to disrupt many traditional hierarchies of power. Not only were they teaching about TikTok and social media but also they were learning from their peers as they planned the lesson to take advantage of the funds of knowledge that existed in the class. They surveyed the class to learn who had the most experience with TikTok to become group leaders and also expert resources for troubleshooting any problems that arose. Prensky (2010) suggests that when incorporating technology, teachers should avoid positioning themselves as the all-knowing expert and become more of a facilitator of learning, what he refers to as "partnering pedagogy." In her final reflection, a peer teacher shared that initially she felt embarrassed that she did not know how to assist one of the groups. She wrote,

> But looking back, this interaction emphasizes that education is transactional. Similar to how students learn from teachers, we also have as much to learn from them. . . . This doesn't make us failures—it makes us human while eliminating the sense of hierarchy that permeates a lot of K–12 education.

This is an important realization; because technology and media are changing so fast, when teachers partner with students in the learning and teaching process, both can benefit.

Figure 27.2 Two still frames from TikTok videos. The one on the left was used by students to create the one on the right. An example of the original TikTok template is available at https://tinyurl.com/yufstnj2. The student remixed TikTok video is available at https://tinyurl.com/7aar55cx.

The peer teachers worked with us to strategically divide everyone into eight groups to ensure equitable groupings that included a TikTok expert and an online participant. The peer teachers prepared the class a week earlier with a 15-minute presentation that explained the instructions and demonstrated examples. On the day of the lesson, students went right to work and used the first 75 minutes to create their TikTok. An example can be seen in the TikTok students created that uses a trending short video which shows a person walking down the street and spotting people doing something unusual with their car. He asks them what they are doing, and they explain "it's an art project," to which he responds, "Ok, I like it, Picasso!" Our students used the audio from the original with a video they filmed of somebody doing something unusual—that is, "teaching about climate change in schools" (Figure 27.2). The last half hour of the class was used to share and debrief the activity. Similar to the previous class, the peer teachers facilitated the final presentation and debrief session, focusing on process over product. Once again, the metacognitive discussion required all the students to reflect on their experiences creating and to name the learning that was gained from the process of collaboratively creating their alternative media.

Conclusion

Research about the benefits and limitations of peer teaching is scant, especially regarding peer teachers' and students' perspectives about how these methods impact their academic and social–emotional development (Deakin et al., 2012). Although our examples are unique to our context, a large U.S. research university during the pandemic, our experiences align with much of the literature (Assinder, 1991; Dawson et al., 2014; Stigmar, 2016). Through our attempts to disrupt the hierarchies of power in the classroom and empower students, we saw many examples of democratic learning and teaching. Students who volunteered to teach their peers experienced the realities of teaching: the thoughtful planning necessary to incorporate active learning and reflection, the practical requirements of coordinating the students and the learning spaces, and the hands-on realities of live teaching in the moment. We learned the importance of the five key ideas mentioned above: (a) building relationships through dialogue, (b) valuing students' assets, (c) providing frequent feedback, (d) offering class time, and (e) prioritizing reflection about the learning process.

The peer teachers commented at the end about how much they enjoyed the experience and learned from the entire process. Some reflected about how those experiences helped them realize how much they enjoy teaching and want to become a teacher. They became leaders among their classmates and created new lessons that we are now incorporating into other classes. Many of the students who benefited from the peer teachers' lesson reported their appreciation of those activities, listing them as their favorites for the entire course. The democratic pedagogies that evolved from this work disrupted traditional classroom hierarchies, centered students' voices and ideas, built community, incorporated multiple literacies, and provided praxis to theorize and enact social and environmental justice.

References

Assinder, W. (1991). Peer teaching, peer learning: One model. *ELT Journal, 4513*, 218–229.

Bath, D., Smith, C., Stein, S., & Swann, R. (2004). Beyond mapping and embedding graduate attributes: Bringing together quality assurance and action learning to create a validated and living curriculum. *Higher Education Research & Development, 23*, 313–328.

Collins, P. H. (2000). *Black feminist thought: Knowledge, consciousness, and the politics of empowerment* (2nd ed.). Routledge.

Cornwall, M. G. (1980). *Students as teachers: Peer teaching in higher education*. Centrum Onderzoek Wetenschappelijk Onderwijs.

Crenshaw, K. W. (1989). Demarginalizing the intersection of race and sex: A Black feminist critique of antidiscrimination doctrine, feminist theory and antiracist politics. *University of Chicago Legal Forum, 1989*(1), 139–168.

Cubbage, J. (Ed.). (2022). *Critical race media literacy: Themes and strategies for media education*. Routledge.

Dawson, P., van der Meer, J., Skalicky, J., & Cowley, K. (2014). On the effectiveness of supplemental instruction: A review of supplemental instruction and peer-assisted study sessions literature between 2001 and 2010. *Review of Educational Research, 84*, 609–639.

Darder, A., Baltodano, M., & Torres, R. D. (Eds.). (2003). *The critical pedagogy reader*. Routledge.

De Abreu, B. S. (Ed.). (2022). *Media literacy, equity, and justice*. Routledge.

Deakin, H., Wakefield, K., & Gregorius, S. (2012). An exploration of peer-to-peer teaching and learning at postgraduate level: The experience of two student-led Nvivo workshops. *Journal of Geography in Higher Education, 36*, 603–612.

Dewey, J. (1938). *Experience and education*. Collier Books.

Durham, M. G., & Kellner, D. M. (Eds.). (2002). *Media and cultural studies: Keyworks*. Blackwell.

Fagen, A. P., Crouch, C. H., & Mazur, E. (2002). Peer instruction: Results from a range of classrooms. *The Physics Teacher, 40*(4), 206–209.

Freire, P. (2010). *Pedagogy of the oppressed* (M. B. Ramos, Trans.). Continuum.

Freire, P., & Macedo, D. (1987). *Literacy: Reading the word and the world*. Bergen & Garvey.

Funk, S., Kellner, D., & Share, J. (2016). Critical media literacy as transformative pedagogy. In M. N. Yildiz & J. Keengwe (Eds.), *Handbook of research on media literacy in the digital age* (pp. 1–30). IGI Global.

Hammer, R., & Kellner, D. (Eds.). (2009). *Media/cultural studies: Critical approaches*. Peter Lang.

Higdon, N., Butler, A., & Swerzenski, J. D. (2021). Inspiration and motivation: The similarities and differences between critical and acritical media literacy. *Democratic Communiqué, 30*(1), 1–15.

Jenkins, H. (2006). *Convergence culture: Where old and new media collide*. New York University Press.

Kellner, D. (1995). *Media culture: Cultural studies, identity and politics between the modern and the postmodern*. Routledge.

Kellner, D., & Share, J. (2007). Critical media literacy, democracy, and the reconstruction of education. In D. Macedo & S. R. Steinberg (Eds.), *Media literacy: A reader* (pp. 3–23). Peter Lang.

Kellner, D., & Share, J. (2019). *The critical media literacy guide: Engaging media and transforming education*. Brill/Sense.

Kincheloe, J. (2007). *Critical pedagogy primer*. Peter Lang.

Ladson-Billings, G. (2021). I'm here for the hard re-set: Post pandemic pedagogy to preserve our culture. *Equity & Excellence in Education, 54*(1), 68–78.

López, A. (2021). *Ecomedia literacy: Integrating ecology into media education*. Routledge.

Mihailidis, P., Shresthova, S., & Fromm, M. (2021). The values of transformative media pedagogies. In P. Mihailidis, S. Shresthova, & M. Fromm (Eds.), *Transformative media pedagogies* (pp. 14–27). Routledge.

Moll, L. (2019). Elaborating funds of knowledge: Community-oriented practices in international contexts. *Literacy Research: Theory, Method, and Practice, 68*, 130–138.

Morrell, E., Dueñas, R., Garcia, V., & Lopez, J. (2013). *Critical media pedagogy: Teaching for achievement in city schools*. Teachers College Press.

National Association for Media Literacy Education. (n.d.). *Media literacy defined*. https://namle.net/resources/media-literacy-defined

Ojeda, A., Ortega, E., Ramos, J., Romero, V., Sandoval-Lopez, N., Thompson, B., Valeriano, M., & Vega Lopez, J. (2024). Disrupting hierarchies of power and uplifting environmental justice through collaborative ecowriting. In J. Share (Ed.), *For the love of nature: Ecowriting the world* (pp. 115–116). Peter Lang.

Prensky, M. (2010). *Teaching digital natives: Partnering for real learning*. Corwin.

Ramasubramanian, S., Riewestahl, E., & Landmark, S. (2021). The Trauma-informed Equity-minded Asset-based Model (TEAM): The six R's for social justice-oriented educators. *Journal of Media Literacy Education, 13*(2), 29–42.

Share, J., & Gambino, A. (2022). A framework, disposition, and pedagogy for teaching critical media literacy. In W. Kist & M. T. Christel (Eds.), *NCTE special issues: Critical media literacy, Volume 2: Bringing critical media literacy into ELA classrooms* (pp. 11–17). National Council of Teachers of English.

Share, J., Mamikonyan, T., & Lopez, E. (2019). Critical media literacy in teacher education, theory, and practice. In *Oxford research encyclopedia of education*. Oxford University Press. https://oxfordre.com/education/view/10.1093/acrefore/9780190264093.001.0001/acrefore-9780190264093-e-1404

Stigmar, M. (2016). Peer-to-peer teaching in higher education: A critical literature review. *Mentoring & Tutoring: Partnership in Learning, 24*(2), 124–136.

Yosso, T. J. (2020). Critical race media literacy for these urgent times. *International Journal of Multicultural Education, 22*(2), 5–13.

Alternative Cultures of Resistance and Collective Organizing in the Platform Economy

Cheryll Ruth R. Soriano

Amid promises of flexibility, and also actively hailed by many governments as a solution to unemployment, location-based or "geographically tethered" platforms (Woodcock & Graham, 2020) offering ride hailing, food, and last-mile delivery platforms have attracted high numbers of workers in the Global South. With rampant displacements in various sectors of the economy during the COVID-19 pandemic, *platform labor* became a primary source of livelihood for many. But amid the opportunity and the promises of flexibility are precarious work conditions that include pay fluctuations, seasonality of work, hypercompetition, exhaustion, high levels of physical risk, lack of safety nets, algorithmic discrimination, and unfair suspensions, as well as the overall lack of control over platform-mediated organization and management of work (International Labour Organization [ILO], 2021; Tassinari & Maccarrone, 2020; Woodcock, 2021; Woodcock and Graham, 2020).

Although research has highlighted the challenges that platform labor poses for the formation of resistant identities and collective organization, scholarly work and news reports have nonetheless drawn attention to the multiple forms of resistance and collective organization among workers that attend to the injustices in the platform economy.[1] Notably, although many labor movements in the past have been driven by traditional unions, new forms of worker collectives and protest repertoires have emerged to reflect the creative and diverse ways workers, especially those from the informal sector in the Global South, enact their contextual *collective agency* (Bessa et al., 2022; Y. Chen & Soriano, 2022; Cini, 2023; Qadri, 2023; Soriano & Cabañes, 2020). Where traditional unions featured more prominently in platform labor protest activities in Europe and North America, this is not so much the case in Asia Pacific and Africa, and with no documented union-led mobilizations in the Arab region (Bessa et al., 2022, p. 23). In addition to the dwindling union membership in countries such as the Philippines (ILO, 2020), it is important to note that in some countries, such as China, unionizing is prohibited (Y. Chen & Soriano, 2022). Yet, multiple articulations of collective mobilizations are documented globally, constituted by collective app turn-offs and strikes, unity parades, protest demonstrations captured in media reports, and driven by both informal worker collectives and traditional (and new) unions (Bessa et al., 2022, p. 24).

This leads to the importance of examining how platform workers articulate what Chun and Agarwala (2016) call "alternative cultures of organizing" that may deviate from and extend traditional expressions of resistance or forms of organizing. In this chapter, I examine alternative cultures of organizing via "new subjects of labor," "targets" workers bargain with, "repertoires

---

[1] Examples: for the Philippines, see Soriano et al. (2022); for Indonesia, see Qadri (2023); for India, see Selvi et al. (2021); for Thailand, see Mieruch and McFarlane (2022); and for China, see J. Chen (2018).

of struggle," as well as the material dimensions of these resistant and organizational forms (Chun & Agarwala, 2016, pp. 635–636). In addition to manifesting new labor subjects that include women, students, ethnic minorities, youth, or migrants, "alternative cultures diversify the spaces and scales of collective organizing beyond the workplace" (p. 636) to include roads, motorbikes, neighborhoods, platform apps, and social media, and they can involve both local and transnational networks. Through these, workers collectively confront capital's attempts to gain ultimate power by combining struggles for redistribution with struggles for recognition of the self-worth of platform workers.

Communication and media technologies play a dual role in platform labor and emergent cultures of organizing. Technology is central to contestation given that worker concerns are primarily tied to the very model of platform-mediated work organization that incorporates multiple mechanisms of unfair labor arrangements (Tassinari & Maccarone, 2020; Woodcock & Graham, 2020). On the other hand, because platform workers require communication technology such as smart devices and internet connectivity to work, technology is also central to worker communication and mobilization processes (Bessa et al., 2022; Soriano & Cabañes, 2020). As I discuss below, some workers and their supporters have used their technological knowledge to develop platforms with more redistributive goals.

My empirical research on platform labor focuses on the Philippine experience. Following the entry of Uber in 2014, many platforms with global and regional presence have followed suit, along with homegrown start-ups that now proliferate throughout the country. High numbers of workers in the Philippines, estimated at half a million (Fairwork, 2022), have joined platform labor amid the lack of viable employment opportunities. Questions about worker perspectives and experience in joining collective action were integrated into our Fairwork (2022) research in the Philippines that involved in-depth interviews with platform workers. Seeking to understand mobilization strategies and the role of media more deeply, we joined and observed social media groups of Filipino ride-hailing and food delivery workers and took notes of resistant expressions and mobilization strategies. As platform worker associations and unions started to form in 2021 and 2022, one-on-one interviews and focus groups with labor organizers were conducted to better understand their aims and targets, strategies, and the facilitating and constraining factors of collective organization. For purposes of this analysis, the Philippine platform labor organizing experience is juxtaposed against news of gig worker mobilizations in other areas of the Global South as well as extant scholarly analyses.

Challenges for Collective Organizing in the Context of "Always-Existing" Precarity

Labor scholars have argued that a sense of community of workers has declined with the fragmentation of workplaces and internationalization of global value chains driven by technological development (Woodcock & Graham, 2020). Amid the lack of regulatory policies and protection, platform workers—often categorized as independent contractors—suffer from the threat of deactivation and termination if they engage in public resistance or mobilization. Furthermore, not only do platform workers lack economic structural power due to their dispersed, seemingly peripheral location in production chains but also their associational power is undermined by occupational contexts that may make ambiguous the target of collective organizing. Here, I pertain to platform business models that engage subcontractors such as fleet companies or smaller entrepreneurs and make ambiguous the target of worker demands.

It is important to nuance the analysis of injustice and precarization among platform workers in the Global South. To do this, I draw from the work of Ronaldo Munck (2013), who argues for the need to counterbalance the tendency of Western scholarship to assume an aura of newness to the precarity that workers in the Global South experience (Soriano & Cabañes, 2020). In the Philippines, for example, precarity has been the always-already condition of workers, and the informality and lack of social protection experienced by platform workers do not necessarily differentiate them from the almost 40% of the Filipino worker population who are in similarly vulnerable forms of employment (ILO, 2020). In the Global South, short-term contractualization and informal arrangements abound, and many workers do not enjoy statutory protections (Chun & Agarwala, 2016).

The everydayness and commonality of worker vulnerability across industries that makes platform labor appear palatable are further compounded by the dominant discursive representation of the platform worker as "free, flexible, and entrepreneurial." The prevailing market and media narrative is that the platform sector will lead to social inclusion, allowing those with limited access to livelihoods to become new-age entrepreneurs who can earn through flexible work schedules, able to expand their earnings according to the scale of effort, and "be their own boss" (J. Chen, 2018; Y. Chen & Soriano, 2022; Fairwork, 2022). This imaginary of free, flexible independent contractors, sometimes embraced by workers themselves, allows platforms to elide employee protections and at the same time poses challenges to collective organizing (Soriano & Cabañes, 2020; Tassinari & Maccarrone, 2020). Connected to the signaling of platform workers as free and entrepreneurial is the identification of them as being more advanced than their counterparts (i.e., other public transport drivers) because they work with technology apps. The attractiveness of the work is conveyed in the media through multiple signs, including the use of celebrities as signifiers in platforms' job advertisements.

At the height of COVID-19 lockdowns, another trope emerged—the promotion of riders as "superheroes" of the pandemic. This works to normalize the difficulties and risks of on-demand work and workers' understanding of it as a viable and even altruistic work opportunity. Moreover, platform workers are expected to overcome the challenges and channel entrepreneurial values to thrive in competitive labor markets by themselves (Soriano & Cabañes, 2020; Woodcock, 2021). This is compounded by the fact that when work is digital, workers are physically dispersed and also take on diverse jobs at irregular times. Despite the above, platform labor precarity has spurred some workers to engage in multiple forms of resistance and collaborative practices, with media being a central space for coordination and communication and also functioning to visibilize and amplify physical protests (Bessa et al., 2022; Soriano et al., 2022).

The role of media in documenting and popularizing worker protests throughout the world has been well acknowledged (e.g., Chun & Agarwala, 2016; Maffie, 2020). The inability of informal and precarious workers to access basic labor rights and protections across national contexts has revived the significance of symbolic power. Traditionally, *symbolic power* has helped reshape terms and conditions of employment by raising public awareness about the unjust conditions that "invisible" groups of workers face in low-paid, precarious jobs (Chun, 2009). These can include "public dramas" staged in the streets but documented in the media for wider viewership (Chun & Agarwala, 2016). The media play a crucial role in facilitating workers' symbolic power because they make visible isolated worker grievances and help amplify their demands for national and international attention, potentially facilitating awareness and local as well as transnational support. This can be instrumental for exerting pressure upon platforms (especially because many of these operate globally or regionally) and government regulators.

But beyond traditional media, there is emerging scholarship theorizing the role of self-mediation and social media interactions in fostering resistance, solidarity, and unionizing among platform workers in the Global South (Bessa et al., 2022; Lehdonvirta, 2016; Maffie, 2020; Mieruch & McFarlane, 2022; Qadri, 2023; Soriano & Cabañes, 2020). Unique to this category of informal workers is that amid the documented precarious conditions, they are fully digitally tethered and have access to internet connectivity at all times as part of their work. It is imperative, therefore, to explore the unique ways platform workers use media spaces to express resistance and solidarity, even those that work in dialectical tension with the power of global capitalism.

Alternative Cultures of Resistance and Collective Organizing Among Platform Workers in the Philippines and Beyond

Platform workers are cultivating innovative strategies and creating novel organizational forms to challenge the conditions of low-paid, insecure, and unprotected forms of work. I discuss these below by examining the subjects, targets, repertoires, and the material dimensions of these resistant expressions and collective organization.

Labor Organizers and (Old and New) Subjects of Labor

Platform workers are waging struggles that directly address the intersectionality of class and other social identities. The occupational diversity of platform labor in the Global South (e.g., automobile ride hailing versus motorcycle taxi; logistics; food and courier delivery; and cleaning, spa, and care services) implies that workers represent a broad range of income, age, gender identities, ethnic and linguistic backgrounds, migration status, and even literacy levels. Although platform workers may be conveniently categorized in the middle- to lower class brackets, it is important to recognize that in the Philippines, and likely many other countries in the Global South, such class brackets represent the largest percentage of the population (Soriano & Cabañes, 2020). Furthermore, our research showed that workers who owned cars and treated gig work as a side gig perceive labor conditions very differently from motorbike courier delivery workers who continually pay vehicle amortization on top of other work-related costs. Still, their experiences somewhat differ from what appears to be the bottom of the pyramid of platform work—bicycle delivery riders—who are confined by platforms to short-distance deliveries, implying much lower rates but nonetheless involving significant physical labor. Similarly, women and migrants alike encounter challenging working conditions as they are exposed to another layer of risks as they engage in platform work (Selvi et al., 2021; Qadri, 2023; Woodcock, 2021). One key challenge for platform labor organizing, therefore, is how to cater to the multiple worker identities encompassed by platform labor, foster solidarity and harmonize demands and grievances, and harness a collective articulation of their demands.

The Philippines' first gig workers' union, United Delivery Riders Association of the Philippines (RIDERS), is still in its infancy, having been formed in August 2022, although within its first few months it attempted to mobilize smaller unions of workers in the provinces. RIDERS is affiliated with a larger labor federation, Sentro ng mga Nagkakaisa at Progresibong Manggagawa, which represents approximately 80,000 workers in the private, public, and informal sectors and which is also associated with the International Trade Union Confederation, one of the largest global labor centers (https://sentrolabor.wordpress.com). However, platform labor organizing in the Philippines was not pioneered by a labor union. *Kagulong (Kapatiran sa Dalawang Gulong),* considered a workers' collective with approximately 5,000 members, has made important representations of workers in lobby meetings with the government's key labor agencies and legislative bodies even prior to the formation of RIDERS. Notably, *Kagulong* started as a mutual aid association of motorcycle-riding enthusiasts, many of whom are platform workers. In interviews, the founder narrated that motorcycle rider members generally belong to the working classes and sympathize with the demands of platform workers for fair pay and basic labor protections. From its initial Metro Manila focus, Kagulong has since expanded its membership to province-based workers and also started to represent the interests of bicycle platform workers (Don Pangan, personal communication, November 2021 and May 2022). On the other hand, RIDERS, due to its affiliation with traditional unions, tends to embrace a more radical political outlook and militant organizing methods. It also uses the strategy of mobilizing a wider array of social actors, including women's organizations and other activist groups, to strengthen the moral weight of platform workers' symbolic struggles by recasting labor disputes as broader issues of social and economic injustice. Although both RIDERS and *Kagulong* have achieved some success in mounting labor campaigns, they both struggle with recruiting platform workers, who perceive themselves as entrepreneurs or have antagonistic perceptions about labor organizations.

Targets

PLATFORMS

Most platform workers aim for greater transparency in pay calculations and improvement in rates, provision of basic safety nets, and fairer management practices. This implies that most often, platform worker resistance and collective organization efforts are directed at platform management in the hopes of influencing important pro-worker platform reforms.

REGULATORY AND LEGISLATIVE GOVERNMENT BODIES

Many instances of documented protests also target policymakers and regulatory bodies. Platform worker unions and collective bodies in many areas of the world have led appeals for legislation that will recognize the existence of employer–employee relationships because this can facilitate workers' access to benefits and protections afforded by existing labor statutes (Bessa et al., 2022). Worker groups and collectives in Asian countries have also protested for governments to provide subsidies amid oil price hikes and the COVID-19 pandemic. In summary, targeting state actors involved calls ranging from direct safety nets and protections amid social and economic challenges (survival) to appeals for legislative response and reforming the platform labor economy (broader structural reforms).

MEDIA

Labor organizers recognize the importance of gaining media attention to document and amplify their demands. Although some news organizations have published stories about gig worker protests, labor organizers lament that relative to other stories that media pay attention to, platform workers' views about their working conditions should be more prominently featured in the news. For example, labor leaders in the Philippines expressed frustration that when a platform worker was reported to have been found dead on his motorcycle and the platform provided limited support, claiming the absence of an employer–employee relationship, news networks gave more privileged interviews to the platform management rather than to the worker's family and labor groups. The labor organizers explained that featuring the worker's side could have helped mainstream workers' demands for platform accountability and meaningful protections from work-related risks. This case of a platform worker's death while in his workplace—the motorcycle—is an example of what Chun (2013) calls "public drama." Public dramas that expand protest repertoires to include occupations of bridges and other public spaces or hunger strikes have become an increasingly salient feature of informal and precarious workers' struggles in Asian contexts and require media attention and support to achieve their goals (Chun, 2013).

Repertoires

"TAKING THE SQUARE"

There has been an increase in platform worker demonstrations throughout the Philippine archipelago, with tactics that include unity parades, strikes, and demonstrations in front of platform offices (Soriano et al., 2022). These align with the strategies of platform labor activists elsewhere where workers (whether union-led or spontaneously driven by self-organized groups of workers) have gathered in front of platform offices, conducted "mass ride-outs" and "unity parades" through city centers to show force, or organized flash mob protests to cause a scene (Cant, 2020; Cini, 2023). Most of these protests focus on the lack of transparency in fare matrices, unfair deactivations, hidden costs, and the absence of protections. However, such public-facing actions by workers are threatened by platform suspensions and deactivations, compelling workers to consider alternative forms of resistance.

COLLECTIVE APP "SWITCH-OFFS"

App-based drivers have used their self-employed status to their advantage when it comes to striking. An example of this is when workers collectively switch off apps or refuse jobs from the targeted app, sometimes at peak times. Because they are not subject to the restrictive strike laws that control formal employees, workers have more freedom to collectively stop work when they wish. Nonetheless, workers who are found by platforms to have participated in such activities can still suffer from deactivation or permanent banning.

MEME AND HASHTAG MOBILIZATION

In addition to physical protests, worker groups also engage in the active exchange of memes and hashtag mobilization. The circulation of memes that cynically poke fun at low pay or directly attack platforms for unfair labor management help make worker grudges visible for other workers across social media groups, while allowing workers to stay anonymous. These also help platform workers interface with broader social actors or draw the attention of larger worker unions and labor federations.

GAMING THE APP

Woodcock (2021) argues that transport and delivery platform workers have "internal" structural power to disrupt the operation of a platform, or even "game" the platforms' rigid algorithmic monitoring and rating systems. This includes a practice known among drivers in China as "pinning the driver" (*zhazhen*; Y. Chen & Soriano, 2022, p. 52), which has also been observed in the Philippines. In pinning the driver, drivers collude with friends or other workers to claim the cash bonus by asking them to send fake ride requests, pretending to have completed the ride without having driven to the destination. In the Philippines, workers would lend the app and collaborate with other workers to gain more recorded rides and increase incentives. Pinning the driver is also engaged during planned strikes, where participant drivers in China request ride service to identify nonparticipants and then cancel the order or offer poor ratings to punish workers who are uncooperative to strikes (Y. Chen & Soriano, 2022).

PLATFORM CO-OPS AND WORKER-OWNED PLATFORMS

Other forms of alternative organizing are platform co-ops (Scholz, 2017) and worker-owned platforms (Grohmann, 2022). These are platforms designed to challenge the capitalist logics of traditional platforms with the aim to embed the principles of shared ownership, decent pay and income security, co-determined work, and worker protections and benefits, among others (Scholz, 2017, pp. 175–185). Yet, the platform cooperativism movement is not without criticism, as it is known for being well-situated in the contradictions between "politics and enterprise" and "activism and entrepreneurship" (Sandoval, 2020, p. 812). For example, although maximizing profit may not be the aim of these platforms, they ultimately rely on commercial income for sustainability or ideologically justify soft algorithmic control. Furthermore, they are often "devised and implemented 'from above'" with very few of those truly emanating from workers (Woodcock, 2021, p. 92). Still, new worker-led cooperative models inspired by some of the principles of platform cooperativism (but deviating from traditional iterations) are being experimented with in the Global South, albeit there is commonly low uptake among workers (Grohmann, 2022). With this increase in attempts to enact labor power through "pro-worker" technology, it is important to question the extent to which they are truly designed and controlled by workers and how pro-worker ideologies are ultimately embedded in their design.

Media and the Materialities of Worker Organization

Because precarious workers face punitive responses when they organize, the affordances of social media offer opportunities for workers to find belonging and build associational power both covertly and publicly. The assumed individualism of platform labor is challenged by the fact that workers are often connected through social media groups in WhatsApp, Viber, Douyin, or Facebook to exchange strategies of coping; crowdsource aid in times of distress; or simply engage in "watercooler talk," in which workers share everyday experiences and struggles through memes, jokes, and light banters.

Platform workers also engage in instrumental communication such as "entrepreneurial solidarities" on social media groups (Soriano & Cabañes, 2020), where they exchange self-help strategies drawn from vernacular knowledge (Y. Chen & Soriano, 2022; Qadri, 2023) about how to survive and thrive in the platform-mediated work environment. The regular and continuous sharing of strategies is important given that platforms constantly change their algorithms, promotional schemes, codes of conduct, material requirements for work, and even incentive and pay matrices. These affordances help contribute to workers' "ambient affiliation" (Zappavigna, 2011) that affirms the common experiences of their conditions and struggles.

Unions and workers' collectives use social media for coordination and mobilization. Most labor organizers are optimistic about the contributions of online spaces to document the history of their struggles, make issues visible and searchable, and facilitate everyday communication and coordination. On social media, it is easier for labor organizers to demonstrate affinity with workers of similar experience globally by sharing their protest activities. Moreover, social media is viewed as useful for those who cannot attend physical gatherings to learn about an event and also to increase support. Given the geographic and occupational diversity, online initiatives can illustrate the scale of shared grievances. These function to rekindle sentiments and create a sense of belonging to construct and sustain mobilization practices.

Another significant component pertains to the materiality of protest representations across the media. The riders' motorbikes not only facilitate riders' ease of mobility during protests and unity parades but also are commonly used in protest materials to signify platform work. Another key source of identification crucial in protests is the gig workers' colored uniforms, which are usually associated with a particular platform. Cognizant of the power of signification and potential impact to their brands, platforms in the Philippines have recently prohibited workers from exhibiting any form of identification (e.g., uniforms, helmets, and bags) during protest activities, whether physical or online. Without uniforms, platform workers are unidentifiable when shown in news reports, and platforms use this ambiguity to argue that protesters are "impostors."

Platform Labor Organizing and Mobilization: Future Directions and Questions

Many previous studies on labor resistance and organizing have highlighted overt forms of activism or well-organized and union-led political engagements as key to addressing the structures of labor injustice. However, there are nuances in platform workers' conditions that complicate the way resistance and collective organization can be understood, as well as the role of media in it.

Collective efforts for mutual support or circumvention of platform labor controls are more often driven by hopes of immediate economic gain or by the threat of income decline. Nonetheless, although many informal organizing efforts on social media have yet to fully translate into institutional changes or sector-wide solidarity, these efforts need to be viewed as part of a continuum of workers' long-term struggles for labor justice. For some workers who are fully dependent on platform labor and embrace their identity as independent contractors, perhaps "entrepreneurial strategies" and expressions of "mutual aid" on social media will be the extent of their collective participation to mitigate immediate challenges. For other workers who recognize the deeper injustices wielded by platform-mediated organizations of work, they would perhaps be attracted to join sustained and public mobilizations that aim to spur policy changes and pressure platforms for much-needed pro-worker reforms. Other workers would be able to draw connections between the injustices of labor platformization and the unbridled profit accumulation in neoliberal economic systems and may wish to affiliate with larger transnational unions to challenge capitalism head on. How to bridge these multiple subjectivities and diverse levels of identification with deeper labor justice issues will be a continuing challenge.

Although not a direct focus of this chapter, intermediaries have historically played an important role in labor organizing. These include critical media but also engaged scholars, research networks, and other civil society actors helping in the amplification of gig worker campaigns, fostering legislative dialogues, or even helping develop alternative platform design. Perhaps crucial for future analysis would be these intermediaries' role and responsibilities in sustaining platform labor mobilization, protecting workers amid the counterpunch of platforms, or crystallizing their efforts to challenge platforms' collusion with media and governments.

It is apparent that although the resistant strategies and tactics of worker collective organizations appear to echo each other throughout the Global South, there is limited observable cross-country or regional organizing among workers. It would be of value to examine the congruences, contradictions, and opportunities for connection by drawing from the comparative experiences of the Global South. As a direction for future research, examining patterns of organization and challenges to build solidarity across national and even regional experience may enrich theoretical debates in terms of the politics, nuances, and actual meaning of these spaces for workers and activists. Practically, this would be useful for supporting and bridging diverse expressions of resistance and solidarity amid continuing technological development and demand for platform reforms.

Acknowledgments

This research was performed with the funding and administrative support of Fairwork/ Deutsche Gesellschaft für Internationale Zusammenarbeit (GIZ) and De La Salle University.

References

Bessa, I., Joyce, S., Neumann, D., Stuart, M., Trappmann, V., & Umney, C. (2022). *A global analysis of worker protest in digital labour platforms* (ILO Working Paper 70). International Labour Organization. https://www.ilo.org/wcm sp5/groups/public/----dgreports/---inst/documents/publication/wcms_849215.pdf

Cant, C. (2020). *Riding for deliveroo: Resistance in the new economy*. Polity Press.

Chen, J. (2018). Thrown under the bus and outrunning It! The logic of Didi and taxi drivers' labour and activism in the on-demand economy. *New Media and Society, 20*(8), 2691–2711.

Chen, Y., & Soriano, C. R. (2022). How do workers survive and thrive in the platform economy: Evidence from China and the Philippines. In M. Graham & F. Ferrari (Eds.), *Digital work in the planetary market* (pp. 41–58). MIT Press.

Chun, J. J. (2009). *Organizing at the margins: The symbolic politics of labor in South Korea and the United States*. Cornell University Press.

Chun, J. J. (2013). *The struggles of irregularly employed workers in South Korea, 1999–2012* [Working paper]. UCLA Institute for Research on Labor and Employment.

Chun, J. J., & Agarwala, R. (2016). Global labour politics in informal and precarious jobs. In S. Edgell, H. Gottfried, & E. Granter (Eds.), *Handbook of the sociology of work and employment* (pp. 634–650). SAGE.

Cini, L. (2023). Resisting algorithmic control: Understanding the rise and variety of platform worker mobilisations. *New Technology, Work and Employment, 38*(1), 125–144.

Fairwork. (2022). *Fairwork Philippines ratings 2022: Towards fair labour conditions in the PH platform economy*. https:// fair.work/en/fw/publications/fairwork-philippines-ratings-2022-towards-fair-labor-conditions-in-the-ph-platf orm-economy

Grohmann, R. (2022). Beyond platform cooperativism: Worker-owned platforms in Brazil. *Interactions, 29*(4), 87–89. https://doi.org/10.1145/3540251

International Labor Organization. (2020). *Informal economy in the Philippines*. https://www.ilo.org/manila/areasofw ork/informal-economy/lang--en/index.htm

Lehdonvirta, V. (2016). Algorithms that divide and unite: Delocalisation, identity and collective action in "micro-work". In J. Flecker (Ed.), *Space, place and global digital work* (pp. 53–80). Palgrave Macmillan.

Maffie, M. D. (2020). The role of digital communities in organizing gig workers. *Industrial Relations, 59*(1), 123–149.

Mieruch, Y., & McFarlane, D. (2022). Gig economy riders on social media in Thailand: Contested identities and emergent civil society organisations. *Voluntas, 30*, 1–11. doi:10.1007/s11266-022-00547-7

Munck, R. (2013). The precariat: A view from the South. *Third World Quarterly, 34*(5), 747–762. doi:10.1080/01436597.2013.800751

Qadri, R. (2023). Algorithmized not atomized: The distributed solidarity of Jakarta's gig workers. *International Journal of Communication (Online), 17*(20), 3899–3918. https://ijoc.org/index.php/ijoc/article/view/17760

Sandoval, M. (2020). Entrepreneurial activism? Platform cooperativism between subversion and co-optation. *Critical Sociology, 46*(6), 801–817. doi:10.1177/0896920519870577

Scholz, T. (2017). *Uberworked and underpaid: How workers are disrupting the digital economy*. Polity Press.

Selvi, S., Maheswari, U., & Kuriakose, F. (2021). *From granular to collective resistance: Rethinking workers' protests in digital cultures*. SSRN. http://dx.doi.org/10.2139/ssrn.3963547

Soriano, C., Binghay, V., Medina, M., Garcia, C., & Badger, A. (2022, October 17). *The rise of worker protests in the Philippine platform economy spotlights unfair work conditions*. Fairwork. https://fair.work/en/fw/blog/the-rise-of-worker-protests-in-the-philippine-platform-economy-spotlights-unfair-work-conditions

Soriano, C. R. R., & Cabañes, J. V. A. (2020). Entrepreneurial solidarities: Social media collectives and Filipino digital platform workers. *Social Media + Society, 6*(2). https://doi.org/10.1177/2056305120926484

Tassinari, A., & Maccarrone, V. (2020). Riders on the storm: Workplace solidarity among gig economy couriers in Italy and the UK. *Work, Employment and Society, 34*(1), 35–54.

Woodcock, J. (2021). *The fight against platform capitalism: An inquiry into the global struggles of the gig economy*. University of Westminster Press.

Woodcock, J., & Graham, M. (2020). *The gig economy: A critical introduction*. Polity Press.

Zappavigna, M. (2011). Ambient affiliation: A linguistic perspective on Twitter. *New Media & Society, 13*(5), 788–806. https:// doi.org/10.1177/1461444810385097

LGBT Activism, Social Media, and the Politics of Queer Visibility in Ghana

Godfried A. Asante, Wunpini Fatimata Mohammed, and Ama Boatemaa Appiah-Kubi

This chapter explores how lesbian, gay, bisexual, transgender, and sassoi (LGBTS) Ghanaian activists use social media to mitigate the tensions around the desire for political visibility and the need for personal safety. Sassoi is a local term used by same-gender-loving people in southern Ghana to identify themselves outside of the dominant Western LGBTQI+ discourse. Therefore, we include sassoi in the LGBTQI+ acronym to highlight the diverse forms of sexualities outside the dominant Western sexual categories. Same-sex sexual relations continue to be a criminal offense in Ghana under the carnal knowledge clause instituted by the British during colonization (Adjepong, 2021; Atuguba, 2019). Although the law does not specifically mention same-sex sexual relations, the carnal knowledge clause criminalizes all forms of non-heterosexual sexual activities, and it is usually used to violate the rights of sexual minorities. The broad entrenchment of heteronormativity as the basis for Ghanaian cultural and sexual citizenship has created room for the legitimation of vigilante and state violence against LGBTS persons (Asante, 2020; Otu, 2021). Simultaneously, LGBTS activists have emerged to resist their erasure from national politics. The clash in meanings on what constitutes African sexual citizenship has sparked intense debates about African subjectivity and sexual rights between religious and political leaders and the local Ghanaian LGBTS activists. Related to the topic of this chapter is the dialectical tensions that activists experience as they navigate the tenuous terrain between the need for political visibility and the necessity for security, safety, and sense of belonging.

Television, radio, and social media continue to play a significant role in framing and influencing the debates around sexual rights and queer visibility throughout the world (Altman & Symons, 2016). In Ghana, such debates are largely shaped by anti-LGBTS media organizations that have partnered with anti-LGBTS politicians and religious fundamentalists such as the Ghana Pentecostalist and Charismatic churches (GPCCs) both in Ghana and in the United States to discursively frame LGBTS rights as part of Western colonial efforts (Asante, 2020; Mohammed, 2022; Tettey, 2016). Hackett (1998) notes that the Pentecostalists were very quick to understand the implications of the liberalization of the media, which entailed a shift from state ownership and control over radio, television, and the press to privatization of these outlets. They realized that broadcasting their messages through radio and television was a perfect way to proselytize in order to attract more people to their church. Therefore, they began to buy more airtime and broadcast their activities through radio and television. Nowadays, early in the mornings, virtually all Ghanaian radio stations offer zealous sermons by Pentecostal preachers. In addition to a wide variety of Christian programs, television viewers encounter advertisements of popular churches inviting viewers to come to their crusades to receive wealth and financial success. In this regard, GPCCs have acted as moral entrepreneurs (Tettey, 2016) to falsely make the case that LGBTQ+ rights will morally bankrupt the nation and further entrench Western imperialist control of Ghana's culture and resources. The discursive framing of LGBTQ+ rights as morally bankrupt and akin to European colonization has created an atmosphere in which homophobic violence and discrimination can be rationalized as protecting African cultural values and therefore LGBTS people should be made politically voiceless.

More contemporarily, LGBTS Ghanaian activists use social media sites such as Twitter, Facebook, and Instagram to navigate the institutional constraints presented by conventional media such as television and radio. For instance, some LGBTS activists are denied access to debunk false statements made about LGBTS people on television and radio. Furthermore, human rights activists are rarely invited to appear on radio and television programs to discuss the illegality and inhumane treatment of LGBTS persons in Ghana. The alternative option has largely been social media as a site to garner political visibility and activism (Mohammed, 2022). Bailey (2021) also notes that social media sites such as Twitter, Facebook, and Instagram are usually represented as queer safe spaces because they allow for the complex maneuvering between visibility and invisibility to occur by creating room for anonymity and privacy. Nonetheless, its features have also restricted their ability to implement a stronger mobilization strategy against anti-LGBTS bills and movements in the country (Gore, 2018). Ultimately, activists have to navigate the dialectical tensions between the need for visibility and invisibility, along with political solidarity, and what constitutes progress within LGBTS activism in the Ghanaian context. In this chapter, we flesh out these tensions.

In the following, we first explore the historical and political context influencing the entrenchment of political homophobia in the Ghanaian sociocultural landscape. We delve into colonial and African perspectives on LGBTS identities. Next, we examine the literature on how social media can be utilized as queer safe spaces. We join other queer and feminist geography scholars and communication scholars to challenge the monolithic construction of virtual queer spaces as liberatory and inclusive and reveal the dialectical tensions that shape activist approaches to activism.

Colonial/African Perspectives on LGBTQ+ Identities

Despite historical evidence to the contrary, same-sex relations continue to be represented as a menace and a Western import. There is ample anthropological evidence of cultural practices that nurtured gender diversity, often in sexual relational terms, among precolonial African societies.

According to Howard-Hassmann (2001), same-sex relations were not always understood as homosexuality in Africa. This means that same-sex relations have never been uncommon in African societies. They had always existed prior to the arrival of the colonialists to the continent. Many studies have shown the diverse nature of sexuality in Africa as elsewhere (Epprecht, 2010). These studies demonstrate the prevalence of same-sex relations in different African contexts in which young and older people, men and women, engaged in same-sex relations for social, cultural, and even personal reasons (Epprecht, 2010; Murray & Roscoe, 1998). Most scholars note that heterosexual relationships coexisted with same-sex sexual practices. For example, Murray and Roscoe (1998) note that in precolonial societies such as the Bafia of Cameroon, young boys engaged in sexual relations with older boys. Through their socialization process, young boys played passive roles with senior brothers, often resulting in penetrations. Although this was done in secrecy and was not known by parents, in some other communities, same-sex sexual relations had been instituted without any form of antagonism.

Among the Mossi of West Africa, Gisu of East Africa, Zande and Pahuins of Central Africa, and Senegalese and Zambians, in addition to others, same-sex sexual relations appeared more like a cultural and social institution legitimized by the norms and values of the society (Hassett, 2007; Heald, 1999; Tauxier, 2012). Both Heald and Hassett assert that transsexuality and homosexuality existed among the Gisu of East Africa without any contention. Attesting to homosexuality among the Zande of Central Africa Republic, Evans-Pritchard (1970) contends that same-sex marriages commanded similar respect as hetero-sexual marriages. Although the Pahuins in Central Africa had wives, young adults continued to have same-sex relations with young boys without facing any repudiation. Also, among the Ashanti in Cote d'Ivoire, enslaved people captured during conquests were used as concu-bines. This means that they became sexual partners of the men of the kingdom. In Senegal, enslaved men engaged in sexual relations with each other due to the absence of females. This was also prevalent among women in Lesotho (Kendall, 1998). According to Murray and Roscoe (1998), female husbands were known among the Sotho, Lovedu, Koni, and Zulus in South Africa. Among the Lovedu, the queen was forbidden from having a male husband and was required instead to have a wife (Murray & Roscoe, 1998). Zabus (2013) argued that female same-sex sexual practices were widespread in almost all African societies where sexual relations between women could be encountered, such as among Hausa women in northern Nigeria. Sodomy has been part of the initiatory process of people in countries such as Zambia (Murray & Roscoe, 1998).

However, beginning in 1957, as several African countries began to obtain independence, knowledge of these cultural practices has been largely grafted over by a neocolonial Christian cisheteropatriarchal narrative that maintains and asserts Africans are inherently heterosexual and, in turn, normatively gendered (Epprecht, 2013). The gradual erasure of precolonial rela-tional formations can be traced back to African oral traditions. Prior to colonial conquest, orality was the primary mode for many African societies to transmit their histories and cultural practices. However, sexual practices were rarely preserved through oral tradition, thus open-ing the way for colonial narratives of sex and gender duality and binarism to gain prominence (Epprecht et al., 2018). Moreover, colonialism introduced formal education and boarding schools that restricted, if not barred, intergenerational familial contact between grandparents, parents, and children. Taken together, precolonial knowledges about gender and sexual diver-sity, and the cultural systems and relational formations that made such diversity possible, largely eroded into a colonial hegemony of cisheteropatriarchy. Currently, the increasing influ-ence of Pentecostalist Charismatic churches, proselytizing against a backdrop of support from African political elites—for whom gender and sexual diversity are equated with "primitive-ness" and amorality and/or, paradoxically, viewed as a Western secular force threatening tradi-tional African culture—play an especially hostile role in the continued demonization of gender and sexual diversity (Epprecht, 2008).

In Ghana, although the laws are not explicit on the illegalities of same-sex relations, the carnal knowledge law criminalizes all forms of nonheterosexual activities, paving the way for homophobic and violent attacks on the LGBTQ+ community (Adjepong, 2021; Asante, 2020; Otu, 2021). The LGBTQ+ community is primarily marginalized and experiences physical and psychological violence (Adjepong, 2021; Dankwa, 2021; Gyamerah et al., 2020; Quarshie et al., 2020). This violence is institutionalized in the sense that educational, religious, political, legal, and social institutions work together to entrench homophobia in the country (Mohammed, 2019). Undeniably, religion, politics, and the media are critical instigators of violence against the LGBTQ+ community in Ghana (Amoah & Gyasi, 2016; Baisley, 2015; Essien & Aderinto, 2009; Tetteh, 2016). These institutions appropriate the media space and use political power to threaten nonheterosexual and queer individuals and deprive them of their freedom of speech. Doing so creates an unwelcoming and unsafe environment for sexual minorities to thrive or exercise their right to agency (Ako, 2021; Amoah & Gyasi, 2016). Hence, there is a drive toward queer safe spaces.

Social Media as Queer Safe Spaces?

As explained above, the LGBTS community in Ghana experiences targeted physical violence. As such, the open expression of same-sex sexuality and its advocacy have largely remained invisible. In this larger context, it is important to explore the overarching literature around queer safe spaces as a site for collective political becoming and activism. Carillo-Rowe (2010) emphasized "the inter of intercultural communication is a capacious site of unfolding interaction across lines of difference. It gestures toward the unknown and unknowable space between unevenly located subjects" (p. 221). Here, we can extrapolate Carillo-Rowe's concerns about alliance building as saturated in power lines and relations to queer safe spaces as well.

Major social media sites such as Twitter, Instagram, and Facebook have predominantly functioned as queer safe spaces where networks can be forged and advocacy efforts can be mobilized. Yet different assumptions underlie the meanings of "queer safe spaces." Pascar et al. (2018) argue that *queer safe spaces* are characterized by (a) underscoring resistance and subversion as significant capacities required in the queer space construction; (b) formulating a space for the community and its culture; (c) constructing subjective boundaries that are known to the members of the marginalized group but do not have to be known to outsiders; and (d) establishing a new organization of temporality, which creates continuous subjective gender experiences and performances rather than producing dissociation. Nonetheless, although digital spaces have offered new opportunities for queer and LGBTQ+ people to network with each other and mobilize, they have also presented pertinent challenges for community consciousness and collective identity production for LGBTQ+ activism and mobilization (Asante, 2017; Boyd & Ellison, 2007; Nash & Gorman-Murray, 2019).

Cavalcante (2019) argues that queer youth have found social community and belonging on social media sites. In a way, social media sites have become new gayborhoods and gay bars for youth. As a result, he explains that LGBTQ+ youth come together on social media to perform essential sociopolitical and sociocultural functions, such as educating themselves on issues related to sexuality, digitally narrating intimate storytelling, and fostering sexual networks and encounters. Furthermore, Asante (2018) explores how social media sites, such as closed Facebook groups, offer spaces of belonging where African immigrants in the diaspora and those on the continent create transnational relations in a virtual space.

Hashtag activism, for example, has become a potent political tool for building public support through social media. It has become a means by which marginalized voices share their opinions, and it has the potential to inject new voices into public discourse and create sociopolitical changes in the real world (Goswami, 2018; Nenoff, 2020). Hashtag activism has been one of the essential tools for challenging and resisting heteronormative and homophobic norms (Freelon et al., 2018; Jackson & Foucault Welles, 2016; LeMaster & Johnson, 2019). Scholars such as Liao (2019) have revealed how the Chinese LGBTQ+ community on Weibo, through the hashtag #IAmGay#, countered censorship of homosexual content. Liao notes that the hashtag allowed users to engage in discursive activism through storytelling that involved personal and particular narratives. According to Liao, the posts shared generated connective actions that generated alternative discourse about LGBTQ+ rights and free speech and consequently challenged the government's hegemonic discourse. Bailey (2021) also reveals how trans women use social media through hashtag activism to counter negative stereotypes about the community. In her book *Misogynoir Transformed: Black Women's Digital Resistance*, Bailey emphasized that Black trans women use digital platforms to create redefined representations of themselves outside the problematic lens of trans misogynoir. Through hashtags such as #GirlsLikeUs, #TWOC, and #FreeCeCe, trans women transform social media into social justice magic that advocates for their lives. These hashtags led to real-life transformations that challenged stereotypes and offered better health outcomes for Black trans women (Bailey, 2021).

In their work on hashtag activism, Jackson et al. (2020) also demonstrate how popular hashtags from 2009 to 2019 provided race and gendered counterpublics opportunities to speak back to power. The authors emphasize how the creation and use of #GirlsLikeUs by a network of transgender women, especially trans women of color, provided them the space to engage and share their experiences beyond stereotypical representations. Through hashtags, they built community, celebrated their accomplishments and visibility, and advocated for trans issues and rights through their voices and sharing of factual information about trans experiences with injustice (poverty, sexism, and racism). The hashtags thus afforded them the opportunity for counter-engagement to center trans politics and normalize trans lives. As argued by the authors, hashtags played an indispensable role in constructing an intersectional digital trans community and radically shifting the representations of and messages about trans people from outside the community (Jackson et al., 2020). Nonetheless, these forms of activism come with different risks in the Ghanaian context that activists have to continually evaluate.

As much as virtual spaces offer a protected space for collective mobilization, it also has the tendency to produce spaces infused with differential power structures (Carillo-Rowe, 2010). Queer safe spaces are defined by different expectations on what constitutes the "LGBTQ+ community," the rules of engagement and the "appropriate" ways to do activism, or what even constitutes queerness. Feminist and queer geographers have astutely observed patterns of inclusion and exclusion within digital queer spaces. Feminist geographers, in particular, have called for the shifting of studies on queer space to focus on the "mutual constitution of gendered identities and spaces" (Bondi & Rose 2003 p. 234). Hartal (2018) contends that current work by feminist geographers has opened the door for the examination of the "mutual construction of LGBT subjectivities and their experiences in space, specifically, queer space" (p. 3).

We are of the view that queer safe spaces are constitutive of the physical, discursive, rhetoric, virtual, material, emotional, and imagined capacities. Virtual queer safe spaces are not outside of, or distinct from, the identity politics engulfing face-to-face interactions. Thus, tensions emerge as community members navigate not only the potential for anti-LGBT violence but also the nuances of building solidarity and alliance within the LGBTS community in Ghana. As such, Ghana presents a particularly useful context for the exploration of queer safe spaces as sites of differential and contested belonging. Next, we explore the three key tensions that LGBTS activists experience.

Navigating Tensions in the Ghanaian Technosphere
Tensions Around Political Visibility and Invisibility

Since many Ghanaian media organizations began to utilize social media in the 2000s to reach a wider public beyond traditional media, there has been an uptick in discussions around LGBTQ+ rights in Ghana. When social media platforms such as Facebook became very popular in Ghana around 2006 and 2007, a cross section of Ghanaians began to use them to discuss various issues occurring in the country. Conversations around sexual identity and "Ghanaianness" gained attention. Even during this time, the wide digital divide meant that these platforms were only accessible to a few Ghanaians, given the high costs of internet data and digital gadgets such as computers and smartphones. Today, Facebook, Instagram, and Twitter are used widely as spaces of public deliberation on essential political and social matters.

As such, there is a vibrant digital public sphere that various organizations affiliated with the government, civil society, and the nonprofit sector have leveraged to reach a wider national and global audience with varying degrees of success. Despite this steady growth, it was not until 2018 that LGBTS organizations such as LGBTQ+ Rights Ghana began to make a concerted effort to utilize social media platforms to bring awareness to issues affecting queer and trans Ghanaians. Although there are other LGBTS organizations in the country, LGBTQ+ Rights Ghana is considered the foremost LGBTQ+ organization because of its large presence on social media, which tends to overshadow the other subtle and (invisible) advocacy tactics adopted by other organizations in the country. Ultimately, tensions arise between the need for political visibility via social media and the cultural expectations of sexual discretion (Dankwa, 2021).

LGBTS issues in Ghana began to gain visibility in the early 1990s. Before then, it was generally reported in both local and international media that there were no "homosexuals" or LGBTS movements in Ghana. In 1998, the silence around same-sex sexuality was ruptured when the British government funded a human rights training workshop for Ghanaian sexual minorities. Andam (2019) explains that after the training, three attendees formed the Gay and Lesbian Association of Ghana. However, the group encountered government opposition to its name and changed it to the Center for Popular Education and Human Rights Ghana. Eventually, it received funding from the Astraea Lesbian Foundation for Justice to purchase stationery and furniture to begin its LGBTQ+ advocacy work in Ghana.

Asante (2022) notes that the establishment of the first LGBTQ+ organization in Ghana portended the establishment of numerous partnerships between Western governments, international nongovernmental organizations, and the already existent grassroots organizations. This moment also initiated the "bureaucratization" of queer social movements from a decentralized grassroots movement that focused on everyday concerns, such as increasing poverty, inadequate health care, and corruption, to the sole focus on the LGBTQ+ community, sexual rights, and visibility politics. The ensuing partnerships that emerged in the hope of advancing LGBTQ+ rights in Ghana also necessitated the desire to construct a deserving "LGBTQ+ community" to attract international donors. However, the desire to make the "LGBTQ+ Ghanaian community" visible to a predominantly international audience prompted the use of specific visibility tactics on social media that ultimately thrust the LGBTS community into international politics which do not always serve the interests of the larger LGBTS community who do not have access to the digital affordances of social media. Eventually, dialectical tensions arose out of the need for political visibility while also being cognizant of the larger implications of such visibility work—no matter how necessary it is.

Although some LGBTS organizations have utilized the digital public sphere to bring attention to issues affecting their community, they have also utilized these platforms to build safe spaces and to strategize about building queer liberatory futures. Twitter is a vital platform on which queer politics are articulated in Ghana. Indeed, other mainstream feminist and gender advocacy organizations have utilized social media platforms to support their organizing work in the country (Mohammed, 2023). Organizations such as Rightify Ghana have utilized Twitter to draw attention to the human rights violations that the queer and trans community is perpetually subjected to. Others, such as the Young Feminist Collective, have used Instagram and Twitter to hold the current president of Ghana, President Nana Addo, accountable for his complicity in state-sanctioned violence directed at the LGBTQ+ community (Mohammed, 2022). It is within this larger context that we bring attention to the way that social media can function as a queer safe space—one in which queer and trans communities in Ghana organize around a queer digital politic, albeit not without consequences of internal rife.

Tensions Around Intersectional Solidarity

While LGBTQ+ communities grapple with institutionalized violence from the state, they often have to navigate complicated relationships with mainstream feminist organizations whose praxes are often exclusionary of the queer and trans community. Mohammed (2022) indicates how mainstream organizations, in their quest to create solidarity with queer and trans people, reproduce harmful narratives that further entrench homophobic norms in the Ghanaian public sphere. Here, we draw parallels between the issues affecting queer communities and other marginalized groups in the country, highlighting the importance of solidarity and accountability in building queer and feminist liberatory futures that center the margins. Recent conversations on intersectionality in Ghanaian feminist movements have shed light on the exclusion of the LGBTQ+ community in gender advocacy in the country (Adjepong, 2021) and the need to build bridges across feminist and queer organizations and activists. These initiatives reveal the tensions within these groups and how it influences their approaches to political advocacy on social media.

LGBTS organizations are strategically positioned to disrupt the exclusionary politics that have long plagued mainstream feminist organizing in the country. For example, Rightify Ghana recently embarked on a social media campaign to provide education about LGBTS identities in Ghanaian languages. Although this campaign attempted to include languages that are often excluded in mainstream feminist organizing, the group inadvertently reproduced the marginalization of certain communities that have historically been disenfranchised. Fox and Ore (2010) argue that omitting intersectionality from the analysis of safe spaces leads to the reliance on a particular identity around which safe spaces are constructed. In this instance, the campaign focused on the Akan, Ga, Ewe, and Hausa languages, which are widely spoken in the south of the country, thus completely excluding the northern half of the country from these representations, including queer individuals. Note that the campaign was popularized by a trans woman who sought to reach the grassroots and subaltern communities, often erased from feminist organizing work. The second author, who is a Dagbana/Dagomba, and whose language and cultural identity were erased from this representation, brought attention to this erasure. Another feminist who witnessed this interaction intervened and offered to pay for the inclusion of northern Ghanaian languages in this campaign. The second author eventually worked together with Rightify Ghana to identify voice-over artists to replicate this campaign in the Waali and Gurune languages.

Stengal and Weems (2010) note that power relations constrain and enable certain ways of speaking and acting. That notwithstanding, this feminist intervention clearly demonstrates the need for accountability systems in queer safe spaces (Russo, 2019). It also draws attention to the issue of ethnopolitics that is often pushed to the periphery in discussions around LGBTS activism. Paying attention to the ways that ethnopolitics informs queer Ghanaian identities shows how certain subject positions are imagined to inhabit the discursive boundaries of safe space in digital spaces.

Although the result of this feminist intervention was more inclusion for a systematically marginalized community in the Ghanaian national space, it is not guaranteed that this result would have been achieved if the critique were directed at a mainstream gender advocacy or feminist organization. Historically, mainstream feminist organizations whose lens of activism is limited to focusing on issues affecting straight, Christian, and southern Ghanaian women have often resisted critiques from queer communities, religious minorities, and people from marginalized ethnic groups (Mohammed, 2023). Feminist and queer solidarity and accountability were achieved in this case because although a member of this queer organization was resistant to the critique provided by the second author, she was open to working with the second author, as well as the benevolent feminist who offered to bear the costs of producing video campaigns that would include northern languages. Ultimately, LGBTS organizations have the potential to propel the feminist movement forward by embodying feminist account-ability and intersectionality praxes in the work that they do. They have the potential to create the liberatory futures that are needed to undo the reproduction of marginalization that has been the norm in Ghanaian feminist spaces for a long time.

Tensions Around Progress and Backlash

Although social media has been used to garner spaces of solidarity between queer, trans, and feminist organizations, its sharing features have produced contradictory and ambivalent situa-tions for queer communities in Ghana. On February 24, 2021, LGBTQ+ Rights Ghana posted images and videos of an LGBTS community center on various social media sites. It noted that the community center was established to act as a safe space for queer Ghanaians to mobilize and seek support. However, anti-LGBTS activists used the Instagram and Facebook posts as evidence of the entrenching reach of LGBTS rights in Ghana and mobilized the Ghana Police Service for its closure. Since this incident, several LGBTS people in the country have become targets of homo-phobic violence. This case speaks to how organizational activities on social media affect the lives of queer individuals outside of the digital technosphere. This incident also shows that although social media sites can be used to create awareness around important and essential political issues for queer individuals in places where same-sex relations are criminalized, such queer visibility tactics can come with risks for all LGBTS persons in the region. This exemplifies the political ramifica-tions of the need for social progress and its larger implications beyond social media.

Social media companies have done little to protect LGBTS people in areas where same-sex sexual relations are criminalized. As such, this increases the ramifications for local social activists who have little power to challenge the increasing incendiary messages about LGBTS people. Two months after the closure of the LGBTS community center in Accra, Twitter announced that it would be establishing its regional headquarters for West Africa in Ghana—a move that could give it some leverage to monitor and regulate the content of anti-LGBTS activists in the region. However, both Twitter and Facebook have failed to moderate anti-LGBTS content and hate speech on their platforms, signaling that such a move might alienate a larger cross section of their market base. Ultimately, although social media allows for the sharing of positive LGBTS messages that signal progress, the backlash against the use of such platforms calls for a careful engagement and celebration of social media as liberatory spaces. For LGBTS people in places such as Ghana, such corporate irresponsibility creates conditions for vulnerability, exposure, and possible violence.

Conclusion

Social media will continue to be a major component of social justice initiatives on the African continent, but its influence on queer visibility politics needs further investigation, especially in the era of neoliberalism. Some scholars have called attention to the precarity of digital feminism in neoliberal contexts that confine the demands of feminist politics to narratives of individual choice and empowerment (Gill, 2007). Here, we see that many of the same material constraints faced by offline queer activists are replicated online, where the desire for the development of radical political interventions exists alongside the general commodification of resistance and the specific consumption of narratives drawn from the most marginal communities.

As we have explained, LGBTS activists in Ghana utilize social media sites to create a queer safe space and seek solidarity with other marginalized groups. Nonetheless, the profit imperative of these sites raises concerns about the negotiations of privacy, data protection, and regulation. As we expand queer social justice efforts in the West African region, it is essential to continue to explore ways to mobilize people beyond the gratification garnered from sharing content on social media. Queer visibility politics creates a limited view of activism from which a particular form of social justice is imagined.

References

Adjepong, A. (2021). *Afropolitan projects: Redefining Blackness, sexualities, and culture from Houston to Accra*. University of North Carolina Press.

Ako, E. Y. (2021). *Towards the decriminalisation of consensual same-sex conduct in Ghana: A decolonisation and transformative constitutionalism approach* [Doctoral dissertation]. University of Pretoria.

Altman, D., & Symons, J. (2016). *Queer wars*. John Wiley & Sons.

Amoah, P. A., & Gyasi, R. M. (2016). Social institutions and same-sex sexuality: Attitudes, perceptions and prospective rights and freedoms for non-heterosexuals. *Cogent Social Sciences*, *2*(1), Article 1198219.

Asante, G. A. (2017). *Reproducing the Ghanaian/African subject: Ideological tensions and queer subjectivities in postcolonial Ghana* [Doctoral dissertation]. University of New Mexico. https://digitalrepository.unm.edu/cgi/viewcontent.cgi?article=1107&context=cj_etds

Asante, G. A. (2018). "Where is home?" Negotiating comm(unity) and un/belonging among queer African migrants on Facebook. *Borderlands*, *17*(1), 1–22.

Asante, G. A. (2020). Anti-LGBT violence and the ambivalent (colonial) discourses of Ghanaian Pentecostalist–Charismatic church leaders. *Howard Journal of Communications*, *31*(1), 20–34. https://doi.org/10.1080/10646175.2019.1590255

Asante, G. A. (2022). "They just need to empower themselves:" reproducing queer (neo) liberalism in LGBTS Empowerment discourses of representatives of LGBTS Human Rights NGOs in Ghana. *Communication and Critical/Cultural Studies*, *19*(4), 344–362.

Atuguba, R. A. (2019). Homosexuality in Ghana: Morality, law, human rights. *Journal of Politics and Law*, *12*, Article 113.

Bailey, M. (2021). *Misogynoir transformed: Black women's digital resistance*. New York University Press.

Baisley, E. (2015). Framing the Ghanaian LGBT rights debate: Competing decolonisation and human rights frames. *Canadian Journal of African Studies*, *49*(2), 383–402. http://dx.doi.org/10.1080/00083968.2015.1032989

Bondi, L., & Rose, D. (2003). Constructing gender, constructing the urban: A review of Anglo-American feminist urban geography. *Gender, Place and Culture: A Journal of Feminist Geography*, *10*(3), 229–245.

Boyd, D. M., & Ellison, N. B. (2007). Social network sites: Definition, history, and scholarship. *Journal of Computer-Mediated Communication*, *13*(1), 210–230.

Cavalcante, A. (2019). Tumbling into queer utopias and vortexes: Experiences of LGBTQ social media users on Tumblr. *Journal of Homosexuality*, *66*(12), 1715–1735.

Dankwa, S. O. (2021). *Knowing women: Same-sex intimacy, gender, and identity in postcolonial Ghana*. Cambridge University Press.

Epprecht, M. (2008). *Heterosexual Africa? The history of an idea from the age of exploration to the age of AIDS*. Ohio University Press.

Epprecht, M. (2010). The making of "African sexuality": Early sources, current debates. *History Compass*, *8*(8), 768–779.

Epprecht, M., Murray, S. O., Andam, K., Miguel, F., Mbaye, A. C., & Gaudio, R. P. (2018). Boy wives, female husbands twenty years on: Reflections on scholarly activism and the struggle for sexual orientation and gender identity/expression rights in Africa. *Canadian Journal of African Studies/Revue canadienne des études africaines*, *52*(3), 349–364.

Essien, K., & Aderinto, S. (2009). "Cutting the head of the roaring monster": Homosexuality and repression in Africa. *African Study Monographs*, *30*(3), 121–135.

Evans-Pritchard, E. E. (1970). Sexual inversion among the Azande. *American Anthropologist*, *72*(6), 1428–1434. https://www.jstor.org/stable/pdf/672861.pdf?casa_token

Fox, C. O., & Ore, T. E. (2010). (Un)covering normalized gender and race subjectivities in LGBT "safe spaces". *Feminist Studies*, *36*(3), 629–649.

Freelon, D., McIlwain, C., & Clark, M. (2018). Quantifying the power and consequences of social media protest. *New Media & Society*, *20*(3), 990–1011.

Gill, R. (2007). Postfeminist media culture: Elements of a sensibility. *European Journal of Cultural Studies*, *10*(2), 147–166.

Gore, E. (2018). Reflexivity and queer embodiment: Some reflections on sexualities research in Ghana. *Feminist Review, 120*(1), 101–119.

Goswami, M. P. (2018). Social media and hashtag activism. In D. Rastogi, M. Kaur, & S. Bālā (Eds.), *Liberty Dignity and Change in Journalism* (pp. 252–262). Kanishka Publishers.

Gyamerah, A. O., Taylor, K. D., Atuahene, K., Anarfi, J. K., Fletcher, M., Raymond, H. F., McFarland, W., & Dodoo, F. N. A. (2020). Stigma, discrimination, violence, and HIV testing among men who have sex with men in four major cities in Ghana. *AIDS Care, 32*(8), 1036–1044. https://doi.org/10.1080/09540121.2020.1757020

Hackett, R. I. (1998). Charismatic/Pentecostal appropriation of media technologies in Nigeria and Ghana. *Journal of Religion in Africa, 28*(3), 258–277.

Hartal, G. (2018). Fragile subjectivities: Constructing queer safe spaces. *Social & Cultural Geography, 19*(8), 1053–1072.

Hassett, M. (2007). *Anglican communion in crisis: How the Episcopal dissidents and their African allies are reshaping Anglicanism*. Princeton University Press.

Heald, S. (1999). *Manhood and morality: Sex, violence, and ritual in Gisu society*. Psychology Press.

Howard-Hassmann, R. E. (2001). Gay rights and the right to a family: Conflicts between liberal and illiberal belief systems. *Human Rights Quarterly, 23*, 73–95.

Jackson, S. J., Bailey, M., & Welles, B. F. (2020). *#HashtagActivism: Networks of race and gender justice*. MIT Press.

Jackson, S. J., & Welles, B. F. (2016). # Ferguson is everywhere: Initiators in emerging counterpublic networks. *Information, Communication & Society, 19*(3), 397–418.

Kendall, K. (1998). When a woman loves a woman in Lesotho: Love, sex, and the (Western) construction of homophobia. In S. Murray & W. Roscoe (Eds.), *Boy-wives and female husbands: Studies in African homosexualities* (pp. 223–241). State University of New York Press.

LeMaster, B., & Johnson, A. L. (2019). Unlearning gender—Toward a critical communication trans pedagogy. *Communication Teacher, 33*(3), 189–198.

Liao, S. (2019). "#IAmGay# what about you?": Storytelling, discursive politics, and the affective dimension of SOCIAL media activism against censorship in China. *International Journal of Communication, 13*, 2314–2333.

Mohammed, W. F. (2019). Deconstructing homosexuality in Ghana. In S. N. Nyeck (Ed.), *Routledge handbook of queer African studies* (pp. 167–181). Routledge.

Mohammed, W. F. (2022). Feminist accountability: Deconstructing feminist praxes, solidarities and LGBTQI+ activisms in Ghana. *Communication, Culture & Critique, 15*(4), 455–462. https://doi.org/10.1093/ccc/tcac031

Mohammed, W. F. (2023). Why we need intersectionality in Ghanaian feminist politics and discourses. *Feminist Media Studies, 23*(6), 3031–3047. https://doi.org/10.1080/14680777.2022.2098798

Murray, S. O., & Roscoe, W. (Eds.). (1998). *Boy-wives and female husbands: Studies in African homosexualities*. State University of New York Press.

Nash, C. J., & Gorman-Murray, A. (Eds.). (2019). *The geographies of digital sexuality*. Palgrave Macmillan.

Nenoff, A. (2020). # MeToo: A look at the influence and limits of "hashtag activism" to effectuate legal change. *University of Illinois Law Review*, 1327.

Otu, K. E. (2021). Queer slacktivism as silent activism? The contested politics of queer subjectivities on GhanaWeb. *Sexualities, 24*(1–2), 46–66.

Pascar, L., Hartal, G., & David, Y. (2018). Queering safety? An introduction. *Borderlands, 17*(1), 1–11.

Quarshie, E. N. B., Waterman, M. G., & House, A. O. (2020). Prevalence of self-harm among lesbian, gay, bisexual, and transgender adolescents: A comparison of personal and social adversity with a heterosexual sample in Ghana. *BMC Research Notes, 13*(1), Article 271. https://doi.org/10.1186/s13104-020-05111-4

Rowe, A. C. (2010). Entering the inter: Power lines in intercultural communication. In T. K. Nakayama & R. T. Halualani (Eds.), *The Handbook of Critical Intercultural Communication* (pp. 216–226). Wiley-Blackwell.

Russo, A. (2019). *Feminist accountability: Disrupting violence and transforming power*. New York University Press.

Stengel, B. S., & Weems, L. (2010). Questioning safe space: An introduction. *Studies in Philosophy and Education, 29*, 505–507.

Tauxier, L. (2012). *Les noirs du Soudan: Pays Mossi et Gourounni*. Emile La Rose.

Tettey, W. J. (2016). Homosexuality, moral panic, and politicized homophobia in Ghana: Interrogating discourses of moral entrepreneurship in Ghanaian media. *Communication, Culture & Critique, 9*(1), 86–106.

Zabus, C. (2013). Anthropological Wormholes from Pederasts to Female Husbands. In *Out in Africa* (pp. 16–51). Boydell and Brewer. https://doi.org/10.1515/9781782041979-003

Indigenous Environmental Media Activism in South Asia

Uttaran Dutta

South Asia is not only the home of nearly one-fourth of the global population but also the home of 165 million Indigenous people, consisting of more than 800 different Indigenous tribes, who speak 700 different tribal languages. In most cases, these enormously diverse populations belong to the lowest socioeconomic strata; therefore, they remain marginalized both materially and communicatively. In the context of the environment and Anthropocene, the tribal people are negotiating with the oppressions, exploitations, and negligence from the governments and dominant structures, which largely satisfy neoliberal agendas and interests. Being geographically isolated and resource-poor, the Indigenous people have experienced several atrocities during the past few decades and continue to do so; these include eviction from ancestral land, deforestation, unsafe mining activities, stealing of environmental resources such as minerals and metal ores, pollution of water sources, controversial construction of industrial processing units in Indigenous territories. Such inhumane and capitalistic environmental abuses, which damage Indigenous environmental resources and health, often trigger resistance and protests from the Indigenous communities and beyond. However, having less access to communicative resources, Indigenous dissent and activism rarely receive adequate media attention and, therefore, often remain unknown in the spaces of discursivity. From the perspective of communication studies, this chapter discusses local and global ways of doing environmental activism by the tribal communities of the "central tribal belt" of India and other areas of South Asia.

In this regard, the chapter discusses several cases from both mediated (i.e., contemporary and traditional media) and non-mediated spaces. For instance, community-level environmental organizations, participatory actions, and interactions are examined. Indigenous voices, delineations, and activities in digital spaces and social media are also discussed. Recent years have witnessed major transformations in the mediascape; notably, online spaces and avenues have triumphed over traditional media. The chapter specifically explores cases of local peoples' mediated participation and the contributions of citizen journalists and community media, the emergence of environmental allies and online activism, as well as Indigenous cinema (or the fourth cinema) and their decolonial and anti-hegemonic communications.

South Asian Indigenous Populations and Their Human Rights

Extant scholarship and reports from international institutions primarily focus on five South Asian countries: Afghanistan, Bangladesh, India, Nepal, and Pakistan (Mamo, 2022). As per the 2011 census, 104 million Indigenous people lived in India; the Indian government recognized 705 ethnic tribal groups that communicate in more than 650 Indigenous languages. Afghanistan and Pakistan are home to 60 Indigenous tribes that speak more than 30 languages. Likewise, in Bangladesh, more than 54 Indigenous groups converse in 35 tribal languages, And in Nepal, 63 tribes comprise more than one-third of the total national population. Limited information is available on Indigenous populations in the rest of South Asia. For instance, less than 0.1% of the Sri Lankan population is Indigenous (primarily the Wanniyala-Aetto tribe, a forest-dwelling community on the brink of extinction).

Overall, the Indigenous population of South Asia is highly diverse geographically, ecologically, linguistically, as well as socioculturally. Despite their cultural richness and unique tribal practices, the nation-states exhibit reluctance in recognizing their Indigenous identities and human rights. For example, in India, many ethnic groups are not yet officially recognized as "Indigenous"; likewise, tribal groups of Bangladesh are still fighting for their Indigenous status. Such administrative strategies not only deprive Indigenous people of their due dignity and rights but also ignore many Indigenous populations by excluding their ethnic groups. For instance, in the case of Nepal and Pakistan, reports suggest that the actual numbers of Indigenous people are higher than the official figures (Mamo, 2022).

While remaining as unrecognized (or inadequately recognized), the Indigenous people of South Asia are perennially experiencing systematic discrimination and subjugation by the dominant structures, as well as exploitation and oppression by the upper-class/upper-caste groups. Consequently, the Indigenous people experience deprivation in various ways, including loss of their land or property rights; lack of access to resources and services; inadequacy (or absence) of Indigenous rights in terms of practicing/celebrating tribal cultures, religions, languages, and customary laws; and limited sociopolitical and economic independence. For example, during the past few decades, in the name of environmental conservation, many Nepalese Indigenous people have experienced human rights violations such as unlawful arrest, torture, killing, forced eviction from their ancestral lands, as well as denial of access to basic survival resources.

Environmental Justice Movement

From the perspective of grassroots engagement and activism, the environment is conceptualized as the space where we live, interact, work, perform, and learn. Pezzullo and Cox (2021) define environmental justice as (a) understanding environmental inequities and addressing the disproportionate burden on underprivileged communities, (b) fighting for inclusion of unheard voices and underrepresented issues in the discursive spaces of decision-making, and (c) co-creating avenues and opportunities for the marginalized toward ensuring healthy and sustainable communities that are culturally and environmentally sound. The issues of environmental injustices are multifaceted and complex, and disadvantaged communities (e.g., Indigenous groups) experience such atrocities more deeply and bluntly. Roberts (2007) aptly notes, "The greatest brunt of climate change's effects will be felt (and are being felt) by the world's poorest people" (p. 295). South Asian Indigenous people are no exception.

Environmental justice movements, a glocal phenomenon, seek to address issues of marginalized (including Indigenous) people and places, particularly those negatively impacted by environmental inequities, the Anthropocene, and insufficient human rights; such movements can be grassroots activism, online activism, or both. Contemporary environmental movements and scholarship are paying more attention to "local" than macro- or policy-level transformations, and such "localism" is paving the way for newer possibilities and avenues.

Transformative movements for environmental justice in Indigenous contexts mostly emerge from the experiential realities of underserved communities whose members live in polluted climates and sacrifice their aspirations and priorities. Indigenous and decolonial perspectives emphasize local ways of envisioning nature-friendly and local-centered approaches as an alternative to mainstream environmental practices; specifically, they focus on grassroots-led Indigenous ways of sustainable development (Mihaylov & Perkins, 2015). Organized by (or in collaboration with) Indigenous communities, such efforts and initiatives focus on situated adversities and help raise voices to foreground realities/concerns at the margins.

Such movements pay attention to pivotal contributions and engagements of Indigenous people to legitimize their struggles and negotiations and to question and resist climate inequalities; thus, Indigenous people communicatively seek to reclaim dignity as a fundamental human right. Notably, Indigenous communities and their grassroots initiatives/aspirations operate with limited cultural and material resources, and they often experience difficulties and/or fail to change the wider structure and power dynamics. Often, to challenge and change situated adversities, the underprivileged communities seek help from people/groups/networks to form and expand coalitions to bring about meaningful transformations.

In South Asia, many of the forest-dwelling Indigenous people have experienced difficulties as their forest rights are denied. For example, in India, tribal people throughout the nation have submitted their forest rights claims individually as well as communally, and some of the applicants' claims have been acknowledged by the government. Importantly, noting the pressing need of environmental justice for the underserved Indigenous people, the Ministry of Tribal Affairs directed the state governments to be careful and cognizant so that rejection of Indigenous claims on invalid ground can be prevented.

Grassroots Indigenous environmental initiatives often foreground causes and effects of a variety of environmental disruptions and threats (including policies and technologies that will have destructive effects); tribal environmental activists examine such injustices from the perspectives and intersections of class, gender, caste, or ethnicity. Moreover, in the Indigenous context, the concepts of locality, rurality, remoteness, and power inequality are intimately associated (Johnson & Frickel, 2011). The rural (and Indigenous) regions are often unfavorably compared to urban spaces; and the tribal communities are often depicted as culturally backward, inferior, and less deserving.

Scholars note that "place" is deeply tied to our materially and socially constructed realities; therefore, our place attachments and environmental identities influence each other (Vorkinn & Riese, 2001). In tribal contexts, place is intimately intertwined to several fundamental aspects of Indigenous existence, including their pro-environmental behaviors and attitudes as well as acts of expressing environmental concerns. Geographically, underserved spaces, including Indigenous lands, that are located outside of urban and mainstream regions are often labeled as "sacrifice zones" because they bear the most burden of unsustainability and environmental damage. Dominant stakeholders fail to understand the struggles at the margins because they never live or experience such realities; local activists and Indigenous communities seek to foreground situated environmental stress and lived realities in discursive spaces.

The following is an example from India: Data research organizations such as Land Conflict Watch report that currently there are approximately 650 ongoing land conflict cases, which affect 7.8 million underserved people in India. Many of these cases involve Indigenous lands. Critics note that although currently unavailable, it is important to develop centralized databases of land disputes to understand the land alienation in tribal regions. Indigenous communities, often with their environmental and human rights allies, file cases to reclaim their lands from the non-tribals. Despite some success in the court procedures, the enforcement support from the nation-state is still a matter of concern for many tribal communities; consequently, many of the tribal lands are still in the possession of non-Indigenous individuals and/or groups. Constitutional bodies such as the National Commission for Scheduled Tribes have also expressed concerns because a large portion of Indigenous populations have experienced detrimental effects due to land grabbing and land acquisitions; as such, these organizations have urged state governments to ensure justice and to restore alienated lands of Indigenous populations.

Indigenous People and Environmental Communication

According to scholars, activists, and Indigenous communities, power inequality is one of the key factors in environmental justice movements. Therefore, scholars suggest that it is important to critically examine the notion of power (including aspects of powerlessness and vulnerability) in Indigenous contexts, specifically how tribal communities are often targeted by the dominant forces/power structure and how these communities experience environmental harms and risks in their everyday existence (Gibbs, 2002).

In the Global South, where tribal communities have a high illiteracy rate and limited access to formal education , Indigenous people are often considered unqualified to represent their own voices in discursive spaces. Moreover, Indigenous voices are often portrayed as emotional, ignorant, and pseudo-scientific; consequently, dominant stakeholders strategically ignore and delegitimize Indigenous discourses in the spaces of decision-making. Such prejudice and discriminatory behaviors from the mainstream prevent Indigenous people's voices from reaching a wider audience and advancing discussions about Indigenous environmental matters.

For instance, in Bangladesh, during the past few years, Indigenous people in the Chittagong Hill Tracts have been experiencing drinking water issues due to illegal stone-extraction activities from water bodies and streams. Specifically, the Marma, Khumi, Mro, and Tanchangya tribes of the Bandarban region have been suffering from portable water shortages, particularly during the summer as the streams, their only water source, gradually dry up. Local Indigenous communities with help from various environmental rights and human rights organizations are raising concerns and fighting against such illegal stone extraction by filing petitions in the High Court. As a result of such activism, stone lifting from areas adjacent to the Sangu and Matamuhuri Rivers of the Bandarban reserved forest has been reduced; however, more community action and governmental support are needed to ensure sustained availability of drinking water.

Increasingly, critical, Indigenous, and decolonial scholars are arguing that the mainstream environmental communication research espouses a top-down unilateral approach in which the dominant stakeholders (including governments, policymakers, corporations, think tanks, etc.) are using media and other discursive apparatus to disseminate messages to the least powerful sections, including Indigenous people. They further note that the hegemonic discourses are selective in nature; that is, such discourses often pay attention to certain issues and strategically ignore (if not erase) others, particularly issues pertaining to powerless groups and their existential struggles. In addition, critical scholars emphasize the necessity of paying more attention to the roles of alternate narratives and nondominant discourses and also how common (and marginalized) people understand the issues of environment, engage in creating contents, as well as organize transformative actions.

Local and Participatory Environmental Grassroots Activism

The evolution of participatory communication is increasingly evident in the growing environmental communication domain. *Participatory communication* embraces decentralized horizontal communication models and focuses on the receiver instead of the sender; thereby, it values the Indigenous autonomy and collective cultural and oppositional identities. Thus, instead of the top-down monologic mode of information dissemination, the participatory approach gives rise to dialogic or two-way communication processes between decision-makers and citizens, giving voice and choice to the people at the receiving end of the dominant environmental agenda (e.g., Indigenous people).

For example, environmental activists and Indigenous organizations in India participated in protests and raised their voices against a government proposed/draft amendment, the

Indian Forest (Amendment) Act 2019. According to grassroots activists, the proposed act allegedly provided administrative authority to violate the environmental and human rights of Indigenous peoples. Later, the central government decided to withdraw the proposed amendment; the Union Minister of Environment, Forest and Climate Change announced, "We are completely withdrawing the draft amendment to the Indian Forests Act to remove any misgivings, the tribal rights will be protected fully and they will continue to be the important stakeholder in forest development" (Press Information Bureau, 2019, para. 1).

Participatory communication scholarship argues that participation is intimately tied to basic human rights; thus, the participatory approach is invested in legitimizing unheard voices and perspectives rather than echoing the intentions and agendas of elites and the dominant stakeholders. Indigenous perspectives opine that marginalized people have the right to use their knowledge and agentic abilities to identify situated needs, articulate vision and aspirations, and make meaningful decisions to improve their lives. Participation of underserved communities in remote/Indigenous regions is constrained by several factors, including illiteracy and linguistic proficiency, technological access, and cultural praxis. However, participatory means of telling their environmental stories/experiences in their own ways help Indigenous people cope/negotiate in the spaces of marginality and find meaningful and mindful solutions.

In addition to grassroots organizations, researchers and academic citizens are also collaborating with Indigenous communities to work on environmental conservation and resource management. Such collaborations, grounded in the values of cultural humility, co-learning, and respect (for people, place, and worldviews), pay reflexive attention to a variety of sociocultural and contextual complexities. Thus, these enduring engagements at the margins not only aim at exploring effective avenues of knowledge production and innovative research outcomes but also seek to build capacities and trust as well as yield/continue sustainable relationships.

One example of such initiatives is a community-led Indigenous effort to conserve a sacred grove—a place that is deeply tied with Indigenous identity, spirituality, and worldviews. Supported by an academic, the Santhal tribal community of eastern India collectively participated and mobilized the engaged environmental action to address situated degradation of natural resources (including deforestation), social–ecological challenges to conserve environmental resources, and overall well-being of community members (Dutta, 2020).

Local Media and Indigenous Environmental Communication

The *mediascape*, both global and local, has witnessed huge transformations in the past few years. As print media is gradually diminishing, common people are relying more on online spaces (including digital news/information platforms [e.g., the webpages of governments and institutions], online news channels, and social media [e.g., Facebook and Twitter]) for news and updates. Moreover, noting the ownership concentration in media businesses (i.e., big tech and multinational corporations are controlling the mediated landscape [including environmental narratives]), scholars argue that the contents and voices from the underprivileged sections are getting delegitimized in the discursive spaces.

Traditional news coverage (print and digital) often fails to adequately represent local communities and their environmental matters; scholars argue that local news reporters and their firsthand accounts are most effective in legitimizing the nuances of everyday negotiations at the margins. Furthermore, scholars specifically emphasize several factors, including "closeness" of local media with communities, their situated knowledge about the geographical surroundings, and local socioeconomic and religiopolitical contexts.

In March 2018, more than 35,000 farmers (mostly tribal farmers) and, in November, 10,000 Indigenous farmers marched in the state of Maharashtra demanding land rights and loan waiver (among other issues). These Indigenous protests and actions received attention from local and mainstream media as well as wider public spheres. Reports suggest that more than 230,000 land dispute cases were pending in Maharashtra alone; Indigenous farmers were denied their rights of land ownership, even if they were cultivating on those lands. As an outcome of these protests and media coverage, the Maharashtra administration promised the tribal people that it would take appropriate measures to ensure Indigenous land and forest rights, as well as to provide compensation for droughts and other natural disasters.

In recent years, community media and peoples' active contributions have changed the mediated spaces, which traditionally were contributed by formal journalists. Such a transformation in turn compelled us to rethink participatory discursive practices around environmental matters (including issues of water, land, pollutants, and climate degradation) and how they are communicated in the spaces of decision-making toward formulating sustainable solutions. Thus, local media can be envisioned as an enabler of participation and democratic decision-making, particularly for communities that are underrepresented.

Examples of such community- and people-led media from South Asia are CGNet-Swara and GramVaani. CGNet-Swara is a voice-based and Web-based citizen network, which envisions common people (not just trained journalists) as potential contributors so that unheard voices from the margins can reach the wider public sphere. Similarly, GramVaani, a voice-activated community platform, is another people's forum from rural India dedicated to legitimizing underserved voices and issues.

Citizen Environmental Journalism

In the contemporary era, common citizens emerge as one of the major sources of environmental news reporting; their eyewitness accounts, reports, and opinions enrich knowledge and perspectives about situated environmental issues. Increasingly, such alternative/underexplored materials of environmental reporting are receiving attention from the scholarly communities; Mythen (2010) notes that such contents "add to the plurality of discourses circulating about hazardous events, provide an alternate agenda from mainstream news and bring into question the political and cultural logics that underpin risk incidents" (p. 49). Citizen journalists mostly use their own devices and resources to create online content (e.g., images, videos, and narratives) and share them using their socially mediated accounts, blogs, and other preferred forms of reportage.

Again, from the perspective of participation, "participatory media" emphasizes the importance of local contexts (sociocultural, historical, political, economic, religious, geographical, etc.), and the processes of mediation encourage and facilitate dialogue, collaboration, and initiatives to solve problems mutually. The aspects of participation and participatory media are not only relevant to environmental communication scholarship but also increasingly recognized in related domains, such as climate change sciences, environmental humanities, and environmental sciences. From a Freirean perspective, Rodriguez (2004) showed that participatory media (she used the term *citizens' media*) are enablers of personal as well as communal conscientization and empowerment, and thereby help Indigenous people reclaim their identity and dignity. Such a media culture and communicative infrastructure not only catalyze transformative exchange of thoughts and encourage collaborative engagements in creating meaningful content but also help community media reach wider audiences within and beyond the rural and Indigenous spaces of the Global South.

One such example is from the Taplejung district of Nepal, where a private company tried to establish a tourism business by renaming a sacred Indigenous site—Mukumlug—without obtaining appropriate consent from local Indigenous communities. In response, representatives of the Yakthung/Limbu tribe and the Lawyers' Association for Human Rights of Nepalese Indigenous Peoples utilized the power of "community media" to spread the word and also lodge complaints to the National Human Rights Commission. In their petition, they urged the government and wider public to help retain the original name of the sacred site as well as to prevent the company from destroying Indigenous spaces, resources, and identity.

Online Environmental Activism

In response to environmental degradation/crisis, many local environmental organizations have emerged; these organizations fight for local sustainability issues, become environmental allies to the communities, and create solidarity to convey and communicate information using various online avenues, including social media. Like the offline activistic initiatives, the online environmental activities represent marginalized (including Indigenous) voices and aspirations, and they seek to provide them a sense of agency toward emancipation and empowerment. Online means help these organizations to work together through shared practices of sustainability and thereby create and bolster networks regionally, nationally, as well as internationally.

Gradual easiness (primarily technological) and economy of communicative infrastructure encourage many environmental nongovernmental organizations and individuals to participate in online environmental activism as well as to connect and communicate with the wider global populations. Some of the prominent forms of online activism are ethical hacktivism; informational (including educational and cultural) campaigns; creating awareness and advocacy to organize, mobilize, and reinforce social movements; and actions for environmental causes (Vegh, 2003). One of the early South Asian examples is the occurrence of the 1984 Bhopal gas leak disaster in India; several local and global campaigns for environmental justice were organized to mobilize online and offline resources toward ensuring justice for the survivors after the disastrous incident.

A recent example demonstrates how online activism and reporting from the Indigenous India was instrumental in revealing that several tribal populations throughout the nation suffered evictions and discrimination during the COVID-19 pandemic. Specifically, it was reported that 32, 81, and 20 families were evicted (often forcibly) from their ancestral lands in the states of Odisha, Telangana, and Chhattisgarh, respectively, between April and October 2020. The evictions made the marginalized tribal families more vulnerable to extreme impoverishment and deprivation. Mediated accounts also suggested that many of the homes (along with standing crops) of tribal people were burnt down as the populations were struggling to obtain basic amenities such as food, medicine, and shelter.

Fourth (Indigenous) Cinema

Indigenous cinema (or fourth cinema) is another activism tool for representing Indigenous environmental narratives, worldviews, and values. Scholars have noted that fourth cinema is an Indigenous response to wide misrepresentation of tribal culture, realities, and situated complexities (Wilson, 2015). Being anti-hegemonic and anti-White, fourth cinema celebrates the power and authenticity of Indigenous visual imagery and epistemologies. Such films are distinctive from the non-Indigenous portrayal of tribal identities, and they essentially challenge attempts of external invasion of Indigenous cultures. Deeply grounded in Indigenous philosophies and ancient value systems, fourth cinemas use experiential narratives (and, in some cases, myths) to highlight situated negotiations and spiritual/sacred relationships of tribal people with nature and environmental resources.

To address inadequate representations of Indigenous identities and culture in the mainstream, South Asian cinema, as well as to foreground Indigenous voices and adversities, some Indigenous filmmakers have created production units to make films and documentaries; one such initiative is Akhra, a tribal documentary and film production house located in eastern India. Since 1995, directors Biju Toppo and Meghnath have produced more than 30 films and documentaries on Indigenous culture, struggles, human rights, and environmental destruction, which were screened at many film festivals in South Asia and beyond.

For example, films such as *Ek Hadsa Aur Bhee* (*Yet Another Accident*; 1997) and *Vikas Bandook Ki Nal Se* (*Development Flows from the Barrel of the Guns*; 2003) depicted how Indigenous people in the "central Indigenous belt" of India were brutally killed and lost their properties and land, particularly from dominant violence and murderous acts against protesters and activists, as well as from evictions in the name of development. Some recent Indigenous films rendered tribal agencies and narrative more poetically. The 2022 film *Dhabari Quruvi* (a mythological bird/sparrow), by Seral Murmu, told stories of silent sufferings at the margins as well as the attempts to dismantle the shackles of oppression. On the other hand, *Jharia* (*The Spring*; 2017) showed the lifelong environmental commitment and actions of an elderly man, Simon Oraon, also known as the Water Man from Jharkhand, who tirelessly fought for water rights and environmental justice.

Indigenous communities and environmental organizations often embrace both offline and online environmental activism to increase their reach and impact. In other words, offline and online campaigns complement and bolster each other when used mindfully and strategically. For example, London-based Vedanta Resources' bauxite mining site in the Niyamgiri hill region of Odisha, India, recently received attention from the scholarly and mediated worlds. The mining activities allegedly destroyed approximately 60 hectares of forest and displaced more than 100 families, and the refinery polluted the local environment, which negatively impacted human (and wildlife) health and local economies. The Dongria Kondh tribe organized in-person protests against such atrocities by blocking roads, forming human chains. The tribe also became an ally of Survival International, a global human rights organization that lobbied for the cause at the governmental level (nationally and internationally) as well as launched online campaigns (e.g., by producing the film *Mine—Story of a Sacred Mountain* and via several socially mediated platforms) to create worldwide awareness.

Conclusion

To study Indigenous environmental activism in South Asian context, this examined both mediated (including contemporary and traditional media) and non-mediated spaces. For instance, the aspects of community-level environmental organizations, participatory actions, and interactions were examined. Indigenous voices and delineations in digital spaces and social media were also researched. In addition, mediated discourses from print and audiovisual media, including reports, films, and documentaries, were explored.

Future research endeavors on environmental activism could include the study of other Indigenous regions and populations of the Global South. Also, it is important to pay attention to (a) specific environmental issues or conditions that Indigenous people are experiencing and/ or (b) specific population groups/subgroups (e.g., in terms of gender, age, sociopolitical scenario, or geographical regions). Again, as technology progresses, numerous opportunities are emerging in digitally mediated spaces, which would open up more possibilities and avenues of activism as well as research in the Indigenous context. Finally, more research on environmental activism from the Indigenous and decolonial perspectives is needed to bring about ethical and responsible transformations at the margins.

References

Dutta, U. (2020). Protecting sacred-groves: Community-led environmental organizing by Santhals of eastern India. *Environmental Communication, 14*(1), 36–51.

Gibbs, L. (2002). Citizen activism for environmental health: The growth of a powerful new grassroots health movement. *Annals of the American Academy of Political and Social Science, 584*(1), 97–109.

Johnson, E. W., & Frickel, S. (2011). Ecological threat and the founding of US national environmental movement organizations, 1962–1998. *Social Problems, 58*(3), 305–329.

Mamo, D. (Ed.). (2022). *The Indigenous world 2022.* International Work Group for Indigenous Affairs.

Mihaylov, N. L., & Perkins, D. D. (2015). Local environmental grassroots activism: Contributions from environmental psychology, sociology and politics. *Behavioral Sciences, 5*(1), 121–153.

Mythen, G. (2010). Reframing risk? Citizen journalism and the transformation of news. *Journal of Risk Research, 13*(1), 45–58.

Pezzullo, P. C., & Cox, R. (2021). *Environmental communication and the public sphere.* SAGE.

Press Information Bureau (2019, November 15). Government clears misgivings of amendment in the Indian Forest Act, 1927. Government of India, Ministry of Environment, Forest and Climate Change. https://pib.gov.in/news ite/PrintRelease.aspx?relid=194511

Roberts, J. T. (2007). Globalizing environmental justice. In R. Sandler & P. C. Pezzulo (Eds.), *Environmental justice and environmentalism: The social justice challenge to the environmental movement* (pp. 285–307). MIT Press.

Rodriguez, C. (2004). The renaissance of citizens' media. *Media Development, 51*(2), 17–21.

Vegh, S. (2003). *Hacking for democracy: A study of the internet as a political force and its representation in the mainstream media* [Doctoral dissertation]. University of Maryland.

Vorkinn, M., & Riese, H. (2001). Environmental concern in a local context: The significance of place attachment. *Environment and Behavior, 33*(2), 249–263.

Wilson, P. (2015). Indigenous documentary media. In D. Marcus & S. Kara (Eds.), *Contemporary documentary* (pp. 87–104). Routledge.

Indigenous Media Organizing

Mohan J. Dutta *and* Christine Ngā Hau Elers

Across diverse global registers, Indigenous media reflect the ongoing struggles of Indigenous people to secure sovereignty over symbolic and material resources. The neo/settler colonial processes that have historically constituted and continue to shape the expulsion and displacement of Indigenous people from land, habits, livelihoods, and ecosystems continue to constitute Indigenous struggles, catalyzed by the accelerated processes of extreme neoliberalism. Even as disciplinary architectures and academic conversations have turned toward the incorporation and co-option of decolonization discourse toward the service of global capital in the form of extreme neoliberal reforms and new forms of climate colonialism, Indigenous communities across global registers offer theoretical anchors for reimagining social, political, and economic organizing, narrated through/on Indigenous media.

In this chapter, we approach the concept of social justice as an anti-colonial register that challenges the forces of racial capitalism–colonialism, embodied in the struggles of the Indigenous body, situated in relationship with land, against the ongoing extractive land grabs that form the frontiers of neoliberal capitalism (Bargh, 2016, 2021; Bargh & Otter, 2009; Kelsey, 2015; Lesutis, 2019; McCormack, 2012). Drawing upon the theoretical framework of the culture-centered approach (CCA) that situates material inequality in relationship with communicative inequality—that is, the inequality in the distribution of communicative resources—we further explore the concept of social justice as struggles for redistribution of communicative resources in the face of settler colonial violence, erasure, and ongoing co-option of Indigenous resistance (Dutta, 2004a, 2004b, 2018a, 2018b). Indigenous media, as infrastructures of resistance to the interplays between neoliberal capitalism and neocolonialism, offer theoretical registers for materializing anti-capitalism practices of organizing.

Culture-Centered Processes of Indigenous Media Organizing

We draw upon the culture-centered approach (CCA) as a meta-theory for exploring the interplays of communicative inequalities and material inequalities in Indigenous struggles against dispossession. As a meta-theory, the CCA turns to the registers for voice infrastructures in conceptualizing anchors for transformation, working alongside Indigenous theories of social change. The relationship between the CCA and Indigenous theories is one of solidarity, with the voice infrastructures amidst Indigenous struggles constituting the sites where Indigenous knowledge is articulated, forming the basis for organizing for structural transformation. Culture-centered processes of creating voice infrastructures in Indigenous communities are situated amidst the ongoing struggles for communicative sovereignty, reflecting the rights of Indigenous people to own communicative resources (Dutta, 2018a, 2018b; Jones et al., 2006).

Communicative Sovereignty

Indigenous organizing draws on communicative sovereignty—that is, the ownership of communicative infrastructures by Indigenous communities—as the basis for challenging the material dispossessions catalyzed by the colonial–capitalist structure. Consider here the organizing of the Ejercito Zapatista de Liberacion Nacional (Zapatista Army of National Liberation [EZLN]) that challenged the hegemonic configuration in Mexico by foregrounding Indigenous claims to sovereignty. Indigenous organizing, voiced through communicative infrastructures owned by the Zapatistas, challenged both the colonial processes of extraction and expulsion, and neoliberal processes of extreme exploitation. The organizing of the EZLN created a communicative infrastructure for Indigenous participation, opening up the spaces of participation to plural voices and diverse popular movements. Indigenous articulation of justice as resistance to the implementation of the North American Free Trade Agreement challenged the role of the Mexican state, working alongside the U.S. Empire, to push neoliberal reforms that catalyzed the further expulsion and exploitation of Indigenous peoples (Dutta & Pal, 2020). The communicative infrastructures co-created by EZLN, in solidarity with global networks of activists and social movements challenging neoliberalism, witnessed the oppression and marginalization of Indigenous tribes in the Chiapas region of Mexico (Dellacioppa, 2009; Dutta & Pal, 2020). EZLN built a digitally networked infrastructure of activists and allies, including connecting with the Association for Progressive Communications to make claims to Indigenous rights in Mexico and resist the genocidal neoliberal policies pursued by the state (Dutta, 2011).

Note that the content generated by the Zapatistas, mediated through their spokesperson Subcomandante Marcos, documented the oppressions experienced by Indigenous Mexicans and generated claims to Indigenous rights (Dutta, 2011; Dutta & Pal, 2020). These narrative frames were circulated through the digital infrastructures of allies, further being pushed into mainstream global print media. The communicative sovereignty enacted by the Zapatistas served as the basis for enacting narrative sovereignty and Indigenous control over the story frame as it moved across discursive registers globally. The digital infrastructure shaped media coverage, foregrounding the question of Indigenous human rights and struggles against neoliberal extractivism on the global stage.

The resistance crafted by EZLN served as the basis for the knowledge infrastructure built around the concept of Zapatismo, building a global theory of social change challenging neoliberal globalization. Communicative sovereignty enacted by EZLN shaped the articulation of knowledge claims rooted in Indigeneity, situated within the context of a local struggle and globally relevant in challenging the violent onslaught of neoliberal globalization on Indigenous communities (Bell, 2018; Dutta, 2011; Holden et al., 2011), one that systematically suggests pathways of transformative politics by emphasizing local autonomy, self-governance, and listening. As noted with the example of EZLN, subaltern participation in discursive spaces at the local level seeks to resist global control of transnational corporations (TNCs).

In India, voice infrastructures on digital spaces co-created by *adivasi* (Indigenous) communities such as *Adivasi Voices Matter* resist the hegemonic colonial neoliberal–capitalist ideology that shapes the mobilization of development to steal Indigenous land, foregrounding adivasi values as the basis of organizing life and relationship with land. Digital platforms such as YouTube and Twitter foster openings for transformation amidst a strictly regulated media environment controlled by capital. These infrastructures, albeit constituted within the broader logics of digital colonialism, also create openings for raising adivasi claims, for being in conversation with Indigenous movements, and for crafting broad solidarities for Indigenous resistance movements amidst the large-scale violence deployed by the state.

Land Occupation and Narrative Sovereignty

In the backdrop of the ongoing expulsions of Indigenous communities from land, Indigenous struggles for justice take the form of land occupations. Culture-centered processes of organizing co-create media infrastructures for Indigenous enactment of narrative sovereignty. Consider, for instance, the role of voice infrastructures in enacting narrative sovereignty in the Indigenous land occupation in Feilding, New Zealand, against a climate adaptation project pushed by the local government without appropriate consultation and through the theft of Māori land (Elers & Dutta, 2023; Mika et al., 2022). Under the umbrella of the Center for Culture-Centered Approach to Research and Evaluation, a community infrastructure we had co-created in the form of a community advisory group, messaging strategies were developed to support the land occupation (Dutta, 2018a, 2018b; Elers & Dutta, 2023). The messaging strategy retained narrative sovereignty, framing the climate adaptation solution being put up on the land as climate colonialism, thus rendering visible the violation of legal processes in the confiscation of the land.

Similarly, the protest at Ihumātao in Aotearoa against land confiscation is constituted around land rights, drawing in Māori participation across Aotearoa. Critical to the movement at Ihumātao, organized under the umbrella of Save Our Unique Landscape (SOUL), is the participation of youth, drawing on the Kaupapa Māori concept of safeguarding land and resources. The presence of Indigenous voices on a wide array of platforms, controlled by Indigenous protestors, disrupted the erasure of Indigenous voices and the colonizing ideology of development (Elers & Dutta, 2023; Elers & Jayan, 2020; Gill, 2021). The land occupation as material intervention into the organizing architecture of settler colonialism was upheld by digital media narratives, mediated through images, sounds, and videos. These multimodal narrative accounts shaped a wide array of educational activities both at the site of the occupation and across geographically distant spaces, creating registers for crafting solidarities. The narrative accounts offered by SOUL shaped media commentaries, complemented by active engagement with mainstream media. The communicative infrastructure supported participation in political processes, submissions of petitions, *hīkoi* (march), and legal engagement. The Protect Ihumātao movement foregrounds the interplays of cultural safeguarding, safeguarding of spiritual linkages, and safeguarding of land as the basis for enacting tino rangatiratanga (sovereignty).

The narrative articulated through the communicative infrastructure of the movement resists the settler colonial construction of the right to determine the ownership and use of *Ihumātao*. It foregrounds the ideology of Whiteness that encloses land as property, rendering visible the legal processes of Whiteness that mobilize land theft. The voices emergent from Ihumātao depict this theft as the core of colonialism, constructing decolonization as resistance to the settler colonial ideology of land as property. It is through the communicative infrastructures that the protestors delineated the original theft of the land that formed the basis of the legal transactions which were subsequently carried out on the land, inverting the legal claim of private capital on the land based on the argument that they had a legitimate right having purchased the property via legal means. The communicative infrastructure of SOUL disrupted the Whiteness of the housing development narrative constructed by the state–capital nexus that positioned the housing development on the land as a response to alleviate the housing shortage. At the heart of the organizing infrastructure of SOUL was the mobilization around land occupation as decolonization.

Similarly, in the mid-1990s, amid the aggressive liberalization of India, the resistance organized by the Dongria Kondh against the Niyamgiri mining project foregrounds the role of voice infrastructures in resisting extractive neoliberal colonialism (Padel & Das, 2010).

Through a range of corporate social responsibility activities, a mining multinational, Vedanta, had development-washed the dispossession of adivasi (Indigenous) people, deploying corporate social responsibility—based community engagement to erase the democratic participation of communities in decision-making processes in *gram panchayats* (village government), protected by the Schedule V of the Indian constitution. Violating the Schedule V that protects Indigenous land, adivasis were not consulted in the decision-making processes that led to the land grab. In this backdrop, the organizing of the Dongria Kondh co-created communicative infrastructures for laying claim to the state, referring to the guidelines of the Schedule V of the Indian constitution to mobilize petitions, legal claims, protest marches, and digital narratives (Dutta, 2015a, 2015b; Padel & Das, 2010). Digital mobilization across platforms such as YouTube and Facebook foregrounded Dongria Kondh voices, co-creating an infrastructure for listening to adivasi articulations, documenting the pollution, environmental degradation, cultural genocide, and threat to Indigenous health and livelihood brought about by the mining project. The resistive processes led to change, with the Supreme Court of India ordering local village councils to make a final decision regarding the development of the mining operations in Niyamgiri, and all of the 12 village councils unanimously rejecting the mining project in 2013.

Organizing for Media Infrastructures

Amidst the neoliberal consolidation of power and control in the hands of capital, the increasing concentration of media power in the hands of White, settler colonial, capitalist structures is resisted through Indigenous organizing. In India, the formation of digital infrastructures such as the platform "Adivasi Lives Matter" secures Indigenous narrative sovereignty. In Aotearoa, Māori struggles for rights over media infrastructures draw upon the organizing principles of *Te Tiriti* as the founding document, depicting the decolonizing power of Te Tiriti as an organizing register for transforming media ownership practices and patterns (de Bruin & Mane, 2016; Mane, 2014). Challenging the anti-Māori racism of settler colonial media spaces (Jackson, 1997), Māori mobilization across Aotearoa sought greater representation, participation, and ownership of media infrastructures (Bell, 2018; de Bruin & Mane, 2016; Matamua, 2014; Matike Mai Aotearoa, 2016). Organizing around the concept of media sovereignty, ownership and control over broadcasting were viewed as vital to the survival of Te Reo and Māori cultural practices. The Te Reo Māori claim was led by the late Huirangi Waikerepuru, leading to the creation of Māori radio and serving as the basis for Māori-language broadcasting (Mane, 2014).

The processes of Māori organizing drew upon legal resources to secure Indigenous rights over media infrastructures (Barrett & Connolly-Stone, 1998). Note here the mobilization of Māori activists around Te Reo Irirangi o Te Ūpoko-o-Te-Ika, organizing alongside claimant groups Ngā Kaiwhakapūmau I te Reo Māori and New Zealand Māori Council to carry out court action against the Crown over the sale of broadcasting assets (Mane, 2014; Ngā Kaiwhakapūmau, 1999), Māori organizing to raise Māori claims before the Waitangi Tribunal (2019) resulted in the securing of radio frequencies by Māori (Barrett & Connolly-Stone, 1998; Matamua, 2006). Critical here is the process of raising claims based on the foundational principles of Te Tiriti, which led to the creation of Māori television (J. Smith, 2015, p. 185). Māori resistance, enacted as challenge to the Crown (J. Smith, 2016), shaped the struggle for justice, securing the rights of Māori to Māori television. The struggles for justice organized by Māori offer a theoretical register for mobilizing Indigenous claims of sovereignty in media infrastructures, depicting the interplays of epistemic, cultural, and communicative registers for organizing social change. Māori organizing through media infrastructures shapes the mobilization for political representation, decolonizing the settler colonial infrastructure of democracies (see Ellis, 2021). Throughout the world, Indigenous organizing to build and sustain media infrastructures in the form of community radio, community-based digital storytelling, Indigenous video productions, and Indigenous films offers registers for challenging the frontiers of neoliberal capitalism as extraction. Hegemonic forms of climate capitalism are challenged through Indigenous stories narrated on Indigenous owned communicative spaces that disrupt hegemonic concepts of what constitutes media, drawing on Indigenous forms of art, performance, and storytelling.

In Canada, Indigenous organizing across diverse contexts has shaped the presence of a plethora of Indigenous-led media spaces since the 1960s, crystallizing in the launch of the Aboriginal Peoples Television Network (APTN) in 1999 as an infrastructure for Indigenous voice (Callison & Hermida, 2015). These Indigenous-led media spaces offer narrative sovereignty, serving as vehicles for self-representation and for building counternarratives that challenge the racist narratives underlying the violence perpetrated by the settler colonial state (Alia, 1999; Ginsberg et al., 2002). The leadership of Indigenous communities in the APTN creates narrative control among Indigenous communities, where Indigenous articulations and reports challenge the racist constructions, frames, and tropes in mainstream media. The visual registers that primitivize Indigenous communities and fix Indigenous cultures in essentialist tropes are challenged, rejected, and dismantled through the narrative control held by Indigenous peoples. Critical here is the role of APTN amidst crises induced by extractive neoliberalism and Indigenous protests against violent neoliberal policies, offering Indigenous frames around critical issues, including challenges to the environment built into the everyday governmentality of neoliberal settler colonialism. The organizing framework of the APTN and alternative Indigenous media have drawn in creative practices, innovating with plural registers of communication and communities and working across a wide array of platform resources such as Facebook, YouTube, and Twitter. Even as digital infrastructures are organized as the basis for upholding Indigenous media infrastructures, it is worthwhile to note the colonizing forms of platform capital that extract and profit from Indigenous data. In this backdrop, organizing for Indigenous sovereignty in the realm of digital infrastructures is critical in raising claims of data sovereignty, regulation of platform capital and its uses of data, and the work of building Indigenous-owned platforms.

Co-Creating and Sustaining Solidarities

Solidarities sutured through mediated spaces sustain Indigenous struggles for rights and at the same time are critical to the sustenance of media infrastructures across globally dispersed spaces (Dutta, 2012; Dutta et al., 2021). The power of the state–capitalist nexus that forms the basis for settler colonial violence calls for sustained strategies of community action. The Zapatista movement described previously offers an example of Indigenous-led solidarities, anchored in Indigenous knowledge systems and values of care and community. One of the salient features in the organizing work of EZLN was the solidarity networks it created, fostered, and sustained, both in catalyzing resistance locally and in drawing upon global networks of support. These global networks of support in turn carried forth the ideas articulated by EZLN, building global registers for resistance to neoliberalism based on values of care and connection. The Italian Ya Basta! and the Irish Mexico group are examples of global support communities that were formed around EZLN, with strong links of solidarity with the movement (Olesen, 2004).

The challenge offered by EZLN to the neoliberal policies of the Mexican state served as the theoretical basis for global struggles against extractive neoliberalism. The global solidarity networks built by EZLN brought together activists from throughout the world, building global resistance to neoliberalism based on Indigenous articulations and anchored in Indigenous articulations of autonomy reflected in Zapatismo (Barmeyer, 2009; Dellacioppa, 2009). Indigenous autonomy offered the basis for building global resistance to neoliberalism, shaping and sustaining locally led community-based struggles against neoliberalism across spaces (Esteva, 2005; Esteva & Prakash, 1998; Olesen, 2004). The first Intercontinental Encounter Against Neoliberalism and for Humanity held by EZLN in 1996 was one of the first international gatherings that brought together activists from throughout the world to organize against neoliberalism (Starr, 2005). It created the People's Global Action, a transnational organization that brought together diverse organizations from throughout the world, including from India, Nigeria, the United States, and Bolivia.

In 2005, EZLN launched the "Other Campaign" as the basis for solidarity building for diverse local struggles across Mexico and the United States, co-creating long-term organic grassroots linkages of support across these diverse local struggles, working across multiple registers and nodes of resistance to neoliberalism (Barmeyer, 2009; Dellacioppa, 2009). Reflecting radical grassroots participation as an organizing framework for resistance, the campaign was launched with listening tours as EZLN moved out into poor communities in various areas of Mexico, listening to the stories of local struggles and mobilizing them. As a cross-border global movement against neoliberal capitalism based on local enactments of autonomy and rationalities of care that challenged neoliberalism, the Other Campaign signed on activist organizations across borders that sought to carry out a Zapatista mandate in their own local struggles, communicating with each other through *encuentros* (gatherings). In Los Angeles, the activist organization Case del Pueblo was formed in 2002 based on Zapatista principles, addressing the housing needs of immigrant families threatened with displacement by gentrification by incorporating Zapatista principles and methodologies (Dutta & Pal, 2020).

Zapatista activism shaped the Indymedia network, depicting the power of alternative imaginaries networked through digital infrastructures in building registers for challenging neoliberalism (Dutta, 2012; Olesen, 2004). The Indymedia network that brought together anarchist and pro-democracy hackers dispersed throughout the world mobilized participation in the global resistance movement against neoliberalism, reflected in "the Battle in Seattle," which was deeply rooted in the organizing features of Indigenous protest. The network mobilized global-scale protest against neoliberalism by being rooted in local action, situated in context and in the everyday cultural organizing of community life. At the heart of the network was the Zapatista principle of autonomy, anchored in Indigenous articulations of sovereignty. The network also served as a media infrastructure for reporting on the protest, from the protest, controlled by voices within the protest (Dutta, 2012). When global justice activists descended on the Seattle meeting of the World Trade Organization in 1999, the large-scale mobilization of local community actions and interconnected community networks, facilitated by the digital infrastructure of Indymedia, shaped the size and impact of the protests. Critical here is the role of Indigeneity as the basis for theorizing and materializing autonomous networks of movements against neoliberalism working across diverse nodal registers, generating political coalitions among activist groups. Critical to the network infrastructure of transformation was the role of technologies such as mobile phones that enable activists to coordinate movement and protest strategies instantaneously.

Dismantling Racist Violence

Across Indigenous struggles globally, the struggle for control over media infrastructures is constituted amidst the systemic erasure of Indigenous voices and Indigenous knowledge systems through racist architectures of knowledge production and circulation (L. Smith, 1999, 2011;

McCormack, 2016). In the postcolonial context of India, for instance, the oppressive hierarchies of caste have historically worked to uphold and perpetuate Brahminical control over knowledge systems while simultaneously devaluing, co-opting, and erasing adivasi knowledge systems. The struggles of adivasis for claims to knowledge making are constituted amidst ongoing mobilization to dismantle the Brahminical racism that forms the postcolonial sites of knowledge production, shaping the violence of erasure and perpetuating extreme racist practices that make the academe uninhabitable for adivasi students. These processes of organizing across media platforms name and label the shallow performances of opportunistic decolonization among upper caste academics, instead calling for an embodied politics of knowledge generation emerging from within adivasi land struggles. Voices such as that of the late adivasi academic and activist Abhay Xaxa (2016) shape the mobilization of resistance against the racist violence of epistemic structures. The following is an excerpt of a poem penned by Xaxa on an online platform:

> I am not your data, nor am I your vote bank,
> I am not your project, or any exotic museum object,
> I am not the soul waiting to be harvested,
> Nor am I the lab where your theories are tested.

Similarly, the struggles of Māori for sovereignty over language, cultural practices, and knowledge generation are shaped in the backdrop of the ongoing racist practices in Aotearoa that systematically undermine Māori knowledge and seek to erase Māori knowledge claims (Abel & Mutu, 2011; Mutu, 2011, 2019a, 2019b). The historic denial of Māori culture, language, and knowledge forms the racist infrastructure of the settler colonial state, continuing to be perpetuated in the form of the organized attacks on Matauranga Māori. Claims to science are deployed to catalyze these attacks.

Conclusion

This chapter offers an overview of Indigenous struggles for, with, and through Indigenous media to lay claims to Indigenous rights in local, regional, and global registers. It draws upon the organizing principles of the CCA to attend to the interplays between communicative inequalities and material inequalities. The processes of building voice infrastructures in Indigenous struggles are crucial to the ongoing resistance against the interpenetrating forces of colonialism and neoliberal capitalism. Moreover, the interconnections between Indigenous media infrastructures offer the basis for transforming extractive neoliberal practices on a global scale, foregrounding knowledge infrastructures that articulate ways of organizing rooted in love, community, and care.

References

Abel, S. (2011). The (racial) political economy of Maori Television. *Australian Journal of Communication*, *38*(3), 125–138.

Abel, S., & Mutu, M. (2011). There's racism and then there's racism: Margaret Mutu and the immigration debate. *MEDIANZ: Media Studies Journal of Aotearoa New Zealand*, *12*(2), 1–19.

Alia, V. (1999). *Un/covering the north: News, media and aboriginal people*. University of British Columbia Press.

Bargh, M. (2016). Opportunities and complexities for Māori and mana whenua representation in local government. *Political Science*, *68*(2), 143–160.

Bargh, M. (2021). Challenges on the path to treaty-based local government relationships. *Kōtuitui: New Zealand Journal of Social Sciences Online*, *16*(1), 70–85.

Barmeyer, N. (2009). *Developing Zapatista autonomy: Conflict and NGO involvement in rebel chiapas*. University of New Mexico Press.

Barrett, M., & Connolly-Stone, K. (1998). The Treaty of Waitangi and social policy. *Social Policy Journal of New Zealand*, (11), 29–48.

Bell, A. (2018). A flawed treaty partner: The New Zealand state, local government and the politics of recognition. In D. Howard-Wagner, M. Bargh, & I. Altamirano-Jiménez (Eds.), *The neoliberal state, recognition and Indigenous rights: New paternalism to new imaginings* (pp. 77–92). Australian National University Press.

Callison, C., & Hermida, A. (2015). Dissent and resonance: #Idlenomore as an emergent middle ground. *Canadian Journal of Communication, 40*(4), 695–716.

de Bruin, J., & Mane, J. (2016). Decolonising ourselves: Language learning and Māori media. *Critical Arts, 30*(6), 770–787.

Dellacioppa, K. Z. (2009). *This bridge called Zapatismo: Building alternative political cultures in Mexico City, Los Angeles, and beyond.* Rowman & Littlefield.

Dutta, M. J. (2004a). The unheard voices of Santalis: Communicating about health from the margins of India. *Communication Theory, 14*(3), 237–263.

Dutta, M. J. (2004b). Poverty, structural barriers, and health: A Santali narrative of health communication. *Qualitative Health Research, 14*(8), 1107–1122.

Dutta, M. J. (2011). *Communicating social change: Structure, culture, and agency.* Routledge.

Dutta, M. J. (2012). *Voices of resistance: Communication and social change.* Purdue University Press.

Dutta, M. J. (2015a). A postcolonial critique of public relations. In J. L'Etang, D. McKie, N. Snow, & J. Xifra (Eds.), *The Routledge handbook of critical public relations* (pp. 272–284). Routledge.

Dutta, M. J. (2015b). Decolonizing communication for social change: A culture-centered approach. *Communication Theory, 25*(2), 123–143.

Dutta, M. J. (2018a). Autoethnography as decolonization, decolonizing autoethnography: Resisting to build our homes. *Cultural Studies ↔ Critical Methodologies, 18*(1), 94–96.

Dutta, M. J. (2018b). Culture-centered approach in addressing health disparities: Communication infrastructures for subaltern voices. *Communication Methods and Measures, 12*(4), 239–259.

Dutta, M. J., & Pal, M. (2020). Theorizing from the Global South: Dismantling, resisting, and transforming communication theory. *Communication Theory, 30*(4), 349–369.

Dutta, M. J., Ramasubramanian, S., Barrett, M., Elers, C., Sarwatay, D., Raghunath, P., Kaur, S., Dutta, D., Jayan, P., Rahman, M., Tallam, E., Roy, S., Falnikar, A., Johnson, G., Mandal, I., Dutta, U., Basnyat, I., Soriano, C., Pavarala, V., . . . Zapata, D. (2021). Decolonizing open science: Southern interventions. *Journal of Communication, 71*(5), 803–826.

Elers, C., & Dutta, M. (2023). Academic–community solidarities in land occupation as an Indigenous claim to health: Culturally centered solidarity through voice infrastructures. *Frontiers in Communication, 8*, Article 1009837.

Elers, C. H., & Jayan, P. (2020). "This is us": Free speech embedded in Whiteness, racism and coloniality in Aotearoa, New Zealand. *First Amendment Studies, 54*(2), 236–249.

Ellis, M. (2021, October 4). *Maori ward advocates plan hikoi protest against 0Ruapehu District Council.* Retrieved February 1, 2022, from https://www.rnz.co.nz/news/ldr/452897/maori-ward-advocates-plan-hikoi-protest-agai nst-ruapehu-district-council

Esteva, G. (2005). Celebration of Zapatismo. *Humboldt Journal of Social Relations, 29*, 127–167.

Esteva, G., & Prakash, M. S. (1998). *Grassroots postmodernism: Remaking the soils of cultures.* Zed Books.

Gill, S. (2021, May 11). *Hundreds of people join historic march for Maori wards in Manawatu.* Retrieved January 27, 2021, from https://www.stuff.co.nz/pou-tiaki/300304206/hundreds-of-people-join-historic-march-for-mori-wards-in-manawat

Ginsburg, F. D., Abu-Lughod, L., & Larkin, B. (Eds.). (2002). *Media worlds: Anthropology on new terrain.* University of California Press.

Holden, W., Nadeau, K., & Jacobson, R. D. (2011). Exemplifying accumulation by dispossession: Mining and Indigenous peoples in the Philippines. *Geografiska Annaler: Series B, Human Geography, 93*(2), 141–161.

Jackson, M. (1997, May). Smashing cups and muriwhenua. *Kiwa Hiwa Ra*, p. 25.

Jones, R., Crengle, S., & McCreanor, T. (2006). How tikanga guides and protects the research process: Insights from the Hauora Tane project. *Social Policy Journal of New Zealand, 29*, 60–77.

Kelsey, J. (2015). *The fire economy: New Zealand's reckoning.* Williams.

Lesutis, G. (2019). Spaces of extraction and suffering: Neoliberal enclave and dispossession in Tete, Mozambique. *Geoforum, 102*, 116–125.

Mane, J. (2014). He reo tautoko: A history of iwi radio broadcasting. In R. Higgins, P. Rewi, & V. Olsen-Reeder (Eds.), *The value of the Māori language: Te hua o te reo Māori* (pp. 319–330). Huia.

Matamua, R. (2006). *Te Reo Pāho: Māori radio and language revitalisation: A thesis presented for the degree of Doctor of Philosophy in Māori Studies at Massey University* [Doctoral dissertation]. Massey University.

Matamua, R. (2014). Te Reo Pāpāho me te Reo Māori—Māori broadcasting and te reo Māori. In R. Higgins, P. Rewi, & V. Olsen-Reeder (Eds.), *The value of the Māori language: Te hua o te reo Māori* (pp. 331–348). Huia.

Matike Mai Aotearoa. (2016). *He Whakaaro Here Whakaumu Mō Aotearoa: The report of Matike Mai Aotearoa—the Independent Working Group on Constitutional Transformation.* Matike Mai Aotearoa.

McCormack, F. (2012). Indigeneity as process: Māori claims and neoliberalism. *Social Identities, 18*(4), 417–434.

McCormack, F. (2016). Indigenous claims: Hearings, settlements, and neoliberal silencing. *Political and Legal Anthropology Review, 39*(2), 226–243. https://doi.org/10.1111/plar.12191

Mika, J. P., Dell, K., Elers, C., Dutta, M., & Tong, Q. (2022). Indigenous environmental defenders in Aotearoa New Zealand: Ihumātao and Ōroua River. *AlterNative, 18*(2), 277–289.

Mutu, M. (2011). *The state of Maori rights.* Huia.

Mutu, M. (2019a). The treaty claims settlement process in New Zealand and its impact on Māori. *Land, 8*(10), Article 152.

Mutu, M. (2019b). "To honour the treaty, we must first settle colonisation" (Moana Jackson 2015): The long road from colonial devastation to balance, peace and harmony. *Journal of the Royal Society of New Zealand, 49*(Suppl. 1), 4–18.

Ngā Kaiwhakapūmau i te reo Māori. (1999). *Māori Broadcasting timeline* [Paper presentation]. A national hui on Māori Development in Information Technology and Telecommunications, Wellington.

Olesen, T. (2004). The transnational Zapatista solidarity network: An infrastructure analysis. *Global Networks, 4*(1), 89–107.

Smith, J. (2015). Māori Television's service to its publics in an era of digital plenty. *International Journal of Digital Television, 6*(2), 185–201.

Smith, J. (2016). *Māori Television: The first ten years.* Auckland University Press.

Smith, L. T. (1999). *Decolonizing methodologies: Research and Indigenous peoples.* Zed Books.

Smith, L. T. (2011). Re-storying the development of Kaupapa Māori. In J. Hutchings, H. Potter, & K. Taupo (Eds.), *Kei Tua o Te Pae Hui Proceedings: The challenges of Kaupapa Māori research in the 21st century* (pp. 10–15). New Zealand Council for Educational Research.

Starr, A. (2005). *Global revolt: A guide to the movements against globalization.* Zed books.

Sykes, A. (2010). *The politics of the brown table.* Te Whaainga Wahine. Retrieved September 17, 2021, from http://whaaingawahine.blogspot.com/2010/11/politics-of-brown-table-annette-sykes.html

Waitangi Tribunal. (2019). *Hauora: Report on stage one of the health services and outcomes kaupapa inquiry* (WAI 2575). Legislation Direct. https://forms.justice.govt.nz/search/Documents/WT/wt_DOC_195476216/Hauora%202023%20W.pdf

Xaxa, A. (2016). I am not your data. *Adivasi Resurgence, 13.* https://agitatejournal.org/article/i-am-not-your-data/

SECTION V

Conclusion

The Future of Media and Social Justice: Resistances, Reckoning, and Reparative Justice

Srividya Ramasubramanian *and* Omotayo O. Banjo

An Antidote to Dehumanization, Destruction, and Despair

As we pen these concluding remarks in early November 2023, the United Nations (UN) and several world leaders are calling for a ceasefire in the Middle East as Gaza experiences unimaginable levels of destruction of civilian lives, homes, schools, and hospitals. More than 25 Palestinian journalists have been killed just this last month. Thousands of children are missing or have been killed, leading the UN to call Gaza a children's graveyard. Palestinian communication scholar Professor Ahlam Muhtaseb was disallowed from giving her speech on Palestine at the presidential address and awards ceremony of the National Communication Association's annual conference. This, just five years after the seminal publication #CommunicationSoWhite (Chakravartty et al., 2018) in the *Journal of Communication* which called our attention to the biases that silence non-White scholars and non-White stories. This volume issues yet, another clarion call.

As mothers, immigrants, women of color, poets, scholars, and activists, we are deeply concerned about how language, media, and culture are being weaponized to dehumanize, destroy, and demolish entire communities of people. Nation-states, the military–industry–prison complex, and fundamentalist organizations continue to use media and technology as tools for surveillance, violence, exploitation, propaganda, genocide, and apartheid. Religious and ethnonationalist movements such as the Hindutva, Zionism, White nationalists, and ISIS are actively recruiting and radicalizing youth into their toxic ideologies. They are targeting progressive voices and initiatives led by activists, scholars, journalists, and other media-makers through intimidation, silencing, imprisonment, and even extrajudicial killings.

A Generative Space Across Geographies and Generations

As co-editors, we view this handbook as our humble offering to the world as an antidote to the despair and distress that so many of us feel at this moment. We hope it can help channel our energies to create a generative space for dialogues across positionalities and perspectives, geographies and generations, theories and methods, as well as issues and identities relating to media and social justice.

Through this collection, we have been incredibly fortunate to work with some of the leading voices on media and social justice scholarship throughout the world, many of whom have experienced multiple stigmatizations and generational violence due to colonialism, imperialism, heteropatriarchy, White supremacy, and related factors. They have been thinking and writing about issues relating to media and social justice within their specific cultural and national contexts for many years. Their collective wisdom emerges from their lived realities of subjugation and oppression but also resistances and resurgences, which have been nuanced and refined over multiple generations. What they could include within a single chapter of

5,000 or so words is merely a small peek into their lives, experiences, and efforts. These chapters are broad brushstrokes intended to provide an overall sense of the wide range of media formats, research methods, social issues, and theoretical approaches that represent this subfield. We encourage you to dive deeper into the scholarship of the contributors whose chapters resonated with and inspired you.

An Inclusive, Interdisciplinary, and Intersectional Approach

Taking an inclusive and interdisciplinary approach to this scholarship is essential because almost every discipline today within social sciences, arts, humanities, and the sciences has to contend with what it means to be part of the larger digital media culture. We have been intentional about including scholar–activists who use a range of methods, paradigms, and approaches. Like ikebana, we have put together theories, methods, and case studies to bring meaning to not just the creators of the collection but also those who engage with it through their lens and values. In doing so, we have tried to center historically marginalized epistemologies and knowledge systems such as Indigenous, intersectional, transnational feminist, and critical cultural approaches to media and social justice scholarship. Doing so helps readers better appreciate the complexities and nuances of intersecting oppressions, social structures, and power networks regarding media ownership, workforce, labor, production, representation, users, and impacts. It is also an attempt to decenter Whiteness, Eurocentrism, and hegemonic social sciences within the media and communication discipline. In these ways, it builds on and is inspired by the #CommunicationSoWhite movement of 2018, the #BlackLivesMatter uprising of 2020, and the ongoing #FreePalestine protests of 2023.

Toward Reckoning, Restoration, and Reparative Justice

We urge scholars, educators, and community leaders to use media and technology as interventions and infrastructure to elevate the voice, agency, and resistance of those in the margins. Our handbook provides many examples and case studies of activism and collective action from throughout the world. As critical media scholars and activists, the ongoing screenwriters and actors strike is an example of collective resistance by creative media workers. Throughout the world, gig workers are also leading the way in the use of media to challenge biometric surveillance, unhealthy workplace conditions, and inequalities in pay structures. Critically examining and resisting technological innovations such as artificial intelligence, ChatGPT, and other forms of machine learning that are poised to serve as the next frontiers of colonialism are essential to this work. Centering intersecting structures of social inequalities such as White supremacy, patriarchy, capitalism, classism, heteronormativity, casteism, fundamentalism, and colonialism within cultural and media systems means that media scholar–activists have to stay vigilant of how social justice is getting weaponized, co-opted, and contained in ways that serve status quo dominant ideologies.

As scholar–activists putting our bodies on the line by speaking out against repression by those in power, we must work collectively to create spaces for solidarity, safety, and sense-making within our classrooms, creative industries, curricula, and communities. In the weeks and years to come, we hope that our handbook can lead to conversations about urgent topics such as climate change; peace in the Middle East; Indigenous sovereignty; inclusion of caste-oppressed groups; and more representations from African, Latin American, and other continents beyond North America and Europe. We stand in solidarity with our comrades and allies in our global networked community of scholar–activists committed to peace, liberation, and justice for all. Together, we must re-envision the role of media and technology in our shared collective futures through reckoning, restoration, and reparative justice for collective healing and flourishing.

Reference
Chakravartty, P., Kuo, R., Grubbs, V., & McIlwain, C. (April 2018). #CommunicationSoWhite. *Journal of Communication, 68*(2), 254–266. https://doi.org/10.1093/joc/jqy003

INDEX

For the benefit of digital users, indexed terms that span two pages (e.g., 52–53) may, on occasion, appear on only one of those pages.

Tables and figures are indicated by an italic *t* and *f* following the page number.

media use/resistances, 75–76
  post-gay era, 75–76
  power relationships, 71
  sexual backwardness theme, 73–74
  transmisogynistic mode of
    becoming, 74
  See also queer/transgender studies
Liao, S., 271
Libya, 160–61
Lifers Behind Bars, 179, 180*t*
Lim, E., 7
literacy counterpublics, 45–46
Littler, J., 23
Lizzie McGuire, 62–63
Lizzo. *See* Jefferson, M. V.
Lizzo's Watch Out for the Big Grrls, 45
Llinares, D., 178
Logo, 75–76
Longoria, Eva, 62–63
López, A., 249
Lopez, Jennifer, 67–68
Lorre, C., 198
Loughead, T., 6
Lovecraft Country, 199
Lovedu, 269–70
Love & Hip Hop Hollywood, 73–74
Love Is Not Violence, 227
Lövheim, M., 88
low-income families studies, 33

Macedo, L. B., 109
Madras, 172–73
Madurai Veeran, 172
Magallanes-Blanco, C., 246–47
Mahabharata, 167
Mahmood, S., 147
Malaysia, 89
Malcolm X, 129
Mallapragada, M., 195–96
Mance, B., 28–29
Mancini, P., 132
Manusmiriti (Laws of
  Manu), 166–67
Māori, 289, 290–91
Maragh-Lloyd, R., 45
Marcus Aurelius, 154
Marcuse, H., 126–28
Markle, Meghan, 23–24
Marma, 281
Married with Children, 156
Martin, A. L. Jr., 73
Martin, Trayvon, 128, 160–61
Martins, G., 244
Marwick, A., 82
Marx, K., 13, 14
McChesney, R., 13, 15
McCune, J. Q., Jr., 73–74

McGowan, C., 227–28
McMillian, M., 6
Means Coleman, R., 5–56, 57, 59
media literacy. *See* critical media
  literacy
media/media research generally
  community-based *vs.* community-
    engaged research, 119–20
  culture-centered approach, 119–21
  importance of, 3–4
  power relationships, 4
Media Reform Coalition, 25
medicalization, 97–98
Mensa, V., 197
mental health interventions/
  migrants. *See* migrants/media-
  based interventions
mentorships, 55
Merrill, K. Jr., 7–8
Me Too movement, 45–46, 160–61
Mexico, 229–30, 288, 291–92
Meyrowitz, J., 29
Microsoft, 16, 237–38
Middle East media. *See* closed
  contexts
migrants/media-based interventions
  cultural adaptation, 221, 222
  demographics/stressors, 216–17
  effectiveness, 220, 221–22, 223
  face-to-face therapy, 220
  health/digital literacy barriers, 222
  ICBT, 219–21, 220n.1
  implementation, 220
  literature review, 217–19, 218*f*
  media/ICT interventions
    for, 217
  mental health interventions
    for, 216
  outcomes, 221
  types of, 219–20
  See also domestic workers
*Misogynoir Transformed: Black
  Women's Digital Resistance*
  (Bailey), 271
Mitchell, D., 99
Mitra, R., 75
Modern Family, 62–63
Mohammed, W. F., 8, 274
Mokhtar, M. F., 89
monopoly capital school, 15
Montgomery bus boycott, 147–48
Moonlight, 23
Morah, D. N., 34
Moreno, Rita, 67–68
Mosco, V., 14, 34–35
Mossi, 269–70
Mothers of the Plaza de Mayo, 231

Moultrie, j. l., 5, 52, 58
Mro, 281
Munck, R., 260–61
Muñoz, J. E., 80
Munro-Bjorklund, V., 181
Murray, S. O., 269–70
Muslim American youth studies, 33
Mythen, G., 283

Nandanar, 169
  (Bhakta) Nandanar, 169
narrative sovereignty, 289–90
narrowcasting, 25n.2
Native Americans marginalization
  studies, 33
Nattamai, 172
Negra, Amara La, 66
Nepal, 278–79, 283–84
Netflix, 16, 179, 180*t*
Neville, H. A., 32
New Labour government, 21–22
New York Times, 162
New Zealand, 289, 290–91
Ng, E., 75–76
Nichols, Tyre, 54n.3
Nieborg, D. B., 16–17
Niederdeppe, J., 34
Nigeria, 34, 143–44, 147, 269–70.
  See also transnational/diasporic
  identities
Nightmare (Emirates, 2015), 155–
  56, 155n.3
Ni Una Menos, 230–32
Nollywood (South Africa), 195
Nwonka, C., 22
Nygren, T., 221
Nyong'o, L., 197

Occupy Wall Street movement, 161–62
Ochonu, M. E., 198
Okoeguale, A., 196
Okoli, A. C., 196–97
Oliver, M., 98
Oloruntobi, T., 7, 198
Oluwo, I., 9
Omojola, O., 34
online *dakwah*, 90
online dating, 92–94
Ono, Kent, 113
Open TV (OTV), 83
Orang, M., 220
Orange Is the New Black, 179, 180*t*
Ore Iravu (One Night), 171
Orientalism, 109
Ornelas, N., 227
Other Campaign, 292
Oz (TV show), 178